THE NEW ENLIGHTENMENT

A Twenty-First Century, Peaceful American Revolution

ROBERT BIVONA

New Enlightenment Citizens Union
NECU Press
PO Box 4103
North Fort Myers, FL 33918
info@newenlightenment.us

Cover: NASA satellite image of the sun on the horizon

Printed in the United States of America

LCCN 2017905732
ISBN 978-0-9967067-0-4 Softcover
ISBN 978-0-9967067-2-8 Hardcover
ISBN 978-0-9967067-1-1 ebook

Advance Endorsements of the Book and Movement

"It's a well thought-out proposal, and if it could get off the ground, it could be significant."

Noam Chomsky, Ph.D., "world's top public intellectual" in a 2005 poll, Institute Professor Emeritus of Linguistics, Massachusetts Institute of Technology, philosopher, historian, political commentator, activist, one of the founders of the field of cognitive science, eighth most frequently cited scholar in history, author of over one hundred books.

"I am very impressed by your project. People who are looking to hear about serious alternatives to the ongoing neoliberal hegemony in U.S. policymaking circles will find your book very useful and even inspiring... a valuable resource for people seeking out a coherent vision of how we get from here to there in the struggle for a more just society...The book is also well organized and well written. Congratulations on the enormous work effort as well as the final product."

Robert Pollin, Ph.D., Co-director, Political Economy Research Institute and Distinguished Professor of Economics University of Massachusetts, Amherst, member of the Scientific Advisory Committee of the European Commission project on Financialization, Economy, Society, and Sustainable Development, selected by Foreign Policy magazine as one of the "100 Leading Global Thinkers" for 2013.

"I just completed your masterful treatise! It is truly the most comprehensive roadmap for national renewal that I have seen! Congratulations!"

James B. Stewart, Ph.D., Pennsylvania State University Professor Emeritus of Labor and Employment Relations, Management and Organization, Former President of the National Economic Association, Former Editor of The Review of Black Political Economy, and Former President of the National Council for Black Studies.

"I want to compliment you on a well thought out progressive economic and political program."

Michael Ash, Ph.D., Chair of Economics Department, and Professor of Economics and Public Policy, University of Massachusetts, Amherst, one of the 100 Leading Global Thinkers of 2013, Foreign Policy magazine.

"A well written, well documented 1) treatise on the structural ills of a global neo-liberalism, 2) a manual for social action in what is essentially an agenda for societal re-democratization and a 3) reference book for fact retrieval and argument building to support his agenda for major societal progress. Robert Bivona has done this in not three, but one book. Easily understood charts, graphs and data clarify and support his descriptions of many social ills and proposals to solve them. I can highly recommend The New Enlightenment as a good read for those looking for solutions to what may seem like intractable and forever unresolvable problems of our era."

Thomas W. Gray, Ph.D., Center Scholar, Center for Study of Co-operatives, University of Saskatchewan.

"Bivona notes that we are the wealthiest country and wealthier than we have ever been, yet we rank close to or at the bottom among advanced countries on many of the most important measures of well-being such as life expectancy, infant mortality, poverty rate, incarceration rate and equality. Our political system no longer responds to the major issues affecting the majority of Americans. Systemic solutions are needed, and The New Enlightenment details some that are powerful and innovative."

Stephen A. Bezruchka, MD, Professor, Department of Global Health, Masters of Public Health Degree Program, University of Washington, political activist. A national authority on the socioeconomic determinants of the health of populations.

"Modern day corporate capitalism directs far too much of the benefits of the hard work and creative ingenuity of workers to a tiny economic elite. A country comprised mainly of worker-owned and democratically run corporations will solve our inequality problem, greatly reduce the tendency for corporations to create negative externalities and have other major positive impacts on society. Bivona provides the clearest vision of exactly how to get there from here. His detailed program, if instituted, will result in worker controlled and owned business enterprises performing most of the economic activity of the country, after a two-decade transition period. It can be of revolutionary importance.

The book also offers many perspicacious recommendations on ways to improve our tax system. If you wish this writer luck, you wish all of us luck. The 1 percenters have to be concerned about a stable society as well."

Carmine Gorga, Ph.D., Political Scientist, Economist, author.

Book Review

This book is dedicated to Noam Chomsky.

Noam Chomsky's clear moral vision and lifelong relentless dedication to serving it, penetrating analysis of social conditions, and vast knowledge has inspired and will continue to inspire countless people to struggle for a more just society.

CONTENTS

In addition to the income and wealth tax, the following Part 2 policies generate sufficient revenues to support all the proposed policies requiring federal funds including those in Part 3, eliminate the $680 billion deficit (2013) and create over a $300 billion surplus. Most of the following policies also provide other benefits.

PART 3

THE WAY TO A GOVERNMENT OF, FOR, AND BY THE PEOPLE **251**

PART 4

INFORMATION AND ARGUMENTS SUPPORTING POLICIES   393

Introduction

Every observer of our society can see we are facing many serious problems. These problems are not isolated; they are connected through political and economic systems serving the majority of Americans increasingly poorly. The New Enlightenment describes some of the ways these systems are descending us into alarming levels of injustice and dysfunction, but its primary focus is on solutions. You will learn how we can create a more prosperous and far more just and democratic society, one in which prosperity will be more equitably shared.

Sometimes paradigm shifts are necessary to solve fundamental problems. Now is such a time, so innovative, transformative solutions are promoted here. They are evidence based to best serve the country as a whole. Few of us want what we have now, a political system mainly serving a small elite most able to influence it, and their dominance is growing. We can have a truly democratic republic through the political system reforms I detail in this book.

The beneficial transformations I design for—some are summarized below—may seem too large to be achievable. Many will believe that no policies can exist that will achieve these goals because if they did exist they would have already been implemented. However, if you consider the policies detailed in this book carefully, you will see that this prejudice is misguided. The detailed program described in this book will:

- End unemployment or reduce it to historic lows.
- Create a minimum tax-free annual income of $34,980 for full-time work. Expanding and reforming the Earned Income Tax Credit (EITC) and raising the minimum wage to $11.10 per hour (which increases the income of the lowest wage full-time worker to the maximum income where the largest EITC will be applied) will accomplish this.
- Reduce full-time work-hours to 36 hours per week. Despite 10% fewer work-hours, and consequently as much as 10% lower compensation from the workplace, people's take-home income whose income now is under $160,000 will rise, and rise proportionally more the lower the income, due to either lower taxes or the expanded EITC.

- Transform the economic system to one where most economic activity will be performed by worker-owned and controlled businesses at the end of the designed 20-year transition period. Loans, grants, tax benefits and subsidies within several detailed programs will accomplish this. By extending democratic practices into the workplace, and substantial capital ownership to the workforce, income and wealth inequality reduction, productivity enhancements, and other important benefits result.

- Eliminate the dominating importance of money controlled by national public office candidates and their allies, and thereby allow a meaningful democracy to exist. This will be accomplished mainly by instituting a TV and radio station license requirement to offer generous allotments of airtime free of charge to four qualified candidates per national public office contest within a thoroughly detailed system. No reasonable need for the purchase of airtime will exist. All airwaves are publicly owned, so they should best serve the public interest. Also, support qualified candidates with postal, newspaper, and internet advertising subsidies, and institute a new Fairness Doctrine.

- Enhance democratic functioning with new, innovative democratic forms. Average citizens in deliberative groups involving 0.1% of the citizenry will develop some public policies.

- Create a vigorous media of, for, and by the people necessary for a well-functioning government of, for, and by the people. This book details these ways to accomplish this: Institute a license renewal requirement for worker-ownership and control of air media companies, and support it with loans, grants, tax benefits and subsidies. Motivate ownership and control by workers of other kinds of media businesses, also through loans, grants, tax benefits and subsidies. Media ownership and control by workers will eliminate important media content selection biases resulting from the character of current media ownership and management, and result in other important benefits. The media's role in the functioning of a democratic society is essential, and our media corporations' current structure is inevitably serving this role poorly. This policy will create a new and vigorous media culture more responsive and accountable to the majority.

- Eliminate tuition for two and four-year public colleges. This will help meet our stated ideal of equal opportunity for all and help create the well-informed citizenry needed for a well-functioning democracy and economy. It will also remove an enormous burden from millions of future college graduates whose education serves the national interest.

- Increase Social Security payments by $500/month to all recipients, and provide it to some who are currently ineligible. The United States ranks 30th among 34 developed countries in the percentage of a median worker's earnings that our public pension system replaces, and private pensions are becoming less common and generous.
- Eliminate the $680 billion deficit (2013) and create over a $300 billion annual surplus. We will maintain this surplus until we eliminate the federal debt and its interest payment. In 2013, this payment was over $250 billion on almost a $15 trillion federal debt. (The budgetary impact of all policies is determined relative to the 2013 federal budget.)

The economic and political system reform program detailed in this book will also have other transformative beneficial impacts if instituted.

Impossibly grandiose goals? They are not—on one condition: Your support and the support of many others for the detailed program in this book and the organization devoted to seeing it be instituted. Please join us so we can reach a critical mass in numbers for this change to be inevitable. Let this time of crisis be a time of opportunity, a time for a New Enlightenment where, unlike during the 18th century Enlightenment, all people independent of race and sex share in its benefits. All of our lives can be improved, for tens of millions of us dramatically so, through policies that will create a far more just and beneficial political, social and economic order. Now is the time to make it happen.

Our current political system needs radical reform because, inherently, policymakers unwilling or unable to serve the majority are its result. When good and capable persons overcome nearly insurmountable barriers to their entry into elected office, they are largely disabled by dysfunctional rules of Congress and colleagues serving narrow, moneyed interests. So further decline or paralysis is inevitable without system change.

The person who may be the most well-informed judge on the relative quality of our election system is the internationally renowned election observer, former President Carter, whose Carter Center has monitored 96 elections in 38 countries. He said, *"We have one of the worst election processes in the world right in the United States, and it's almost entirely because of the excessive influx of money."* For this and other important reasons, the U.S. Congress's approval rating reached a historic low in 2014 of 9%.[1] Only 9% of Americans think Congress is mainly influenced by the voters they represent.[2]

The outcomes of our economic system are to a large degree determined by the regulation, tax, and government expenditure policies created by our political system, so major economic injustices and hardships are evident. A 2013 Gallup poll found that 20% of the U.S. population did not have enough money to buy the food they or their family needed at least once over the prior year.[3] In 2013, about 50 million, that's over one in every seven, Americans lived in poverty, a higher fraction than at any time since 1966, a higher number than ever. Our per capita Gross Domestic Product (GDP) was $52,800 in 2013, but in 1966 it was $28,680 in 2013 dollars. So on average, each person in the United States had an income almost two times higher in 2013 than in 1966, yet about the same fraction of the population was in poverty because nearly all the country's income gains have gone to a small economic elite.

The average wealth of the poorest 40%, 126 million Americans, was negative $10,800 in 2013, but as our GDP per capita indicates, we are a wealthy country, not a poor one.[4] The total wealth of just 400 people, less than .00013 % of our population, was over $2.3 trillion in 2013.[5] This is approximately the total wealth of the least wealthy 190 million Americans or 60% of the country and is about the GDP of Italy, the eighth largest national economy in the world. The top 400 people have wealth equivalent to 12.8% of U.S. GDP in 2013. In 1980, the wealthiest 400 Americans had wealth equal to "*only*" 2.8% of U.S. GDP.

The Gini coefficient measures inequality, with numbers between 0 and 100 that rise with greater disparities. The UN-Habitat Monitoring and Research Division defines an income Gini coefficient of 40 as an "*international alert line*" indicating that a society's "*Inequality [is] approaching dangerously high levels*" that could "*lead to sporadic protests and riots.*" Our income Gini coefficient is now about 48 and has risen to about 80 for U.S. wealth.[6] Our economic inequality is the highest in the developed world and our economic mobility the lowest.

We cannot have a functioning economic system if income or wealth is divided equally, but disparities so large that the top 1% of Americans have 24% of the nation's income is unjust and economically, politically and socially harmful.[7] The average income of the top 1% of U.S. households in 2011 was $1,530,773, while the average income of Americans in the bottom 20% was $9,187. The highest income for an individual was $4.9 billion. Part 4, Note 1 details why this degree of income disparity is unjustifiable and harmful.

With the huge disparity in economic power inevitably comes a huge disparity in political power, resulting in greater economic disparity. This vicious cycle of growing power disparities will lead to disaster unless it is consciously and forcefully interrupted and reversed. Yet it seems we are continuing to run on this path of predictable outcome, like lemmings over a cliff.

Increasingly, people are aware of their powerlessness, so they no longer bother to vote. If people believe their interests will not be served whoever is elected, they have little motivation to vote. We have, by far, the lowest voter turnout in the developed world.

Concurrent with the decline in trust in our political system and leaders is a decline in trust in our business leaders and media. And this decline in trust is extending not just to our most important institutions, but also to one another as individuals. The percentage of Americans who believe that other people can generally be trusted fell from 46% in 1974 to 33% in 2012. Trust is essential to social cohesion and political stability, and it is negatively correlated with economic inequality. Trust in a democratic system of government requires trust in the few who represent the interests of the many.

These ominous signs for the future of our country and many other signs of societal dysfunction and decay we urgently need to address with robust policy solutions. Some of these other signs I describe in Part 1 of this book. For decades, both major political parties have allowed the development of, or created, a long list of shocking economic, political and other societal conditions. Why are we tolerating this?

We are a creative people, yet little creativity has been applied to the most important domains of ensuring that our economic and political systems best serve the majority of people. The debate on all the important related issues has been too narrow, due mainly to a dysfunctional media. But the problem runs deeper to those in our academic institutions' political science and economics departments, where adherents to failed dogmas are common— dogmas that, not coincidentally, have served a narrow elite, to the detriment of the majority. Academic economists have commonly supported or actively promoted the policies of removing important and necessary regulations on corporations, and of lowering taxes on high-income households and corporations that have been instituted over the last few decades. These policies have served the country poorly. However, some members of these academic disciplines have had clearer vision or higher purpose, and some of the policy proposals in this book use ideas of some of these and other exceptional people.

Clearly, a mass movement is needed for fundamental change, and I hope this book attracts you to be part of the one in the direction it defines. Recent history gives the Occupy movement and the Tea "Party" as examples of important political forces that rose unexpectedly and quickly to great prominence. These movements are far from the limit of what can be accomplished, and what has been accomplished by political movements in the past.

I chose the name The New Enlightenment mainly because economic inequality was one of the most important motivations for the Enlightenment period's societal transformations, including the one that created the United States. Data from medieval England and today indicate it is more extreme now than it was before the Enlightenment. For this reason and others, it is time for a New Enlightenment. These data and this analysis are in Part 1, *Now Is the Time for The New Enlightenment.*

If you are aware of the evidence that our economic and political systems require major reforms, you can skip most of Part 1 with little loss of continuity. The data from England before the Enlightenment are rarely seen, though, and their analysis and comparison with conditions today is original here, so I recommend that no one skip this Part 1 information and other historical and essential information in the first ten pages of Part 1. The facts in Part 1 may cause despair, but do not despair. The rest of the book is designed to create hope by providing the major part of a foundation for a New Enlightenment.

Robert Bivona

The New Enlightenment was written over about a five-year
period beginning in December 2011

Part 1

Now Is the Time for
The New Enlightenment

Now Is the Time for The New Enlightenment

During the Enlightenment, people imagined and acted on a vision of a radically more just world

The original Enlightenment period in the 18th century was a time when many people in Europe, and later in the American colonies, shared a vision of a transformed world. The more widespread use of printing presses, more extensive roadways, and newly created postal services needed to distribute periodicals and other print media allowed their means of mass communication, print media, to dramatically increase public awareness of societal issues. There was an explosion in the number of books and other publications. Literacy rates increased greatly, and debating societies and other public forums were used to discuss the important issues.

As a result, many people were able to imagine the possibility of a fundamentally more just world order than the one in which they were living. An order based on reason, the ideals of equality for all, democracy and fundamental individual human rights. More importantly, they also acted on their new and radical vision. During this period of revolutionary transformations, the powers of monarchy, the privileges of the nobility, the political power and authority of the Catholic Church were overturned. There were also dramatic revolutions in science and philosophy. The American Revolution (1775–83) was an integral part of the Enlightenment period.

Enlightenment revolutionaries strove to create more egalitarian societies

The awareness of the importance of economics to politics was a fundamental part of the Enlightenment. The Enlightenment revolutionaries experienced the injustice of the majority of the wealth of their society being controlled by a tiny fraction of the population. This small minority used their vast wealth to control the political and social order. So Enlightenment revolutionaries formed more egalitarian societies where political leaders were accountable to the majority, and governments were designed with the intention to ensure that public policy served the ideals of democracy, equality for all, reason and basic individual human rights. America was one of these societies.

America was the most egalitarian society in the world

In America's early years it was the most egalitarian society on the planet, and our Founders were proud of these conditions. In a letter from Monticello dated September 10, 1814, Thomas Jefferson wrote:

"We have no paupers .... The great mass of our population is of laborers; our rich, who can live without labor, either manual or professional, being few, and of moderate wealth. Most of the laboring class possess property, cultivate their own lands, have families, and from the demand for their labor are enabled to exact from the rich ... such prices as enable them to be fed abundantly, clothed above mere decency, to labor moderately and raise their families .... Can any condition of society be more desirable than this?" Jefferson contrasted these conditions with an England of paupers and plutocrats: *"Now, let us compute by numbers the sum of happiness of the two countries. In England, happiness is the lot of the aristocracy only; and the proportion they bear to the laborers and paupers you know better than I do. Were I to guess that they are four in every hundred."*[8]

George Washington, nine months before his inauguration as the first president, predicted that America *"will be the most favorable country of any kind in the world for persons of industry and frugality, possessed of moderate capital, to inhabit ... it will not be less advantageous to the happiness of the lowest class of people, because of the equal distribution of property."*[9]

After Alexis de Tocqueville's famous journey to America in the 19th century, he returned to France and wrote that nothing *"Nothing struck me more forcibly than the general equality of conditions... the influence of this fact...has no less empire over civil society than over the Government; it creates opinions, engenders sentiments, suggests the ordinary practices of life, and modifies whatever it does not produce...the equality of conditions is the fundamental fact from which all others seem to be derived, and the central point at which all my observations constantly terminated."*[10]

Early America was the world's most egalitarian society.[11] Today, we are the outliers in the other direction—we are the most unequal of all the developed countries. On a per capita basis, we produce over 30 times the amount of goods and services per year than when the country was founded.[12] Yet, in 2012, almost 50 million Americans were in poverty and over 20 million were severely poor, with incomes less than one-half the official poverty income.[13]

During America's early years England's 1% were so rich that the country's average national income was nearly as high as that of the colonies, despite the much greater prosperity of the majority of Americans. Today, America's 1% are taking a greater share of national income and wealth than the old English aristocracy did, and a larger percentage of the country's income and wealth than any other advanced country.

The Enlightenment era's ideals were far from fully realized: The tolerance of the atrocity of slavery and the near extermination of Native Americans

The Enlightenment era ideals of freedom and equality for all, democracy, basic individual human rights and using reason to determine action, advanced societies greatly. But they had (and we still have) a long way to go. Many Enlightenment era Europeans' and Americans' understanding of who was fully human was tragically deficient. Racist atrocities during the Enlightenment era resulted from faulty information and evil people, not Enlightenment ideals.

Slavery pre-existed the Enlightenment era, but the large Transatlantic slave trade was facilitated during the era by advancements in weaponry and their production processes, the ability to travel, and to produce ships that could carry large numbers of people. Unfortunately, advancements in science and technology, a major characteristic of the Enlightenment era, have always resulted in advancements in the abuse of science and technology.

The Enlightenment transformations were imperfect and incomplete advancements, as have been all others. Basic individual human rights were not extended in the U.S. and Europe to races other than the white race, and to women, until well after the Enlightenment, and even in the 21st century this extension is far from complete.

Social orders dominated by elite powers of monarchy and nobility were inhumane, and eliminated based on Enlightenment philosophy. We now are in a period where a kind of aristocracy is again dominating our social order. This book will describe some of the resulting dysfunction and injustices.

So we need a New Enlightenment, one where all people independent of race and sex share in its benefits. But these benefits will be largest for those currently most disadvantaged by the unjust social order now.

If African Americans were justly compensated for their labor as slaves, what would the assets received then be worth today? Also, a hundred years of Jim Crow laws and economic oppression from other forms of discrimination followed the theoretical emancipation of the slaves. The result is that African Americans now have 1/20 the per capita wealth of whites.

Although not targeted to benefit any specific race, New Enlightenment reforms will reduce disparities between the races. But to what degree should we further correct disparities resulting from injustices of the past? This will best be answered after the true democracy and other social reforms of the New Enlightenment.

We have moved far from our founding ideals

We are far from the degree of egalitarianism that existed at our founding, of which Jefferson was so proud. The inequality and injustice in our society is extreme and its extent is not commonly reported. Important parallels exist to our conditions now and those that existed prior to, and that motivated, the Enlightenment revolutions.

Wide agreement exists that some degree of economic inequality is necessary and just, and that there is a limit on how extreme it should be. But most people are not aware how extreme our economic inequality is, and that it is beyond this limit. In Part 1 and Part 4, Note 1, I will describe further how extreme our economic inequality is and why it is not economically or morally justifiable. It is economically, politically and socially harmful.

Although most people, both on the left and the right, feel that some things are fundamentally wrong in the country now, most do not know the extent and seriousness of the wrongs. Whether you already knew them or learn of some here, we hope you will join us in imagining a more just world order and in acting on this new vision. Together, we can accomplish the institution of the innovative solutions of the New Enlightenment, just as those of the original Enlightenment acted by instituting visionary and innovative solutions needed for their time.

Most Americans greatly underestimate our economic disparities

The chart on the next page, created using national poll data, well summarizes important information on how our country's wealth is distributed and how little most people know about it.[14] It is worth exploring.

The bottom bar, labeled "ideal," represents what most people believe would be the ideal wealth distribution—different shades of gray represent the different quintiles (fifths of the population). The chart shows that the average American believes it is justified for people to have different levels of wealth. Average Americans believe that people who contribute more to the welfare of the country deserve more than an average amount of the country's wealth. People in the bottom quintile, on average, contribute less and therefore deserve less, in their view. (But, as we will see later, at the extremes of the wealth distribution, wealth and degree of societal contribution may not be positively correlated.)

As you can see, the average opinion is that people in the bottom quintile deserve about half of what they would have if wealth were distributed equally into each quintile, or about 10% instead of 20% of the country's wealth. The opinion is that people in the top quintile justifiably or ideally should have about 60% more than what they would have if wealth were distributed equally into each quintile (about 32% instead of 20%).

Actual U.S. Wealth Distribution Plotted Against
the Estimated and Ideal Distributions

■Bottom 20%   ■Second lowest 20%   ■Middle 20%   Second highest 20%   ■Top 20%

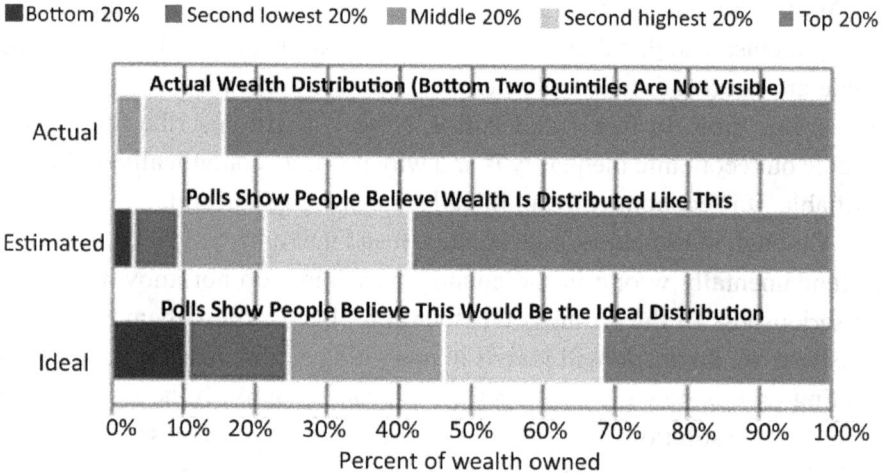

The middle "Estimated" bar shows the average of what people estimate is the actual distribution of wealth. It expresses awareness that inequality is far more extreme than is considered ideal. People estimate the bottom 20% to have only about 2% of the country's wealth—a small fraction, one-fifth, of what would be ideal, and the top 20% have almost double what they consider ideal.

Now look at the top bar, which expresses the facts of the wealth distribution. It seems there has been an error because only three quintiles are showing, so two quintiles are missing. But as I mentioned in the introduction, the total wealth of the poorest 40% of Americans is negative. The bottom two quintiles are invisible because they are negative or too small to appear on the chart. The bottom 20% has -1.4% of the country's wealth (has debt greater than assets), and the next 20% has 0.3% of the country's wealth, so the bottom 40% has -1.1% of the country's wealth.[15] They are in a condition worse than having no wealth at all.

In 2013, Forbes magazine researchers found that the wealthiest 400 people had over $2.3 trillion. Using Federal Reserve data for the rest of the population, this is more than the total wealth of the bottom 60% or 190 million Americans—a level of inequality far worse than most people imagine could exist. It is almost incomprehensible, so if you would like to have a better sense of how vast this disparity is, consider the analogies in Part 4, Note 10.

If you have only one penny and have no debts, you have more wealth than the total wealth of the 128 million poorest Americans. Most people would consider someone with more wealth than the total wealth of 128 million Americans to be very wealthy. So if you have a penny and no debts, congratulations; now you are considered wealthy. But likely not as wealthy as any of the 400 Americans with total wealth that exceeds the total of all the GDPs of 121 of the 189 nations for which the World Bank records GDP. Wealth disparities result from, and contribute to, income disparities, which are also very large and growing.

The majority of Americans are not aware of how concentrated wealth is because the extremely wealthy live isolated from the rest of society; most people will have no contact with this small economic elite, nor will they ever have any sense of what that elite controls. Also, our mass media do not express many facts related to this issue, either at all or with the emphasis, detail or repetition that many far less important issues receive.

As part of an international study by scholars at the Harvard Business School and Thailand's Chulalongkorn University, a U.S. survey revealed that Americans estimate that the ratio of CEO pay to median worker pay is about 30 to 1. In reality, the average S&P 500 company CEO earned 354 times what the median U.S. worker did in 2012. Americans said that ideally that gap would be 6.7 to 1.

Performance bonuses, stock options, and exorbitant salaries are tax deductible, so taxpayers are subsidizing the CEO pay gap. And CEOs routinely receive performance incentives even when they fail to hit the productivity targets that were supposed to trigger the bonuses. How does this happen? The corporate CEO compensation process in public companies CEOs commonly strongly influence, directly, or indirectly, through allied board members. Also, dozens of the largest American corporations routinely set performance targets for huge bonuses so low that they're effectively meaningless.[16]

Media "pundits" often express the view that American voters care little about inequality, but to the degree this is true, it is mainly due to the fact most Americans don't realize how extreme inequality is. Today's public policy rests on a foundation of ignorance. A large majority of Americans have no idea what our society is really like.

Now, one-third the U.S. population is either in poverty or low-income (less than two times the poverty level income) and one-fifth are food insecure.

Our national definition of poverty is not generous. In 2015, the official poverty line for a family of four was $24,250, or $6,062 per person per year, or $505 per month.

Food insecure households are those in which some days there is not enough money to purchase food needed to maintain normal activity levels or health. The percentage of Americans saying they did not have money for food they needed at least once in the 12 months prior to a Gallup poll more than doubled from 9% in 2008 to 20% in 2013. (6% of Chinese in 2011 said the same, down significantly from 16% in 2008.)[17] Certainly, most of these people could not buy food many more times than once over the prior 12 months.

Official government statistics have 14.3% of U.S. households food insecure for the same time period. However, this statistic excludes households in their category "marginal food security." This category has as part of its definition "Households had problems at times ...accessing adequate food, but the quality, variety, and quantity of their food intake were not substantially reduced." If people have problems at times accessing adequate food they are food insecure, therefore the Gallup poll statistic is a better measure of the true level of food insecurity.

Researchers from the Harvard School of Public Health, Brandeis University, and Loyola University, in an update of their report *The Economic Cost of Domestic Hunger* calculated the direct and indirect cost of adverse health, education, and economic productivity outcomes associated with hunger as $167.5 billion for 2010. They also found that expanding the Supplemental Nutrition Assistance Program to all food insecure households would cost about $83 billion a year. Our nation pays $84 billion more per year for hunger to exist than we would pay to eliminate it.

Fifty-one percent of Americans experience poverty at some time before age 65.[18] But our official definition of poverty does not expose the true number of Americans in extreme economic hardship. The National Center for Children in Poverty at Columbia University estimated in 2008 that *"families typically need an income of at least twice the official poverty level ($42,400 for a family of four) to meet basic needs."* The Economic Policy Institute has also determined that although the income to meet basic needs depends on local living costs it averages 2.4 times the official poverty income.[19] According to a University of Massachusetts study, the share of prime working-age adults who can't generate enough income to meet their basic needs shot up from 31% in 2000 to 38% in 2010.[20] In the years leading up to the recession, the bottom 80% of the American population had been spending around 110% of its income.[21]

The average income of the bottom 20% in 2011 was $9,187, while the average income of about the top 1.7 million households was $1,530,773, and one person had an income of $4.9 billion—he paid a tax rate lower than the average schoolteacher.[22]

The tax, regulation and government expenditure policies created by a political system determine how an economic system functions. If we had a functioning democracy, the best interests of the majority would be served by the economic system through the political system. What polls indicate most people consider the "ideal" wealth and income distributions would not only be possible; it would not be possible for ones significantly different from them to exist in a well-functioning democracy.

The graph on the left compares the income gains from 1980 to 2008 of the top 1% to the bottom 90%. The graph on the right shows that the middle and lower classes have done poorly relative to the upper class since 1970. Middle class is defined as those with an income 67% to 200% (two-thirds to double) of the overall median household income after incomes have been adjusted for household size (totals not equal to 100% due to rounding).

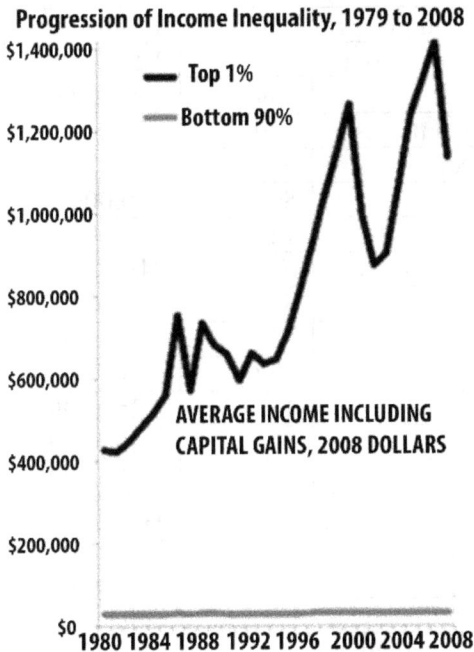

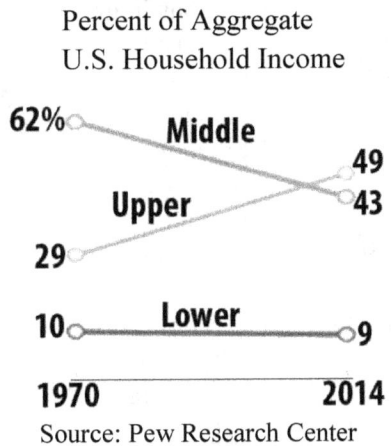

Progression of Income Inequality, 1979 to 2008

— Top 1%
— Bottom 90%

AVERAGE INCOME INCLUDING CAPITAL GAINS, 2008 DOLLARS

Percent of Aggregate U.S. Household Income

62% Middle 49
Upper 43
29
10 Lower 9

1970   2014

Source: Pew Research Center

Greater economic disparities exist now than before the Enlightenment, as the table shows, for income inequality. The first three columns of the table include data from Gregory King's classic early study of British income inequality that published the information on 26 classes of persons in England and Wales in 1688. The fourth column is calculated by multiplying the first and third columns.

Income Distribution in 17th Century Britain

Number of Families in Class	Class	Yearly Income Per Family (£)	Total Income in Class
160	Temporal lords	3,200	512,000
26	Spiritual lords	1,300	33,800
800	Baronets	880	704,000
600	Knights	650	390,000
3000	Esquires	450	1,350,000
2000	Eminent merchants & traders by sea	400	800,000
12000	Gentlemen	280	3,360,000
5000	Persons in greater offices and places	240	1,200,000
8000	Lesser merchants and traders by sea	198	1,584,000
10000	Persons in the law	154	1,540,000
5000	Persons in lesser offices and places	120	600,000
40000	Freeholders of the better sort	91	3,640,000
5000	Naval officers	80	400,000
2000	Eminent clergymen	72	144,000
15000	Persons in liberal arts and sciences	60	900,000
4000	Military officers	60	240,000
120000	Freeholders of the lesser sort	55	6,600,000
8000	Lesser clergymen	50	400,000
50,000	Shopkeepers and tradesmen	45	2,250,000
150000	Farmers	42	6,300,000
60000	Artisans and handicrafts	38	2,280,000
50000	Common seamen	20	1,000,000
364000	Laboring people and out-servants	15	5,460,000
35000	Common soldiers	14	490,000
40000	Cottagers and paupers	6	240,000
30000	Vagrants, beggars, gypsies, thieves and prostitutes (per head)	2	60,000

Medieval Britain Income Inequality Summary and Analysis with a Comparison to Income Inequality in 2011:

	Medieval Britain	2011 U.S.
Maximum household income	3,200(£)	$4.9 billion (hedge fund manager John Paulson)
Median household income	38(£)	$51,413
Ratio of maximum income to median	84.2 to 1	95,307
Top 400 highest income household's average income	1835(£)	$202,400,000
Ratio of top 400 average income to median	48 to 1	3,937
The highest 1%'s income percent of all income	11.3%	24%

INCOME INEQUALITY IS FAR MORE EXTREME NOW THAN IN MEDIEVAL TIMES.

Economic inequality was one of the most important motivations for the Enlightenment period's societal transformations—one compelling reason for a New Enlightenment. And as you will see, more reasons exist. Political inequality also motivated Enlightenment revolutions and our public policies bear almost no relationship to the preferences of the poor and the middle class.

Adam Smith was one of the key figures of the Scottish Enlightenment, and he is widely considered the father of modern economics. His work was important to many other very influential thinkers, including David Ricardo and Karl Marx in the nineteenth century and John Maynard Keynes and Milton Friedman in the twentieth. Smith's "An Inquiry into the Nature and Causes of the Wealth of Nations" (1776) is one of the most influential books ever written. In it he wrote:

"Wherever there is great property there is great inequality. For one very rich man there must be at least five hundred poor, and the affluence of the few supposes the indigence of the many."

"All for ourselves, and nothing for other people, seems, in every age of the world, to have been the vile maxim of the masters of mankind."[23]

"Our merchants and masters complain much of the bad effects of high wages in raising the price and lessening the sale of goods. They say nothing concerning the bad effects of high profits. They are silent with regard to the

pernicious effects of their own gains. They complain only of those of other people."

Societies require systems that moderate tendencies for distributions of wealth and income to be highly skewed toward a small economic elite.

The term "economist" did not exist in the time of Adam Smith. He considered himself to be a moral philosopher dedicated to understanding ways for society to be organized to best serve the majority of people and the ideal of justice.

People should be taxed *"as nearly as possible, in proportion to their respective abilities; that is, in proportion to the revenue which they respectively enjoy under the protection of the state."* Taxation should *"remedy inequality of riches as much as possible, by relieving the poor and burdening the rich."* Adam Smith

Smith maintained that sharing the feelings of others as closely as possible is ideally one of our main drives in life. The meaning of his famous "invisible hand" reference has been grotesquely distorted to justify individual greed as the driving force within society.

Good governments in the past have controlled, through the regulatory and tax systems, extreme economic disparities. They instituted policies to create and maintain a large and prosperous middle class. Now our government has lost its capacity to do so to a large and growing degree.

From 1936 to 1980, the top marginal tax rate was between 70% and 94%, and the average was 82%. Now it is 39.6%. When the U.S. occupied Japan and Germany and set up new democratic governments, it set a top marginal tax rate of 85 and 90% respectively, as part of the civilizing and democratizing process. U.S. top rates were 91% at the time. We knew then that concentrated income and wealth creates undemocratic and unjust societies, like aristocratic "Old Europe."

Higher top tax rates are correlated historically with higher growth, contrary to the claims of so-called supply-side economists. They are also associated with periods of lower *before* tax top incomes and the wider sharing of prosperity. When top tax rates are high, executives have less motive to bargain for exorbitant compensation since the government will receive most of the gains (to use to serve wider public interests). When upper management takes a smaller portion of corporate income, workers can take a larger portion.

The average S&P 500 CEO's pay was 27 times the median worker's pay in 1973, even then arguably an unreasonable and unjust disparity. The 354 times the median worker's pay in 2012 that CEOs received represents a gain of 1,211% in share of median pay. Some CEOs receive hundreds of millions of dollars per year in compensations, and most S&P 500 CEOs receive well over $10 million per year. The CEO of the country's largest health insurer, United Health Care, received $109 million in compensation in 2009. Is this where our health care dollars should go, rather than healing the sick? In 2012, JC Penney's CEO received 1,795 times its average worker's pay and benefits.

Public corporations' CEO compensations are determined either by the executives themselves or by the board of directors' corporate compensation committees, whose members, in many corporations, the CEO has considerable power to choose, and who usually earn comparable salaries (as senior executives of other large corporations).

Directors of large corporations have a very lucrative part-time job. Meeting just three or four times per year, the average S&P 500 director was paid $251,000 in 2012, so they are highly motivated to be generous to the CEO, who to nominates directors.[24] Sometimes executives sit on one another's compensation committees. Sometimes, executives are members of the committee that determines their pay. Since it is impossible to give a precise estimate of each manager's contribution to the firm's output, inevitably, a system determining compensations that uses closely aligned associates benefiting from each other's generosity will yield extreme compensations. The size of which is only limited by cultural norms and the high degree of freedom of those involved to serve their interests. Cultural norms now, instead of restraining the growth in top management pay, as they once did, encourage it, so they have exploded.

The great majority (60% to 70%) of the top 0.1% of the income hierarchy consists of top managers.[25] Adam Smith's "invisible hand" metaphor has been interpreted to mean (incorrectly) that markets result in beneficial and just outcomes without the intent of the participants. However, senior executive's income can more appropriately be described as resulting from having their "invisible hands in the till,"[26] than described using Adam Smith's "invisible hand" metaphor as it has been interpreted. This is a better metaphor because the process is an obscured taking of money from others, in this case, other stakeholders, without their permission.

Our corporate governance laws do not require firms to give shareholders a say in management compensation, which would normally be expected since they own the firm. This would, as would higher top tax rates, be a restraint on the explosion of executive salaries.

The relatively low top income tax rates and capital gains rates now result from influence on our political system, media, and even on segments of academia, by the wealthy to serve their interests. To compensate for the reduced taxes on the rich, taxes have been increased on the middle class and the poor, government services and investments have been cut, and the government has had to borrow vast amounts of money, mainly from the wealthy.

The George W. Bush tax cuts alone, which mostly benefited the wealthy, reduced federal revenue by $1.9 trillion just between 2002 and 2011. The decade's long trend of reducing taxes on the wealthy has reduced revenue far more, creating an enormous national debt and starving the government of the resources needed to support public services, including the maintenance of our infrastructure, sometimes with catastrophic results. For example:

Most people think of the Hurricane Katrina disaster as one of the worst natural disasters in our history, but it was not. 1,500 people died, close to $100 billion in damage resulted, and whole neighborhoods were wiped out in one of America's most historic cities.[27] It was primarily not a natural disaster, though, it was a disaster caused by our economic and political systems. Most of the tragedy occurred when levees in New Orleans failed *after* the storm had passed because the levees collapsed, which caused most of the flooding. The levees were known to be in poor repair so allocating inadequate resources for the levee system caused most of the destruction.

A higher concentration of the poor lived in flood prone areas than in other parts of the city. The Lower Ninth Ward, with a poverty rate of 36%— three times the national average at the time—was especially vulnerable and was devastated. Even though there were several days of warning, thousands of the poor could not flee because they lacked a car, money for a motel room, or friends and family in safe locations. Then when the levees collapsed, the world saw the depths of poverty in which these people were living. They also were shocked by the awareness that in the wealthiest country in the world there was extreme neglect of our public infrastructure, and neglect of our professed ideals of justice, equality for all, and basic individual human rights. Even reason was neglected since reasonable actions would have made the disaster far less costly to everyone, not just the poor.

What defines a society is a set of mutual benefits and duties. Public schools, public libraries, public transportation, public hospitals, public parks, public museums, public recreation, and public universities provide some of these mutual benefits, but increasingly we are ignoring the duty to publicly support these institutions. Even some of our public highways and public bridges are trending toward effectively being "privatized" with new or higher tolls.

As we withdraw public funds, public schools and roadways deteriorate, public playgrounds and pools decay, public hospitals decline, and fees increase for people to access some public goods (publicly provided services or things for the shared benefit of all members of a society). This trend is progressing as an increasing amount of the country's income and wealth is going to a small elite, so the rest of society is increasingly unable to support these public goods. This elite is controlling the political system to withdraw their support also because they send their kids to private schools, buy memberships in private tennis and swimming clubs, pay premium rates for private health care, and substitute other private goods for public goods.

In a report of a study led by the nation's leading scholar of residential segregation, Princeton's Douglas Massey, he summarized the findings this way: *"During the late twentieth century... the well-educated and the affluent increasingly segmented themselves off from the rest of American society"* by residing where they are surrounded by the similarly privileged. Robert Reich, Chancellor's Professor of Public Policy, UC Berkeley, and former U.S. Secretary of Labor labeled this trend *"the secession of the successful."*

Massey's study used incomes at least four times the federal poverty threshold to define affluence. Since this income was within the top few deciles, segregation of the affluent so defined from the poor, though extreme and growing, is far from complete. But the more extremely affluent have almost entirely segregated themselves from just about everyone not as rich as themselves.[28]

Tocqueville observed a very different America in the 19th century:

"In the United States, the more opulent citizens take great care not to stand aloof from the people. On the contrary, they constantly keep on easy terms with the lower classes: they listen to them, they speak to them every day."

Today, the opposite is true. And the proportion of the upper class that is third generation upper class is growing. With that increase has come increasing ignorance of the experiences and concerns of the people in the world outside their bubble. This is the essence of the major part of our political, economic and social problems because this small economic elite is using their power to determine the political, economic and social course of the country to serve their narrow interests to a large and increasing degree. The mass media have major impact on the social course of the country, and its control by this small and segregated economic elite is an important obstacle to needed social reforms.

Without good public schools, affordable higher education, good roads, adequate health care for everyone and other public goods, societal dysfunction and decay is inevitable. Outside of defense, domestic discretionary spending is down sharply as a percent of the economy. With declines in state and local spending, total public spending on education, infrastructure, and basic research dropped from 12% of GDP in the 1970s to less than 3% by 2011.[29] This decline can be reversed only using funds that our economic system is directing to a small segment of the population. A dysfunctional political system that has allowed them to succeed in influencing government to reduce their taxes needs fundamental reforms.

Most of the income of the very wealthy we tax at the much lower capital gains rate than the labor rate. From 2003 to 2012 this tax rate was 15%. In 2013 it was raised to 20% for people in the 39.6% income tax bracket, still far below the labor tax rate. The inequality in capital gains is far greater than that in any other form of income, so giving a tax break to capital gains is giving a tax break to the very rich. The bottom 90% of income earners get less than 10% of all capital gains. The top 1% get almost half of all capital gains. The four hundred highest-income taxpayers in 2007, each with an average income of over $300 million, paid only 17% of their total incomes in taxes that year because most of their incomes were treated as capital gains when the capital gains rate was 15% and the top labor tax rate was 35%. Only 8.8% of the top 400's income came from wages.[30]

The lower capital gains tax rate is not economically justified. No correlation exists between lower capital gains rates and higher growth historically.[31] It serves the interests of the wealthy, not society. To compound this injustice, about half of all capital gains are never subject to tax because the capital gains tax is forgiven at death. If a taxpayer holds onto an asset until he or she dies, neither the taxpayer's estate nor the heirs pay the tax.

Our tax system has grown more regressive over the last few decades. An income tax is regressive if it takes the same percentage of income from everyone regardless of income. Progressive taxation is widely accepted as a superior way to fund government services because it takes a progressively higher percentage of income based on the ability to pay or the size of income. All developed countries use progressive taxation for economic and moral reasons.

An extensive international study using data from the Gallup World Poll found that respondents living in a nation with more progressive taxation evaluated their lives as being closer to the best possible life, and they reported having more positive and fewer negative daily experiences than did respondents living in a nation with less progressive taxation. The association between more progressive taxation and higher levels of subjective well-being was mediated by citizens' satisfaction with public goods, such as education and public transportation, that was provided by the funds generated by the tax system.[32]

Our payroll tax would be regressive solely for the reason that only one tax rate is levied on incomes. But a further injustice has compounded this injustice. The 6.2% Social Security portion of this tax is levied only on the first $113,700 of income. The top four hundred people whose average income was $202.4 million in 2011 paid not the same percentage of their income in tax, but the same amount of tax as someone making $113,700. They paid less than 0.0035% while everyone with incomes $113,700 or less paid 6.2%, or greater than 1,780 times the percentage that people paid whose average income was $202.4 million. We need to invent a stronger word than "regressive" for this tax. How about "retrogressive"? Democratic governance is intended to serve the interests of the majority. Do we have democratic governance?

Corporations are hoarding a record $4.75 trillion that is not being used productively; in the third quarter of 2012 corporate earnings were $1.75 trillion. While making something on the order of $200 million each, six American families paid no federal income tax in 2009.[33] Meanwhile, we cut government services, exploded the deficit and left 23.2 million people unemployed.[34] Would these conditions exist if wealthy and powerful corporations and the wealthy individuals who are their primary investors did not have a disproportionate influence on government policy?

The graph on the following page displays what has happened regarding sources of government revenue since 1950. The graph uses the term "employment taxes" instead of the more commonly used term "payroll taxes" that I have used. As the graph shows, there has been a rise in the share of federal revenue supplied by the extremely regressive payroll tax by several multiples, from about 10% to 40%, while there has been about a proportionately huge fall in the share of federal revenue from corporate taxes, from about 30 to 6%.

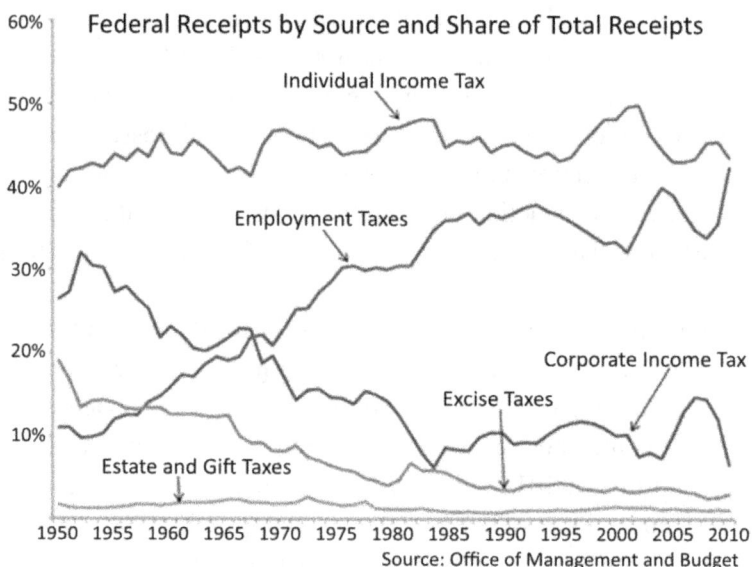

Federal Receipts by Source and Share of Total Receipts

Source: Office of Management and Budget

The Excesses of the Plutocrats of 2012

In our 1920's, historic concentrations of wealth and income in a small economic elite and a kind of plutocracy existed in the United States. Their enormous inequalities played an important role in creating the 1929-1939 Great Depression and its New Deal response that greatly reduced inequality and resulted in relatively stable economic growth for decades.

Although wealth and income concentration in terms of percent are similar today as in the 1920s, we are a much wealthier country now, so the wealth and income of our "plutocrats" (which for the following purpose I define as the top 1%) is much larger.

If the average member of our top 1% in 2012 would have limited himself to the same amount of wealth and income (inflation adjusted) as the average plutocrat of 1928, for example, and the total of the excess above this amount that they actually received were distributed to the rest of the nation, 99% of the population would have had $16.1 trillion more in wealth and $2.48 trillion more in income.[35]

All students in public colleges paid $125 billion in tuition in the 2012-2013 academic year. If the excess $2.48 trillion income of our plutocrats were used instead to make college tuition free for students, $2.35 trillion would have remained. If this remaining portion of the nation's income were progressively distributed (the poorest receiving the most) to households in the bottom

80% in income, on average, they each would have had $24,325 more income. Consider the following as a way to understand the significance of this additional $24,325 in income:

The BLS's 2012 Consumer Expenditure Survey shows that mean per household cost per year for food was $6,599; health care, $3,556; transportation, $8,998; apparel and services, $1,736; electricity, 1,388; natural gas, fuel oil, other fuels, $496; water, other public services, $525.[36] These costs for the most important necessities of life, excluding shelter, total $23,298—$1,027 less than the $24,325.

What about shelter? Most people prefer owning their own home. If you buy a home with cash, it's a one-time, not annual, expenditure, but the 2012 median house value of $153,000 is a large amount of cash.[37] If the $16.1 trillion excess wealth in the top 1% were progressively distributed within the bottom 80% of households in wealth, on average, each would have received $166,230—$13,230 more than needed to buy a median value home. This remaining $13,230 is almost three times the median American's retirement savings, which is $5,000![38]

If the bottom 80% of households had $24,325 more income and $166,230 more wealth, on average, and students did not accumulate another $125 billion in debt (that now totals $1.2 trillion), far more goods and services would have been purchased, so GDP would have been substantially larger and unemployment substantially lower. And the adults receiving much more money would have better been able to support children and save for retirement.

The excesses of modern-day plutocrats continue to grow. However, the wealth and income of our top 1% would not exist if they did not live in a society with well-functioning public systems and a vast commonly inherited knowledge base that is a powerful social resource. So it is not just up to them to decide whether or not they will accept "only" the huge amounts of income and wealth of the plutocrats of the 1920's. (I discuss in some detail the important impact of the social resource side of the partnership in which we all participate to create wealth in Part 4, Note 1.) We are in a democratic society where systemic issues that impact the lives of everyone we all should decide on democratically.

As a result of the New Deal, and the ideals it established for subsequent policymakers, we raised taxes on top incomes as high as 94% as one of the policies that reduced inequality. New Deal policies began in 1933 and their impact began in 1934. In the 20 years from 1934 to 1953 GDP growth rates averaged 6.42% and top tax rates averaged 83.2%. From 2005 to 2015, growth rates averaged 1.75%, and top tax rates averaged 35.9%.[39]

The New Enlightenment policies would not result in limiting the average wealth and income of our top 1% to that of the plutocrats of 1928. Like today it would be a few multiples larger, just somewhat reduced due to higher top income tax rates and a wealth tax. But this reduction will be substantially moderated (or eliminated) due to the resulting improved national economic conditions.

Inequality & Hardship Grows as Economic Mobility Declines

America's gross national income of $16.4 trillion in 2013 makes it the wealthiest nation in the history of the world. Over the course of the twentieth century alone, real (adjusted for inflation) income per capita increased roughly eightfold. A system that would divide national income equally would be unjust and harmful to national economic performance. But a limit exists on how large inequalities can grow before the system creating them is also unjust and harmful to national economic performance. To get a sense of how unequally our economic system distributes national income, consider: If it were divided equally among all employed persons, including those working part-time, each person would have earned $115,520 per year, or their annual work-hours could have been cut in half with their income reduced on average to $57,760.[40] This is over two times the median personal income of $28,030 in 2013.

Huge increases in the income of corporate managers and major shareholders of corporations are the main drivers of the rapidly rising income disparity. Capital income for the wealthiest 1% of Americans has risen enormously, from about 31% to 54% of national capital income, as the following graph shows.

Among the upper 1%, the real winners are the upper 0.1%, whose share of national income increased from 3.1% (1972) to 11.3% (2012). Had the share of the upper 0.1% remained as it was 30 years prior, the income for all other Americans, including the rest of the upper 1%, would have increased by about 8% in the last three decades.[41] If the income distribution were the same as it was in 1979, families in the bottom 80% of the income distribution would make $11,000 more per year, on average, than they're earning today.[42]

Capital income, the income from stocks and bonds dividends and interest, of the country's top 400 taxpayers, who make up .00028% of all persons filing individual tax returns, even more clearly displays a country out of balance. In 2013, the 400 households earned 5.3% of all dividend income and 11.2% of all income from sales of capital assets.[43]

Increasing share of income from wealth claimed by top 1 percent

Concentration of capital incomes, by income group, 1979–2010

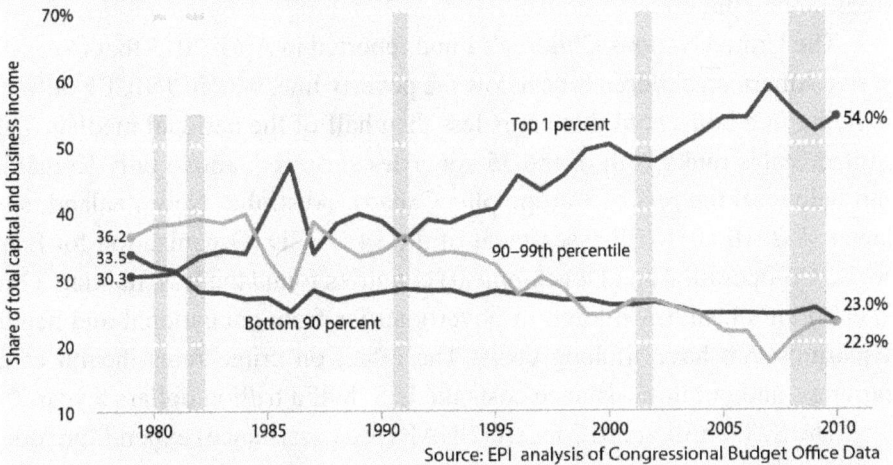

Source: EPI analysis of Congressional Budget Office Data

Economic gains are far more top-heavy than these numbers indicate because the vast majority of the top's gains are not taken as income. They are held in appreciated asset values that income statistics do not reveal, so extreme wealth inequality is growing far larger.

From the end of the recession in 2009 through 2011, the wealthiest 7% of households saw their aggregate wealth rise by about $5.6 trillion, while the rest of us saw aggregate wealth decline by about $669 billion.[44]

Extreme and rising inequality is transforming our political and economic system, from one that created a broad middle class to a feudal society dominated by a small number of super-wealthy "lords of the manor."

The truth of Adam Smith's statement that great wealth in the possession of a few implies great inequality and the indigence of the many is being demonstrated in modern America:

Our nation's families in poverty do not cluster just below the poverty threshold. 44% have incomes of less than half the poverty line. In our wealthy nation, more than one in seven live in poverty, but even more shocking; one in sixteen are "severely poor," or live in "deep poverty," and their ranks have been growing for decades. During the pre-recession 2000-2005 period, the number of the severely poor grew by 26%, over 50% faster than the overall population in poverty. Since then, the recession has caused the growth of the population of the severely poor to increase 28% to 20.4 million in 2012. A higher percentage of Americans are severely poor now than at any time since the government has kept records, starting in 1975. Almost 7% are severely poor, but children's likelihood of living in severe poverty is far worse—10% are in severe poverty.

The United Nations Children's Fund reported in April 2013 that over one in five American children falls below the poverty line, which UNICEF defines as living in a household that earns less than half of the national median. The United States ranks 34th of the 35 countries surveyed, above only Romania and below all the rest of Europe plus Canada, Australia, New Zealand, and Japan. A 2010 UNICEF assessment of the 34 OECD (Organization for Economic Co-operation and Development) countries found the U.S. ranking 22nd in children's health. Children in poverty suffer from educational and health disparities that have lifelong costs. The effect on crime rates, health care, earnings, and public assistance costs the U.S. half a trillion dollars a year.[45]

The $78.4 billion 2012 federal SNAP (food assistance) expenditure does not meet the needs—almost 40 million Americans depend on food pantries to live. Meanwhile, just 20 rich Americans made as much on their investments in 2012 as the entire 2013 SNAP budget that serves 47 million people.[46] The 400 wealthiest increased their wealth by an amount more than the total amount spent on all federal food, housing and education programs, plus veterans' disability and healthcare programs combined.[47]

A kind of large "tax" substantially increases the burdens of the poor. The lack of savings and the need for immediate access to cash for survival needs forces many to use the services of greedy payday lenders, check cashers, and subprime high-interest lenders. These and other excess costs for services and goods for about forty million low income households results in an average "poverty tax" on their income of around 10%.[48]

Our poverty statistics for African Americans and Latinos should be even more alarming to a nation expressing the ideal of justice for all. 25.3% of Latinos (one in four) live in poverty, 10.5% in deep poverty; and 27.6% of African Americans (10.9 million) live in poverty, 12.8% in deep poverty. 39% of African American children and 32% of Latino children live in poverty.[49]

Poverty in America not only robs people of adequate or decent food, it also forces many people out of their homes, and homelessness is especially harmful to children. One in 45, or over 1.6 million, children experience homelessness in America each year.[50] While homeless, they experience high rates of acute and chronic health problems. The constant barrage of stressful and traumatic experience also has profound effects on their development and ability to learn. The Children's Defense Fund's 2014 annual report *The State of America's Children* revealed that 1.2 million public school students were homeless in 2011-2012, 73% more than before the recession. A study conducted by the U.S. Conference of Mayors found that 12 of the 23 cities surveyed had to turn away people needing shelter, due to a lack of capacity. The National Law Center on Homelessness and Poverty states that approximately 3.5 million people experience homelessness in a given year.

We all know that the 2008 financial crisis was economically devastating to many millions of Americans and caused many bankruptcies and foreclosures, forcing millions from their homes, but these signs of serious economic system dysfunction existed and were growing well before the devastating financial crisis. Personal bankruptcies rose from fewer than 300,000 in 1980 to two million in 2005, and home mortgage foreclosures increased fivefold between the early 1970s and 2005.[51] From 2006 to 2014 there were over 22 million foreclosure filings.[52]

How can any reasonable person believe that the structure of a society and economic system that creates these results cannot and should not be radically improved?

What do these statistics mean in terms of real human lives?

- Hundreds of homeless wait outside the Star Hope Homeless Mission in Houston, and when they reach the two hundred limit hundreds are turned away to spend the night on the street.
- People who cannot afford sufficient food to feed their families camp in the cold overnight at San Jose's Sacred Heart Community Service food pantry to be sure to get food before the food bank runs out. Some bring their small children and a tent. A 2009 Feeding America survey found that 55% of food banks had to turn people away in the prior year.[53]
- Thirty-five hundred people in Wise, West Virginia, wait as long as fourteen hours for medical care from the Remote Area Medical Corp., an organization that once served only the desperately poor in Third World countries and now operates in the United States.

Since Adam Smith's time, productivity (the amount of goods and services produced per man-hour) has increased enormously due to knowledge and technological advancements, making per capita income and wealth proportionately enormously greater here, in his country, and throughout the developed world. During some of this period, we more equitably shared these gains. In the mid-1970s, a disconnection began between productivity growth and nonsupervisory wage growth, as this graph displays:

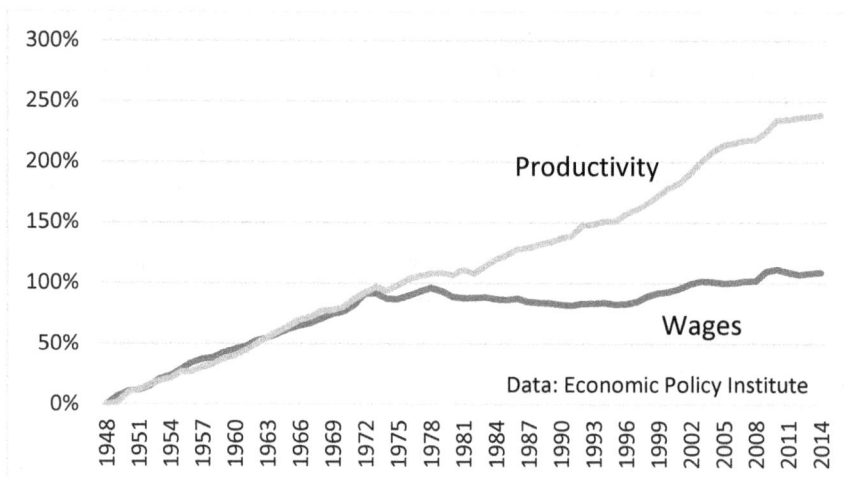

Since workers produce about double the goods and services per hour, isn't it reasonable to expect to earn at least close to double in wages than in 1979? Instead, median wages are about the same, and the median wage of a male worker is down 7%.[54]

Imagine the difference in your life and the country if wages doubled with the rising productivity. *The resulting vast increase in national income and wealth went to just a small economic elite.*

From 1981 to 2008, 96% of the income gains in the U.S. went to the top 10%. The bottom 90% shared 4%.[55] This period had a $7.2 trillion or 120% increase in real GDP. From 1997 to 2008, all the income gains in the U.S. went to the top 10%. The bottom 90% lost income. This period had a $3.3 trillion or 34% increase in real GDP. Most of the gains in GDP result from the increase in average worker productivity, which almost doubled since 1981 (up 93.4%),[56] yet 90% of the workforce has benefited little from the great advances that are responsible for the productivity gains.

Government policies played a major role in this injustice, yet our policy-makers continue to avoid dealing with this injustice constructively, while it grows. From 2009 to 2011 the bottom 99% lost income. GDP gains over this recovery period, though, were about $1.3 trillion, but since the bottom 99% lost income, effectively 121% of the income gains went to the top 1%. The top 10% share of income in 2012 was equal to 50.4% of all U.S. income, a level higher than 1928.[57] The great economic disparity then was an important part of the systemic failures that caused the 1929-39 Great Depression, as ours was in the systemic failures causing our Great Recession.

Economic expansions are supposed to be the good times, the periods in which incomes and living standards improve. But who benefits from rising incomes in an expansion has changed drastically over the last 60 years, with progressively less benefit, and in the most recent expansion a loss, to the bottom 90%. A Bard College economist created the following graph that vividly shows that "trickle down" economics is more appropriately called "trickle drown" economics for the bottom 90%.

Distribution of Average Income Growth during Expansions

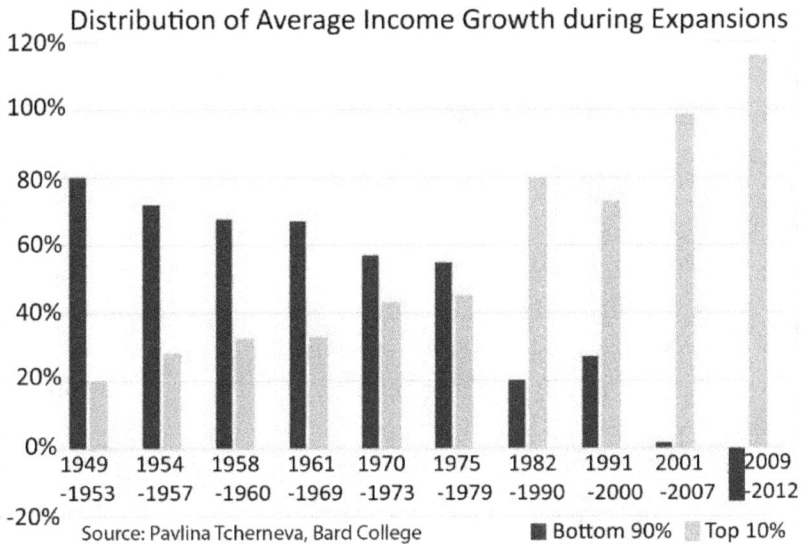

Source: Pavlina Tcherneva, Bard College   ■ Bottom 90% ▒ Top 10%

The United States has a record level of inequality of income from labor, probably higher than in any other society at any time in the past, anywhere in the world. This includes societies in which skill disparities were extremely large, such as those with an educated class and a large fraction of the population illiterate. We have greater labor income disparities than what existed in apartheid South Africa, and India when it had a large illiterate portion of its population with a small educated class.[58]

Our income inequality is also substantially larger than official statistics indicate because large amounts of capital income are directed to tax havens, and substantial amounts of capital income that are tax-exempt are not reported, so are not included in the income tax records. These records are generally the source of income statistics. Tax-exempt capital income would substantially raise income inequality measures if accounted for. It would likely add about 2 percent to the top 1 percent's share of national income.

Household wealth reached $77.3 trillion in September 2013.[59] This is $657,000, or about two-thirds of a million dollars' average wealth per U.S. household, while the poorest 40% had a total wealth less than zero. A recent Federal Reserve survey found that 47% of respondents either could not cover an emergency expense costing $400 or would cover it by selling something or borrowing money.[60] Wealth inequality is even more extreme than income inequality and is more rapidly growing. Between 2010 and 2013, average incomes for the bottom fifth dropped 8%; average wealth dropped 21%.[61]

Analysis of hundreds of years of historical evidence shows that the rate of return to capital generally exceeds the growth rate of the economy.[62] This results in exponentially increasing inequalities of wealth and income as income from capital grows at an exponentially faster rate than income from labor. Only two world wars and the Great Depression interrupted the process through both the destruction of capital and radical policy changes, much of which have been undone. The top 1% now has more investment capital or financial wealth (total net worth minus the value of one's home) than the bottom 95% combined.[63] Growing economic disparities will now continue to proceed with terrifying results unless we interrupt it again with vigorous public policy solutions, ideally of a more effective, systemic, and therefore more enduring character, such as those I will describe in Parts 2 and 3.

Equality of educational opportunity, although not sufficient, is one of the most powerful converging forces for reducing our extreme and diverging economic disparities. On average, the higher a person's educational attainment, the higher the income and the lower the likelihood of being unemployed. Our country is now abdicating its responsibility to serve one of its most important stated ideals of equality of opportunity by erecting huge financial barriers to a college education. Over the last few decades, states have been withdrawing public support for higher education and raising tuitions.

This problem has grown more rapidly since the recession. Many people now are deciding not to get a college education for financial reasons, and those that choose college often leave with overwhelming debt. The student debt total of over $1.2 trillion is more than the total national credit card debt.

Education not only benefits society by creating a workforce that creates wealth, pays taxes, and needs fewer government services, it also allows people to be more informed and effective participants in a democracy. Unjust barriers to education will harm our economy and democracy for many years into the future. The United States is now ranked twelfth internationally in the percentage of young people with college degrees, an area where we once led the world. Fewer than 60% who start college finish with degrees, often for financial reasons.

For most of our history, America was known as the land of opportunity. If you were poor or born into a poor family, your chances of rising to high income or wealth were greater here than anywhere else in the world. Now, if you are poor or born into a poor family, your chances of staying poor through-out your life are higher in the United States than in any other advanced country, except possibly the UK (some sources report the U.S. with lower economic mobility than the UK).

"If Americans want to live the American dream, they should go to Denmark." Richard Wilkinson, whose research demonstrated a strong correlation between inequality and social and health problems, made this statement, and for good reason: upward mobility is the essence of the American dream, and as the graph shows, Denmark has the highest income mobility.

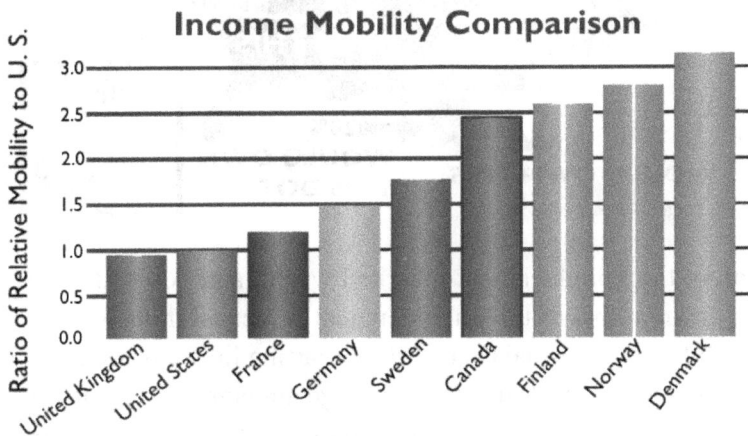

Income Mobility Comparison

Ratio of Relative Mobility to U. S.

| United Kingdom | United States | France | Germany | Sweden | Canada | Finland | Norway | Denmark |

Source: Pew Charitable Trust Economic Mobility Project

Inequality of opportunity is demonstrated using the extreme example of the Walmart dynasty. The six heirs of Walmart have wealth of $145 billion, greater than the bottom 42% of the U.S. population, or 133 million people combined. Walmart's profits ($28 billion in 2013) and its major owner's wealth is made through the unfair compensation of the essential labor of the many low wage Walmart workers. This abuses the workers and taxpayers, since many of their workers cannot survive on Walmart's wages, so they need food, housing, energy and health care subsidies to survive.

The fact that six heirs can inherit a dynasty of this much wealth and power is one of the most devastating indictments of our economic and political systems. These six heirs did nothing exceptional, except get born into their extraordinary circumstances, and a large fraction of their wealth results from paying a large fraction of their workforce below a living wage.

The Walmart heirs are just one extreme example of a growing trend. A study by the Boston College Center on Wealth and Philanthropy projects that $36 trillion will be passed down to heirs from 2011 to 2061. This will create a new aristocracy with unprecedented wealth, and therefore power.

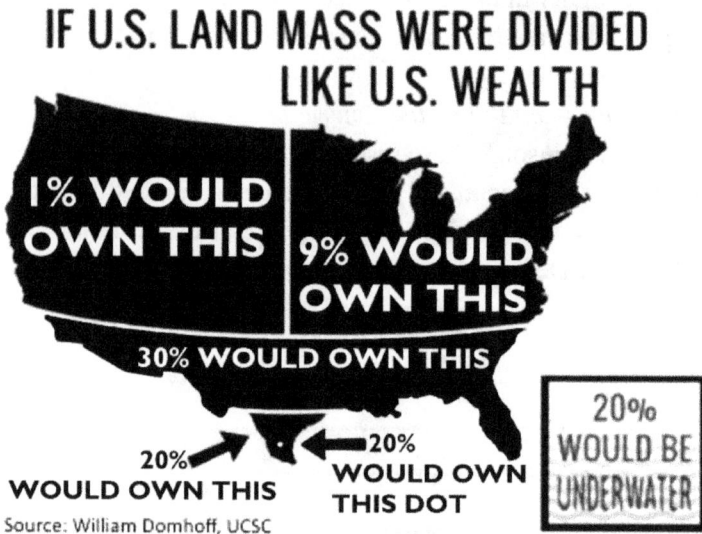

IF U.S. LAND MASS WERE DIVIDED LIKE U.S. WEALTH

1% WOULD OWN THIS

9% WOULD OWN THIS

30% WOULD OWN THIS

20% WOULD OWN THIS

20% WOULD OWN THIS DOT

20% WOULD BE UNDERWATER

Source: William Domhoff, UCSC

Before the Enlightenment inherited wealth and power dominated. This was the main motive of the Enlightenment's societal transformations. Is the ideal of all having an equal chance at the starting line now gone? It seems we are moving back to the 15th century. Large amounts of inherited wealth and gross concentrations of wealth, inherited or not, characterize aristocratic, not free and democratic societies. The above chart shows a level of wealth disparity that is unjust and a threat to democracy. The combined wealth of the bottom 20% and the next 20% would put 40% underwater, and thus not even on the U.S. map.

An economy and society cannot continue to function indefinitely with social groups that continue to diverge. As is the case with our economic system, signs of severe political system problems are clear. Our political system is becoming increasingly corrupted in the process of advancing the cycle of economic and political system decline.

Political Inequality Grows with Economic Inequality

The U.S. Congress has a 9% approval rating, now reaching a historic low, as it has several times over the last five years. A Gallup poll found that 77% of Americans believe Congress is causing *"serious harm to the country."*[64]

Congresspersons spend over half of their time in office raising money for their next election.[65] Instead of focusing on developing policies to reduce unemployment, poverty, and our huge and unjust economic disparities, on policies to ensure long-term national prosperity, on health care and foreign policy, including wars, elected officials spend most of their time asking for campaign contributions. Much of this time they "dial for dollars"—make phone calls to the wealthy for money. When the people called agree, they then expect their interests to be served—interests commonly not aligned with the public interest.

Only 9% of Americans think Congress is mainly influenced by the voters they represent. Yet in 2012, over 90% were reelected. Clearly, we live in a country with a failed political system.

A 2012 Rasmussen Poll found that 43% of likely voters believe the U.S. Congress would be better chosen through a random selection of members from the pages of a phone book than through our current system, and 19% were unsure.[66] So almost two-thirds of likely voters at least suspect that the "phone book system" beats our current system. This would be an easy, effective and inexpensive way to choose a "representative" legislative body.

Our present legislatures are not truly "representative" in the way a randomly selected legislature would be. Women, for example, constitute 51% of the adult population but comprise only 24% of the 114th Congress. Blacks, Hispanics, and other minorities are also far from proportionately represented. About half of the electorate, which does not vote, could be considered to be completely unrepresented. Slightly over 50% of Congress are millionaires, compared to 4% of U.S. households.[67]

But if you have a clear view of the level of knowledge of politics or public policy of the average person you likely would believe that putting the average person in a powerful governmental position through a random selection process would be unwise. However, in an appropriate environment with access to necessary information, it may be advantageous. And if systems were in place that demonstrated that ordinary people could have a substantial impact on public policy it would probably increase public engagement.

New Enlightenment policy is not for the random selection of our legislature. An elected representative body has value as an institutional arrangement. However, supplementing and assisting our representative legislature with systems that give average citizens substantial influence on policy also has value. Policy 28 details an innovative democratic form which uses randomly selected citizens in policymaking processes, and Policy 30 also opens policymaking processes to the view and participation of average citizens. Other policies remove the need for candidates to raise campaign money.

Our current political system is extraordinarily dysfunctional, largely as a result of our election system. As I noted in the introduction, the most internationally renowned election observer, former President Carter, whose Carter Center has monitored 96 elections in 38 countries, said, "*We have one of the worst election processes in the world right in the United States, and it's almost entirely because of the excessive influx of money... unlimited political bribery [has resulted in] a complete subversion of our political system as a payoff to major contributors.*"

$6.3 billion was spent in the 2012 election. It was the most expensive election in U.S. history by $1.0 billion, until the 2016 election, which is estimated to have cost $6.9 billion.[68] Because of the high cost of elections, elected officials and challengers are forced into the pockets of wealthy "special interests" donors, giving them enormous influence on the direction these policymakers take our nation.

But the essence of the problem is not the large amounts of money required in the election process. It is the source of, and motives behind, the dominant portion of its supply.

Consider the relative social value of the $180 billion spent in 2014 on U.S. advertising to that of "advertising" the policies and character of public office candidates. Procter & Gamble alone spent $4.6 billion mostly on advertising Bounty paper towels, Crest toothpaste, and Tide laundry detergent, arguably products of little distinguishing characteristics worthy of being communicated on limited airwaves of enormous public value. Devoting even more than triple the resources Procter & Gamble does on advertising to our election process would not be unreasonable. New Enlightenment policies do not reduce the resources used in the election process, they change the source of and motives behind its supply.

Because of the Citizens United Supreme Court decision, there was historic spending of approximately $1 billion in the 2012 election by outside groups dominated by a small number of individuals, organizations, and corporations making large contributions. Fewer than 40 donors to these "Political

Action Committees" (PACs) that advocate for or against the election of candidates gave over $200 million to those groups. PAC spending increased from $15 million in 1974 to $546.5 million in 2012, a 3,543% increase.

The 2010 Citizens United Supreme Court decision determined that corporations have the constitutionally guaranteed right to make unlimited contributions to Super PACs, 501(c)(4) "social welfare" nonprofits, and 501(c)(6) trade associations. These organizations can spend unlimited amounts to influence election outcomes, and it is even possible for foreign entities to abuse this decision. 93% of super PACs funding came from 3,318 people—one tenth of one tenth of one tenth of one tenth of one tenth of Americans, or one-hundred thousandth of Americans.[69] Super PACs, which are required by law to operate independently of candidates, often have more money and so more influence over election outcomes than the candidates themselves do. In 2012, over 40% of all campaign spending came from the top .01%, or Americans in the top one ten-thousandth of incomes.

Before Citizens United, the huge financial resources of corporations and wealthy individuals were a corrupting influence on our democracy. Look at the following graphs and decide if the trends indicate that we will no longer have any remnants of a meaningful democracy if we allow them to continue.

The 2014 McCutcheon Supreme Court decision eliminated the $123,000 cap on the amount an individual can contribute to federal candidates and political parties. The Supreme Court seems oblivious to the corruption of our "democracy" by the wealthy resulting from their decisions. If the Supreme Court does not change, their majority view that money is speech, corporations are people, and using large amounts of money to support candidates for public offices' campaigns in exchange for access and influence once elected does not constitute corruption will result in advancing the decline we are experiencing. The semblance of a democracy we once had will further descend into a plutocracy or aristocracy serving elites at the expense of the rest of society. Far more important than changes in the Supreme Court, though, are substantial changes in our Constitution.

A poll performed by Lake Research Partners for the public interest group Public Citizen found that 78% of voters feel that reducing the influence of money in politics and elections is important. Sixty percent think we need major changes or a complete overhaul of our campaign finance laws. Despite the critical importance of this issue to our nation, and widespread awareness of this, no solutions are being seriously considered by policymakers as the problem grows. Part 3 describes policies that would radically beneficially transform our political system, allowing a true government of, for, and by the people to exist.

Spending by Non-Candidate, Non-Party Groups

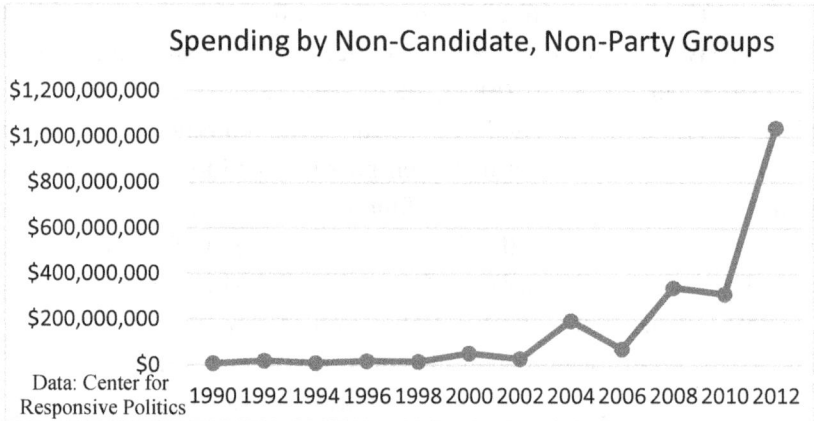

Data: Center for Responsive Politics

1990 1992 1994 1996 1998 2000 2002 2004 2006 2008 2010 2012

Percent of All Campaign Spending with Percent of All Income for the Top .01% of Americans

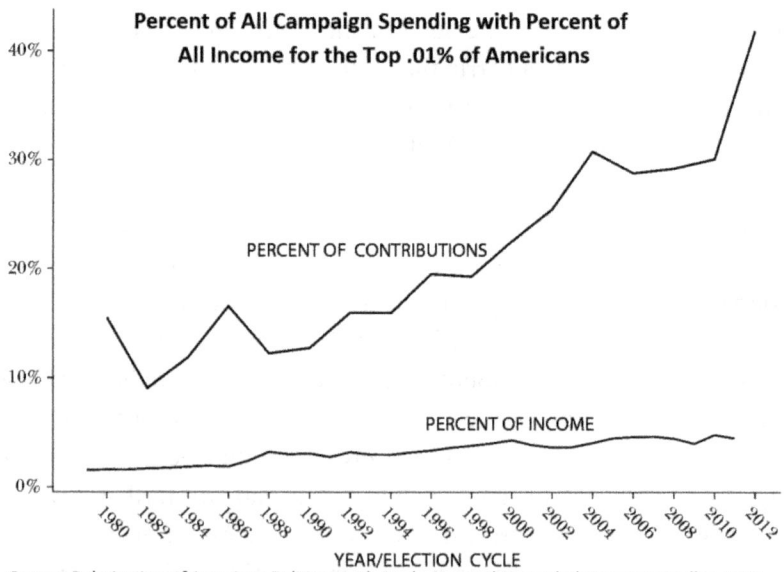

PERCENT OF CONTRIBUTIONS

PERCENT OF INCOME

YEAR/ELECTION CYCLE

Source: Polarization of American Politics, Keith Poole, Howard Rosenthal, Carnegie Mellon Univ.

Both of our major political parties have been corrupted by the system we have now. The concentration of wealth, income, and power into a small segment of the population has progressed at about the same rate during both Democratic and Republican administrations and congresses for over 30 years, yet incumbents rarely lose elections. Are most people voting for candidates they know are not serving their interests because they have no choice?

In 2012, 95.2% of incumbent senators and 91.2% of incumbent congressional representatives who ran for office won re-election. Incumbents commonly get re-elected largely due to the enormous advantages of incumbency in raising campaign cash.

A Princeton University study using almost two thousand survey questions on proposed policy changes between 1981 and 2002 (that also includes 2005-2006 and 1964-1968 data) found that when Americans with different income levels differ in their policy preferences, actual policy outcomes strongly reflect the preferences of the most affluent but bear virtually no relationship to the preferences of poor or middle-income Americans.[70] A more recent study report made available for preview (before official publication) describes the results of this study's detailed analysis of the relationship between voter preferences and policy results this way:

"In the United States ... the majority does not rule—at least not in the causal sense of actually determining policy outcomes. When a majority of citizens disagrees with economic elites and/or with organized interests, they generally lose…even when fairly large majorities of Americans favor policy change, they generally do not get it. …policymaking is dominated by powerful business organizations and a small number of affluent Americans… America's claims to being a democratic society are seriously threatened. The preferences of the average American appear to have only a miniscule, near zero, statistically non-significant impact on public policy."[71]

In other words, America is a society ruled by, and exclusively serves the interests of, the wealthy and corporations. The U.S. is not a true democracy or a society organized in the interests of its people. The study exposed the severity of the problem before the Supreme Court's Citizens United and McCutcheon decisions opened the floodgates for campaign cash, so the power of moneyed interests in our elections, and therefore in determining public policy, is now even larger than the study indicated.

Although most Americans are not aware of this research, they know its conclusion is correct. Many have lost hope that the political system will serve their interests, so they do not bother to vote. Why vote if your interests will not be served by whoever wins? In 2010, 21% of eligible voters between the ages of 18 and 24 voted and 41% of all eligible voters voted. This is the lowest voter participation rate in the developed world by far, and just slightly better than Zimbabwe, which is far from being a beacon of democracy. In the late 1800's, several times we had a voter participation rate of over 80%, and it was generally about 75%. In Denmark and Sweden in recent elections, it was about 82%.[72]

Our historically high levels of citizen disengagement from our political system and historically high disapproval ratings of Congress are part of a long-term decline in trust in our fundamental institutions and our fellow citizens. The General Social Survey, the major periodic assessment to monitor societal change, found that the percentage of Americans who believe other people can generally be trusted fell from 44% in 1980 to 32% in 2006, the lowest level ever recorded by the survey. A recent study found that only "*18% trust business leaders to do the right thing.*"[73] A 2012 Gallup poll found that Americans' distrust in the media hit a new high, with 60% saying they have little or no trust in the mass media to report the news fully, accurately, and fairly.[74] Trust is essential to social cohesion, political stability, and commerce, and it is negatively correlated with economic inequality.

Corporate Influence on Government

Corporations serve many important functions in our society. They provide the majority of workers' income and make the products we consume, use, and defend us. They have contributed to advancements that have improved productivity. (The largest productivity advances resulted from government funded research, mainly in public research institutions. Evidence for this is in Part 4, Note 1). But the current corporate form is also resulting in harm to society. Its anti-democratic structure is causing vast inequalities, low and declining average job satisfaction, corruption of our political system, and other negative societal impacts, making necessary the reforms I will describe in *The Way to Prosperity for All* and the corporate media reforms in *The Way to a Government of, for, and by the People*. New Enlightenment corporate structural reforms will result in far more benign and beneficial corporate behavior. The benefits will include increasing the pace of productivity advancements that the corporate sector contributes to society.

Disproportionate influence in determining who holds government office is one way public policy has been corrupted to serve corporate interests and the interests of wealthy individuals. Lobbying is another powerful way where similarly massive amounts of resources are corrupting public policy to the detriment of the majority. For example:

Between 2008 and 2010, thirty large corporations spent more money lobbying Washington than they paid in taxes. Twenty-nine paid zero in taxes and instead received tax rebates over those three years. General Electric received $5 billion, while it had profits of $10.5 billion. The total value of the rebates received by the 30 corporations was nearly $11 billion. Combined lobbying expenses during the period were $475 million. They received an excellent, 2,216%, rate of return on their investment! Combined profits during the same period were $164 billion.[75] From 2009 to 2013, about $17 billion was spent on lobbying because it brings a large return on investment for corporations, often resulting in unnecessary government or consumer costs.

Our Founders would be vehemently opposed to the power we have allowed corporations to gain. Americans of the Revolutionary generation disliked and distrusted corporations. Britain's East India Company was the largest corporation of its day; its dominance of trade angered the colonists so much that they dumped East India's tea products from one of the company's ships into Boston Harbor, an act now known as the Boston Tea Party. At the time, in Britain, large corporations funded elections generously, and large corporations' stock was owned by nearly everyone in Parliament.

James Madison, the "Father of the U.S. Constitution," wrote, *"The growing wealth acquired by [corporations] never fails to be a source of abuses."* That it is *"an evil which ought to be guarded against." "The power of all corporations, ought to be limited in this respect."*[76]

President Dwight D. Eisenhower made probably the most famous warning of influence on public policy by corporations to serve their interest to the detriment of the public interest, in a particular industry. His famous farewell address warning the American people about the *"military-industrial complex"* originally identified a *"military-industrial-congressional complex."* The *"congressional"* part was dropped because Eisenhower prided himself on the strength of his relations with a Congress of the opposing party; he did not want to risk harming them with an implication of vulnerability to undue influence or corruption. Unfortunately, we were deprived of Eisenhower's insight into the complex that has dominated a mindset in which our government tends to view many situations abroad as military challenges instead of mutually beneficial diplomatic or assistance missions. One result is a U.S. military budget nearly equal to the size of the rest of the world's military budgets combined.

Corporate contractors received $320 billion to perform work for the federal government in 2010. The Project on Government Oversight's (POGO) analysis found these contracts cost taxpayers, on average, 1.83 times more than if federal employees had done the work. That's $145 billion wasted in 2010 alone through overcharges by private corporations for their contract work with the federal government. POGO found that Department of Defense service contracting cost **2.94 times more** than an average Department of Defense civilian employee performing the same job. 27,000 Pentagon contractors, one in nine, evaded taxes and still continued to get Defense Department contracts, according to a 2004 Government Accounting Office (GAO) study. The contracting process, frequently no-compete arrangements, encourages corruption on an unprecedented scale, wasting hundreds of billions of dollars of public money. The power of money in elections and lobbying has resulted in this outsourcing of government function, in deregulation and massive, unnecessary public costs. This power is growing and creating increasingly severe societal dysfunction.

Corporate influence on public officials has also harmed the public through getting artificially low prices for our public resources. For example: The Powder River Basin (a geologic structural basin in southeast Montana and northeast Wyoming) provides approximately 40% of the nation's coal. The highest bid ever received on a federal coal lease there was just $1.10 per short ton, although it sells for approximately $10 per short ton, and even more when exported. Tracts are rarely competitively leased, depriving us of fair market value. In the Powder River Basin, there have been 25 coal lease sales over the last two decades, and 20 had only one bidder. The Bureau of Land Management is allowing the coal industry to determine the leasing process and essentially the price of our publicly owned resources. Also, coal companies receive billions of dollars in taxpayer subsidies via preferential tax treatments such as tax deductions to cover the costs of investments in mines and favorable capital gains treatment on royalties.[77]

The burning of coal produces more CO_2 and other harmful emissions per BTU than any other commonly used fuel. Therefore, public policy that would best serve the public interest rather than the interests of coal companies would be exactly the opposite from what it is now. Coal companies would pay a market determined price, at least, and would not be given subsidies.

Corporate influence on policymakers has also been an important factor in the stagnation and decline of median wages. Wages decline as the rights of labor erodes through lack of enforcement of labor laws. The National Labor Relations Act, NLRA, protects the rights of employees to discuss organizing and workplace issues with co-workers, engage in collective bargaining, and participate in strikes and other activities supporting demands including those for fair wages and benefits. It requires employers to engage in collective bargaining with the workers' union. However, reported violations of the NLRA skyrocketed in the late 1970s and 1980s. During the 1980s, one in 20 workers who voted for a union were illegally fired. There was little enforcement of the laws to protect workers. This is a major reason for the decline of unions, a major cause of the rise in income inequality, as the strong correlation shown in this graph suggests.

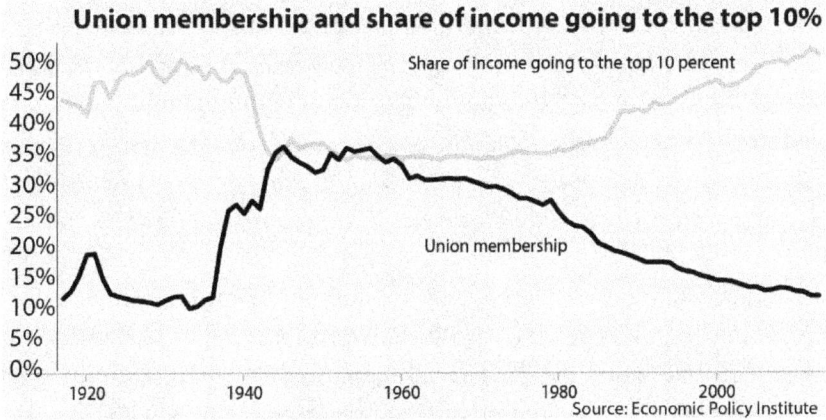

Union membership and share of income going to the top 10%

Share of income going to the top 10 percent

Union membership

Source: Economic Policy Institute

Corporate Influence on Health Care Policy

The private insurance industry's influence on health care policy is creating the most inefficient health care system in the world. The system is causing major economic harm to our country. It is also unjust, and it's an international embarrassment. A World Health Organization detailed study measured overall health system performance for 191 countries. It found that France has a health care system with the best outcomes and highest satisfaction rates in the world; France spends less than half per capita than we do, and we had over 50 million people uninsured in 2012, and substantially inferior health outcomes and satisfaction rates.[78]

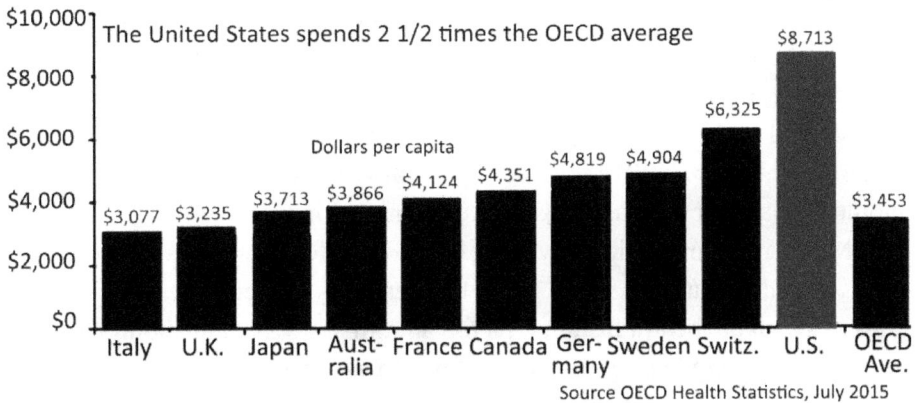

The United States spends 2 1/2 times the OECD average

Dollars per capita

Italy	U.K.	Japan	Australia	France	Canada	Germany	Sweden	Switz.	U.S.	OECD Ave.
$3,077	$3,235	$3,713	$3,866	$4,124	$4,351	$4,819	$4,904	$6,325	$8,713	$3,453

Source OECD Health Statistics, July 2015

A press release by the Commonwealth Fund, a private foundation that studies international health care systems, on its major 2014 study on health care systems around the world stated: *"Despite having the most expensive health care system, the United States ranks last overall among 11 industrialized countries on measures of health system quality, efficiency, access to care, equity, and healthy lives. The other countries included in the study were Australia, Canada, France, Germany, the Netherlands, New Zealand, Norway, Sweden, Switzerland, and the United Kingdom. While there is room for improvement in every country, the US. stands out for having the highest costs and lowest performance-the US. spent $8,508 per person on health care in 2011, compared with $3,406 in the United Kingdom, which ranked first overall."*[79]

The Affordable Care Act is not a solution. 23 million Americans will remain uncovered, and national health care costs will increase about $311 billion between 2010 and 2019.[80] The sales, marketing, and underwriting activities of many poorly regulated private insurance companies with diverse billing and review practices, unnecessary testing and procedures due to perverse financial incentives of caregivers, and very high doctor pay all will continue to unnecessarily drive up costs under the Affordable Care Act.

Also, semi-monopoly power of insurers and giant hospital systems is driving prices up, as is the shortage of doctors. The U.S. is already short 20,000 doctors, a number expected to increase over six-fold by 2025. Both the high cost and a restricted number of medical school slots is the cause. The average new medical school graduate carried $166,750 in debt in 2012.[81]

Chief executive officers at Fortune 500 health insurance companies, who have opposed new regulations under the Affordable Care Act, have emerged as one of the ACA's greatest beneficiaries. Average compensation for the top nine health insurance CEOs rose by over 19% in 2013 to $13.9 million, while some of the largest insurers more than doubled CEO pay. Aetna's CEO received over $30.7 million.[82] The disclosures of higher CEO pay coincided with several of the same companies announcing better than expected earnings in the first quarter of 2014, even as they warned that patients and businesses should prepare for increased insurance premiums in 2015.

Medicare, our public, universal, health plan for all seniors, is more efficient, provides better financial protection, and has higher patient satisfaction rates than private health insurers. Its top administrator is paid about $200,000 per year. Directing huge amounts of money to upper management in for-profit corporations is incompatible with achieving the imperative of a cost effective, ethical health care system. Funds diverted from patient care results in a loss of access to affordable health care.

If we had France's highest health care system satisfaction rate and per capita costs we would save over $1.35 trillion per year, an amount far larger than our huge federal fiscal deficit, *and greater than the total amount of federal income taxes collected in 2011.* The graph shows per capita health care costs for some OECD countries and the OECD average.

Great increases in corporate wealth have inevitably led to great increases in corporate political and media propaganda power. And our corporate media is one of the most influential segments of the corporate elite directing public attention away from critically important issues and influencing the direction of public policy away from majority interests. Six giant companies control 90% of what we read, watch, or listen to. This is why most of the conditions described in Part 1 are not widely known. They are not given an appropriate degree of exposure with policy solution discussions and debates, which in addition to an otherwise corrupted political system, is why we are not beneficially acting on them. The managers of these huge conglomerates are not representative of the general population and values elite interests over majority interests.

Fundamental media reform is necessary. It is interdependent with broader social and political reform. They will rise or fall together. For more information on the critically important media problem and its solution, see The New Enlightenment media reform proposal in *The Way to a Government of, for, and by the People*, Policy 29.

The Founding Fathers experienced the destructiveness of wealthy corporations being allowed to have great influence in government, which is why they put restrictions upon them after our government was organized. Corporations were granted charters by the state as they are today, but unlike today, corporations could exist only 20 or 30 years and could deal in only one commodity. They could not hold stock in other companies, and their property holdings were limited to what they needed to accomplish their business goals, and any political contribution by corporations was a criminal offense. Thomas Jefferson said:

"I hope we shall ... crush in it's birth the aristocracy of our monied corporations which dare already to challenge our government to a trial of strength, and to bid defiance to the laws of their country."[83]

A University of Zurich study reported that a small group of companies—mainly banks—wields huge power over the global economy (and therefore much of the world's political systems, media, and so wider social structures). The study is the first to look at all 43,060 transnational corporations and the web of ownership among them. The researchers' network analysis identified 147 companies that form a "*super entity*," controlling 40% of the global economy's total wealth. The close connections mean that the network could be prone to "*systemic risk*" and vulnerable to collapse.[84]

In the modern world, it is necessary that people join together in stable organizations to accomplish economic ends, but the resulting organizations must be sized, structured and regulated to ensure serving the best interest of society results. New Enlightenment policy will support the widespread transformation of corporate structures to a form that will result in far more beneficial corporate behavior (Policy 3 and Policy 29).

Large Economic Disparities Have Little-Known Consequences

Our large and growing economic disparities are causing pervasive harm, extending into our society and our personal lives in ways not widely known. Health and social problems are strongly correlated with income inequality. The graph shows this strong correlation. It is from the book *The Spirit Level* by research epidemiologists Kate Pickett and Richard Wilkinson. The indicators that make up the Index of Health and Social Problems are: life expectancy, math proficiency and literacy, infant mortality, homicides, imprisonment, teenage births, trust, obesity, mental illness, drug and alcohol addiction, and social mobility.

Studies have shown more than a correlation: Inequality has a causal relation to health and social problems. One study suggested that the loss of life from income inequality in the U.S. in 1995, before the larger disparities we experience today, was the equivalent of the combined loss of life due to lung cancer, diabetes, motor-vehicle accidents, HIV-related causes, suicide, and homicide.[85]

One explanation for income inequality's apparent effect on health and social problems is "status anxiety." Wide economic disparities exacerbate status competition and cause stress, which can lead to poor health and other negative outcomes. Some research has compared different groups in different countries and found that those in lower socio-economic groups in more equal countries sometimes do better than those in higher socio-economic groups in more unequal countries.

The U.S. is 30th in life expectancy. The population of Cuba, which has a per capita GDP of $6,790 compared to our $52,980 (about one-eighth of ours), has a higher life expectancy and a lower infant mortality rate than we do. Social determinants of health and poor access to health care for tens of millions of Americans are responsible. As Pickett and Wilkinson's research details, the social determinants of health are associated with economic inequality.

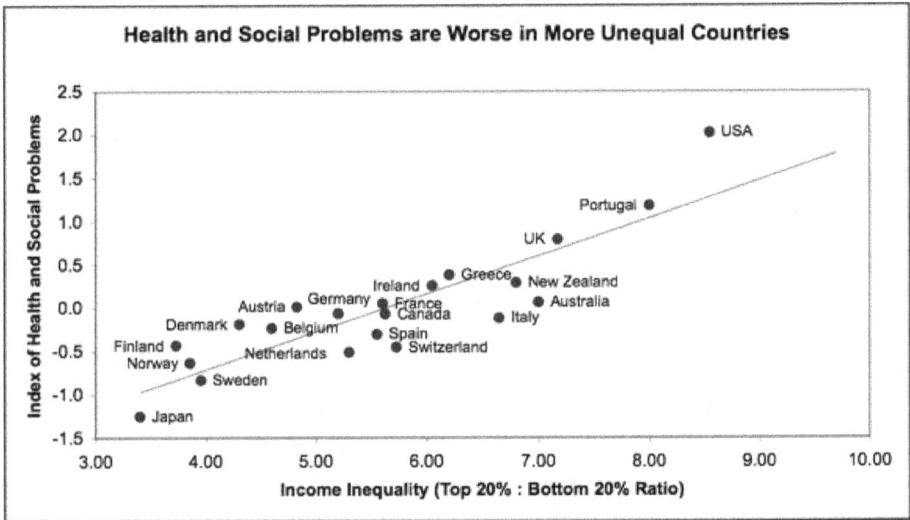

Health and Social Problems are Worse in More Unequal Countries

The Great Recession also resulted from our large and widening economic disparities. Part of the character of our increasing inequality was stagnation or decline of the purchasing power of the lower and middle classes, which inevitably either depressed their spending or caused people to take on debt, sometimes to maintain a lifestyle similar to that of others whose income and lifestyle was diverging from their own. As I noted earlier, in the years leading up to the recession the bottom 80% of the American population had been spending around 110% of its income. Since unscrupulous banks and financial intermediaries were freed from regulation and were eager to earn good yields on the enormous savings injected into the system by the wealthy, credit was offered indiscriminately. Loan originators often sold the loan, so they did not care if the borrower could pay it back. This led to the default of massive values in loans and derivatives devastating our financial system and economy.

Warnings on Concentrated Economic Power

Several of our Founders warned against highly concentrated economic power. Leaving economic elites free to pursue their private interests regardless of the public interest, including through influencing our political system, they knew would be a threat to our country. John Adams, the second president of the United States and the first vice president, wrote: *"Property monopolized or in the possession of a few is a curse to mankind: We should preserve not an absolute equality—this is unnecessary, but preserve all from extreme poverty and all others from extravagant riches.*[86]

"Power is a Thing of infinite Danger... No simple Form of Government, can possibly secure Men against the Violences of Power... Aristocracy will soon commence an Oligarchy, and Democracy, will soon degenerate into (a state where) *every Man will do what is right in his own Eyes, and no Man's life or Property or Reputation or Liberty will be secure and every one of these will soon mould itself into a system of subordination of all the moral Virtues, and Intellectual Abilities, all the Powers of Wealth, Beauty, Wit, and Science, to the wanton Pleasures, the capricious Will, and the execrable Cruelty of one or a very few."*[87]

".... power always follows property." If *"the Multitude will have the Ballance of Power, ... the Multitude will take Care of the Liberty, Virtue, and Interest of the Multitude in all Acts of Government,"* Adams wrote.[88]

And Adams, observing the conditions in old Europe warned of its dangers, and saw the need for radical change—essentially for the Enlightenment revolutions. In some ways, the disparities that he refers to below are now more extreme here than they were in Europe then:

"The people find themselves burdened now by the rich, and by the power of the crown now commonly wielded by the rich. And as knowledge and education ... have been increasing among the common people, they feel their burdens more sensibly, grow impatient under them, and more desirous of throwing them off. The immense revenues of the ... the crowns, and all the great proprietors of land, the armies and navies must all be paid by the people, who groan and stagger under the weight. The few who think and see the progress and tendency of things, have long foreseen that resistance in some shape or other must be resorted to, some time or other. They have not been able to see any resource but in the common people; indeed, in ... democracy; because the whole power of the aristocracy, as of the monarchies ... must be wielded against them." Adams wrote.[89]

If Adams were today to observe the enormous resources going to our military industrial complex and tiny elite, and the power this elite exerts on our government, wouldn't he say essentially the same thing of the United States today, and so advocate for a New Enlightenment? For example: In 2014 we spent on military expenses (including veterans) $689 billion. The poorest

50% in wealth in the country were important contributors to the creation of the goods and services needed to support this expenditure. This $689 billion is the total accumulated wealth of the poorest 50% of Americans.

James Madison, "Father of the Constitution" and the author of the U.S. Bill of Rights, also wrote that great inequality is an evil and that government should prevent *"an immoderate, and especially unmerited, accumulation of riches."* He favored the *"operation of laws which, without violating the rights of property, reduce extreme wealth toward a state of mediocrity, and raise extreme indigents toward a state of comfort."*[90]

The threat of the ascendancy of economic elites in the financial industry was strongly warned against. Madison warned of the *"daring depravity of... the stock-jobbers* [big investors who] *will become the pretorian band of the Government, at once its tool and its tyrant; bribed by its largesses and over-awing it by its clamours and combinations."*[91] We did not heed Madison's warning.

Nor did we Thomas Jefferson's. He warned of *"a government of an Aristocracy, founded on banking institutions and monied in corporations ... riding and ruling over the plundered ploughman and beggared yeomanry."*[92]

Jefferson strove to *"form a system by which every fibre would be eradicated of ancient or future aristocracy; and a foundation laid for a government truly republican."* One way to accomplish this that he advocated for was through *"laws of entail [inheritance, that] would prevent the accumulation and perpetuation of wealth in select families, and preserve the soil of the country from being daily more & more absorbed in Mortmain."*[93] *I am conscious that an equal division of property is impracticable. But the consequences of this enormous inequality producing so much misery to the bulk of mankind, legislators cannot invent too many devices for subdividing property, only taking care to let their subdivisions go hand in hand with the natural affections of the human mind."*[94] *Another means of silently lessening the inequality of property is to exempt all from taxation below a certain point, and to tax the higher portions of property in geometrical progression as they rise. Whenever there is in any country uncultivated lands and unemployed poor, it is clear that the laws of property have been so far extended as to violate natural right,"*[95] Jefferson wrote.

As previously noted, George Washington wrote that America *"will be the most favorable country of any kind in the world for persons of industry and frugality, possessed of moderate capital, to inhabit ... it will not be less advantageous to the happiness of the lowest class of people, because of the equal distribution of property."* Although not a warning, it could be consid-

ered Washington's recommendation against allowing large inequalities in America.

Abraham Lincoln, in a letter to Colonel William F. Elkins Nov. 21, 1864, wrote of the Civil War's devastating impact and of what he saw would be an even greater danger for our nation: "I see in the near future a crisis approaching that unnerves me and causes me to tremble for the safety of my country. As a result of the war, corporations have been enthroned and an era of corruption in high places will follow, and the money power of the country will endeavor to prolong its reign by working upon the prejudices of the people until all wealth is aggregated in a few hands and the Republic is destroyed. I feel at this moment more anxiety for the safety of my country than ever before, even in the midst of war."

Theodore Roosevelt pointed out the dangers of allowing the existence of an elite driven greed that successfully accumulates vast wealth, which will inevitably result in a further corruption their character. *"There is not in the world a more ignoble character than the mere money-getting American, insensible to every duty, regardless of every principle, bent only on amassing a fortune, and putting his fortune only to the basest uses—whether these uses be to speculate in stocks or ... allow his son to lead a life of foolish and expensive idleness and gross debauchery, or to purchase some scoundrel of high social position... Such a man is only the more dangerous if he occasionally does some deed like founding a college or endowing a church, which makes those good people who are also foolish forget his real iniquity. These men are equally careless of the working men, whom they oppress, and of the State, whose existence they imperil.... a very great number of men who approach more or less closely to the type, and, just in so far as they do so approach, they are curses to the country."*[96] Roosevelt wrote.

Franklin Delano Roosevelt witnessed a similar percentage of the nation's wealth going to the top 1% in the Roaring Twenties as exists today, yet, as detailed previously, the amounts the top 1% owned then was far less than the amounts today. He wrote: *"The first truth is that the liberty of a democracy is not safe if the people tolerate the growth of private power to a point where it becomes stronger than their democratic state itself. That, in its essence, is Fascism—ownership of Government by an individual, by a group, or by any other controlling private power. The second truth is that the liberty of a democracy is not safe if its business system does not provide employment and*

produce and distribute goods in such a way as to sustain an acceptable standard of living. "[97]

Better regulation of the private banking system and a public banking sector is needed

Reckless "financialization" of our economy has been harmful and at times has
caused devastating harm, even in our nation's earliest years. Here is Thomas
Jefferson's description of the problem in 1792, most of which rings strangely
familiar: Financial speculation *"withdraw[s] our citizens from the pursuits of
commerce, manufactures, buildings, and other branches of useful industry to
occupy themselves and their capitals in a species of gambling, destructive of
morality, and which had introduced it's poison into the government itself."*[98]
*Ships are lying idle at the wharves, buildings are stopped, capitals withdrawn
from commerce, manufactures, arts, and agriculture to be employed in gambling; and the tide of public prosperity almost unparalleled in any country is
arrested in its course, and suppressed by the rage of getting rich in a day. No
mortal can tell where this will stop, for the spirit of gaming, when once it has
seized a subject, is incurable. The tailor who has made thousands in one day,
though he has lost them the next, can never again be content with the slow
and moderate earnings of his needle. "*[99]

When a financial bubble burst in early 1792, Jefferson was not surprised.
*"At length our paper bubble is burst.... In New York ... the bankruptcy is
become general. Every man concerned in paper [is] broke, and most of the
tradesmen and farmers who had been laying down money ... have lost the
whole. It is computed there is a dead loss at New York of about five millions
of dollars, which is reckoned the value of all the buildings of the city; so that
if the whole town had been burned to the ground it would have been just the
measure of the present calamity. "*[100]

The financial industry is now taking an extraordinarily large and increasing portion of the country's income, and has caused a modern-day *"calamity."* The sector accounted for about 14% of GDP in 2007, up from about
4% in 1950. The vast wealth of this industry has translated into great power
to influence our political and policymaking process, which it has used to the
detriment of the rest of society, and its wealth and power are growing. For
example:

For the decades since the Depression era, the Glass-Steagall Act pro-
tected the country from the kind of financial crisis that triggered the Great
Depression. The act separated commercial banks that used depositors' money

to make loans to businesses and individuals from investment banks that used bank money to make investments. Making risky investments using money received from commercial banks' depositors was prohibited.

The influence of thousands of the industry's lobbyists on government officials, and the industry's funding of election advertising to support candidates who would serve their interests, eventually led to the repeal of this act in 1999. Within eight years of the combining of commercial and investment banks into huge *"too big to fail"* institutions, we had another depression era-like crisis. When investment banks' bets were paying off, these banks made enormous profits and some of their executives became billionaires, but when the bets failed, our society took the devastating losses. The losses total $22 trillion of wealth through reduced economic output and the real estate price crash.[101]

The total value of all real estate in New York City in 2016, including the value of the land the buildings are on, is $1 trillion, so the *"calamity"* was far greater than twenty times *"that if the whole town had been burned to the ground."*[102] The economic cost of the 9/11 terrorist attacks is estimated to be $3.3 trillion; financial industry practices caused economic harm just to our nation alone, neglecting the international harm, similar to seven 9/11 terrorist attacks.

The political harm resulting from severe financial crises can also be devastating. German researchers' analysis of a dataset covering 20 advanced economies and more than 800 general elections revealed that, on average, extreme right-wing parties increase their vote share by 30% after a financial crisis. They state: "Importantly, we do not observe similar political dynamics in normal recessions or after severe macroeconomic shocks that are not financial in nature. Preventing financial crises also means reducing the probability of a political disaster."[103]

The industry's influence also led to these policies with important roles in causing the financial crisis and recession:

- A ban on regulating credit-default swaps (which is insurance against nonpayment of a debt).
- Major increases in the leverage allowed to investment banks.
- Little regulatory enforcement from the Securities and Exchange Commission.
- International agreements to allow banks to measure their own riskiness
- A failure to update regulations to keep up with the tremendous pace of financial innovation, such as for mortgage derivatives.

- Lax lending standards.

Financial industry predators freed from regulation received large commissions from lenders for steering Americans into the riskiest subprime mortgages imaginable. Sometimes called "liars loans" where no job and no income was required, or the loan writers would fabricate, or encourge the borrower to fabricate, job, asset, or income information. The banks bundled those mortgages into almost worthless and unregulated derivatives until the inevitable crash.

As a result of the 2008 financial crisis, more than 9 million American jobs were destroyed. Real unemployment skyrocketed to more than 17 percent, as more than 27 million workers were unemployed, underemployed, or had stopped looking for work altogether. The American dream of homeownership turned into a nightmare of foreclosure for 15 million households. And a third of the remaining homeowners were underwater—owing more on their mortgages than their homes were worth. A huge spike in homelessness resulted in thousands of Americans setting up tent cities in Sacramento, Fresno, Tampa Bay, Reno, and elsewhere because they had no place else to live.[104]

The financial crises also destroyed millions of American's retirement dreams, sometimes completely wiping out life savings, and made it impossible for many families to afford to send their kids to college.

In 2008, Wall Street investment firms awarded almost $18 billion in bonuses. In the fall of 2008, Congress authorized a $700 billion taxpayer rescue of the financial system. Many financial company executives got tens of millions in bonuses while they were taking tens of billions in bailout money from the government. Joseph Cassano, AIG financial products executive, got a $34 million bonus and 72 other AIG executives got $131 million more in bonuses in 2008, while AIG took $182 billion in government bailout. Wall Street bonuses rose to $20.3 billion in 2009.

I would not think an observer of our society unreasonable for concluding that these actions were an expression of insanity. Political satirist Roy Zimmerman described well in a song what financial company executives essentially told our society after the devastating financial and economic system crash of 2008:

> *We charted out this course*
> *That left us broken on the ice*
> *But there's no need to thank us*
> *A hefty bonus will suffice*

Then, insanely, we complied. From another perspective, the scenario was not insane, but a predictable outcome of a political and economic system of a design that inevitably serves a small elite extraordinarily well, at the expense of the majority.

In 2008, an analyst from the credit-rating agency Standard & Poor's that consistently and knowingly gave AAA ratings to near-worthless mortgage-backed securities, said, "Let's hope we are all wealthy and retired by the time this house of cards falters."

Even the Federal Reserve has been hijacked by the bankers it is in charge of regulating. For example, Jamie Dimon, CEO of JPMorgan Chase, served on the board of the New York Fed at the same time that his bank received a $391 billion Fed bailout. At least eighteen current and former Fed board members were affiliated with banks and companies that received emergency loans from the Fed during the financial crisis.[105]

The public was told that it was necessary to spend trillions of public monies to bail out financial institutions to support essential lending functions to businesses, but the banks decreased lending after the bailout, as the graph shows. Instead of using the money to increase lending, they bought risk-free Treasury bonds and other government-guaranteed securities with the money, essentially lending the money back to the government. The banks have also been collecting interest on money they are not lending—the "excess reserves" they have at the Fed. The Fed helped bail out the banks by paying them interest on this money that they're not lending, and they are still collecting it.

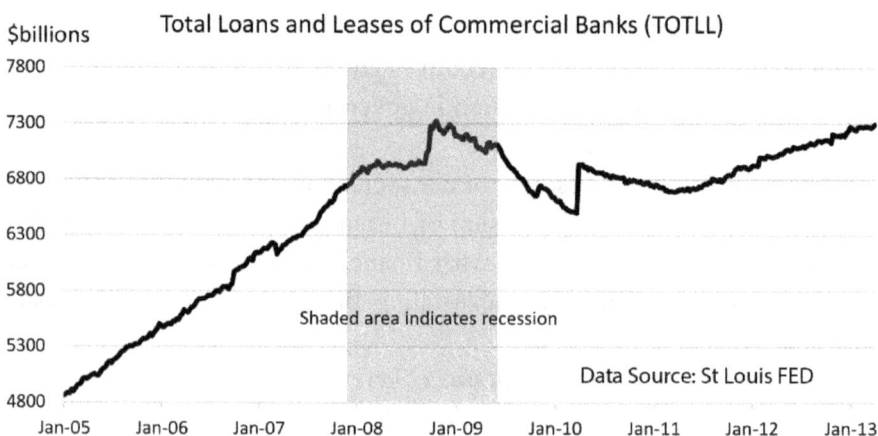

Total Loans and Leases of Commercial Banks (TOTLL)

$billions

Shaded area indicates recession

Data Source: St Louis FED

University of Missouri research in collaboration with the Levy Research Institute of Bard College revealed that the combined total value of all Federal

Reserve financial industry loans, guarantees and outright purchases of financial assets in response to the financial crisis was greater than $29 trillion.

No serious discussion occurred of directing a substantial portion of the massive amounts of public money that went to the banks to help homeowners that were "underwater," and to large, urgently needed infrastructure expenditures. Thirty-two percent of America's major roads are in poor or mediocre condition and twenty-four percent of America's bridges are structurally deficient or functionally obsolete. These unsafe conditions are costing drivers about $67 billion annually for increased fuel consumption, body dents, worn tires and premature wear wrought by pitted roads, about $324 per driver.[106] Studies show that for every dollar we invest in infrastructure we can expect a return of $2 - $4 in economic gains. The higher amounts occur during economic downturns.[107]

The Federal Highway Administration found that a $1.25 billion infrastructure investment supports 34,779 jobs related to the project.[108] A $450 billion investment in badly needed infrastructure improvements would have created about 12.5 million jobs. In July 2013, the official number of unemployed persons was 11.5 million; the investment would have ended the unemployment problem, and most of the investment we would have recovered in added tax revenues from the economic stimulus effect. The American Society of Civil Engineers estimates $3.6 trillion is needed for infrastructure maintenance, repair, and renovation. $450 billion is a minor fraction of what was given to the financial industry. (The Bush tax cuts, 43.1% of which went to the top 20%, reduced revenue by $1.9 trillion just between 2002 and 2011.[109])

In the 1930s, the federal government made it possible for everyone, even those in very rural areas, to have electric power at their homes, and now it is of major importance to virtually every American's life. But today, America's aging electrical grid results in hundreds of major power failures each year, many of which are avoidable. It is unnecessarily vulnerable to extreme weather events and cyberattacks. The World Economic Forum ranks our electric grid at twenty-fourth in the world in terms of reliability, just behind Barbados.[110]

The financial industry spent $2.2 billion on lobbying during the period of development of the Dodd-Frank legislation designed to limit the financial industry practices that triggered the Great Recession. Over 3,000 lobbyists worked on financial reform legislation in 2010 as Dodd-Frank was being debated. Half of them had previously worked as Capitol Hill aides, members of Congress, or executive branch staffers. The resulting legislation is so weak that most experts consider another financial crisis to be inevitable.[111]

Eric Rosengren, the president of the Federal Reserve Bank of Boston, said that the continued prevalence of overnight financing to keep banks solvent is one of the *"financial stability issues that still really scares me."* The "heads, I win; tails, you lose" compensation system also remains in place. Bankers' and traders' incentives result in high risk/reward trades to get multimillion-dollar bonuses. They get the rewards of a successful trade but don't suffer the losses if it fails, their bank does, and ultimately we all do if the losses are big enough to require a bailout due to systemic risk.

The Dodd-Frank Act promises no more bailouts, but the four largest U.S. banks—now JPMorgan Chase, Bank of America, Citigroup, and Wells Fargo—control $8.2 trillion in assets, an increase of 28% from the time before the crash of 2008. The assets of these banks alone are nearly half the size of America's gross domestic product. Does anyone believe that the federal government would allow any of these big banks and other big banks that are bigger than ever to fail?

The market for risky financial products has undergone a great revival. As happened in 2005 and 2006, investors are searching for better returns on their investments than minuscule savings accounts and high-quality bonds returns. A record $345 billion of junk bonds were sold in 2012.

One particularly dangerous result of weak regulation is that the derivatives market is steadily growing. The total notional value, or face value, of the global derivatives market when the housing bubble popped in 2007 stood at around $500 trillion. It has grown to at least $700 trillion by the end of 2011. That is over ten times the size of the entire world economy! Incredibly, we have little information about it or its implications for the financial strength of any of the big banks.[112]

Funding armies of lobbyists to enact policies to serve their industry's interests regardless of the public interest is very effective. So is funding candidates' campaigns. In the 2008 campaign, Senator Barack Obama got about $1 million from employees of Goldman Sachs and he received $9.9 million from the financial industry. Most of his original economic team's prior policies or actions played an important role in creating the crisis. They were chosen because the financial industry favored them. For example:

President Obama's Treasury Secretary Timothy Geithner was one of our nation's top regulators during the subprime scandal. He took no effective action even in response to the FBI warning that there was an epidemic of fraud. Jack Lew replaced Geithner as Treasury secretary after he returned to Wall Street as president of the private equity firm Warburg Pincus. Lew had been chief operating officer of Citigroup's Alternative Investments division, dedicated to proprietary trading. Lawrence H. Summers, head of President Obama's National Economic Council, collected roughly $5.2 million in compensation from hedge fund D.E. Shaw in 2008 and he was paid over $2.7 million in speaking fees by several troubled Wall Street firms and other organizations. Mr. Summers, as Deputy Secretary of the Treasury in the late 1990s, blocked the efforts of regulators to regulate the financial derivatives market that became the principal cause of the global financial crisis.

The problem of inappropriate influence from the financial sector is systemic. I mention President Obama because when in office he was at the top of our political system. The problem is more severe in the opposing Republican Party. The industry's cash has gone to Republicans at about a two-to-one ratio for decades; however, Democrats received 56% of the industry's donations in the 2008 election cycle for the first time since 1990.[113] Senator Dick Durbin said, *"And the banks – hard to believe in a time we're facing a banking crisis that many of the banks created –are still the most powerful lobby on Capitol Hill. And frankly, they own the place"*

Martin Wolf, named in the top 100 lists of global thinkers by *Prospect* and by *Foreign Policy* magazine, and associate editor and chief economics commentator at the *Financial Times* (regarded as the most credible and important publication internationally in reporting financial and economic issues) said this about the financial sector: *"An out-of-control financial sector is eating out the modern market economy from inside, just as the larva of the spider wasp eats out the host in which it has been laid."*

As the finance industry has risen, manufacturing industries have fallen as a percentage of the economy, as the following graph shows. The financial industry has played a role in this process through its sole interest of profit maximization. Sending manufacturing jobs to low wage, low tax countries where lax environmental and labor standards exist maximizes the profits of their business investments. It also depresses worker compensation here. Meanwhile, the compensation of Wall Street bankers soars. Just in bonuses alone, the $26.7 billion distributed to them would have been enough to more than double the pay of the 1,085,000 minimum wage workers in 2013.

Members of the financial industry are a large and growing segment of our economic elite. The 25 highest paid hedge fund managers' income in 2013 was $21.15 billion, two and one-half times the $8.5 billion all America's 158,000 kindergarten teachers made. These hedge fund manager's compensation far in excess of their societal contribution (if any) and their income is taxed at the much lower capital gains or "carried interest" rate than labor rate. No true democracy would allow this massive tax loophole for the super wealthy.

Manufacturing and financial sectors as share of private economy 1948–2009

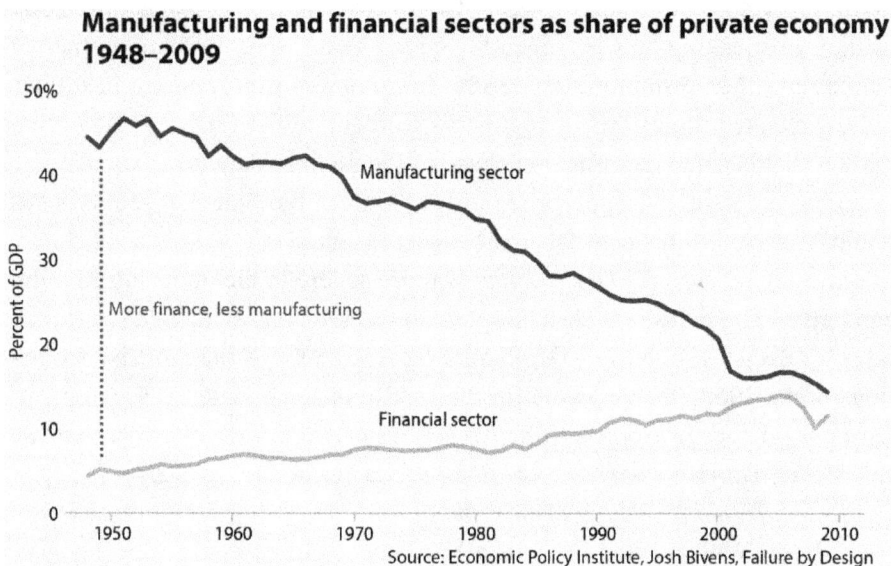

Source: Economic Policy Institute, Josh Bivens, Failure by Design

Hedge fund traders played a role in the devastating financial crisis that wiped out $22 trillion of wealth. Trillions of dollars in public funds were used to stabilize financial markets so stock prices are back to pre-recession levels. Stocks are the primary asset of the wealthy, including these hedge fund managers. The main asset of the middle class, housing, has been little supported by public money and has risen less and at a much slower rate. Also, many of the middle class were forced out of their homes since 2007. Over 10 million families lost their homes or entered foreclosure in the crisis and recession that followed.[114] Although some have repurchased homes, the result is a homeownership rate decline from 2007 to 2015 of over 7%. The homeownership rate declined to a 48-year low in the second quarter of 2015.[115] This has resulted in an increase in wealth inequality.

Without billions of dollars in public funds, executives of some financial companies could not have received millions of dollars of personal compensation during and after the crises, yet they showed no regard for the public, violating even fundamental human rights. They instituted corporate policies that threw homeowners by the millions out of their homes, often illegally and fraudulently. Many thousands of false foreclosure affidavits were filed with the courts, all of which were felonies. No one has been criminally prosecuted.

Although there was a $26 billion settlement between the U.S. government and five major banks in compensation for their illegal foreclosures, this was not a sufficient governmental response. These institutions were given far over $26 billion in public bailout money, so essentially they did not pay any penalty, the taxpayers did. The Courts approved the $26 billion foreclosure settlement on April 10, 2012, but thousands of people had been thrown out of their homes illegally in 2008. Out of that $26 billion fund will come payments of $1,500 to $2,000 to some homeowners who lost their homes through illegal foreclosures, if they can be found or can do what is necessary to make a claim for this relatively insignificant amount of money.[116]

The rule of law and accountability, actions based on reason, freedom and equality for all, and basic individual human rights. Are these obsolete ideals to our government policymakers and financial companies?

Bill Black, Ph.D., the former director of the Institute for Fraud Prevention, and a central figure in exposing congressional corruption during the late 1980's and early 1990's savings and loan crisis, now professor of economics and law at the University of Missouri, Kansas City, said, *"The (financial) system is ungovernable . . ."* He added that just one financial company, JP Morgan, committed frauds *"epic in scale, unprecedented in world history. . . $23 billion we're talking about, these are frauds that made Jamie Dimon* [the CEO] *and other senior officers incredibly wealthy by creating fictional income that led to very real bonuses."* Lehman Brothers executives committed the fraud of moving billions of dollars off the bank's books at the end of each quarter, then replacing them at the beginning of the next quarter to hide the firm's financial weakness.[117] No one has been criminally prosecuted.

In July 2014, Citigroup reached a $7 billion settlement for mortgage fraud. Then-attorney general Eric Holder said Citigroup's "activities contributed mightily to the financial crisis that devastated our economy in 2008... The bank's misconduct was egregious. As a result of their assurances that toxic financial products were sound, Citigroup was able to expand its market share and increase profits." Richard Bowen, a former Citigroup executive turned whistle-blower, added, "In July of 2008, I gave the SEC a thousand pages documenting fraud and the false representations given to investors in many securitizations.... In light of the huge losses this behavior caused our country, it is outrageous that, six years later, a settlement of only civil fraud charges would be announced, with no individuals being held accountable and no real admission of wrongdoing or true penalties assessed."

In April 2011, Wachovia (since acquired by Wells Fargo) was fined for laundering billions of dollars in illegal drug money. The federal prosecutor said, "Wachovia's blatant disregard for our banking laws gave international cocaine cartels a virtual carte blanche to finance their operations." The fine was less than 2 percent of the bank's $12.3 billion profit in 2009. In July 2016, JPMorgan Chase paid $200 million to settle criminal and civil charges related to bribing foreign officials. These are just a few examples that demonstrate that criminal activity is part of the business model of Wall Street, yet no one has been criminally prosecuted. Bank of America, Goldman Sachs, Wells Fargo, Morgan Stanley, and HSBC have settled for many billions of dollars in fines for fraud and other criminal activity that has included money laundering, currency manipulation, bribery, conspiracy, and rate tampering. [118] The fines, though large, were a small fraction of their profits, and major criminal laws were not enforced.

Is it possible that financial company insiders being in top positions in the administration, and paying for elected officials' campaigns, had anything to do with laws not being enforced? Certainly, undue influence on the laws enacted exists. The following are some other examples of this.

For hundreds of years, civilized societies all over the world have instituted usury laws to protect borrowers by limiting interest rates charged by lenders. Taking advantage of others' misfortunes was considered unethical and against the public interest. In 1980, Congress passed the Depository Institutions Deregulation and Monetary Control Act. Among the act's provisions, it exempted federally chartered savings banks, installment plan sellers, and chartered loan companies from state usury limits. Now, for credit card lenders and payday loan companies, the sky is the limit. Payday loan borrowers, over just several months, can easily spend far more on fees than they ever received in cash and some borrow from multiple sites to pay off other payday lenders. At annual rates, the fees typically exceed 300% and sometimes reach four digits—resulting in the average 10% *"poverty tax"* for the roughly forty million households noted earlier.

The 2005 bankruptcy law made it impossible for students to discharge their debt even in bankruptcy, even if their educational institution was incompetent and their education was worthless. Since banks are supposed to be financially sophisticated, the system is supposed to be designed for them to have an interest in determining the likelihood that the borrower will be able to pay back the loan based on the value of the education it purchased. But the banks had little financial interest in being responsible, so they were not. The system is designed to serve the banks—for the banks to get paid with little risk, either through government insurance or the lifetime pursuit and garnishing of wages of the borrower. Also, the resulting much lower risk to the bank than other types of loans did not lower the interest rates to a commensurate level.

Many of the poor and middle class used the loans for education in private for-profit colleges that provided poor quality coursework that was not useful in the job market. Private for-profit colleges enroll about 13% of higher education students and account for 50% of the loan defaults. Many for-profit schools are owned partly or mostly by Wall Street firms and the for-profit banks. If the lender will get paid whether or not the students get an adequate education, and the lender owns the school whose profits increase based on lowered costs for faculty and facilities, it's inevitable that students will be poorly served, and Wall Street will be well served.

Even for-profit school fraud is common. Federal investigations found that recruiters would lure students, often members of minorities, veterans, the homeless, and low-income people, with promises of quick degrees and post-graduation jobs and then leave them poorly prepared and burdened with staggering federal loans. For-profit schools spend heavily on advertising, and their students are far more likely to borrow money to pay for tuition. Students at for-profit schools often do not realize that cheaper alternatives exist through public community colleges and trade schools.

Only 9% of the first-time, full-time bachelor's degree students at the University of Phoenix, the nation's largest for-profit college, graduate within six years. Twenty-two percent of the first-time, full-time bachelor's degree students at for-profit colleges graduate within six years, compared with 55% at public institutions and 65% at private nonprofit colleges.[119] Compared with traditional, nonprofit schools, both public and private, for-profit schools disproportionately enroll low-income and minority students who qualify for government aid to cover the relatively high tuitions.

Some for-profit colleges provide a good education, and some have introduced innovative teaching methods, so they are worthy of government-backed student loans. But standards are necessary because most are serving students, the future of our country, poorly. The government proposed standards in 2010, where only if there were adequate completion and student satisfaction rates, and a reasonable fraction got the jobs that were promised, would the school qualify for government-backed loans. The schools' and the banks' lobbying and campaign cash succeeded in weakening the proposed regulations.

The final standards leave a maximum of 5% of schools facing financial sanctions. The original plan would have meant penalties against about 16%, and penalties were pushed from 2012 to 2015.[120]

Our government couldn't reasonably regulate an industry many of whose members are causing significant harm to the future of the country, even though the industry largely exists because of the federal government. Schools in the $30 billion-a-year for-profit education industry receive as much as 90% of their revenue from federal student loan programs and federal aid.[121]

Many students who graduated from good quality schools couldn't find employment for long periods or had to settle for work that did not require a college degree because of the recession the financial companies created. Due to the poor job market, nearly half of America's recent graduates have settled for working in a job that does not require a college degree. Long periods of unemployment, or employment outside of the field in which you are trained, damage future good employment prospects, making any loan more difficult to pay back.

But low-income or not, good education or bad, bankruptcy or not, one thing is certain: Students will be hounded to pay their dues for doing what they thought was necessary to best contribute to our nation's economy—the loan for their education, with interest.

Financial companies' practices in lending and foreclosures targeted the weak, the poorly educated, the poor. Moral scruples were set aside in massive efforts to move money from the bottom to the top—not a new problem, but one that can be solved or alleviated only by good government.

Here is Thomas Jefferson's description of the problem: *"It seems to be the law of our general nature, in spite of individual exceptions; and experience declares that man is the only animal which devours his own kind; for I can apply no milder term... to the general prey of the rich on the poor."*[122]

The finance industry is mainly intended to supply capital for businesses to make investments in plants and equipment or *"fixed investments."* But as the graph shows, as finance has about tripled as a fraction of our economy, fixed investments have fallen.

The finance industry has to a large degree captured our government. What is remaining has mostly been captured by other wealthy corporate or wealthy individual interests. The deficit that is in most urgent need of attention and remedy is our democracy deficit.

Fixed investment and finance sector value-added as shares of GDP, 1948–2009

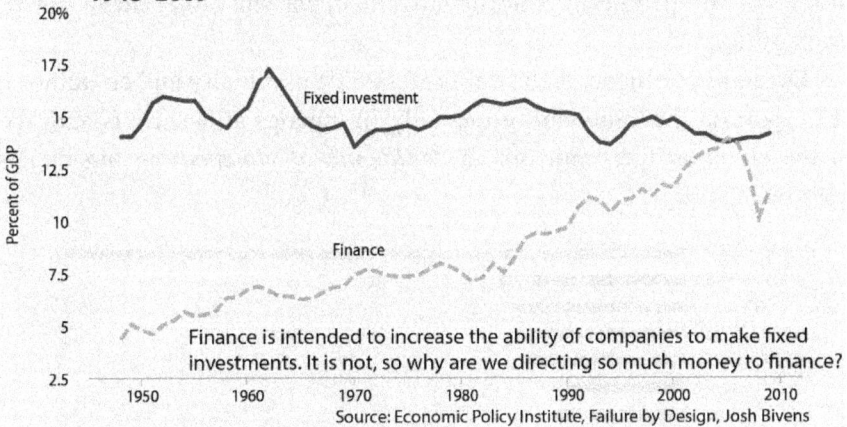

Finance is intended to increase the ability of companies to make fixed investments. It is not, so why are we directing so much money to finance?

Source: Economic Policy Institute, Failure by Design, Josh Bivens

New Enlightenment policies institute a public banking sector required to serve purposes essential to our program to create a true government of, for, and by the people, and prosperity for all.

Mass Incarceration: Further evidence for major political system dysfunction

Mass incarceration? If true, a violation of founding principles stated in our Declaration of Independence of *"unalienable Rights, that among these are Life, Liberty and the pursuit of Happiness."* Mass incarceration we normally associate with brutal foreign tyrannies, widespread oppression and great crimes against humanity, such as Hitler's network of concentration camps. We are not Nazi Germany, but we are tolerating mass incarceration and state sanctioned barbarism in the United States. Lack of appropriate mass media attention to the issue is playing an important role, but the problem now is more widely cultural.

2.4 million people are incarcerated in the U.S., often under horrific conditions. This is an incarceration rate of 760 prisoners per 100,000 population, or over **seven** times higher than the median rate for the 34 OECD countries. Conditions in some of our prisons should not exist in any civilized society.

In New York City's Riker's Island jail complex, which houses a daily population of nearly 12,000 inmates, in just the first 3½ months of 2014, 12 inmates were slashed or stabbed, eight in the neck or face, and many others suffered broken bones, concussions, punctured eardrums or other serious injuries. Some resulted from inmate on inmate violence, but inmates have also reported arbitrary and wanton abuse by correction officers.[123] Some inmates leave the facility physically and/or mentally crippled for life from injuries sustained in the facility. Riker's Island is mainly a pretrial facility, so a large majority of the people in it are legally innocent since they have not been proven guilty.

Dr. James Gilligan, a clinical professor of psychiatry and co-author of a 2013 report on the treatment of mentally ill inmates at Riker's Island, wrote that the situation there mirrors an *"epidemic of violence"* in big city jails across the country.

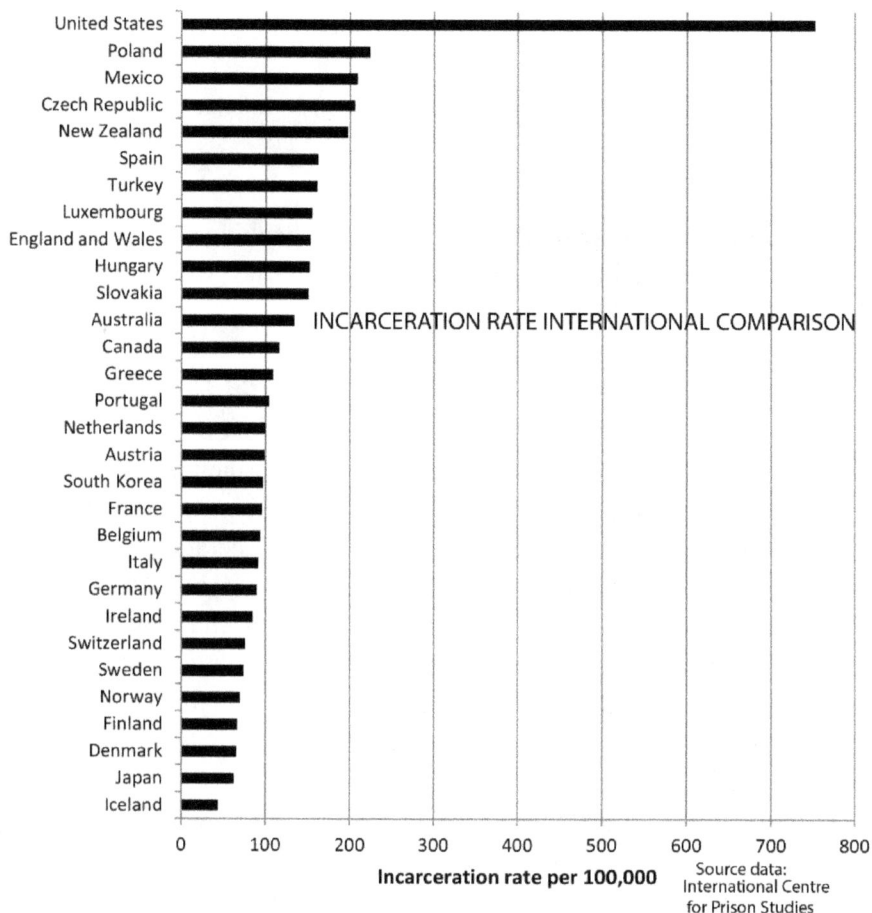

INCARCERATION RATE INTERNATIONAL COMPARISON

United States, Poland, Mexico, Czech Republic, New Zealand, Spain, Turkey, Luxembourg, England and Wales, Hungary, Slovakia, Australia, Canada, Greece, Portugal, Netherlands, Austria, South Korea, France, Belgium, Italy, Germany, Ireland, Switzerland, Sweden, Norway, Finland, Denmark, Japan, Iceland

Incarceration rate per 100,000

Source data: International Centre for Prison Studies

Over seventy thousand prisoners are raped each year, so common it is held out as a threat as a potentially routine part of the punishment.[124] An un-cooperative suspect being threatened with rape in prison is commonly repre-sented on television as ordinary, often as if this state of affairs is humorous. The normalization of prison rape indicates that our society is descending into more widespread and dangerous social decline.

International human rights experts and bodies have condemned some of our incarceration practices, including indefinite or prolonged solitary confinement, and have recommended that the practice be abolished entirely. The devastating psychological and physical effects of prolonged solitary confinement are well documented by social scientists. The United Nations Special Rapporteur on torture and other cruel, inhuman or degrading treatment or punishment concluded that even 15 days in solitary confinement constitutes torture or cruel, inhuman or degrading treatment or punishment. After just 15 days irreversible harmful psychological effects can occur, but many in U.S. prisons are held in solitary confinement for months, even years.

Inmates can be placed in solitary confinement not only for violent acts, but also for acts such as possessing contraband, using drugs, ignoring orders or using profanity. At least 80,000 are in solitary confinement or some type of segregated housing.[125] Every state holds some people in solitary confinement—as does the federal government, and eight states keep between 5% and 8% of their prison populations in isolation.

The percentage of inmates diagnosed as mentally ill has risen from 20% to 40% over the last eight years.[126] Harsh prison conditions exacerbate mental illness (or sometimes create it in those not previously mentally ill), yet our prisons are being used to a large degree to warehouse the mentally ill.

State spending on corrections is growing six times faster than state spending on higher education. Several states now spend more on prison systems than they spend on universities. State spending for corrections reached $52.4 billion in fiscal 2012 and has been higher than 7% of overall general fund expenditures every year since fiscal 2008.[127] It has nearly quadrupled over the last two decades. One in every 31 adults, or 7.3 million Americans, are either in prison, on parole or probation.

The devastating impact of our mass incarceration policies on many millions of Americans is lifelong because a criminal record, especially for a felony, creates lifelong discrimination in employment, housing, and other areas. Villanova University sociologists calculated that if the mass incarceration trend had not occurred, the poverty rate would be 20% lower today, and five million fewer people would have fallen below the poverty line.[128]

The number of prisoners in private facilities increased by 350% over the last fifteen years. Studies show that private facilities perform badly compared to public ones on almost every metric—prevention of intra-prison violence, jail conditions, and rehabilitation efforts. Any savings in costs are mainly attributed to lower worker salaries and benefits that sometimes cause higher government expenditures later to support the employee health care or other needs that are not accounted for.

The Geo Group is the U.S.' second largest private detention company. Its CEO received $5.7 million in compensation in 2011, far higher than an equivalent public sector manager's pay. Generally, though, private detention companies pay their workforce much lower wages than equivalent public sector employees, some barely above minimum wage, with few benefits.

So in some ways, this industry is typical of much of corporate America— depress salary and benefits for most workers to increase profits and to direct funds to upper management and owners, and to influence our political and policy-making process to serve corporate interests, often to the detriment of society's interests. But there are important differences: These practices in the prison industry are supported solely by public funds, and the industry thrives when large numbers of people are deprived of their freedom.

The two largest private detention companies had about $20 million in lobbying expenditures and $5 million in total political contributions from 2003 to 2012. The promise of a high paying job to government policymakers after they leave office is another way this industry can exert influence on policy decisions.

These companies have a financial interest in maintaining criminalization laws for minor drug offenses, and harsh sentencing for relatively minor and non-violent crimes, including some "three strikes" crimes with mandatory lifetime sentences, and for our country to not resolve the illegal immigration problem so that millions of illegal immigrants are subject to imprisonment. These policies often lead to unnecessary harm to minor offenders, the hardening of minor offenders into serious criminals, and calls for even more draconian law enforcement and punishment protocols. The resulting social and economic costs are large and is another indication public policy development is not guided by reason or a moral compass.

The 2005 annual report of the biggest of these firms, the Corrections Corporation of America (CCA), cautioned its investors about their risks, which they work to minimize through their influence on policymakers:

"The demand for our facilities and services could be adversely affected by the relaxation of enforcement efforts, leniency in conviction and sentencing practices or through the decriminalization of certain activities that are currently proscribed by our criminal laws. For instance, any changes with respect to drugs and controlled substances or illegal immigration could affect

the number of persons arrested, convicted, and sentenced, thereby potentially reducing demand for correctional facilities to house them."

In 2015, CCA and the Geo Group made a combined $361 million housing prisoners. CCA made $3,356 a year in profit for each prisoner, while GEO Group made $2,135 a year in profit per prisoner.[129]

CCA sent letters recently to 48 states offering to buy up their prisons as a remedy for "challenging corrections budgets" and recession caused budget shortfalls. In exchange, the company requires that the prisons remain at least 90% full. So if we manage to reduce our incarceration rate to "just" double the OECD average, CCA owners and managers will be very upset with us, and take us to court for damages from violating their contract.

Private detention enterprises feed on misery and are motivated to do all they can to ensure that nothing is done to decrease that misery. Is it rational or just to allow this industry to influence our political and policymaking process and to continue to grow in influence as it is doing? Although private prisons house slightly over 8% of prisoners now, this percentage and the industry's influence is growing rapidly. Profiteering from the imprisonment of human beings corrupts justice and compromises public safety. New Enlightenment policies will end all incarceration for profit.

The influence of private detention companies on our political and policymaking systems is not yet the primary cause of the explosion in prison populations. The primary causes are a dysfunctional political system, the media that allow distortions and lies to be promulgated, and racism. Since the 1980s, political opportunists used the work of pollsters and political strategists that found that by using *"get tough"* rhetoric on issues of crime and associating drug crimes mainly with African Americans, many whites would support them, and this strategy was *"successful."*

Crime rates have fluctuated over the last 30 years, and they are at historic lows. But imprisonment rates have quintupled, mainly due to the war on drugs. Drug offenses account for about two-thirds of the increase in the federal inmate population, and more than half of the increase in the state prison population. The following graph shows the explosive growth in the number of incarcerated Americans since President Nixon's " War on Drugs", 1984 Sentencing Reform Act and President Clinton's War on Drugs.

The drug war has been brutal. The onslaught has involved SWAT teams, military equipment, and sweeps of entire neighborhoods, mainly in poor African American communities. Elsewhere, few people know about this war and its devastation.

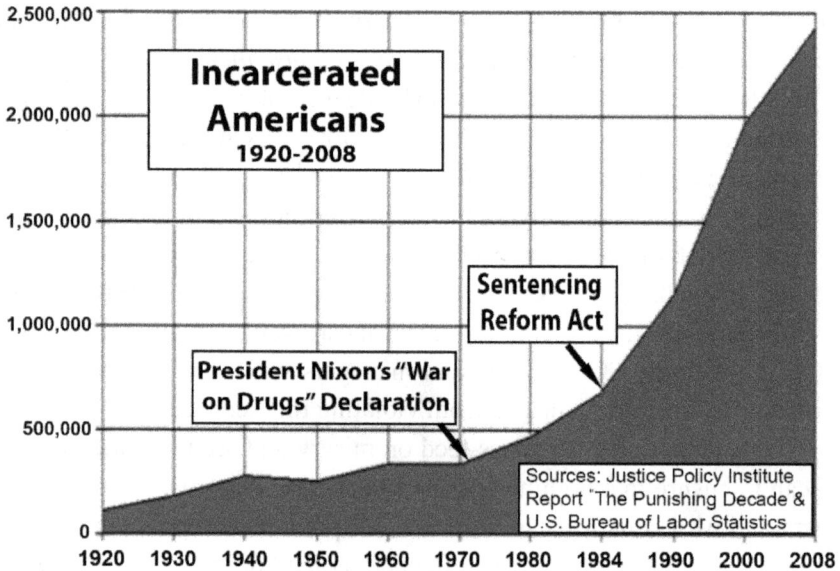

Studies show that people of all colors sell illegal drugs at similar rates, However, white youths have about three times the number of drug-related visits to the emergency room as their African American counterparts indicating African Americans use drugs less frequently. In some states, African Americans comprise 80%-90% of all drug offenders sent to prison. A large majority of African American men in some urban areas have a felony record. As a result, they can be legally discriminated against in employment, housing, access to education, food stamps, and public benefits, denied the right to vote, and be excluded from juries. The system seems designed to send people back to prison, which is what happens about 70% of the time because of the immense challenges created by the system for survival on the outside.[130]

Federal laws motivated the onslaught by allowing state and local law enforcement agencies to keep 80% of the cash, cars, and homes seized from drug suspects, and by providing funding based on the number of drug arrests. In 2005, four out of five drug arrests were for possession only. During the 1990s—the period of the most dramatic expansion of the drug war—nearly 80% of the increase in drug arrests was for marijuana possession. Studies have shown that marijuana is less harmful than alcohol or tobacco and at least as prevalent in middle-class white communities as in the inner city where the vast majority of drug war resources and arrests have been focused.

The election of Barack Obama to the presidency was an important milestone toward racial equality, but this milestone is blocking our view of how far we still have to go. President Obama has admitted to using illegal drugs in his youth. If he had not been raised by white grandparents in Hawaii and instead by black parents in a poor black neighborhood on the mainland, his fate likely would have been radically altered. In Chicago, where nearly 80% of African Americans are labeled "felons" and where he started his family and launched himself toward the White House, based on the 80% statistic and his use of illegal drugs, the odds are he would have been arrested at least once. Likely, he would have been convicted of felony possession, been stripped of the right to vote, and been in and out of the prison system unable to find a job or housing. It is unlikely he would have become president of the United States. How many lives have we destroyed in our misguided "drug war" with equal or greater potential than President Obama?

African Americans are doing no better than they were when Dr. Martin Luther King Jr. was assassinated and uprisings swept inner cities across America. Nearly a quarter of African Americans live below the poverty line today, approximately the same percentage as in 1968. The black child poverty rate is higher now than it was then. Unemployment rates in black communities rival those in Third World countries. In major cities nationwide, about 50% of black men are jobless. In 1968, Martin Luther King decried the black unemployment rate when it was about 9%.

Instead of creating good schools in all communities, we declared a war on drugs and embarked upon the greatest expansion of a prison system in world history. Only 35% of black boys nationwide graduate from high school. The United States imprisons a larger percentage of its black population than South Africa did at the height of apartheid. In our nation's capital, it is estimated that 75% of young black men can expect to serve time in prison.[131]

For children, the era of mass incarceration has meant broken homes, poverty, and hopelessness as many see loved ones cycling in and out of prison. Children who have incarcerated parents are far more likely themselves to eventually be incarcerated. Twenty-five percent of African Americans who grew up in the last three decades have had at least one parent locked up during their childhood.[132]

People have a false understanding of what our legal system is like from shows like "Law and Order," which suggest that lawyers are always available and do tremendous investigative work on the behalf of clients in even routine cases—this is not true. Many thousands of people go to jail or prison every year without even meeting with an attorney because they can't afford one. Prosecutors use the threat of harsh sentences and the promise of a lesser sentence to get defendants to plead guilty, which many innocent people do because they are afraid of doing ten or more years in prison if they do not.

A place where the majority of the population has insignificant influence on public policies and where the law is a brutal tool of control rather than a foundation for the majority's prosperity is a place not unlike what existed under the British before the American Revolution. Our Founders and their contemporaries were willing to die to end such a social order.

A social order poorly serving or disserving the majority requires fundamental reforms

I can continue to provide examples from a virtually endless list exemplifying malfunction and injustice, and the violation of our most important ideals. We are now too far from the conditions that the Enlightenment revolutions sought to achieve, or that would exist in a society with a truly democratic government. We do not have to tolerate these conditions or wait for them to get worse before we effectively act.

A more just and better-functioning society based on reason, the ideals of democracy, fundamental human rights and progress is attainable and necessary. People of the Enlightenment period, including most of America's population at that time, acted on this judgment when they confronted systemically created injustices with a vision for a radically more just social order. Now is the time for us to act again on the ideals of the Enlightenment with a new vision for a radically more just social order because again extensive and extreme systemically created injustices exist. Some of our Founders warned against some of them, and they are similar to the ones they fought to overcome. This book provides a vision, in substantial detail, for a radically more just social order that will facilitate further advancement; essentially a social order for a New Enlightenment where, unlike the 18th century Enlightenment, all people independent of race and sex share in its benefits.

Over the last few decades, a vast wealth transfer has occurred to our modern-day small economic elite whose dominance in wealth and power now is in some ways more extreme than the old English aristocracy against which we revolted to establish a more egalitarian society.

Three facts alone indicate that we have descended into a new aristocratic social order:

- Our political system has allowed the wealthiest 400 Americans, or about .00013% of the U.S. population, to accumulate wealth in total that exceeds that of the bottom 60% or 190 million Americans combined. The wealth of these 400 totals $2.3 trillion, not counting substantial amounts hidden in tax havens.

- We have the lowest intergenerational economic mobility of any advanced nation.

- When Americans with different income levels differ in their policy preferences, policy outcomes bear virtually no relationship to the preferences of poor or middle-income Americans. Policy outcomes commonly benefit a small elite at the expense of the rest of society, just as in the case of the aristocracies before the Enlightenment.

Most people are not aware how far economic disparities are departing from reasonable bounds, and how extensive is the resulting harm to all of us. If most people knew the facts, sufficient numbers would find them unacceptable to motivate major social change, so, unlike some claiming adherence to Enlightenment principles during the original Enlightenment period, we will be devoted exclusively to the peaceful means of education to effect change. In the New Enlightenment we will appeal to reason, and if necessary, take other nonviolent political actions to achieve our goal of eliminating the inherent injustices of our aristocratic economic, political, and social order.

More equal societies benefit not just the poor and all those in the bottom half of the wealth and income distribution, they benefit everyone, including the wealthy in profound ways, some not widely known. As we've seen earlier, health and social conditions are negatively impacted by economic inequality. Although the poor suffer more from these negative consequences, the perhaps surprising evidence is that the wealthy also are harmed. For example, the lifespan of the wealthy in more equal societies tends to be higher than it is in more unequal societies.

Extreme material rewards have often not resulted from a similar degree of social contribution. Sometimes they have resulted from socially destructive actions. But however large an individual's positive societal contribution, the degree of compensation must be justified based on the Enlightenment ideal expressed in Article 1 of the 1789 Declaration of the Rights of Man and the Citizen: "Social distinctions can be based only on common utility." The degree incomes rise above average must be beneficial to society. The degree we have is not socially valuable; it is destructive.

As detailed in Part 4 Note 1, even when an individual's constructive social contributions played a role in creating some his or her large amounts of wealth, enormous social resources were essential to the process. It is justifiable that the portion of wealth for which these social resources are responsible be returned to its source; society.

Creating an environment where intrinsic rewards (the enjoyment of doing the work itself) and the rewards of status, prestige, and appreciation are more dominant motivators would be beneficial and potentially of great importance. For this reason, among others, some policies I detail in this book if instituted could be transformative.

Too many people have lost hope that major beneficial change is possible. This widespread hopelessness comes from the feeling that the system is controlled by a powerful class that has "captured" the two major political parties dominating our government and captured our mass media, and that these institutions will not allow major system change. It seems we have lost the "can-do" spirit that defined America, but we can renew it.

The New Enlightenment Citizens Union

With your support of New Enlightenment policies, equal opportunity for all and equal justice for all (which the 14th Amendment to our Constitution is supposed to guarantee) will be more than pious pronouncements of what America offers. The New Enlightenment Citizens Union (and eventually Party) is devoted to serving these ideals with the detailed policies described in Part 2 and 3 (and a few others in development). All New Enlightenment Citizens Union or Party policies, now and in the future, will enhance egalitarianism to the degree practical, and improve democratic functioning. This will also serve other important ideals.

Before forming an official party we will support candidates running within any party label that support New Enlightenment policy to a sufficient degree that they would characterize themselves, and we would characterize them, as New Enlightenment candidates. This would be similar to what many candidates have done with the "Tea Party" label. They ran within the Republican Party and called themselves "Tea Party" Republicans.

Labor unions were once important forces for social justice, but with only 11% of the total workforce and 7% of the private sector workforce now unionized, they are no longer. The bargaining power of unions helped keep executive pay in check and made possible regular wage increases that allowed factory workers to purchase their homes as well as some of the expensive goods such as cars that they helped produce. This resulted in faster economic growth and lower unemployment on average during the years when unions were strong. Unions also mobilized people to vote in support of government policies that redistributed wealth, such as high taxes on the upper-income brackets and on corporations in the postwar years, and regular increases in the minimum wage. To a large degree, the labor movement created the economic stability and economic mobility that we experienced in earlier decades when unions were strong.

Labor union's impact on the welfare of both unionized and non-unionized workers historically has been major. It has also included substantially improving worker benefits and labor protections, ensuring safe workplace conditions and limiting full-time work days to five eight hours. The unions provided a democratic voice for workers at the workplace, and in the larger society. The New Enlightenment "Citizens Union" will compensate for the loss of labor unions as an important force for social justice. More than that, it will enhance and extend the value this important civic institution has had historically as a force for social justice.

The New Enlightenment Citizens Union, in addition to being an organization formed in support of New Enlightenment policies, will be the vehicle of a renewed public spiritedness. Ultimately, it will likely be necessary to develop the organization into a new formal party.

There are many examples in history, including our own, where large numbers of people striving for justice overcame great odds to achieve their goals. If we renew our can-do spirit and join together, we can do it again. We can achieve more shared prosperity and truly have a government of, for, and by the people.

An October 2013 Gallup poll found that 60% of Americans say that a third major party is needed, the highest Gallup has measured in the 10-year history of this question. Most of us know it's time for major societal changes. We need a clear blueprint for creating a far more just and democratic society, one that motivates and facilitates further advancement. I hope you will judge this book to contain an important portion of such a blueprint.

No other party or organization has a similarly focused and detailed blueprint of the fundamental reforms needed for the establishment of a true government of, for, and by the people, and prosperity for all. I designed all public policies in The New Enlightenment to serve one or the other or both of these goals. If we achieve these goals, all other societal problems will be far easier to solve than they currently are, and solved in a way that serves the best interests of the majority. It will be a new, peaceful American revolution—a transformation to a radically more democratic and beneficial government, and just society, if the proposals in The New Enlightenment are instituted.

New Enlightenment goals in summary are:
- Institute innovative, effective, and efficient ways to prosperity for all—a moral imperative and practical goal for world history's wealthiest country.
- Institute innovative, effective, and efficient ways to a true government of, for, and, by the people.

If we institute New Enlightenment policies, they will:

- **End unemployment, or reduce it to historic lows.**
- **Lift tens of millions of Americans out of poverty to a standard of living that now exists in the middle class and substantially improve the standard of living of tens of millions more.**
- **Reduce full-time work-hours 10%, to 36 hours per week.**
- **Transform the economic system over a two-decade transition period to one where worker controlled and owned business enterprises will perform most of the economic activity of the country.**
- **Eliminate the dominating importance of money controlled by national public office candidates and their allies in elections and thereby allow a meaningful democracy to exist.**
- **Enhance democratic functioning with new, innovative democratic forms. Average citizens in deliberative groups involving 0.1% of the citizenry will develop some public policies.**
- **Transform the ownership and management structure of many media corporations, through regulations and incentives. This will create a new media culture more responsive and accountable to the majority. We will create a vigorous media of, for, and by the people that are necessary for a well-functioning government of, for, and by the people.**
- **Eliminate tuition for public colleges. This will help meet our ideal of equal opportunity for all and help create the well-informed citizenry needed for a well-functioning democracy and economy.**
- **Eliminate the deficit and create over a $300 billion annual surplus.**

If instituted, the policies detailed in this book will have these and other transformative beneficial impacts. These are not exaggerations or idle claims. I will show the evidence for these impacts. But only if the policies detailed are widely known and supported will they be instituted. Only a mass movement can result in the major change that we now need.

It is time for a New Enlightenment.

Restoring and Reinventing Ways to Realize Our Ideals of Democracy, Human Rights, Reason, and Progress

THE NEW ENLIGHTENMENT

"The End of all Government is the happiness of the People ... the greatest happiness of the greatest Number is the point to be obtained."

John Adams, Founding Father, Second President of the United States, the first Vice President of the United States, Enlightenment political theorist.

"Power concedes nothing without a demand. Find out just what any people will quietly submit to and you have found out the exact measure of injustice and wrong which will be imposed upon them."

Frederick Douglass (1818-95) escaped from slavery in Maryland at age 20 and became a world-renowned abolitionist, social reformer, author, and orator.

Part 2

The Way to Prosperity for All

"The most important problem that we are facing now ... is rising inequality."

Robert Shiller, Nobel Prize in Economic Sciences, 2013

The Way to Prosperity for All

On a per capita basis, our country is wealthier than ever. In spite of this, a record 50 million poverty-plagued people makes the poverty rate among the highest on record. The percentage in "deep poverty" (half the official poverty income) is the highest on record. Our per capita GDP ($52,800) is almost two times that of 1966 ($28,680 in 2013 dollars), yet about the same fraction is in poverty now as in 1966 because almost all of the country's income gains have gone to a small economic elite.

As I described in Part 1, conditions now are too far from the level of egalitarianism that our Founding Fathers considered ideal and therefore wanted to be maintained by the government they created. Economic inequality was one of the main motives for the societal transformations of the Enlightenment. It is now greater than it was before the Enlightenment, of which the American Revolution was a part. Below is a review of a few more facts indicating that it is time for a New Enlightenment.

Wealth Inequality

Inequality of wealth is even more extreme than our extreme income inequality. U.S. household wealth reached $77.3 trillion in September 2013.[133] This is about a $657,000 (about two-thirds of a million dollars) average wealth per U.S. household. Considering this fact, is it acceptable for our economic and political system to result in a negative total wealth of the least wealthy 40% of the country, or about 128 million people?

In 2013 the top 400, or 0.00013% of Americans, had over $2.3 trillion in wealth, more wealth than 190 million or 60% of the least wealthy Americans combined.[134] Most people are aware that economic inequality is extreme, but not aware it is this extreme. If you have a penny and no debts, you have more wealth than the total wealth of about the 128 million poorest Americans combined. When a large portion of our ship of state is underwater, even though part of the ship is still rising, there is cause for concern about the eventual fate of the ship.

It has been known for thousands of years that extreme economic inequality is a threat to stability and democracy:

Aristotle (384-322 B.C.), one of the most influential philosophers in history, who made contributions to logic, metaphysics, mathematics, physics, biology, botany, ethics, politics, agriculture, medicine, and other fields, concluded in "The Most Practical Type of Constitution":

"Good government is attainable in those states where there is a large middle class—large enough ... to be stronger than both of the other classes...The reasons why democracies are generally more secure and more permanent than oligarchies is the ... middle class.... is more numerous and is allowed a larger share in the government than it is in oligarchies."

The ancient Greek Platonist philosopher and prolific author Plutarch (A.D. 45-120) observed:

"An imbalance between the rich and the poor is the oldest and most fatal ailments of all republics"

Income Inequality

America's gross national income of $16.4 trillion makes it the most prosperous nation in the history of the world. Over the course of the twentieth century alone, real income per capita (adjusted for inflation) increased roughly eightfold. If national income were divided equally today among all employed persons, including those working part-time, each person would be earning $115,520 per year, or their annual work-hours could be cut in half with their income reduced on average to $57,760.[135] This is over two times the median personal income of $28,280 in 2012.

We cannot have a functioning economic system if we divide income or wealth equally, but disparities so large that the top 1% of Americans have 24% of the nation's income are unjust and economically, politically and socially harmful. The average income of the top 1% of U.S. households in 2011 was $1,530,773, while the average income of Americans in the bottom 20% was $9,187. The highest income for an individual was $4.9 billion. Part 4, note 1, details why this degree of income disparity is unjustifiable and harmful. The New Enlightenment policies would strongly incentivize formation of corporate structures that would create more egalitarian outcomes without redistribution. Also, more robust redistributive and other New Enlightenment policies will reduce extreme disparities with their widespread harmful consequences.

Our huge disparity of income is widening, and the rate at which it is widening is increasing. Despite a $1.3 trillion GDP increase over the 2009-2011 recovery period, the bottom 99% lost income, so effectively **121%** of the income gains went to the **top 1%**.[136] The top 10% share of income in 2012 is equal to 50.4% of all U.S. income, a level higher than 1928 right before the Great Depression. The great economic disparity then was an important part of the systemic failures that caused the Great Depression, as ours was of the Great Recession. The United States has a record level of inequality of income from labor, probably higher than in any other society at any time in the past, anywhere in the world. This includes societies in which skill disparities were extremely large, such as those with an educated class and a large fraction of the population illiterate. For example: We have greater labor income disparities than apartheid South Africa did, and India did when it had a large illiterate portion of its population with a small educated class.[137]

The share of prime working-age U.S. adults who can't generate enough income to meet their basic needs shot up from 31% in 2000 to 38% in 2010.[138] Over 150 million people are either in poverty or with low-income (less than two times the poverty level). Families in poverty do not cluster just below the poverty threshold. 44% have incomes of less than half the poverty line. These over one in sixteen Americans are the "severely poor," or live in "deep poverty," the highest on record. During the pre-recession 2000-2005 period, the number of the severely poor grew by 26%, over 50% faster than the overall population in poverty. From 2005 to 2012 the population of the severely poor increased by 28%, to 20.4 million.

Inequality of Opportunity

For most of our history, America has been known as the land of opportunity. If you were poor or born into a poor family, your chances of rising to high income or wealth were greater here than anywhere else in the world. Now, if you are poor or born into a low-income family, your chances of staying low-income throughout your life are higher in the United States than in any other advanced country.

Another Important Negative Outcome of Our Economic and Political Systems

Our nation's productive capacity is creating unprecedented national wealth and income. Due to advances in knowledge and the resulting technology and systems involved in economic performance, productivity has doubled since

1974. This could have resulted in our working half the number of hours for the same income as in 1974, or the same number of hours with two times the income, if we had an economic system designed to best serve the majority of the population. (One extreme example of a way productivity improved through technological advancement is through the almost universal use by businesses of spreadsheets on microcomputers. With these tools a person can do calculations, and analyze and organize data, in minutes, that could have taken that same person in 1974 months to accomplish.)

Instead of working fewer hours for the same income, the median household with children is working nine more hours per week, an increase from 58 to 67 hours or 15.5%; the median household income is about the same; the income of the bottom quintile has declined; and a larger fraction of the population is living in poverty.[139] The graph on the following page shows the upward progression in the number of hours worked for families both with and without children. The increase in work-hours of the median household has served mainly to increase the concentration of income and wealth in small economic elite.

Liberty and the ability to participate in a democracy are extremely limited when people are compelled to work almost all of their waking hours, as is now commonly the case—and unnecessarily so given our levels of productivity. The more time available for judgments on public policy issues, and to otherwise participate in the democratic process, the better we can participate.

Our productive capacity allows for a reduced full-time work-hour standard, while substantially increasing the standard of living of most people, including tens of millions of Americans in severe hardships—some typical of much poorer countries, including those mentioned earlier, such as: 20% of Americans in a Gallup poll said in 2013 that they did not have enough money to buy the food they needed on at least one occasion over the prior 12 months. Most of these people had the problem much more often than once, many who never thought it possible they would ever need emergency food assistance.

Dysfunction of our economic system is harming the great majority of Americans. And if we don't measure quality of life purely in terms of personal wealth, harm is caused to everyone. Everyone benefits from living in a decent, just, and well-functioning society. Part 1 and Part 4, Note 1 describes some of the ways even the "1%" is harmed by our economic system.

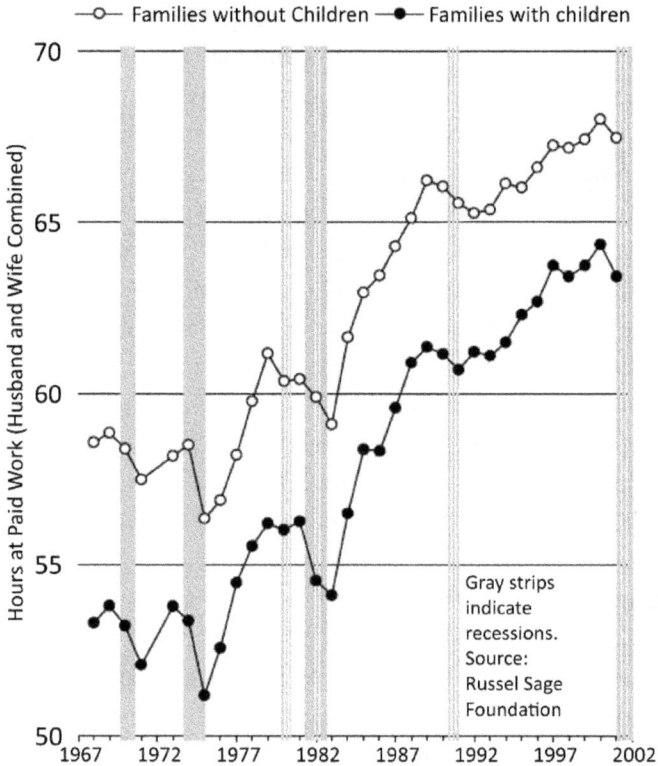

New Enlightenment economic policies, which include policies that motivate and support a transformation of the ownership and management structure of business enterprises, ensure that our economic system far better serves the country as a whole. They are designed for greater prosperity and a more just sharing of it, and for realizing some of the potential for widespread reduction of work-hours due to productivity advancements.

An important benefit of a system-wide per-person work-hour reduction is a reduction in unemployment. Without the advances of a shorter workweek, vacation time, earlier retirement and later labor force entrance, the economies of the OECD would never have attained the "golden age" of high employment that prevailed after the 1930s Depression. Between 1870 and 1970, work-hours of workers fell roughly by half. As productivity increased these countries instituted laws that reduced average work-hours per worker, in effect distributing work in a more economically beneficial and just way, as we should do now.

Limits to Growth

Between 1950 and 2000, world population more than doubled; world agricultural production tripled; world GDP and energy use quadrupled. World economic output continues to increase exponentially—the OECD projected, in 2012, growth at about a rate of 3% per year through 2030. If this growth rate continues, world GDP will be double 2012 levels in 2035.

At current levels of production, environmental and resource depletion problems are serious. Depletion of finite resources is likely to impact on world GDP before the worst impacts of global warming. Critics of the pessimistic position on growth limits have pointed out that new resource discoveries, new technologies for extraction, and the development of substitute resources as well as expanded recycling all extend the horizon of resource use. It is highly unlikely that these advances will do more than delay inevitable major resource limit problems sometime within this century.

Food production's worldwide land use is causing massive species extinction, soil erosion, and greenhouse gases emissions—more than all forms of transportation combined (largely from cattle and rice farm methane emissions and CO_2 from the cutting of rain forests), and is environmentally destructive in other ways.

An important issue will also be the environmental impacts of increased resource recovery. The highest quality and easiest to access mineral ores are exploited first, then as lower quality ores are accessed, the energy requirements to obtain processed metal, as well as the volume of related industrial waste, will rise. Our present mining operations have left a legacy of scarred earth and polluted water—how will we deal with future higher impact requirements? As world population grows, environmental degradation is likely to increase.

The New Enlightenment describes policies to mitigate global warming and the pollution created by economic activity, but policies that deal with resource limit projections are beyond the scope of this book. The economic policies of this book will create increased prosperity in the short to medium term—prosperity that is far more equitably shared. Eventually we will need to deal with resource limits, which will require social planning and international agreements. If governments anticipate resource constraints and act in a constructive manner these problems will be manageable.

As with all public issues, if the public interest is to be best served it will require a true government of, for, and by the people. New Enlightenment policies will create such a government. Both through their representatives and directly, the citizenry will be enabled to be much more effective participants in social planning decision-making processes.

The austerity economics that says "work longer and retire later" is exactly wrong. It will exacerbate the unjust trend of increasing the number of people unemployed, lowering wages of the majority of the population, and concentrating vast wealth and income in a small minority. Working less and sharing prosperity more equitably will be a great societal advance.

Although productivity advances are temporarily disruptive to some people, they should ultimately benefit everyone. This would be the outcome in an economic system designed by a well-functioning democracy. When productivity reaches levels that cause undesirable levels of unemployment, the country is best served by national labor regulatory reforms that reduce average system-wide work-hours per worker, while maintaining or increasing average incomes. And educational opportunities should be made easy to access for learning the skills needed for new work requirements that productivity advancements create.

Other nations have acted on the vision that reducing average work-hours per worker best serves their citizenry. Dutch workers have the world's shortest working hours—over 400 fewer work hours per year than American workers. The Dutch economy has been very productive, and their unemployment rate was 5.8% in December 2011, compared to 8.5% in the United States. The Netherlands has a positive trade balance and high personal savings. A Gallup survey ranks the Dutch third in the world in life satisfaction, behind only the Danes and Finns, and well ahead of Americans.[140] In 2000, the French government introduced a maximum work week of 35 hours. Wage subsidies support it.[141]

According to the OECD, in 2015, Americans worked 419 hours more than Germans; 308 more than the French; 125 more than Australians; 116 more than the British; 84 more than Canadians; and 71 hours more than the Japanese.[142]

The most effective, straightforward and beneficial way for society as a whole to share in the advantages of the enormous and rapidly growing productive capacities of modern mechanization and other technologies is through widespread ownership of businesses by their workers. These advantages will continue to increase with the creation of new technologies, so ideally, we all, or as many as possible or practical, need to have a piece of the business assets that create them. I will detail The New Enlightenment's practical 20-year program to largely accomplish this in Policy 3.

The falling costs and growing sophistication of robots have the potential to increase productivity rapidly. This can be a great benefit to the majority or be devastating through the high level of unemployment that could result. A small elite can make huge profits replacing people, or we can all reduce work-hours and share in the benefits of the enhanced productive capacity more equitably through The New Enlightenment policies to ensure a widespread establishment of worker-owned business enterprises and other policies.

Economists at the Massachusetts Institute of Technology, Erik Brynjolfsson and Andrew McAfee, believe rapid transformation to an extensive use of robots will occur. They wrote: *"The pace and scale of this encroachment into human skills is relatively recent and has profound economic implications."* In one example, a robotic manufacturing system initially cost $250,000 and replaced two machine operators, each earning $50,000 a year. Over the 15-year life of the system, the machines yielded $3.5 million in labor and productivity savings.[143] Only public policy can ensure that productivity advancements benefit the majority, rather than harm it.

Wasting an important advantage of our large and growing productivity by working unnecessarily long hours has negative impacts that will reach far beyond the present. When parents work long hours it harms children, and thus the future of the country. A 2007 UNICEF study ranked children's welfare in the Netherlands as the highest in the world. The United States was next to last of twenty-one wealthy countries studied. When parents commonly have little time for their children, this will naturally be the result.

The research on the effects of early life suggests that roughly half of our health as adults is programmed from conception to about the age of two.[144] The importance of these "first thousand days" is the subject of increased interest and study. Countries with healthier populations make it easier for parents to parent through fewer work-hours, including paid maternal during this formative period. Everyone in society gains when children grow up to be healthy adults. The rest of the world seems to understand this simple fact, so most developed and many developing countries have healthier populations.

What will be the future social cost of leaving children alone with today's television programming and video games, or with low-paid, poorly trained child care workers? We pay child care workers on average less than we pay animal caretakers and parking lot attendants. Children commonly experience a series of "bonding breaks" resulting from high child care worker turnover rates. Also, a shocking 16 million, or 22%, of children in the United States live in poverty, 7.3 million of whom are in deep poverty.

A shorter work-week will allow us to spend more time with family and friends, better participate in the political system, volunteer, take classes, do art or other activities that are creative, exercise more, sleep more, drive less, and engage in any other preferred leisure activities such as gardening. Rising incomes have failed to increase happiness. Working long hours as we have in the past to keep on doubling and redoubling our gross domestic product, even if there were no resource limits to continue to do this, would result in environmental disaster. *I will detail New Enlightenment programs for a better way forward toward more leisure time, no or very low unemployment, and a more equitable sharing of prosperity, and for creating a political system that will facilitate further advancements.*

This better way involves moderate increases in taxes on high income and wealth households. Since the requirement to pay taxes is a restriction of freedom, I would like to point out: The New Enlightenment holds the ideal of freedom as a high priority as well as the Enlightenment ideals of democracy, human rights, reason, and progress. Societies require that freedom must have some constraints, though, in the process of serving the other ideals or the greater good, in the form of rules determined through democratic processes, if cultural mores are not sufficient. The requirement to pay taxes is one of these necessary rules. We, and especially the wealthiest among us, cannot be free to shirk the financial responsibilities for the support of a just and prosperous society.

Can anyone deny that freedoms are denied to those tens of millions of Americans who are in poverty most of whom are food insecure, or unable to get treatment for illness due to lack of funds, or compelled to work long hours due to low pay, or lack opportunities for advancement? Or deny that some of these freedoms are far more significant than the lost freedom from society's insistence that the wealthy contribute their fair share to the society that not only allowed them to accumulate large amounts of wealth but was an active participant in the process? Or that all our freedoms would be greatly diminished if our infrastructure, public education system, and other government services did not exist or were made dysfunctional? Some of these services are poorly functioning now, withdrawing funds further is not likely to be part of the solution to the problem of how best to improve them.

The moral and economic and other justifications for higher taxes on high income and wealth I describe in more detail in Part 4, Note 1, rather than here, to avoid a large diversion from the focus on explaining the details of The Way to Prosperity for All. Also included is an exploration of other important justifications for higher taxes on high income and wealth, including reducing our "democracy deficit," other social problems, and even the health problems caused by conditions associated with inequality.

On moral and economic grounds, and to serve the advancement of democratic governance and other social values, from those with large amounts of income and wealth a justifiably large debt is owed to our society. If paid to support New Enlightenment economic and political reform policies, transformative beneficial impacts beyond and including the economic and political will result.

The New Enlightenment taxes will not significantly affect the lifestyle of the wealthiest in our society. Most of this book describes how we will use the resulting public funds for great benefit to all of society.

During the Age of Enlightenment, society advanced with radical ideas for economic, political and social development, and a common sense of shared responsibility to improve their world. It's time to re-clarify the importance of having an economic, political and social structure based on the Enlightenment ideals of democracy, human rights, reason, and progress. Applying the public-spiritedness, thoughtfulness, and dedication of many during the Enlightenment, we can solve our modern day fundamental economic, political, and social problems that are separating us from those ideals, and advance into a New Enlightenment. The social reforms detailed in this book is intended to be an important part of its foundation.

Evaluate New Enlightenment public policy proposals in Part 2 based only on whether they will, if instituted, achieve the goal of prosperity for all—not on whether the extent of the reforms is too large to be practically achievable by our political system. A new definition of practicality regarding public policy is required, one that would exist in a true democracy: If it benefits the majority, it should be considered practical, and only if it does not should it be regarded as impractical. The New Enlightenment political system reforms in Part 3 will ensure that we meet this ideal.

I developed New Enlightenment policies over about a five-year period beginning in December 2011. The policy details of Part 2 are based on data that change frequently, and some policy details require large amounts of calculation time. As the writing of the book progressed, it became clear it would be a multi-year project so I chose to write the policies using 2013 data and to determine their budgetary impact relative to the 2013 federal budget. The essential character of all the policies remains as beneficial as when they were written. When implemented, relatively minor adjustments will need to be made in some details based on conditions at the time. So far, we are taking a very different path than the one leading to the major social advancements I detail in this book. But it is not yet too late, though such a time could come. An elite that cannot see beyond their narrow self-interest is unprecedentedly wealthy and powerful so it is possible to descend into very extraordinary levels of injustice and dysfunction.

"We can either have democracy in this country or we can have great wealth concentrated in the hands of a few, but we can't have both."
Louis Brandeis, U.S. Supreme Court Justice (1856-1941)

The Most Immediate Way to a More Just Sharing of Prosperity, While Increasing Economic Activity, Reducing Full-time Work-hours, and Eliminating Unemployment

The most immediate way to establish a far greater degree of shared prosperity is through a greatly expanded earned income tax credit (EITC) or subsidy. The New Enlightenment EITC will eliminate the problem of the "working poor"—tens of millions of employed Americans with insufficient income to meet basic needs—and nearly eliminate poverty by creating many millions of new jobs. The wages of people whose income is below $50,000 per year will no longer pay income taxes; instead, the government will add money to their paychecks.[145] Also, as part of our labor regulatory reforms, we will reduce the full-time workweek to 36 hours from 40. Among the benefits will be a substantially reduced unemployment rate.

In 1850, the average number of weekly work-hours of an industrial worker was roughly 66 hours, or 11 hours per day, six days per week. Eventually, popular movements and productivity advancements led to a 44 hour-a-week standard, decreed by the 1938 Fair Labor Standards Act. This act required that beyond the 44-hour workweek limit, pay would be at one and a half times the base rate in covered industries, and it set a federal minimum wage. In 1940, Congress amended the Fair Labor Standards Act, reducing the federal workweek limit to 40 hours.

Based on Bureau of Labor statistics, the productivity in the nonfarm business sector increased from 1947 to 2014 by a factor of about 4.25 (data for 1940 were not available).[146] So we could work less than ten hours per week to have the same standard of living we had seven years after the 40 hour-a-week standard was established, and when the country was two years into the post-World War II boom. Although most of us would prefer a standard of living higher than the average of 1947, probably most of us would settle for double its standard of living, which should require less than 20 hours of work per week. So we are well past due for a popular movement to reduce work-hours and distribute the results of our enormous productive capacity more equitably. A reduction to 36 hours per week is a very conservative one.

All work-hours over 36 hours per week will be required to be paid at the time-and-a-half rate, and over 40 hours at double time. This will motivate corporations to reduce work-hours and make up the lost work-hours by hiring more people, reducing the unemployment rate to 2.8% (excluding this and other New Enlightenment policies' economic stimulus impact, which will eliminate it). A 2.8% unemployment rate is the lowest it's been since at least 1947, the farthest back U.S. Bureau of Labor Statistics data go. (The next lowest was in 1953, when it was 2.9% and, possibly not coincidentally, the top marginal income tax rate was 92%, among the highest in our history, second only to the 94% rate from 1944-45.) For the analysis determining the 2.8% unemployment rate, see the text boxes on the following two pages. If you prefer not to see the somewhat technical details, you can skip the text box content with no loss of continuity.

Despite the 10% reduction in work-hours resulting in as much as 10% less compensation from the workplace, everyone's take-home income covered under this overtime rule (less than $100,000 income) will rise, and rise proportionately more the lower the income due to either lower taxes or an expanded earned income tax credit. Not all companies will reduce full-time worker income an equal percentage as the 10% full-time work-hour reduction. Some companies will reduce it less, due to what research has revealed regarding worker productivity: Average worker productivity increases when full-time work-hours are reduced. Productivity increases because when people work less they have more energy and motivation during the time they are working. Corporate profits may increase from this effect, or preferably

Estimate for unemployment rate resulting from work-hour reduction (excluding reduction from stimulus impact)

In July 2013 there were 117.7 million full-time jobs (a decline since the start of the recession of four million) while part-time jobs grew by 2.6 million, to 27.4 million. Of the 117.7 million full-time jobs, 107.8 million were salaried and hourly workers, about 86.2 million of which will be covered by this new overtime rule. A 4 hour/week reduction in the work-hours of each of these 86.2 million full-time workers would yield 345 million work-hours/week to be supplied by new workers (or increased work-hours of part-time workers).

Not all workers will have their work-hours reduced by 4 hours. Assuming a conservative 70% of the 345, or a reduction of 241 million work-hours/week, this will require 6.7 million new full-time, 36 hour/week workers. However, the roughly 43 million salaried workers not covered under current overtime rules that will be covered under this new rule will have on average a much greater than 4 hour/week reduction. These workers now work on average 49 hours/week. Assuming a conservative additional average 3 work-hours/week reduction for these workers yields an additional 129 million work-hours/week. The total work-hours reduced that will be needed to be supplied by the new full-time workers is about 370 million, if the work-hours of part-time workers are not increased. This requires 10.3 million new full-time workers. Another conservative assumption we will make in determining the positive employment impact of the new fulltime 36 hour/week standard is that work-hour reductions in the top 20% will not occur, since overtime pay is not mandated for them. However, some reduction of work-hours requiring more workers in the top 20% will likely occur, due to pressures to maintain some work-hour parity.

Experience in other countries indicates that businesses will likely be able to satisfy labor requirements with about 94% of the increase in employment projected based on just reduced work-hour considerations, due to the productivity increases of workers working fewer hours.

Also, the number of persons employed part-time who would like a full-time job if one were available was 8.2 million in July 2013. We seek to assure that these people can have full-time employment also. Assuming the average number of hours per week of these workers is 25 hours, the number of total work-hours needed to provide full-time employment for them is 90 million.

Accounting for the work-hours needed for full-time employment of those now working part-time and for productivity increases leaves 258 million work-hours per week for new full-time workers. This is sufficient for 7.2 million new full-time workers (either hired or as partners in newly formed worker owned and self-directed companies, as detailed in Policy 3).

The July 2013 official number of unemployed persons was 11.5 million. So the official unemployment rate would be reduced to the difference between 11.5 and 7.2 million, or 4.3 million, divided by the size of the labor force in July 2013 of 155 million, or 2.8%. This analysis assumes that all new workers would be full-time, but if some are part-time more would be needed, reducing the official unemployment rate further.

corporations would increase hourly pay. Competitive pressures in the full employment environment created by this and other New Enlightenment policies will motivate businesses to at least account for the productivity increase with higher pay.

The reduced taxes will include both reduced income taxes on incomes under $160,000 and the elimination of the worker half of the payroll tax on all workers. Policy 2 specifies the income tax rates for all incomes.

The payroll tax elimination alone will give all workers covered by this new overtime rule, a take-home pay increase in an amount almost sufficient to compensate for the possible 10% reduction in workplace income without subsidies or an income tax cut. These workers now pay 7.65% of their income in payroll tax. As I describe in *Now Is the Time for The New Enlightenment,* the payroll tax is extremely regressive, which is why I propose that we extensively reform it by replacing the worker half of it with progressive taxes and eliminating the top income cap on the employer portion of the tax.

A large majority of businesses are covered by the Fair Labor Standards Act and we would extend coverage of this new overtime rule to all businesses. Currently, salaried workers can be excluded from the Act's overtime rule if they earn over $23,660 a year.[147] In 1975, 62% of full-time U.S. salaried workers were eligible for overtime; now fewer than 8% are eligible. This has resulted in employers abusing by many low and middle-income people by demanding over 40 hours per work-week for no overtime pay. For example, some of the nation's largest chain restaurants and retailers, including Starbucks, Chipotle, Walmart, and Ralphs supermarkets, have expected salaried employees to work long hours while denying them overtime because they were classified as managers with pay over $23,660 per year. An August 2014 Gallup poll found that the average number of hours worked per week by a salaried worker is 49.

New Enlightenment policy will extend the overtime requirement to all salaried and hourly workers under the 80th percentile in income, now about $100,000 per year. Although this new rule will not cover workers earning between $100,000 and $160,000, social pressures will reduce work-hours in this income group to maintain some parity with covered workers. However, any in this group not receiving a work-hour reduction will receive a take-home pay increase resulting from lower taxes.

Federal regulation will allow pay reductions up to 14% for workers having work-hour reductions of 14% or more to meet the requirement of 36 hours without overtime pay. Corporate profits have soared with upper management pay due to both the suppression of worker pay and the increase of their work-hours. Companies most abusive of the excessive work-hour tolerance of salaried workers in corporate culture earning less than $100,000 per year will be relatively disadvantaged by this policy (but justifiably so). They would need to reduce profits and/or upper management pay to compensate for the higher costs from reducing the work-hours to 36 hours of salaried workers working over 42 work-hours per week. (42 to 36 hours is about a 14% reduction.)

Financial and social pressures on businesses to institute full-time work-hour reductions as soon as possible after the policy is implemented will be substantial for those eligible for the mandated overtime pay. Although financial pressures will likely be sufficient, additionally, we will promote the policy as a full employment policy where business's civic duty would be to reduce full-time work-hours to the new 36-hour standard to the degree practical. And ignoring their civic duty will be costly in another way: Many workers will prefer to work for businesses that do not require work over 36 hours per week.

As a further incentive to reduce full-time work-hours and to mitigate additional expenses to corporations resulting from this policy, $500 per month will be the subsidy for each new full-time worker over the number of employees prior to the institution of this policy for a period of one year. To receive the subsidy, we will require that full-time work-hours be reduced to 36 hours for nine or more full-time workers for each subsidized new hire. For companies with fewer than nine additional full-time workers, the requirement will be reduced to the number they have. Businesses that are prosperous and growing their workforce without reducing work-hours will also add the additional employees resulting from the work-hour reduction.

Redirected unemployment insurance funds will support most of the corporate subsidies. If all the 10.4 million unemployed persons in December 2013 and the 3.5 million "missing workers" who have dropped out of the labor force because they have lost hope of finding employment are hired, the subsidy cost would be $83 billion, which is less than federal expenditures on unemployment insurance in 2012, and the federal government will be responsible for only a portion of the subsidy cost according to the system described shortly.[148]

The economic stimulus effect of the wage subsidy and other New Enlightenment policies will be large, substantially increasing demand for workers. This increased demand will be more than sufficient to employ all in the official labor force and the 3.5 million "missing workers."[149] As we will show, the number of workers required to supply the work-hours lost by reducing full-time work-hours, in addition to the stimulus impact of this and other New Enlightenment policies will eliminate unemployment and could result in a labor shortage requiring some businesses to employ some workers over 36 hours per week at the overtime rate.

Likely, though, most of the excess demand for workers will be met by more people entering the workforce than indicated by the 3.5 million "missing workers" estimate, considering our 62.8% labor-force participation rate. For unemployment reduction estimate calculations, see *Economic Stimulus Including Employment Impact of All Policies*, Note 2 of Part 4. After the year the subsidies are in effect, these New Enlightenment policies would save the federal government about $50 billion per year in unemployment benefit costs if unemployment is eliminated.

However, some relatively short-term unemployment is unavoidable due to business failures, normal labor market churning, and possible skills mismatches. We will assume a conservative $40 billion annual unemployment compensation expenditure saving in our federal budget calculations. The saving in state budgets will be similarly large, reducing or eliminating deficits, allowing infrastructure and additional education and other expenditures that would not have been possible otherwise.

Since productivity continues to increase and median wages continue to stagnate, the long-term trend in the number of people wanting to work but not able to find suitable employment is not likely to be down without major public policy changes such as this one. The 62.8% labor-force participation rate in 2015 is a 36-year low and it is expected to trend lower. The unemployment rate is not the best measure of the amount of involuntary unemployment since it excludes those who gave up looking for work due to lack of opportunities.

The corporate $500/month subsidy will require the cooperation of the states since unemployment insurance is mainly a function of the states and the subsidy will be considered part of the unemployment insurance system. The federal government paid $185 billion of the total $434 billion paid in unemployment benefits from 2007 through 2011. This average 43/57 federal/state unemployment funding support partnership will be applied to the subsidy funding support. Any state that chose not to participate would lose federal unemployment funds and the stimulus impact of the corporate subsidies. The states would support 57% of the $500 subsidy, or $285 for the official number unemployed when this policy is implemented, to corporations for new hires over the course of the year the subsidy policy is in effect. The federal government will pay the balance and pay 100% of the subsidy for any number of new hires above the official number unemployed when this policy is implemented. The many benefits of this policy will likely motivate state cooperation. Corporations in states that cooperate will have a competitive advantage over those in states that do not—another reason that likely all states will cooperate.

The possible benefit reduction per worker supplied by corporations due to the reduced work-hours per worker and increased number of workers will be compensated for by a national health system and a substantial increase in Social Security benefits. I will detail these policies, including their funding supports, later (the Social Security reform in this book and the health system reform in a subsequent document).

To solve the potential problem of requiring more facilities such as office space for the increase in number of workers, the standard 8-hour workday for five days per week per worker could be changed to a 9-hour workday for four days per week per worker, while maintaining the five workdays to accommodate the increase in the number of workers. This increases by 12.5% the number of people that can use existing facilities, more than sufficient for the approximately 10% increase resulting from the work-hour reduction. It also reduces commute costs per worker in time, money and effort, and commute environmental costs.

Supporting income below a defined level using government funds was also proposed by the Nobel Prize winning "conservative" economist Milton Friedman, and we now provide this for low-income workers through the Earned Income Tax Credit. In its original form the EITC was signed into law by President Ford in the 1970s. President Reagan, who deemed it *"the best anti-poverty, the best pro-family, the best job creation measure to come out of congress,"* substantially expanded it. The EITC has been supported and expanded by both Republican and Democratic administrations and congresses.

Studies have shown that the EITC has a positive labor supply effect. One recent study found that the EITC leads about one in ten parents who would not otherwise be working to enter the labor force. Another study, reported by the National Bureau of Economic Research, showed that lower tax rates and bigger tax credits helped low-income families more than other government programs did, and confirms that the Earned Income Tax Credit increases labor-force participation.[150] As a result, its full effects on poverty and hardship may be even greater than its direct effects.[151]

Although this expanded EITC program is expensive, and is the most expensive New Enlightenment program, it will almost eliminate poverty directly through the subsidies, and by solving the problem of the decline in labor-force participation. The Congressional Budget Office (CBO) projects the labor-force participation rate will fall to 60.8% over the next decade. Several factors are causing this decline, among them are federal policies that discourage work. The best anti-poverty programs encourage work. This policy will eliminate the need for many other less beneficial anti-poverty programs.

The current EITC has not only lifted millions of people out of poverty, it has also increased the incomes of families most likely to spend that additional money. In the 2013 tax year, over 27 million working families and individuals received the EITC.

In summary, increasing the EITC and extending it upward, while reducing work-hours and unemployment is justified because:

- Productivity has soared while lower and middle-class wages have declined or stagnated.
- Many remain in poverty, including many millions of "working poor."
- The average number of work-hours of the employed, and the number unemployed have increased.

The following EITC will eliminate the problem of the "working poor" and nearly eradicate poverty by creating many millions of new jobs. Full-time workers earning between $10,000 and $20,000 will receive an income supplement of $15,000. This supplement will incrementally decline to $10,000 for full-time workers earning $30,000; to $5,000 for full-time workers earning $40,000; and then to zero for full-time workers earning $50,000. All tax rates and income supplement amounts we will determine using the sum of all forms of income from labor and capital. Capital gains or "carried interest" will not get preferential treatment, as it now does. The tax rate for full-time workers with incomes between $50,000 and $90,000 will be cut to 10% of income. The taxes for people with incomes of between $90,000 and $160,000 will be cut to 20%. All marginal tax rates and income supplement amounts are detailed in the table in Policy 2.

We will require that only filers reporting income over $10,000 per year will qualify for the increased EITC. This requires at least half-time (18 hours/week annual average) work at the minimum wage ($11.10 under New Enlightenment policy, initially) and proportionately less work time for higher wage workers. Since New Enlightenment policy will create a full employment labor market, many opportunities for work will exist. (For those unable to work, New Enlightenment policy will substantially increase Social Security disability payments, as detailed later, and for anyone earning less than $10,000 the current EITC will apply.)

Current law stipulates that only the filing statuses in the categories single, head of household, married filing jointly, or qualifying widow or widower can be eligible for the EITC. Taxpayers who file as "married filing separately" cannot get the credit. Although the qualification and credit amounts when filing jointly somewhat reduce the marriage penalty, some remains and is unjust.

We will eliminate any marriage penalty for the expanded EITC by allowing the "married filing separately" status. If disallowing it is maintained under this proposal, an unjust marriage penalty will exist far greater than currently exists, that would motivate many people not to marry who otherwise would. It would also greatly disadvantage children of married couples. Under New Enlightenment policy each partner in a married couple would get the same credit as if they were single, using the filing status "married filing separately." Also, we will eliminate the child tax credit, which costs about $57 billion per year.[152] The benefit to married couples with children from the expanded EITC will be far greater than that existing from the child tax credit.

The lowest income two-parent households with both working full-time will have $70,000 tax-free income per year: $40,000 from the workplace and $30,000 in EITC, from two $15,000 credits. The lowest income two-parent households working half-time will have $50,000 tax-free income per year, $20,000 from the workplace and $30,000 in EITC. These are worst-case situations; rarely will both parents in a household be working at minimum wage.

In addition to the full-time work-hour reduction freeing up time for leisure and raising children, this greatly expanded EITC will do so for many millions of people by allowing them to work less than full-time for a livable income. Currently, two parent households working half-time at minimum wage have a workplace income of $14,500 and an EITC of $3,373 for a total income of $17,873, so the New Enlightenment EITC and $11.10 minimum wage will almost triple their income (increase it by a factor of 2.8).

In 1968, the minimum wage in 2015 dollars was $10.65 per hour.[153] However, it could and should be far higher today—we are a far wealthier country, with a far higher GDP per capita than in 1968, due to productivity increases. According to Bureau of Labor Statistics, productivity grew by a factor of 2.35 since 1968.[154] If we all shared in the benefits resulting from these gains, the 1968 minimum wage would be $25 per hour today.

Full-time workers under New Enlightenment policy would have an effective minimum wage of $19.40 per hour, but since the subsidy amount is the same for half-time workers their effective minimum wage would be higher, $27.80 per hour. Based on our nation's experience in 1968, and productivity increases since then, our economy can support an effective minimum wage between $19.40 and $27.80 per hour. In fact, the economy would boom based on the increased purchasing power of many tens of millions of Americans.

The yearly cost to the federal government of the income supplements will be $904 billion.[155] This cost will be supplied by higher taxes on approximately the top 8% of incomes and lower taxes on the 49th through 92nd income percentile if the revenue increase resulting from the economic stimulus effect of this policy is included. Middle and lower income people will spend money received as a result of this "reverse income tax" policy that they currently do not have. This will cause further increases in employment to satisfy rising demand and higher incomes to some of those currently employed, which will result in higher tax revenues. The payroll tax elimination on workers will reduce government revenues by about $420 billion per year and will be replaced by eliminating the cap on the Social Security tax the employer pays and progressive taxes I describe later.

Mark M. Zandi, Ph.D., a frequent advisor to policymakers and the chief economist of Moody's Analytics, where he directs economic research, found that for every dollar the federal government spends on increased food stamps, work share programs, or unemployment benefits, U.S. economic output increases by $1.71, $1.64, and $1.55 respectively. (The process that results in more than $1 in output increase from $1 in spending I describe in Part 4, Note 2). The stimulus effect of this policy will yield about $275 billion in additional federal tax revenue, assuming the 1.55/1 ratio. However, this does not take into account the relatively small decrease in spending from the high-income groups that will pay taxes on their income at a higher rate. I take into account the various economic impacts of this policy in the comprehensive budget analysis in Part 4, Note 2. This policy will also increase revenue on the state and local levels.

Some will say that both the wage subsidy and reduced work-hours are reforms that are too "radical" and not "practical," or politically not achievable because too many people, especially the prominent "pundits" and those currently in government will view them as too radical. Good reasons exist to have an entirely contrary view regarding how radical[156] the proposals are.

Between 1870 and 1970, work-hours fell by half, due to advancements in productivity. Since 1970, productivity has more than doubled, so work-hours could again have fallen by half for anyone who wanted to maintain the same material well-being as existed in 1970. It could have if we had an economic and political system that served the interests of the great majority of the people. This proposal, and the following one detailing income tax rates, some may reasonably consider to be too timid, moderate or conservative. Neither proposal will change the fact that some people will continue to have an after-tax income for a few minutes of work, or even no work, exceeding that of tens of millions of other people working full-time for a year. So you decide if the proposals are an appropriate step toward a more just and equitable society.

The $904 billion expanded EITC cost is less than 10% of the total adjusted gross income reported in 2013, and slightly over 5% of GDP. Considering the enormous income inequalities existing, it is a moderate measure for this proportion of national income to be used to create a more just income distribution, mainly by benefiting workers in the bottom half of the distribution.

If instituted, these policies will greatly enhance the well-being of the large majority of people, and really everyone if you measure well-being using a more appropriate measure than dollars exclusively. If we had a functioning democracy, it would be considered "impractical" to stop the implementation of these policies because functioning democracies are designed for instituting policies that serve the majority well. The New Enlightenment political system reforms, in concert with our economic system reforms, will create a functioning democracy. We then can decide together on how best to reduce workhours and enhance egalitarianism further. Egalitarianism is more vigorously promoted in *A System to Facilitate Widespread Establishment of Worker-Owned Enterprises* (Policy 3), and to some degree in all other New Enlightenment policies.

---

*The New Enlightenment: Ideals of Democracy, Human Rights, Reason, and Progress * Policy 1*

Increase Marginal Tax Rates on the Wealthy

In a nation with a widening chasm between the wealthy and everyone else, it is reasonable for those at the top to pay more in taxes. We need public funds for programs that create greater equality of opportunity, for supporting the provision of public goods, and to lift tens of millions of people out of poverty and greatly reduce economic hardship for tens of millions more. These higher taxes on the wealthy are fully justified on the moral, economic and other grounds detailed in Part 4, Note 1. However, it is important to dispel here one successfully established myth created by advocates of lower taxes for the rich and corporations, that the wealthy are the job producers, so anything that reduces their income will reduce their ability and incentive to create jobs.

Lack of funds is not holding back job creation. America's corporations are sitting on over $4.75 trillion in cash.[157] And it is not our dysfunctional financial sector's inability to find profitable ways to invest the cash. What is holding back job creation is the lack of demand for products and services. If more demand existed, firms would respond with investment and hiring. Many decades of experience exist where unemployment rates were far lower and business investment rates were far higher when tax rates were very much higher than they are now (as they were for decades until 1980). It is demand that creates jobs, so it is our high level of inequality that is destroying jobs because it is characterized by many tens of millions of people with too little money to purchase the goods and services they would if they could afford to.

The table summarizes the New Enlightenment income supplements and tax rates. The income supplements and tax rates apply to all income, from whatever source: wages, capital gains, or "carried interest."

It is well justified to treat income from capital gains no differently from income derived from wages and salaries. The inequality in capital gains is greater than that in any other form of income. Giving a tax break to capital gains is mainly giving a tax break to the very rich. The bottom 90% of the population gets less than 10% of all capital gains. The 400 highest-income taxpayers in 2007, each with an average income of over $300 million, paid only 17% of their total incomes in taxes that year because most of their incomes were treated as capital gains when the capital gains rate was 15% and the labor tax rate was 35%.

Income	Marginal tax rate
$410,000+	55%
$260,000 - $410,000	50%
$160,000 - $260,000	40%
$90,000 - $160,000	20%
$50,000 - $90,000	10%
$40,000 - $50,000	0% Tax 0-$5,000 Income supplement
$30,000 - $40,000	0% Tax $5-$10,000 Income supplement
$20,000 - $30,000	0% Tax $10-$15,000 Income supplement
$10,000 - $20,000	0% Tax $15,000 Income supplement

Also, capital gains tax cuts motivate corporations to pay out dividends leaving fewer funds inside the corporation for investment.

For more information justifying equalizing the capital gains and labor tax rate, and on eliminating a capital gains tax avoidance technique the wealthy sometimes use, see Part 4, Note 1, page 448.

Nobel Prize-winning economist Peter Diamond and the American Economics Association's John Bates Clark Medal winner, Emmanuel Saez, did an analysis to determine the tax rates that would maximize federal revenues and provide other social benefits. They found that the optimum federal tax rate on incomes over $400,000 is between 48% and 76%. The higher rate applies if tax avoidance and evasion opportunities are minimized. They base their calculations on their maximum estimate of how responsive high-income taxpayers are to the top tax rate, so an optimum range is likely higher. They also determined optimal rates higher than our proposed rates for incomes over $100,000.

The analysis by Diamond and Saez does not take into account the variable effectiveness of the use of the resulting tax revenues in economic stimulus. Economic stimulus impacts proportionately increase incomes. If our policies are unusually economically stimulative compared to the previous use of tax revenues, which there are good reasons to believe they will be, the optimal rates determined by Diamond and Saez would be higher. When revenues resulting from higher taxes on high incomes are mainly directed to people with low incomes, this is the most direct and immediate way to increase demand and the resulting incomes.

Also, their calculations do not reflect the benefit of productivity enhancements from increasing the perception of fairness. The sense that our economic system is unfair undermines trust and motivation, which is essential for the functioning of our economy (and our democracy).

New Enlightenment rates are at the low end or lower than the optimal income tax rates determined by Diamond's and Saez's analysis because they provide a sufficient amount of funds to accomplish our goals in combination with other New Enlightenment tax and expenditure reduction policies (and to minimize controversy over the increased rates).

Economist Thomas Piketty, a renowned expert on the character of economic inequality within and among nations worldwide, estimates an optimal top tax rate in the developed countries of above 80%. He wrote: *"The evidence suggests that a rate on the order of 80% on incomes over $500,000 or $1 million a year not only would not reduce the growth of the U.S. economy but would in fact distribute the fruits of growth more widely while imposing reasonable limits on economically useless (or even harmful) behavior…The idea that all U.S. executives would immediately flee to Canada and Mexico* [if his recommended tax rates were instituted] *and no one with the competence or motivation to run the economy would remain is not only contradicted by historical experience … it is also devoid of common sense."*[158]

Highly progressive taxation maintains free competition and private property while individual incentives are modified according to democratically determined rules. They allow an ideal compromise between social justice and individual freedom. The United States, which has always highly valued individual liberty, earlier in our history adopted tax systems more progressive than those in any other country.

From 1936 to 1980, the top marginal tax rate was 70% or more, and the average was 82%. Since 1987, the official top rate has remained below 40%, and the effective rate, after all deductions and credits, between 18% and 25%.

When the U.S. occupied Japan and Germany after World War II and set up new democratic governments, it set a top marginal tax rate of 85 and 90% respectively, as part of the civilizing and democratizing process. U.S. top rates were 91% at the time.

Analysis of historical data reveals a positive correlation between economic growth and top tax rates. Contrary to the claims of "supply-side" economists, economic growth tends to be greater in years when top tax rates are higher. This graph makes the positive correlation clear.

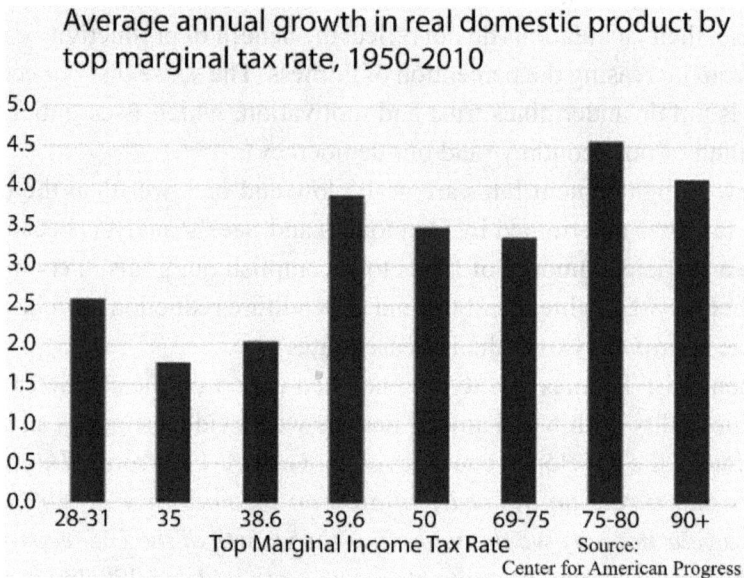

Average annual growth in real domestic product by top marginal tax rate, 1950-2010

Top Marginal Income Tax Rate

Source: Center for American Progress

From 1951 to 1980, when the top rate was between 70% and 92%, average annual growth in the American economy was 3.7%. These tax rates that many of the most prominent "pundits" and politicians claim would cause economic disaster are associated with the opposite, economic boom. The growth rate over the decade 2006 through 2015 averaged 1.4%.[159] "Supply-siders" claim that Ronald Reagan's 1981 tax cuts caused the 1980s economic boom. In fact, that boom followed Reagan's 1982 tax increase. Similarly, most of the 1990s boom followed Bill Clinton's 1993 tax increase.

Many factors are involved in economic growth. Correlation does not prove causation; however, the positive historical correlation of growth and top tax rates proves that higher top tax rates are not incompatible with higher growth rates, as the most prominent "pundits" in the media would have you believe. Some of the resulting increase in funds from the increase in top tax rates were used to support research and development, infrastructure improvements, serve the ideal of equal opportunity for everyone, and reduce inequality, so causal factors are involved in the positive correlation. These kinds of policies are economically stimulative. (see Part 4, Note 1, for more details).

These taxes on incomes over $50,000 will raise $758 billion more than our current tax system per year assuming pre-tax incomes remain the same as in 2013. However, pre-tax income will increase from the stimulation of economic activity from the income supplements. The resulting tax revenues will be about the amount needed for the income supplements proposed. The economic stimulus impact of New Enlightenment policies I take into account in Part 4, Note 2.

The New Enlightenment wage supplements and tax reductions for the middle class will enable them to spend more. This increase in spending will increase employment, corporate profits, stock prices, and tax revenues. Although the rich will pay higher taxes and thereby receive a somewhat smaller share of the economy's overall gains, those overall gains will be larger than they would be otherwise. Wealthy Americans may come out ahead compared to where they were before.

*The New Enlightenment: Ideals of Democracy, Human Rights, Reason, and Progress * Policy 2*

A System to Facilitate Widespread Establishment of Worker-Owned and Self-Directed Enterprises

For democracy to survive, the institutions within democratic societies must not be antithetical to it, and if any institution becomes so, we must reform or reinvent it.

Corporate capitalism as currently practiced is anti-democratic. Workers in most corporations are told what to do and have no influence on corporate policy, including how corporate income is distributed among workers, management, and owners. For five days per week, most adults devote most of their waking hours (including commute time) to these anti-democratic institutions, and partly as a result, democracy is also disappearing from our political system. Corporations and the economic elites that control them are having an undue and extremely disproportionate influence on public policy.

Widespread employee ownership and control of business enterprises will create a more democratic society. Democratic control will eliminate wide income disparities and the resulting negative economic, political and social consequences and eliminate other injustices resulting from an anti-democratic, hierarchical form; develop a sense of community within businesses and between businesses and their local communities; and motivate more productive work. This can be more than just a utopian ideal. This policy is a detailed, practical route to widespread worker-ownership and control of business enterprises.

Our corporate capitalist form violates basis property rights. Most owners or shareholders of public companies have no say on how much of the profits of the corporation they will receive. Property rights normally imply access to the fruits of the property. Public companies' shareholders also generally have no say in the pay of the people running the company they own, which would also normally be part of an owner's property rights. And they have no say in how corporate funds are used to influence our political system through campaign contributions and lobbying. In general, it is difficult for public company shareholders to challenge what management does with the business they own. The essential character of employee-owned and controlled businesses includes basic property rights for the business enterprise owners.

Also, property rights are now commonly violated because in our knowledge-based economy the value of knowledge is a substantial part of the value of businesses, and much of this knowledge resides in workers. Essentially, workers embody company value to a far greater degree than the value of the company's financial capital they own. To estimate this value consider: As of November 24, 2014, the ratio of market value to book value (the total of the value of the company assets shown on its balance sheet or accounting records) for the S&P 500 was 2.88, so off-balance sheet intangible assets comprised 65.3% of the total market value of those firms. On Nov 24, 2014, the total market value of all publicly-traded U.S. firms was $21.7 trillion. Assuming the market value to book value ratio for the total market is the same as that of the S&P 500, intangible assets totaled $14.2 trillion for public companies. Not all intangible assets reside in workers, though. Intangible assets include the intellectual property of patents and copyrights; the intellectual capital of databases and general business methods; and the knowledge and practices of workers, or their "economic competencies."

One extensive study found that about 44% of the intangible asset value resides in employee's "economic competencies" or about 29% of total firm value.[160] *That is $6.2 trillion just in public company value alone.* (This does not include the value of other components of intellectual capital that current workers may have contributed to.) Workers embody or possess this capital in a limited sense because financial investors capture the market or financial value embodied in the workers. If workers were the financial owners of the firm, their economic competencies' associated financial capital would go to the rightful owners of this capital.

If it were common that businesses were wholly owned by the workers in them, our large and growing economic disparity would be substantially reduced because businesses are a major form of national wealth and the relatively low labor income disparity inherent in worker-owned and controlled enterprises. Also, widespread capital ownership allows widespread sharing of the appreciation of asset values. Among the reasons this is important is asset values tend to grow more rapidly than the economy.

An extensive study of international historical data found that although return on capital, r, depends on many technological, social, and cultural factors, it has resulted in an average return of roughly 4% - 5% for centuries. The economic growth rate, g, has been less. The long-term disparity between r and g results in growing inequalities of wealth and income. Income inequalities grow with wealth inequalities because income from investments grows at a rate exponentially faster than income from labor, whose growth rate is associated with the economic growth rate. However, over the last few decades, median labor income has been growing much more slowly than the economic growth rate, creating a more rapid than average growth in inequalities.

The two world wars and the Great Depression and their policy responses interrupted, for about three decades, the general trend of r being greater than g through the destruction of capital, high inflation, and radical policy changes; many of which have been undone.[161] This process will now continue to proceed with terrifying results unless it is interrupted again with vigorous public policy solutions. This New Enlightenment policy will solve the growing economic disparity problem and reverse the trend while increasing national prosperity. It will do so more effectively than any policy instituted in the history of the United States, and it will be more enduring because of its systemic nature.

Probably the most beneficial and valuable form of capital or wealth that individuals can possess is the value of the business enterprises in which they work. In addition to business value appreciation, worker-owners gain profits, which can be larger than appreciation or the average gains on stocks. Corporate profit margins vary by industry, but on average, they were 13.6% in 2012, a post–World War II high.[162]

The top 1/100 million highest wealth holders in the world received an average rate of return of 6.8%, much higher than the average adult who received a 2.1% return from 1987 through 2013 (adjusted for inflation).[163] The profit percentage is relative to sales and the asset appreciation rate is relative to asset values so these numbers are not directly comparable, however, based on sales to asset value ratios it is common that profits exceed asset appreciation of even the super wealthy.

Receiving both profits and asset appreciation brings the greatest return on capital. r being greater than g is less important if the majority of people have a significant amount of the kind of capital—the business enterprise in which they work and that they control—that brings the greatest return.

Beyond greatly reducing economic inequality is a justification for the widespread establishment of worker-owned and self-directed enterprises of even more fundamental importance. Our nation's most important ideal is that those in power should not be able to take away any of our fundamental rights without due process of law. Many lives have been lost to acquire and defend these rights, and we will continue to spend many trillions of dollars presumably to defend them. But the structure of the enterprises dominating our society requires that most of us sacrifice some of our fundamental human rights to live.

In addition to "bosses" grabbing an increasing portion of corporate income for themselves by using their power to depress median wages and benefits as much as the market will bear for workers, bosses can choose to end any worker's income and often pension and healthcare entirely for almost any reason, with workers having no recourse. 150,000 people are fired without legitimate reason per year.[164] Also, "bosses" have knowingly devastated the lives of many people by firing all or a substantial fraction of their companys' workers to move operations to a foreign low wage, low regulation country.

Workers sometimes must submit to control of their off-job time because their livelihood is in jeopardy if they don't. However, many workers have been unable to avoid being fired based on behavior off the job. Workers have been fired for their political views, their blog content, whether they drink or smoke off job, associate with any group their boss disapproves, and other behaviors their boss disapproves (such as riding a motorcycle off work, which, to reduce healthcare cost risks, can be against company policy).

In addition to video, GPS and computer activity monitoring at work, workers are commonly required to access the company server at home, which gives access to personal information on their home computer. Many known cases exist where employers monitor personal emails of workers at work, and the power to access personal information likely is also abused at worker's homes. 25% of employers have fired employees based on email content.[165] Your boss can require you to have with you a GPS enabled company cell phone evenings and weekends, which allows your boss to know where you are always. Privacy has also been obscenely violated during indiscriminate urine tests for drugs where workers have been required to allow a person watch as they give the sample, to guard against urine substitution.

Some "little tyrannies" that are the economic enterprises that dominate our larger society abuse their top-down structure less than others, but all such social structures where some people can dominate others unaccountable to any kind of democratically determined system of justice are unjust to varying degrees.[166] We must restructure at least most of them to a democratic form if we are to live in a truly democratic country.

Worker owned and democratically controlled enterprises exist in our economy and interact normally with conventional business, which facilitates successful transformation to a society where worker-owned and self-directed enterprises are the predominant kind of business enterprise in the country. The new society can gradually develop within the old. Worker owned and self-directed enterprises currently are in all sectors of our economy, from banking, finance, and insurance to education, manufacturing, retail, and agriculture. Nationwide, 223 worker cooperatives having 7,500 worker-owners now exist.[167] All worker cooperatives are worker-owned and self-directed enterprises (WSDEs). Also, in the United States, 13.8 million worker-owners are in Employee Stock Ownership Plan corporations (ESOPs) that are generally not worker self-directed.

Economic democracy does not reject the role of markets, rather it tempers the profit maximization motive that currently drives the way in which businesses engage with the market with a greater emphasis on worker and community interests. For example:

A non-worker board of directors directs conventional corporations; they make the decisions on all important corporate policies. They decide how to distribute corporate income, including among the workers as pay, or select managers that determine worker pay. Public company managers often decide on their own pay or influence the selection of those who do, which is responsible for much of the explosive growth in income inequality. This results in harmful consequences, including the corruption of our political system. In cooperatively owned businesses the workers make all the important decisions through democratic processes, both directly and through an elected board of directors from among the workers. The workers choose the maximum level of wage disparity among workers that they consider the most just and beneficial, which results in far lower disparities.

One of the most serious, common and well-justified criticisms of conventional capitalism is that its design intrinsically motivates enterprises to create "negative externalities" (costs associated with a product or service that the provider does not pay so are not incorporated in the price) to maximize profits. With worker-ownership and control, this tendency is reduced for some kinds of negative externalities and eliminated in others.

One example of a negative externality: A business pollutes the environment to save pollution mitigation costs. Associated cleanup and possible harm to health and other costs are paid by others rather than the business. Another example is when a business leaves a community for lower labor or regulatory costs, or tax or subsidy advantages elsewhere, conventional businesses ignore the economic and social costs to the abandoned community, and the community pays. All the harmful consequences of inequality are also negative externalities of businesses of conventional corporate form.

A board of directors in a remote city may not be concerned with their decision's resulting harm to the environment of their business. They tend to base their decision purely on the profit motive, but workers in control of their business would make more beneficial decisions because they have to live with the consequences.

Worker-ownership also keeps resources from being transferred from local communities to multinational corporations and their owners, which can also be considered a negative externality. Supreme Court Justice William O. Douglas decried the *"effect on the community when independents are swallowed up by the trusts and entrepreneurs become employees of absentee owners."* The result, Douglas wrote, *"is a serious loss in citizenship. Local leadership is diluted. He who was a leader in the village becomes dependent on outsiders for his action and policy. Clerks responsible to a superior in a distant place take the place of resident proprietors beholden to no one."[168]* In Fireside Chat 6, Franklin D. Roosevelt warned of a *"definition of Liberty... where a free people* (are) *gradually regimented into the service of the privileged few."*

Almost everyone considers democracy the best way to govern our society. In democracies, people participate in decisions that affect their lives either directly or through their representatives. As you will see, it is eminently practical to realize democratic ideals in our economy or work life, through widespread business enterprise worker-ownership and control.

Cooperatively owned businesses can range from small-scale to multibillion-dollar businesses. The worker-owned Mondragon Corporation (a conglomerate of cooperatives) in Spain has over 83,000 full-time and over 15,000 part-time workers. It is one of the most successful corporations in Europe. Their highest paid worker is compensated in amount about 6.5 times that of the lowest paid worker. In the U.S., the top to median pay ratio for corporations of similar size is over 350 to 1, top-to-bottom over 750 to 1. As are all worker cooperatives, the Mondragon Corporation is both worker owned and worker self-directed.[169]

The number of Americans involved in worker-owned ESOP firms has increased, from 250,000 in 1975 to about 13.8 million working in over 11,000 firms today. These firms are not "worker cooperatives" or WSDEs, or democratically run to the degree that Mondragon Cooperatives are, and most are not 100% worker-owned. However, their degree of worker-ownership has revealed some important advantages of workers sharing in the ownership of the firms in which they work:

Each year Fortune magazine publishes the results of surveys on "100 Best Companies to Work For." Corporations with broad-based employee ownership or profit sharing, although only 10% of the Fortune 500, regularly represent over half the winners.[170] Publix Supermarkets is the largest ESOP, with 160,000 employees. It was named as one of Fortune magazine's "100 Best Companies to Work For" (1998–2014) and "Most Admired Companies" (1994–2014) and was ranked as one of the top ten companies on the Forbes list of the largest private companies (1996–2013). Publix also scored higher than any other supermarket for customer satisfaction in a national survey conducted by the American Customer Satisfaction Index (1995–2014).

ESOPs by the end of 2012 generated $1.059 trillion in assets for 13.8 million employee-owners—a per capita retirement account balance of about $77,000,[171] about 2.5 times the retirement assets of employees in non-ESOP companies.[172] 12.1% of all working adults in the private sector reported getting laid off in 2010, but just 2.6% that were part of an ESOP.

Because workers own at least part of ESOP corporations they benefit directly from increases in company income and value, so they tend to be more productive. In the largest study of the performance of ESOPs, Rutgers University researchers found that they increased sales/employee by about 2.3% to 2.4% per year over what would have been expected absent an ESOP.[173] If ESOPs are structured as WSDEs, productivity will be further enhanced.

From the earliest days of our country's founding, it was known that businesses where workers share in the profits are more productive. Research commissioned by Thomas Jefferson found that when fishermen shared in the profits of fishing operations they were more efficient. Paying workers a share of profits helped build the fortunes of many of the most successful businessmen. John D. Rockefeller of Standard Oil, George Eastman of Eastman Kodak, William Cooper Procter of Procter & Gamble and grain merchant Charles A. Pillsbury all used profit-sharing to attract the best workers, reduce turnover and give employees a greater incentive to make their businesses prosper.[174]

Democratic participation brings important advantages above those of just some sharing in profits, so we will take all practical measures to direct the expected large increase in the number of ESOPs that will be formed over the next 15 years resulting from "baby boomer" business owner retirement, instead to the formation of corporations with the WSDE structure. This process will be important in achieving the goal of widespread WSDE establishment.

More Evidence of the Superior Performance Resulting from Worker-Ownership and Self-Direction

Many studies have shown that participatory ownership, when combined with participatory work practices, greatly improves business performance, as indicated by higher sales and sales growth per worker. The consistency of the results of the many studies demonstrates this definitively. One study found that ESOP companies had sales growth rates 3.4% per year higher and employment growth rates 3.8% per year higher in the post-ESOP period than would have been expected based on pre-ESOP performance. When the companies were divided into three groups based on the degree of participative management, the most participative companies showed a gain of 8% to 11% per year faster than they would have been expected to grow. Other studies have shown similar results.[175]

Studies have revealed that workers in these companies have greater company loyalty and pride in working for the firm, so turnover is reduced. This creates a competitive advantage by reducing the costs of recruiting, training, and integrating new employees in money, time, and effort. Also, workers in firms with participatory ownership and participatory work practices express a willingness to work harder and innovate more, and they are more willing to co-monitor other worker's performance which, in addition to workers being more motivated to perform well, reduces the need for supervisors.[176]

Studies have found much higher failure rates for conventional capitalist companies than worker cooperatives in North America.[177] A study conducted by Quebec's Ministry of Industry and Commerce in 1999 concluded that *"Co-op startups are twice as likely to celebrate their 10th birthday as conventionally owned private businesses."*[178] An international survey of studies on business survival time of worker cooperatives compared to conventional firms discovered worker cooperatives early survival and median lifespan meet or exceed that of conventional firms, and that worker cooperatives are uncommon mainly due to difficulty in securing capital.[179]

- In France, the three-year survival rate was 80-90% for cooperatives converted from "in crisis" or "sound" enterprises, respectively. The average three-year survival rate for all French enterprises is 66%. The five-year survival rate of cooperatives formed from existing businesses was 61-82%, for all French businesses it was 50%.[180]
- Cooperatives in British Columbia between 2000 and 2010 had a five-year survival rate of 66.6% (100 out of 150), compared to conventional Canadian businesses which had a 43% and 39% 5-year survival rate in 1984 and

1993, respectively. Alberta cooperatives created in 2005 and 2006 had a three-year survival rate of 81.5% compared to 48% for conventional Alberta businesses. A 2008 study in Quebec showed that co-ops had a five-year survival rate of 62% and ten-year survival rate of 44%, compared to 35% and 20%, respectively, for other Quebec businesses.[181]

- Cooperatives in Italy have shown a lower mortality rate and incidence of bankruptcy than conventional businesses.[182]
- In 2005, 1% of German businesses were declared insolvent, but the statistic for cooperatives was less than 0.1%.[183]

The major reason for the success of worker cooperatives has been superior labor productivity. Studies comparing square-foot output have repeatedly shown higher physical volume of output per hour, and others show higher quality of product and also economy of material use.[184]

Some people claim that co-ops are impractical due to their inability to attract good managers. But this claim is false, and the mythology of super-managers being mainly responsible for the performance of well-performing companies is just that, mythology. Studies have found a negative correlation between CEO pay and long-term profitability of companies. Researchers from the University of Utah, Purdue University and the University of Cambridge studied 1,500 company's performance compared to other companies in the same field from 1994 to 2011. They found "The (stock value) returns are almost three times lower for the high paying firms than the low-paying firms" and that the longer the highly paid CEOs were in office, the more their firms underperformed.[185]

Analysis of the cooperatives that comprise the Mondragon Corporation found that productivity and profitability are consistently higher for the cooperatives than for comparable traditional capitalist firms. A study in 1974 found the worker turnover rate in Mondragon was 2% compared to 14% in similar traditional capitalist firms.[186] One particularly successful Mondragon company, Irizar, has been awarded prizes for being the most efficient company in its sector; in Spain, it competes against ten private enterprises, but its market share is 40%.[187] It manufactures products for transportation, from luxury coaches to city buses.

Each cooperative in Mondragon has its own workplace structure, though they share some common characteristics. Irizar's structure is especially interesting and important to learn from. To encourage innovation and the diffusion of knowledge, it has a flat organizational structure based on work teams with a high degree of autonomy, and there are no bosses. Rather, each team sets its own targets, establishes its own work schedules, and organizes the work process as they choose. The teams also work with each other, so that knowledge is transmitted efficiently. Participation also occurs in a general assembly, which meets three times a year rather than the one time common in other Mondragon firms, where they approve the company's strategic plan, investments, etc. These participatory structures have enabled Irizar to surpass its competitors in profitability and market share.[188]

The Emilia-Romagna region of northern Italy is an excellent example of a successful cooperative economy, with 40% of its region's GDP deriving from cooperative enterprises. The region of four million people, one of the richest and most developed areas in Europe, rose from poverty only a few decades ago based on its development of a cooperative economy.[189] Per capita GDP is 129% of the European Union average. The region is based on a dense network of 420,000 small and medium-sized firms. Agricultural, manufacturing, building and construction, mechanical engineering, robotics, biomedicine, graphic arts, wholesale trade, brokering, hotels, catering, transport, communications, banking and insurance, and business-related services, among other kinds of firms, comprise the network.[190]

Worker cooperatives are uncommon in Europe and the United States due in large part to difficulties in securing capital, but there's also lack of knowledge and support systems. Widespread awareness of the viability of worker-owned and self-directed enterprises and knowledge of successful organizational structures is necessary for widespread establishment. This can be best accomplished in our educational institutions, especially colleges. Within The New Enlightenment's free college education proposal, we recommend that the basic skills and knowledge needed for cooperative business enterprise management and direction be a part of the core curriculum of two and four-year colleges.

However, we do not need to wait for all college graduates to have this knowledge. Sufficiently effective educational and support systems can be put in place before the optimal situation of large numbers of college graduates having detailed knowledge of the character of WSDEs. With education, capital, technical support, and other policy changes—all of which have been important for the success of conventional capitalist businesses—the widespread establishment of businesses with participatory management and ownership could be the next great movement of American history, and ultimately world history.

Another obstacle to widespread establishment of WSDEs, especially in modern America, is an atomized population where collective civic engagement is uncommon and withdrawal from our political democracy is occurring. Pervasive feelings of disempowerment, interpersonal alienation, and mistrust exist and must be overcome. Also, many people assume that participating in the decisions of directing a business requires sophisticated entrepreneurial instincts and other skills or knowledge too difficult for them to acquire. Most people have never considered the possibility.

Widespread knowledge dissemination in colleges and our mass media on the advantages and nature of workplaces with collective ownership and direction can overcome these obstacles. This will not only result in an improved and more just economy, but also improve our democracy and social relations. The more that people hear about worker-ownership and self-direction, know about it, learn of its successes and potentials, the more they'll be open to it, including those who might now reject it as "foreign," "socialist," "idealistic," or "impractical." The New Enlightenment's media policy will result in a media that will focus on issues that serve the best interests of the country, including the character of WSDEs, of which many media corporations will be important examples.

Some see the fraction of the time it takes for a boss to decide on and hand down a bureaucratic order, compared to the time it would take a group to decide the issue democratically, implies superior efficiency in undemocratic structures. But those who would implement the policy are less likely to overlook unforeseen contingencies if they participated in its development, and any democratically determined policy is likely to be implemented more effectively since workers would be more committed to it.

Hierarchical bureaucracies are commonly criticized for inefficiency because of their undemocratic, inflexible, uncommunicative, uncreative character. In centralized organizations, change can come only from the top—but at the top are people who often do not learn of "errors" at the bottom. Information does not flow efficiently to bureaucrats, who are isolated from the consequences of their actions. And workers who can expeditiously and effectively correct an "error" instead wait for dictates from on high. These and other failures of bureaucracy do not apply to democracy.

In the literature, one finds descriptions of workers in cooperatives who do not have the desire to participate in the governance of the firm, who want only to get their paycheck and not deal with the challenges of deciding policy. Workers in a WSDE may participate in its direction to the degree they choose.

But if too many choose not to participate, or participate reluctantly, this can undermine the WSDE's democratic functioning. This problem can be overcome by well-designed democratic structure that will invite participation. Almost everyone craves new challenges periodically, and rarely would people choose a job bereft of challenges or opportunities for growth, if the opportunities were well understood. Many studies have shown that control over one's work is positively associated with job satisfaction, which, as previously noted, is low and trending lower.

Our wage subsidy policy (Policy 1) would not be necessary for an economic system that did not create large, unjust income disparities, and ideally will be a temporary policy until we develop an economic system that did not require income redistribution. An economic system mainly composed of worker-owned and self-directed enterprises would be such a system. It would have inherently smaller and more just income disparities and the other beneficial characteristics described in this policy proposal.

The awareness of the importance of widespread worker-ownership and self-direction of businesses has been growing. In the U.S., among the many groups that have made important contributions in advancing the movement toward widespread worker-ownership and self-direction of businesses are The Sustainable Economies Law Center, Democracy at Work, the Federation of Southern Cooperatives and The Democracy Collaborative. The Democracy Collaborative, co-founded by Gar Alperovitz, one of the intellectual leaders of the movement, has helped create several within a system designed to add to their numbers over time. But the system, though innovative and valuable, as is the work of the other groups, will not result in pervasive WSDEs. Progress is far too slow if we are to achieve the ideal we seek. We need major national public policy changes.

Total business sales value in 2014 was $30.9 trillion.[191] The total value of all U. S. businesses is over $54 trillion.[192] Only about 250 cooperatives (or WSDEs) exist in the US. Their total business and sales value was not available, but it is certainly an insignificant fraction of a percent of that of all U.S. businesses. Based on current growth rates, establishment systems, and financing options, it is very unlikely that this basic fact will change in anyone's lifetime reading these words in 2017.

If we are to achieve the imperative of widespread worker-ownership and self-direction of businesses within a tolerable time frame two formidable obstacles must be removed: Lack of access to sufficient capital and lack of knowledge in the majority of the citizenry.

More than half of our population have little, no, or negative wealth, making business investment under current circumstances difficult, and over 95% know little or nothing about worker-ownership and self-direction of businesses. Even when people have the necessary knowledge and want involvement the necessary financing is often not available, or burdensome obstacles to it exist (such as through crowdsourcing). A massive increase in worker-owned business financing availability and knowledge are necessary.

New Enlightenment policies overcome the obstacles of lack of financing and lack of knowledge in the majority of the citizenry. The following policies are designed to facilitate a gradual transformation over about two decades to an economic system where employee owned and self-directed enterprises will be the predominant type of business enterprise in the country. The creation of new businesses organized as WSDEs and the conversion of existing businesses, both privately and publicly owned, to worker-owned and worker self-directed enterprises we will vigorously support by various systems. We begin with a modified version of a system proven successful over decades in Italy.

Improving One of Italy's Successful Worker-Owned Business Establishment Policies

The following part of The New Enlightenment's comprehensive WSDE establishment policies is adapted and improved from a long-term policy in Italy, under its "Marcora" Law.[193] Since 1985, the Marcora Law has succeeded in promoting the establishment of prosperous, worker-owned and worker self-directed enterprises by unemployed workers. It does this by providing two or three years' total unemployment benefits in advance to groups of ten or more unemployed workers that present an acceptable business plan (a detailed description of the business including projected cost and revenue streams) for a worker-owned enterprise. These workers are required to forgo rights to these benefits if the enterprise fails. The success rate of businesses established under the Marcora Law has been 90%, and only 5% of capital supplied was lost through failures.[194] This compares favorably to the rate of 37% of new businesses surviving four years in the U.S.[195]

We propose the following way of adapting and improving Italy's successful Marcora law in the U.S.:

Our unemployment compensation currently runs for 73 weeks maximum including federal unemployment insurance extensions. Supplying just this total amount instead of a two-year benefit amount in advance is not likely to be adequate in many cases. Manufacturing businesses, for example, have higher than average capital requirements. Also, since the individual states supply unemployment compensation for the first 26 weeks, any policy to adapt the Marcora law to the U.S. would require state cooperation.

To solve both problems, the 26-week unemployment benefits that states typically provide will be supplemented by grants and loans from the federal government of an amount equal to 78 weeks (totaling two years) of benefits for any state willing to cooperate by lending (not granting) 26 weeks of benefit amounts to qualified worker-owner groups. The federal grants will be in an amount equal to eight weeks of unemployment benefits, and loans in an amount equal to 70 weeks of benefits. This federal money, and that the state money is provided as a loan, not a grant, as is now the case with any provided unemployment benefits, will motivate most states to cooperate, and likely all of them, as the success rate in Italy is duplicated or exceeded here.

We will not limit eligibility for this program to those at the start of the unemployment benefit period. All receiving benefits will be eligible, so in some cases, unemployment benefits will increase under this program. However, the benefits are mainly in the form of loans, not grants, as are current unemployment benefits. Also, the costs of this program will decline quickly as we institute New Enlightenment policies because little or no unemployment will result.

In some cases, the loaned and granted amount, plus any other contributions the worker-owner group can make with personal funds, or loans or grants from sources they could find independently, may be insufficient capital to satisfy the funding needs of the planned business. In these cases, the federal government will partner with a local community credit union or bank if it lends a minimum of 20% of the additional WSDE funding requirements.

Current law stipulates that federally insured credit union loans to businesses cannot be above $50,000 and that the personal liability and guarantee of the principal is required.[196] New Enlightenment policy will eliminate these restrictions, which do not exist for commercial banks, on credit union loans to WSDEs.

The federal loans will originate in a newly established national "Commonwealth Bank" with ten regional branches. ("Commonwealth" is derived from the conjunction of the words "common" and "wealth" since the companies so assisted will hold the wealth of the company in common by the workers.) I will describe the Commonwealth Bank further in a Banking Reform and Public Banks policy (to be detailed in a future document).

Many qualified local credit union or bank loan officers exist nationwide. They are a valuable and widely dispersed resource that will be essential in determining the likely viability of proposed WSDEs nationwide. We will institute policies to incentivize local credit union or bank involvement financially in this and most of the following WSDE establishment programs. In addition to facilitating the widespread establishment of WSDEs, this will reduce the relative power of the big national banks, which is also an important New Enlightenment goal.

The federal partnership with local community credit unions or banks will direct public funds most effectively because local financial institutions would generally be in the best position to evaluate proposals of local businesses for further Commonwealth Bank evaluation. They would also be most conveniently located for evaluating the proposals of local residents for businesses whose customer base would extend beyond the local community and would offer funds only for businesses determined worthy of the risk.

Greatly financially leveraging the result of local credit union or bank loan officers' loan decisions will be a highly advantageous way to facilitate the widespread establishment of WSDEs. In addition to local credit union or bank loan officer's knowledgeable evaluations, the second level of evaluation at the Commonwealth Bank will ensure a low risk for the loans.

Loan rate bidding by banks will determine the WSDE loan interest rates. As success rates become more commonly established with time for WSDEs formed through this policy, the rates would go down. Rates will vary for each WSDE, based on the bidding process. The Commonwealth Bank loan term and interest rate will be 20 years, typically at an interest rate 0.25% lower than the loan rate of the bank with the winning bid. However, the Commonwealth Bank will have the discretion to choose up to a 1% lower interest rate if it determines that the lowest rate resulting from the bidding process is unreasonably high.

The business assets will collateralize the loans and the likelihood of long-term viability will be high, based on both private and public bank evaluations and the superior performance resulting from the character of WSDEs relative to conventional enterprises. After three years, WSDE success rates will be widely established and known, allowing refinancing at lower rates based again on bank bidding. Federal policy would incentivize this by paying a reasonable refinancing fee to the original lender.

To assure equal opportunity to the poor, we will require for the partnership, which includes a loan fee, that banks evaluate worker-owner loan applications solely on the merits of the proposed business, and whether the experience and knowledge or education of the applicants will meet operational requirements. These are the important criteria for predicting business success. This New Enlightenment policy will not allow wealth or assets and prior income data as loan approval criteria. However, all workers will have a significant amount of wealth for investing in WSDEs because we will offer federal grants to economically disadvantaged households for WSDE investment. This will reduce an unjust consequence of our enormous wealth inequalities.

The federal government will provide to the credit union or bank, a WSDE loan origination fee of 2% of the amount lent as an incentive to give some preferential attention to loans for this purpose. This will largely insure against the risk for a typical loan for the bank. The New Enlightenment's Banking Reform and Public Banks policy will also offer preferential federal funds access to credit unions and community banks organized as WSDEs, with discounted rates for this purpose, at approximately a .25% discount. The rate would vary depending on the Federal Reserve Discount Rate. The Federal Discount Rate in 2015 was 1%, so a .25% discount would have reduced this rate by 25% [197] The discount would give a competitive advantage to credit unions and community banks organized as WSDEs while allowing them to offer lower rates for WSDE establishment loans.

The 2% fee incentive to make worker-owner loans would not lead to injudicious lending because 98% of the capital lent by the credit union or bank would be at risk, and the loan review at the federal level will further assure this.

If no community banks or credit unions will make a loan to a specific worker-owner group, governmental support for this worker-owned business will be limited to the grant and loan amount total equal to two years of unemployment compensation. In which case, the workers would need to develop an alternate business plan that this amount would satisfy or seek other lenders for additional funding, or use more of the group's personal funds. New Enlightenment policy also motivates municipal governments to assist in the formation of WSDEs with loans. The substantially different local government partnership system I detail later.

Within all New Enlightenment WSDE establishment systems we will also motivate support from local sources in the following way, which will minimize the need for federal loans and increase community involvement with local businesses: We will determine federal loan requirements after bonds to support WSDE funding needs are offered for purchase only by community members or the municipal government. These bonds will be made available through the lending credit union or community bank for a period of three weeks. The bonds, with a detailed description of the recipient business and specific purpose of the bond funds, will also be offered on a website where only local residents will be eligible investors. This will allow community members to vote with their dollars on what kinds of businesses are most worthy of support. Bonds will only be offered if the bank partnership requirements are met.

Although funds sourced outside the community have equivalent financial value, part of the purpose of this policy is for the community to be involved with the establishment, practices, and success of businesses in their community. New Enlightenment policies will motivate community members to seek local businesses for investment support through bond purchases by exempting the first $1,000 of bond interest from income taxes for each of the WSDEs an individual supports with bond purchases within this and all of our WSDE establishment programs. For example, if someone invests $22,000 in each of eight local WSDEs at 4.5% interest, their interest payment from each WSDE would be $990, and this person's total $7,920 interest annual payment from the WSDEs will be exempt from tax. (A 4.5% bond interest rate is the average of the 20-year rate for A and AA rated corporate bonds in April 2014.)[198]

Municipal bonds are also exempted from federal tax, but these WSDE corporate bonds will pay the higher rates typical of corporate bonds with the advantage of tax exemption included. This will be an important incentive for local investors to support local WSDEs. The maximum interest payment per WSDE that is tax-free will motivate wealthy investors to invest in a large number of WSDEs. This policy will also help to insulate local resident assets and savings from national and international speculative tumult and reduce the amount of money that participates in creating the bubbles and crashes, thereby reducing their severity.

Annual bondholder meetings will be required and will also be open to the community members other than bondholders, if space is available, for community input on business practices. Among the bond purchasers and other members of the public would be individuals with expertise relevant to the WSDE's operations, so these meetings could serve an important advisory function that may lead to significant productivity improvements, in addition to helping to minimize negative impacts of businesses' practices on the community.

This government bank and community credit union or bank sharing of the capitalization of loans for businesses arrangement is similar to the state-owned Bank of North Dakota's arrangement with community banks in that state (although not generally for WSDEs), and their success rate has been excellent. In 2012, the Bank of North Dakota produced record earnings for the ninth consecutive year. It contributed these earnings to the state treasury. Meanwhile, the big banks had $4.05 trillion in losses and required trillions of dollars in federal funds to bail them out, and largely devastated the world economy in the process.[199]

As in Italy, unemployed workers accepting advances in unemployment compensation will be required to forgo rights to additional unemployment compensation if the business fails. Workers in control of their business typically are highly motivated to make the business succeed, and this financial risk adds to their motivation, making failure unlikely.

Extending Community Credit Union or Bank Partnerships for More Widespread WSDE Establishment

The same partnership agreement with community credit unions or banks to capitalize worker-owned enterprises will extend beyond lending to the unemployed, to any WSDE comprised of ten or more people that presents a worker-owner business plan acceptable to a community credit union or bank for a loan of at least 20% of the total capital requirements of the WSDE. (Also, in all loan partnership systems, the loan partner could be the local government.)

Under the federal granting system for investment in WSDEs, 83% of Americans will be eligible for some grant up to $14,700. This maximum would be available to anyone with no or negative wealth, solely for investing in his or her WSDE, and would be the most anyone could receive in their lifetime (except under extraordinary circumstances such as when facilities are destroyed by a natural disaster).

For the partnership agreement, all WSDE workers will be required to contribute $14,700 or their equal share of the funding needs of their WSDE, whichever is less. All workers will be able to make this contribution based on the federal grants and/or their wealth. This worker contribution requirement will also apply to the prior and subsequent WSDE establishment programs.

Enterprise ownership would be equal. However, the necessary economic disparities based on the level of skill and amount and difficulty of work will be accomplished both by the level of pay and company contributions to individual capital accounts (described later in *Summary of Recommended WSDE Structure*). This allows any compensation disparity that the company's members feel is necessary to attract competent people and serve the ideal of fairness. Equal ownership implies the equal voting rights essential to democratic governance and is analogous to equal citizenship.

For businesses requiring staffing in addition to the applicants under this, the prior, and subsequent New Enlightenment WSDE establishment programs, the following would apply:

- The directors of the WSDE in its first four years will either be all the applicants, or some, chosen by the applicants by vote.
- The directors select, for approval by all the applicants, additional workers who would be employees for the standard trial period of nine months before membership (worker-ownership status).
- Funding requirements over $14,700 per worker that workers could not supply the WSDE will source through the bank partnership and bondholders and lend to applicants with insufficient funds to purchase their equal share of the WSDE.
- The equal share will be determined using the planned worker total after a 6-month establishment phase (this 6-month period could be extended for large businesses).

Funds lent to the workers they would make payments for through deductions from the portion of business income they receive as compensation for their work. The WSDE will use these payments to make its loan payments.

The applicants will determine initial wages by vote. Based on their foreknowledge of the character of WSDEs, and that all workers will determine maximum company-wide wage disparities after their trial period before ownership by vote, they would be unlikely to create huge disparities between the applicants and any additional workers who they hire.

After four years, the WSDE will institute directorship elections in a General Assembly of all workers, as they would every four years subsequently under standard WSDE governance practices.

Licensed consultants will be available for the WSDEs created through this, the prior and subsequent establishment programs to assist them during their establishment phase. The consultants will have completed federal government certified training programs that we will offer in colleges and community colleges. They will have detailed knowledge of WSDE governance practices, including variations for different sizes and types of enterprises, and would also evaluate and advise on educational institutions for improving relevant skills.

WSDEs will select consultants from official registries, and 80% of their salaries we will federally subsidize for any that agree to maximum pay rates or schedules. Also, widespread knowledge of WSDE structure and function will exist resulting from the New Enlightenment free college education policies detailed in Policy 7, and the media content of a New Enlightenment reformed media (Policy 29). The Small Business Administration will provide additional support that could include on-site technical consultant assistance. The SBA's funding will be substantially increased for this and other WSDE support services, as detailed later.

Supporting the Conversion of Pre-existing Privately Owned Businesses to WSDEs

We will also offer the federal loan partnership agreement to WSDEs formed by workers purchasing a business from a private owner (or owners). Under current law when owners transfer a business to its workers within Employee Stock Ownership Plans corporations (ESOPs), they receive important tax advantages. We would maintain and add to these advantages for owners selling to WSDEs.

Under current ESOP law, any capital gains the seller has on the sale to an ESOP is tax deferred if these gains are reinvested in qualified investments. We will maintain this provision for WSDEs, and in addition, $20,000 per year in seller note interest will be tax-free and free of any conditions on how the funds are used. It is common in sales to ESOPs for the seller to lend some funds needed for the sale and it will be more common in sales to WSDEs based on the additional tax advantages. But most importantly, $20,000 per year tax-free income would be a motive for sellers to prefer WSDE over ESOP transfer or would allow the purchase of the business at a lower price by a WSDE for an equivalent financial benefit to the seller. (For sellers in the New Enlightenment 55% tax bracket $20,000 per year tax-free income would increase their take-home income by $11,000 per year.)

Also, as a motive for owners to sell to a WSDE it may be advantageous for WSDE buyers to offer the possibility of including a sales provision that would allow the seller to speak for a short time at company general assemblies. This provision will also motivate WSDE sales since owners often like to maintain some involvement with the business they devoted many years to build. Sellers will have no control, just the opportunity to be heard, which many owners may find desirable. It would not be a significant intrusion on the WSDE owners for the prior owner to speak for possibly up to 10 minutes at a General Assembly, most commonly held once per year, and the WSDE may benefit from the prior owner's input.

To determine company value an appraiser could be used, as is done on ESOP transfers now. However, to lower the expense of, and to standardize and facilitate, the transfer process, a standardized evaluation system will be developed that could be used nationally, with exceptions made for unusual circumstances. Smaller companies could benefit significantly from such a process. The system would use asset values, and some function of annual profits and earnings growth rate estimates for public companies in the same industry, and possibly some dependence on price per sales ratio of public companies in the same industry would be included.

The claim that only an appraiser can determine a private company's value is dubious. Businesses are notoriously difficult to evaluate, as has been demonstrated with many studies on public company valuations by stock analysts. Based on future stock prices, the analysts' determinations of company long-term value relative to the value of other companies on the market, on average, are no better than random guesses.

A standardized evaluation formula will be worthwhile at a minimum as a starting point for negotiations. If it is sufficiently flexible, it will be useful to apply in most cases.

The movement to establish the ESOP corporate form we intend to be just a preliminary stage of a more just and democratic worker-ownership movement. Most ESOP corporations are only partially worker-owned (through company funding with tax-deductible cash contributions to the company's ESOP trust, which the trust then uses to purchase the worker-owners' shares). And as I mentioned earlier, ESOP corporation's management and direction are not under democratic worker control. They are structured so that the trust votes the shares owned by the workers.

Although ESOPs distribute the advantages of business ownership more equitably than conventional capitalist businesses, that they are not worker self-directed results in unreasonably large disparities in income and asset allocation among workers, and little or no worker control over other business policies—major deficiencies the WSDE form will correct.

If the ownership transfer process facilitated it, ESOP companies could have been formed as both 100% worker-owned and worker self-directed enterprises. New Enlightenment federal policies are designed so that in the future WSDEs will be formed as a superior alternative to ESOPs. Instead of a trust voting the shares on corporate policy, the workers would do the voting, on a one-worker, one-vote basis. Essentially, workers would be equal citizens in their enterprise, and this equality also would be expressed through an equal share in its ownership (but not equal amounts contributed to, and therefore value in, their capital accounts, or equal incomes).

Most ESOPs are created when owners retire and do not have an heir who wants to run the business because of the substantial tax advantage owners receive that sell to employees in an ESOP. The owners of over 70% of American middle-market business owners anticipate selling their businesses because there is no family successor. The estimated wealth transfer per year over the next 11 years is $240 billion, totaling $2.6 trillion.[200]

In addition to the tax advantages, retiring owners are often motivated by other than personal financial gain when they transfer their businesses. How they will be remembered as a contributor to the well-being of their community and colleagues, and ensuring the integrity of the business that they created, can exceed maximizing financial gain as a priority. If they sell to an outside owner company, workers may lose income or their jobs. The new owner may sell off assets and end operations or use some of the assets for other purposes that would better serve the needs of the buying corporation. In any case, it is likely that workers will have the stress of dealing with major changes.

Giving workers ownership in a worker self-directed enterprise is the most beneficial way of expressing gratitude for the contribution their work made to the owner's success by ensuring their dignity and respect in a work environment that will also make them more prosperous. Also, it stabilizes the economy of the community in which the owner and workers live. Most owners would sacrifice some financial gain for these outcomes.

To further facilitate directing this vast wealth transfer to the formation of WSDEs, the federal government loan requirement for a bank partnership we will waive where owner retirement motivates the pre-existing company sale. These businesses are generally successfully operating by the workforce seeking ownership, and the motivation for the sale is less likely related to any business or business prospect deficiency than sales from non-retiring owners, and worker-ownership status will generally improve performance. A minimum age of 60 years for the seller owning the company for at least ten years will be the determinant of whether the bank partnership will be required.

Historical evidence indicates that loan risk is low for loans to workers buying out a retiring owner, so business evaluation from a local financial professional is not likely to be advantageous. The default rate on bank loans to ESOP companies during 2009-2013, most of which originated during the transfer process from retiring owners, was only 0.2% annually, compared to mid-market companies in the U.S. that typically default on comparable loans at an annual rate of 2.0% to 3.75%.[201] Due to the low risk, local community credit unions and banks would also offer loans for this purpose, if the low risk was known. The loan risk is likely to be even lower for WSDE loans, due to the improved performance from the democratic structure and the commitment of funds by each worker.

Workers rarely would not participate in the WSDE by not contributing $14,700 (if this much is needed) toward its funding under the modified federal loan partnership system for a retiring owner's sale to WSDEs. A relatively small financial commitment (with a one-time lifetime grant available for those who cannot afford it) will generally be well worth sharing in the profits and ownership of their firm.

Since most ESOPs now are formed on owner retirement, we would expect this to also be the case for transfers from existing owners to WSDEs, at least until the competitive advantage of businesses with WSDE structure was commonly demonstrated and widely known. We expect that eventually, many operating owners will choose the WSDE structure due to competitive pressures. The superior performance of WSDEs and the preference of many consumers to purchase goods and services from WSDEs will likely result in taking market share from conventionally owned and managed businesses. Also, some owners will want to benefit their workers and community in this way just for the personal satisfaction it will bring them, after witnessing other thriving WSDE businesses.

We will also encourage participation from local citizens in the funding of local WSDE businesses formed as a result of sales from retiring owners as we do in the bank lender partnership systems. We will exempt the first $1,000 of bond interest from income taxes for each of the WSDEs an individual supports with bond purchases. This will minimize the need for federal loans and increase community involvement with local businesses. As in the lender partnership systems, annual bondholder meetings will be required and will be open to the community members other than bondholders, if space is available, for community input on business practices.

The amount of federal funds needed for loans in this system will depend on how large a fraction of the capital requirements on average that retiring owners will take back in loans and how much will come from other sources, including community bond purchases. Assuming $240 billion per year in value is to be transferred, the following are rough estimates of the impact on federal government resources of the policy to direct ESOP formation to WSDEs. If half of the value of sold businesses is taken back in loans by the retiring owner seller to support the owner's retirement income, that leaves $120 billion per year that must be supplied from other sources. If half of this amount was supplied by banks, community member bond purchases, personal funds of workers including from grants and miscellaneous sources, that leaves $60 billion in loans from the federal government. The federal government's bond tax exemption cost will total approximately $208 million per year.[202]

ESOPs also offer tax advantages to the corporation and workers. In addition to the previously described supports, we will create somewhat greater but similar tax advantages for WSDEs and their workers. Under current law, ESOPs are structured as either IRS C corporations or S corporations, with S corporations having tax advantages for companies with fewer than 100 employees. We will establish a separate category for tax purposes for WSDEs of any size.

As described in *Summary of Recommended WSDE Structure*, a large portion of business profits is distributed in worker capital accounts, in proportion to their wages, and to the enterprise's Collective Reserve Fund. Workers will pay no tax on funds allocated to their capital accounts until they receive distributions and their portion of the business value upon terminating employment; then they are taxed on the distributions and capital gains. The WSDE will pay no tax on the standard contribution to the Collective Reserve Fund.

WSDE contributions to the capital accounts will be tax-deductible up to a limit of 50% of wages or $200,000 per year, whichever is smaller. Interest and principal on the loans that the WSDE is paying and that workers are paying to the WSDE will be paid with pretax income.

Also, The New Enlightenment's inheritance tax (Policy 9) that replaces the estate tax allows an exemption of $300,000 per inheritor. If an owner bequeaths his firm, or any portion of it, to his employees, for any who receives less than $300,000 in value no tax would be owed.

ESOPs are required to establish a trust with periodic reporting requirements. The trust is a separate entity with fiduciary responsibilities to the workers. A separate trust would not be involved with WSDEs because the workers would direct the company, so they would have fiduciary responsibility to themselves. This would reduce administrative cost relative to ESOPs.

After we institute this policy to promote business succession with superior tax advantages to ESOPs to worker-owned and self-directed businesses, worker-ownership transfer by owners on retirement will be both more common and more valuable to society. But it will only happen if business owners know of the availability of this alternative. We will, therefore, widely publicize this option to maximize the projected transfer of ownership of businesses valued at trillions of dollars to WSDEs over the next couple of decades. Such companies, many of which would have been absorbed by big corporations, will instead be taken over as part of a new direction in democratized worker-ownership.

Supporting the Conversion of Companies Declaring Bankruptcy to WSDEs

The Community Credit Union or Bank Partnership policy will also apply when companies declare bankruptcy. Management problems often cause business failures, and employee owners are more likely to rescue the business than the management previously selected by the investor's board of directors. If the workers and owners do not agree on a price prior to Chapter 7 bankruptcy proceedings, the workers will be given first choice of ownership at a price equal to the liquidation value of the business assets determined in the proceedings, plus the obligation to pay whatever debts the court does not discharge. If they have a willing community credit union or bank lender providing sufficient funds for the federal loan partnership system, the system will apply. The assets would not have to be used to provide the same goods or services that the bankrupt company provided. Workers may find more productive uses for the assets.

Chapter 11 bankruptcy law stipulates that the business can continue operations. We will change current law to require worker-ownership and self-direction for the reorganized company if the workers choose ownership and if they have a willing bank partner within the federal partnership system. In the cases of large national or multinational company bankruptcies, we will allow the large national banks to be federal partners within the system, and offer them the same financial incentives as we do to local banks when they provide WSDE establishment loans. When a traditional capitalist enterprise fails, the best use will be made of the opportunity to advance the movement toward widespread worker-ownership and self-direction of business enterprises by not limiting financing options when financing needs are large, however maintaining a bank partnership requirement is worthwhile.

If prior owners are relieved of most or all responsibility for debts to the workers, as bankruptcy often allows, the workers can decide how these debts to fellow workers could be paid out of future business proceeds. This will allow retirement pension responsibility that is often either drastically reduced or eliminated in bankruptcy proceedings, with devastating impact on people's retirement income, to be assumed by the workers to the degree they chose.

According to data from bankruptcydata.com, the failure incidence of public companies from 2000 to 2011 averaged 143 companies per year, with an average total value of all bankrupt companies' assets per year of $257 billion. Since public companies total about 7,000, this represents a failure rate of about 2.0%. Also based on data provided by bankruptcydata.com, on average, about 84% of public company bankruptcies result in a reorganized company rather than liquidated assets.[203]

Applying these averages yields an average of 120 reorganized public companies with a total asset value of $216 billion per year. All these companies had sufficiently good prospects for long-term viability to be reorganized, so it is likely a bank partner could have been found in all these cases for the federal loan partnership for WSDE formation. These good prospects, and the depressed price of a company in bankruptcy offering the potential for large gains, will motivate workers to choose ownership.

About 1.7% of public companies were reorganized per year over the 2000 to 2011 period. Assuming this same rate over the next 20 years, about one-third of public companies will be reorganized, so in 20 years about one-third will be converted to WSDEs, just based on this policy alone. (Somewhat less, because presumably in the latter years some bankruptcies will be of WSDEs.)

Although bankruptcy data for privately held companies were not available, it is likely to be similar. Assuming it is, in 20 years about one-third of privately held companies also will be converted to WSDEs, just based on this policy alone.

Initially, some banks may be reluctant to lend to reorganized bankrupt businesses with an unfamiliar structure, but after learning of the evidence and witnessing participatory work practices and ownership improving business performance compared to conventional businesses, prejudices will dissipate. Companies would not be restructured unless prospects for profitability were good, and participatory work practices and ownership will increase the likelihood of long-term viability. Also, the WSDE loan origination fee of 2% of the amount lent will largely insure against the risk for a well-considered loan by the bank. A per worker commitment of $14,700 will further reduce the risk, so further motivate bank involvement.

General Motors, one of the largest corporations in American history declared bankruptcy and was reorganized in 2009, and the failure of other large corporations is not uncommon. *Would GM have failed if decisions of corporate management largely responsible for its failure were instead made democratically within a WSDE system with a worker elected board of directors? This is unlikely, mainly for the following reasons:*

Public company managers often have short-term profits as a top priority. High profits in the next quarter raise stock prices, and so the value of their bonuses, option awards, stock awards and other non-equity incentives. The total value of these incentives for S & P 500 CEOs on average was about $9.2 million in 2012—what the median wage worker would earn in 334 years.[204] Workers have as a higher priority long-term concerns, such as whether they will have a job with gradually increasing wages in a company that is prosperous ten years or more into the future.

A conventional corporation's transformation to a WSDE will require an adjustment period. It should not be excessively disruptive though, because the workers will remain in place and most will gain a substantial advantage in the new structure, so they would be motivated to have it succeed, and consultants to assist in the transition process will be supported with federal funding.

Obviously, workers could choose not to participate in the WSDE and leave the company, but this is not likely to be common, and any that do would be easily replaced by outsiders that would be excited by the opportunity. Many would see that the depressed price of a corporation in bankruptcy could increase by multiples if profitability returns, which is likely, due to the bank evaluations and the superior performance on average of WSDEs. Some in the highest level of management may more often leave, but sufficient numbers of qualified managers would likely remain, tempering any disruption. Members of the top management are often responsible for the failure, so their departure may be advantageous in some cases.

Bankrupt public companies will sometimes be of a size that is not an ideal WSDE size, but a beneficial transformation to shared ownership and direction can occur at large sizes. It is more difficult to establish a desirable degree of democratic participation in large corporations than in corporations with fewer than 500 workers, so we recommend this limit when practical unless larger sizes would result in significant economies of scale that could not be otherwise achieved.

Contrary to their claims of efficiency, most large conventional capitalist corporations wastefully direct large amounts of society's resources to exorbitant executive perks and salaries, transportation and communications to far-flung corporate empires. Most depend for their profits and survival on public subsidies, tax exemptions, and externalized costs. Often they receive indirect subsidies when they pay less than a living wage, maintain substandard working conditions, market hazardous products, dump untreated wastes into the environment, and extract natural resources from public lands at below-market prices. Dr. Ralph Estes, co-founder and vice president of the Center for Advancement of Public Policy, emeritus trustee at the Institute for Policy Studies, and emeritus professor of business at American University, estimated that corporations extracted over $2.6 trillion in 1994 in such subsidies in the United States alone— roughly five times their reported profits.[205]

It is one of the basic principles of efficient market function that the full costs of a product or service be borne by the seller and passed on to the buyer. We don't have free and efficient markets because many conventional corporations in it would not be if they had to bear the true full costs of their operations. WSDEs will not extract the social costs that many conventional corporations do.

Bankrupt companies are often purchased by larger companies, increasing their size and power with all its attendant problems. As I noted earlier, Supreme Court Justice William O. Douglas (Time magazine called Douglas *"the most committed civil libertarian ever to sit on the court"*) correctly pointed out that local autonomy is diminished by large national and international corporate structures resulting from corporate mergers. And as FDR said, it results in *"people (being) gradually regimented into the service of the privileged few."* We ignored their observations. The consolidation trend continued so that now several industries are dominated by monopolies or semi-monopolies.

Economies of scale are used to justify large size. In some cases, such efficiencies exist, but we must weigh the social costs against these advantages, instead, we are ignoring them. Large size entails bureaucratic inefficiencies, greater likelihood of negative externalities, large economic inequalities, political corruption, and "people regimented into the service of the privileged few." Sometimes the social costs of mergers and acquisitions include those of semi-monopolies and monopolies. In industries dominated by semi-monopolies and monopolies, prices can be artificially high and innovation is stifled. For more information on monopolies see pages 395-7.

When economies of scale from large size would be advantageous, we should accomplish it, when possible, by combining WSDEs with 500 or fewer workers into groups along geographic or functional lines.

How to approximate this ideal by giving some autonomy to groups within a WSDE reorganized large bankrupt conventional corporation will vary based on circumstances. I will use Kmart's bankruptcy as an example. Kmart filed for Chapter 11 bankruptcy in 2002, by far the largest retail corporation in history to do so.

The Kmart Bankruptcy and Hypothetical WSDE Transformation

Each store could have been organized using much of the governance structure of an independent WSDE, but within the restrictions set by a companywide, worker elected board of directors. A worker elected "governing council" for each Kmart store, elected from among the store's workers by the workers, would have similar responsibilities as a board of directors would have in an independent WSDE. In addition, for most corporate level policy decisions, they would act as representatives of their store. On the most important decisions, or the ones democratically determined to require a direct vote by all the workers, the governing council would not have more than a standard worker vote. A petition signature standard for requiring a direct vote on a corporate level decision, possibly one-half of the workforce of any one store, within a virtual "General Assembly" (described later) will be established.

The impact of Kmart's reorganization as a WSDE on its competitive position relative to Walmart and other retailers would have been substantially positive. The workers would all own an equal piece of one of the largest corporations in America and would share in its profits to varying degrees determined by democratic processes within the corporation. This would likely result in a level of feelings of excitement, solidarity, and devotion to their jobs that would be unprecedented in a corporation of its size, which would likely result in substantially improved customer service. Since the workers would all share in the profits, their compensation would be substantially higher than that of workers at Walmart. It is well established that workers in this kind of work environment are more productive. Federal funds will be provided for the hiring of consultants to assist in WSDE structure transition processes to ensure that this potential is realized.

New Enlightenment policies will also improve the competitive position of WSDEs by strictly enforcing labor laws, some of which Walmart has violated to gain competitive advantage, including firing workers trying to unionize. Store managers also have often been abused by requiring over 70 workhours per week for their salary. New Enlightenment overtime pay requirements for salaried workers will eliminate this problem.

Throughout the country, dozens of lawsuits allege that store managers, apparently expecting a similar sacrifice by hourly workers, routinely forced hourly employees to punch out at the time clock and then return to work, putting in hours of unpaid labor. Also, Walmart settled a federal investigation of its use of hundreds of undocumented migrants to clean its stores, making a record-setting payment to the federal government.

One factor that is claimed to be partly responsible for Walmart's success is instilling an entrepreneurial spirit and decentralized management style in each store. An entrepreneurial spirit and decentralized management style would be inherent in the recommended hypothetical structure for Kmart and would exceed any that could exist at Walmart.

Mismanagement by the so-called "frat boys," the CEO Conaway and his team, were mainly responsible for the bankruptcy. One important factor in the failure was a slow investment in computerized inventory management systems (unlike Walmart and Target). Also, Kmart failed to keep its stores looking clean and attractive, driving away customers.

With workers in control and sharing in the profits, the stores would all be better maintained and attractive because workers would be highly motivated to attract customers. The knowledge of, and pressures from, tech savvy workers, presumably some with computer science degrees, would result in sophisticated computerized inventory management systems as effective as Walmart's because they all would be benefiting from the resulting increases in profits. Software to serve this purpose is not extraordinarily difficult to produce, but if they did not have sufficient in-house expertise (or if it would be less expensive), they would have sufficient expertise and motivation to choose a qualified outside software vendor.

Senior management of Kmart lived a life like that of rock stars and divas. They had gated estates, yachts, company jets, and they saw their perks, bonuses, and loans increase while their company reported losses of about $3.9 billion in just the five quarters before bankruptcy. Over 70,000 workers lost their jobs, and millions of stockholders lost their retirement plans because of the actions of Kmart senior management.

A manager at a Texas store told the Free Press organization (a lobbying group that advocates for press freedom and increased government oversight of telecommunication service providers) that the company bankruptcy announcement *"was devastating, just devastating. It's just that you're never ready."* Employees, he said, were hurt, angry and afraid, *"all those emotions that come with uncertainty."*

After restructuring, the new board operated under the "good-old-boys" framework and awarded their former colleagues "golden parachutes," despite the mismanagement and rampant allegations of fraud, deceit, and corruption. CEO Conaway got $9 million in severance and loan forgiveness, and four others in top management received several million each.

Imagine if the option to take ownership control was open to the workers.

Workers would not have wasted corporate money on "golden parachutes." Instead of being "hurt, angry, afraid and devastated," they would be excited by the possibility of being an equal owner with their fellow workers in one of the largest corporations in America.

Financial advisors for the reorganization plan estimated that the value of the reorganized Kmart in a Chapter 11 reorganization was between $2.25 billion and $3 billion.[206] With 240,000 employees, using the average value estimate, $2.625 billion, this is about $11,000 per employee, which is less than the maximum lifetime grant of $14,700 allowed for workers with no or negative wealth.

To estimate the pay benefits Kmart workers would gain in a WSDE Kmart, consider how much Walmart workers' pay would increase if it were a WSDE: Walmart had an income after expenses except taxes of $25.7 billion in 2013 and taxes of $8 billion. If it were a WSDE, most of its profits would be distributed among the workers. *If 70% of its profits were, on average each would receive per year about $9,000, or about $750 per month above their current pay.*

Kmart is not Walmart, which is well known for exceptional business performance. But no competitive advantage of Walmart could not eventually be exceeded by a Kmart with an organizational form known to produce superior performance. The workers' equal share of one of the largest corporations in America would increase in value by multiples if the corporation performed well. To estimate this increase, consider that Walmart has a market value of about $250 billion, with about two million employees. This is about $125,000 per employee. If Kmart workers could match the performance of Walmart per worker, it would likely be valued per worker about the same, resulting in about $114,000 above their initial investment, which represents a gain of over 1000%.

The levels of motivation and excitement that would exist in the workers would make taking market share from Walmart a near certainty. On average, a few hundred thousands of dollars in additional total income and capital gains per Kmart employee after 20 years of work would be likely, compared to the average Walmart worker.

The amount of federal funds needed for public company reorganization as WSDEs for loans will depend on how large a fraction of the capital requirements on average will come from banks and other sources, including community bond purchases. Assuming $216 billion per year will be required, the following are rough estimates of the impact on federal government resources of the policy to direct public company reorganization to WSDE formation. If half of the value of $216 billion were supplied by banks, community member bond purchases, personal funds of workers including from grants, and miscellaneous sources, that leaves $108 billion in loans from the federal government, well within practical limits. If community member bond purchases supported 25% of the remaining $108 billion, 20% that would qualify for the tax-free interest income, and the bond interest averaged 4.5%, the tax exemption cost would be $292 million per year.[207]

The bankruptcy data for nonpublic companies were not available. For budgeting purposes, we will use the rough estimate of approximately the same budgetary impact as public companies, so we will budget $292 million in tax exemption costs for WSDEs formed on private company bankruptcies.

"Sociable Takeovers" Not "Hostile Takeovers" of Some Public Corporations

"Hostile" corporate takeovers are takeovers of corporate control against the wishes of current management. The interests of the workforce are ignored.

Usually, with a shift of control/ownership to another corporation comes lots of organizational change, often new bosses, loss of jobs and an overall attitude of "out with the old, in with the new," with workers as pawns in a game only the wealthy can play for their profit. When the takeover results in a privately held firm, using mainly borrowed funds, the process is called a leveraged buyout. Research indicates that worker wages on average are reduced after leveraged buyouts, even though productivity often rises. Financial gains from higher productivity are converted into returns for owners rather than salary increases for employees. Private equity companies are the practitioners of leveraged buyouts, and the companies they buy are twice as likely to file for bankruptcy as comparable public companies.[208] These companies' owners more commonly abuse lax regulation by paying themselves more than the firms are worth and then defaulting on debt obligations sometimes causing massive job losses and associated social harm.

Sometimes hostile takeovers result in replacing all employees; other times, the new corporation maintains some employees temporarily, mainly to train their people. Whatever the decision, the takeover can have a negative impact on employee morale because they have no control or say in a process that can have major impacts on their lives. The employees are likely to have some repercussions or big changes to deal with, job loss or not.

The following New Enlightenment policy facilitates *"sociable takeovers"* as an alternative to *"hostile takeovers"* or conventional leveraged buyouts. A sociable takeover is a worker takeover. In a hostile takeover or conventional leveraged buyout, the few decide the fate of the many, with disregard of the many if it leads to the financial gain of the few. In a sociable takeover, the many decide their own fate, based on democratic processes and federal policy support under this condition: The market capitalization of the company is sufficiently low that, after a minimum $14,700 investment from each worker, the loan payments on the remaining balance to buy out the shareholders could be supported by projected profits.

As in all WSDE establishment systems, all workers will be able to make the $14,700 investment based on the granting system and/or their personal wealth. The bank partnership (or in some cases a city partnership agreement as detailed later) we will use to ensure a robust federal government loan risk evaluation. In the cases of large national or multinational company sociable takeovers, we will allow the large national banks to be federal partners within the system, and offer them the same financial incentives as we do to local banks when they provide WSDE establishment loans.

A vote of 80% of the workforce approving the sociable buyout will initiate the process. Workers can base their votes on the public information included in company financial statements, and any other information available to them as employees. Most workers will likely vote based on recommendations from fellow employees.

A voting system is needed that assures that votes are confidential because some workers may fear that if their vote for a sociable takeover were known it might negatively affect their relationship with current management if the 80% threshold is not reached. Also, if the votes were publicly known it may impact the stock price. We recommend that a division within the central office of the Commonwealth Bank receive the confidential votes to tally for each public company.

No specific date for voting will be set; instead, we will accumulate votes for each company, and any vote that is more than one-year-old we will drop from the tally. We will require every public company to provide the Commonwealth Bank a complete list of all its employees, and this list will be available on a Commonwealth Bank website for employees to check. Also, we will require voter identifying information with any vote to confirm its validity. If and when a company's worker vote tally reaches the 80% threshold, the Commonwealth Bank will do a loan approval analysis based on company financial statements and any other relevant public documents. If the loan is approved, we will halt stock trading and seek a bank partner.

Rarely will the Commonwealth Bank's approval not result in finding a bank partner. A bidding process will be used where banks would compete for the loan based on interest rate. Trading is halted after the Commonwealth Bank approval rather than the private bank because once the Commonwealth Bank approval became publicly known it would most likely impact the stock price. If no bank will offer an acceptable rate, trading would resume in the public shares, but this would be rare, especially as the benefits of the WSDE structure became more widely known.

Shareholders could convert their shares' value to bond value at the interest rate of the private bank winner of the bidding process. However, if the original loan is refinanced at a lower rate in the future, the bond rate would again be made equal to the private bank loan rate. As in all WSDE establishment systems, the first $1,000 of bond interest will be tax-free. (This would apply to their interest on their total portfolio value, not on each company's bonds in which they owned stock.) Any shareholder that chooses not to convert will be paid the value of their shares.

When a bank partner is found, an election process for a new board of directors will begin. This process will vary based on company size. For large companies, part of the process would involve workers meeting regionally two or three times over two months in assemblies before a company-wide vote for company directors. Also, a website will be available as a forum for those seeking a directorship position to provide qualifying information to WSDE members. Other practices of WSDEs, which I describe later, will also be instituted regionally, with more representative democratic practices at the corporate level.

Current management would remain in place during the transfer period to transfer any necessary and useful information they have. Likely a few weeks would be sufficient, and some managers may choose to remain in the WSDE beyond the transfer period. However, it will generally be at a much lower pay based on the far more equitable distribution of corporate income inherent in WSDEs.

Managers have a fiduciary responsibility to the company that we will ensure is met. Federal law 18 U.S.C. § 1346 has been used to prosecute public company executives for breaching their fiduciary duties. Either this law or other relevant existing laws would be enforced (or we will propose other laws if these prove insufficient) to ensure that the major transition to WSDE status is done without harm to business operations during the transfer period.

During the transition period, before board elections, the fifteen most senior members of the company's staff directly involved in providing the product or service the company markets will be the most directly involved with the licensed WSDE establishment consultants assisting in the transition period, and the Commonwealth Bank and private bank. For example, if the company designs, manufactures and sells machinery, the longest term engineers, shop floor workers, and sales people would be the company liaisons with the outside entities assisting the WSDE formation (possibly five from each division). These people would, as would all workers, be among those eligible for election to the board of directors for the standard four-year term.

Normally, when public companies are taken private in a leveraged buyout, the shareholders are offered a price above the share price at the time of the buyout. This will not be done in sociable buyouts. The prospects for the success of the newly formed WSDE is higher the lower the price, and it is in the country's best interest to facilitate the establishment of WSDEs to the degree practical and reasonable. The market price is a fair price, and if a premium above a market price is offered, possible rumors of a sociable buyout will artificially raise the stock price because investors will buy company stock just to get the sociable takeover bump-up in price.

The sociable takeover loan interest rates may be higher than most WSDE bank partnership rates. The loans most often being made in amounts above the company net asset values, since market values for the great majority of companies exceed net asset values, and the novelty of the situation may result in the loans being viewed as more risky. As success rates become established with time, the rates will go down based on success rate data being available to banks in the competitive bidding process. After three years, WSDEs' performance after a sociable takeover will be known allowing refinancing at lower rates, based again on bank bidding. As in all WSDE loans, federal policy will support refinancing based on WSDE performance by paying a reasonable refinancing fee to the original lender.

Federal Reserve data reveals that commercial and industrial loans over a 1-year term made by domestic banks averaged 3.52% in 2015.[209] For the purpose of the following case studies of the feasibility of public companies' conversion to WSDEs, I assume that banks will require a premium over average rates. Rates will likely be lower than that of the case studies.

The loan interest in the partnership agreement I assume to be 6% on 20% of the loan, from private banks. Although 6% is significantly higher than average, it is not an uncommon business loan rate.[210] Since the Commonwealth Bank could charge up to 1% less than the bank partner, 5% on the 80% of the loan from the Commonwealth Bank is assumed in the case studies, so the loan interest in total is 5.2% for the first seven years. Thereafter just the 5% Commonwealth Bank loan will remain on the loan balance.

The case studies also assume another worst case situation: no refinancing at lower rates as success rates are established. Average WSDE loan rates almost certainly will be at or lower than average business loan rates as success rates are established with time within the system, based on historical WSDE performance evidence outside the system. Three years will likely be sufficient. As a result, the high probability of success and large advantages to workers shown in the following sociable takeover case studies will likely be larger.

To find the case study corporations I used the results of "stock screens" (computerized searches of stocks meeting detailed financial and other criteria) and found many good prospects for sociable takeovers. I describe the screening processes in the following text box. (You can choose not to read the text box's somewhat technical content with no loss in continuity.)

The following are case studies of public companies of widely varying industries and sizes, selected from those resulting from the stock screens. The studies indicate that the companies could easily service their loans even at the high end of the likely range of winning interest bids by their bank partners.

All of these are preliminary studies, but they indicate that the potential for sociable takeovers is large.

To be conservative in my analysis, in addition to using high loan rates, I do not take into account that significant potential exists that the more beneficial WSDE corporate structure would improve business performance, making the servicing of the loans needed for the buyout easier than what the following evaluations project based on the past performance of the conventional corporation.

Screening Process Information

Since the net corporate profit rate on sales averaged over 8.3 percent over the last 30 years and over 1,800 public companies have a market capitalization less than annual sales revenue, significant potential exists for "sociable buyouts" even at the high loan rates. All companies with a price per sales ratio of one or less and an average profit rate are possible sociable buyout prospects since the 8.3 percent profit is significantly greater than the 5.2 percent loan cost. However, price per sales ratio varies greatly by industry and within industries and averaged 1.56 in January 2014. Industries with price per sales ratio of 1 or less tend to have lower prices relative to sales due to lower than average profit rates.

Stock screening tools exist where both price per sales ratio and profit rate resulting from continuing operations can be used as criteria. Presumably, all stocks that result from a search of price per sales ratio less than one and profit from continuing operations greater than, let's say, 9 percent, to have a substantial amount of profit remaining after 5.2 percent is used to pay loans, are good prospects for sociable takeovers. 114 companies met these criteria.

Stock screening tools can also discover companies with low price earnings ratios. Any companies with a price earnings ratio less than about 11 earned 9 percent of the value of the stock in a year. 655 companies met these criteria. The earnings used to determine these ratios can include non-recurring income, so sometimes these companies will not be good prospects for sociable takeovers because earnings from continuing operations are the best determinant of that, but an additional criterion, projected price earnings ratio of less than 11 the following year, resulted in 304 companies meeting both these criteria.

The following are more detailed evaluations on some of the companies resulting from these stock screens.

The following companies are just a sampling of many other possible "sociable takeovers." In these cases, the preliminary evaluations reveal that business profits far exceed loan servicing costs. Seventy percent of what remains after the loan payments would support a substantial and, in some cases, very large average raise per worker. Workers would decide whether more or less than using 70% was appropriate for raises, based on their judgment of how much revenue the corporation needs to maintain to insure against down times, unforeseen expenses, and for future expansion. Individual workers would receive more or less than the average raise based on WSDE governance practices. The raises could be in current wages or as distributions into member capital accounts. In several cases, a "sociable takeover" would result in workers receiving a raise of several thousands of dollars per month.

The source of company financial data used in the evaluations is Yahoo Finance, on October 6, 2014, or within a day or two of it.

Appliance Recycling Centers of America Inc.

Appliance Recycling Centers of America Inc., stock symbol ARCI, is the nation's largest recycler of major household appliances. It provides appliance recycling and replacement services for electric utilities and other sponsors of energy efficiency programs and the general public. The company was founded in 1976, is based in Minneapolis, Minnesota and has 329 employees. It also sells new household appliances through a chain of 18 retail stores under the ApplianceSmart name in Minnesota, Ohio, Georgia, and Texas.

In the four quarters ending June 2014, it had income or profits from continuing operations before taxes of $5,139,000, which amounts to $1,302 per month per employee. If the employees owned the company, they could do what they choose with these profits.

The company has a market value or "capitalization" of $16.9 million. In a sociable buyout, after deducting the $14,700 investment from each employee, $12.1 million remains that requires financing. Eighty percent at five percent interest and 20 percent at six percent interest yields a total monthly payment for the loans of $301 per employee initially and $194 after seven years when the remaining portion of the 20-year loan remains due. These amounts are easily payable from the $1,302 per month profits per employee from continuing operations. The company would be able to support a raise in varying amounts for the workers, decided by standard WSDE practices, and they would wholly own the company at the end of 20 years when the loan payments would end. The company has a net asset value or "book" value per employee of $52,956 per employee and a market value of $51,368 per employee. If 70% of the remaining profits after the loan payments were distributed to the workers, it would support an average raise of $701 per month, and after seven years $776 per month, or $8,408 and $9,308 per year, respectively.

MFRI Inc.

MFRI (stock symbol MFRI) manufactures and sells filter bags for industrial air pollution control systems known as baghouses. The company also engineers, designs and manufactures specialty piping systems and leak detection and location systems. The piping systems include those for transporting chemicals, hazardous fluids, and petroleum. It sells its products primarily in the United States, the Middle East, Europe, Canada, and India. MFRI, Inc. employs 1,013 people, was founded in 1989, and is headquartered in Niles, Illinois.

In four quarters ending July 2014, it had income or profits from continuing operations before taxes of $13.5 million, which amounts to $1,110 per month per employee. The company has a market value of $67.1 million.

In a sociable buyout, after deducting the $14,700 investment from each employee, $52.2 million remains that requires financing. Eighty percent at five percent interest and 20 percent at six percent interest yields a total monthly payment for the loans of $423 per employee, and $272 after seven years, easily payable from the $1,110 per month profits per employee from continuing operations. The company could also support a worker pay raise, in amounts decided by standard WSDE practices. If 70% of the remaining profits after the loan payments were distributed to the workers, it would support an average raise of $480 per month, and after seven years $586 per month, or $5,770 and $7,031 per year, respectively. The workers would wholly own the company at the end of 20 years when the loan payments would end. The company has a net asset value or "book" value per employee of $80,815 and a market value of $66,269 per employee.

Travelcenters of America LLC

Travelcenters of America LLC. (stock symbol TA) is a full-service national travel center chain in the U.S., with nationwide locations serving hundreds of thousands of professional drivers and other highway travelers each month, including virtually all major trucking fleets. Its travel centers operate under the TravelCenters of America, TA and Petro brand names. It offers diesel and gasoline fueling services, restaurants, heavy truck repair facilities, stores and other services with 20,670 employees. You have probably seen some of its travel centers on highway exits in your neighborhood or travels.

In four quarters ending June 2014, it had income or profits from continuing operations before taxes of $21,930,000, which amounts to $88 per month per employee. The company has a market value of $348.8 million.

In a sociable buyout, after deducting the $14,700 investment from each employee $44.95 million remains that requires financing. Eighty percent at five percent interest and 20 percent at six percent interest yields a total monthly payment for the loans of $18 per employee and $11 after seven years, easily payable from the $88 per month profits per employee from continuing operations. The company could also support a worker pay raise, in amounts decided by standard WSDE practices. If 70% of the remaining profits after the loan payments were distributed to the workers it would support an average raise of $49 per month and after seven years $54 per month, or $593 and $646 per year, respectively. The workers would wholly own the company at the end of 20 years when the loan payments would end. The company has a net asset value or "book" value per employee of $22,204 per employee and a market value of $16,875 per employee.

Omega Protein Corporation

Omega Protein Corporation (stock symbol OME), headquartered in Houston, is one of the nation's leading producers of edible fish oil, which is high in nutritionally desirable Omega-3 fatty acids and is used in many food products. Omega Protein also produces specialty fish meals for livestock feeds, and fish solubles which are used as an organic fertilizer and in other applications. The Human Nutrition segment offers various products, including Omega-3 fish oils, and other ingredients to the nutraceutical industry. The company sells its products in the United States, Mexico, Europe, Canada, Asia, and South and Central America. Omega Protein Corporation was founded in 1913 and has 450 employees.

In four quarters ending June 2014 it had income or profits from continuing operations before taxes of $58,170,000, which amounts to $10,771 per month per employee. The company has a market value of $265.3 million.

In a sociable buyout, after deducting the $14,700 investment from each employee, $258.7 million remains that requires financing. Eighty percent at five percent interest and 20 percent at six percent interest yields a total monthly payment for the loans of $4,715 per employee, and $3,035 after seven years, easily payable from the $10,771 per month profits per employee from continuing operations. If 70% of the remaining profits after the loan payments were distributed to the workers, it would support an average raise of $4,240 per month, and after seven years $5,415 per month, or $50,875 and $64,984 per year, respectively. They would wholly own the company at the end of 20 years when the loan payments would end. The company has a net asset value or "book" value per employee of $601,610 per employee and a market value of $589,578 per employee.

Alaska Communications Systems Group Inc.

Alaska Communications Systems Group Inc. (stock symbol ALSK) provides communication services comprising voice and broadband services; and managed services, including data network hosting, IT management, cloud-based services, billing and collection, and long distance services to business customers, government customers, including municipal, local, state, and federal government, school districts, libraries, rural health care hospitals, and wholesale customers, such as other telecommunications carriers. It also provides voice and broadband services to residential customers, voice and broadband termination services to inter- and intrastate carriers, support services, wireless voice and broadband services, and wireless devices. The company offers its products and services through its retail stores, a direct sales team, and a network of agents. Alaska Communications Systems Group was founded in 1998, is headquartered in Anchorage, Alaska, and has 850 employees.

In four quarters ending June 2014, it had income or profits from continuing operations before taxes of $196.2 million, which amounts to $19,236 per month per employee. The company has a market value of $72.8 million.

In a sociable buyout, after deducting the $14,700 investment from each employee $60.3 million remains that requires financing. Eighty percent at five percent interest and 20 percent at six percent interest yields a monthly payment for the loan of $581 per employee, $374 after seven years, very easily payable from the $19,236 per month profits per employee from continuing operations. If 70% of the remaining profits after the loan payments were distributed to the workers, it would support an average raise of $13,058 per month, and after seven years $13,203 per month, or $156,700 and $158,440 per year, respectively. They would wholly own the company at the end of 20 years when the loan payments would end. The company has a net asset value per employee of $161,509 per employee and a market value of $85,600 per employee.

The company had extraordinarily high income from continuing operations in the quarter ending September 2013 for reasons I did not investigate.

However, to determine if this unusual quarterly performance were not repeated how good a prospect it would be for a sociable buyout, I took the average of their before tax income from continuing operations in the prior two years as their projected income. This average was $17.7 million, which amounts to $1,731 per month per employee, also far greater than the loan payments.

Renewable Energy Group, Inc.

Renewable Energy Group Inc. (stock symbol REGI) operates through two segments, Biodiesel and Services. The Biodiesel segment acquires feedstock, manages construction and operates biodiesel production facilities and marketing, selling, and distributing biodiesel, glycerin, free fatty acids, and other co-products of the biodiesel production process. This segment produces biodiesel from various feed stocks, including inedible corn oil, used cooking oil, inedible animal fat, and from virgin vegetable oils, such as soybean oil or canola oil. It also purchases and resells biodiesel and raw material feedstocks,

The Services segment provides biodiesel facility management and operational services to biodiesel production facilities and other clean-tech companies, and acts as a construction management and general contractor for the construction of biodiesel production facilities. Renewable Energy Group, was founded in 1996, is headquartered in Ames, Iowa, and has 188 employees.

In the four quarters ending June 2014, it had income or profits from continuing operations before taxes of $72.9 million, which amounts to $32,310 per month per employee. The company has a market value of $427.3 million.

In a sociable buyout, after deducting the $14,700 investment from each employee, $424.5 million remains that requires financing. Eighty percent at five percent interest and 20 percent at six percent interest yields a total monthly payment for the loans of $18,520 per employee, $11,922 after seven years, easily payable from the $32,310 per month profits per employee from continuing operations. If 70% of the remaining profits after the loan payments were distributed to the workers, it would support an average raise of $9,650 per month, and after seven years, $14,270 per month, or $115,823 and $171,242 per year, respectively. They would wholly own the company at the end of 20 years when the loan payments would end. The company has a net asset value or "book" value per employee of $3,607,649 per employee and a market value of $2,272,819 per employee.

FAB Universal Corporation

FAB Universal (stock symbol FABU) distributes digital entertainment products and services worldwide through intelligent kiosks, retail stores and franchises, and online through Apple iTunes and Google Android, using subscription sales for mobile devices, smartphone apps and Netflix-like subscription models. The company has three business units: Digital Media Services, Retail Media Sales, and Wholesale Media Distribution. FAB Universal, formerly known as Wizzard Software Corporation, is based in Pittsburgh, PA, and has 188 employees.

In the four quarters ending June 2014, it had income or profits from continuing operations before taxes of $21.42 million, which amounts to $9,493 per month per employee. The company has a market value of $12.48 million.

In a sociable buyout, after deducting the $14,700 investment from each employee, $9.72 million remains that requires financing. Eighty percent at five percent interest and 20 percent at six percent interest yields a total monthly payment for the loans of $424 per employee, $273 after seven years, very easily payable from the $6,938 per month profits per employee from continuing operations. If 70% of the remaining profits after the loan payments were distributed to the workers, it would support an average raise of $6,349 per month, and after seven years $6,454 per month, or $76,184 and $77,452 per year, respectively. They would wholly own the company at the end of 20 years when the loan payments would end. The company has a net asset value of $737,590 per employee and a market value of $66,383 per employee.

FONAR Corporation

FONAR Corporation (stock symbol FONR) is a developer, manufacturer, servicer and seller of MRI scanners. The company introduced the world's first commercial MRI in 1980, and went public in 1981. FONAR's most extraordinary product is the Upright MRI, also known as the Stand-Up MRI, the whole-body MRI that scans patients in numerous weight-bearing positions like standing, sitting, in flexion and extension, as well as the conventional lie-down position. The company also offers management services to diagnostic imaging facilities and leases office space, facilities, and medical equipment. It also provides related supplies, staffing, training, and supervision of non-medical personnel, legal services, accounting, billing, and collection. In addition, it assists medical offices in the development and implementation of practice growth and marketing strategies. As of June 30, 2014, it managed 11 diagnostic imaging facilities in New York state and Florida. Fonar was founded in 1978, is based in Melville, New York, and has 430 employees.

In the four quarters ending June 2014, it had income or profits from continuing operations before taxes of $11.05 million, which amounts to $2,141 per month per employee. The company has a market value of $66.4 million.

In a sociable buyout, after deducting the $14,700 investment from each employee, $60.1 million remains that requires financing. Eighty percent at five percent interest and 20 percent at six percent interest yields a total monthly payment for the loans of $1,146 per employee, $738 after seven years, easily payable from the $2,141 per month profits per employee from continuing operations. If 70% of the remaining profits after the loan payments were distributed to the workers, it would support an average raise of $697 per month, and after seven years $982 per month, or $8,358 and $11,788 per year, respectively. They would wholly own the company at the end of 20 years when the loan payments would end. The company has a net asset value of $58,947 per employee and a market value of $154,442 per employee.

REX American Resources Corporation

REX American Resources Corporation (stock symbol REX) operates in two segments, Alternative Energy and Real Estate. The Alternative Energy segment is engaged in the production of ethanol, dried and modified distiller's grains, and non-food grade corn oil. Its dry distiller grains with solubles are used as proteins in animal feed. The Real Estate segment leases real estate properties. The company was formerly known as REX Stores Corporation and changed its name to REX American Resources Corporation in 2010. The company was founded in 1980, is based in Dayton, Ohio, and has 105 employees.

In the four quarters ending June 2014, it had income or profits from continuing operations before taxes of $122.4 million, which amounts to $97,169 per month per employee. The company has a market value of $559.3 million.

In a sociable buyout, after deducting the $14,700 investment from each employee, $557.8 million remains that requires financing. Eighty percent at five percent interest and 20 percent at six percent interest yields a total monthly payment for the loans of $43,567 per employee and $28,046 after seven years, very easily payable from the $97,169 per month profits per employee from continuing operations. If 70% of the remaining profits after the loan payments were distributed to the workers, it would support a very large average raise of $37,522 per month, and after seven years $48,386 per month, or $450,258 and $580,631 per year, respectively. They would wholly own the company at the end of 20 years when the loan payments would end. The company has a net asset value per employee of $3,097,010 per employee and a market value of $5,326,857 per employee.

Meritage Homes Corporation

Meritage Homes Corporation (stock symbol MTH) is engaged in the designing and building of single-family detached homes in the United States. The company operates through two segments, Homebuilding and Financial Services. It offers a range of homes for various home buyers, including first-time, move-up, active adult, and luxury. Meritage Homes Corp. is one of the nation's largest single-family home builders. The company provides its homes under the Meritage Homes, Monterey Homes, and Phillips Builders names. It also offers title insurance and closing/settlement services for its home buyers. The company primarily builds and sells its homes in Arizona, Texas, California, Colorado, Florida, North Carolina, South Carolina, and Tennessee. As of December 31, 2013, Meritage offered its homes in 188 communities. The company was founded in 1985 and is based in Scottsdale, Arizona. It has 1,050 employees.

In the four quarters ending June 2014, it had income or profits from continuing operations before taxes of $162.4 million, which amounts to $12,890 per month per employee. The company has a market value of $1.4 billion.

In a sociable buyout, after deducting the $14,700 investment from each employee, $1.38 billion remains that requires financing. Eighty percent at five percent interest and 20 percent at six percent interest yields a total monthly payment for the loans of $10,815 per employee, $6,962 after seven years, although a higher percentage of the profits than the prior cases, these amounts are also easily payable from the $12,890 per month profits per employee from continuing operations. If 70% of the remaining profits after the loan payments were distributed to the workers, it would support an average raise of $1,453 per month, and after seven years $4,150 per month, or $17,440 and $49,802 per year, respectively. They would wholly own the company at the end of 20 years when the loan payments would end. The company has a net asset value per employee of $959,230 per employee and a market value of $1,333,330 per employee.

Take-Two Interactive Software Inc.

Take-Two Interactive Software Inc. (stock symbol TTWO) is a leading worldwide developer, publisher and distributor of interactive software games. The company's software operates on multimedia personal computers and video game console platforms. It is one of the largest distributors of interactive software games in the United States and one of the top publishers of interactive software games in Europe. The company delivers its products through physical retail, digital download, online platforms, and cloud streaming services. Take-Two, founded in 1993 and headquartered in New York City has 2,530 employees.

In four quarters ending June 2014, it had income or profits from continuing operations before taxes of $396 million, which amounts to $13,040 per month per employee. The company has a market value of $1.74 billion.

In a sociable buyout, after deducting the $14,700 investment from each employee, $1.70 billion remains that requires financing. Eighty percent at five percent interest and 20 percent at six percent interest yields a total monthly payment for the loans of $5,520 per employee, $3,553 after seven years, easily payable from the $13,040 per month profits per employee from continuing operations. If 70% of the remaining profits after the loan payments were distributed to the workers, it would support an average raise of $5,267 per month, after seven years $6,643 per month, or $63,203 and $79,721 per year, respectively. They would wholly own the company at the end of 20 years when the loan payments would end. The company has a net asset value per employee of $307,030 per employee and a market value of $687,747 per employee.

Mechanical Technology Inc.

Mechanical Technology, Inc. (stock symbol MKTY) products include electronic gauging instruments for position, displacement, and vibration applications in the manufacturing, research, design, and process development markets. It also provides precision measurement tools for semiconductor wafers including solar wafers, and engine balancing and vibration analysis systems for military and commercial aircraft. The company serves the electronics, aircraft, aerospace, automotive, semiconductor, and research industries. Mechanical Technology markets its products through direct sales and representatives in the Americas, and through distributors and agents in Europe and Asia. Mechanical Technology, founded in 1961, is headquartered in Albany, New York, and has 31 employees.

In four quarters ending June 2014, it had income or profits from continuing operations, before taxes, of $3.05 million, which amounts to $8,210 per month per employee. The company has a market value of $5.6 million.

In a sociable buyout, after deducting the $14,700 investment from each employee, $5.16 million remains that requires financing. Eighty percent at five percent interest and 20 percent at six percent interest yields a total monthly payment for the loans of $1,366 per employee, $880 after seven years, easily payable from the $8,210 per month profits per employee from continuing operations. If 70% of the remaining profits after the loan payments were distributed to the workers, it would support an average raise of $4,789 per month, $5,129 per month after seven years, or $57,462 and $61,551 per year, respectively. They would wholly own the company at the end of 20 years when the loan payments would end. The company has a net asset value per employee of $106,018 per employee and a market value of $181,290 per employee.

The bond tax exemption costs would be about $16 million per year for the sociable buyout program.[211]

Supporting WSDE Establishment When Companies Relocate or Factories Are Abandoned

The Community Credit Union or Bank Partnership policy will also apply when a factory plans to close and relocate operations out of state or overseas. Current employees could present a business plan to a community credit union or bank (or to the local government under the system I describe subsequently) to provide funding under the partnership agreement to transfer the enterprise to worker-ownership under these conditions:

If the factory and/or other building facilities aren't sold three months before ending operations, the city will hire an independent appraiser to determine a value (or possibly a standardized evaluation formula will be used). A bidding process that includes the workers will not be required to determine fair value because an agent of the owner could bid the price up to get a higher than fair market price from the workers. Preferably, the workforce and owner will agree on the price before or after the appraisal, but if not, we recommend that the city applies eminent domain laws for the sale of the facilities that are in process to be abandoned. These laws are designed for governments to force sales of private property when a compelling public interest exists, as it will in these cases if the workers and the local financing partner will accept the resulting price.

The city could discount the appraisal by as much as 20%, to account for some of the social costs of abandonment. This appraisal and discounting process will generally make the investment sufficiently attractive to motivate the partnership with a community credit union or bank, or the city government itself. If the workers are not interested in a buyout, the facility could remain on the market beyond the 3-month period before relocating.

Abandoned factories or other business facilities sometimes sit idle and decay for years, becoming a blight, and sometimes a hazard to a community. After a six-month warning, if the owner of any abandoned facility does not sell it we will promote taking the property under eminent domain laws by cities. Fair compensation to the owner will be made in consideration of the social costs of abandonment. Cities will grant, or provide at a discounted price, the property to groups seeking its use for a worker-owned business. Federal financing will be available for the sale price.

The assets purchased would not have to be used to provide the same goods or services that the original company provided. Workers may find more productive uses for the assets.

We will also offer community members the opportunity to purchase bonds under the business abandonment and relocation programs. Total values of company assets abandoned were not available. Although it will likely be less, we will use the estimate of half the tax exemption costs as in bankrupt public company conversions to WSDEs to be conservative in our budget analysis, so we will budget $146 million per year.

Credit Unions—an Important Part of a Democratized Economy

The credit unions that will support WSDE formation, although not WSDEs themselves, are cooperatively owned businesses—by far the largest number of cooperatively owned businesses that exist. Credit unions are democratized, one-person, one-vote banks that their customers own. More than 106 million Americans belong to credit unions; their total assets are over $1.25 trillion.[212] The Community Development Financial Institutions (CDFI) Fund at the Treasury Department has helped create a national network of over 1,000 community development banks, credit unions, and loan funds.

New Enlightenment policies will expand this program in its "Banking Reform and Public Banks" proposal (to be detailed in a future document), but even at current asset levels when leveraged 4/1 with federal and community members' funds, credit unions and community banks can be important partners in our efforts in establishing worker-owned businesses. As previously noted, we will offer preferential federal funds access with discounted rates to credit unions (and WSDE banks) for lending to WSDEs to further support the growth and importance of credit unions, and WSDEs.

Widespread support exists for increasing the number and relative financial power of credit unions and local community banks. Popular support for local banking has increased since the major bank caused financial crisis, and activists have encouraged this process with "move your money" efforts, shifting billions of dollars away from Wall Street and large banks and into credit unions and smaller banks. New Enlightenment policies will support this trend.

Federal and local government WSDE establishment partnerships

As we have described, we use the judgment and financial commitment of local credit unions or community banks to select worker-owned businesses with sufficiently good prospects to be worthy of federal government loans and/or grants. To further support widespread establishment of worker-owned and self-directed enterprises, we will use the judgment and financial commitment of city governments, for the following reasons and under the following conditions:

Cities are forced to endure great financial and social costs when traditional capitalist enterprises abandon a city because operations relocated elsewhere would allow higher profits either through lower labor, tax, or environmental or other regulatory compliance costs, or through government subsidies. One estimate is that taxpayers spent roughly $65 billion (2001 dollars) to pay for the infrastructure and other capital costs needed to serve individuals who moved out of declining cities to other locations just over the 1980 to 1999 period. Research by University of Maryland researcher Tom Ricker found that adding private costs (e.g., redundant houses, stores, factories, etc.) brings the figure to over $350 billion—not including lost tax revenues and increased social spending by communities when jobs decline and citizens leave town.[213]

Almost every city or state also spends large amounts to bribe big corporations to locate operations in their city or state. Big companies often extract public subsidies of between $100,000 and $200,000 per promised job brought to a city, and these kinds of bribes sometimes cause additional harm. Companies locate in the city until another locality offers a bigger bribe. The company then moves in response to the new city's bribe, causing economic harm and waste of resources to the abandoned city, and to the country.

It is also common for cities to make equity investments in local businesses. In 1989, 20.4 percent of cities surveyed were making direct investments in local businesses. By 1996 a majority, 56.3 percent, were doing so as part of their routine development strategy.[214] Focusing these investments on worker-owned businesses will be especially beneficial for cities. In addition to creating greater egalitarianism, prosperity, and democracy, it will allow long-term planning and minimize the enormous waste and costs created when company management decides to abandon factories, workers, and communities. Worker owned businesses are rooted in the community.

To encourage cities to direct funds to local worker-ownership of businesses, this New Enlightenment policy offers a loan origination partnership with cities. This partnership will also include grants to participating WSDEs in the city. If the city purchases bonds or provides loans to supply 10% of the total WSDE funding requirements for the establishment of a WSDE, the WSDE will be eligible for the grants and loans. The WSDE grants will be 50% of the bond or loan amount (5% of the capital). Funds under this system can be provided to WSDEs formed as new businesses or formed from pre-existing businesses sold to a WSDE.

We will limit the loan amount to 10% from the city to maximize the number of WSDEs worthy of support that the city can select while requiring a sufficiently large minimum commitment of city funds to assure careful selection. This will minimize the risk of loss of federal funds. Loan appraisals will also be performed in the Commonwealth Bank; it could reject a city approved loan.

The maximum total amount of city loans to all WSDEs under the federal partnership program will be $130 per city resident. We will use mailing address city for population counts, not just population within official city limits. (For example, if one million people have a city's residential mailing address, the city could provide $130 million total per year for establishing WSDEs, and total available funds for WSDEs in the city would be $1.3 billion.) Limiting city loans also has the advantage of encouraging the supplying of funds from local citizens. This policy will motivate the redirection of city funds previously directed to conventional businesses to WSDEs, and substantially increase the amounts provided.

Just as in partnership bank loans, to assure equal opportunity to the poor, New Enlightenment policy will require for the city partnership that cities evaluate worker-owner loan applications solely on the merits of the proposed business and whether the experience and knowledge or education of the applicants will meet operational requirements. These are the important criteria for predicting business success. Wealth or assets and prior income data will not be allowed as loan approval criteria.

Prior financial status as a loan criterion will be allowed when cities want to target funds to the poor. Some cities may prefer to provide loans with the associated federal support to help the poor establish businesses. This will minimize social service costs and the costs associated with crime more often committed by people economically disenfranchised. The most benefit from the program will likely be realized by cities that support businesses with loans that will best serve city development needs or have important social value for the city, independent of the prior wealth of the prospective owners

As in the partnership with community credit unions and banks, only applications by groups of ten or larger will be accepted, and the same policy would apply to businesses that would require staffing in addition to the applicants.

The federal partnership agreement will include a requirement to establish a City Development Agency (CDA) division, with a director appointed by the mayor (or city manager) who will evaluate applications for city loans. This director, and the mayor since he will have supervisory responsibilities, will both be responsible for the CDA's actions.

The federal partnership agreement will require that a portion of the city's website be devoted to describing the businesses that were funded, with the reasons the city selected them for support, and the business applications that were rejected, with the reasons they were rejected. The average national new WSDE success rate, and the city success rate of new businesses of other types, could be used as benchmarks to evaluate the CDA director's judgment on the WSDE businesses that he or she used city funds to support. The voters when evaluating the mayor's judgment in the following election will also use these criteria. Presumably, mayors will select directors with a good record of managing public funds.

We will determine federal loan requirements after bonds offered for purchase only by community members to support any additional funding needs are made available on the city's website with a detailed description of the recipient business and specific purpose of the bond funds. We will also offer grants of 50% of the bond amount purchased by community members up to a maximum of 5% of total capital requirements, in addition to the grants associated with city supplied funds. Also, the same tax benefits will apply as in the partnership with local credit unions or banks system. For the advantages described previously, the required annual bondholder meetings will also be open to the community members other than bondholders, if space is available.

Since the federal grants support for the establishment of WSDEs supported by cities is proportional to both the city government and direct citizen's support, it maximizes the benefits of these federal funds to local communities. The total annual WSDEs grant amount associated with both city government and citizen support will be a maximum of $130 per person in the city population. Considering the funds that will be available from citizen bond purchases, bank loans, city loans and personal funds, including the grants to the economically disadvantaged, the total federal loan amount is likely to be much less than $200 billion per year. The following table details limits and estimate ranges of the various sources of funds to support WSDE establishment that cities select for support.

This program is designed to support the formation of city selected WSDEs with funding of $410 billion total maximum amount from all sources per year. Assuming full utilization of the granting program associated with city loans or bond purchases, the annual grant cost will be about $21 billion. Assuming that citizen bond purchases will support at least the same portion of WSDE capital requirements as city governments' loans or bond purchases or 10% of total funding requirements, $41 billion, the grant support associated with these bond purchases will also be about $21 billion. These and the remaining available funding support amount details are in the table.

Any city desiring to fully utilize this federal granting and lending support program for WSDEs with insufficient funds could partner with its county or state governments to provide the additional funds. The total revenues of all municipalities in 2009 was about $400 billion. Using $41 billion total for all cities, or $130 per city resident, as an investment to increase revenues directly through the loan interest and indirectly through the economic stimulus impact of newly established businesses structured as WSDEs will be within practical bounds for many cities.

New York City between 1994 and 2001 paid $2.26 billion in subsidies to corporations that threatened to leave the city without them.[215] These were subsidies, not loans that are paid back with interest as in The New Enlightenment policy. This is an annual average of $282 million per year or $34 per resident.

The federal funds and beneficial economic impact of the policy from other causes will likely motivate county or state governments to participate where cities have insufficient funds. A New York Times investigation found that cities, counties, and states combined provide $80 billion per year in subsidies to corporations or over $250 per person.[216] Loans of $130 per person are clearly within practical bounds for city-state partnerships if local government giveaways are now almost twice as large.

Established WSDEs seeking expansion including through absorption of conventional firms will be allowed to offer bonds to finance the expansion with the same tax advantages as in our WSDE establishment proposals.

Allocated or Estimated Financial Support of City Supported WSDEs from All Sources

Funding Source	National Total Min ($ Billions)	National Total Max ($ Billions)	Per City Resident Min ($)	Per City Resident Max ($)	% Of Funding Min	% Of Funding Max
City Loans	41	41	130	130***	10%	10%
Federal Grants (CL)*	21	21	65	65	5%	5%
Local Citizen Bond Purchases	41	123	130	390	10%	30%
Federal Grants (B)* (Max.)	21	21	65	65	5%	5%
Bank Loans	41	123	130	390	10%	30%
Personal Funds**	41	82	130	260	10%	20%
Federal Loans	0	205	0	651	0%	50%

*(CL) Limit, Based on City Loan Amount (B) Limit, Based On Citizen Bond Amount
** This includes funds granted to the economically disadvantaged through the system
    I describe in the next section
*** Limit within federal partnership agreement

Grants to the Economically Disadvantaged for Investment in Their WSDE

Grants will be available to economically disadvantaged individuals for investment in WSDEs meeting The New Enlightenment WSDE establishment and structure standards. All individuals between the ages of 18 and 64 with below average wealth will be eligible.

The most detailed wealth data available are in the Survey of Consumer Finances (SCF) by the Federal Reserve, and these data are for households only. The Federal Reserve estimated all 118 million American households' wealth using a large survey and statistical projections from the survey data. The granting system will use these data in this way:

The average wealth per household is $495,000, using the 2010 SCF data. (Updating to 2013 SCF data would not change the character of the policy.) Because the country's wealth is heavily skewed toward the highest quintile, 83% of households had below average wealth. The total population between 18 and 64 years old is 198 million, amounting to an average of 1.68 per household in this age range. For this policy, we assume that all the wealth of households is held equally by those members between 18 and 64 years of age. Dividing $495,000 by 1.68 gives the average wealth per 18 to 64-year-old of $294,000. The grant amount will be 5% of the difference between each person's wealth in the age range of 18 and 64 and $294,000.

We will determine each eligible person's wealth by dividing their household's wealth by the number of people in their household between 18 and 64 years old. (When the New Enlightenment wealth tax system, Policy 5, is instituted, we will use the more specific and comprehensive wealth data than the current Federal Reserve data that will be established for individuals and households, just as comprehensive income data is established now under the income tax system.) To determine the grant amount, negative wealth will be considered zero wealth. This will result in grants up to $14,700 for individuals with zero or negative wealth, for the sole purpose of investing in a qualified WSDE. This amounts to an expenditure of $96.5 billion per year for 20 years, assuming the maximum participation rate.[217] Grantees will need to be careful in their WSDE selection because the grant maximum per person in their lifetime will be $14,700.

This policy will be another strong motive for widespread establishment of WSDEs, since the funds will be available only for this purpose, and 83% of Americans aged 18 to 64 will be eligible. This granting system will be an important part of creating a far more equal opportunity and egalitarian society.

Although the average wealth per adult in the United States is about the average of 20 OECD countries, its median is about 58% of the average of their medians because of our much larger wealth disparities. U.S. average wealth per adult is $248,395 (2011), but our median wealth is only $52,752. The average of the 20 countries per adult wealth averages is $249,308, and the average of their medians is $91,663. Nine of the 20 other countries have a higher average wealth per adult, and we are near the bottom in median wealth. Sixteen countries have a higher median wealth per adult than the U.S.

This is true despite America's vastly greater land and natural resources per person than Europe (just as Norway's high oil and gas earnings account for its higher GDP per person than the U.S.). America has far more oil, gas, and coal per capita than Europe, for example. Despite America's vast resource advantage, we have a lower quality of life in many ways than countries in northern Europe.

Median and mean wealth per adult in 20 advanced countries, 2011*			
Country	Median	Mean	Mean/median
Australia	$221,704	$396,745	1.8
Austria	$88,112	$194,207	2.2
Belgium	$133,572	$275,524	2.1
Canada	$89,014	$245,455	2.8
Denmark	$25,692	$239,057	9.3
Finland	$86,286	$174,895	2.0
France	$90,271	$293,685	3.3
Germany	$57,283	$199,783	3.5
Greece	$43,571	$105,843	2.4
Ireland	$100,351	$181,434	1.8
Italy	$,953	$259,826	1.7
Japan	$128,688	$248,770	1.9
Netherlands	$66,056	$186,449	2.8
New Zealand	$68,726	$167,957	2.4
Norway	$87,377	$355,925	4.1
Spain	$71,797	$130,179	1.8
Sweden	$43,297	$284,146	6.6
Switzerland	$100,901	$540,010	5.4
United Kingdom	$121,852	$257,881	2.1
United States	$52,752	$248,395	4.7
Averages	$91,663	$249,308	3.2
U.S./Average	0.576	0.996	1.5
(Data source: Economic Policy Institute, State of Working America)			

We have much room for improvement both in wealth creation per adult and far more so in its more equitable distribution. This is more obvious when you consider that the other countries in the comparison have far from an ideal distribution. Providing investment funds that will yield higher than average returns to the majority of the population will eventually raise median and mean wealth to higher levels than the 20 country averages, motivating other countries to establish similar policies.

WSDE Support after Establishment

The U.S. Small Business Administration (SBA) will give business management training, provide technical consultants including on-site consultations if requested, and make referrals to approved technical training institutions to newly formed worker-owned companies when needed. We will increase the SBA's budget by $450 million to meet this increased responsibility. This approximately doubles its salaries and expenses budget. The Council of Cooperatives, a new kind of local institution, will also provide these services, using the SBA as a partner when needed. A National Cooperative Congress and Research Institution will also be an important part of the support system.

When possible, federal agencies will choose WSDEs when purchasing goods or services. Based on current needs for infrastructure expenditures alone, this will be a very important additional means of support. In 2013, the American Society of Civil Engineers gave the country a grade of D+ on its physical infrastructure and determined that we need $3.6 trillion worth of infrastructure improvements. For example, one in nine bridges were characterized as structurally deficient. Because of current low-interest rates and high unemployment (real unemployment, not necessarily official unemployment that excludes those who have dropped out of the labor force), there will never be a better time to make progress on making the infrastructure improvements. Many WSDEs will be formed to satisfy these needs, so this will be an important component of our widespread adoption of WSDEs program.

Much of the decision-making on the WSDEs to contract for the infrastructure work can be made in partnership with local governments. States and municipalities can conduct an inventory of their maintenance and construction needs for schools, including preschools, roads, bridges, and dams for federal funding support. WSDEs will supply the necessary labor and materials within an 80/20 federal/local funding partnership system.

We will phase in the requirement that all federal purchases from businesses be from WSDE's, and incentivize state and local governments to do so, possibly by federally covering 5% of the WSDE goods or services price.

Also, WSDE products and services will be labeled or otherwise officially identified so that people would be free to support these more beneficially structured enterprises with their purchasing choices.

Extensive Beneficial Impacts

These policies of promoting worker-owned and self-directed enterprises are important for reasons in addition to the economic ones resulting from the additional motivation that workers feel in workplaces where there is democratic control and shared ownership, facilitating the transition of unemployed workers back into productive employment, empowering people previously unable to invest in business enterprises, and greatly reducing economic disparity. Enterprises of this type will help complete modern society's limited democratization. For most workers, no democracy exists in their workplaces, where they must spend much of their lives. Retaining the hierarchical and undemocratic organization of enterprises is obstructing meaningful democracy in our lives.

Workers required to learn the skills of participating fully in directing their worker-owned enterprises will be much more inclined to demand equal participation in their community and national politics, strengthening the democratic processes that create well-functioning democratic governments.

Another important benefit of worker-owned and self-directed enterprises: Studies have shown that when people's work lives are dominated by the decision-making of others, it negatively affects health. The psychological impact of having little control over what a person does for a large part of the day has physical effects.

Do the following statements indicate that both Abraham Lincoln and Ronald Reagan would support the widespread establishment of WSDEs that New Enlightenment policies will accomplish?

During the period of major debates and conflicts over the morality of slavery, and for a period after the Civil War, the common view was that working for wages was not much superior to slavery if extended over long periods. Abraham Lincoln expressed this view:

"If any continue through life in the condition of the hired laborer, it is not the fault of the system, but because of either a dependent nature which prefers it, or improvidence, folly, or singular misfortune."

Unfortunately, President Lincoln did not foresee that it would eventually be a fault of the system, and as this fault has become more pervasive, it has become more often ignored. We will work toward correcting this fault with this major system reform.

Ronald Reagan said:

"In the future we will see in the United States and throughout the Western world an increasing trend toward the next logical step, employee ownership. It is a path that befits a free people."

New Enlightenment policies will rapidly advance us along the path that befits a free people toward widespread employee ownership. For an economic system to work for the majority of people, the majority of people must control the economic enterprises that comprise it.

Successful examples of worker-owned and controlled enterprises can offer useful ideas on practical WSDE governance structure. Below I recommend basic WSDE governance structure and support institution ideas, mainly adapted or duplicated from the most studied WSDE examples. These ideas are open to optimization and development during the debates on the details of the major and beneficial transformation to an economic system where worker controlled and owned business enterprises are the predominant business enterprise structure in the country.

Understanding the basic character of well-studied and successful examples is an important foundation for these debates, so I have included a summary description of some examples in Part 4, Note 7. They include the Plywood Cooperatives in the Pacific Northwest, the Mondragon Cooperatives of Spain, and the Lega Cooperatives of Italy. (Cooperative and WSDE are used interchangeably, with a few exceptions that I will specify).

Summary of Recommended WSDE Structure

Governance structure would vary based on size. Small WSDEs need little or no formal governance structure or have little need of managers or directors. Occasionally a nominal "board of directors" is useful in small WSDEs for some decisions, or for administrative matters with which other members do not want to concern themselves. Other decisions can be made by consensus or by workers themselves regarding their own work.

New Enlightenment WSDEs of all sizes share ownership equally, and share authority equally in determining governance policies, and will have the capital accounts system described below for all workers. The necessary economic disparities based on the level of skill and amount and difficulty of work are accomplished both by the level of pay and company contributions to individual capital accounts. This allows any degree of compensation disparity the company's members feel is necessary to attract competent people and serve the ideal of fairness. Equal ownership implies the equal voting rights essential to democratic governance and is analogous to equal citizenship.

The following is the recommended structure of WSDEs of a size greater than about 20 workers. This structure could vary somewhat depending on how large the WSDE is and other democratically determined considerations:

Workers meet in a General Assembly one to three times per year as they see fit. With large corporations, such as some of those formed from public company sociable takeovers, the General Assembly could be virtual where speakers' proposals could all be considered simultaneously by workers, either individually or, preferably, in groups using large screens to display speakers making presentations and proposals and answering questions, if an assembly hall for all workers was not practical.

In general, a maximum size of 500 workers is recommended, to facilitate democratic processes. When possible, larger economies of scale will be accomplished by gathering individual co-ops into groups defined by geography or product line.

The General Assembly elects the board of directors, about ten directors (varying between three and fifteen depending on WSDE size or preferences), approves large capital expenditures, admits new members, and considers other major proposals. Workers would receive a packet of information about the firm's operations and the issues to be decided in advance, possibly a month before General Assembly.

New members are admitted based on the candidate getting a 75% positive vote. This recommended threshold can be adjusted based on circumstances. Applicants for membership are screened carefully not only for skill and education but also for interest in the ethics of cooperation. A nine-month probationary period is required for new members. Every worker-owner has an equal vote on all General Assembly decisions and may see whatever data or documents he or she wishes.

The General Assembly also decides the wage ratio between the highest and lowest paid worker in the WSDE. The position of any individual member on the wage scale depends on a system of points awarded for qualifications, responsibility, the difficulty or danger of work, and social integration. Funds distributed to worker capital accounts will be in proportion to pay. Reportedly, WSDEs of similar structure have up to a nine to one pay ratio from the highest to lowest paid worker. No disparity standard will be established since democratic processes within each WSDE are more likely to determine optimal disparities for the particular WSDE's circumstances.

Directors serve four-year terms and are regular workers, generally from a wide variety of job categories, since all workers are eligible. Their directorship duties are performed on their regular work time for no extra pay. The directors meet at least once per month and appoint managers for four-year terms to manage day-to-day operations. Contract renewal is contingent on a performance review. Managers cannot be dismissed except with the approval of the General Assembly. Mutual monitoring, and the fact that workers all share in the economic benefits of their work, will result in a greatly reduced need to employ supervisors or lower level managers.

Committees dealing with innovation, grievances, and other matters will be formed for anyone choosing to participate. Social committee directors are elected by the membership to deal with safety, wages, workplace conditions, grievances, and related issues.

Serious disciplinary problems are reportedly rare in cooperatives with similar structure. If a disciplinary action is needed, managers would refer the issue to the social committee for the imposition of penalties including suspension, loss of income for up to sixty days, or in extreme cases, expulsion. For the more serious penalties, WSDEs may choose to require the approval of the General Assembly.

A committee of managers, sometimes augmented by outsiders, advises the board of directors. A "watchdog council" that consists of three elected members of the General Assembly monitors everyone else.

Only in exceptional circumstances, such as when people with special skills are needed temporarily, will a WSDE employ non-members, and these workers will be limited to 10% of the workforce, excluding workers in their probationary or trial period of nine months.

Annual bondholder meetings are open to the public.

After deducting wages, interest, and depreciation from net income, 30% is allocated to a Collective Reserve Fund, which is used for reinvestment or to help support the WSDE in down times, and 70% is credited to the individual capital accounts of the members. When losses occur, 30% are covered out of reserves; any remaining losses are debited from individual accounts. Individual capital account funds are dispersed on departure, but up to 30% can be withheld if the capital withdrawal is a threat to the enterprise. Departing members will also receive the value of their ownership share.

To further promote egalitarianism and possibly increase productivity, for any worker who would require little training to do the job of another worker I recommend limited training time for this purpose. This will be especially beneficial where it would be practical to train workers for management duties. If workers from a wide variety of backgrounds could rotate through management positions, this would eliminate a permanent management class. Initially this training time would result in some productivity losses, but long-term productivity will probably increase because:

- The varying perspectives and knowledge of the different workers rotating through varying positions may inject ideas for improvements in business practices that would not have otherwise occurred.
- Varying work experiences can reduce burdensome monotony, and thereby increase performance motivation.

An Important WSDE Support Institution: The Council of Cooperatives

We will establish one Council of Cooperatives (CC) modified WSDE per city, or region if city size is inappropriately small, that any WSDE in the city or region can join voluntarily. The CC will serve mainly an advisory role. It will seek out possible synergies between member WSDEs that could result in economies of scale advantages, including the sharing of some personnel and research and development costs, and the exchange of services. It will also advise on legal and financial issues, perform management training, assist in conflict resolution, offer recommendations on local technical training institutions, and either create advertising material or advise on its creation for the member WSDEs. At the request of any member WSDE, it will perform a comprehensive financial audit every two years, using the resulting information to advise on improving operational efficiency.

The CCs' operating funds will be supplied by a small tax deductible fee from the member WSDEs and a federal government annual operating grant maximum of $8 per city resident (the amount will depend on the number of citywide WSDEs), or a maximum annual federal expenditure of $2.5 billion. Commonwealth Bank loans will be available for startup funding. The ten-person directorship of the CC in its first year will be chosen from among community members (if ten or more CC workers are appropriate for the city or WSDEs population size) who offer their qualifications to the city. Cities will make these qualifications available to citywide WSDE members for their judgment. Meetings with members at their General Assembly could also be part of the CC staffing decision-making process when practicable. Citywide WSDE members will elect the ten directors on a one member, one vote basis.

The initial directors would hire additional workers, if needed. After the establishment of the initial workforce (within six months), WSDE governance practices, except directorship elections and those related to worker-ownership (Collective Reserve Fund and individual capital accounts), will be instituted. Two years after this establishment period, half the directorship of the CC will be elected by the CC workforce and half by the member WSDEs for four-year terms.

The CC will not be worker-owned but will be a modified worker self-directed enterprise. The average wage of all CC workers will be set at 30% higher than the average effective wage, including distributions into capital accounts, of all the workers in the member WSDEs, because of the CC's important role in promoting the prosperity of all its members and the disadvantages of not being worker-owned. The CC workers and directors will determine the maximum wage ratio.

The CC will also organize an annual Citywide Cooperative Congress where representatives of all city WSDEs will be eligible to attend. The Citywide Cooperative Congress will be especially useful for industrial and technology WSDEs to facilitate alliances for sharing research & development expenses to innovate production practices or products. Allied WSDEs may also decide it is advantageous to form an independent banking WSDE to offer clients credit for the purchase of their products and for depositing their surplus funds. Federal policies to assist WSDE banks will be described in The New Enlightenment Citizens Union or Party's Banking Reform and Public Banks future document.

The CC will also organize and participate in alliances of WSDEs for the shared funding of one or more health clinics staffed with general practitioners and support staff for free medical services to the WSDE members. General practitioners can serve most of the health care needs of most workers. Sufficiently large alliances will be able to support more extensive care and specialist services, for possibly a small fee per service to workers. The resulting lower health care costs will give a substantial competitive advantage to WSDEs, at least until The New Enlightenment Citizen Union's or Party's more comprehensive health care system reform (to be detailed in a future document) is instituted. These clinics, plus catastrophic cost insurance coverage, will bypass most of the large administrative and insurance industry costs. Administration costs consume 31% of U.S. health spending.[218]

Also, a substantial portion of health care dollars is wasted in fee-for-service relationships where doctors are incentivized to sell more tests and procedures to raise their income. Essentially, doctors are paid like salespersons, with lucrative commissions. Some of the resulting unnecessary tests and procedures not only waste health care dollars, they also harm health. (For example, studies have shown that many CT scans, angioplasties, and back surgeries performed were unnecessary, so they caused more harm than benefit, sometimes serious harm. One study found that one-third of adults are unnecessarily exposed to CT scans.[219] Another study found that one in 1200 patients 45 years old or younger who undergo just one full body CT scan will die from radiation induced cancer, and one in 50 will who receive annual scans for 30 years.[220]) Doctors compensated with a salary paid from the earnings of their patients as a group will have interests far better aligned with the interests of their patients, minimizing unnecessary tests and procedures.

The shared medical facility will be a modified WSDE of this character: The facility will be paid for by the member WSDEs in proportion to the number of members in the WSDE. Although the doctors and support staff will not own the facility, they will share in the direction of its operations. The CC directors will hire the initial staff. After two years, 50% of the board of directors of the health facility will be member WSDE elected representatives and 50% elected representatives of the health facility staff. Otherwise, standard WSDE governance practices, except those related to worker-ownership, would apply.

This modified WSDE structure medical facility will likely only be necessary in the early stages of widespread WSDE establishment. As WSDEs become more common, it may be preferable for groups of WSDEs to contract with WSDE health care facilities to provide services for an annual fee.

The National Cooperative Congress and Research Institution

After establishing WSDEs under our policy for two years, New Enlightenment policy is to establish an annual National Cooperative Congress of industrial and technology WSDEs. A major purpose of the National Cooperative Congress will be to decide on the character and funding levels of a National Institute of Cooperative Research and Development. Free access to all product and production process innovations developed by this institute will be given to all participating WSDEs.

The federal government will match any funding provided by the partici-pating WSDEs on the condition that other non-participating WSDEs be free to use all research results for a reasonable return on investment fee. Other than WSDEs, standard patent restrictions (though reduced under New Enlighten-ment policy)[221] will apply. This free or easy access to innovations to improve products or processes will help stimulate the widespread adoption of the WSDE structure. No one conventional corporation will be able to match econ-omies of scale of an alliance of all WSDEs in R&D expenses. Federal ex-penditure on R&D is well justified based on the high returns it has brought historically.

This policy will also result in a significant economic stimulus. Currently, corporations patent their innovations and use their patents to exert monopoly power to extract large amounts of money from the economy. With widespread sharing of innovation, the country will be better served through lower costs and more widespread sharing of prosperity.

Our Founders and other visionary leaders considered widespread ownership of productive capital of the highest importance

Massive support for worker-ownership of economic enterprises using federal resources to serve the best economic and other interests of our nation is not unprecedented. Several Homestead Acts gave away large tracts of land for homesteaders, for little or no cost, to farm or produce timber. Between 1862 and 1934, the federal government granted 1.6 million homesteads and distrib-uted 270 million acres (420,000 square miles) of federal land for private own-ership, most of which were operated by family owners that marketed some of their farm products. This was 10% of all land in the United States. Anyone, including freed slaves and women, 21 or older, or the head of a family, could apply to claim a federal land grant.

The Southern Homestead Act of 1866 sought to address land ownership inequalities in the South during Reconstruction.[222] The first Homestead Act was proposed by Northern Republicans before the Civil War but was blocked in Congress by Southern Democrats who wanted Western lands open for set-tlement by slave-owners.

Land was the main form of productive capital at the time of the Home-stead Acts; today, it is corporations or business enterprises. Massive federal support should be adapted appropriately to the worker-ownership of the pro-ductive capital of modern times, to create the widely shared prosperity our

Founders intended for the United States.

John Adams, Thomas Jefferson, and James Madison wanted the government to ensure that the productive capital of their time was widely shared for a decent, democratic and well-functioning society. They wrote:

"...power always follows property. The only possible Way then of preserving the Ballance of Power on the side of equal Liberty and public Virtue, is to make the Acquisition of Land easy to every Member of Society: to make a Division of the Land into Small Quantities, So that the Multitude may be possessed of landed Estates. If the Multitude is possessed of the Ballance of real Estate, the Multitude will have the Ballance of Power, and in that Case the Multitude will take Care of the Liberty, Virtue, and Interest of the Multitude in all Acts of Government," wrote Adams.[223]

"But it is not too soon to provide by every possible means that as few as possible shall be without a little portion of land. The small landholders are the most precious part of a state," wrote Jefferson.[224]

In his only book, *Notes on the State of Virginia*, Jefferson argued that as the proportion of citizen landowners went up, political corruption went down. He wrote to Madison in 1775 that those excluded from property ownership needed to have this *"fundamental right"* returned to them. Like other Founders, he believed property owners were more likely to protect liberty.[225]

Jefferson wrote in his Proposed Constitution for Virginia:

"Every person of full age neither owning nor having owned 50 acres of land, shall be entitled to an appropriation of 50 acres or to so much as shall make up what he owns or has owned 50 acres in full and absolute dominion."

And Madison wrote in a letter to Jefferson:

"I have no doubt that the misery of the lower classes will be found to abate wherever the ... laws favor a subdivision of property"

As previously noted, George Washington predicted that America *"will be the most favorable country of any kind in the world for persons of industry and frugality, possessed of moderate capital, to inhabit. ... it will not be less advantageous to the happiness of the lowest class of people, because of the equal distribution of property."*

And Noah Webster wrote, *"a general and tolerably equal distribution of landed property is the whole basis of national freedom."*[226]

Another indication that our Founders wanted equitable sharing of the advantages of productive capital, within practical and reasonable bounds, but to a substantial degree, is: Washington instituted a cod fishing subsidy to help the then-integral industry (it was the fourth largest) recover from the Revolutionary War, which required any businesses that received the subsidy to have a profit sharing agreement with their workers and pass along five-eighths of their subsidies to their workers.

Economic inequality is now more extreme than before the Enlightenment and American Revolution. Our Founders revolted against a social structure characterized by great inequality and would not want one to be re-established in this country.

Our federal government's first attempt at massive support of widespread ownership of economic enterprises, the first Homestead Act, was blocked by a 19th-century economic elite. A 21st-century economic elite will also be a powerful force blocking vigorous support of worker-ownership of today's economic enterprises. Only massive popular support will be able to overcome their obstruction.

The Founders of our country and their successors with vision throughout U.S. history knew that a thriving middle class with ownership of the productive capital needed for their livelihood is necessary for liberty. We have lost this vision, and now relatively few workers receive significant capital ownership of the enterprise in which they work. Since the early 1990s, American companies on average have given almost 30% of stock options to their top five executives. Nearly all the rest of the options go to the top 2% or so of company employees.[227]

Most of our citizens are hired laborers in corporations dominated by this tiny elite in a system creating massive inequality in income and wealth. Political domination and corruption by this small economic elite are a reality and a developing trend that cannot continue if the country is to survive. "Crony capitalism" is common where corporate elites extract privileges from the government through lobbying, political donations, and the revolving door between high political office and highly paid corporate jobs.

The people and institutions dominating our economic and political systems are entrenched, powerful, and will not welcome widespread productive capital ownership policies. A mass movement supporting New Enlightenment policies is needed to be able to use federal resources to serve the best economic and other interests of the country, as they have in the past to great benefit.

Thomas Jefferson knew the future would bring the need for major changes in the laws. He wrote,

"...laws and institutions must go hand in hand with the progress of the human mind. As that becomes more developed, more enlightened, as new discoveries are made, new truths disclosed, and manners and opinions change with the change of circumstances, institutions must advance also, and keep pace with the times."[228]

In summary, New Enlightenment policies promote the widespread establishment of worker-owned and worker self-directed enterprises with programs in these categories:

- Italy's Marcora Law adaptation for unemployed workers
- New businesses established as WSDEs
- Existing privately held businesses' conversion to WSDEs
- Bankrupt businesses' reorganization
- Public companies' "sociable takeovers"

In addition to the federal government, funding mechanisms involve community members where the WSDE is located and local credit unions or banks, or involve local governments.

These programs will gradually transform the economy to one where worker-owned and worker self-directed enterprises are the predominant business enterprise structure in the country over about two decades.

Worker-ownership and self-direction improve productivity, substantially reduces economic disparities, promotes meaningful democracy, improves workers' job and life satisfaction, and even has a positive impact on the health of workers. The great importance of the widespread establishment of worker-owned and self-directed enterprises justifies and requires The New Enlightenment policies for extensive national support.

In consideration of the low unemployment rate that will result from New Enlightenment policies, grant funding requirements plus the origination fee total to community banks under the modified Marcora Law will be small. This amount, plus the fee amount for other WSDE loan originations, will likely be significantly less than the federal government's profits on all the loans made under the system to facilitate the establishment of worker-owned enterprises. To be conservative in our budget analysis, I assume loan profits will not exceed this amount to cover any of the grants to support WSDEs that cities support with bond purchases or loans, tax exemption, Council of Cooperatives, increased SBA, economically disadvantaged grants, and default costs.

However, loan profits likely will exceed modified Marcora Law related costs and loan origination fees, possibly by over ten billion dollars per year.

Whatever this excess is, it will be deposited each year in separate and restricted individual accounts of all citizens under 18 years of age in equal amounts. Only on a citizen's 18th birthday will he or she have access to the account balance. Ideally, it would most commonly be used to help purchase a WSDE or home.

Assuming the midpoint of our estimated range of amounts of funds from community investors in city supported WSDEs, the annual cost of the community investor tax exemption policy is about $2.0 billion. This assumes that the bond investor population will have a 30% average tax rate, higher than the 18% average overall tax rate of the general population. The tax exemption cost for the retiring owner sales to WSDEs will be about $46 million. The funding requirement for the Council of Cooperatives will be about $2.5 billion. The increase in the SBA budget is $450 million. The funding requirement for the grants to the economically disadvantaged is $97 billion. The total federal expenditure per year to support the widespread establishment of worker-owned and self-directed enterprises are these amounts, plus the $41 billion in WSDE grants in our city partnership system, or about $143 billion. Eventually, the cost of The National Cooperative Congress and Research Institution will also be substantial, but the return on investment will be large.

Modified or Partial WSDE Structure Establishment When Full WSDE Establishment Is Not Practicable

Although it is far from the ideal that is more closely approximated elsewhere, and that the prior New Enlightenment policies will create, a partial or modified WSDE structure is widespread in Germany, and to a lesser degree in Sweden, Denmark, Norway, Austria, and Luxembourg. In Germany, modified WSDEs of this character are required by law: For firms over 2000 workers, one-half the board of directors must be workers, and between 500 and 2000 workers, one-third must be workers. Researchers have found that this policy increased productivity through better communication between management and workers. Most Germans favor this policy because it reduces conflict, downsizing and plant closures through mutually agreed on compromises and improvements.

Since 1985, Germany's median wage went up nearly 30%, versus only 6% in the United States. The highest income 1% in Germany takes about 11% of German income.[229] In the United States, the 1% takes about 24%. Germany generated $2 trillion in trade surpluses from 2000 to 2010, while the United

States accumulated $6 trillion in trade deficits. Germany has 21% of its work-force in manufacturing; we have 9%. During the 2008 economic collapse, big German companies adopted a "short work" policy to spread the pain of the recession. Instead of laying off masses of workers, German companies short-ened everyone's workweek, saving 500,000 jobs, so Germany's unemploy-ment rate went down during the recession while America's rose sharply and stayed high.[230] Labor's integration with the directorship of industry was the major factor in Germany's success.

For firms that are not WSDEs, we will institute a similar legal require-ment in the U.S.

The New Enlightenment: Ideals of Democracy, Human Rights, Reason, and Progress * Policy 3

Raise the Minimum Wage

New Enlightenment policy raises the minimum wage to $11.10 per hour. We will also adjust it each year by at least the inflation rate. If the productivity growth rate is higher than the inflation rate we will adjust it by the average of the two, to ensure that low wage workers share in the benefits of nationwide productivity advancements. This hourly wage for the full-time work-hours of 36 hours per week will raise the annual workplace income of the lowest wage full-time worker to about the maximum income ($20,000/year) where the largest expanded earned income tax credit (Policy 1) will be applied. The EITC will then raise the income of minimum wage full-time workers to an effective minimum wage of $19.40 per hour, but since the $15,000/year EITC subsidy amount is the same for half-time workers their effective minimum wage would be higher, $27.80 per hour. Also, workers earning less than $50,000 per year pay no payroll or income taxes.

A minimum wage of $11.10 per hour is not an unreasonably burden-some wage for businesses to pay. The minimum wage in 1968 was about $11 per hour in 2013 dollars, 52% higher than today's $7.25 minimum wage. Considering that we were a much poorer country in 1968, with about 43% of current worker productivity, it should now be more than double the 1968 wage to maintain the same income disparity levels that existed in 1968. However, since some industries are now in international competition with low wage countries that were not in 1968, being cautious in selecting a minimum wage increase while supporting higher incomes with an EITC expansion seems the most prudent way to increase minimum incomes to desirable and practical levels.

The experience of other countries also indicates that a minimum wage of $11.10 per hour is not an unreasonably burdensome wage for businesses to pay. These countries have a minimum wage of about $11 per hour or higher: Australia, Luxembourg, Monaco, France, Belgium, San Marino, New Zealand, Ireland, and the Netherlands. Australia has a $16.88 minimum wage and escaped the recent international recession, hasn't had a recession in 20 years and had a 5.7% unemployment rate, far lower than the 7.3% rate in the U.S. in November 2013. Clearly, the most prominent media pundits' and politicians' claim that a higher minimum wage would lead to higher unemployment is incorrect.

The commonly expressed theory is that if labor costs more, business would more aggressively cut their workforce to minimum levels, or raise prices to cover the wage increase, which reduces demand and the need for workers. But this ignores that when large numbers of workers have more money, they purchase more goods and services, and this increases business income and creates the need to hire more workers. Businesses would also benefit from the positive correlation between worker productivity and wages when wages are unfairly low. Studies have shown both positive and negative effect, but mostly no significant effect on unemployment based on minimum wage changes in the past internationally, indicating that the positive and negative employment effects have canceled each other out.

Consider the impact on our largest private employer, Walmart, of a higher minimum wage: Walmart spent $7.6 billion buying back shares in 2012, driving up the company's share price, further enriching the Walton family, and consolidating its control by capturing over half of Walmart stock. The heirs have more wealth than the poorest 42%, or 133 million, of Americans combined. Walmart's profits ($22 billion in 2016) and its major owner's wealth is made through the unfair compensation of the essential labor of the many Walmart low wage workers, and the abuse of taxpayers. Taxpayers pay food, housing, energy and health care subsidies to Walmart workers who often cannot survive on Walmart's wages. (Our country's largest nongovernmental employer, and many others, support their workers to a lesser degree than slaveholders did their slaves. Slaveholders had to be sure to provide a minimum standard in food, housing, and medical care to protect their investment, and so that their slaves would be as productive as possible.)

If these buyback funds were *"redirected to Walmart's low-wage workers, they would each see a raise of $5.83 an hour,"* according to a Demos think tank study. Over a million Walmart workers earning $5.83 more per hour would have a significant stimulus impact on the economy and lead to raised wages for many millions of workers throughout the economy. A 2011 Chicago Federal Reserve Bank study found that for every dollar increase in the hourly wage of a minimum wage worker, the result is $2,800 in new consumer spending per year from that worker's household.

Even if Walmart, whose CEO made $22.4 million in 2016 (about $10,000/hour), uses none of the buyback money or tens of billions in profits to pay for the wage raises, and instead raised prices to pay for them, prices would rise very little. The University of California, Berkeley Center for Labor Research and Education determined that by raising the wages of all Walmart workers to a minimum of $12 per hour, the average impact on a Walmart shopper would be a 1.1% increase in prices, or $12.49 per year, for the average consumer who spends approximately $1,187 per year at Walmart. However, most or the entire raise could be paid for by the resulting increased worker productivity that is known to occur when workers are paid more fairly, and profit increases from increased sales, so even this small price increase would not be necessary.

Australia's system allows for lower minimums for trainees entering the workforce, as The New Enlightenment policy will, according to the guidelines in this table.

Minimum Hourly Wage Schedule

Year of training	Workplace Hourly Wage	After EITC Wage Full-time	After EITC Wage Half Time
0-1	$10.00	$18.30	$26.65
1-2	$10.50	$18.80	$27.15
2+	$11.10	$19.40	$27.75

No payroll or income taxes deducted.

An increase in the minimum wage would also raise the wages of millions of low wage workers not receiving the minimum wage because employers would need to maintain disparity levels to some degree. About 35 million workers, or 30% of the workforce, would benefit from a minimum wage increase.[231]

Also, directing money from corporate owners and managers to low wage workers will reduce the speculative financial practices that led to the 2008-09 Wall Street crash and subsequent Great Recession.

The New Enlightenment Party or Citizens Union will lead efforts for an international agreement to raise minimum wages to reduce international inequality and minimum wage disparities. Signatories will set their minimum wage to no lower than 40% of the country's average wage (not the median wage which is generally much lower). This will reduce inequality worldwide. A provision will include agreement participation for tariff free access, to the markets of other countries in the agreement.

As the world's most influential country, we have an obligation to focus attention on, and contribute to the solution of, the world's most serious problems. According to an Oxfam report, *"The cost of inequality: how wealth and income extremes hurt us all,"* the $240 billion net income in 2012 of the richest 100 billionaires worldwide would be enough to eliminate extreme poverty four times over. [232] Oxfam's executive director wrote: *"Without a concerted effort to tackle inequality, the cascade of privilege and of disadvantage will continue down the generations. We will soon live in a world where equality of opportunity is just a dream. In too many countries economic growth already amounts to little more than a 'winner takes all' windfall for the richest."*

Here is another example demonstrating the problem: Jorge Paulo Lemann, the co-founder of the company that owns Burger King, 3G Capital, has a net worth of more than $31 billion. He is the richest person in Brazil. Many of his Burger King employees earn just $7.25 an hour.[233]

Oxfam found in 2015 that the richest 85 people in the world, less than one-fifth the passenger capacity of the most commonly flown passenger jet (the Boeing 747), control as much wealth as the poorest half of the global population, or 3.6 billion people, put together! (It's more appropriate to have exclamation points that would fill an entire page here instead of just one, but if you've come with me this far you probably know this, so I'll save the ink and paper.)

But now global inequality is even more extreme. Oxfam reported in 2016 that just 62 people own as much wealth as the 3.6 billion people. If global inequality continues to increase so that the rate of decline in the number of people whose wealth equals that of 3.6 billion people stays the same as the last year, in 2.7 years one person will own the wealth of 3.6 billion people. To suppress movements to reduce inequality will he then advance a related trend? Will he buy all the world's media outlets and use his money to influence our formal educational institutions to propagandize us with the view that he deserves the wealth of 3.6 billion people because he is highly productive?

Oxfam research also revealed that the richest 1% share of global wealth increased from 44% in 2009 to 48% in 2014, and then to over 50% in 2015.[234] Do we want to live in a world where the 1% own more than the rest of us combined?

Ideally, the international agreement and our trade policy reforms will eventually eliminate or greatly reduce the need for wage subsidies by creating conditions where the minimum wage could be raised to $19.00/hour without significantly disadvantaging companies in international competition. Also, our system to facilitate the establishment of worker-owned enterprises will result in a higher minimum wage within these enterprises without government regulation.

Recently a movement for a $15 minimum wage has been gaining prominence and has had success in some cities. So far Seattle, Los Angeles, and New York City have adopted at least a phased-in $15 minimum, and several other cities and states have also adopted a higher than federal minimum wage. The New Enlightenment $11.10 minimum wage, in combination with an expanded EITC that creates an effective $19.40 minimum wage (with no payroll or income taxes deducted) has these advantages:

- It results in a higher than $15 minimum wage.
- It ensures an increase in low wages that are above the minimum.
- It reduces the potential for negative impact on industries in international competition with low wage countries.
- It reduces the potential for negative impact on startups since they generally have little or no profits. Essentially, the New Enlightenment EITC will sometimes be used with a highly progressive corporate and personal tax system to transfer some income from high-income businesses and people to support businesses trying to establish themselves pay a fair wage.

However, a better-regulated market (and a democratic corporate structure) has advantages over government income transfers. So to minimize ongoing local dependency on outside agencies, even well-functioning democratic ones, after two years at the $11.10 minimum, we will support a gradual increase. In $1 per year increments, based on the observed impact of this incremental rise, we will increase the minimum wage until it reaches $16/hour. Our international agreements and trade policy reforms will minimize job losses due to competition with low wage countries. More beneficial ways to help underdeveloped countries advance exist than by having them produce our goods and services. Also, based on the observed impacts of the gradual rise in the minimum wage we will consider continuing the incremental rise to a minimum wage of $19 per hour or higher. As the workplace minimum wage rises, costs for the New Enlightenment expanded EITC (Policy 1) will fall.

> *The New Enlightenment: Ideals of Democracy, Human Rights, Reason, and Progress* * *Policy 4*

A Small and Highly Progressive Wealth Tax

Our grotesque degree of income inequality is greatly exceeded by that of our wealth inequality, and it is increasing. We need to address this with public policies. It threatens our democracy and is unjust. The shocking disparity between the conditions of the poorest 40% of Americans, whose combined wealth is less than zero, and the 400 people who report over $2.3 trillion in wealth, which is equal to the total wealth of the bottom 190 million Americans, is even worse than official statistics indicate. Official statistics are based on surveys in which wealth is self-reported with no penalties for underreporting so they almost certainly substantially underestimate the largest fortunes.

One estimate of the amount of unreported financial assets held in tax havens is between 10% and 30% of global GDP, or up to $24 trillion.[235] However, Oxfam and the Tax Justice Network report that tax havens hold as much as $32 trillion, a vast amount of money hidden from government records, and so from taxation.[236] At the time, this represented 13% of global wealth. (Our income inequality is also larger than official statistics indicate, because significant amounts of income are directed to tax havens and substantial amounts of capital income is tax exempt, so are not reported or included in the income tax records. These records are the source of income statistics.)

The immoral and antisocial behavior of individuals that grow wealthy from "free trade" policies, the country's infrastructure, educated workforce and other resources and then after accepting their society's generosity to them, cause their neighbors to pay society's bill must be strongly constrained by national and international law. This behavior is essentially theft and is contributing to our extreme inequality. If we all set our own tax rate, as tax evaders do, our society would disintegrate.

A common statistical measure of inequality is the Gini coefficient, a number between zero and 100 that rises with greater disparities. Our income Gini coefficient in 1970 was 40; today, it is about 48. It has increased to about 80 for U.S. wealth as of 2010. A Gini value of 100 means one person has all the wealth. The richest 0.1 percent, ranked by wealth, have 22% of wealth of U.S. household wealth.[237]

The proportion of income from capital for the top 0.1% increased from 64% to 70% from 1996 to 2006.[238] An important cause of our dangerous and growing income inequality is our dangerous and growing wealth inequality.

In 1992, the top tenth of the population controlled 20 times the wealth controlled by the bottom half. By 2010, it was 65 times. As previously noted, the top 1% of Americans own a staggering 40% of the wealth. The U.S. has the greatest degree of wealth and income inequality in the developed world.[239]

Extreme wealth concentration threatens the very existence of democracy is one tragic lesson of Latin American history. Economic oligarchs that feel threatened by majority rule have repeatedly thwarted democratic reforms there, sometimes violently. In the U.S., so far, economic elites have damaged our democracy by corrupting our election process and dominating our governmental policy process in other ways, but as rifts widen, political unrest and violent repression are possible here also. Wealth inequality in the U.S. today far exceeds that in Europe; it is now in the Latin American range. I describe in *Now Is the Time for The New Enlightenment* how Americans of increasingly divergent socioeconomic strata are living ever more different lives, with dangerous results for society including the erosion of meritocracy, empathy, and democracy.

The global financial crisis initially reduced the assets of most of the wealthiest American families, but since most of their wealth tends to be in stocks and the stock market has recovered, their wealth generally has recovered or exceeds pre-recession levels. Its effects for the bottom half continue to be devastating. The number of owner-occupied homes has fallen by over a million since 2007.[240] And average housing values have increased less than stock values. Since housing is where most of the wealth of the middle class tends to be, wealth inequality has increased substantially since before 2007.

Even "conservative" institutions with a dominant "free market" ideology such as the International Monetary Fund have warned that our high income inequality could damage our long-term economic growth, but an even larger risk is our larger and faster-growing wealth inequality, partly because it is an important contributor to our growing income inequality. Major economic implications of its eventual destabilizing political impacts exist. Before this more catastrophic outcome, tens of millions of people at the lower end of our wealth distribution have limited or no access to economic opportunities, such as the ability to invest in business ventures, and limited access to educational opportunities, so their ability to contribute economically is impaired. Also, they are easily made destitute with short periods of no or reduced income. Since large wealth disparities are widening, terrifying outcomes will inevitably occur unless we recognize the trend and reverse it.

New Enlightenment policy to facilitate investment by workers in cooperatively owned businesses will give the ability for business investment to unprecedented numbers of people, including the poor. I will describe later The New Enlightenment free college education proposal that will greatly reduce disparities in educational opportunities. The New Enlightenment inheritance tax supports free college education and substantial funding increases for K-12 schools. However, we need to have other sources of funds to facilitate the widespread establishment of worker-owned businesses and for other New Enlightenment programs. A very small percent wealth tax will raise an enormous amount of revenue for these and other important public needs, including slowing the explosive growth in wealth disparities.

High earners add much more to their wealth every year than low earners, so wealth inequality increases even if income inequality stays the same. But long-term trends show income disparities growing, contributing to our explosive growth in wealth inequality.

Wealth's rate of return is greater than the growth rate of the economy or the growth rate of wages from labor, and the trends indicate that this difference will increase over the 21st century. Since total wealth is enormous and far more concentrated than income, income from capital gains is substantially overrepresented in the upper decile of the income hierarchy, and even more so in the upper centile. However, capital appreciation generally far exceeds capital income for the extremely wealthy. It is generally enough to take a few million a year in dividends (or some other type of payout) while leaving tens or hundreds of millions, or even billions, of dollars more of the return on one's capital to accumulate. Some of the super wealthy increase their wealth by billions of dollars in a year. The graphs show the explosive relative and actual growth of the wealth of the super wealthy. These graphs use data from self-reported wealth surveys, so significantly understate their wealth.

Forbes 400 Wealth Total 1982-2013 (2013 $ Billions)

Total private wealth is growing two to three times faster than GDP in the U.S., and its growing size and power is being concentrated in a small economic elite.

Ratio of average top 1% household wealth to median wealth, 1962–2010

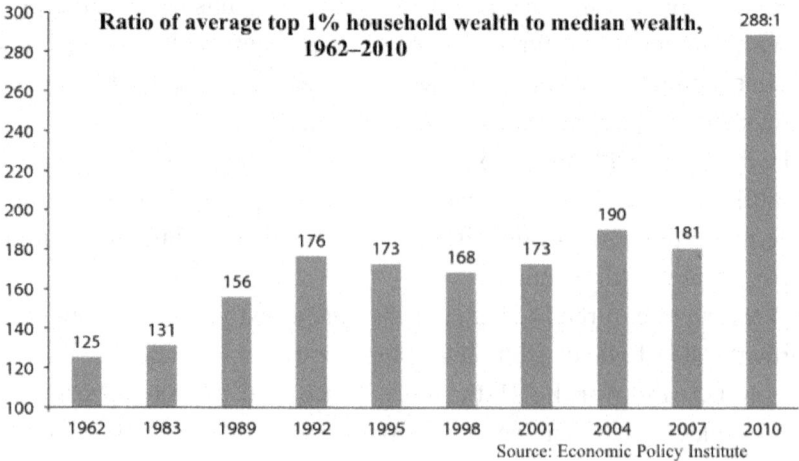

Source: Economic Policy Institute

Number and wealth of billionaires 1987-2013

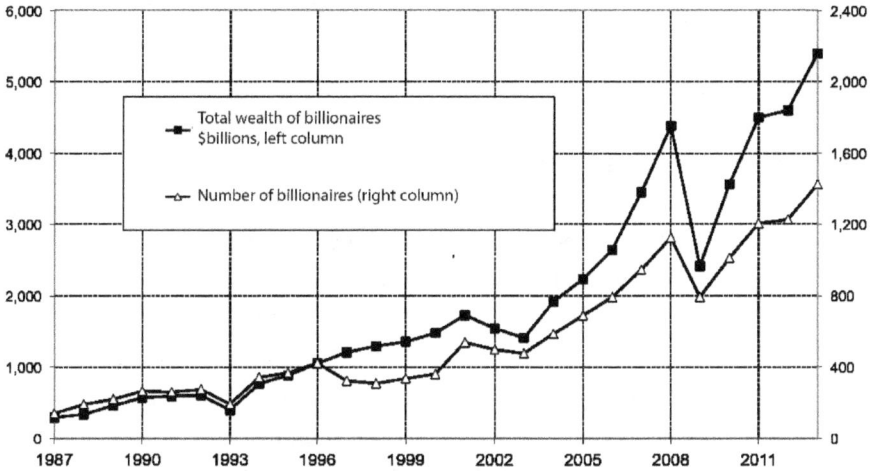

Between 1987 and 2013, the number of billionaires rose according to Forbes from 140 to 1400. Their total wealth rose from 300 to 5,400 billions of dollars Source: piketty.pse.ens.fr/capital21c

Billionaires as a fraction of global population and wealth 1987-2013

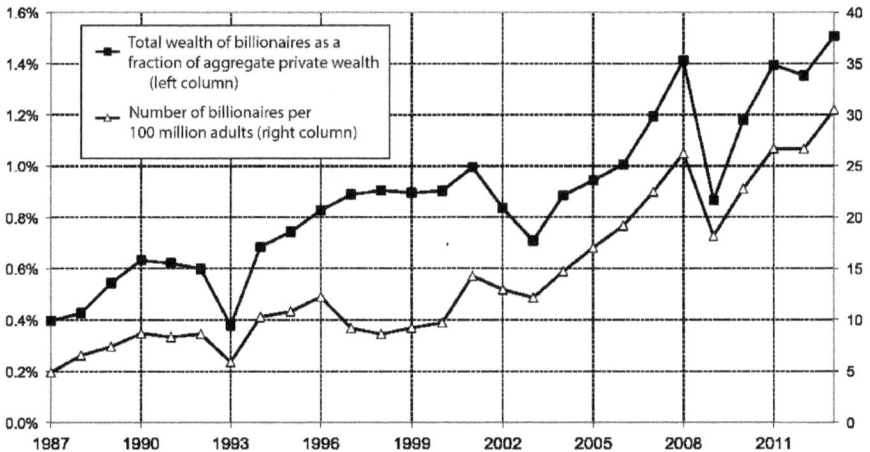

Between 1987 and 2013, the number of billionaires per 100 million adults rose from 5 to 30, and their share of aggregate private wealth rose from 0.4% to 1.5%. Source: piketty.pse.ens.fr/capital21c

In March 2013 there were 1,426 billionaires worldwide from 66 countries, with a combined net worth of $5.4 trillion, which was more than the combined GDP of 152 countries. The United States had the largest number of billionaires by far of any country, with 442 in 2013. A record 1,645 billionaires made the 2014 List of the World's Richest People with an aggregate net worth of $6.4 trillion. In 2015, the U.S. had a record-breaking 540 billionaires, with a combined net worth of $2.4 trillion.

If the very wealthy are taxed on the basis of declared incomes that are a minor fraction of their economic incomes, then by taxing that income at a rate of 55% or even 99% results in taxing their total economic gains at an extremely low rate. It is low relative to what the rest of the population pays on their economic gains, and the wealthy's ability to pay, and their debt to society. For example:

Households with a billion dollars in wealth on average receive about 6% returns, or gains of about $60 million per year on their investments. If they take $2 million in income and keep the rest invested and are taxed at 55% only on this income, this $1.1 million tax amount is only 1.8% of their total economic income, excluding any labor income. (No one would need to work to support the household with this level of capital gains.)

This very low tax rate means only taxing income puts an unfair burden for the support of government on the middle class, and even high and very high-income people whose wealth is not extreme. Since tax rates as expressed as a percentage of economic income are extremely low at the top of the wealth hierarchy, our current tax system accentuates the explosive growth of inequality resulting from the rate of return on wealth exceeding the growth rate of the economy. This problem is especially extreme because larger fortunes can garner larger rates of return. A system that includes a progressive wealth tax will attenuate this dynamic. Even a system with the much more progressive New Enlightenment income tax rates will not significantly slow the explosive economic disparity growth, without a wealth tax.

Taxing wealth directly, not merely high incomes including capital income, will be important for the support of programs to assist tens of millions of Americans under unnecessary and often extreme hardship. The resulting revenues will also serve our professed, but far from realized, ideal of equal opportunity and justice for all, and otherwise improve overall economic, political, and social conditions.

A tax on wealth is also justified for these reasons:

- It is an incentive to seek the best possible return on one's capital. For example, a tax of 1.5% on wealth is relatively low for an entrepreneur who earns a return on capital of 10% a year. But it is high for someone who earns 2% or 3% return a year. A wealth tax will motivate people who use their wealth inefficiently to find more productive use, or to sell assets to pay their taxes, thus transferring those assets to investors who may use it more productively. Making more productive use of assets or increasing their commercial value benefits society, including through creating demand for labor.

- A tax on wealth can be seen as a property rights use fee. Protection of property rights is a primary purpose of government, so the more "property" or wealth a person holds of all types including stocks, the more the person enjoys the existence of government and its property rights support systems.

- Currently, localities tax wealth in the form of real estate. Important defects exist in current property taxes. One is that property is taxed at its market value regardless of debt; a heavily indebted person is taxed the same as a person with no debt. Another is that it is generally taxed at a flat rate, or close to it. Many people have been forced out of their homes as a result of the property tax, and the prior defects played a contributing role. Property taxes generate significant revenue, over 1% of national income.[241] No good reason exists to exempt other kinds of assets from taxation, and a progressive tax on net wealth that accounts for debts is a more just tax. When a real estate tax was first introduced, real estate was the main form of wealth. Just as our Founders instituted a tax on the main form of wealth in their times, we need a wealth tax appropriate for the major forms of wealth in ours.[242]

- Wealth is created in partnership with socially created resources. As I detail in Part 4, Note 1, these resources are the predominant contributor to the processes that create wealth, so it is justified for more of the wealth created by this partnership to serve social needs than is currently the case.

A small percentage wealth tax will raise an enormous amount of money. The marginal rates shown in the table, on financial assets, housing, cars, and business ownership, and other wealth will raise $516 billion per year.

Wealth ($)	Tax Rate
10 million +	1.50%
1 million – 10 million	1.00%
0 – 1 million	0%

This estimate uses the Federal Reserve's 2013 Survey of Consumer Finances data (the most extensive and detailed source of wealth data available) and 2013 Forbes 400 data, which is intentionally excluded from the FED survey. Also, it assumes that previously hidden financial assets held in tax havens will be revealed as a result of reforms of U.S. law and international asset ownership transparency agreements. Based on the previously noted estimates, it is reasonable to assume that 13% of private U.S. wealth is currently hidden in tax havens. However, some estimates are significantly lower, so to be conservative we assume tax havens hold 10% of private U.S. wealth. Our tax revenue estimate assumes that this hidden wealth is distributed proportionately with other wealth but since it is skewed toward the higher end of the wealth distribution, tax revenues will be higher than our estimate.

Both our wealth tax and our income tax require, to be most effective and just, international asset ownership transparency. Any taxes existing in other countries, including those with income and no wealth taxes, require the same, so negotiations initiated by the U.S. to create transparency would likely result in a robust agreement.

The wealthy want records to show that they own their assets when they want to claim them. Why should societies tolerate systems that then allow them to hide the fact they own their assets to shirk their responsibility to support the democratically determined needs of their society? Without their society they would have no assets. The injustice of and dysfunctions resulting from this shirking of responsibility likely about 99% of the world's population would like to see end, so it should and can end.

The U.S. has recently taken an important step toward creating more international asset transparency. The Foreign Account Tax Compliance Act (FATCA) adopted in 2010 was scheduled to be phased in by stages in 2014 and 2015. It requires all foreign banks to inform the Treasury Department about bank accounts and investments held abroad by U.S. taxpayers, along with any other sources of revenue from which they might benefit.

This advance requires improvement because the only penalty for noncompliance is a 30% surcharge on income that the noncompliant bank derives from the U.S. This will likely be sufficient for compliance of the large international banks, but will likely lead to the creation of smaller banks that specialize in overseas portfolios. International agreements and sanctions on countries that refuse to require financial institutions to provide the required information, possibly including a large tariff on their exports, will be needed. With the ability of modern electronic record keeping and tracking of economic transactions, and advancements in our international agreements, we can largely eliminate the problem of capital flight to avoid the tax.

The increasing globalization of the world economy suggests that we should partly globalize taxation. The New Enlightenment Citizens Union (or

Party) will advocate for a progressive globalized wealth tax with rates determined by international agreement. A global standard wealth tax, in conjunction with international asset reporting agreements, will minimize tax avoidance problems.

International wealth tax negotiations could take place within the Global Forum on Transparency and Exchange of Information for Tax Purposes, the United Nations, the International Monetary Fund, the World Bank, or the G20. (The G20 is a group of finance ministers and central bank governors from 19 of the world's largest economies and the European Union.) Signatories might also agree to devote the resulting revenues to support solutions to high priority international problems, such as reducing global poverty and achieving the Millennium Development Goals, combating climate change by financing alternative energy projects and reforestation, and repaying national debts incurred during the post-2008 financial crisis. Insufficient resources have been the main barrier to solving the most important problems worldwide. But the money is available—in abundance. Economic globalization and technological developments are making the rich mega-rich, as the fact that there are now over 1,600 billionaires with over $6.4 trillion in wealth demonstrates.

The Oxfam report referenced earlier found that people in countries around the world believe that the rich have too much influence over their country's economic and political systems. The wealth of the 1% richest people in the world amounts to $110 trillion, or 65 times as much as the poorest half of the world, of whom 1 billion suffer from malnutrition.

A 1% international tax on wealth above $1 million would generate more than $2 trillion per year worldwide for urgent public needs. Our advocacy to serve these needs through the public revenues this tax generates will be an important way we can lead the world in solving its most serious problems

Even without a globalized tax, The New Enlightenment's level of national taxation is unlikely to motivate a significant expatriation problem. To minimize this potential problem we would bar entry into the country to anyone with over $1 million in wealth who gives up U.S. citizenship to avoid tax responsibilities. Only if the person could prove he did not expatriate to avoid tax responsibilities would he be allowed 30 days per year in the U.S.

Based on 2013 data, about 90.5% of households have less than $1,000,000 in wealth, so would not have paid any tax. The business or stock investment and other assets taxed, on average, increase in value far more than the amount of tax per year. Often the investment funds that the wealthy use to invest their money take a far higher percentage in fees than this tax will.

If the increased government revenues are used to stimulate economic activity, as they are in New Enlightenment policies, the wealth of wealthy individuals will not be reduced to the same degree as the tax, and often will be increased as a result of the positive impact on their income and asset values of the improved economy. Essentially, the amount paid in tax will be an investment that will not only bring the return of a more just and better functioning society in which to live, it often will bring financial returns.

Banks, insurance companies, and stockbrokers within the U.S. are already required to inform the IRS on assets they administer for clients. Evaluating privately owned businesses will be less straightforward, but a standardized system could be developed to evaluate these businesses as well. Possible evaluation systems could use comparisons to similar public companies, or use asset values and some function of annual profits and possibly revenues. Localities maintain real estate values that are regularly updated based on market conditions; this information could also be easily available.

In rare cases, people with almost all their wealth tied up in property and businesses might have trouble coming up with enough cash to pay the tax. We can solve this problem by making payment periods flexible with a government loan on the tax amount, with just interest due. All or part of the principal payment could be deferred until the asset was sold, or before then when funds were available. People with sufficient wealth for the tax to apply rarely will not have the tiny percentage available for the tax in cash or liquid assets.

A general wealth tax is not unprecedented in American history. Throughout the first half of the 19th century, states expanded their use of the property tax to include land, equipment, household goods, cash, and stocks. If the United States institutes a wealth tax, European countries would likely all institute one or expand any existing.

In 2008, France, Norway, Switzerland, and five other members of the Organization for Economic Cooperation and Development imposed wealth taxation, and Italy is considering one. Spain dropped such a tax several years ago but now plans to reinstate it as part of a deficit-reduction effort.

For the advocates of the income tax in the early 1900s, their challenge was larger than ours since at the time an income tax was unconstitutional. Some argue we have a similar barrier, but better arguments exist that a wealth tax is not unconstitutional.[243] But either way, we should be able to overcome any barriers to the implementation of a tax that will be as extraordinarily beneficial to the nation as a progressive wealth tax.

A wealth tax will be an important part of The New Enlightenment's program to create a more prosperity and far more just and democratic society.

(As this book was going to publication, the FED released its detailed survey data on 2016 household wealth. Analysis of this data reveals a substantial increase in household wealth and in wealth inequality, and that the proposed wealth tax system would generate $777 billion per year in public funds. I detail how the $516 billion per year could beneficially transform our nation. A $777 billion annual increase in tax revenues we could use for a further advance to a fundamentally superior society.)

Based on 2013 data, The New Enlightenment wealth tax will raise about $516 billion per year, which is the amount we use in our budget analysis.

Thomas Jefferson suggested a progressive tax on property or wealth to reduce inequality:[244]

"Another means of silently lessening the inequality of property is to exempt all from taxation below a certain point, and to tax the higher portions of property in geometrical progression as they rise. Whenever there is in any country, uncultivated lands* and unemployed poor, it is clear that the laws of property have been so far extended as to violate natural right."

Benjamin Franklin wrote this regarding the rights of the public to excessive wealth:

"All the Property that is necessary to a Man, for the Conservation of the Individual and the Propagation of the Species, is his natural Right, which none can justly deprive him of: But all Property superfluous to such purposes is the Property of the Publick, who, by their Laws, have created it, and who may therefore by other Laws dispose of it, whenever the Welfare of the Publick shall demand such Disposition. He that does not like civil Society on these Terms, let him retire and live among Savages. He can have no right to the benefits of Society, who will not pay his Club toward the Support of it."[245]

* "Uncultivated lands" is analogous to our underutilized industrial capacity today. We have about 29% unutilized manufacturing plant capacity,[246] which will be better utilized due to the increased demand created by the more equitable sharing of prosperity that a wealth tax will allow.

The New Enlightenment: Ideals of Democracy, Human Rights, Reason, and Progress * Policy 5

A Reemployment System

Of the 11.5 million people unemployed in 2013, 4.3 million were long-term unemployed over six months.[247] In addition, at least 3.5 million had given up hope, so were not looking for work, so were not counted in these statistics.[248] People unemployed for long periods have difficulty getting back into the job market. High levels of long-term unemployment damage and destroy lives and strain our social safety nets.

The New Enlightenment's adaptation of Italy's Marcora Law to support the establishment of worker-owned and self-directed enterprises by unemployed persons that I described in Policy 3 will help reintegrate some of the unemployed into the workforce. And Policy 1 and other New Enlightenment policies will greatly reduce the number of unemployed. We will also institute this reemployment system to support early reintegration into the workforce and less economic hardship for people that do experience unemployment.

One part of the reemployment system will be wage insurance. Any job loser who takes a new job that pays less than his or her former job will be eligible for 90% of the difference, for up to two years. The maximum wage subsidy will be 90% of the difference between nine times the median income and the new income. After two years, many workers will have acquired enough on-the-job training to render them sufficiently productive to warrant wages similar to the wages they had on the job they lost.

Wage insurance will speed the movement of laid-off workers into new jobs because it will induce them to take jobs that pay less, rather than wait for ones that pay as much as the job that was lost. It will thereby save the costs of unemployment benefits and will generate added revenues as re-employed workers pay income taxes earlier than otherwise.

For workers who need additional skills, we will provide income support for up to a year while a worker is engaged full-time in approved training or education programs. Longer-term training is more effective than short-term, especially when it gives people the tools to continue learning on the job. If job seekers enroll in programs that prepare them for fields in which labor is likely to be in short supply, such as nursing or teaching, they will receive income support for an additional year of training and education. Since participants will acquire the kinds of skills rewarded well in the new economy, and fill positions for which there are labor shortages, we will reap the benefits of this program in the longer term through stronger economic growth, higher tax revenues, and less dependence on social safety nets.

The total new costs of the reemployment system are about $3 billion a year.[249] Costs will decline greatly as New Enlightenment policies are instituted, since they nearly eliminate (or do eliminate) unemployment, and result in a much better-trained workforce.

> *The New Enlightenment: Ideals of Democracy, Human Rights, Reason, and Progress * Policy 6*

Provide Free College Education

We have in the past had very low or no tuition for everyone meeting admission requirements to public colleges, and no resource shortage exists now to do so. Our nation is wealthier than it has ever been.

Several countries require little or no tuition for a college education. In Finland, Denmark, Ireland, Iceland, Norway, Sweden, Italy and Mexico, public colleges and universities are free. In Denmark, not only is college tuition-free, college students actually get paid. In Germany, the public colleges are free not only for Germans but also for international students, which is why every year more than 4,500 students from the United States enroll in German universities.[250] Some of these countries have among the best educational outcomes in the world. These countries' policymakers have had the vision to see the importance of having a well-educated citizenry so they have essentially removed financial barriers to a college education.

Education not only benefits society by creating a workforce that creates wealth, pays taxes, and needs fewer government services. It also allows people to be more informed and effective participants in a functional democracy. A national investment to provide free college education is well worth the cost.

Higher education in an authoritarian, undemocratic country needs only to cultivate obedient and productive workers. As a democracy, we depend on a knowledgeable, public-spirited, and engaged population. Increasingly, we are losing sight of this fundamental truth. Higher education has a vital role to play in the renewal of U.S. democracy.

Many United States students avoid pursuing a college education for financial reasons. A national survey by Northeastern University found that 67% of students born in the mid-1990s or later are concerned about being able to afford college.[251] And many who overcome the disincentive of the high cost will have their college loan payment as a substantial burden on their finances for many years. Due to the poor job market and declining wages, many will never be able to pay back those loans. The national student loan default rate is about 14% per year.[252]

The average student debt load for the class of 2012 is $29,400, and student debt totals over $1.2 trillion. According to the Federal Reserve Bank of New York, 10% of all debt in the U.S. is in student loans, second only to mortgages, and more than the total national credit card debt. To burden millions of students with often overwhelming debt is unjust and unwise. Our society should support education as an investment that pays large dividends.

The number of people who have made and are making decisions not to get post-secondary education for financial reasons is not known. But it is likely large enough to have a significantly detrimental impact on our economy and democracy far into the future. Internationally, the United States ranks twelfth in the percentage of young people with college degrees, an area where we once led the world. South Korea now has taken the global lead. Over 60% of its citizens under age 34 in 2009 earned a degree, while the U.S. had only 40%. Fewer than 60% who start college finish with degrees in the U.S., often for financial reasons.

Enhancing Civic and Economic Functioning

Too few postsecondary institutions offer programs that prepare students to engage the questions Americans face as the world's most powerful democracy. Civic learning and democratic process engagement should be an educational priority for all higher education institutions, public and private, two-year and four-year. Writing ability and science literacy is not optional for college graduates, nor should civic learning be.

All graduates should have familiarity with the branches of government and with basic information about U.S. history, including the historical and sociological understanding of several social movements and debates about democracy, both in the U.S. and abroad. Cultivating the ability to think critically and collaborate with people of differing views and backgrounds to resolve complex public issues based on shared values of liberty, justice, ethical integrity, equality and empathy must be an essential objective of all colleges.

Experience with the group deliberative process at the foundation of New Enlightenment Policy 28 should be a part of core college curriculum.

An interesting and important basic difference between the 18th century and the 21st century was the degree of what might be called "social consciousness." A feeling of obligation to society was prevalent then. People of the Enlightenment era believed that shared beliefs were important and public life mattered more than one's private life. Also, people of the Enlightenment believed that a well-defined code of manners and behavior was necessary to allow men to live in harmonious groups. These are ideals worthy of the effort to reestablish and extend to all groups, not just white men as in the Age of Enlightenment, so we are all part of a harmonious human family, and our colleges could play a major role in this.

Also, to facilitate creating a more democratically structured economy primarily comprised of worker self-directed enterprises, basic skills and knowledge needed for cooperative business enterprise management and direction should be acquired by all two and four-year college students.

Basic understanding of law pertaining to the relatively more common contingencies of personal and business life should also be included in core college curricula. Knowing the relevant rules of our society is important. It is of particular importance to know our legal rights and how to protect them. For example, millions of people since the start of the financial crisis were thrown out of their homes or apartments, despite the fact that legal protections existed that could have stopped the process if they knew of them. Often people cannot afford a lawyer or do not know that one would be helpful in their circumstances. Basic legal self-defense, as part of other commonly relevant law coursework, should be part of core curricula.

The tendency for the rate of growth of wealth to be larger than the rate of growth of the economy and labor income is a powerful force of divergence that will continue to create widening inequality unless interrupted with vigorous policy solutions. But forces of convergence also exist. An important one is the diffusion of knowledge and skills. This force is being diminished while the forces of divergence are increasing because barriers to education are being erected. The New Enlightenment policy will eliminate financial barriers to a college education as an important way of enhancing a force of convergence, while also improving national economic performance.

The Harvard Business School's 2013–14 Survey on U.S. Competitiveness report "An Economy Doing Half Its Job" states, *"Skills shortages make it hard for firms operating in the United States to increase their productivity consistently, the major driver in sustaining their ability to compete and rais-ing their capacity to pay workers. Thus, skills issues are at the heart of the aspect of U.S. competitiveness that worries us the most: the stagnation of liv-ing standards among most Americans."* About 52% of U.S. employers re-ported difficulty in filling positions due to skills deficiencies in applicants with *"lack of technical skills"* among the top causes.

On average, the higher a person's educational attainment, the lower the likelihood of being unemployed and the higher the income, as the following table shows. Note that the graph shows educational attainment has been grow-ing in importance. Gallup's polling data revealed that 72% of the top 1% wealthiest Americans have a college degree, compared to 31% of those in the bottom 99%.

Although most jobs filled over the previous decade were filled by work-ers who did not have bachelor's degrees, and the U.S. Bureau of Labor Sta-tistics projects that to continue, its projections assume that the educational characteristics of occupations will not change.

High-paying occupations sometimes only require training that has in-cluded a few college courses, an associate degree, apprenticeship programs, or vocational classes at a technical school. But when an occupation includes workers with different levels of education, workers with more education often can better compete for jobs, and more jobs are likely to require a degree in the future. This is particularly true if the occupations require academic skills, such as mathematics or science.

Healthcare occupations are expected to be among the fastest growing and highest paying (in most categories) in the economy, and most require a col-lege degree. For some that do not, such as health aide and nursing aide, it may be beneficial to require a two-year degree to prepare for their work. Home health aides and nursing aides now typically have much less education.

Due to greater interaction through easier travel, communications and global trade, the field of international studies and relations, including the study of languages, will be a part of postsecondary education of large and growing importance. Knowledge in all subject areas has increased substan-tially and will continue to since free high school education was instituted. A college education allows a similar level of competence in dealing with the knowledge of importance in the contemporary world as a high school educa-tion did decades ago.

Earnings and Unemployment Rates by Educational Attainment		
Education attained	**2012 Unemployment rate (%)**	**Median earnings/ week**
Doctoral degree	2.5	1,624
Professional degree	2.1	1,735
Master's degree	3.5	1,300
Bachelor's degree	4.5	1,066
Associate's degree	6.2	785
Some college, no degree	7.7	727
High school diploma	8.3	652
No high school diploma	12.4	471
Note: Data are for persons age 25 and over. Earnings are for full-time wage and salary workers. Source: U.S. Bureau of Labor Statistics		

The Widening Earnings Gap of Young Adults by Educational Attainment

The difference in median annual earnings of high school and college graduates when members of each generation were 25 to 32

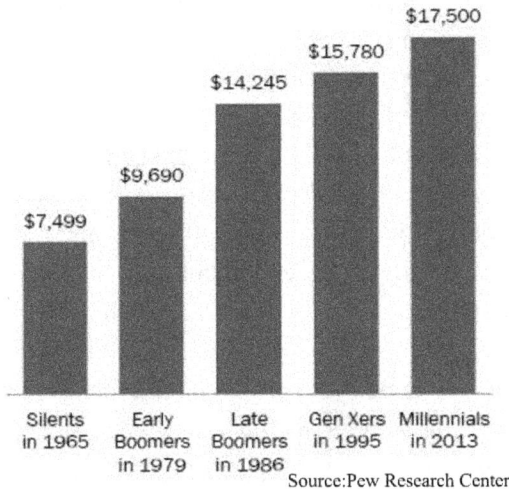

Silents in 1965	Early Boomers in 1979	Late Boomers in 1986	Gen Xers in 1995	Millennials in 2013
$7,499	$9,690	$14,245	$15,780	$17,500

Source: Pew Research Center

Basic knowledge of the sciences is especially important since science is the foundation for understanding our world. With scientific knowledge we have some power to predict and control our environment. Science is involved in choosing what to eat, how to best protect and improve our health in other ways, and how to best protect and enhance the quality of our environment. The world has changed in such a way that science literacy has become necessary for everyone, not just a privileged few. Scientific literacy is also important because as Charles Darwin put it, *"there is grandeur in this view of life."*

Widespread scientific literacy is important within a citizenry that participates in decisions (or selects representative that do so) on the levels of public funding for basic research and where basic research public funds should be spent and on other significant public policy decisions. Public spending on basic research has been and will continue to be of major importance in productivity advancements. The nature of business requires that their research funds are focused on areas likely to bring useful results in the short term. Only government can have the long-term horizon in view when making research investment decisions. The long-term returns of these investments have historically been very large, between 30% and 100% or more.[253]

Harmful public policies based on ignorance of science, such as those influencing action on climate change, would be less common if the voting public had a better understanding of the tremendous explanatory power of the natural sciences.

Also, postsecondary education in the sciences, in addition to extending knowledge, reinforces knowledge previously learned, enabling more people to better participate in the education and stimulation of the interest of children in these fields, which could help motivate future professional interest. This will help meet the increasing demand for technically skilled workers and contributes to the process that will lead to future scientific advancements, which will allow the productivity advancements of great importance to the future of the country and the world. If properly managed, productivity advancements will enable further reductions in work-hours, and help lift more people out of poverty worldwide.

World knowledge is now doubling about every two years, and the rate of increase is increasing. Among the most important skills that a college education develops are research and independent learning skills needed for a lifetime of learning in many occupations, and for full democratic participation.

College also serves a secondary societal purpose of delaying workforce entry where there are high levels of unemployment. Fewer jobs are needed to satisfy the employment requirements of a smaller workforce. If all students in college were instead added to the number of people looking for work, the unemployment rate would more than double.

Some Necessary Policies to Reduce College Costs

An important cause of the large increase in college costs over the last few decades is a disproportionately large increase in the number of administrative staff, and in the pay of higher level administrative staff. It is not uncommon now for schools to have more administrators than faculty members. Reducing administrative costs and bureaucracy should be part of any university reform.

Just five years ago, $500,000 was a high salary for a university president. Today, a growing number make $1 million or more, and the average salary is $421,395. In 2011, most public-college presidents earned between two and four times the average salary of their full professors. Some made much more. Chief financial officers of universities who made $175,000 five years ago often make $300,000 or more today.[254]

University administrators argue that their salaries must be competitive with private sector salaries. But universities offer benefits including higher job security that are not available in the private sector, and for decades could attract very competent administrators for salaries far lower than they are today. Also, the explosion in top salaries in the private sector is part of an unjust trend in our economy that the public sector should avoid further supporting with tax dollars to a public sector economic elite. The funds can be much more effectively used to serve the essential functions of colleges.

The rapid rise in administrative staffs has resulted in a decline in employee productivity. We can measure administrative staff productivity in two ways: (1) students per administrative employee, and (2) degrees awarded per administrative employee. Regarding enrollment, administrative employee productivity in the non-profit sectors declined by between 23.2% and 27.6% between 1987 and 2007. With regard to the number of degrees awarded, administrative employee productivity in the non-profit sectors fell by between 15.8% and 19.1% between 1987 and 2007.[255] College and university administrators decide the number of staff, and it's clear that they love to hire people like themselves who can reduce their workload while they expand their empires.

A 25% reduction in administrative and support staff is achievable based on historical experience and on the fact that the bursar's office personnel will no longer be necessary for collecting tuition. This will result in a saving of $3.7 billion per year. These substantial savings colleges could use for whatever instructional purpose they determine to be in the best interest of their current students, to save for future instructional purposes, or to contribute to the elimination of tuition in public colleges that have higher than the average tuition of $8,646 federally granted per student.

Publicly funded institutions should decide on the pay of administrators based on the best interests of the public, not the administrators, as the trend has been. We will limit the salary of the highest paid administrator, typically the college president, to whichever is greater, the 50th percentile of the faculty salaries or the percentile of the faculty salaries equivalent to the college's percentile of enrollment compared to all colleges. For example: If the college has enrollment greater than 60% of all public colleges, the salary of the college president would be limited to a salary at the 60th percentile of the faculty salaries.

The size of the college, to a degree, relates to the level of responsibilities of the college president, but larger colleges typically satisfy any excess responsibilities with varying numbers of vice presidents or other administrators, depending on college size. All other high paid administrators' salaries would also be reduced in an appropriate relation to that of the college president.

If current administrators decide this change is unacceptable, many other qualified candidates could administer a college at these salaries. Students working part-time could fill many administrative positions, and faculty on temporary leave from teaching duties could fill higher level ones, as was not uncommon decades ago. Other capable people could also be found for this level of pay. Administrative duties are far less intellectually demanding than the duties of faculty and require far less training to perform.

The college president salary limits we propose are maximums only, not recommended salaries. The faculty performs the essential function of colleges which should focus their resources on their essential function, education, not building dynasties with unreasonably high paid leaders at the top. Although pay of top administrators would be cut by as much as 80% or more in some cases, upper mid-level administrators' pay would be cut less, and mid- and lower-level not at all. If overall savings in administrative pay averaged 20%, the resulting saving colleges could redirect to educational purposes is about $2.2 billion. In total, the administrative cost saving will be about $5.9 billion per year that colleges could redirect to instructional purposes.

Full Public Support for the Costs of College Education

Public universities had 13.35 million students in 2012-2013 with an average tuition cost of $8,646.[256] The total tuition paid was $115 billion. The American Association of Community Colleges fact sheet states that total tuition paid to community colleges in 2013 was about $9.8 billion, with an average tuition of $3,300. New Enlightenment policy will make college education free to qualified students. We will give direct federal grants to public four-year colleges of $8,646, and to public two-year colleges, $3,300 per student per year under these conditions:

1.   The college eliminates tuition for all students meeting admission requirements.
2.   Administrative staff is reduced by 25 percent.
3.   The salary of the highest paid administrator, the college president, is limited to whichever is greater, the 50th percentile of the faculty salaries or the percentile of the faculty salaries equivalent to the college's percentile of enrollment compared to all colleges.
4.   Civic learning and engagement with democratic processes, including those within WSDEs, coursework is required for graduation.

Conditions 2 and 3 could be satisfied by using a proportional three-year phase-in period.

Current college scholarship granting agencies will be able to redirect all scholarship money to private colleges that in the past supported public college student tuition. The probability and size of scholarships to students wanting to attend a private college will then be substantially larger when we institute this free public college policy.

At current enrollment levels, the total increase in federal funding for college education would be $125 billion. However, this policy will result in more students enrolling in college, and we will budget for a 10% increase requiring about $138 billion.

We will not decrease funding for the federal Pell Grant award and the Federal Supplemental Educational Opportunity Grant Program, which totaled about $39 billion in fiscal year 2012. We will direct these funds to the support of book and living expenses for students in public universities based on income guidelines.

Our university system has been the best in the world, one of the drivers of American prosperity. We will ensure that it remains excellent and unsurpassed in quality by supporting with federal funds an 80/20 federal/state sharing of expenses in additional facilities that the individual states determine worthy of state funds to improve instruction or research capabilities.

Arizona State University president, Michael M. Crow, estimated a need for a one-time $45 billion investment in public university infrastructure nationwide. In 2008, he recommended that this expenditure be part of a stimulus package, and only $2 billion was budgeted and spent over two years for this purpose.[257] We will support 80% of the remaining college infrastructure up-grade expenditure over ten years with federal dollars. $3.5 billion per year we will budget for this purpose within our $300 billion annual infrastructure/public works budget.

Considerable potential exists for increasing educational efficiency or lowering the costs per student for the same or better level of education through new techniques, including the use of computers and the Internet. We will encourage innovative techniques as follows:

The federal grant amount per student will remain the same independent of efficiency improvements so any efficiency improvements the states make they will benefit from. They could use the saved funds for any other purposes. Student and faculty satisfaction rates with any educational reforms will be the most important determinant of the value of the reform.

Also, after a three-year period based on in-depth studies of student and faculty satisfaction rates with any educational reforms nationwide, the most effective will be selected for national use, and any performing poorly will be eliminated. Standardized tests will be a part of this process, but will not be the primary criterion because of the problem of motivating excessive resources to "teach to the test," and test results are often not a good measure of capacity or value received from the educational experience. This analysis will likely lead to national educational efficiency improvements.

The New Enlightenment: Ideals of Democracy, Human Rights, Reason, and Progress * Policy 7

"Laws for the liberal education ... are so extremely wise and useful, that, to a humane and generous mind, no expense for this purpose would be thought extravagant." "Liberty cannot be preserved without a general knowledge among the people." John Adams[258]

"In every wise struggle for human betterment one of the main objects, and often the only object, has been to achieve in large measure equality of opportunity. In the struggle for this great end, nations rise from barbarism to civilization, and through it people press forward from one stage of enlightenment to the next." Theodore Roosevelt[259]

Increase Social Security Payments:
Social Security Plus

As the following graph shows, our Social Security benefits are low by international standards. The United States ranks 31st among 34 developed countries in the percentage of a median worker's earnings that the public-pension system replaces. For someone who worked all of his or her adult life at average earnings and retires at 65 in 2012, Social Security benefits replace about 41% of past earnings. The OECD average is 57.9%.

Social Security Benefits Are Low Compared With Other Advanced Countries

Social Security benefits for median worker as a percentage of earnings

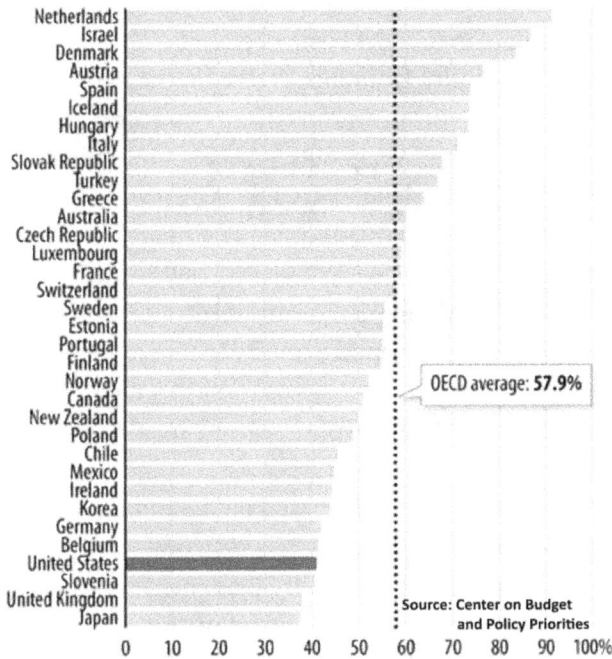

OECD average: **57.9%**

Source: Center on Budget and Policy Priorities

This "replacement rate" will decrease to about 36% for a median earner retiring at 65 in the future. The full retirement age, which has already risen to 66, will climb to 67 over the 2017-2022 period.

Sixty-two million elderly and disabled people receive Social Security benefit payments. Many depend on them to meet basic needs, but inadequate support is common. For 65% of elderly beneficiaries, Social Security provides the majority of their income. For over 36%, it provides more than 90% of their income. For 24% of elderly beneficiaries, Social Security is the sole source of retirement income. Among those aged 80 or older, it provides the majority of income for 76% of beneficiaries and nearly all the income for 45% of beneficiaries.[260]

About 5.4 million Social Security recipients live in poverty. Four percent of those over sixty-five, or 1.6 million people, are ineligible for Social Security, 44% of whom, or 700,000 people, live in poverty. In 2011, Social Security paid 41.6% of retired workers receiving benefits an amount under $1,000 per month, and 62.6% of retired workers under $1,400 per month. In June 2012, the average Social Security retirement benefit was $1,234 a month, about $14,800 a year.[261]

Our low benefits are reduced further due to high health care costs. Most retirees enroll in Medicare's Supplementary Medical Insurance and have premiums deducted from their Social Security checks. As the rise in health care costs continue to outpace general inflation, those premiums will increase the number of recipients unable to meet basic needs.

Social Security Disability Insurance (DI) benefits make up over 90% of income for nearly half of non-institutionalized recipients and over 75% of income for the vast majority of recipients. Almost one-fourth or 3.5 million people receiving DI fall below the poverty line. Most of the 14 million receiving DI live below 200% of the poverty line. The monthly benefits to 56.2% of the disabled receiving benefits were under $1,000 per month and 74.6% under $1,400 per month. About 13% of disabled-worker beneficiaries also collect Social Security's Supplemental Security Income (SSI), which indicates that they are very poor, with few or no assets. SSI lifts them to just over three-fourths of the poverty line. The average SSI payment is less than $550 per month.[262]

Our low benefits are not justified based on the proportion of our population requiring support. Because of the U.S.' comparatively high birth and immigration rates, we are graying less rapidly than many other nations. People age 60 or older will make up about a quarter of our population in 2040, a figure that several European countries and Japan have already surpassed.

Many "pundits" express that we need to keep Social Security benefits low because of a future "demographic crisis," but this "crisis" is exaggerated. As there are more non-working older people, there will be fewer children or below working age people to support, due to lower reproduction rates. Also, productivity continues to increase, allowing fewer workers to produce more, and a sufficient amount even if the proportion of the dependent population rises. The Congressional Budget Office projects average productivity growth through 2033 of 1.66% per year. The Social Security Administration projects that in 2033, the number of workers per recipient will be 2.1; today it is 2.8. However, based on the CBO productivity growth projection, 2.1 workers will produce then what 2.82 workers produce today.

The Center for Strategic and International Studies Global Aging Preparedness index rates various nations' readiness for future demographic changes. CSIS assigns a low priority to reducing Social Security benefits in the United States. Its top priority for the United States is reining in future health-care costs and growth. As I noted previously, our health care costs are more than twice the per capita costs of the average of OECD nations.

Among all workers, including those offered and not offered a retirement plan at work, only 39.6% participated in a retirement plan in 2009, the first time in 15 years that it dropped below 40 percent.[263] In 1999, 69% of employers offered their full-time workers some form of retirement benefits. Now, just 62% of employers or unions provide a pension or retirement savings account, and this downward trend is expected to continue. This trend away from defined benefit pension plans to defined contribution retirement plans is projected to reduce average retirement incomes.[264] The Employee Benefits Research Institute's Jack VanDerhei estimates 45% of the next generation of retirees will fall short of meeting their basic financial needs—not a comfortable retirement, but basic needs.

Social Security is well managed, with less than 1% of its expenditures for administration. It is more efficient, secure, and fair in its distribution than any private sector counterpart is or could ever be. It is an excellent example of government working well, and reducing inequality. Without Social Security, poverty among those over 65 would jump from 9% to 50%.[265]

Social Security benefits more than just the recipient. Knowing that one's parents will have Social Security frees up the generation in the middle to direct more family resources to their own children.

The Social Security system's funding mechanism requires modification. It is based on a work-related, contributory system in which workers provide for their own future economic security through taxes paid while employed. Since inequality has increased greatly and is characterized by tens of millions of Americans with below a living wage, a just retirement system cannot provide only some fraction of this inadequate amount. We should source some portion of the benefit from general funds supported by progressive taxes.

New Enlightenment policy institutes a $500 per month benefit increase for all current Social Security recipients and a $500 per month payment to all

citizens over age 65 not currently eligible for Social Security. This will substantially reduce poverty levels and substantially improve the standard of living of an additional tens of millions of people. And tens of millions of low-
income people having substantially more disposable income for the consumption of goods and services as a result of this policy will have a stimulus effect
on the economy that will increase federal revenue.

The annual cost of the Social Security Plus program will be $382 billion,
about half of which will be paid for by raising the cap on the income on which
the Social Security tax is applied. In addition to eliminating the worker half
of the Social Security tax (included in policy 1), we will eliminate the
$133,700 income cap on the employer portion of the tax. This will raise $189
billion per year.[266] We will fund the other half of the cost through progressive
New Enlightenment taxes.

*The New Enlightenment: Ideals of Democracy,
Human Rights, Reason, and Progress * Policy 8*

Increase Funding for Public Defenders, Reform Criminal Laws, and Support Inmate Rehabilitation

Unnecessarily harsh crime laws and a dysfunctional criminal justice system
have caused devastating harm to millions of Americans, especially those least
able to defend themselves. Criminal justice system reforms are an important
part of economic policy reforms because of the unnecessary economic harm
to individuals, local communities, and our country caused by our unjust and
dysfunctional criminal justice system.

About 2.4 million people are now incarcerated, often under horrific conditions. This is an incarceration rate of 760 prisoners per 100,000 population,
or more than **seven** times higher than the median rate for the 34 OECD countries. One in every 31 adults, or 7.3 million Americans, are either in prison,
on parole or probation.[267] Imprisonment rates have quintupled over the last 30
years, mainly due to the war on drugs. In fact, this war has been waged to a

large degree on the poor, and disproportionately on African Americans. However, evidence indicates that people of color aren't any more likely to commit drug crimes than whites are.

The drug war has been brutal. The onslaught has involved SWAT teams, military equipment, and sweeps of entire neighborhoods, mainly in poor African American communities. Little is known elsewhere about this war and its devastation. Federal laws motivated these enormously destructive practices by allowing state and local law enforcement agencies to keep 80% of the cash, cars, and homes seized from drug suspects, and by providing funding based on the number of drug arrests. In 2005, four out of five drug arrests were for possession only.

During the 1990s—the period of the most dramatic expansion of the drug war—nearly 80% of the increase in drug arrests was for marijuana possession, a drug less harmful than alcohol or tobacco and at least as prevalent in middle-class white communities as in the inner city where the vast majority of drug war resources and arrests have been focused.[268]

Accounting for both those in and out of prison, a large majority of African American men in some urban areas have been labeled felons for life, mainly resulting from the drug war. People with a felony record can be legally discriminated against in employment, housing, access to education, food stamps and other public benefits, in addition to being denied the right to vote and to be excluded from juries. The system seems designed to send people back to prison, which is what happens about 70% of the time because of the immense challenges created by the system for survival after prison release.[269]

As I noted previously, Villanova College sociologists determined that if the mass incarceration trend had not occurred in recent decades, the poverty rate would be 20% lower today and five million fewer people would have fallen below the poverty line.[270] By age 48, the typical former inmate will have earned $179,000 less than if he had never been incarcerated. Incarceration significantly depresses total lifetime earnings, so it is a significant factor in economic inequality, especially between minorities and whites.[271]

The National Institute of Mental Health estimated that a clinical diagnosis of mental illness would exist for nearly two-thirds of inmates (64.2%) in local jails, and an average of over 50% in state and federal prison.[272] Prison conditions can exacerbate mental illness, and create it in some of those not previously mentally ill, yet our prisons are being used, to a large degree, to warehouse the mentally ill.

There is an epidemic of violence in big-city jails across the country.[273]

Rape is shockingly common in prison. Over seventy thousand prisoners are raped each year. These conditions threaten both the physical and mental health of many prisoners, and should not be tolerated in any civilized society.

How many lives have we destroyed throughout this period of mass incarceration? Aside from the moral implications, and the funds wasted on prisons, how much has this cost us all in wasted human resources that could have benefited us all?

Prisons are necessary for public safety, both by keeping dangerous criminals off the streets and by deterring would-be offenders. However, the overuse and inappropriate use of incarceration and brutal prison conditions are harmful to society. And when prisoners are released, a decent, functional society must help them fulfill their responsibilities to their victims, their families and their communities by helping them find and keep legitimate employment.

For children, the era of mass incarceration has meant broken homes, poverty, and hopelessness, as they see their loved ones cycling in and out of prison. Children who have incarcerated parents are far more likely to be incarcerated themselves. 25% of African Americans who grew up in the last three decades have had at least one parent locked up during their childhood.[274]

A false view of our legal system is widespread, due to shows like "Law and Order," which suggest that everyone accused of a crime has a lawyer who appears on demand, willing to do tremendous investigation and background research for the defendant in even the most routine cases. This is not true. Hundreds of thousands of people go to jail or prison every year without even meeting with an attorney because they cannot afford one and a public defender was not provided. In one California county alone, in 2002, there were over 12,000 guilty pleas entered by people who had no lawyer.[5]

Many plead guilty based on a promise of a lesser sentence by prosecutors and the threat of a harsh sentence, such as ten or more years in prison. Knowing they will not be properly defended, and rightly suspecting that the judge or jury will believe the police officer's word over theirs, innocent people plead guilty. Those who speak to a public defender often get nothing more than a few minutes of time and a hurried guilty plea recommendation because of overwhelming caseloads. More than 90 percent of criminal cases are never tried before a jury. Most people charged with crimes forfeit their constitutional rights and plead guilty.[275]

Public defense caseloads frequently far exceed national standards, which limit felony cases to 150 a year per attorney. Felony caseloads of 600 or more are common. A New York Times investigation found defenders with a total caseload of over 1,600 cases annually.[276] Access to investigators, experts or scientific testing is commonly lacking. Governments often spend three times as much on prosecution as on public defense. Rates for assigned counsel (private lawyers appointed when there is no public defender available) are often set at $25 or $30 per hour, even though the average cost of running a law office is much higher.

If societies are judged based on how they treat their most vulnerable people, ours will not be judged well. When people are threatened with losing their freedom and being branded for life with the crippling label of "felon," and they do not have the resources to defend themselves, New Enlightenment policies will ensure that sufficient resources are provided so they can be properly defended.

The 6th Amendment to the Constitution requires this: *"In all criminal prosecutions, the accused shall...have a compulsory process for obtaining witnesses in his favor, and to have the assistance of counsel for his defense."*

New Enlightenment policies require all jurisdictions to meet national caseload maximum standards for public defenders with appropriate investigative, expert and scientific testing support. About $5.3 billion is spent per year nationally by state and local governments on public defender and assigned council programs.[277] We will include in the federal budget an additional $4.5 billion per year for the public defense of individuals who cannot afford an attorney. These funds will be provided within a 50/50 federal/local jurisdiction sharing of expenses to meet New Enlightenment national standards. For local jurisdictions with median incomes less than 80% of national median income, where excessive hardships would be produced in raising the taxes to participate in the 50/50 funding partnership, the federal government will provide 90% of the additional funding needed to meet the standards.

Net costs for this policy will be reduced by the reduction in costs from the reduction in false imprisonments. False convictions happen regularly, but we don't know how often because most false convictions never see the light of day. We know only about the rare ones that are discovered and corrected (at least in part) by exoneration. Exonerations are unlikely and unrepresentative of the mass of invisible false convictions, and we don't have nearly a full count of exonerations. Because the average time from conviction to exoneration is about 13 years, only those sentenced to serious crimes with decades-long prison terms are likely to even bother undertaking the long, arduous, and resource-intensive process of proving their innocence.[278] Exonerations are used as a measure of the percentage of convictions that are false, but it is a very poor measure.

We will never know the accurate number of false convictions, but some studies estimate that between 2.3% and 5% of all prisoners in the U.S. are innocent.[279] These estimates can be wildly inaccurate because exonerations are just the tip of an iceberg of wrongful convictions; it is not unlikely to be significantly higher than 5%. Assuming 5%, the number of innocent people in prison is about 120,000. If a better functioning public defense system could reduce this number by 30%, 36,000 fewer innocent people would be in prison. At the average cost of $31,000 per prisoner, this yields a saving of $1.12 billion per year. However, even if we ignore these savings, the approximate total $7.2 billion policy cost (this assumes that $2 billion of the $4.5 billion in federal dollars will be spent covering 90% of the policy cost), including the costs to local jurisdictions, is about $23 per capita. Equal justice for all, which is supposed to be one of our most important ideals, and which the 6th Amendment and 14th Amendment to our Constitution *("...nor shall any state deprive any person of his life, liberty, or property without due process of law, nor deny to any person.... the equal protection of the laws)* is supposed to guarantee, is well worth this cost.

Also reducing costs will be New Enlightenment policies that will treat drug use as a public health problem requiring treatment and community service, and not use jail time for those guilty of drug possession. Prohibition has exploded the prison population and bred more serious crimes by suppliers and dealers, including violent crimes and the corruption of officials.

State and local drug laws should change; the following facts and grants will motivate this change:

Federal grants of $3 per state resident will be provided to states that institute statewide addiction treatment programs instead of prison time for drug possession. The states would distribute the funds to local jurisdictions as appropriate.

According to several conservative estimates, every dollar invested in addiction treatment programs yields a return of between $4 and $7 in reduced drug-related crime, criminal justice costs, and theft. When savings related to healthcare are included, total savings can exceed costs by a ratio of 12 to 1. Major savings to the individual and to society also stem from fewer interpersonal conflicts; greater workplace productivity, and fewer drug-related accidents, including overdoses and deaths.[280] The federal grants require an annual budgeted amount of $950 million.

New Enlightenment policies will vigorously support successful reintegration of released inmates into society. To do so we, will motivate jurisdictions nationwide to adopt the following Pew Charitable Trusts policy recommendations with grants and education campaigns, and institute these policies in federal cases:[271]

- Reconnect former inmates to the labor market through education and training, job search and placement support and follow-up services to help former inmates stay employed. In-prison vocational programs produced net benefits of $13,738 per offender (a return of $12.62 for every dollar invested), and adult general education produced net benefits of $10,669 per offender (or $12.09 per dollar invested). Employment and job training services for offenders in the community yielded $4,359 per offender, the equivalent of $11.90 per dollar invested. When the other New Enlightenment policies are instituted, the workforce will be fully or nearly fully employed, so former inmates will find it far easier to find employment on release than under current labor market conditions.

- Enhance former inmates' economic condition by capping the percent of an offender's income subject to deductions for unpaid debts (such as court-ordered fines and fees), and expanding the Earned Income Tax Credit. An extensive EITC expansion is in Policy 1.

- Screen people convicted of crimes by the risks they pose to society and divert lower-risk offenders into high-quality, community-based mandatory supervision programs. "Technical violators," offenders who have broken the rules of their probation or parole but have not committed new crimes, make up as much as half to two-thirds of prison admissions in some states and are a particularly large target for diversion. Every day spent under community supervision rather than behind bars is an opportunity for a sentenced individual to build vocational experience, to care for children, and to pay victim restitution and other fines and fees, rather than drain resources from the public coffer. Statistics indicate that the average cost per day in state prison is near $80 compared with a day on probation supervision, which costs just $3.50. The $76.50 difference per day per person is a 96% saving.

- Use earned-time credits, a proven model that offers selected inmates a shortened prison stay if they complete educational, vocational, or rehabilitation programs that boost their chances of successful re-entry into the community and the labor market. A study of states that used earned-time credits found that offenders who earned the credits had fewer new felony convictions and that prison stays for the eligible offenders dropped by over two months, saving the state money on incarceration costs. Similar earned time credits to shorten supervision terms should be offered to offenders on probation and parole to encourage compliance and avoid incarceration for violations.

- Use swift and certain sanctions other than prison, such as short but immediate weekend jail stays, to punish probation and parole violations, holding offenders accountable while allowing them to keep their jobs.

The community-based supervision programs and in and out of prison training and rehabilitation programs will result in jurisdictions having a large net saving in funds. This alone should motivate the establishment of these policy changes nationwide. To further motivate this we will offer a $10 per state resident grant to states that meet federal guidelines for community-based supervision programs, and in and out of prison training and rehabilitation programs, in all jurisdictions statewide. The states would distribute the funds to local jurisdictions statewide, based on prison population or financial need as appropriate.

This policy will significantly improve state and local budgets, both through more efficient use of funds and the large subsidy. Neglecting savings at the federal level the subsidy would cost the federal government $3.2 billion per year.

Besides drug laws, other criminal laws also need reform including "three strikes" and mandatory minimum laws. Our goal is to put an end to excessively harsh crime policies that result in mass incarceration and stand in the way of a just and equal society. When large numbers of people are unnecessarily torn from their families, those families, their communities, and our entire society are degraded in many ways. Usually, where incarceration is now used, better ways than harsh prison sentences exist to instill a sense of responsibility.

We will also eliminate public benefit and rights restrictions on those with a felony conviction. Society's best interest is served by supporting released prisoners' reintegration into society, not by erecting unnecessary barriers to it, as current public policy does.

Additional specific reforms require further development, which we would accomplish by motivating the debate needed for determining more effective and humane policies to deter behavior where there is wide agreement that it needs to be deterred and the level and nature of rehabilitation efforts.

The public defender policy cost of $4.5 billion, the drug treatment subsidy of $950 million, the community-based supervision programs, and the in and out of prison training and rehabilitation program's cost of $3.2 billion total about $8.7 billion. Since most of the resulting savings will be at the state and local level, and we ensure that we are conservative in our federal budget analysis, we will use this $8.7 billion as the net additional federal cost. This amount is also conservative since the level of crime will likely decrease as a result of the more just and prosperous economic conditions resulting from New Enlightenment policies.

One indication that crime rates are associated with economic and political injustice: Although the number of guns per capita in Switzerland is the highest in Europe, it is about half that in the U.S. But they have 0.5 gun homicides per 100,000 inhabitants and we have about 5 firearm killings per 100,000 people, or ten times as many.[281]

We need major reform of gun laws but the gun homicide rate disparity indicates most of the problem is cultural. Just changing the gun laws will not solve the problem. These cultural factors likely include economic inequality, poverty rates, incarceration rates, food insecurity rates, poor quality of K-12 education in low-income areas, access disparities to health care and college education and other social support disparities, and a political system that ignores the preferences of the vast majority of the population. These problems either do not exist or are much less severe in Switzerland. When people are treated like their lives don't matter, it is more likely for them to treat others like their lives don't matter, sometimes violently. Our gun laws and gun violence rates are symptoms of more fundamental social problems that require solution.

*The New Enlightenment: Ideals of Democracy, Human Rights, Reason, and Progress * Policy 9*

In addition to the income and wealth taxes described previously, the following Part 2 policies generate sufficient revenues to support all the proposed policies requiring federal funds, including those in Part 3, eliminate the $680 billion deficit (2013) and create a $300 billion surplus. Most of these policies also provide other benefits.

Replace Estate Tax with a
Progressive Inheritance Tax

Large amounts of inherited wealth, and gross concentrations of wealth, inherited or not, characterize aristocratic, not free and democratic societies. We can and should use the tax system to support broad-based economic and political opportunity and substantially reduce dynastic wealth.

Inheritance is an important driver of the huge and growing wealth disparities. Gratuitous gifts and bequests represent between 35% and 45% of household net worth.[282] This estimate is based on surveys where respondents are asked whether they have received any inheritances, gifts, or other types of wealth transfers, such as trust funds, in the past, and the value of the transfer. This method is likely to result in substantial under-reporting. Inheritances as a fraction of total wealth, especially of the largest fortunes, are likely to be much more than we know.

We tax these wealth transfers through our estate tax, raising less than $12 billion, or just 1% of the $1.2 trillion transferred annually.[283] Many people inherit wealth so vast they never need to work or do anything of value to society. They can live off the investment proceeds of their inherited wealth at an income far greater than the majority of the full-time working population, Sometimes their inherited assets value increases more than their income.

Six of the ten wealthiest Americans are heirs to major fortunes. As I noted previously, the six Walmart heirs have $145 billion, more wealth than the bottom 42% or 132 million Americans combined. We are at the beginning of the largest intergenerational transfer of wealth in history. A Boston College Center on Wealth and Philanthropy study projects that $36 trillion will be passed down to heirs from 2011 to 2061. This will create a new aristocracy with unprecedented wealth, and therefore power.

For economic inequalities to be tolerable, they need to be, to the degree practical, associated with merit, or contributions to society, and be within reasonable bounds. Inequalities must be useful to all, and only then can they be justified. (An important Enlightenment ideal: "Social distinctions can be based only on common utility," according to Article 1 of the 1789 Declaration of the Rights of Man and the Citizen.)

In old Europe, a relatively small group of wealthy families lived lavishly on the fruits of inherited wealth, and the rest struggled to survive. It would be a cruel and ironic fate if the United States, once known in old Europe and throughout the world to be the land of opportunity and egalitarianism, reversed roles with old Europe. Without vigorous policy solutions to change direction, this is our destination.

The advantages that vast intergenerational wealth transfers provide are based not on merit, but on luck. Clearly, public funds are needed, and should be raised by taxing inherited income, especially large amounts, at a higher rate than earned income. Also, taxing bequests and gifts more heavily than other income will limit or reduce dynastic wealth, a purpose of value in itself, in addition to the value created by a large increase in public resources. Society can direct these resources to purposes that will maximize benefit to all. Also, this tax can be paid by people more easily able to bear the burdens of government finance. It will provide funds sufficient to support free college education, and substantially increase the funding of relatively low funded K-12 schools.

"A just man will rejoice" in excessive wealth being returned to society upon his death

In *Agrarian Justice*, Thomas Paine offered an estate tax proposal as a remedy to economic injustice in the old Europe of his day. He justified it by pointing out that as hunter-gatherers, or for the vast majority of human existence, we all were equal inheritors of the Earth. *"It is a position not to be controverted that the earth, in its natural uncultivated state was, and ever would have continued to be, the common property of the human race. In that state every man would have been born to property. He would have been a joint life proprietor with the rest in the property of the soil, and in all its natural productions, vegetable and animal,"*[284] he wrote.

Paine believed that civilization should provide advantages to everyone and that a person in poverty or with no wealth is in a worse state *"than he would have been had he been born in a state of nature, and that civilization ought to have made, and ought still to make, provision for that purpose* [of providing everyone the value of their lost natural inheritance], *it can only be done by subtracting from property a portion equal in value to the natural inheritance it has absorbed"* from other people, to be provided in compensation to them.[285]

He proposed an estate tax to accomplish this, using the funds generated to provide everyone at age 21 sufficient wealth to start a farm to earn a livelihood, and a pension sufficient for a decent livelihood starting from age 50, and to support the disabled. He chose to tax wealth upon death for these purposes *"because it will be the least troublesome and the most effectual, and also because the subtraction will be made at a time that best admits it* [since it] *is at the moment that property is passing by the death of one person to the possession of another. In this case, the bequeather gives nothing: the receiver pays nothing. The only matter to him is, that the monopoly of natural inheritance, to which there never was a right, begins to cease in his person. A generous man would not wish it to continue, and a just man will rejoice to see it abolished."*[286]

A tax to enhance the productive capacity of the following generation

Rather than acting on Paine's vision of everyone starting adulthood with wealth sufficient to begin a productive life, today we force many young people to start adulthood with mountains of student loan debt, from under which many will never dig out. In The New Enlightenment, we will act on Paine's vision for young adults in a way appropriate for our times. In Paine's time, acquiring what was necessary to farm was the main way to earn a living. Today knowledge acquisition is most important, so society should offer resources for this purpose, and provide it, as Paine likely would, using a tax on wealth transfers at death.

The major contribution that knowledge makes to wealth creation today, unlike in Paine's time (although it was important then also), is discussed further in Part 4, Note 1. To use much of modern society's large accumulation of inherited knowledge and advance it to further improve our capacity to create wealth requires widespread knowledge acquisition. Society should now facilitate this with free access to post-secondary education and more federal support for an improved and more equitable K-12 system. In The New Enlightenment, we also provide funds for business (not necessarily farm) acquisition, with public funds sourced elsewhere—a policy that Paine's writings indicate he would also likely approve (policy 3).

Our large and growing income disparities are to an important degree created by our huge and growing inherited wealth disparities. Since 2009, corporate profits, dividend payouts, and the stock market have all risen sharply, but for most people wages have stagnated or declined. As previously noted, the proportion of income from capital for the top 0.1% increased from 64% to 70% from 1996 to 2006.

In the United States in 2013, the richest 10% of households owned 75% of all the country's wealth and the top 1% of households owned 40% of the wealth. The bottom half of households owned just 1.1% of the country's wealth. But, as I noted previously, large amounts of some of the wealthy's wealth are hidden in tax shelters, and even when not in tax shelters self-reporting likely results in these statistics under-representing our huge wealth disparities. The largest fortunes are almost certainly higher than we know.

As an important way to reduce the growing economic divide and increase opportunity for all, we will replace the estate tax with an inheritance tax, using the progressive income tax rates defined earlier plus 5%, with an exemption. An estate tax taxes the donor, which is inappropriate, and taxing the donor has allowed this tax to be denigrated with the term "death tax," even though it is essentially a tax on the living heirs. The "death tax" label also implies that everyone who dies has to pay the tax, but under current law, only 0.14% of estates owed the tax in 2013.[287] We should tax inherited wealth more appropriately, based on each heir's ability to pay, using a progressive inheritance tax on the heirs.

The unjust and irrational exclusion of capital gains for taxation at death under the estate tax will be virtually eliminated by replacing the estate tax with The New Enlightenment's inheritance tax; the heir will pay the tax on the full asset's value on transfer, including any gains, above a $300,000 inheritance. For example: Now over half the value of assets transferred by estates worth over $100 million is comprised of capital gains.[288] An insignificant fraction of their capital gains will escape taxation using the New Enlightenment system.

Under The New Enlightenment income tax system, federal income tax revenue will be about 18% of national income. The New Enlightenment inheritance tax is designed to yield about 21% of inherited income. Since the distribution of inherited income is skewed toward much higher incomes than other income, taxing inheritances without an exemption will yield over 21% because the highest tax rate of 60% (55% income tax plus 5%), and the tax rates of 55% (50% income tax plus 5%) and 45% (40% income tax plus 5%), will be applied to a much larger fraction of inheritance tax payers than income tax payers. However, an exemption will be used below which inheritances will not be taxed.

The value of this exemption that will yield a 21% average tax is $300,000. This estimate is based on bequeathed wealth being of the same distribution as the 2010 Federal Reserve Survey of Consumer Finances wealth distribution and the assumption that on average five heirs will receive equal inheritances or portions of this bequeathed wealth. If the average number of heirs after the New Enlightenment inheritance tax is instituted is fewer than five, fewer than five exemptions would be applied, so over 21% of bequeathed wealth would be collected. If there are over five heirs less than 21% would be collected. However, if the average is over five heirs, an important purpose of the tax will still be served by distributing dynastic wealth to larger numbers of people in smaller portions. This inheritance tax will be a motive to do so to minimize the total tax paid that does not exist under the estate tax. For example:

For someone who bequeaths $30 million to one person, that person would pay the tax based on his income on $29,700,000, almost all of which would be at the 60% rate or about $17.8 million in taxes. If he bequeathed this amount to 100 people equally, no tax would be paid because each person would get $300,000 which is exempted. One hundred people receiving $300,000 would reduce inequality, and would generally increase consumption and associated economic activity much more than one person receiving about $12 million after tax. Assuming five heirs per estate, about 95% of the population will pay no inheritance tax.

Also, an increase in the inheritance tax will induce some of the wealthy to consume more, since less benefit to heirs will occur from money they do not spend, and this will stimulate the economy.

To prevent the avoidance of the tax through gifts by donors throughout their lives, the total of lifetime gifts and bequests below the exemption will not be taxed, then the inheritance tax is applied on the cumulative total of all prior year gifts above the $300,000 exemption, and applied on the amount not previously taxed. For example:

If a person receives $300,000 total in gifts over five years, no tax would be paid. If a $100,000 gift is received in the sixth year, our income tax schedule shows that from zero to $50,000 is not taxed, essentially lifting the exemption to $350,000, from $50,000 to $90,000 or $40,000 would be taxed at the income tax rate of 10% plus 5% or 15%, yielding $6,000 in tax, and from $90,000 to $100,000, or $10,000, would be taxed at 20% plus 5%, or 25%, yielding $2,500 in tax, or a total of $8,500. If a $100,000 gift is received in the seventh year, the tax rate for this $100,000 would be determined starting from the prior $100,000 above the exemption as a base. So the $60,000 from $100,000 to $160,000 would be taxed at a 20% plus 5% rate yielding $15,000 and the $40,000 from $160,000 to $200,000 would be taxed at a 40% plus 5% rate, yielding $18,000, or total $33,000 in tax.

In the past, the failure of estate tax supporters to address what exceptions should be made for family farms and family owned businesses was a prime reason for the success of estate tax opponents. Most people consider that forcing the sale of a farm or business to pay the tax is unjust because sometimes it could disrupt the heirs' lives. However, this concern is unjustified for our current estate tax. Only a handful of family farms and businesses owe any estate tax at all, and none have had to be liquidated to pay the tax.[289]

The New Enlightenment inheritance tax policy will eliminate the possibility of forced sales of family farms and family owned businesses by allowing heirs, when necessary, to defer taxes due on the value of inherited farms and businesses, no matter how far in the future, by giving a loan on the tax amount, or any necessary portion of it, to the heir, with only interest payments required at a market rate of interest until disposition. Paying down principal will not be required until the sale of the business, or the time that cash or liquid assets are acquired sufficient to pay the remaining portion of the tax. Of course, business value will be appraised in consideration of any outstanding business loans. This will make the loan on the tax amount affordable using business income. This deferral option will be available only to the extent that the tax could not be paid with other inherited liquid assets, including excess cash in the business's accounts and assets owned by the business that it is not using for business operations, after leaving a reasonable cushion.

Another perspective on this arrangement is: The government would immediately receive the business value of the tax amount by the heir in all cases, but when necessary would lease back the portion of the business whose value is the tax amount. The annual lease fee would be equal in value to what would be the interest and principal payment on a standard business loan on the tax amount, until the time that the loan would have been paid.

If the heir held onto a business for life and ultimately bequeathed it, the new heir will owe the remaining portion of the loan on the tax of the previous owner. The deferral with interest will again be available on the remaining value in the business in consideration of all its outstanding loans.

Frequently, heirs sell family businesses because they do not wish to continue operating them, and the evidence indicates that businesses owned or managed by heirs tend to perform relatively poorly.[290]

Land or collectibles or other illiquid (not easily or quickly sold) assets will also be provided the deferral option with interest. However, since these assets may not be income generating, the loan will have to be supported by other income, or the asset could be sold to pay the tax.

This inheritance tax will yield $253 billion or $241 billion more per year than the estate tax it will replace (assuming an average bequest is to five heirs). Our inheritance tax satisfies the total funding requirements for free college education and the following federal education expenses. The resulting increase in federal funds will be "earmarked" or devoted exclusively for these purposes to make the benefits of this policy more obvious.

There continue to be many underperforming schools, and international comparisons indicate we need to do far more to assist schools in low-income neighborhoods, where the property taxes that are a large source of funding for schools are inadequate. In contrast to European and Asian nations, which fund schools centrally and equally, the wealthiest U.S. school districts spend nearly ten times more than the poorest, and spending ratios of three to one are common within states.[291]

Of the 1.8 million high school graduates who took the ACT test in 2013, only 26% reached the college readiness benchmarks in all basic subjects. Only 5% of Americans ages 25 to 34 whose parents didn't finish high school has a college degree. 23% is the average of 20 rich countries in an OECD study.[292] Both unequal access to good quality K-12 education because of the huge funding disparities and huge financial barriers to a college education are mainly responsible for this enormous and ominous international disparity.

Thirty years ago, the average gap on SAT-type tests between children of families in the richest and poorest 10% of Americans was about 90 points on an 800-point scale. In 2014, it was 125 points, one of the worst gaps in the 65 countries participating in the Program for International Student Assessment.[293]

In addition to reversing our nation's decline in the educational status of our citizenry and ensuring a well-educated citizenry through free college education, New Enlightenment policy is to provide substantial additional support to relatively poorly funded K-12 school districts.

We will provide an additional $90 billion to meet the goal of ensuring that every child receives an education that prepares him or her for success in college, careers, and life. We spent $621 billion in 2011–12 on public education in total at all levels of government.[294] Considering per-student spending disparities as large as ten to one between some school districts, and the inadequacy of the $51 billion total federal spending under the No Child Left Behind Act and Elementary and Secondary Education Act in eliminating education quality disparities, $90 billion could be well used to raise the quality of education in our lower funded schools. This funding will include a requirement that all students participate in physical education and the study of nutrition. We can best address the problem of the explosion in obesity and diabetes nationwide through education of the young.

The reduction in administrative costs and the promotion of evidence-based education reforms will be a part of this reform, as in the college education reform.[295] Experimental reforms should include more individualized instruction using newly developing technological tools, and greater freedom by students to be engaged in planning their own learning experiences based on their interests and learning pace. World knowledge is now doubling about every two years, and the rate of increase is itself increasing, so the most important skills to learn in school are independent learning skills. Allowing students to pursue their own interests to a larger degree will help develop the independent learning skills needed for a lifetime of learning in many occupations, as well as for full democratic participation. It also motivates and facilitates the learning process.

The total additional expenditures budgeted for K-12 education, and the $138 billion expense for free college education, is $228 billion, which the revenue from this inheritance tax will satisfy, with $13 billion remaining for other purposes.

*The New Enlightenment: Ideals of Democracy, Human Rights, Reason, and Progress * Policy 10*

James Madison and Thomas Jefferson said this referring to limiting inheritance:

"The evil of an excessive & dangerous cumulation of landed property in the hands of individuals is best precluded by the prohibition of entails, by the suppression of the rights of primogeniture," wrote Madison.[296]

"I am conscious that an equal division of property is impracticable, but the consequences of this enormous inequality producing so much misery to the bulk of mankind, legislators cannot invent too many devices for subdividing property, only taking care to let their subdivisions go hand in hand with

the natural affections of the human mind." Thomas Jefferson, who cited Adam Smith in his writings on the subject:

"A power to dispose of estates for ever is manifestly absurd. The earth and the fulness of it belongs to every generation, and the preceding one can have no right to bind it up from posterity. Such extension of property is quite unnatural." Adam Smith [297]

Corporate Tax Reform Including the Ending of Tax Haven Abuse

Corporate tax revenue has fallen from about 6% of gross domestic product in the 1950s to less than 2% today.[298] This enormous decline resulted from the reduction of statutory rates, and an increase in tax loopholes including the use of offshore tax havens. In fiscal 2011, total corporate federal taxes paid fell to lowest level since at least 1972, 12.1% of profits earned from activities within the U.S. Companies paid on average from 1987 to 2008 a 25.6% effective rate, far below the 35% top statutory corporate tax rate resulting from decades of corporate lobbying reducing it from 52% in the 1950s.[299] Corporations have exploited loopholes in our tax system and have lobbied successfully to increase those loopholes—a lucrative activity for lobbyists and their firms, with high social costs.

As noted earlier, between 2008 and 2010, thirty large corporations spent $475 million lobbying Washington, and as a result, twenty-nine paid zero in taxes and instead received tax rebates over those three years. General Electric received $5 billion, while it had profits of $10.5 billion. The total value of the rebates received by the thirty corporations was near $11 billion. Since the combined lobbying expenses during the period were only $475 million they received a 2,216% rate of return on their lobbying investment.

Multinational corporations complained that the higher rates of earlier decades made them "less competitive," so we "reformed" rates down to 35%. Then they went from country to country, complaining that their tax rates made businesses "less competitive," so these countries also "reformed" their tax rates. So now our statutory rates again are higher than rates in many other nations. This "downward spiral" has shifted tax burdens worldwide away from the wealthiest and reduced governments' resources.

As shown on page 24's graph, since 1950, there has been a dramatic rise in the share of federal revenue supplied by the extremely regressive payroll tax from about 10% to 40%, while there has been a dramatic fall in the share of federal revenue from corporate taxes, from about 30% to 6%. Meanwhile, corporate profits are at a 60-year high, well above where they were before the Great Recession hit.

Publicly listed corporations are hoarding a record $4.75 trillion that is not being used productively, and in the third quarter of 2012 corporate earnings were $1.75 trillion.[300] Meanwhile, we cut government services, exploded the deficit, and left 23.2 million people unemployed.[301] At the same time that corporations are making huge profits, workers' wages are declining. Between 2007 and 2012, wages fell for the entire bottom 70 percent of the wage distribution, despite productivity growth of 7.7 percent.[302]

Corporate shareholders are the beneficiaries of the reduced taxes. In 2007, the top 10% owned 81.2% of all corporate stock. The bottom 60% of us owned 2.5%. Taxes on corporations are taxes on those with the greatest ability to support the democratically determined needs of society. Taxes on corporations are also well justified because they and their major owners are benefiting the most from the vast resources of society.

U.S. companies that earn profits outside our borders pay tax on their income minus any taxes they pay to other countries. So if a company pays a tax rate of 10% in the other country, it has to pay a tax rate of only 25% here. But they need not pay any tax until they "repatriate" the money, or bring it back to the U.S. To take advantage of this loophole, companies move jobs, factories and profit centers to tax havens out of the country to keep their profits outside the U.S.

Multinational corporations are holding about $2 trillion outside of the country to "defer" their taxes. The largest U.S.-based companies expanded their untaxed offshore stockpiles by 14.4%, or $183 billion, in just one year, according to data compiled by Bloomberg.[303] Microsoft, Apple, and Google each added to their non-U.S. holdings by over 34%. Combined, these three companies alone plan to keep $134.5 billion untaxed by our government, over double the $59.3 billion they withheld two years earlier. Apple alone has over $100 billion outside the country. Google reported $10 billion in profits in Bermuda in 2011.

The accumulation of offshore profits—totaling $1.46 trillion for the 83 companies Bloomberg examined—is increasing, because of the incentives in the U.S. tax code for booking profits offshore and leaving them there. A Government Accountability Office study reported that of the 100 of the largest publicly traded companies, 83 reported operating in tax havens, often in several simultaneously.[304]

What makes these actions by our tech companies especially galling is that they profit greatly because of costly investments in basic research by our government, for instance, in developing the Internet, the browser, and microelectronics. They take from what our society has provided, and then diligently work to abdicate their democratically determined responsibilities for supporting our society.

Investing abroad means creating jobs abroad. With trade liberalization, the goods produced by American multinationals abroad can then be sold in the U.S. We provide multinationals with American innovations and profitable American markets. A rational and democratic government would not then allow them to not only escape paying taxes to the U.S. but also encourage them to create jobs and income abroad.

More than 70% of Fortune 500 companies use offshore tax havens to avoid paying U.S. taxes. America's leading companies have set the example for others to follow. One scheme involves transferring intellectual property (patents, etc.) to a subsidiary registered in a tax-haven country, whose main overseas physical location is often just a mailbox. They do this to make it appear that a big part of customer costs are intellectual property license fees paid to that subsidiary, so profits can be made in a country with no tax.

Another, relatively new, and increasingly popular, scheme involves renouncing corporate citizenship entirely. The company merges with a foreign rival in a country with lower taxes and then reincorporates there while continuing its business in the United States. Many corporations have committed, and many more are considering, this unconscionable betrayal of their homeland.

Thomas Jefferson warned us, *"Merchants have no country. The mere spot they stand on does not constitute so strong an attachment as that from which they draw their gain."*[305]

The federal government loses over $150 billion in revenues each year through tax haven abuse, and this amount is likely to increase substantially.[306] Tax haven abusers benefit from our markets, infrastructure, educated workforce, government sponsored research and security, but then they avoid responsibility for paying for these services by using tax havens. To compensate for the loss, we have to increase revenues from other sources, cut public spending priorities, or increase the national debt. Also, multinationals' ability to transfer profits overseas unfairly disadvantages small businesses.

Tax havens also deprive state governments of billions of dollars. In 2011, the states lost approximately $39.8 billion in tax revenues from corporations and wealthy individuals who sheltered money in foreign tax havens. Multinational corporations account for over $26 billion of the lost tax revenue, and wealthy individuals account for the rest.[307]

Corporate tax haven abusers in the past have influenced government officials to give them a very low tax rate or a "repatriation tax holiday" to bring their huge accumulation of profits back to the U.S. and use it to "create jobs." The companies brought the money back, and not only didn't "create jobs," they moved even more jobs, factories, and profit centers out of the country, assuming they will eventually get another "repatriation tax holiday." The multinational corporations holding $2 trillion in subsidiaries outside the country, untaxed, have said that they will not bring the money back without another "tax holiday."

This untaxed $2 trillion represents about $700 billion in government revenue we could use to put people to work repairing our roads, bridges (24% of America's bridges are structurally deficient or functionally obsolete), and schools, and for our other policy proposals that require funding that will improve all of our lives.

The Solution

Taking production or corporate headquarters location out of consideration in determining corporate tax would end the harmful practices of locating factories, dummy subsidiaries and corporate headquarters in low or no tax countries. This New Enlightenment policy does this by taxing corporations on the same percentage of their total profits as their percentage of revenue from sales in the U.S., initially at a flat tax rate of 35%. For example:

- Exavoid Corporation has $100 million of sales worldwide in 2012.
- $15 million of those sales (15% of total sales) are made in the U.S.
- Exavoid Corporation's total worldwide profits are $10 million.
- 15% of Exavoid Corporation's worldwide profit, $1.5 million, will be taxed as U.S. income at a flat tax rate of 35%. It will pay $525,000 in tax.

Using this method, it will not matter whether the Exavoid Corporation is a U.S., multinational or foreign corporation. Corporations will be taxed based on where they sell, instead of where they claim profits. This will eliminate tax avoidance by locating profit centers in tax havens and eliminate a motive for foreign countries to lower their corporate tax rates to get U.S. corporations to expatriate or otherwise move jobs, factories and profit centers out of the U.S. to keep their profits from being made here.

If a foreign company wants to do business in the U.S. it will be required to be taxed using this method on sales in the U.S. Profits and revenues of all subsidiaries worldwide of corporations selling products in the U.S. will be included in determining the tax, so corporations could not avoid the tax by transferring profits to subsidiaries not doing business in the U.S.

Some argue that we shouldn't tax corporations because they just "pass through" taxes to their customers through higher prices. But corporate taxes are on profits, and companies optimally price their products to maximize profits. If they increase prices to cover taxes, they will reduce profits, which would be counterproductive. There will, therefore, be little or no effect on prices.

A possible reason prices may be reduced by the policy exists if corporate behavior mirrors to some degree individual behavior in response to higher taxes. As I showed in Part 1, historical evidence indicates that CEOs are less likely to take exorbitant incomes when top tax rates are high because they get a smaller portion of their pretax income above the income on which the top rate is applied. Excess corporate profits often result from abusing anti-competitive positions. Just as with CEOs, if taxes are higher, corporations will get a smaller portion of their pretax income, so they will have less of a motive to abuse anti-competitive positions to increase their income, in this case through abusively high prices.

Taxing corporations on their profits at a higher rate increases any motivation that corporations may have to pay workers higher wages since higher wages would reduce profits, which would reduce taxes. In effect, 35% of any wage increase will be paid by the government if corporations pay taxes at a 35% rate. However, we will reform current law to limit the deduction of compensation over 12 times the pay of lowest paid worker in a corporation. Currently, some CEOs are paid annual compensation in the tens, and even hundreds of millions of dollars, or thousands of times the pay of their lowest paid worker. Corporations get to reduce their taxes by fully deducting these exorbitant amounts from their taxed profits.

No current limit exists on this deduction if the compensation is paid in stock options, pension, and deferred compensation, or if it meets the conditions of a non-equity incentive plan. A regular salary limit of $1 million for tax deductibility exists, but this limit is routinely exceeded by using the loopholes of the prior compensation types.

The unlimited tax deductibility of top management compensation is an important cause of the enormous rise of income inequality, which, in effect, the government is subsidizing. New Enlightenment policies will eliminate this abuse of tax law and decrease inequality by motivating corporations to raise the lowest paid worker's salary, stock or stock option compensation value if compensation increases at the top are desired. Corporations will still be free to pay higher than 12 times what goes to the lowest paid worker, but compensation in excess of this will no longer be essentially subsidized by the government through reduced taxes. (A mark-to-market capital gains tax for stock gains will be instituted, as described in Part 4, Note 1, pages 448-449.)

We will lead efforts to have an international agreement to tax corporations using this method. All countries have been damaged by corporate use of tax havens, and the race to the bottom in corporate tax rates, and rising inequality. Wouldn't other countries welcome the U.S.' lead in correcting these injustices?

Unfortunately, potential schemes also exist to avoid taxes using this tax system, but regulations could eliminate or greatly restrict them. However, the most beneficial way to eliminate avoidance possibilities is an international agreement on this taxing method. This method is the most just method of taxation since companies would, in essence, be paying for access to the market of the country or countries they would sell to. The more sales to a country, the more tax to that country is appropriate. If enough countries agree and put a high tariff on goods from countries that don't participate in the agreement, this would be effective. If the U.S. advocated for such an agreement that would be in the best interest of all countries, it can be accomplished.

Great increases in corporate wealth have inevitably led to great increases in corporate political and media propaganda power. This trend is turning on its head the view that all reasonable people have had, that the purpose of the corporate form and the businesses that use it (and our entire economic system) ultimately is to serve the economic best interests of all of society. This policy will be an important part of turning it right side up again.

With the initial flat corporate tax rate of 35%, this method of taxing corporations will raise approximately $550 billion per year or about $350 billion more than the current system. These estimates are the result of District Economics Group's detailed analysis of 2010 data.[308] Since corporate profits of corporations taxable at the corporate level (C corporations) have increased by

20% from 2010 to 2012 the revenue gains will be higher.[309] To be conservative in our budget analysis we use the $350 billion District Economics Group determined. In Part 4, Note 6, we make a "ballpark" estimate of revenue gains that results in a similar, but somewhat lower, value to that resulting from the detailed analysis of the District Economics Group.

The top corporate tax rate in the 1950s and 1960s was between 51% and 52%, during a period of economic boom and before the period when giant multinationals motivated the spiral down in international corporate tax rates. After the international agreement on The New Enlightenment corporate tax method, we will seek agreement on a gradual increase in the rate to 55% of profits, equivalent to the New Enlightenment top marginal income tax rate on individuals. This will increase revenues by $713 billion per year. In our budget accounting, we use the $350 billion increase that will result from a 35% rate.

*The New Enlightenment: Ideals of Democracy, Human Rights, Reason, and Progress * Policy 11*

Reduce Military Spending

The United States spends far more than any other country on defense and security. Since 2001, the base defense budget has soared from $287 billion to $530 billion, without even counting the costs of the Iraq and Afghanistan wars, which raised the total to $718 billion. This does not include the $127 billion of benefits for the veterans.

One Trident nuclear submarine could destroy 200 cities around the world with its multiple warheads before reloading. We have 18 of these submarines, each of which overwhelmingly deters any military attack. They can remain submerged for long periods without surfacing, are virtually undetectable when submerged, and are the nation's most survivable nuclear strike capability. Of course, these submarines represent a very tiny fraction of our military capabilities.

Using a nuclear weapon in a world where nine countries possess approximately 16,300 nuclear weapons, though, risks an unintended consequence: destroying most of the life on the planet.[310] (But it is mad to continue to rely on MAD (mutually assured destruction) to save us from this fate)

President Eisenhower's famous farewell address, warning the American people about the *"military-industrial-complex"* originally was a warning about the *"military-industrial congressional complex."* The *"congressional"* part was dropped because Eisenhower prided himself on the strength of his relations with a Congress of the opposing party, so he chose not to say anything that might harm that relationship. Unfortunately, we were thus deprived of Eisenhower's insight into the complex that has created a mindset in which our government tends to view many situations abroad as military challenges instead of, more beneficially for both our and foreign interests, preventive, diplomatic, and assistance missions. Lives will be saved by not having our soldiers patrol the world to the degree that exists now, provoking the populace into adverse responses in which they would not have otherwise engaged.

President Eisenhower, a West Point trained five-star general, also made this statement on the real costs of the military: *"Every gun that is made, every warship launched, every rocket fired signifies, in the final sense, a theft from those who hunger and are not fed, those who are cold and are not clothed...This world in arms is not spending money alone. It is spending the sweat of its laborers, the genius of its scientists, the hopes of its children."* Unfortunately military spending is necessary but most expenditures now are not. They are wasteful and harmful.

In November 2011, Admiral Ryan decried the *"gross mismanagement and cost overruns in expensive weapons programs, few of which have any relevance to the wars our troops are fighting today."* In a Senate floor speech, Senator and former presidential candidate John McCain accused the Pentagon of *"a shocking lack of any accountability"* for cost overruns and matching new weapons to actual combat needs.

Billions of dollars of contractor looting have been exposed by Pentagon audits and investigations by the GAO. No matter how obsolete, unnecessary, hazardously designed, or redundant (each military service has its own specially designed vehicles and aircraft), contracts keep getting renewed and overruns reimbursed year after year. Robert Gates, former Secretary of Defense and CIA director, described military spending after 9/11: *"What little discipline existed in the Defense Department when it came to spending has gone completely out the window,"* and *"America's civilian institutions of diplomacy and development have been chronically undermanned and underfunded for far too long, relative to what we spend on the military."* Former Air Force Chief General Merrill McPeak said, *"If we can't defend this country for $300 billion a year, we ought to get some new generals."*

By the time you read this, the war in Afghanistan will likely be over. The Obama administration requested $86 billion in military spending for this war in the 2013 fiscal year. That included only funds expended specifically for the costs of the war. This does not include soldiers' regular pay, only combat pay. The $86 billion also excluded the costs of future medical care for soldiers and veterans wounded in the war or the additional interest payments on the national debt that will result from higher deficits due to unfunded war spending.

The war is not likely to have made us safer, but instead put us at greater risk from the fury created in response to U.S. caused casualties. In every year of the war Afghan civilians died in higher numbers, many by drones the U.S. used illegally there and in Pakistan, Somalia, Yemen, and beyond. Our adversaries in Iraq, Afghanistan, and Pakistan had no air force, no navy, no artillery, no tanks or armored personnel carriers, no elaborate logistics, no battlefield communications, and no nighttime vision. They had little training, and their principal weapons were rifles, improvised exploding devices, and suicide belts.

About 25,000 to 30,000 Taliban fighters in sandals held at bay the world's most powerful military force, which has deployed over 130,000 soldiers plus an equal number of contractors in the field. It is hard to believe that U.S. soldiers were there to fight for our freedom and safety. We will organize a new opposition to ruinous runaway militarism.

We support these policy recommendations of the Institute for Policy Studies as conservative measures to reduce annual military spending while maintaining or increasing national security:

- Reduce the U.S. nuclear arsenal – a $20 billion saving per year:
  Reducing the nuclear arsenal to no more than 311 warheads will save $20 billion per year. An arsenal of that size would provide more than enough nuclear deterrence against current and future threats, according to the faculty of the Air War College and the School of Advanced Air and Space Studies. If we make this reduction, Russia has agreed to match it. This reduction will also give rise to major savings by saving on operations and maintenance costs—an under-recognized and huge portion of the Pentagon expense account.

- Eliminate two active Air Force wings and two carrier groups that are not needed to address current and probable future threats – a $8 billion saving per year.
- Scale back outsourcing – a $40 billion saving per year: A 15% decrease in non-Pentagon national security federal service contracts will save $3.3 billion per year, and the same decrease on military contracts would have saved $37.2 billion in 2013. These reductions could easily be achieved without reducing national security.[311]
- Close one in three U.S. military bases in Europe and Asia – a $10 billion saving per year:
- The United States maintains roughly 1,000 military bases worldwide. We support closing many, but in the near-term, bases in Europe and Asia, which serve what are now outdated Cold War purposes, should go first. We recommend that at least 50,000 troops be withdrawn from military bases in Europe and Asia. This will save $10 billion per year.
- End Foreign Military Financing – a $5 billion saving per year. The State Department spent $5 billion in 2013 on grants for foreign governments to buy U.S.-made weapons. This arms trade often fuels conflicts and contributes to human rights and international law violations. Ending this arms trade will save $5 billion per year.

When the wars in Iraq and Afghanistan are ended, the additional reduction in military spending resulting from the above policies from the current baseline of $530 billion will bring military spending to $447 billion. However, former Air Force Chief General Merrill McPeak's judgment that the country could be easily defended for $300 billion a year we believe is almost certainly correct, likely by a large margin because General McPeak would include one in any estimate he gave. The extreme waste and inefficiency has been discovered despite the fact that the GAO has determined the Defense Department budget to be unauditable. Donald Rumsfeld complained when he was Defense Secretary that about $3 trillion could not be traced.

The Center for American Progress discovered wasteful spending in these areas among others:

- Our spending on military R&D is significantly higher than that during the height of the Cold War.
- V-22 Osprey helicopters, despite bipartisan support to scrap production due to safety concerns and ongoing technical problems, continue to be purchased at $90 million each.

- A new nuclear research facility (CMRR-NF), has been budgeted, even though the House Appropriations Committee recommended delay because it has "*no coherent mission,*" and it would cost fifteen times more to maintain than the existing facility.
- We continue to purchase the Virginia class submarine, "*though it is ill-suited to fight today's asymmetrical wars*" at $2.6 billion each.[312]

The military budget is about half the entire discretionary budget of the U.S. government, yet it is not audited. This leads to enormous amounts of waste. One year the GAO caught the Air Force buying billions of dollars in spare parts because it did not know these parts were already purchased and in a warehouse. New Enlightenment policy requires the Department of Defense budget to be audited annually to discover waste and abuse.

Although we believe General McPeak's estimate is probably correct, and possibly an overestimate on the level of spending best for the country, we will not make this judgment without intelligence information that we cannot have in our current position. To be conservative, we will assume that waste reduction could be accomplished to bring spending down to the midpoint of our $437 billion and General McPeak's $300 billion estimate, or to a $368.5 billion annual expenditure, yielding a $161.5 billion saving per year.

*The New Enlightenment: Ideals of Democracy, Human Rights, Reason, and Progress * Policy 12*

Reduction of Other Wasteful Spending

The New Enlightenment Citizens Union (and eventually, Party) supports the "Green Scissors campaign" spending reduction recommendations. For over 18 years the Green Scissors campaign has been a collaboration between budget and environmental groups aimed at eliminating wasteful spending that is harmful to the environment. Its 2012 report is a collaboration between environmental organization Friends of the Earth, budget watchdog Taxpayers for Common Sense, and free market think tank R Street. Their views diverge significantly on most public issues and the role of government, but they joined together around one shared goal: exposing and eliminating wasteful and environmentally harmful spending. The recommendations in the Green Scissors report have been arrived at by consensus between all of the groups. We support the following of their policy recommendations:

- Considering the massive budget deficits and other important needs for federal revenue, and oil company revenues and profits reaching new highs, and the need to reduce carbon emissions, subsidies provided to the fossil fuel industry are irrational. It is time to eliminate subsidies for fossil fuels for these and other environmental reasons. The approximate saving per year in federal revenue that will result is estimated to be $15.8 billion.

- The environmentally risky nuclear industry receives enormous federal subsidies. Since the 1950s, it has benefited from federal supports for insurance, research and development, production tax credits, and borrowing or loan guarantees. These subsidies and others are for costs that should be borne by industry, not taxpayers. When eliminated, they will save the federal government $7.8 billion per year.

- Revenue savings and gains from policy reform on public lands: Profitable industries that extract resources on publicly owned lands benefit from outdated and unnecessary subsidies, or very low fees to the government for access to publicly owned resources, far below the value of the resource. For example: The 1872 general mining law allows companies that mine for precious metal on public lands to pay no royalties to the federal government for the right to profit from the precious metals. The price of gold is at all-time highs, over $1,600 an ounce as of April 2012. So while mining industries, such as the gold, copper and silver industries are busy filling their coffers, taxpayers are getting next to nothing. As a result, we lose billions of dollars in revenue per year.

The Powder River Basin area provides approximately 40% of the nation's coal. New Enlightenment policy is for the federal government to receive at least a market price for this coal. Instead, the highest bid ever received on a federal coal lease there was just $1.10 per short ton, despite the fact that coal from the region sells at approximately $10 per short ton, and even more when exported overseas. A higher than market price is justified to discourage its use since coal burning is an important source of carbon pollution. If the social costs of carbon were fully accounted for in the price little or no coal would be purchased and burned.

In many cases, the U.S. Army Corps of Engineers and the Bureau of Reclamation construct water resource projects are not economically justified and have serious negative environmental impacts. We will eliminate unnecessary and harmful projects.

The total savings and gains from policy reforms on public lands will yield to the federal government about $2.5 billion per year.

One Green Scissors subsidy reduction recommendation deserves special mention because of the size of its budgetary impact and its importance for our nation for other reasons, and its extraordinary importance for developing nations unjustly harmed by current policy:

Washington wastes billions of taxpayer dollars each year on misguided agricultural policies. Instead of providing a safety net for America's family farmers—the reason many political leaders say they support the programs— federal agricultural policy mainly provides subsidies on favored crops and to large-scale agricultural businesses that can thrive without governmental support. Other crops and small-scale U.S. farmers are then disadvantaged. Large corn growers just in the fifteen years between 1995 and 2009 received $73.8 billion in subsidies. Much of this corn is used to produce high fructose corn syrup at artificially low prices, motivating consumption in quantities that contribute to the explosion of diabetes among young people.

Agricultural subsidies have long-term detrimental effects on the global food system, and is especially harmful to food security in less developed countries. Subsidies result in some U.S. crops on the world market at below the cost of production and others at a price so low that developing world producers cannot survive on farm income at the artificially reduced crop prices, so are forced off their farms.

The impact of developed country cotton subsidies alone is devastating. Oxfam International found that the over ten million people in central and western African countries who rely on the production and sale of cotton, lose up to $250 million every year due to subsidies in developed countries. The Congressional Research Service found that the United States spent about $24 billion just on cotton subsidies over the past ten years. The World Trade Organization (WTO) ruled that U.S. cotton subsidies are illegal, yet we continue to violate WTO commitments seven years after that ruling.

Subsidies allow retaliation under WTO rules. In 2009, a WTO arbitration panel granted Brazil the authority to collect $147.3 million in damages, to impose punitive tariffs, and to lift patent protections on $829 million worth of United States goods.

In 2002, industrialized countries in the Organization for Economic Co-operation and Development (OECD) spent $300 billion on crop price supports, production payments and other farm programs. Countries with unsubsidized goods are essentially shut out of world markets, devastating their local economies.

In pursuit of subsidies, farmers often cultivate marginal farmland, where the nutrient depleted soils require intensive fertilization, or where the soil is on easily erodible hillsides. The resulting soil erosion, and overuse of fertilizers and pesticides both on nutrient depleted soils and to farm fertile croplands more intensely, is environmentally harmful.

If developed nations eliminated their subsidies and eliminated trade barriers, such as import tariffs protecting domestic producers from international competition, foreign aid may be unnecessary and rural poverty would be significantly reduced. Every subsidy dollar paid into the agriculture sectors makes developing countries' farm sectors that much less competitive. The International Food Policy Research Institute found that every year *"protectionism and subsidies by industrialized nations cost developing countries about US$24 billion."*[313]

The Research and Policy Program at the Global Development and Environment Institute at Tufts University found that in Mexico, due to U.S. agricultural subsidies, *"an estimated 2.3 million people have left agriculture in a country desperate for livelihoods."* The study estimated that the cost to Mexican producers was around $12.8 billion in a nine-year period, over 10% of annual U.S.-Mexico agricultural trade value. A major cause of the problem of illegal immigration from Mexico is our agricultural policy forcing Mexican farmers who can't compete with subsidized U.S. crops off their farms.

If developed country farm subsidies were eliminated, developing countries would have more funds for urgent public needs, such as providing safe water sources; every year, 2.5 million people die from dysentery and other intestinal diseases due to the lack of clean drinking water. Countries could also afford better medical care and access to tools to fight diseases. Over two million people, mostly in sub-Saharan Africa and Asia, die from malaria each year due to lack of access to effective pesticides and the high costs of effective malaria treatments. In Uganda alone, malaria kills about 400 people per day.

Additional revenues from agriculture would also allow poor countries to invest in the infrastructure to deliver electricity and natural gas to rural areas.

Millions of Africans die each year from cardiovascular diseases caused, in part, by poor indoor air quality, often a direct result of burning dung and wood for cooking fires and heat. Acute lower respiratory infections claim 4.5 million lives per year, mostly in developing countries.[314]

Also, wildlife populations in developing countries are devastated because of agricultural subsidies. At current prices, poaching often provides more revenue than farming.

Ending agricultural subsidies would benefit the federal budget, Third World farmers and countries, the environment, endangered species, and reduce our illegal immigration problem. The International Monetary Fund estimates that eliminating various agriculture subsidies in rich countries would raise global welfare by $100 billion.

New Zealand, a nation four times more economically dependent on farming than the United States ended its farm subsidies in 1984. The changes were initially met with fierce resistance, but New Zealand farm productivity, profitability, and output have increased since the reforms.[315]

Eliminating misguided agricultural subsidies will save the federal government $17.7 billion per year.

*The New Enlightenment: Ideals of Democracy, Human Rights, Reason, and Progress * Policy 13*

A Carbon Tax

The scientific evidence for warming of the climate system is overwhelming. Below is some noted on NASA's website:[316]

1) Global sea level rose about 17 centimeters (6.7 inches) in the last century. The rate in the last decade, however, is nearly double that of the last century.

2) All major global surface temperature determinations show that Earth has warmed since 1880. Most of this warming has occurred since the 1970s, with the 20 warmest years having occurred since 1981 and with all 10 of the warmest years in the last 12 years. Even though the 2000s witnessed a solar

output decline resulting in an unusually deep solar minimum in 2007-2009, surface temperatures continue to increase.

3) Greenland lost 150 to 250 cubic kilometers (36 to 60 cubic miles) of ice per year between 2002 and 2006, while Antarctica lost about 152 cubic kilometers (36 cubic miles) of ice between 2002 and 2005.

4) Glaciers are retreating almost everywhere around the world — including in the Alps, Himalayas, Andes, Rockies, Alaska, and Africa. Satellite observations reveal that the spring snow cover in the Northern Hemisphere has decreased over the last five decades and that the snow is melting earlier.

5) Statement on climate change from 18 scientific associations: "Observations throughout the world make it clear that climate change is occurring, and rigorous scientific research demonstrates that the greenhouse gases emitted by human activities are the primary driver."

CO_2 accounts for about 82% of all U.S. greenhouse gas emissions from human activities.[317] Our emissions will eventually cause a catastrophic degree of global warming, if we do not substantially reduce current emission levels. A carbon tax will reduce greenhouse gas emissions by reducing the burning of fossil fuels, which is the primary source of carbon emissions, and provide the additional benefit of reducing associated pollutants.

An interagency workgroup of the federal Government determined that the "social cost of carbon" (SCC) is $25 per ton (about 21 cents per gallon of gasoline).[318] The results were widely criticized for failing to account for the uncertainty about potential catastrophic outcomes. The Stockholm Environmental Institute U.S. Center published findings that accounted for the uncertainty about potential catastrophic outcomes. Its peer-reviewed report, "Climate Risks and Carbon Prices: Revising the Social Cost of Carbon," determined that SCC can be *"as high as $893 per tonne."* A carbon tax is needed to reduce and cover some of these costs.

U.S. oil imports remain astronomically high, and about 1.5 million barrels a day come from the troubled Persian Gulf.[319] A reduction in our consumption of oil by raising its price closer to its true cost through a carbon tax will improve our balance of trade and reduce our dependence on Middle East oil.

New Enlightenment policy is to tax fossil fuels (coal, oil, and gas), based on how many tons of carbon dioxide such fuels produce when burned, at the rate of $35 per metric ton of carbon dioxide or its equivalent. If the revenues from the tax went into New Enlightenment policies that require federal expenditure, middle-and lower-income Americans will come out far ahead.

A carbon tax will push energy companies and businesses to invest in new ways to reduce greenhouse gases through lower carbon fuels and products, and through energy conservation and efficiency improvements. Since this tax will lead to less carbon emissions, it will result in less tax over time. However, the tax rate per metric ton will be increased to keep the annual revenue constant, and to put increasing pressure on the market to lower carbon emissions.

Several European countries, including Denmark, Finland, Germany, Italy, the Netherlands, Norway, and Sweden, have imposed carbon taxes up to $89 per ton. Most are using the revenue to lower taxes on the majority of their labor force, producing modest increases in job creation.

A carbon tax is easy to administer because it is levied at the points where fossil fuels enter the U.S. economy. It will be applied to only a few thousand points of entry, such as mine mouths, well heads or ports, rather than hundreds of millions of downstream smokestacks and tailpipes. A tax of $35 per metric ton of carbon dioxide or its equivalent will raise about $210 billion per year.[320]

> *The New Enlightenment: Ideals of Democracy, Human Rights, Reason, and Progress * Policy 14*

Equal Charge for Nuclear Power Plants

The carbon tax will give a competitive advantage to renewable energy sources, which is desirable. Nuclear power results in serious disposal and other environmental problems so it should not be allowed to gain a market advantage over power using fossil fuels after we institute carbon taxes. Nuclear waste remains dangerously radioactive for hundreds of thousands of years, and no geological structure can assure stability that long. Also, nuclear plants are vulnerable to accident and sabotage, and nuclear material coursing its way through our roads makes it vulnerable not just at the plant to terrorists.

In March 2011, a massive earthquake and tsunami hit Japan and caused the worst nuclear accident since Chernobyl, and made the dangers of accidents clear. Public opinion polls show that only 39% support nuclear power.

New Enlightenment policies include a tax per BTU of energy produced by nuclear power equal to the average tax per BTU resulting from the $35 per metric ton carbon tax on oil, coal, and natural gas. This will maintain nuclear power's competitive position with power from fossil fuels after the institution of carbon taxes. This tax will raise about $24.1 billion per year.

> *The New Enlightenment: Ideals of Democracy, Human Rights, Reason, and Progress * Policy 15*

Hazardous Emissions/Release Taxes

Because of the adverse health and environmental consequences of toxic pollutants, we will impose a fee on the pounds of toxic pollutants released into the environment (air, water, or land) by manufacturing or processing facilities. This will motivate industry to reduce these pollutants. It will also raise the price of some products commensurate with their real cost, reducing demand for products that release toxins in their production process.

Metal mining facilities accounted for 30% of the total toxic releases in 2008, while electric utilities accounted for 23%. Also, smelting and refining are important sources. Among the toxic releases are lead and mercury.

Lead and mercury are known neurotoxins that cause brain damage in fetuses and children. They never degrade into safe compounds, but rather bioaccumulate in the food chain, especially fatty tissues of fish and animals, including humans. All mothers' milk contains these metals in varying levels, with the potential to harm nursing babies. There is no "safe" level of these toxins.

Coal-burning power plants are a leading source of both mercury and lead emissions due to the metals embedded in the coal. Technologies exist to remove these metals from waste gases, but power plants might increase the use of alternative fuels including renewables instead of installing new scrubbers or other controls.

The table shows toxic release amounts released per year by industry, with tax revenue based on a $5/lb. charge on toxic releases.

These taxes will motivate emissions/release reductions, and help pay for their harmful health and environmental consequences. They will yield $7.88 billion per year.

Toxic Release Amounts Released Per Year

(Value added, revenue estimate in $billions, toxic releases in millions lbs.)

Industry	Value added	Toxic releases	Revenue estimate	As % of value
Chemical & allied	355	468	2.34	0.66%
Primary metal	94	440.6	2.20	2.34%
Paper & allied products	79	186.1	0.93	1.18%
Transportation equip.	252	38.4	0.19	0.08%
Rubber & misc. plastic	91	40.2	0.20	0.22%
All others	1403	401.8	2.01	0.14%
Total	$2,274	$1,575	7.88	0.35%
(Source: Statistical Abstract of the United States: 2011, tables 1006 and 378)				

*The New Enlightenment: Ideals of Democracy, Human Rights, Reason, and Progress * Policy 16*

Financial Transactions Tax

The New Enlightenment's financial transactions tax will raise a substantial amount of revenue for public needs, serve an important regulatory role, and compensate for some of the harm that industry practices have caused. In these ways, it is similar to a pollution tax.

Before the recent financial crisis, large financial companies' bets were often paying off, and many made large profits, enabling some of their executives to become billionaires, but when their bets failed, our society took the devastating losses. The losses totaled $22 trillion of wealth through reduced economic output and the real estate price crash.

It is reasonable for the financial sector to play a significant role in deficit reduction because of the large role it played in creating the current debt crisis worldwide, both through the costs of the bailouts and the lost revenues from the extended recession. The recession has been a major cause of the increase in the national debt since 2007. But, despite the evidence that it has imposed large costs on society, the financial sector has succeeded in escaping taxation.

Before the crisis, 40% of the total of all profits of all U.S. corporations went to the financial industry. The vast wealth now being directed to this industry is attracting many bright young people, some of the country's best minds. Instead of going into some profession that serve others, such as medicine, teaching, public service, or scientific research, they are increasingly choosing finance because of the possibility of extreme financial rewards. Just before the financial crises, almost half of Harvard's graduating class took jobs on Wall Street.[321] The percentages are similar at other Ivy League colleges.

With so many talented young people in finance, it's not surprising that there would be innovation in that industry. But many of these "financial innovations" that circumvented regulations lowered long-run economic performance. Many of the nation's most highly trained and intelligent people spend their time and talent finding the most effective ways to squeeze more money out of assets, or take the assets or income of others. One way is through short-term or "flash" stock trading, which essentially takes the value of assets from others. Nothing of value is created, instead, money is moved to those with the most effective computer algorithm, and fastest connections and computers. These activities are a poor use of many of our nation's most talented minds. They are incentivized to produce a social value that does not compare with that of real innovations like the transistor, computer, laser, or the Internet that increased our standard of living.

This industry for many years has been taking an unjustifiably large and increasing portion of the country's income, accounting for about 14% of GDP in 2007, up from about 4% in 1950. The resulting governmental policy influence derived from their vast wealth has been used to the detriment of the general population. A recent dramatic example was the industry's influence resulting in financial deregulation, which was the primary cause of the worst financial crises since the Great Depression.

As the finance industry has risen, manufacturing industries have fallen as a percentage of the economy, as the graph on page 58 shows. The financial industry has played a role in our manufacturing sector's decline through its sole interest of profit maximization. Sending manufacturing jobs to low wage, low tax countries where lax environmental and labor standards exist, maximizes the profits of their business investments. Thomas Jefferson's warning has repeatedly proven to be prescient: *"Merchants have no country. The mere spot they stand on does not constitute so strong an attachment as that from which they draw their gain."*

Ideally, the financial industry serves an important role in our economy by providing payment systems, and by directing and providing information and opportunities for others to direct capital where it can be most productively used. We need policies to ensure that it well serves these roles; some financial industry practices have not. The recent crisis was a rude awakening to this fact that should long ago have been clear.

Our financial sector often misallocates capital, prioritizes exploitation and market manipulation and has created an unnecessarily expensive payment mechanism. Modern technology enables the transfer of money from a consumer to a merchant for a fraction of a cent. Instead, banks are charging merchants 1% - 3% or more of the purchase price. We all pay this exorbitant charge because merchants must pass on this cost through the price.[322]

As I noted previously, Martin Wolf, named in the top 100 lists of global thinkers by Prospect and by Foreign Policy magazine, and associate editor and chief economics commentator at the Financial Times (regarded as the most credible and important publication internationally in reporting financial and economic issues), wrote: *"An out-of-control financial sector is eating out the modern market economy from inside, just as a the larva of the spider wasp eats out the host in which it has been laid."*

Finance is intended to increase the ability of companies to make fixed investments. But as the graph on page 63 shows, as finance has tripled in share of GDP from about 4% to 12% between 1950 and 2009, fixed investments have slightly declined.

The financial industry and some of its wealthy investors motivated the institution of several public policies that led to the recent crisis. Some are described in *Now Is the Time for The New Enlightenment*. These same interests motivated the institution of a much lower capital gains and "carried interest" tax rate than a labor tax rate. Wall Street financiers pay taxes at a much lower "carried interest" or capital gains tax rate on income that comes from managing assets for private equity funds or hedge funds—about half what other high-income people pay on their labor income.

The financial sector is a prime source of rising inequality; worldwide, one in five billionaires comes from that industry. In the U.S. in 2005, 13.9% of the top 1% were financial professionals, up from 7.7% in 1979. They increased their share of the top 0.1% from 11% to 18%, and accounted for 70% of growth of the top 0.1%'s share of national income over the same period.[323] One cause is the unjustly restricted taxation in this sector.[324]

Policies serving the financial industry have resulted in shifting costs to the rest of the population. A financial transactions tax, equal treatment of capital gains and "carried interest" with the labor rate in the tax code, a public banking sector, support of credit unions and worker-owned banks, and an improved regulatory structure are New Enlightenment policies to help ensure that the financial industry best serves society.

A financial transactions tax will raise large amounts of revenue to serve the public good, and it will also be an important regulatory measure for the following reason:

The Dodd-Frank legislation was intended to limit practices that triggered the Great Recession but did not do so sufficiently. Some industry practices continue to place us at risk of devastating harm, now one in a new way.

In the few years since the collapse of Lehman Brothers nearly led to the collapse of the global financial system, new technologies have made markets less transparent, and faster than ever before. Stock exchanges can now execute trades in less than a half a millionth of a second. Financial firms use sophisticated algorithms to execute trades sometimes at 10,000 times a second, seeking tiny financial gains per trade and ending the day not owning the stocks that they traded.

Bizarrely, high-speed trading algorithms are now responsible for over half of U.S. trading. This "flash trading" wiped out nearly $1 trillion in stock market value on May 6, 2010, in a matter of minutes, and then rose almost as rapidly, closing down 3% from the previous day. Prices determined by this kind of trading process are not based on research of company or market fundamentals, on which prices in a well-functioning market are intended to be based.

The financial industry spent $2.2 billion on lobbying during the period of development of the Dodd-Frank legislation. *More than 3,000 lobbyists* worked on financial reform legislation in 2010 while Dodd-Frank was debated. Half of them had previously worked as Capitol Hill aides, members of Congress, or executive branch staffers, and their influence resulted in that law doing almost nothing to regulate high-speed trading.

Studies have revealed that short-term financial transactions contribute to economic volatility without enhancing long-term economic performance and have previously caused financial crises.[325] They also lead firms to focus excessively on the short term. Such "short-termism" contributed to the recent crisis and shifts attention away from the longer term investments essential for long-term productivity increases and economic growth.

Flash trading will likely lead to another financial crisis if not regulated or otherwise discouraged. The New Enlightenment financial transactions tax will strongly discourage flash and other short-term trading. It will also raise large amounts of revenue in a highly progressive way due to the income distribution of the investor population, especially those doing speculative trading, being highly skewed toward high incomes.

We tax all products and services in the United States when they go through a public transaction, from daily necessities to luxury items, except stocks, bonds and derivatives. This inconsistency is irrational and means we're subsidizing speculation in financial instruments. The inconsistency is also unjust because it essentially subsidizes mainly wealthy financial transaction practitioners. We are compounding this injustice by taxing any resulting gains at a much lower capital gains rate than the rate on labor income and not taxing capital gains before heirs receive assets.

A financial transactions tax will help solve important societal problems. Researchers at the Political Economy Research Institute of the University of Massachusetts, Amherst analyzed a tax of the following design, which we propose be instituted.[326] The table shows the revenue generated if trading volume fell by 50% in all financial markets as a result of the tax. The researchers believe it will fall no more than 50% relative to current levels of trading, so the revenues generated could be higher than shown in the table.

Other researchers have determined different amounts of revenue generated, some much less, but the Political Economy Research Institute's estimate is most likely to be closest to the actual revenue generated. However, to be conservative, we will use a revenue generated amount of $300 billion in our budget analysis.

Financial Instrument	Proposed Tax Rate	Revenue Generated
Stocks	0.5%	$62 billion
Bonds	0.15%	$170 billion
Derivatives	0.005%	$120 billion
	Total	$352 billion

Over 30 countries, including Australia, Hong Kong, Singapore, Switzerland, and the U.K., have some form of a financial transactions tax. Of the G20 nations, 16 have a financial transactions tax, and the U.K. has a 0.5% tax. The European Union recently voted to implement a financial transactions tax in at least 11 member nations. With so many European, and several Asian, countries with the tax, there's little chance that trading will move overseas as a result of the U.S having one. The U.K. has had a tax on stock trades for centuries, throughout periods when its volume of trading has grown robustly.

The New Enlightenment Party or Citizens Union would advocate for the United States to lead efforts for an international agreement on a uniform financial transactions tax to serve important public needs globally.

> *The New Enlightenment: Ideals of Democracy, Human Rights, Reason, and Progress * Policy 17*

Real Property Transfer Tax

New Enlightenment policy will also apply a .5% financial transaction tax to real estate transactions—justified for a reason the financial transaction tax is: All other products and services in the United States are taxed when they go through a public transaction. This tax will be collected on the sale and transfer of commercial and residential real property. Sales of real estate in 2013 totaled $1.61 trillion.[327] A tax of 0.5% will yield $8.1 billion per year. The tax is progressive because most of the value of real estate transactions is from high value transactions by corporations and wealthy individuals.

> *The New Enlightenment: Ideals of Democracy, Human Rights, Reason, and Progress * Policy 18*

Mortgage Interest Deduction Elimination

Real estate and building industry groups have opposed proposals to reduce or eliminate the mortgage interest deduction (MID). They have succeeded in convincing the public of disproportionate value to the middle class. This perception, though prevalent, is not accurate. Most taxpayers do not benefit from the deduction because they do not itemize deductions on their federal income tax returns. Only about 30% of taxpayers itemize, rather than take the standard deduction, the majority are upper-middle and upper-income households.

The wealthiest Americans regularly take advantage of the mortgage-interest tax deduction to finance their mansions, luxury vacation homes, and yachts. Yes, even yacht interest can be deducted if it has a sleeping, cooking, and toilet facility and an individual lives in it (or claims to) for at least two weeks a year. So taxpayers are subsidizing the owner of the yacht in the following picture. This table details how benefits are distributed by income level.

Population segment	Income Upper Limit	Income Mean[328]	Average annual savings from MID per taxpayer[329]
lowest quintile	$20,262	$11,239	$0
second quintile	$38,520	$29,204	$22
middle quintile	$62,434	$49,842	$68
fourth quintile	$101,582	$80,080	$200
highest quintile		$178,020	$811
top 1%		$1,530,773	$3,333

The Congressional Budget Office found that 73% of the $70 billion tax loss expenditure in 2013 of the MID went to the top income quintile, with 38% going to the top 5% and 15% to the top 1%. The average taxpayer in the top 1% saved over 111 times what the average taxpayer saved in the bottom 60%.

Homeowners are paying for the tax subsidy when they buy their homes because the mortgage interest deduction is built into the price. That means the majority of homeowners have paid for the benefit of the mortgage interest deduction when they bought their house but received no benefits, and for many of those who did, the small benefit did not compensate for the increase in price.

The claim that the deduction encourages home ownership is not borne out by the evidence. No association exists between homeownership rates and the deduction internationally. Research shows that the tax deduction just rewards behavior—buying a home—that would happen anyway. The resulting large loss in revenues from this deduction will be eliminated by New Enlightenment policy to help support our shared prosperity policies.

This and the prior policy will have the effect of slightly lowering real estate prices, but the effect of the far greater sharing of prosperity of New Enlightenment policy changes would be to raise real estate prices to a larger degree. This policy and the prior policy will have a beneficial moderating effect on real estate price increases. They will also be important in supporting the funding requirements of our *Prosperity for All* and *Government of, for, and by the People* policies. Eliminating the MID will result in about a $70 billion increase in revenue per year.[330]

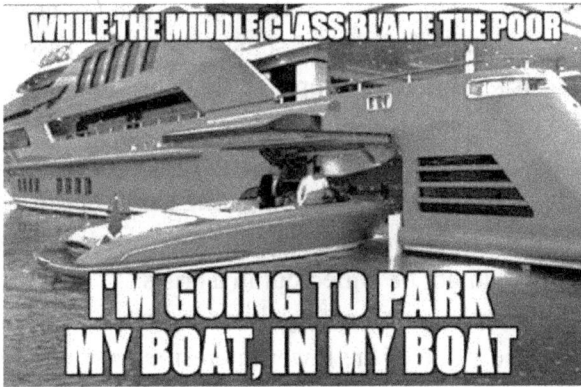

WHILE THE MIDDLE CLASS BLAME THE POOR

I'M GOING TO PARK MY BOAT, IN MY BOAT

(This image was posted on the image-sharing site imgur.com on 4/8/15 and reached the number 1 slot on reddit.com after being upvoted by thousands of people in just a few hours. This indicates a growing awareness that an unjust portion of our nation's enormous wealth is going to a tiny elite. Meanwhile, some lawmakers and media pundits promulgate fictitious anecdotal stories of extravagant spending by welfare and food stamp recipients and other people on government aid to stoke middle class resentment and help motivate tax reductions on the wealthy. Welfare and food stamp recipients can barely survive on what they receive, and qualifying requirements for government assistance limit recipients to those in serious need. Also, U.S. Department of Health and Human Services statistics show that the Temporary Assistance for Needy Families Program and the Food Stamp Program have participation rates of 50% and 60%, respectively, of the people eligible. The image is of a massive 196-foot yacht with a gym, a floating indoor boat garage, and an aquarium.)

---

*The New Enlightenment: Ideals of Democracy, Human Rights, Reason, and Progress * Policy 19*

"Too Big to Fail" Bank Fee

An annual $9 billion fee on banks with revenue over $50 billion annually has been proposed to pay for the TARP bailout funds that are not expected to be repaid and to pay a small fraction of some other costs associated with the recent financial crisis. This fee is opposed by banks and has not been instituted. These "too big to fail" banks should have to pay this fee, and also compensate for the insurance value resulting from their "too big to fail" status. They have an advantage over smaller competing banks because they can raise funds at lower interest rates than they would otherwise be able to if investors thought that they would not be bailed out in a crisis.

Based on International Monetary Fund research and calculations by Bloomberg News, the value of the lower interest rates resulting from the implied government supplied insurance policy is $83 billion annually. This estimate is consistent with those of other researchers. However, economists from New York University, Virginia Tech, and Syracuse University determined that the subsidy value is likely far higher.

Since the 1970s the share of industry assets held by the top five banks grew from 17% to 52%.[331] They take virtually all companies public, were involved in all mergers and acquisitions, play key roles in the pricing of commodities, and handled most of the trading in derivatives.[332] Allowing them to maintain their size and power poses systemic dangers and is a corrupting influence on our political system. Eventually, they should be broken up. A substantial tax on the biggest banks will motivate them to do so voluntarily.

Since some controversy exists over the insurance subsidy's exact value, we will institute a fee at the low end of a 10% error margin around the $83 billion estimate or a conservative $75 billion subsidy fee, in addition to the $9 billion for the past uncompensated financial harm to the country, or an $84 billion fee on the "too big to fail" banks per year. If this tax is not sufficient to motivate them to downsize within five years, the "too big to fail" banks should be required to downsize.

> *The New Enlightenment: Ideals of Democracy, Human Rights, Reason, and Progress * Policy 20*

Miscellaneous Taxes, Fees and Expense Reduction

Airline Fees
Airlines, or ultimately air travelers, should have to pay for the air traffic control system, and there should be an auctioning of airport landing and takeoff slots at airports. Currently, airlines or air travelers are subsidized for these costs, which inappropriately disadvantages rail transport. Disadvantaging rail transport has negative environmental consequences since rail travel has lower CO_2 emissions and other pollution costs per mile. This policy will yield approximately \$3.1 billion per year. [333]

Cigarette Tax
In 2009, the federal excise tax on cigarettes increased to \$1.01 per pack, primarily as a funding source for the State Children's Health Insurance Program. As an additional disincentive to start or continue this harmful habit and to raise revenue needed for the associated health costs, we will institute an additional 20 cents per pack tax. Higher taxes are especially effective disincentives to teenagers. Since taxes are already imposed on tobacco products, the administrative costs of increasing the tax will be negligible. 274 billion cigarettes (13.7 billion packs) were smoked in 2011. Some European countries and Canada tax tobacco at substantially higher rates than does the U.S. This tax will raise \$2.74 billion per year.

Alcohol Tax
We will increase alcohol taxes by 50%. The tax on beer is \$0.58 per gallon, on distilled spirits \$13.50 per proof gallon, and on wine, it varies from \$1.07 to \$3.40 per gallon depending on the alcohol content. The tax increase will therefore be \$0.29 per gallon for beer, \$6.75 per proof gallon for distilled

spirits, and on wine, from $.54 to $1.70 per gallon. Many European countries and Canada tax alcohol at substantially higher rates than those in the United States. Since alcohol taxes are already levied, the administrative costs of a rate increase are negligible. This tax will raise $4.75 billion per year.

The total revenue gain from these miscellaneous taxes and fees is $11 billion per year.

Current Anti-Poverty Program Expense Reduction Due to Poverty Reduction

Current federal government anti-poverty programs are duplicative and complex, many of which New Enlightenment policies will eliminate the need for. A March 2014 House Budget Committee report, "The War on Poverty: 50 Years Later," stated that at least 92 federal programs exist to help lower-income Americans. For instance, there are dozens of education and job-training programs, 17 food-aid programs, and over 20 housing programs. The federal government spent $799 billion on these programs in fiscal year 2012. The report also states that many anti-poverty programs, with little coordination between them, often work at cross purposes.

Unlike New Enlightenment policies, some current federal policies discourage work. The CBO found that some low-income households face implicit marginal tax rates of nearly 100%.[334] Our expanded EITC greatly encourages work, and it alone will eliminate the need for many other anti-poverty programs. And the availability of many worker-friendly, democratically run work environments resulting from Policy 3 will also encourage work.

Although many New Enlightenment policies require large federal expenditures, since they allow the elimination of many current programs and the costs of many others, and greatly advance our economic and political systems, the policies are well worth the costs.

Some of the larger current anti-poverty program categories where expenditures will be greatly reduced through New Enlightenment policies are in the table. Some savings in other programs the table does not account for. The savings are likely to be substantially larger. A large federal subsidy expenditure category not included is medical subsidies. We spent $250 billion on Medicaid alone in 2012. The New Enlightenment policies detailed in this book will greatly reduce these expenditures. We do not account for these savings because they will be accounted for in our health system reform proposal detailed in a future document.

Program category	2012* expenditures ($billions)
Temporary Assistance for Needy Families	16.7
Low Income Home Energy Assistance Program	3.8
Food Aid	105.0
Housing	49.6
Total costs	175.1

*most recent data available

Our wage subsidy, reemployment system, free college education, and increase in Social Security payments and minimum wage policies, and our policies to facilitate and support the establishment of worker-owned enterprises and other New Enlightenment policies, will reduce poverty incidence by over 90%. We will budget for a conservative percent reduction of the above anti-poverty expenditures of 70%. This results in a total savings per year of $123 billion.

*The New Enlightenment: Ideals of Democracy, Human Rights, Reason, and Progress * Policy 21*

The New Enlightenment policies' additional federal expenditures (-) and revenues (+) and savings (+) relative to 2013 federal expenditures and revenues

Estimate ($billions)	Description
-904	Income supplements
-420	Worker half payroll tax elimination
-300	Infrastructure, public works (estimate per yr. for 10 yrs. details TDB)
-382	Social security plus
-138	Free college education
-90	Elementary and Secondary Education
-143	Grants, tax and SBA expenditures to promote worker-ownership
-11.1	Free municipal broadband subsidy
-8.7	Public defenders and inmate rehabilitation
-3	Reemployment system
-2.3	Candidate postage cost subsidy
-1.7	"Primary" candidate newspaper subsidy
-2.2	New Democratic Forms
-6.3	Journalism subsidies
516	Wealth tax
350	Corporate tax reform, including the ending of tax haven abuse
758	Income tax increase
70	Mortgage interest deduction elimination
271	Revenue increase from increased economic activity
300	Financial transactions tax
241	Inheritance tax
210	Carbon tax
189	Eliminate $133,700 income Social Security tax cap
161.5	Military spending reduction
123	Anti-Poverty Program Expense Reduction Due to Poverty Reduction
40	Federal unemployment compensation savings
84	"Too big to fail" bank fee
8.1	Real estate transfer tax
24.1	Equal charge for nuclear power
17.7	Agricultural subsidy elimination
15.8	Fossil fuel subsidy elimination
7.9	Toxic releases tax
7.8	Nuclear industry subsidy elimination
4.75	Alcohol tax
2.74	Cigarette tax
3.1	Airline fees
2.5	Revenue savings and gains from policy reform on public lands
995	**Total**

The deficit in 2013 was $680 billion. The New Enlightenment policies will raise sufficient revenue to eliminate a $680 billion deficit and create over a $300 billion annual surplus. New Enlightenment policies also will:

- End unemployment or reduce it to historic lows.
- Lift tens of millions of Americans out of poverty to a standard of living that now exists in the middle class and substantially improve the standard of living of tens of millions more.
- Reduce full-time work-hours by 10%, to 36 hours per week.
- Transform the economic system over a two-decade transition period to one where worker controlled and owned business enterprises will perform most of the economic activity of the country.
- Eliminate the dominating importance of money controlled by national public office candidates and their allies in elections and thereby allow a meaningful democracy to exist (described in Part 3).
- Enhance democratic functioning with new, innovative democratic forms (described in Part 3).
- Transform the ownership and management structure of many media corporations, through regulations and incentives. This will create a new media culture more responsive and accountable to the majority. We will create a vigorous media of, for, and by the people necessary for a well-functioning government of, for and by the people (described in Part 3).
- Eliminate tuition for two and four-year public colleges. This will help meet our stated ideal of equal opportunity for all and help create the well-informed citizenry needed for a well-functioning democracy and economy.

If instituted, the policies detailed will have these and other transformative beneficial impacts.

> **Will you support and help develop an organization that will have these impacts if it had sufficient support?**
>
> **Is it time for a New Enlightenment?**
> **Will you be a part of it?**

Policies in these areas are under development:

- Health system reform (large revenue gains will result that are not yet accounted for).
- Infrastructure, public goods investment ($300 billion annual cost accounted for).
- Trade policy reform.
- Federal chartering of corporations.
- Labor regulatory reform.
- Additional banking and financial system reform.

The surplus will be much larger than $300 billion when savings from health system reform under development are accounted for. In 2011, we spent $2.7 trillion on health care. If we spent the same per capita as the country with the highest health care system satisfaction rate in the world, France, which spends less than half per capita that we do, we would have saved over $1.35 trillion. This is greater than the total amount of federal income taxes collected in 2011! Many billions of dollars in revenue gains will also result from the reduced interest on the debt. The interest on the $16.7 trillion debt in 2017 was $395 billion. After five years of confirming large surpluses for debt reduction, we will expand our most successful policies that require federal expenditure. We will determine success by evaluation of popular support levels.

If you would like to be a part of the New Enlightenment movement, see www.newenlightenment.us

---

The New Enlightenment

The Way to a Better America

Its blueprint for a more democratic society, and well-functioning and prosperous economy, will guide

A New, Peaceful American Revolution

Part 3

The Way to a Government of, for, and by the People

"The great object (of government) should be to combat evil by establishing a political equality among all."

James Madison, the "Father of the Constitution," author of the Bill of Rights, the fourth President of the United States and Enlightenment political theorist.

The Way to a Government of, for, and by the People

- Eliminate the dominating importance of money controlled by national public office candidates and their allies in elections—a necessary condition for a meaningful democracy to exist.
- Realize the great potential of our airwaves to serve as a public forum for candidates and others communicating on public issues.
- Reform other election systems to ensure more democratically determined outcomes.
- Institute a new democratic form to supplement our elected representative government.
- Create a more representative management of our "Fourth Estate" (the press).
- Reform lobbying and other governmental systems.
- Use the Internet to make policymaking processes more transparent and democratic.

Fundamental reforms of our political system are necessary to create a true government of, for, and by the people. This goal is too important to accept constraints in our efforts to accomplish it, including the provisions of an outdated Constitution. I, therefore, ignore any Constitutional constraints in my focus on developing policies for establishing a well-functioning democracy.

Our Constitution has been inadequate as a foundation of a democracy, and its interpretation by a right-wing Supreme Court has to an important degree turned the First Amendment to it into a kind of powerful weapon against the majority of our population through equating money with speech. Unlimited outside spending by wealthy individuals and corporations in support of the election of candidates as a result of the recent Supreme Court's *Citizens United v. FEC* and *McCutcheon v. FEC* decisions, has created a government even more extremely serving wealthy interests at the expense of the majority than it had in prior years.

We should not be surprised that a society based on our Constitution has not resulted in a well-functioning democracy. Our Constitution was not written to create a democratic society. Here is what Woodrow Wilson, the 28th President of the United States (from 1913 to 1921), wrote of its intent in "Division and Reunion" *"The Federal government was not by intention a democratic government. In plan and in structure it had been meant to check the sweep and power of popular majorities.* [In 1800, only 25% of white males were eligible to vote.] *The Senate, it was believed, would be a stronghold of conservatism, if not of aristocracy and wealth. The President, it was expected, would be the choice of representative men acting in the electoral college, and not of the people. The federal Judiciary was looked to, with its virtually permanent membership, to hold the entire structure of national politics in nice balance against all disturbing influences, whether of popular impulse or of official overbearance. Only in the House of Representatives were the people to be accorded an immediate audience and a direct means of making their will effective in affairs. The government had, in fact, been originated and organized upon the initiative and primarily in the interest of the mercantile and wealthy classes."*

The words "democracy" or "democratic" do not appear in the Constitution. Another important "undemocratic" aspect of the original Constitution: The tolerance of slavery.

Amendments since then have improved the Constitution, but amending it is overly burdensome, and much needs amending. Ideally, a constitution should ensure political equality among all citizens, and it should foster consensus building and promote effective problem solving. And as Thomas Paine wrote, *"When it shall be said in any country in the world, my poor are happy; neither ignorance nor distress is to be found among them; my jails are empty of prisoners, my streets of beggars; the aged are not in want, the taxes are not oppressive, ... then may that country boast of its Constitution."*[335] It is past due for us to take an honest look at the deficiencies of our Constitution and do what is necessary to create a Constitution that best serves our citizenry.

When amendments improved our Constitution we had a diverse media, which allowed and helped motivate these major reforms. We now have a highly concentrated, elite-dominated media that is stifling public debate and widespread exposure to policy reforms that would greatly benefit the majority to maintain a social structure that is grotesquely benefiting elites. This is a fundamental social problem that when solved will greatly facilitate further advancement.

Thomas Jefferson would believe that we are far overdue for a Constitutional Convention to rewrite the Constitution. He wrote in 1816: *"Each generation is as independent as the one preceding, as that was of all that had gone before. It has then, like them, a right to choose for itself the form of government it believes most promotive of its own happiness,"* Jefferson recommended a Constitutional convention every *"nineteen or twenty years,"*[336] so that every generation would have the opportunity to create its own system of governance. Ten 20-year periods have elapsed since Jefferson wrote this, so according to him we have had at least ten too few Constitutional conventions and rewrites. Jefferson's rewrite interval was determined based on a much shorter average lifespan in his time, but the essential point remains valid: Jefferson would believe we are far overdue for rewriting the Constitution.

Jefferson played an important role not only in the first American Revolution, but also what many consider to be the second American revolution, the period of his very contentious election to the presidency in 1800. *"The Revolution of 1800,"* as Jefferson described his party's successful election that year was *"as real a revolution in the principles of our government as that of 1776 was in its form."*[337] The defeat of the Federalists ended their attempt to lead America on a less democratic course. He may again play an important role in an American Revolution, the one now beginning in the 21st century, through his writings on the importance of rewriting the Constitution and some of his other writings.

As I argue in *Now is the Time for The New Enlightenment,* the essence of our election system problem is not the large amounts of money required in it. It is the source of, and motives behind, the dominant portion of its supply. Relative to the social value of the $180 billion spent in the U.S. in 2014 on advertising, the cost of "advertising" the policies and character of candidates for public office is low. $6.7 billion was spent in the 2012 election for all national offices. Procter & Gamble alone spent $4.6 billion on advertising, mostly for

Bounty paper towels, Crest toothpaste, and Tide laundry detergent, in 2014. Devoting even more than triple the resources that Procter & Gamble does on advertising to our election process would not be unreasonable. New Enlightenment policies increase the resources used in the election process, and they change the source of and motives behind its supply.

Election system reform

Policy changes that would best serve the majority require a government that is responsive to the majority; instead, corporate and other moneyed interests are dominating. Many members of Congress are among the moneyed interests—268 are millionaires, about 50%, and at least ten have wealth exceeding $100 million.

The net worth of the members of Congress continued to rise, regardless of the economic recession. An analysis of financial disclosure forms by Roll Call magazine, using the minimum valuation of assets, revealed that members of the House and Senate in 2010 had a collective net worth of $2.04 billion—a $390 million increase from 2008—and an average of about $4 million each. But their wealth is actually substantially larger than this because disclosure forms do not include non-income-producing assets.

Campaigns are getting increasingly expensive, allowing, more than ever, a tiny fraction of our most wealthy citizens to corrupt our democratic process to serve their interests through the use of large amounts of corporate and personal wealth. Despite the large amounts of average wealth of our representatives, they generally use relatively little, most comes from other moneyed interests. We now have a government *"of the 1%, by the 1%, for the 1%,"* as Nobel Prize winning economist Joseph Stiglitz has called it. Senator John McCain, the Republican presidential nominee in 2008, described our election and lobbying systems as *"nothing less than an elaborate influence-peddling scheme in which both parties conspire to stay in office by selling the country to the highest bidder."* Conservatives, progressives, and anyone else who knows of the torrent of cash flowing into our political system can see this obvious fact. Keith Ellison, co-chair of the Congressional Progressive Caucus expressed it this way: *"We don't have elections; we have auctions."*

Many injustices and unnecessary hardships for tens of millions of Americans have resulted from a political system of a design that inherently results in public policy being determined by a small economic elite. 86% of people in a CNN poll said that *"our system of government is broken,"* implying that the best interests of the majority are poorly served or disserved, and an urgent need for fundamental political system reforms.[338]

We now have historic levels of political system dysfunction, with a 9% and declining approval rating for congress, and historic levels of inequality. Both our election and lobbying systems greatly advantage an elite of unprecedented economic power.

Among the policies that corporations and the wealthy have successfully influenced are those that reduced their taxes, reducing our ability to support important public needs. Their influence also has resulted in inappropriate government expenditures and regulatory changes, some of which have resulted in anticompetitive advantages for the funder, and some that have been very costly to our nation. Policies and the politicians who promote them, that maintain and increase their power and privilege are supported, as are attacks on politicians that promote policies that would empower the majority. But, attacks on candidates promoting fundamental policy changes to best serve the majority are rarely needed, because without sufficient money to be heard by the majority they have little influence.

Money has always strongly influenced election outcomes, but now its influence is greater than ever and growing rapidly.

In the 1960 highly contested Kennedy–Nixon election the candidates spent $153 million in 2012 dollars, and in the 2012 Obama–Romney election the candidates spent $1.12 billion for all campaign expenses, a 630% increase. Because of the 2010 Citizens United Supreme Court decision, there was historic spending of approximately $970 million in the 2012 election by outside groups dominated by relatively few individuals and organizations making large contributions. That's over three times the previous record of $301 million in 2008.[339]

Fewer than 40 donors to Political Action Committees (PACs) that advocate for or against the election of candidates for public office gave over $200 million to those groups. PAC spending increased from $15 million in 1974 to $546.5 million in 2012, a 3,543% increase. In 1972, the total amount spent on television political advertising for all local races nationwide and national races combined was about $200 million in 2012 dollars. In 2012, it was about $6.7 billion—a 3,230% increase.[340] As I noted in *Now Is the Time for the New*

Enlightenment, in 2012, over 40% of all campaign spending came from the top .01%, or Americans in the top one ten-thousandth of incomes. Corporations and wealthy individuals can now use large amounts of wealth to shape governments like never in our nation's history.

A New York Times investigation, reported on 10/10/15, found that in the first phase of the 2016 presidential campaign just 158 contributors, with companies they own or control, provided almost half of all the seed money raised to support presidential candidates, $176 million.[341] They are overwhelmingly white, rich, older, and male. Those investing the most in presidential politics contributed tens of millions of dollars to support Republican candidates who have pledged to pare regulations; cut taxes on income, capital gains and inheritances; and shrink government programs that help the middle class and poor. Most made their fortunes in just two industries: finance and energy, where huge public expenditures in bailouts and subsidies play a significant role in their fortunes. But regardless of industry, the families investing the most in the early phase of presidential politics overwhelmingly lean to the right politically.

The Koch brothers are planning on spending $889 million of their funds and a network of donors' funds on the 2016 presidential elections. This is about as much as each of the major parties will spend on their presidential nominee's campaigns.[342] The money will be used to make "contributions" to candidate campaigns—more accurately called "investments" that pay large returns through the resulting public policies. Unlike the parties, their network is constructed mainly of non-profit groups not required to reveal donors, and the Koches have worked to influence policy to keep a system allowing donor identity to remain secret. Their 2016 efforts will be unprecedented in scale by coordinated outside groups to shape an election that will be the most expensive in history. The $889 million will be used not just to influence the outcome of the presidential election but also to ensure that Republicans continue to control the U.S. Senate and U.S. House, and win elections in state and local races all across the country.

Instead of making themselves available to reporters for questioning, as was once common, candidates now often just buy, mainly with the money of wealthy individuals and corporations, the communication services of consultants, then buy political ads they design. Candidates thereby avoid the risk of going off-message or exposing weaknesses. Once elected, they know they need to serve the interests of those who allowed them to win and will enable them to win office in the future.

In 2008, Barack Obama's *"Change You Can Believe In"* and *"Hope and Change"* advertising campaign won Advertising Age's *"Marketer of the Year"* award, based on the voting of members of the Association of National Advertisers. The runners up were *Nike and Coors beer.* Research has shown that most candidates have little or nothing to do with the marketing of their campaigns, including the content of their ads. Marketing consultants determine advertising content. Their job it is to win by using the most effective advertising techniques. Is this a sane way to choose the leader of the most powerful nation on Earth or any of our government office holders?

U.S. Senate candidates must raise the equivalent of $3,300 every day for six years to have enough campaign cash to match that spent by the median Senate race winner.[343]

Our current system results in members of Congress spending, on average, over half their time in office raising money for their next campaigns.[344] Most of this money purchases influence, often to the detriment of the public interest, which then is used to purchase access to airwaves already owned by the public.

By a five to one margin, campaign cash goes to incumbents. In 2008, 80% of the $5.3 billion spent on federal races came from 1% of the population; 60% from only 0.1%.[345] Knowing these facts, it is not surprising that the extensive study noted earlier found that when Americans with different income levels differ in their policy preferences, actual policy outcomes strongly reflect the preferences of the most affluent; they bear virtually no relationship to the preferences of poor or middle-income Americans. America is a society ruled by, and exclusively serves the interests of, the wealthy and corporations. The U.S. is not a true democracy or a society organized in the interests of its people.

Inevitably, a political system that creates this result has low and declining voter participation. Only 36.4% of eligible voters voted in 2014's midterm elections, down from 40.9% who voted in 2010. The last time voter turnout was that low was 1942 when only 33.9% of voters cast ballots, according to the United States Elections Project, when a large share of the voting population was involved in World War II. Voter turnout in presidential elections is higher than in midterms—58.2% of eligible voters voted in 2012, still low and trending lower. The United States has the lowest voter participation rate in the developed world. Why bother participating in a system offering choices none of whom will serve your interests?

As Adlai Stevenson said when running for President in 1956: *"The hardest thing about any political campaign is how to win without proving you are unworthy of winning."* Because of the many hundreds of a percent increase in the need for raising cash for campaigns, now it is not just hard, it is almost impossible.

Thomas Ferguson, University of Massachusetts political science professor and a member of the advisory board for the Institute for New Economic Thinking, described each election cycle throughout the country in this way: *"The evils of two lessers determine who's picked as the lesser of two evils by a declining share of the electorate."*—that's a very clear and concise explanation why we urgently need fundamental election system reform. It's sheer poetry, packing a lot of meaning into very few words—a short poem on our "democracy" descending into the depths of a dystopia.

Our elections system declines in quality each election cycle; it's an international disgrace. As I noted in *Now is the Time for the New Enlightenment*, former president Jimmy Carter, the world's most famous election observer, said, *"We have one of the worst election processes in the world right in the United States, and it's almost entirely because of the excessive influx of money."*

After New Enlightenment policy of making the best use of the publicly owned airways is instituted, elected officials will be free and able to spend all their time in office serving the general public. As it is now, elected officials may be free to spend all their time serving the general public, but they are not able to if they want to stay in office. And new candidates will be made viable that otherwise would not be.

Although several well-intentioned election system reform proposals to reduce large contributors' influence on our election process have been proposed in the past, they have failed to become law because:

- Altering a system in which incumbents are reelected over 90% of the time to a more democratic one puts current policymakers' jobs in jeopardy.
- A dysfunctional media does not give appropriate coverage to system reform proposals that would serve the majority, and to candidates that make or support these kinds of proposals.
- Some reform proposals have involved free airtime. These are especially unlikely to get the broadcast media coverage or degree or character of coverage that is necessary to develop the popular support levels to pressure policymakers to support these reforms. Although our broadcast media companies are required to serve the public interest in exchange for the

free use of the publicly owned airways, they have used their influence to block free airtime proposals in the past, despite its great public service value, because free airtime policies would reduce their profits. This reduces shareholder value and management salaries and bonuses, which are priorities for air media corporate managers when making decisions on media content and on how to use their power to influence public policy.

- Corporate and economic elites, including media elites, who believe their interests are best served by avoiding true democratic governance, are dominating the legislative process through our election and lobbying systems.
- The proposals had defects that would limit their effectiveness. This is not the main cause of their failure to pass since some would have made improvements to the system somewhat, which is better than not at all.

Past election system proposals share three important flaws, including the recently proposed "Government of the People Act" (whose other defects are described in Part 4, Note 9):

- The influence of the mass media filter (its capacity to screen out otherwise viable candidates that it chooses to, through no coverage, an insignificant amount of coverage, or biased coverage) is ignored.
- Public funds will inevitably be used to buy 30-second broadcast media ads.
- Most proposals including the *Government of the People Act* have ignored the excessively restrictive, anti-democratic ballot access laws.

I will detail better, more fundamental reforms.

Past proposals including the Government of the People Act under consideration describe ways of publicly financing candidates for public office. Who qualifies for this assistance is determined by popular support levels, but these levels are to a large degree determined by mass media coverage. These reform proposals would use public funds to multiply the power of corporate mass media coverage decisions. The mass media are poorly serving the public interest now; this will not change when their importance as a candidate filter, enormous now, increases as a result of election system reforms.

Although some prior election system reform proposals would have helped some candidates who otherwise could not compete, a disproportionate influence would have remained in the hands of the relatively small group of people managing our mass media companies. *Six large corporations control 90% of our media content.[346] The defect of the current system is that a tiny fraction of the country, the major campaign funders, largely determine for whom the rest of us can vote. Past election system reforms would have modified this system to one where the funders reduced influence would be largely replaced by mass media managers and major owners increased influence in determining for whom the rest of us can vote. I will describe later the general nature of these interests, how they are aligned with other corporate interests or the interests of our current major campaign funders, and how they are communicated and generally not significantly violated throughout the mass media corporate hierarchy, within The New Enlightenment media proposal.*

Also, we need substantial improvements to ballot access laws. I describe in the *National Ballot Access Standards for Elections to National Office* policy proposal the ballot access problem with The New Enlightenment solution.

Another problem with our current election system and current and prior reform proposals that we must address is that they motivate the use of 30-second ads because of the high cost and limited nature of airtime. Substantive candidate policy proposals cannot be expressed in 30-seconds, so shallow, misleading, and often negative content on other candidates is commonly used for this time. The more that ads of this type fill the airwaves, the less people respect or like any of its contestants, and even the contest itself. Thirty-second political ads disserve or poorly serve our democracy. All prior public financing proposals of which I am aware would inevitably result in mainly funding more of them.

Larger blocks of time on these most powerful media are needed to far better communicate policy proposals and the character of the candidates. Since airtime is limited and valuable, a system is required that selects a limited, yet sufficient number of candidates to provide a wide spectrum of solutions to our nation's problems. For a vibrant, well-functioning democracy, we must enable candidates with various philosophical approaches to public issues to express their views to the majority of the population. Qualifying for the free airtime must be accomplished through democratic processes free of the influence of private sources of money. The following policy proposals serve these ideals and will create a government of, for, and by the people.

Free Candidate Airtime

A Necessary and Just Broadcast Stations' Requirement

The information disseminating power of the Internet notwithstanding, broadcast media remain the most effective way for candidates to reach and influence the majority of the population. This is why far more campaign dollars are spent on broadcast media than any other.

New Enlightenment policy is to institute a TV and radio broadcast license requirement to offer, free of charge, generous allotments of airtime to qualified candidates for public office. The allotments will be large enough so there would be no reasonable need for the purchase of airtime. Many hours per qualified candidate in debates, question and answer public forums, and policy speeches are necessary and provided by The New Enlightenment system. All this content will also be on YouTube, Vimeo and the FEC website.

Air media companies do not financially compensate us for using our publicly owned airwaves. We give access in exchange for public service requirements. No more important obligation exists for air media companies than to allow the airwaves to best serve our election process.

Air media companies are also obligated to serve the public because in granting broadcast rights we are also granting semi-monopoly status. A limited number of on-air stations can exist in an air media market, so none of these markets can be fully competitive.

Also, public funds are largely responsible for broadcast companies' profits. NASA and other government research institutions' work in developing satellite delivered networks, digital electronics, robotic technology, computers and other devices has allowed commercial broadcasters to extend their programming range, automate operations and increase their profits, at taxpayers' expense.

The New Enlightenment's free airtime system will to an important degree treat the airwaves as a kind of public square for qualified candidates for national office to address the nation during campaign season. In the modern world television is a necessary tool for this purpose, and it is also justified to remedy some of the harm it has caused.

Television has played a major role in our citizenry's abandoning the real "town square." Beginning in the 1940s, the exceptional powers of television dispersed members of social groups by sending them home from the town square to instead be with their TV sets. In 1950, only 9% of households had a television, but by 1960 the number reached 87%, the fastest adoption of a new technology in history, with major social consequences.[347]

As early as the 1960s, a shocking five hours per person per day was spent on TV watching, now it is 8.5 hours.[348] This shifted our lives from public gatherings in the bowling alley, the park, playground, and other public places to the privacy of our own homes. Families separated from other families, and over time the TV in the living room became TVs in separate bedrooms, isolating family members from one another. The political scientist Robert Putnam found that the time spent in front of the TV is the most powerful single characteristic accounting for the decline in time devoted to civic responsibilities.

This powerful technology can have redeeming social value by using it to help us meet our civic responsibilities with this policy and The New Enlightenment media reform policy.

Both exposures to new ideas and new people are necessary for our political system. However, increasing the number of people given airtime diminishes the ability for each candidate to have sufficient time to adequately express new or important ideas. Using an equitable qualification process, the New Enlightenment's system limits the provision of most of the free airtime to four candidates per national office contest because this maximizes the number of candidates for the desirable amount of airtime that can be practically offered per candidate. Candidates participating in our free airtime system will not use 30-second ads.

The New Enlightenment election process reforms will result in officials that truly represent the people. They will:

- Allow all qualified people, as judged by a suitable number of their potential constituency, seeking national elected office to have ballot access with an appropriate degree of effort in an equitable selection process. The ballot access selection process should require little or no candidate funds (the ballot qualification process is detailed in Policy 24).

- Extensive information on the ballot-qualified candidates and the policies they propose or would otherwise support should be widely disseminated. Reforms should create conditions where the majority of votes will be cast based on far more information given wide exposure than is currently the case.

- The wide dissemination of extensive candidate, policy, and related information should not require candidate funds. Candidate's free speech to their potential voters should in fact be "free" (unlike today when only people with large amounts of money are truly free to speak because only they are heard by the majority of voters).

Achieving these goals is necessary for a well-functioning democratic republic to exist. Evaluate the following New Enlightenment proposals based on whether they achieve these goals, not on whether the extent of the changes is too large to be practicable. A new definition of "practicable" regarding public policy is required, one that exists in a true democracy: If it benefits the majority, it should be considered practicable; only if it does not should it be considered not practicable.

A free airtime qualification process will be necessary because New Enlightenment less burdensome national ballot access rules will likely lead to over four ballot-qualified candidates in most contests for national offices. To express their policy proposals and character, the four free airtime qualified candidates will receive a large and equal amount of public exposure. This will end the dominance of our two major parties, which will be another beneficial outcome of the system.

Historically, candidates other than those of the two major parties have played critical roles in our democracy by introducing popular and groundbreaking issues that were eventually co-opted by major parties, such as: the abolition of slavery, women's right to vote, social security, child labor laws, public schools, the direct election of senators, paid vacation, unemployment compensation, and the formation of labor unions. The excessively restrictive ballot access laws we now have exclude third-party and independent candidates who could make contributions of similar or greater importance.

The New Enlightenment election system reforms will break the long-term bipartisan lack of action or even discussion on important issues, some where it is well established that the major parties have ignored the will of most of the American people. In a Gallup poll on Oct. 11, 2013, 60% of Americans, the highest that Gallup has measured in the 10-year history of this question, said the Republican and Democratic parties *"do such a poor job that a major third-party is needed."* A record high percentage of voters are now identifying as independent from the Democratic and Republican parties.

Four qualified candidates able to prominently and fully express their views with substantial explanatory content to the majority of voters, using a large and equal value of airtime and other media exposure, would be an advancement of great consequence over our current system. Large postal and other subsidies will also allow this. The four candidates will be democratically selected based on their ideas, not their fundraising ability.

In addition to eliminating the influence of money to the largest degree practical, this New Enlightenment reform will accomplish what no prior election reform proposal (as far as I know) would have accomplished: It will reduce the influence of mass media coverage decisions of the candidates to the largest degree practical.

It's likely that candidates made viable by this New Enlightenment policy will have fundamental philosophical differences on public policy, so the public debate on how best to solve our most important challenges will be greatly widened and stimulated.

Ballot qualified candidates can choose not to participate in the system, but would forfeit all of its advantages, including the likely preference of voters for candidates that do not use money to promote their candidacies. Participating candidates will be required to not run ads during the qualification process. This system will reduce the influence of ads by outside groups, as will a new "Fairness Doctrine." Anyone choosing to participate would have to agree to all the system's provisions.

Candidate Qualification Process for Participation in the Main Free Airtime System

The following equitable system will be used to qualify the four candidates for the large amounts of free airtime. This system gives no advantage to any party and allows candidates to be evaluated on their merits only, as judged by voters. It requires no candidate funds. The qualifying process will be a kind of national primary.

On what we will call week one, 30 weeks before general election day, each ballot-qualified candidate puts a maximum 12,000-word summary of their platform with explanatory content on a portion of the Federal Election Commission (FEC) website created for this purpose. Each candidate will also include up to ten questions that they believe would be most important for the public to have all the candidates answer. This "primary" system allows voters to select the top ten questions from among all the candidate's chosen questions to be used in part of the free airtime system.

The FEC website will allow links to the candidate's website within the candidate's summary; unlimited amounts of information on the candidates would be conveniently available. Broadcast stations will be required to air frequent public service announcements on this candidate supplied information and the civic responsibility to read at least the FEC website content.

Likely, broadcast stations would devote programming to this content, and we will require public broadcasting stations to do so.

We will also offer each ballot-qualified candidate for president, the Senate, and the House space to express their views in all local daily newspapers in the nation, state or congressional district, respectively. Sufficient space would be offered for a 4,500-word description per edition of portions of the candidate's platform, produced by the candidate, with any explanatory content the candidate chooses. 4,500 words are slightly less than the number of words in a typical page of a broadsheet newspaper similar to the New York Times' page size. This content also will be included in the papers' online edition.

Newspapers would group up to ten candidate's content into one print edition. Possibly two or as many as three editions per week with candidate supplied content may be needed in some election years, depending on the number of races, and the number of ballot-qualified candidates per race. New candidate supplied content will be offered in each of five weeks. New Enlightenment media reforms, detailed later, emphasize the support of local media because the dangers and dysfunction of the concentrated media we have require remedy. We will subsidize only the local daily newspapers for the candidate content, both for its financial support value and to increase local medias' prominence and importance, as one part of our more extensive program for the support of local media.

The ink and paper costs for printing the 4,500 words is approximately $.01 per newspaper copy (generally slightly less). We will provide newspapers ten times this cost, or $.10 per candidate plus $3 per newspaper if it is offered free on newsstands or retail outlets on the days the paper has the candidates' supplied content. For example, if the newspaper has 100,000 circulation with eight candidates who supply content, each paper printed would be subsidized with $3.80, so the total subsidy to the newspaper would be $380,000. This subsidy expenditure amount would typically be slightly greater than the amount for purchasing this much advertising space plus purchasing the newspaper at the newsstand price, so the subsidy will substantially benefit the newspapers that cooperate. The subsidy will be valuable not only to the candidates and our election process but also to an important part of our Fourth Estate.

The subsidy would likely be a sufficient motive for all or nearly all local newspapers to cooperate. However, to further support newspapers and encourage their participation, while serving the purpose of well-informing the electorate, we will require on-air public service announcements of all local broadcast stations to inform the public of the day that candidate newspaper content would appear and which newspapers are offering it. These announcements will be a free advertising campaign for the participating newspapers. These and the FEC website information announcements will be public service license requirements for broadcast station.

Based on the widespread and growing concern over our nation's problems, and interest in candidates offering unconventional policies to solve them, this free advertising will likely substantially increase their circulation and online readership on the day the candidate supplied content is printed, with some positive carryover impact on future circulation and online readership. (As this policy was being written the unconventional presidential candidates Bernie Sanders and Donald Trump were drawing historic numbers of people to their campaign appearances and televised debates.)[349]

The total circulation of all U.S. daily newspapers, about 40 million, minus the circulation of nationally distributed daily newspapers, about six million, or approximately 36 million newspapers would be subsidized if circulation did not increase. However, I assume circulation will double on the days candidates supply content under the system, based on the promotional campaign for citizen participation, the importance of the content, and that the newspaper will be free, in budgeting for the subsidy. Assuming the standard of national elections occurring for the House, the Senate and president every two, six and four years respectively, this requires budgeting about $1.7 billion per year for the five weeks of candidate newspaper content.

Also, we will use a broadcast series of eight and seven debates, respectively, for the candidates for president and the Senate. For the House, we will use six debates: three broadcast and three on DVDs, whose mailing and duplication costs will be subsidized. DVD recordings are substituted for some airtime because air media market areas often overlap more than one congressional district so airtime messages by congressional candidates would often be broadcast to voters not in the candidate's district, inefficiently using valuable and limited airtime.

All candidates on the ballot could participate. If a race has over ten ballot-qualified candidates, we will divide the candidates into two groups for two series of debates, to allow more substantive information on their views and policy proposals in the debates. The debates will be two hours twenty-minute variations of the three debate types used for the debates between the generally four free airtime system qualified candidates per contest that I describe later.

Unlike the debates between primary winners, we will permit limited commercial time within these debates. A ten-minute intermission will be included at the 1½ hour point for commercials. No public policy or candidate advocacy will be allowed during the intermission, and market prices could be charged to the commercial advertisers. Likely, a higher than standard rate could be charged based on audience size of recent primary debates. A recent prime time Republican primary debate had 23.1 million viewers, making it the most-watched program in CNN's history.

In each media market, the largest annual average audience size station will be required to air the debates. Also, public TV and radio will air them and any other broadcast, cable or Internet station that chooses to could also do so. Considering the recently large debate audience sizes, and that programming costs will be largely eliminated, and the time for commercials, the provision of debate airtime will not be a significant or unreasonable burden on broadcast media companies.

We will schedule these debates for Sundays. If a race has over ten ballot-qualified candidates, and three national offices are contested, we will add Saturday debate times. As for all on-air candidate appearances, the debates will be available for viewing throughout the campaign on YouTube, Vimeo, and the FEC website.

In addition to the debates, we will offer two 14-minute airtime blocks per candidate for speeches. The 14-minute speeches will also be given on the largest annual audience size commercial TV and radio station in each media market as a license requirement, and on public TV and radio stations. We suggest that speech times be scheduled for Monday, Tuesday, and Wednesday at 9 to 9:30 PM EST with two minutes available for commercials between them. They will run from week 2 through the number of weeks necessary for all candidates to have their first 14-minute speeches in random order, and then their second speeches in random order. Since 12 weeks will be available for this content, sufficient time is available for 36 candidates before primary election day. This would likely be more than sufficient even in years when all three national offices are contested since it is unlikely more than an average of 12 ballot-qualified candidates per race will exist.

The percentage of the population not familiar with the Internet to the degree necessary to cast a fully informed vote is small and diminishing, and New Enlightenment reforms described later will create virtually universal broadband Internet access. However, judgments made just on the other media content by the candidates in this "primary" election will be better informed than most based on our current system in the general election.

We will offer online training programs for librarians, to prepare them to offer regular classes at public libraries on FEC and candidate website access and use, to ensure that everyone can fully participate. Public libraries also generally have public Internet access. If few people require instruction, individual instruction on public computers may be sufficient. Also, frequent on-air public service announcements will be made regarding the system, library assistance, and the civic responsibility of all citizens to participate.

Based on an evaluation of their website and newspaper entries, speeches and their debate performance, and any other information voters seek out elsewhere, they will vote for their top four candidates in order of preference for each national office contested. Using the results, we will use an instant runoff voting process (IRV process detailed in policy 26) to determine the most preferred candidate. Then, using these same vote results, eliminate this candidate from the next runoff to determine the second most preferred. Then eliminate this candidate from the next runoff to determine the third most preferred and so on until the four candidates are selected. This process has important advantages to just immediately ranking the top four that are described in the New Enlightenment instant runoff voting proposal.

Voters could also select from the questions submitted by all candidates, the ten they would most want to be answered by all the candidates in order of preference. We will use the same process described above to select the ten questions most important to the public for the candidates to answer during a portion of their free airtime. The candidate and question preference votes will be cast at regular election polling centers 14 weeks before the general election day. The newspaper entries will begin 29 weeks before Election Day. The following table summarizes the scheduling for all New Enlightenment election process activities, including those after the "primary," that I detail next.

This approximately 6½ month concentrated campaign period will result in the great majority of voters making much better-informed votes than after the seemingly interminable (especially in presidential election years) campaign period we have now.

Candidates wanting to participate in the selection process for free airtime system would be required to agree not to run ads during this process, to level the playing field for being awarded the free airtime. Even before the large amount of information widely disseminated after the qualification process, much better informed "primary" votes will be cast than is typically the case in our current general elections.

Week No.	Characterizing Activity	Week No.	Characterizing Activity
1	Newspaper/FEC Website Entries	16	Primary Election Day
2	Newspaper Entries, Speeches	17	Break
3	Newspaper Entries, Speeches	18	Qualified Candidate Speeches, Debates, Mailings
4	Newspaper Entries, Speeches	19	Qualified Candidate Speeches, Debates, Mailings
5	Newspaper Entries, Speeches	20	Qualified Candidate Speeches, Etc.
6	Primary Debates, Speeches	21	Qualified Candidate Speeches, Etc.
7	Primary Debates, Speeches	22	Qualified Candidate Speeches, Etc.
8	Primary Debates, Speeches	23	Break
9	Primary Debates, Speeches	24	Qualified Candidate Speeches, Etc.
10	Break	25	Qualified Candidate Speeches, Etc.
11	Primary Debates, Speeches	26	Qualified Candidate Speeches, Etc.
12	Primary Debates, Speeches	27	Qualified Candidate Speeches, Etc.
13	Primary Debates, Speeches	28	Break
14	Primary Debates, Speeches	29	Break
15	Break	30	Election Day

The four candidates selected for free airtime will be required to not run on-air ads after the selection process for the free airtime also. In addition to large amounts of additional free airtime exposure and primary campaign supplied information, dissemination of information on each primary winner we will further support in these ways:

- Matching with public funds the spending of the highest spending candidate in a race on print and Internet ads up to a reasonable limit.

- Providing a postal subsidy for nine free mailings per candidate, which is detailed in a separate proposal (Policy 23).
- Reinstituting and improving the Fairness Doctrine, as described later in this proposal and the media reform proposal (Policy 29).

Knowing these facts, and that on-air exposure will be large, there will be little or no incentive for excessive spending by any candidate on advertising.

In 2012, a presidential election year, approximately $120 million, and in 2010, a non-presidential election year, about $15 million, was spent on print and Internet advertising by candidates for national office. The average is about $67 million every two years, so budgeting $34 million per year would likely be sufficient.

Free Airtime System for Qualified Candidates

The following free airtime policy for qualified candidates applies to elections for president and senator. House candidates will be supported with less airtime and more postage subsidy for direct mailing constituents. For campaigns for president and senator, New Enlightenment policies require all air media companies to provide candidates with airtime in these categories over nine weeks:

- Many three-minute blocks per candidate will be offered within the time allotted for commercial ads within normal programming. About 7.5 hours of airtime per candidate will be offered in three-minute blocks.
- Four half-hour blocks per candidate for the Senate for speeches.
- Four 1½ hour debates by the candidates for Senate.
- Five half-hour blocks per candidate for president for speeches.
- Seven 1½ hour debates by presidential candidates.

All the above airtimes will be uninterrupted by commercials. The debate videos and the videos of the three-minute and half-hour speeches aggregated by candidate will be available for viewing throughout the campaign on YouTube, Vimeo, and the FEC website, for easy reference by voters and the press.

Three-minute Block Allotment System

One of the reasons 30-second ads are effective is their political message is delivered "where people are." Substantial numbers of people either cannot or do not want to devote the time to hear extended political speeches or debates. We need to reach these people "where they are" with more substantive messages than occur in 30 seconds. Three minutes is a practical amount of time within the normal commercial time of programming that people choose to watch that can deliver reasonably substantive political messages. Viewing many of them can result in a lot of important information being communicated, alone enabling reasonably well-informed judgements.

The three-minute blocks that will replace commercial time within normal programming we will allot according to the following system:

The main operative factors in determining the value of this airtime to candidates are audience size and message time length, and I will call the product of these two factors, V, or value to the candidates of the airtime within a program. New Enlightenment systems would apportion airtime each week in this way:

Each half-hour program has about nine minutes of commercial time. This time varies by station and program and it is not uncommon for it to be eleven minutes, but is rarely less than six minutes. (Radio commercial times are slightly greater than television.) For nine weeks before an election, in each of the 336 half hours in a week, on all air media, we will require that six minutes be allotted for possible selection by candidates for their 3-minute messages. Not all 336 half-hours will have six minutes of candidate messages, just those selected by the candidates using this accounting system:

The V will be calculated for each program in a one-week period, and all these Vs will be summed to determine the total V of the week's programming on a station. Specifically, the first half-hour of the week program has an audience size we'll call A_1 so its V, which we'll call V_1, is A_1 times six minutes or $6A_1$ minute persons (all Vs are in minute persons units so I will omit the units from now on). Similarly, the second half-hour of the week has a V_2 equal to $6A_2$ and so on. The total value to the candidates of all the available airtime in the week on any station is the sum of the value of time available in each half hour, which equals six times the sum of the audience sizes of all the station's programs.[350]

We will require that each station offers in total to all candidates 20% of the total V per week when a race for both president and senator exists, for the nine weeks before an election. This total will be equally divided among eight candidates, four for president and four for senator. The four maximum would likely run in each race because prospective candidates would know that the value of their ideas, not their bank account or fundraising ability, will determine their success. Specifically, each candidate will get 2.5% of total V for each station each week. In the years when only one office is contested, the candidates would get the same amount, so only 10% of total V will be needed.

Their weekly allotment could be spent only within the week. It would not be transferable to other weeks. Candidates could spend their V allocation as they wish, either for fewer 3-minute blocks on larger audience programs or more 3-minute blocks on smaller audience programs. Audience size and demographics are typically estimated for all programs.

Candidates will select the time slots they want in advance. If two or more candidates choose the same time, we will select the candidate for the time slot at random. Candidates will have available a more than sufficient amount of programming time devoted to voting age populations. If more than one candidate chooses a high voting age audience show for a message, the one that gets it would pay a disproportionately large fraction of their V allotment on it. This would disproportionately reduce their ability to have messages on other programs with a similar number of voting age viewers, so the candidate would not be advantaged. All unit V's are equal in value within the segment of programming the candidates would select.

The total amount of airtime each candidate would have would depend on the average audience size of the programming within which his ads appear. If this average is equal to the average audience size of the station, the candidate will receive about 50.4 minutes of airtime per week, or about 7.5 hours over the course of nine weeks. Since we will allot airtime in 3-minute blocks, the candidate would receive 48 minutes in 16 three-minute blocks in the week, so the candidate would likely choose programming with a different than average audience size to make full use of the candidate's airtime V.

Only the candidate could appear in the 3-minute segments, with instructional charts, graphs or pictures if needed. No one representing the candidate could be used. Some segments would likely be part of a running debate with other candidates. Candidates would be free to direct questions to, or respond to, the other candidates. But at least one-half of the candidate's V allotment per week will be devoted to answering questions from the voters that were determined to be the ten most important in the system that was part of qualifying the candidates for the free airtime described earlier. The answers would likely be part of some or all of running debates between the candidates. All candidates must answer, or elaborate on their answers to, all ten questions during one-half of their total V allotments.

For most of the several hours in 3-minute blocks, each candidate would be answering the questions voters select as their top priority questions or responding to other candidates in a kind of extended debate. These three-minute block responses, exchanges or speeches will be easily available to voters throughout the election at any time of their choosing on websites, in addition to their original airing time.

Half-hour Allotment System

Four half-hour blocks per candidate will be allotted for the Senate, and five per candidate for president, which results in 18 hours of total program time over the nine weeks for major speeches. This assumes the four candidate maximum for free airtime per contest and an election for president and senator in the state. Stations will allot in the first week the prime time hours of 8:00 to 9:00 PM, Monday and Wednesday, the second week 8:00 to 9:00 PM Tuesday and Thursday, and so on, alternating between 8:00 to 9:00 PM on Monday and Wednesday and Tuesday and Thursday for eight weeks. The ninth week would have presidential candidate speeches on Monday, Tuesday and Wednesday.

Candidates will be assigned speech times according to the schedule in the following table. It would advantage no candidate significantly. If any chance exists of a slight advantage, it would be for the "underdog" candidate because it allows him or her to speak last. The table also includes the schedule for the debates. P1 stands for the candidate for president selected in the first instant runoff vote for free airtime; P2 stands for the candidate for president selected in the second instant runoff vote, and so on, up to P4, who was selected last. Similarly, S1 stands for the candidate for Senate selected in the first instant runoff vote for free airtime; S2 stands for the candidate for Senate selected in the second instant runoff vote, and so on up to S4. VP stands for the candidate for vice president; C stands for the candidate for the House in the debate schedule. No commercial time will be allowed during any of the speeches or debates.

The FC time slots are for fact check results of all prior policy speeches, debates and ads. If few statements of fact are in dispute, some of this allotted time could be used for policy position analysis.

Both Politifact and Factcheck.org do fact-checks, as do the New York Times and Washington Post. Representatives of these organizations or members of academia, other policy experts, and journalists would point out inaccuracies or false statements made by the candidates, and do the policy analysis.

Stations could devote more programming time for fact checking throughout the nine weeks, but these two dedicated time slots would be a part of the

On-Air Speech and Debate Schedule on Commercial and Public Media (no commercial breaks)

Week	Day	Candidate speech times		Debate times
		8:00-8:30 PM	8:30-9:00 PM	8:00-9:30 PM
18	Monday	P1	S1	
	Wednesday	P2	S2	
	Tuesday			P1-P4
	Thursday			P1-P4
19	Tuesday	P3	S3	
	Thursday	P4	S4	
	Monday			S1-S4
	Wednesday			C1-C4
20	Monday	P1	S1	
	Wednesday	P2	S2	
	Tuesday		FC	P1-P4
	Thursday			VP1-VP4
21	Tuesday	P3	S3	
	Thursday	P4	S4	
	Monday			S1-S4
	Wednesday			P1-P4
22	Monday	P1	FC	
	Wednesday	P2	S1	
	Tuesday			C1-C4
	Thursday			P1-P4
24	Tuesday	P3	S2	
	Thursday	P4	S3	
	Monday			S1-S4
	Wednesday			VP1-VP4
25	Monday	P1	S4	
	Wednesday	P2	S1	
	Tuesday			S1-S4
	Thursday			P1-P4
26	Tuesday	P3	S2	
	Thursday	P4	S3	
	Monday			P1-P4
	Wednesday	P1	S4	
27	Monday	P2	FC	
	Tuesday	P3		
	Wednesday	P4	FC	

official scheduling to assure on-air exposure of inaccurate, misleading or false statements. The candidate's knowledge that careful fact checking and prominent reporting of the results will be done will likely reduce the number of inaccurate, misleading and false statements compared to prior candidate debates, speeches, and ads.

The candidates for president and senator half-hour speeches and debates will be broadcast simultaneously on all radio and television stations, nationally or statewide, respectively, creating an air media programming *"roadblock"* that air media viewers and listeners could not avoid. At public office campaign time, for a significant amount of time, the airwaves should be a kind of public square of our national village. Anyone going to the public square at the specified times will serve a central responsibility of citizenship by best informing him or herself before the important vote.

The common public square character of airtime is now especially important because of the new, dangerous and growing trend of Internet ad microtargeting. Candidates are using voters' browsing history to determine their interests, allowing candidates to target ads to voters based on those interests. Targeted ads can distort policy positions in one way for some voters and another way for other voters, and the potential exists to change positions of ads entirely based on voter profile. We would guard against this by putting all online candidate ads on a public website. The candidate's prominent public airwaves statements in the New Enlightenment systems will also minimize the potential for this deceptive practice.

Debate Formats

Sometimes debates now more resemble joint campaign appearances where candidates recite talking points to predictable questions. Sometimes the questions are not substantive. But always the questions are chosen based on the biases of a non-representative media elite and their allies, or major party operatives.

The Commission on Presidential Debates has relegated our presidential debates to stage managed campaign events arranged by the two major political parties for over 20 years. The Commission, created and managed by representatives of the two major parties, is committed to preserving the viability of the Republican and Democratic parties by minimizing the potential for the will of the people to choose a third-party candidate. Each party also works to minimize the likelihood that its candidate will be forced off rehearsed talking points.

Debates have been too far from the ideal of debates offering a concentrated period of time when diverse candidates can stimulate voters with a clash of detailed and thoughtful ideas. Voters need to learn the most significant details of what more than two candidates would do with the power of office to resolve the nation's most important problems, or create a more just and better functioning society. Debates can and should be an important part of this learning process.

In most developed nations general election debates are multi-candidate, multi-party affairs. It is not uncommon for five or six candidates to participate. Those countries have significantly better functioning democracies, with higher levels of political engagement than the United States has seen in decades. The barriers that the United States maintains to entry into debates by so-called "minor-party" candidates characterize those of authoritarian states.

New Enlightenment policy is for the following format types for presidential debates, which would create real, far more informative and lively debates: Single Moderator, Town Hall, Expert Panel. All candidates eligible for free airtime would be eligible to participate. Since senatorial and congressional candidates would have fewer debates, rather than have all these debate formats, they would choose from among them. As the scheduling table shows, candidates for the Senate have four debates, for the House two on-air debates, and for president seven debates. We motivate congressional candidates to participate in additional debates by subsidizing DVD debate recording duplication and mailing costs.

Single Moderator

In watching past presidential and vice presidential debates you may have thought that if you moderated the debates, the choices of questions for the candidates would have had significant differences from those chosen. We would all have our own biases in making these selections. Since the questions selected by the moderator determined, to a large degree, the nature of the debate, undemocratically chosen individuals have had an inappropriate amount of influence on this potentially decisive kind of event in our democratic process.

The challenge is to create a system where debate topics are more democratically selected. In some cases, it may best serve the public interest for topic selection to be influenced by people extraordinarily knowledgeable in particular areas of policy. It would also serve the public interest to learn what the candidates consider most important.

Some may argue that past moderators have met the criterion of being people most knowledgeable about particular areas of policy, but this is not correct. Past moderators generally have been chosen from among members of the mass media who are not policy experts, but news announcers or "anchors," and their priorities were determined by the same people making the poor choices regarding news report content I will describe later with The New Enlightenment media reforms.

The New Enlightenment single moderator format will maximize the freedom of the candidates to express what they consider most important, and to respond to questions and challenges from one another within an equitable structure. Getting the candidates' views on each of the other candidates' top priority issues and proposals would be of high value in the voter selection process—far greater value than getting candidates' views on topics chosen based on the biases of an unrepresentative, mass-media-industry-designated moderator.

The format would be a structured conversation between the candidates of the design where the moderator has no influence on the content of the debate—enforcing time limits will be the moderator's only responsibility. This design assumes the maximum four candidates per national contest. This maximum would almost always exist. Candidate number refers to their position in the instant runoff vote selection sequence:

Candidate 1 makes a 5-minute introductory speech, which includes two or three questions the responses to which he believes to be among the most important for the voters to know from all the candidates. Each of the other candidates is given a maximum of 3-minutes to respond in their instant runoff vote selection order. After Candidate 2's response to Candidate 1's questions, candidate 1 has a maximum 1½ minute rebuttal that may include a follow-up question, Candidate 2 then has one minute for response or counter rebuttal. Then candidate 3 responds to the same candidate 1 questions with a 3-minute maximum response and again Candidate 1 has a 1½ minute rebuttal and Candidate 3 has a 1-minute counter rebuttal and so on until all three candidates respond to Candidate 1. Candidate 2 then starts his sequence, and so on until all candidates have all their question and response sequences. If the process is unclear, the following charts will clarify.

The system will allow all candidates to have equal total time and an equal or similar amount of time to address each question. The receivers of questions get four minutes, three initially then one in counter rebuttal. The questioners get 4.5 minutes to address the questions in three 1½ minute rebuttals. (This excludes any time spent addressing the questions in the opening statements).

Single Moderator Debate Structure Charts

After Candidate 1 gives a 5-minute speech ending in two or three questions, the candidates do the following in left to right order. When the process indicated by the top two rows in the chart is completed, move to the next two row entries, and so on:

Candidate 2	Candidate 1	Candidate 2
3-min. response to questions	1.5 min. rebuttal	1 min. counter rebuttal
Candidate 3	Candidate 1	Candidate 3
3-min. response to questions	1.5 min. rebuttal	1 min. counter rebuttal
Candidate 4	Candidate 1	Candidate 4
3-min. response to questions	1.5 min. rebuttal	1 min. counter rebuttal

Then Candidate 2 gives 5-minute speech ending in two or three questions, and the candidates do the following in left to right order. When the process indicated by the top two rows is completed, move to the next two row entries, and so on:

Candidate 1	Candidate 2	Candidate 1
3-min. response to questions	1.5 min. rebuttal	1 min. counter rebuttal
Candidate 3	Candidate 2	Candidate 3
3-min. response to questions	1.5 min. rebuttal	1 min. counter rebuttal
Candidate 4	Candidate 2	Candidate 4
3-min. response to questions	1.5 min. rebuttal	1 min. counter rebuttal

Then Candidates 3 and 4 have their questions for the same response and rebuttal process.

If any candidate's top priority questions are asked by another candidate, he could ask another high priority question or, if he believes the prior discussion on the topic needs further development, he could ask the same or a variation of the same question.

If all candidates take their maximum time for their questions and statements and all their responses, rebuttals or follow-up questions, which is unlikely, completing this process would take 86 minutes. The process would probably take less than 82 minutes which would allow two minutes or more equal time in closing statements by each candidate. One debate in this format will be devoted to domestic policy questions, one for foreign policy, and a third open to any subject for the presidential debates. Senatorial or congressional candidates can choose from among any of these three or the following debate format types (adapted for the geographic area of their constituencies) for their on-air debates.

Town Hall Formats
Young Adult Questioning

A debate forum controlled by young adults could inspire millions of them to tune in to the presidential debates and raise atypical subject matters for national discourse. It will also stimulate the interest of, and educate, almost everyone.

The burdens of those in this age group are unusually serious, and they are voting in historically low percentages, indicating a profound disaffection with the country's political system. This is an ominous sign for the future of the country.

It is likely this will be the first generation in American history whose average economic wellbeing over their lifetimes will be lower than that of the prior generation. For March 2013, the unemployment rate was 16.2% of workers under age 25, over twice as high as the national average. These are people not in school or at work, and are often not doing something positive.

For young people entering the workforce, wages and benefits are declining significantly. As noted previously, students have over $1.2 trillion in student loan debt, more than the total national credit card debt. More than half of America's recent college graduates are either unemployed or working in a job that doesn't require a bachelor's degree. Historic levels of inequality are growing. Potentially devastating environmental developments may have a major disruptive impact on their lives, which may not significantly affect the lives of older Americans. And young people are the future of the country. This demographic deserves special attention.

One way to select young adult participants is:

College student government presidents are elected representatives of a segment of this demographic. We will make use of the value of this representation by asking all student government presidents from colleges in the top 100 highest enrollment colleges (colleges with an enrollment over about 29,000) to attend a town hall debate with a prepared public policy related question for the candidates. (We will ask airlines to donate the trip as a public service and for the public relations value. If none will, the federal government will pay for their flights to the town hall.) Ideally, the presidents would get opinions from fellow students and select what they consider to be the most important policy question for the candidates to answer. They would be obligated to keep the question they chose confidential.

If this format is used for debates in contests for the Senate, the student government presidents in the number of colleges existing in the state would participate. If used for congressional races, student government presidents and all other student elected officials of the colleges in the district would participate. However, for both congressional and senatorial debates, in some cases, this would not result in a sufficient number of participants. We will then include political science, sociology, economics or government studies majors, starting from students with the highest grade point average percentile in each school, and working down until the total of 100 students is reached.

We will randomly select student government representatives at the debate hall for a maximum 30-second question and preface, and they will be allowed a short follow-up question. Each candidate will be given a maximum of 3-minutes to respond to each question and a 2-minute maximum response to each follow-up question, in each case, with the possibility of a 1-minute time extension at the discretion of the moderator.

The random order of questioners would be determined immediately prior to the debate, and a volunteer panel of seven peers will decide if any in the order have a question sufficiently similar to a prior one to be excluded, or if any other overriding concern exists that would cause the question to be excluded. They will also help the questioners edit their questions for conciseness. We will randomly select these seven peers from volunteers among all the participating student representatives sufficiently far down the selection order for questioning the candidates that they would not be a questioner. A question will be rejected only if, after discussion among the panel members, five or more panel members reject it.

Another option for a debate forum controlled by young adults is to choose participants at random from citizens between the ages of 18 and 30. Anyone randomly selected to participate of course can choose not to, in which case another person will be randomly selected until the 100 total is reached. Random selection will likely result in a group that is representative of the general population, or nearly so. Even if a person selected knows little about public policy almost everyone has more knowledgeable family, friends or acquaintances that would likely make suggestions for questions.

Undecided Voter Questioning

Cities with especially severe problems should get more national attention. We will locate one of the town hall debates in the city with a population over 100,000 whose median income is the lowest in the U.S. We will contract the Gallup organization to find undecided voters in this city and randomly select 100 who choose to play a role in a town hall debate. These voters will select what they consider to be the most important policy question for the candidates to answer and would be obligated to keep the question they chose confidential.

We will randomly selected questioners at the debate hall for a maximum 30-second question, and preface if necessary, and will allow a short follow-up question. Each candidate will be given a maximum of 3-minutes to respond to each question and 2-minutes to respond to each follow-up question, in each case with the possibility of a 1-minute time extension at the discretion of the moderator.

As in the young adult format, the random order of questioners would be determined immediately prior to the debate. A volunteer panel of fellow participants will decide if any in the order have a question sufficiently similar to a prior one to be excluded, or if any other overriding concern exists that would cause the question to be excluded. They will also help the questioners make their questions concise. We will randomly select the seven peers from volunteers among the 100 participants sufficiently far down the selection order for questioning the candidates that they would not be a questioner. A question will be rejected only if, after discussion among the panel members, five or more members reject it.

We will also locate another identically formatted debate in the city with the largest population whose population has a median income within three percent of the U.S. median income.

Expert Panel Questioning

Many people have devoted almost all their adult lives to the detailed study of topics relevant to public policy. This is the case for professors of political science, economics, government studies, and sociology. To select our panel, we will request that each university with departments in any of these subject areas collect secret ballots of all professors in these four subjects with their ranked top five votes for panel members of these qualifications:

The panel candidates are members of their discipline or any of the other three related disciplines, who have won an award for their professional work from any relevant professional association or reputable award-granting agency. (For example, a sociology professor could have among his five choices one or more winners of the American Economic Association's annually awarded John Bates Clark Medal, or an economics professor could have among his five choices one or more winners of the American Sociological Association's annually awarded W.E.B. DuBois Career of Distinguished Scholarship Award).

These ballots will then be mailed to the Federal Election Commission, where the votes would be tallied. We will selected five panel members using the instant runoff vote process. If someone selected chose not to participate, we will offer the opportunity to the next highest vote getter.

Panelists will each choose four questions they determine to be the most important for voters to know the response to of each candidate. Internet voting, with a system that will authenticate registered voter's votes or representative sample polling will then be used to select the most preferred questions. Each voter will rank up to seven questions from among the total of 20 questions of the five-panel members.

Using the results of this vote or poll, we will use an instant runoff voting process (IRV process detailed in policy 26) to determine the most preferred question. Then, using these same vote results, eliminate this question from the next runoff to determine the second most preferred. Then eliminate this question from the next runoff to determine the third most preferred and so on until at least seven questions are selected. It is unlikely more than seven questions could be asked in the allotted time.

The voter selected questions will then be asked in ranked order by the panelist who suggested the question, and this panelist will be allowed a short follow-up question. Each candidate will be given a maximum of 3-minutes to respond to each question and 2-minutes to respond to each follow-up question, in each case with the possibility of a 1-minute time extension at the discretion of the moderator.

Elections for the House

We will provide congressional candidates airtime for two debates to minimize the inefficient use of valuable and limited airtime due to air media market areas often overlapping more than one congressional district, while still offering an important amount of on-air exposure. We will use the single moderator format unless the candidates agree on a local adaptation of the other debate types described above. TV and radio stations with the largest audience in the district will be required to carry the debates of the district's congressional candidates. Also, public television and radio stations will carry the debates. We will be use Sunday evening time slots since they are not used for the other candidate debates.

We will provide large subsidies for postage for all candidates for national office, and larger for congressional candidates, because of the more restricted airtime. Their mailings will include two DVDs for two debate recordings and additional policy speeches, as a substitution for on-air debates and policy speeches.

As for the debates and speeches of the candidates for president and the Senate, candidates for the House debates and speeches would also be put on a portion of the Federal Election Commission website, YouTube, and Vimeo.

Additional Free Airtime on Public Media

1½ hour debate times will also be provided exclusively on public media on Friday evenings during all nine weeks of debates on all air media. Two Fridays will have a debate between the candidates for president, three Fridays a debate between the candidates for the Senate, and four Fridays a debate between the candidates for the House. The debates will be of the single moderator type unless a majority of the candidates choose otherwise.

Free Airtime for the Other Ballot-Qualified Candidates

In addition to the above main free airtime system for the qualified candidates (which is combined with internet, print, and postal subsidies) we will provide the opportunity for the other ballot-qualified candidates to have free airtime on public media. On Saturdays, for all nine weeks of the main free airtime system, we will schedule two-hour debates for each national office contest, on public media. (So in some states in presidential election years as much as six hours on Saturdays will be devoted to debates) Any candidate that did not qualify for the main free airtime system will qualify for the Saturday debates. The debates will be of the single moderator type unless a majority of the candidates chooses otherwise.

If only one candidate in a contest did not qualify for the main free airtime system, any of the four main system candidates could participate in the Saturday debates. If none chooses to, the one candidate in a contest that did not qualify for the main free airtime system will receive one-half hour of speech time in each of the nine weeks.

New Enlightenment candidate free airtime will overcome, to a large degree, the impact of corporate and wealthy donor supported super PAC advertisements. Candidates would not only be free to fully express their policy positions, they would also be free to respond to super PAC ads created by opposing interests in the prominent public settings provided by these media. This could include making a wide audience aware of the super PAC's major funding sources, possibly further discrediting any inaccurate ad claims, and potentially the super PAC. However, The New Enlightenment Fairness Doctrine will also result in substantially reducing the number and influence of super PAC ads.

In summary, New Enlightenment election system reforms uniquely beneficial impacts include:

The importance of mass media coverage judgments is minimized. Past election system reform proposals, including the Government of the People Act, would use public funds essentially to multiply the power of corporate mass media coverage decisions.

30-second ads are eliminated and replaced by a minimum of 3-minute blocks of time for communication directly from the candidates. Past election system reform proposals would substantially increase the number of 30-second ads. Half-hour candidate speeches and one-and-a-half-hour debates are also major components of The New Enlightenment system.

New Enlightenment free airtime allotments are sufficiently generous to eliminate the need for raising large amounts of national public office campaign money because candidates' airtime demands the most money, and airtime is the highest power tool for reaching the majority of the population. Also, we will provide large postage subsidies and match the spending of the highest spending candidate in a race on print and Internet ads with public funds, up to a reasonable limit.

Policy debates will be significantly widened because some candidates will be able to fully express to a wide audience important views and policies that would not have otherwise been considered by a large number of voters.

The critically important problems of the corrupting influence of large amounts of money and the dominating influence of mass media coverage decisions is solved by this system. If any additional funds are needed, it would put the candidates on a far more equal footing to raise them.

This New Enlightenment free airtime policy will be transformative, and it should be widely supported because it is based on an obvious truth: Since we all own the airwaves, we should use them to optimize democratic functioning (instead of destructively distort it, which their use does now).

As described within New Enlightenment media reform policies, we will reinstitute the Fairness Doctrine and strengthen it to further level the playing field between candidates. We will require on-air media to provide free equal time immediately following a purchased public policy related ad for an opposing view. If the ad advocates for the election of a particular candidate, all other candidates will be given equal time. This sacrifice would be part of air media's public service responsibility for the use of our airwaves. The value to the public of these ads far exceeds the value of commercial ads, so we need to use the publicly owned airwaves to provide this value.

The commercial airtime sacrifice will be greatly moderated by the foreknowledge of wealthy funders wanting to support the candidacy of an individual that the funds they supply to do so will assist their preferred candidates' opponents to the same degree as their preferred candidate—likely few ads will be funded.

Broadcast stations will object to all New Enlightenment free airtime requirements, but their objections will not be based on losing a substantial fraction of their revenues. And New Enlightenment comprehensive media reforms subsidize, and transform the character of, our media.

Any broadcast stations' sacrifice required by this policy will be small relative to the advantages we confer to them. Broadcasters' exclusive rights to use our public airwaves for free commonly result in over 30% profits. Television stations regard 30% profit as "low." Media executive Barry Diller said of TV stations: *"This is a business where if you are a birdbrain you have a 35 percent margin. Many good broadcasters have 45 to 60 percent margin."* The publicly owned television and radio spectrum is estimated to be worth hundreds of billions of dollars.

Broadcasters in the past acted on their requirement to serve the public interest in exchange for free use of our airwaves by providing free candidate airtime, but they progressively lost sight of this obligation as political advertising increased. The average number of free messages fifteen minutes or longer that broadcasters gave to presidential candidates fell from sixty in 1952 (15 hours total), to twenty in 1972, to five in 1988, to zero thereafter.[340]

Not only do air media companies not give free air time, ad rates substantially increase during campaign season.[351] The law of supply and demand rules, rather than the mandated obligation to the public whose airwaves they are using. During times of peak demand, stations sell political ads at rates many times higher than other ads. Political advertising is now about 12% of average revenue and its growing fast.[352] Political advertising is up 122% from January through May 2016 over that spent over the same period in 2012—about $408 million on television advertising in the presidential race.[353] To summarize in three words modern air media's response to our expressed requirement that they meet public service responsibilities: shirk, then gouge.

Our corporate media are especially powerful barriers to the media reforms needed for improving an election system that is producing a government increasingly unable or unwilling to serve the majority. They control the most influential coverage of the public debate, and to a large degree its content, and their interests are commonly far removed from majority interests, as we will see in more detail within The New Enlightenment media reform policy proposal. A system that uses candidates as conduits of vast amounts of campaign cash into corporate media coffers, though serving their financial interests well, is resulting in progressively more severe societal dysfunction, and common and widespread injustices.

For the four qualified candidates for the large amounts of free airtime, in election years when there is an election for president, the Senate, and the House (when there are the most contested national offices) about 2.75% of the total annual available time for advertisements on air media would be taken so we can have fair elections and good governance. This excludes the time taken to provide equal time to candidates under the Fairness Doctrine. This time is not likely to be substantial for the reason previously mentioned.

In years when there is just a congressional race, about .05% of the total annual available time for advertisements on air media would be taken for this purpose of essential importance to our democracy.[354] In odd-numbered years, there are no national elections, so no candidate airtime would be needed. On average, over all years, about .8% of all time currently devoted to commercials would instead be given free for use by qualified candidates. Although commercial time will be eliminated during candidate speeches and debates, so will station programming costs to a large degree.

Since annual ad time would be reduced, rates for the remaining time available could be slightly higher to compensate for any lost revenue. However, a .8% average commercial time loss is a small price to pay for air media company use of our airwaves that is needed for this policy.

The commercial time allowed within the airtime provided in the qualification process for the large amounts of airtime for four candidates is sufficient broadcast station compensation for this time since program creation costs are eliminated.

Also, New Enlightenment policies include air media subsidies that compensate for some of the loss of ad revenue from this policy. The New Enlightenment comprehensive media policy will reform the essential character of much of the media to align them to a far greater degree with their important public service role.

In the past, proposals for generous allotments of free airtime for qualified candidates have failed because congresspersons serving media companies, other moneyed interests, and their own self-interest have chosen to maintain a system that results in the probability of their reelection being over 90%. Incumbency provides enormous advantages in raising campaign cash. Only a mass movement can result in the major change that is now needed.

This policy is an important part of more comprehensive New Enlightenment media (and other) policies requiring clear majority support to be instituted. Organizing large numbers of people to support media reforms with little or no mass media cooperation, at least initially, is necessary and is possible, through alternative media and other grassroots routes. If the policy reforms are part of a more comprehensive reform movement, the mass media will be compelled to provide significant coverage. The New Enlightenment is designed to be the foundation of such a movement.

As in all the great societal advancements throughout history a mass movement is necessary. Some recent examples include mass movements in the middle of the 20th century without which little or no progress would have been made in advancing the civil rights of women and blacks. Another example of a mass movement resulting in major public policy reforms was the environmental movement of the late 1960s and 1970s when a broad segment of the middle class participated.

On Earth Day in 1970, in the largest one-day grassroots demonstration this country has ever seen, twenty million Americans marched and held rallies and teach-ins to demonstrate their outrage over the industrial poisoning of our environment. They were appalled by incidents such as the Santa Barbara oil spill in 1969, acid rain in the Midwest, the choking smog over Los Angeles, toxic waste in the rivers, to the point where some were catching on fire, and lead paint or asbestos in their own homes.

Governmental response was swift. During his first year in office, President Nixon set up a White House Council on Environmental Quality, naming environmentalist Russell Train as its chairman. Bipartisan majorities in Congress rushed through a flow of environmental legislation: the Clean Air Act; the Clean Water Act; a bill establishing the Environmental Protection Agency; the Federal Insecticide, Fungicide, and Rodenticide Act; the Noise Pollution and Abatement Act; the Coastal Zone Management Act; the Marine Mammal Protection Act; the Endangered Species Act; and the Safe Drinking Water Act.

If we join together, we can move the country in a positive direction again—this time in more fundamental ways into a New Enlightenment.

*The New Enlightenment: Ideals of Democracy, Human Rights, Reason, and Progress * Policy 22*

Support Free Candidate Mailings

New Enlightenment policies will subsidize the full cost of one mailing of an eight-page standard newsletter-sized document per week for all the candidates who qualify for free airtime, for all the weeks of free airtime. The mailings will be to each household of the potential constituency of the candidates. For congressional candidates, included in these nine mailings we will additionally subsidize the cost of two of the mailings to include DVDs (including DVD replication costs) with recordings of their speeches and debates not given airtime similar to that offered candidates for the Senate.

Also, for the House *"primary"* contests DVD recordings are substituted for some airtime. Three debates on DVDs will have mailing and duplication costs subsidized.

The Internet and air media have reduced, but not eliminated, the value of printed material to voters. Many of the poor do not have Internet access, except in public libraries, and many people with Internet access at home also consider printed material a more convenient way to read and share information on a candidate. Unlike air media, print media offer a permanent and easily accessible record of candidate information. Also, receiving candidate material in the mail will be a useful reminder to some people that time needs to be devoted to the important responsibility of deciding whom they want in public office.

An annual budgeted amount of $2.3 billion, of which $1.1 billion is Post Office costs and $1.3 billion in packaging and duplication costs would support the postal subsidy policy. This is based on the mailings going to the addresses of all households within the relevant district or state, or the entire nation in the case of presidential candidates, using the Post Office's EDDM service.

In addition to this policy being important to the process of creating a *government of, for, and by the people*, it will be important to an institution that deserves more public support because it is serving the public well, despite being under attack in an apparent attempt to discredit it, to try to privatize it: the Postal Service. (For some information on why the Post Office deserves this support, see Part 4, note 8.)

---

*The New Enlightenment: Ideals of Democracy, Human Rights, Reason, and Progress * Policy 23*

National Ballot Access Standards

U.S. voting rates decline year after year as our government becomes increasingly unresponsive to the interests of the majority. In 2012, although it was a presidential election year, only 58.2% of eligible voters participated, the lowest voter turnout rate of any advanced country. As I noted previously, in the U.S., in the late 1800's, often over 80% of eligible voters participated; generally, about 75% did. In Demark and Sweden in recent elections it was about 82%.

Our electoral system and government need the new people and new ideas resulting from improving our ballot access laws. Extensive media exposure to the policy proposals of several ballot-qualified candidates of diverse philosophies and priorities will stimulate the voter interest and participation needed for a true *government of, for, and by the people.*

The United States has the most severe ballot access laws of any democracy in the world; it's been criticized by the Organization for Security and Cooperation for them. These laws are designed to minimize the potential for the will of the people to choose a third-party candidate.

The great political theorist C.B. Macpherson said, *"When there are so few sellers (two parties) they need not and do not respond to buyers' demands as they must do in a fully competitive system."* More competition is needed, yet the Supreme Court has ruled that state ballot access laws can require independent presidential candidates and third-party nominees to obtain the signatures of 5% of the number of registered voters. 5% of the number of registered voters in the U.S. is over 7,600,000.

Since petition gathering costs about $1 per signature, the Court's ruling means that it is constitutionally permissible for states to erect ballot access barriers of over $7,600,000 for candidates. Each state selects its own ballot access requirements for presidential and other national office candidates, and ballot access laws invariably greatly advantage major party candidates, mostly with discriminatory rules, but even in states with the same rules for all, the rules greatly advantage the larger financial and organizational resources of major party candidates.

Our Founders opposed the kind of political party system we now have. No mention exists of political parties anywhere in the Constitution, and James Madison warned against partisan "factions" in Federalist No. 10. *"By a faction, I understand a number of citizens, whether amounting to a majority or a minority of the whole, are united and actuated by some common impulse of passion, or of interest, adversed to the rights of other citizens, or to the permanent and aggregate interest of the community"* [He warned against]*an attachment to different leaders ambitiously contending for preeminence and power ...[who] have, in turn, divided mankind into parties, inflamed them with mutual animosity, and rendered them much more disposed to vex and oppress each other than to cooperate for their common good."*

John Adams wrote, *"There is nothing which I dread so much as a division of the republic into two great parties, each arranged under its leader, and concerting measures in opposition to each other. This, in my humble apprehension, is to be dreaded as the greatest political evil."*[355]

In President George Washington's Farewell Address in 1796, he said, *"Let me now ... warn you in the most solemn manner against the baneful effects of the spirit of party.... It serves always to distract the public councils and enfeeble the public administration. It agitates the community with ill-founded jealousies and false alarms, kindles the animosity of one part against another ..."*

And here is Thomas Jefferson's opinion of the value of political parties: *"If I could not go to heaven but with a [political] party, I would not go there at all."*[356]

The New Enlightenment Party will not be a party of the kind that our Founders warned against. We will be a group of people united to support instituting, maintaining and improving programs designed to create a government of, for, and by the people, and prosperity for all. Neither the Democratic nor Republican Party is a group of people devoted exclusively to serving these purposes.

Ideally, voters would vote for candidates whose proposed policies, or policies they support or would promote, would in their judgment, based on sufficient and accurate information, best serve their interests in consideration of the interests of the majority. This judgment should be made independent of any group to which the candidate belongs, including party. The New Enlightenment's ballot access policy proposal is designed to not significantly advantage any party or group of any kind.

Ballot access is the first step to real viability, which results from the other necessary condition of media exposure. Our candidate free airtime and postal, newspaper, and other media subsidies give real viability to candidates through the widespread provision of extensive information on those meeting the following ballot access requirements:

Candidates for Congress Ballot Access

We will institute a petition signature system that includes minimum standards. Candidates will provide printed information to anyone choosing to sign a petition in support of their candidacies. This information will generally include references to other information sources. The signer would then be free to spend the time to determine the value of any information provided and referred to. If the candidate receives enough petition signatures that 150 of the signers, after considering the printed and other information, are sufficiently motivated to appear at the local election office to show identification and sign the following statement, the candidate will be ballot-qualified:

I (voter), after *carefully considering information on the policies that* (candidate) *has developed, or would otherwise support and promote to serve the public interest if elected, believe it would be in the best interest of the citizens of the* (district number) *Congressional District and the United States if* (candidate) *was on the ballot for the (year) election for Congressperson representing the (district number) Congressional District.*

Candidates would need substantially more than 150 petition signers before 150 signers, after more careful and thorough consideration than they made at the initial signing, are sufficiently motivated to go the local election office to sign such a statement. The 150 petition signers standard could be adjusted based on public input, and experience, as could the following recommended number of signers standards for candidates for the Senate and president.

Statement signers will be required to sign an oath that they were not paid or offered any form of compensation to sign their candidate statement. Also, the candidates would be required to sign an oath that they did not pay or offer any kind of compensation, including employment, to anyone to sign their support statement. In both cases, falsely signing their oath will be a felony. The statements in support of candidates of other national office will also require this oath, with the same penalty if false.

This is an appropriate and far lower barrier than current ballot access barriers. It likely would not lead to an excessive number of candidates on the ballot.

This type of requirement is similar to that in some other countries. In Canadian elections to the House of Commons, either 50 or 100 petition signatures are required depending on the electoral district. In the Republic of Ireland, candidates may be nominated to the European Parliament by 60 members of the electorate.

Candidates for Senate Ballot Access

Candidates or their supporters will provide printed information to anyone choosing to sign a petition in support of their ballot access. The information will generally include references to other information sources. The signer would then be free to spend the time to determine the value of any information provided and referenced. If the candidate receives a sufficient number of petition signatures such that 700 signers, after considering the printed and other information, are sufficiently motivated to appear at the local election office to show identification and sign the following statement, the candidate will be ballot-qualified:

I (voter), *after carefully considering information on the policies that (candidate) has developed or would otherwise support and promote to serve the public interest if elected, believe it would be in the best interest of the citizens of the* (state) *and the United States if* (candidate) *was on the ballot for the* (year) *election for senator representing the* (state).

Candidates would need substantially more than 700 petition signers before 700 signers, after more careful and thorough consideration than they made at the initial signing, are sufficiently motivated to go the local election office to sign such a statement.

Elections for President

As for the candidates for the House and Senate, candidates for president petition signers will be given printed information and references to other information sources at the signing. After considering this and other information, the required number detailed below would need to appear at the local election office to show identification and sign the following statement:

I (voter), *after carefully considering information on the policies that* (candidate) has *developed or would otherwise support and promote to serve the public interest if elected, believe it would be in the best interest of the citizens of the United States if* (candidate) *was on the ballot for the (year) election for President of the United States.*

The more extensive Presidential candidate ballot access requirements:

- One state: 1000 election center statements confirming support and prior petition signing.
- Five additional states: 700 election center statements confirming support and prior petition signing.
- Twenty additional states: 150 election center statements confirming support and prior petition signing.

Presidential candidates so qualified will be on ballots nationwide.

Ballot-qualified candidates will be eligible to put a maximum 12,000-word platform summary on the FEC website, and for the other parts of the voter selection process for the main free airtime system, and postage and other subsidies.

The New Enlightenment reforms will result in a greatly widened diversity of candidates and public policy proposals for solving our most important challenges. Issues of concern to the average American and our least powerful citizens will no longer be ignored. We will have a more just and prosperous nation, one where prosperity will be far more equitably shared.

*The New Enlightenment: Ideals of Democracy, Human Rights, Reason, and Progress * Policy 24*

Eliminate Gerrymandering

In a normal democracy, voters choose their representatives. In the United States, to a shocking degree, it is the other way around. For example, the Republican controlled Florida legislature created election district map resulted in the election of 17 Republican and 10 Democratic congressional representatives in 2012, a 70% advantage for Republicans. But in Florida, 4.2 million are registered Republicans and 4.7 million, Democrats, a 12% advantage for Democrats. The map was skillfully designed to avoid a democratic (and Democratic) outcome to favor Republicans.

To accomplish this, district boundaries are bizarre. Florida's 22nd District is 90 miles long and never over 3 miles wide. Other districts look like donuts, embryos or Rorschach tests. Most other states, including those with Democrats in control, draw similarly bizarre partisan boundaries, but overall Republicans have benefited most from this anti-democratic practice. Democrats won 1.4 million more votes for U.S. congressional representatives than Republicans in 2012, yet Republicans had a 33 seat advantage, mainly because of Republican gerrymandering following the 2010 census.

The problem has gotten more extreme recently since the Census Bureau puts out digitized maps, called TIGER/Line files. New geographic information systems for mapping and analyzing demographic data cost only a few thousand dollars, work on ordinary Windows operating systems, and can draw up partisan maps automatically. This has turned gerrymandering from an art into a science.

Gerrymandering is one reason an already change resistant Congress is even more immutable. Only 23, or 5%, of sitting congressmen were defeated in the general election in 2012. The combination of larger numbers of gerrymandered safe seats and the need for candidates to have increasing enormous amounts of cash for their election campaigns is undermining our democracy.

House incumbents on average outspend challengers by five to one. If they can make their election more certain by using party operatives in their state to redraw boundaries favoring their election, they further ensure their reelection. This is another reason we have the lowest voter turnout in the developed world. Also, gerrymandering is resulting in a more polarized Congress since districts are more polarized—an important cause of congressional gridlock.

All countries, in the interests of equal representation, periodically adjust their electoral boundaries to reflect population changes, but no other country allows the process to be abused to instead grotesquely violate democratic principles.

We propose to eliminate gerrymandering and have fair and rational re-districting procedure be the national standard. The most important criterion will be minimizing the sum of the perimeters of all districts because this would create the most compact districts. However, county and city boundaries and other criteria may warrant consideration also. We consider these criteria less important than compactness; however, we propose allowing criteria other than compactness to be considered.

In each state, we will use a contest where participants will submit redis-tricting proposals, with the winner having the lowest sum of perimeters, while also including other factors they consider important or desirable. Contestants can be any political party, qualified public interest group, and the political sciences department of public universities in the state that choose to partici-pate. We would provide the best software for assisting in the redistricting pro-cess to participating political sciences departments, which any political party or qualified public interest group could also access if it chose not to spend its funds to purchase its own.

If a submitted proposal is gerrymandered or deviates from compactness too much, it will be outcompeted by more compact proposals. Each group has an incentive to come close to a maximally compact partition while including deviations it considers appropriate. If a group chooses the minimum perimeter without other considerations, just to maintain its reputation it would have to justify this to other members of their organization and the public. Even if some consider maximally compact partitions not optimal, they would be far superior to what typically exists, and the process will not favor any group, including party.

The option of a nonpartisan commission creating district boundaries also exists, but the conflicts in selecting commission members that all will agree are nonpartisan will sometimes be difficult to resolve, so the method proposed is likely a better option.

To eliminate gerrymandering and to achieve more legislative diversity and other public interest goals, multimember districts with proportional representation we should consider eventually. This would be a more radical reform that we do not advocate for now, except to advocate for its more widespread consideration and debate as a possible reform after we have the government of, for, and by the people resulting from the New Enlightenment reforms.

> *The New Enlightenment: Ideals of Democracy, Human Rights, Reason, and Progress* * *Policy 25*

Voting System Reform: Instant Runoff Voting

New Enlightenment policy is to change our voting system to one where "instant runoff voting" determines the winner. We elect our government officials using "plurality voting," whereby the candidate with the greatest number of votes wins. In races with only two candidates, the winner will receive the most votes. However, with three or more candidates the winner can be elected with far less than the majority, and may even be strongly disliked by the majority of the population. When there are three candidates two may have much more similar positions on all important issues than the third, thereby splitting the vote and giving the election to the least preferred candidate. In a worst-case three candidate scenario, a candidate with just 34% of the vote can win, despite being strongly disliked by 66% of the voters. With four or more candidates, the result can be even more anti-democratic.

A more democratic system would use "instant runoff voting," which ensures that the winner is the most preferred by the majority of voters. Instant runoff voting (IRV) gives voters the opportunity to rank as many or as few candidates as they wish in order of preference (i.e., first, second, third, and so on). The system allows them to do so without fear that their most preferred choice will help a candidate they least prefer to win the election.

After a vote is taken, first choices are tabulated. If over two candidates receive votes, the candidate who receives the fewest first choice rankings is eliminated. All ballots are then recounted, with each ballot counting as one vote for each voter's highest ranked candidate not eliminated. Specifically, voters who chose the now eliminated candidate will have their ballots added to the totals of their second ranked candidate. The weakest candidates are successively eliminated, and their voters' ballots are added to the totals of their next choices until two candidates remain. At this point, the candidate with a majority of votes is declared the winner.

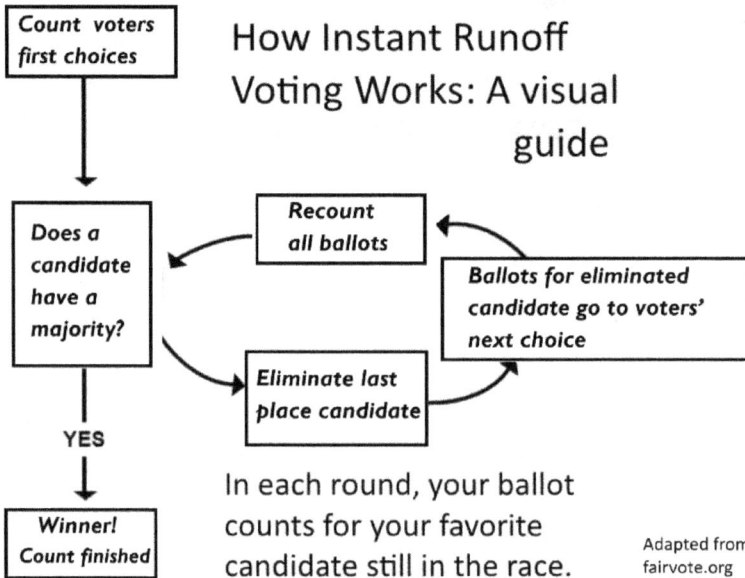

How Instant Runoff Voting Works: A visual guide

Count voters first choices

Does a candidate have a majority?

Recount all ballots

Ballots for eliminated candidate go to voters' next choice

Eliminate last place candidate

YES

Winner! Count finished

In each round, your ballot counts for your favorite candidate still in the race.

Adapted from fairvote.org

Instant runoff voting allows the winning candidate to be the one most preferred by voters and gives voters the freedom to vote for a preferred third-party (or fourth of fifth etc. party) candidate without concern that their vote may give the election to their least preferred candidate if their most preferred candidate loses. It ensures that a winner enjoys majority support when matched against the most preferred opponent. The system now used in national elections does not meet this basic requirement for a fair and democratic election system. Our plurality voting system has resulted in the election of candidates who most voters preferred not be elected.

Compared to traditional runoff elections, instant runoff voting saves tax dollars, reduces money and other resources needed for elections, and elects winners when turnout is highest.

The Electoral College system can result in a president without majority support even if individual states use IRV. However, since IRV ensures majority support in each state, it will substantially reduce this possibility. Individual states can adopt instant runoffs without a Constitutional amendment. Each state's electors could still be appointed through a winner-take-all method, but the IRV states would now be guaranteed to have a winner with majority approval.

We also support abolishing the Electoral College and the election of the president based on a national instant runoff vote. However, this reform we recommend be democratically determined after our more fundamental reforms are instituted.

---

*The New Enlightenment: Ideals of Democracy, Human Rights, Reason, and Progress * Policy 26*

Other National Election Standards Reforms

- **Create A Permanent Voter Registration System**:
  New Enlightenment policy is to use existing government databases to register voters automatically and provide a national permanent voter registration card and number to all citizens upon reaching 17 years of age. (Nineteen states permit 17-year-olds to vote in primary elections and caucuses if they will be 18 by Election Day). The system will eliminate the requirement to re-register upon changing residence. We will use the Post Office change of address database to automatically change voter registration databases.

  Complete and accurate voter rolls are the international norm, yet in the U.S. nearly one out of every three eligible citizens are not registered, and thus unable to vote on Election Day. This is not the only shocking fact related to our current system. Our current decentralized voter registration system is the main reason fictitious names appear on voter rolls, voters are doubly registered, and partisan organizations can manipulate voter rolls. For example, during the 2004 election, a partisan organization in Nevada threw away voter registration forms filled out by citizens who supported the opposing party.[357]

A 2006 nationwide survey concluded that voting age citizens earning less than $35,000 in annual income were more than twice as likely to lack government-issued ID needed to register to vote as those making over $35,000.[358] This policy will allow every citizen to participate in our election process and minimize registration abuses and the disenfranchisement of people most poorly represented by our current government.

- **Facilitate Casting a Vote with National Standards**:
New Enlightenment policies will make Election Day a national holiday. In addition, citizens could vote for 15 days before Election Day at poll locations and vote by mail. Millions of people who are forced to work long hours and take on many responsibilities are unable to vote due to insufficient time. 3% of the electorate waited longer than an hour in the 2012 election. There was a wide variation in wait times by state and precinct, but Florida's voters waited the longest to vote in 2012, nearly 40 minutes on average, and African Americans waited nearly twice as long as whites nationally.[359] We need the participation of all citizens in the democratic process, so this policy will make casting a vote easy for every citizen.

- Require that voting equipment meets national standards on how the equipment processes a vote using a paper ballot.

- Require maintenance of the paper ballot record for a period after the election.

- Require ballots, ballot counting and tabulation minimum standards.

- Restore voting rights to otherwise eligible citizens who have been convicted of a felony after they have served their sentences.

- To ensure accountability, one central, high-ranking official in each state would oversee the entire election process and ensure that it conforms to established national standards.

- The federal government's monitoring function before and on Election Day will be expanded to enable the Department of Justice to prevent discrimination.

*The New Enlightenment: Ideals of Democracy, Human Rights, Reason, and Progress * Policy 27*

Enhancing Democracy with New Democratic Forms

The extraordinary Occupy movement is largely gone, but its spirit has not been extinguished. Severe social injustices will cause it to rise again in a more beneficial, powerful, and enduring way. This renewed spirit will base actions on lessons from the Occupy movement and from several other innovative expressions of democracy internationally, and be part of the essence of the New Enlightenment.

Occupy brought to widespread public awareness the vast economic and political power disparities between the "1%" and the "99%." Now tens of millions of Americans see this issue as the most important of our time. Occupy also brought to widespread public awareness the great importance of public spaces for people to express discontent with public policy and to discuss public issues. Integral to some of these discussions was a decision-making process, also of potentially great importance. If the process (or possibly a modified version of it) that was used—a form of "consensus" decision-making among average citizens—can be a routine part of our policymaking process, the result is likely to be policy far better aligned with the public interest than exists now. This New Enlightenment policy details how we can accomplish this.

Also, Occupy demonstrated the great power of the Internet in social movements, which has continued to be applied to great effect. However, Occupy's core message regarding the injustice of the vast economic and political power disparities between the "1%" and the "99%," expressed about five years ago, remains unaddressed with policy solutions, despite the fact that the majority of our citizenry sees that developing and instituting policy solutions should be a high priority policymaker goal.

Political system dysfunction and wider social dysfunction is growing in a long-term trend with disillusionment with, and distrust of, our form of "democracy." Confidence levels in our democratic institutions are now at historic lows. Competitive elections for the leadership of legislative and executive offices, even when the process was not corrupted by the vast amounts of money of modern-day elections, has tended to not result in truly democratic outcomes. New Enlightenment reforms of our election system, media, and lobbying system, and policies for the widespread establishment of worker-owned enterprises will advance democratic functioning greatly. But we also need the following system, which will integrate average citizens in groups into some public policy development processes.

Average citizen involvement in public policy development will satisfy an essential human need: to be engaged with others in cooperative efforts to improve their and their social group's conditions. Through dialogue and consensus building, average citizens can help develop policies for a more just and egalitarian society. However, despite its faults, representative government with elected officials advised by professional members of the citizenry has value as an institutional arrangement, so I propose supplementing, not replacing it.

In our current cultural environment, most people know little about politics. One reason is that they have an insignificant amount of political power. But it is also true that the average person possesses valuable knowledge and skills and the desire to use them to have some control over the important aspects of his or her life. And this and other New Enlightenment policies will substantially increase the desire and capacity of average citizens to actively participate in the democratic processes determining societal conditions of great importance to their quality of life. The assumption that only professionals can possess the skills to govern well is plainly false, just considering current levels of dysfunction alone.

I describe some evidence that new democratic forms may be needed in *Now Is the Time for The New Enlightenment,* but far more exists. Although other New Enlightenment reforms will advance democratic functioning greatly, the one detailed in this policy proposal may ultimately result in the largest advance. This would be more certainly true if its success motivates further reforms along the same lines.

Among the deficiencies of our current democratic systems are their tendencies to place too little emphasis on systemic reform options when seeking solutions to problems, even when the evidence for the need for them is clear. The need for systemic improvements is evident in these systems:

- A food system based on agricultural practices that are unnecessarily environmentally destructive and that generates health problems through public policies that result in large numbers of people consuming excessive amounts of high calorie, low nutrient density foods.
- A health system that has overwhelming financial barriers to the care needed by tens of millions of Americans and financially destroys many that do access the system. Mental and dental health care are especially commonly inaccessible. The system is dominated by hospitals and places little emphasis on the cost effective and otherwise beneficial methods to

prevent disease. The system has over two times the OECD average per capita costs.

- Energy systems designed to produce and distribute energy, but not to use it efficiently, and designed with too little consideration of the environmental impact of the means of energy production.

- A transportation system dominated by resource inefficient, relatively high pollution generating automobiles. And 42% of America's major urban highways are congested, costing the economy about $101 billion in wasted time and fuel per year. Meanwhile, 45% of American households lack any access to mass transit, and millions more have inadequate service levels.[360] Many sufficiently densely populated areas exist where we could more extensively deploy mass transit for greater resource efficiencies and convenience. Also, the greater resource efficiency and convenience potential of high-speed rail relative to air transport in the densely populated east coast region (and elsewhere) has not been realized.

- An economic system that leaves large amounts of resources unused, while widespread and serious unmet needs exist, and that is generating vast inequalities. Our economic inequality is particularly vicious since it is characterized by historically vast societal wealth and historically vast amounts of it concentrated in a tiny elite while tens of millions of Americans are in poverty. And poverty levels for children are disproportionately high and will likely result in lifelong negative impacts for many millions of children.

- A political system where public policy has no relationship to the preferences of the average citizen.

In 2014, policy scholar Paul Light performed a comprehensive study of the effectiveness of a hundred presidential and congressional investigative commissions on the governmental response to crises. Light found that only thirty-nine inquired into systemic causes, and the quality of their work was sometimes poor, lacking even in basic fact-finding, and often produced no results. For example, despite widespread attention to the BP oil spill in 2010, an investigatory commission and other advisory committee work, there has been no congressional action. The leaks continue (at least until the 2014 report).[361]

The large reservoir of discontent and skills in our citizenry can and should be tapped in new ways for public policy ideas, and for the vision needed for systemic change when such change is called for. Current policymaker advisors and policymakers are often heavily invested educationally, professionally and financially in existing systems so are less open to systemic changes as solutions to problems than the average citizen would be.

Whether systemic reforms are involved or not, substantial benefits will result from a system where average citizens perform some public policy development. Those most likely to be affected by a problem are average citizens who sometimes have information relevant to determining a solution that professionals do not have. They also have the strongest motive to solve it, most immediately see the impact of any solution implemented, and they are best situated to sometimes assist in its implementation.

Currently, letter writing, emails, and phone calls by citizens have little or no impact on policy. The main route of contact by the citizenry on government policymakers with impact is through advisory committees and think tanks where relatively few policy professionals are involved, who commonly pursue ideologically biased points of view in favor of current systems and power structures.

Public policies have too often been based on guesses founded on prejudices, not evidence, and many have been designed to best serve a small elite in disregard of the majority. Well-designed deliberative systems that allow average citizens a significant impact on policy development can create better policy outcomes. Substantial evidence for this exists from policy development systems implemented in Denmark, Germany, Brazil, Australia, Canada, India, even some parts of the U.S., and elsewhere.[362] Also, the research of Daron Acemoglu and James Robinson reported in their book *Why Nations Fail*, shows that successful societies have institutions that are inclusive and promote the use of citizens' talent, ingenuity, ambition, and ability.

The following policy will improve the civic skills of, and tap the capacity of, the average citizen in the development of public policies that best serve their interests and those of the wider society in which we all live. It will create the opportunity for groups of average citizens to participate in the policymaking process. The process incentivizes citizens to develop the capacity to make good decisions, mainly through an awareness that it may result in their having to live with the consequences. However, financial incentives are also involved.

Educational processes, dialogue, and consensus building in small groups of average citizens are at the core of the proposed democratic form. It is designed to be used for both decisions on local issues such as the quality of schools, the environment, policing, local government budgeting, plans for bike lanes, highway routes, etc., and major national and state issues. Despite the great importance of decisions on major national issues, the level of knowledge to make wise policy choices is generally not impractically large for the average citizen to attain when he or she does not already have it.

The proposed process would not be appropriate for creating rapid response policies or policies that require a high level of technical expertise, such as how to best deal with failure of the power grid. But for the ultimately most important policy decisions regarding our energy system, for example, those influencing the proportions of our energy supplied by local renewable sources, energy efficiency measures, and fossil fuels, average citizens can practically gain the knowledge that arguably would result in wiser choices than the ones that current policymakers have made. Also, society may be more willing to accept a policy decision if it were created by groups of average, non-privileged citizens.

The process described below injects into the policymaking process the diversity of knowledge possessed by individuals whose knowledge currently would not be recognized or valued by elite power holders and experts. And this newly utilized knowledge, which the process also enhances, can result in productive innovations that otherwise would not have been achieved. As the process becomes more widely utilized, the exercising of capacities of argument, planning, and evaluation will result in average citizens who are better deliberators.

National Deliberative Processes in Citizen Groups

I propose that 0.1% of the U.S. population (slightly over 0.1% as a result of the details of the proposed selection process) be randomly selected to participate in formal county (or county equivalent) based, but nationally funded, deliberative processes in groups of 25 citizens, called Councils. Taking 0.1% of the population in many counties would result in their having no Councils of the standard 25-member size. So we will round up to the nearest whole number of 25-member Councils after taking 0.1% of the population of each county to determine the number of participants or Councils in the county. This will result in about 358,000 citizens participating nationwide—a large number that I recommend be even larger through voluntary groups outside the official, federally funded system. Washington, D.C. and other cities not part of counties, such as exist in Virginia, will be treated as counties.

Anyone randomly selected to participate of course can choose not to, in which case we will randomly select another person until the desired number is reached. On average, over all councils, random selection ensures that participants are representative of the general population. The lowest 99% in the wealth, income, and power hierarchy will have 99% of the influence on the determined policy recommendations. Random selection gives the same influence over the policymaking process to the poorest 20% of Americans as it gives the wealthiest 20%, unlike existing policymaking processes. However, normal statistical variability will result in the random selection process creating many unrepresentative councils (for example, some with 21 men and 4 women).

To ensure the selection process results in the demographic makeup of each Council fairly reflecting the population of the citizens of the county regarding these characteristics: gender, above or below the 45th percentile of county income, and race, we will require that no less than 12 participants be of one gender (or necessarily no more than 13 participants) and that 13 participants be of the lower income category (or necessarily no more than 12 participants in the higher income category). This will slightly skew the selections toward lower incomes.

To ensure a representative racial diversity, if the population has between 4 and 8% of a particular race we will require between one and two participants be of that race, for races between 8% and 12% of the population they will be represented by between two and three participants, and so on. If a member of a race that represents less than 4% of the population is randomly selected that person would be a participant. (The quota range for a race is determined by dividing four into the race's percent of population and rounding up to the nearest whole number for the upper limit, and down for the lower limit.) Mixed race individuals could identify with a race they consider most appropriate or be included in a separate mixed race category.

For details on the selection process, see the following text box. You can choose not to read the level of detail in the text box with no loss of continuity.

The slight bias towards lower than median income participants is justified based on this group being otherwise poorly represented. The above quotas will be standard for all counties; however, counties would be free to include additional demographic criteria that they consider appropriate in the selection process as well.

In addition to other New Enlightenment policies that will increase the desire and capacity of the citizenry to actively participate in democratic processes, educational programs for the participants also will. But if economic conditions remain as they are, due to the time working to earn a living, too many people will be unable to commit the time and energy that the New Enlightenment deliberative process will require. However, New Enlightenment economic policies will alleviate this problem by reducing the full-time work-hour standard by at least the amount of time per week that the proposed system requires for the people who participate, even without considering that higher wages will allow many people to further reduce their work-hours.

Selection Process for the 25 Council Members

We will use postal records of the residents within county boundaries for the random selections. Random selections will proceed until we select the maximum in any quota category. Further random selections will deselect any in this category that has already reached its maximum until 25 participants are selected. This process will necessarily result in the gender and income category quotas being met.

If after 25 participants are selected the quota for a particular race has not been met further random selections will seek participants to meet this quota who will replace previous selections in the majority selected race of their gender and income category. Those replaced we will also randomly select. In the cases where both income category and gender cannot be matched, previously selected participants in their income category will be replaced regardless of gender.

Each participant must agree to take part in four hours per week, 40-week deliberative processes that will result in public policy recommendations, and in many cases, instituted public policy. They will be paid $100 per week. This amounts to $25 per hour for the official time spent in the process, which, in addition to the personal satisfaction they will receive from influencing policy which impacts their lives, seems fair and reasonable compensation for their time (which will generally involve preparation time in addition to the four-hour meeting time). This payment will help motivate participants to take seriously their responsibility to make their best effort in the process. And it will be a more significant motive for people at the lower end of the income spectrum to participate than at the higher end, which is desirable to help ensure that the resulting policy proposals will serve people who currently have the least economic and political power.

The people choosing to participate will spend their first 4-hour session in standardized instructional programs on the deliberative process itself. Eventually, this will be unnecessary after improved high school and college instruction standards make familiarity with the process widespread. (Also, media coverage of the process may make this introduction unnecessary.)

The instructional programs will emphasize that serving the best interests of as many people as possible that are affected by the issue under deliberation, or serving "the greater good," is important, and that without adhering to this ethos any proposal they make will likely not reach sufficient levels of support to be adopted. For the process to function well, each participant cannot vote for the policy option that advances only his or her self-interest, but rather for the choice that seems most reasonable in consideration of the interests of all concerned. Although some participants may have little in common—some may even have histories of animosity—they are united in a major effort seeking how best to improve the situation or solve the problem on which they are deliberating in a way that is considered fair and reasonable to as many participants as possible.

After the selection of an issue on which to deliberate, using the process we describe below, educational programs on the issue will begin. As part of the educational process, questions may be posed to experts on the issue either by email, in person, or in web conferences. Because a large part of the process involves informing participants about all sides of an issue, they will have (or have access to) the knowledge needed to create their own unique policy recommendations, or evaluate those of others.

All the participants will commonly review any participant's briefing material recommendations based on input from representatives, interest groups or any other source. The importance of selecting material with verifiable facts will be emphasized. For complex issues where excessively large amounts of content results, a minimum level of agreement determined by vote (possibly at least one-third of the members) that the material is from a reliable source will be required for inclusion in the official briefing material. Participants would be free to mention statements from sources of his choosing during the deliberative process but would have to defend their legitimacy if they are to impact the process.

Discussion will follow the educational programs, then a participant will make a policy proposal that he or she finds desirable and believes, based on the discussion, may receive the widest support for improving the situation or solving the problem discussed. Since the goal is to get as many participants as possible to support their proposal, participants will seek and present to the group what they consider would be widely appealing justifications for it.

After a policy proposal is presented each participant then votes to reject or accept it. Anyone who rejects the proposal will detail the reasons. The Council will then, if possible, modify the proposal based on these reasons and retest it for approval by all members. Even if a participant does not entirely approve the proposal, if the disapproval is not strong he or she can allow it to proceed. Any participant with a proposal will be given the opportunity to present it, or meet its requirements based on influencing another participant's proposal. The process is agreement seeking and cooperative, but even when compromise cannot be achieved it motivates constructing fundamentally new proposals based on new ideas.

If after improving a proposal no further compromises can be made, and one or more persons remain who find it unacceptable, the proposal is blocked, at least temporarily. A participant who has another, possibly fundamentally different, proposal can then test it for consensus. If it too cannot achieve consensus, then another proposal is considered and so on. If no proposal achieves consensus, then the one with the fewest number of participants choosing to block it will be adopted. In the case of a tie, a vote (an IRV vote if more than two proposals are tied) will determine the proposal that will be adopted. Ideally, a proposal can achieve consensus, and this will generally be the outcome of the deliberative processes designed to serve this ideal.

A visual guide to the essential part of process follows.

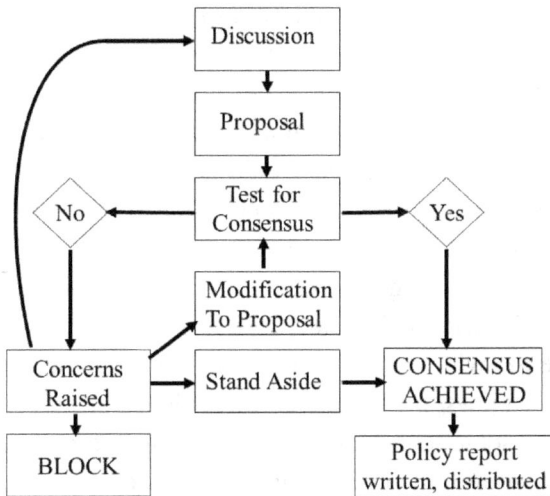

For the process to be effective, each participant must understand that remaining open to new information and proposals is necessary, even if it does not best serve his or her interests. This practice is familiar to everyone. We often discuss issues and resolve conflict by accepting a reasonable and fair outcome for all concerned, rather than ignoring the interests of others in an attempt to best serve our own narrow interests.

The ability of any participant to block a proposal forces participants to negotiate with those having minority views, and to modify proposals to make them at least tolerable for everyone, and when this is not possible, desirable or tolerable to as many participants as possible. Our current democratic forms systematically ignore or discount this important function of democracy. Even when a participant's proposal is rejected through deliberative processes, the participant will at least know why.

An impartial moderator and assistant will keep the discussion on track and make sure that anyone wanting to speak may do so. They will be selected by Council member vote, typically either from among employees of the county chosen by the county manager (or equivalent) or from New Enlightenment Citizens Union members trained for these roles. (Facilitating and improving democratic processes will be an essential function of the New Enlightenment Citizens Union and ultimately Party).

In counties where no county official or trained New Enlightenment Citizens Union member is available, participants will choose a moderator and assistant by vote from among citizens who register their interest with qualifying information on the county government, or if not available, state government website. The essential importance of having an impartial and reasonable moderator thoroughly familiar with the deliberative process will be emphasized in the instructional programs.

The assistants will take minutes, including notation of any requests for information in the meeting that would later be sought and presented at the next meeting or emailed to participants prior to it. Moderators and assistants will also be paid $25 per hour.

Citizens brought together to discuss public policy in a setting that emphasizes equal participation, mutual respect, and reasoned argument will likely bridge the wide chasms existing in the larger society. More sympathy with opposing views, more respect for evidence based reasoning rather than opinion, more social cohesion between people from different backgrounds, and a greater commitment to the public policies developed will result from this system.

A criticism of this kind of deliberation process is that potentially it allows those most rhetorically skilled to have a disproportionate influence on it and its outcome. This may be true to some degree. However, perfection is not achievable with any system, and people with little rhetorical skill can also express the most important determinants of outcomes: facts and reasons. This system is extraordinarily egalitarian. All participants will know that they have equal opportunity for an equal role in determining the functioning of an important part of the world in which they live.

Issue Selection

Each county will have all Councils within it deliberate on the same issues at their own pace in sequence based on this issue selection frequency ranking system:

Each participant chooses his or her top priority issues or problems requiring a public policy change for the ranking process. Their choices can be made in consideration of suggestions from their elected representatives and any interest group they choose. Likely, many interest groups will create a list for consideration in this process. Each elected national, state and local representative can also provide a list to Councils with his or her constituency of up to a recommended maximum of five national, up to five state, and up to five local issues or problems that the representative judges to be the most important requiring a public policy solution. A summary of each issue in 40-words or less is recommended, with any other information the source provides. The recommended maximums will keep review time of recommendations from these sources within reasonable limits.

After considering any suggestions, each participant will either choose from among them or state priorities independent of them. He or she will state up to three national issues, up to three state issues and up to three local issues most preferred for their Council's deliberation in 40-word or less summaries of each issue. The 40-word limit will facilitate the following selection process for the issues on which they will deliberate.

For the participants' choices on all local, state, and national issues that are stated differently but are essentially the same as, or very similar to, others, the system requires that they be included in narrowly defined categories to be stated uniformly. We will modify some issue statements in the category so that the category is represented by one statement. Councils will deliberate on these uniformly stated issues. They will be uniformly stated statewide for the state and national issues (and ultimately nationwide on national issues), and countywide on local issues. I call this process "unifying" the issues statements., The examples I detail below will clarify the process..

Unifying the issues statements will be done by employees of a state agency, possibly the state's election commission or equivalent, and then this agency will rank the unified issue selection frequency in each county separately. After ranking, the issue statements will be returned to the Councils in unified form.

Uniformly stating issues that are essentially the same or similar, but stated differently by different participants, serves the purposes of facilitating selecting high priority issues on which to deliberate, and it simplifies analyzing deliberative process results countywide, statewide, and nationwide. Also it plays an important role in other parts of the proposed system. Often participants will choose issue statements of their representatives or widely known interest groups, so many issue statements will not require alteration to create uniformity of expression.

Below are examples of how individual participants' issue choices could be slightly altered to create uniformly stated issues for Council deliberations. The issue statement unification process will both clarify and uniformly state similar issue choices:

Example 1

- Participant 1 issue: Should climate change be mitigated using a carbon tax?
- Participant 2 issue: How high would gas and other energy costs rise if the U.S. adopted the same tax per ton on carbon as Finland ($89/ton), and is it worth the cost?
- Unified issue statement: Should climate change be mitigated using a carbon tax, and if so, how large can it be before it is unacceptably economically harmful or inequitable?

It is highly unlikely that either participant would object to deliberating on the unified issue statement rather than their own since it is essentially the same as theirs. Although some discretion is involved in creating the unified statements, and in some cases may result in a significant alteration in a participant statement, if it is done reasonably, participants will be very unlikely to find them unacceptable. The purpose of serving the ideal of as many people as practical deliberating on equivalently stated high priority issues would generally be considered worth any compromise involved.

Example 2

- Participant 1 issue: Should the minimum wage be raised to $12/ hour?
- Participant 2 issue: Would raising the minimum wage to $15/hour be harmful to the economy?
- Unified issue statement: How high can the minimum wage be raised before it would be unacceptably economically harmful?

Example 3

- Participant 1 issue: Is a flat tax type of income tax proposed by some Republican candidates for president in their primary contest the most just and economically beneficial type of tax, and which of their proposals is the most just and beneficial?
- Participant 2 issue: Should income taxes be raised on taxpayers with incomes in the top 5% to eliminate the deficit?
- Participant 3 issue: Should income taxes be lowered on the middle class and poor, while making up for the reduced revenue by raising taxes on high incomes?
- Unified issue statement: Considering both economic impacts and fairness, what are the most beneficial marginal tax rates proposed by interest groups, policy experts, and politicians, and can we improve on the best choice among them?

These are complex issues. Each may take the full 40 weeks of some of the Councils that deliberate on them to come to a conclusion. Many issues on which Councils would deliberate would not be nearly as complex. Some less complex, and local, issues may include:

Should funding be increased for?:

- repairing or paving roads
- expanding evening and weekend hours of libraries
- adding more benches in commercial strips
- converting a little-used street segment into a plaza
- enhancing a local park or playground
- preserving the community's beaches from erosion and flooding
- creating a new composting site, etc.

Before returning the state unified national issue statements, they will also undergo a unification process at the national level. States will submit their unified national issues statement to a federal agency, possibly the federal election commission, for national level unification. This agency will then return to the states the national level unified issue statements with the associated issue statements determined by the states, which the states would have associated with the original participant statement for return to the Councils in ranked order based on countywide frequency of selection.

The complexity of the process would be greatly limited by many people choosing the limited number of issues statements recommended by their representatives or popular interest groups. Also, a limited number of issues exist that otherwise would attract the public attention. A visual guide to the issue unification process follows.

UNIFIED ISSUE STATEMENTS TO THE COUNCILS PROCESS

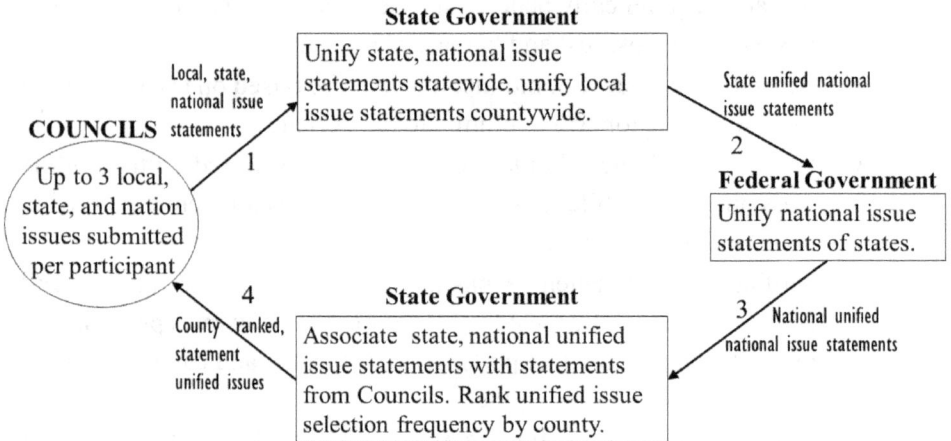

State Government

Local, state, national issue statements

COUNCILS

Unify state, national issue statements statewide, unify local issue statements countywide.

State unified national issue statements

Up to 3 local, state, and nation issues submitted per participant

1

2

Federal Government

Unify national issue statements of states.

4

County ranked, statement unified issues

State Government

Associate state, national unified issue statements with statements from Councils. Rank unified issue selection frequency by county.

3

National unified national issue statements

All participants' issue choices with their unified version will be included in a publicly available database on state and federal websites so the press (or anyone else) can evaluate the reasonableness of the issue statement unification process.

Prior to the Council members' selection of their top priority issues, some issues of concern at all levels of government will be emphasized for their consideration. One is this:

What proportion of local public revenues should originate from the federal government? Localities cannot tax citizens with the degree of progressivity that would be most just and beneficial because if they raise tax rates on the wealthiest or highest income people it will motivate them to move to the neighboring locality, causing a race to the bottom problem where no locality can appropriately fund public priorities. It is very easy to move to a neighboring locality, and even to a neighboring state causing a race to the bottom problem among states. Only the national government has the power to tax using appropriate levels of progressivity because it is far more difficult for high income or wealth people to move to another country than another locality or state to avoid taxes. It is possible, though, so as I have mentioned in some New Enlightenment tax proposals, in an increasingly globalized world, we eventually need to have international agreements on tax systems to avoid the race to the bottom problem among countries.

In each state, we will create a publicly accessible registry of topics in

deliberative processes statewide so that Councils deliberating on the same issue can share educational materials if they choose to, and Councils deliberating on an issue at the same time may also share informational web conferences
with experts. This would make more efficient use of educational materials
and expert time. Members from different Councils could also communicate
to benefit from one another's knowledge.

Each Council will work on its county's concerns in ranked order at their
own pace, going through as many as it can in the 40 weeks. Local, state, and
national issues will be ranked as a group. For some counties, national issues
would be top priority issues, some, state or local, and the mix would vary
depending on the county. Ranking priorities countywide so all Councils in the
county will deliberate on top priority issues as determined by all participants
in the county will make more common the sharing of informational resources
among local people in different Councils. Also, the results of more deliberations on top local priorities countywide will more likely result in a stronger
and more beneficial impact on local government policies than would be the
case if some Councils deliberated on lower priorities according to the countywide majority view.

After a policy proposal is adopted, the Council will produce a report on
it, which it submits to its members' representatives and the press. In counties
where two or more Councils exist, after any local policy decision, each Council will elect three Council members to present and justify the decision to a
county level "Collaborative Council." For up to four eight-hour days, as necessary, over one to four weekends, Council representatives will meet in an
issue specific Collaborative Council to attempt consensus on a policy proposal that is selected and possibly improved from those of the individual
Councils. Collaborative Council participants will be compensated $200 per
day for their time in the process.

Before the Collaborative Councils, the Council representatives would familiarize themselves with the reports of the other Councils on their issue. Collaborative Councils would begin with discussions, then questions and answer
sessions by participants explaining their Council's proposal, and then a vote
(IRV when three or more proposals exist) on the most preferred policy of the
Councils represented. This policy will then be used in the consensus process
so it could be improved by removing as many objections to it as possible.
Some policies with the most votes may have no significant objections to be
removed. (In the case of a tie, participants can determine an optimal proposal,
or one with the fewest significant objections by considering both proposals in

the consensus process.)

When a significant objection exists, a modification suggested to overcome it would be tested for consensus, and if the modified proposal achieves consensus or creates a proposal with fewer objections, the modified proposal will replace the originally selected one. Other suggested modifications to overcome objections would go through the same process. Since an improved version of the most preferred policy proposal will result, it will be the one officially adopted by the Collaborative Council, on which it then writes a report.

Media coverage likely would be extensive on the results of the Collaborative Councils or the Councils when they make a final policy decision, but we will require coverage for broadcast media companies as a license requirement.

For local government policy proposals of Collaborative Councils, or Councils when a Collaborative Council did not decide the issue, a referendum will be taken on the proposals, and for any that a supermajority (60%) approves, it will be required that the local government institute the policy.

For state and national policies, local representatives to the state and federal government will have the discretion to support and advocate for the Council's or Collaborative Council's recommended policies, or not, but would have to justify their decisions. Press coverage will likely result in substantial pressure to comply with the public will as expressed through deliberative processes. If a representative doesn't comply it likely will significantly reduce the representative's re-election chances. However, state and national policies I recommend be influenced more strongly by other levels of the citizen deliberative hierarchy that I describe in the next sections.

Ideally, New Enlightenment policies will be among the policies considered by the Councils, so ideally, this policy would be the first, or among the first, New Enlightenment policies instituted. Moral justifications described in Part 4 should be central to the deliberations on the most important policies designed to greatly enhance egalitarianism. Historically, major social and political reforms such as those regarding slavery and women's suffrage were founded on moral consideration discourse that affected large numbers of people. When decisions must be largely determined by moral considerations, a consensus decision by average citizens generally will be closer to the ideal than those of a small elite. Decisions by a small elite tend to not be made based on serving the good of the whole of society, which is an important consideration in moral decisions. Instead, they are often based on serving their narrow interests.

After the official federally funded 40 weeks of deliberation, both their newly developed civic skills and relationships would likely motivate some participants to form new, voluntary Councils.

Statewide Council Representative Assemblies — "Forums"

State and national officials could use all Councils' policy proposals to determine a majority opinion or a compromise among the state and national proposals. However, in some states and for the federal government the number of Councils will make this process unwieldy. The following process is more systematic, and would likely result in the institution of a superior policy. It uses deliberative processes of representatives from the Councils.

After any state or national policy decision, each Council will elect (using IRV) three Council members to present and justify the decision, in ranked order, to a state level Council, or Forum. For a week, Council representatives will meet in issue specific Forums to select and improve a policy proposal from among those determined by the Councils.

In any case, where the total number of representatives would exceed 200, we recommend limiting Forum size by selecting the top one or two representatives from the ranked order of the Councils as needed to meet the 200 limit. Where after selecting one representative per Council further reductions are required to meet the limit we will randomly select 200 representatives from the top ranked representatives of the Councils for the Forum. Only the largest states may sometimes require this limitation. Forum participants will be compensated $200 per day and their travel and lodging expenses will be paid for within reasonable limits.

Before the Forums, representatives of the Councils would familiarize themselves with the reports of the other Councils on their proposal by reading at least their executive summaries if it is impractical to read all report content. Forums would begin with discussions, then questions and answers sessions by participants explaining their Council's proposal, and then a vote on the most preferred policy of the Councils represented. This policy will then be used in the consensus process so it could be improved by removing as many objections to it as possible, and ideally, achieve consensus.

As in the Collaborative Council process, a modification suggested to overcome an objection would be tested for consensus, and if the modified proposal achieves consensus or creates a proposal with fewer objections, the amended proposal will replace the originally selected one. Other suggested modifications to overcome objections would go through the same process. In the uncommon cases where consensus is not achieved, an improved version of the most preferred policy proposal will result, so it will be the one officially adopted by the Forum.

The Forum then produces a report on this optimized proposal, which it submits to state and national representatives, as appropriate, and the press. As with the Council reports, media coverage would likely be extensive, in this case statewide, but coverage will be required for broadcast media companies as a license requirement. For policy proposals intended for state government implementation, a referendum will be taken on them, and for any that a supermajority approves, we will require that the policy is instituted by the state government.

Nationwide Forum Representative Assemblies — "CSE Congresses"

After any national policy decision, Forum participants will elect three Forum members to present and justify their decision to national level forums. We call these forums CSE Congresses for this reason: The participants will all have progressed through a citizen selection hierarchy based on their expertise and ability to express it on the issue on which they will deliberate. So their conferences will be of citizen selected experts, thus they are Citizen Selected Experts Congresses or CSE Congresses.

For up to a week, Forum representatives will meet in separate CSE Congresses on each issue to select a policy proposal from those of the Forums for improvement using the deliberative process.

Before a CSE Congress, participants would familiarize themselves with the reports of all other Forums on their issue. The CSE Congress would begin with discussions and questions and answers sessions by participants explaining their Forum's policy proposal, then proceed through the same process as described in the Forums to develop an optimal policy proposal. The CSE Congress will produce a report on the proposal, which it submits to national representatives and the press.

As with the Council and Forum reports, media coverage should be extensive, in this case nationwide. Coverage requirements for broadcast media companies will likely not be necessary on these top level deliberative process results (and possibly on other levels also).

For CSE Congress policy proposals, national referendums will be taken on them, and for any policy a supermajority approves it will be required that the policy is instituted by the federal government.

After the 40-week Councils and a one-week break, a second cycle will begin of 40-week Councils, Collaborative Councils, one-week Forums and one week of CSE Congresses. Eventually, we recommend experimenting with a mix of 40-week and 60-week Councils (with a four-week break) as an alternative.

The estimated cost for the Councils nationwide is $2.0 billion per year. The estimated cost for the Collaborative Councils is $37 million, for the Forums $180 million, and for the CSE Congresses $4.6 million, per year. This totals about $2.2 billion per year.

Public Space

Many pre-existing public spaces could be provided for the Councils, Collaborative Councils, Forums and CSE Congresses. For Councils and Collaborative Councils, public colleges and universities typically have many empty classrooms and empty auditoriums on the weekends, as do K-12 schools. Meeting or conference rooms in public colleges and universities, libraries, government office buildings and government owned conference centers are possibilities for the Forums and CSE Congresses. Public buildings commonly have Wi-Fi Internet, and projectors may be available, which would sometimes be useful. In the unlikely event these spaces are not sufficient, churches often have available spaces, and some may offer them.

New Enlightenment policy will facilitate political events, both in and out of the formal federally funded deliberative systems, by instituting a variant of eminent domain laws. Current eminent domain laws allow the government to take private property for compelling public purposes, with fair compensation to the owner. I propose an analogous federal law requiring that unoccupied public spaces in public schools, colleges and universities be provided at no charge to groups that want their use for discussing, deliberating on or educating on public issues if no other space is available for the group. This would be a temporary taking of public space for a compelling public purpose: enhancing democracy. The compensation would be the federal funds that provide a portion of the funding for these institutions.

Systems would be necessary to determine which group can use a particular space, and for assigning people for monitoring each space's use. However, the possibility of vandalism or theft in a building, now often an overriding concern, should not be a barrier to making the best use of public space. Vandalism and theft laws will be enforced, and violators should be held legally and financially accountable.

Since facilitating democratic processes will be an essential function of the New Enlightenment Citizens Union, volunteers among union members could act as monitors, or possibly when a group applies for space the group could assign other persons for monitoring responsibilities. We should not allow local governments to thwart democratic processes needed for the nation to be a well-functioning democracy by unreasonably barring them from available public space that could be well utilized for this purpose.

To increase voluntary deliberative groups' attendance outside the federally funded system, some groups may list their events on event calendars of local media. For events held at universities and colleges, they could be listed on their calendars. I also recommend that all localities have a calendar for listing public educational and deliberative events.

So far, I have described political action or educational events that generally will not occur in publicly prominent places. But as Occupy and many other social movements have made clear, publicly prominent public space for political action and public claim making is necessary. Some other recent examples where social movements relied on prominent public space for their impact are:

Cairo's Tahrir Square was the focus of the movement to overthrow Egypt's Mubarak regime. Prague's Wenceslas Square was the focus of the movement to oust an oppressive regime, which also played an important role in bringing down other totalitarian Communist governments. Those protests were inspired in part by events in Beijing's Tiananmen Square when democracy activists unsuccessfully challenged the power of China's dictatorship. The state capitol in Madison, Wisconsin, where thousands of workers protested the governor's attacks on collective bargaining rights, is another case of a prominent public space becoming a staging ground for political change or resistance. The Boston Common has been a site for protests and public gatherings for nearly three centuries. These examples demonstrate the importance to democracy of having prominent Commons—a square, park or plaza that is open to all, for citizens to rally, voice their discontent, show their power, and sometimes ultimately express a new vision for their country.

We lost some of our public voice when corporate run shopping malls replaced downtowns as the center of action. You can't organize a rally, hand out flyers, or circulate a petition in a shopping mall without the permission of the management, and they generally will refuse to allow this kind of activity. As we have lost places to join together to voice our views as citizens, we have become more passive about what is happening to our country.

It would be unreasonable to require allowing mass demonstrations or rallies on private property, including malls. However, we believe it is necessary to institute national laws that would require allowing the handing out of flyers in malls, privately owned public plazas, and store parking lots announcing a rally or political event elsewhere. This is a kind of eminent domain issue, where private property would not be taken, as current law allows, but some of the owners' pre-existing rights would be, for a compelling public purpose. These places (or vicinities, in the case of parking lots) are where the largest number of people gather, so this is where we must facilitated democratic processes to the degree practical.

Also, a national law analogous to eminent domain law is necessary to ensure public access to publicly owned parks and plazas for political purposes. Public parks do not commonly have unreasonable restrictions, but in some jurisdictions, a permit is required, with application fees, security deposits for clean-up, or fees to cover overtime police costs and administrative costs being charged. National law should ban financial barriers to participating in political or public policy related events in parks. A permit requirement would be acceptable to allow the scheduling of events to avoid conflict between groups. Of course, participants will be required to comply with littering and vandalism laws, and they will be held legally and financially accountable for violating them. Taxes should cover any other expenses resulting from the citizenry exercising assembly and speech rights in public parks, not the participants at the event.

Enhancing democracy with new (and old) democratic forms in existing public space will be an important part of the New Enlightenment's renewal of U.S. democracy.

---

*The New Enlightenment: Ideals of Democracy, Human Rights, Reason, and Progress * Policy 28*

"The deliberative sense of the community should govern."[363]

Alexander Hamilton

"I consider the people who constitute a society or nation as the source of all authority in that nation, as free to transact their common concerns by any agents they think proper, to change these agents individually, or the organization of them in form or function whenever they please."[364]

Thomas Jefferson

Reforming Our Fourth Estate

Widespread worker-ownership and self-direction of media corporations will create a new media culture far more responsive and accountable to the majority. Regulations and incentives can accomplish this.

Why Fundamental Reform Is Needed

The way a media system is structured, controlled and financially supported is of central importance to any society. In non-democratic societies, those in power invariably dominate the media to maintain their rule. Control the means of widespread communication of ideas and information, and you largely control the political structure and broader social structure of the society. The biggest problem facing all who seek a more just society is media that do not express well, or at all, injustices that exist and policies to remedy them to the majority of the population. Media reform is interdependent with political and broader social reform. They will rise or fall together.

Our mass media poorly serve, or disserve, our society

A well-informed populace on public issues is essential to a functioning democracy. Medias' responsibility to create it is why they are called "the Fourth Estate." Yet our most powerful media, our mass media, avoid informing adequately on fundamental public problems and solutions. Ownership and upper management all being members of a wealthy elite is why.

A mass media prominently reporting on fundamental problems and their possible solutions, and instilling a sense that we all have a responsibility to learn about the important issues to enable us to best serve our role in our democracy, would motivate public pressures for public policy that would best serve the majority. This would diminish the relatively privileged position of this elite; it's avoided because too few can see beyond narrow self-interest, to see that a more just society would benefit everyone, including themselves.

The following is one example demonstrating that our highly concentrated corporate media are poorly serving our nation and are a barrier to the fundamental social reforms we need:

In *Now Is the Time for The New Enlightenment* we saw study results showing that on average people believe that the poorest 20% of the American people should have about 10% of the country's wealth, and the poorest 40% should have about 25%. We also saw that most people realize that the country is far more economically divided than their ideal. They believe the poorest 20% have only about 2% of the country's wealth, a small fraction, one-fifth, of what they consider ideal, and the top 20% have almost double what they consider ideal. But the facts are very different, and the difference is of major importance: The bottom 20% has -1.4% of the country's wealth (debt greater than assets) and the next 20% has 0.3% of the country's wealth; in total, the bottom 40% has -1.1% of the country's wealth. The bottom 40% of the country, or 128 million people, have total debts greater than their total assets. Meanwhile, 400 people have over $2.3 trillion, more than the bottom 60% or about 190 million Americans—a level of inequality far worse than most people imagine could exist.

I also described in Part 1, survey results of an international study by scholars at the Harvard Business School and Thailand's Chulalongkorn University indicating that most Americans have no idea how extreme our income inequality is. Americans on average estimate that the ratio of CEO pay to unskilled worker pay is about 30 to 1. In reality, the average S&P 500 company CEO earned *354 times* what the median U.S. worker did in 2012. Americans said, ideally, that gap should be 6.7 to 1. (Performance bonuses, stock options and other forms of exorbitant compensation are tax deductible, so taxpayers are subsidizing the unjust CEO pay gap.)

These poll results indicate that the facts regarding our huge economic divide would be news to most people. But by what reasonable criteria do these facts reach a threshold of importance to be reported, and reported with the high degree of repetition that many stories are reported? And by what reasonable criteria do these economic conditions deserve prominent analytical coverage and policy solution debate?

Among the most important qualities of a society are how its economic system divides the society's economic product among its members, and how large the economic product is. So extreme economic inequality is news of the utmost importance because it directly relates to the first quality and indirectly relates to the second. When economic disparities are extreme, there's a depressing effect on economic activity resulting from the depressed purchasing power of large numbers of people.

If widespread awareness existed of severe economic injustice, then public policy to beneficially deal with the problem would be motivated by public pressure. Today's public policy rests instead on a foundation of ignorance—the public has no idea what our society is really like.

Have you seen on the front page of a major newspaper, or as the lead story on the national network TV news, the 2013 Gallup poll result that 20% of Americans did not have enough money to buy the food they needed at least once over the prior one-year period? What would members of this group put on the front page or present as a lead story if they were in control? It would often differ substantially from what is chosen by current management.

They would certainly have stated this poll result in a front page headline or lead story, with details and analysis on why this level of hardship exists despite the fact that the country, as a whole and on a per capita basis, is extremely wealthy and wealthier than ever. On other days, they would likely include, for example, front page headlines and lead stories on a University of Massachusetts study that found that the share of prime working-age Americans who can't generate enough income to meet their basic needs shot up from 31% in 2000 to 38% in 2010.[365] Or that an Urban Institute study found that over 51% of Americans experience poverty at some time before age 65. This was determined using pre-1999 data. Including post-Great Recession data will likely indicate significantly more than 51%.

Our official definition of poverty does not expose the true number of Americans in severe economic hardship since families typically need an income of twice the official poverty level to meet basic needs, according to research by the National Center for Children in Poverty and the Economic Policy Institute. The living wage varies based on the cost of living and taxes where families live. MIT's Living Wage Project researchers found that in most metropolitan areas, where the U.S. economy and jobs are increasingly concentrated, the living wage is higher than the national median.

So far more than the one-fifth of Americans who are food insecure are under a significant level of unnecessary economic hardship. Most of these people would prioritize mass media report topics very differently than it is now. Common content would include detailed proposals from various sources on ways to make our economic system both more just and able to generate greater overall prosperity.

People read and listen to the news to learn information of importance to society and their lives, so the demand exists for content describing symptoms of serious economic system dysfunction and the ways the economic system could meet their ideals. The supply has not been forthcoming to meet the demand because of inherent media biases. When some facts related to our economic system allowing unnecessary and severe economic hardships for many tens of millions of Americans are mentioned, they are given inappropriately little prominence and repetition, and important solutions are ignored.

Tens of millions of economically distressed Americans would also include headlines and or lead stories on the report that the six heirs of Walmart, who did nothing extraordinary except win "the womb lottery," now have wealth over $145 billion, more wealth than the total wealth of all Americans in the bottom 42%, or 132 million people. That the country is forming an enduring aristocracy is a story of major importance. As I noted previously, we are at the beginning of the largest intergenerational transfer of wealth in history. $36 trillion will be passed down to heirs from 2011 to 2061. This will create a new aristocracy with unprecedented wealth, and therefore power. Few people know this.

Also, few people know that in 2014 over ten million more people have fallen into poverty since 2006 and that approximately 3.5 million people, 1.35 million of them children, experience homelessness per year.[366] A large majority of the people under economic hardship are of working age and either works full-time or would if employment were available. Considering the social importance of the level of economic system dysfunction that all these facts imply, coverage decisions on are made using other criteria.

In the early twentieth century, every medium to large city had five or more competing newspapers with a broad range of politics, right, center and left, so at least one would focus on issues of economic injustice. A diverse media are also important because the United States is a large and diverse country, with an extraordinary number of local self-governments. Local self-governments can be well served only by a locally controlled "Fourth Estate." Instead, we have media consolidation, across all media forms, at historic levels. As I noted in Part 1, six giant companies control 90% of what we read, watch or listen to. The people who control these companies have, on important issues, interests far removed from majority interests. This extreme level of consolidation is serving the country poorly and poses significant dangers.

Extreme wealth has created enclaves of privilege, where the wealthy live isolated from most experiences and concerns of the average American, often to the point of living essentially in a different society, where they have no interest in motivating significant changes in the status quo. This is the society of the controlling owners and managers of our huge mass media conglomerates. (Some mass media owners or top managers are members of a society within ours that some have called "Richistan," where citizens have armies of staff, multiple jets, yachts and 30,000 square foot mansions.) And a sharp division doesn't exist between the wealth and interests of those that control 90% of what we read, watch or listen to, and the people who control much of the remaining 10%.

Although the average reporter does not experience economic hardship as often as the poorest half of America, they are more embedded in the reality of the lifestyle and concerns of the general population than wealthy ownership and management of most of our media corporations. Without pressures, sometimes subtle, sometimes not, transmitted from upper management and owners, report content on economic system dysfunction related subjects would be much more common. Selection processes for reporters and especially commentators, and for editors and lower management, are also responsible for the biased content.

The same biases against appropriate levels of report content on economic and political system dysfunction and policy solution debates exist in the owners and managers of the corporations that are the major advertisers, which further ensures that they will determine media content.

Mass media ownership and management also is more white and male than the community as a whole, leading to biases toward deficient reporting on issues important to women and minorities. In all the important public policy domains, important omissions and distortions that serve elite interests are the rule rather than the exception.

The Pew Research Center's Project for Excellence in Journalism found that in 52 major mainstream news outlets, far less than 1% of news space was devoted to coverage of the topics of inequality or poverty. Philip Bennett, managing editor of PBS's "Frontline" public affairs series, assessed media coverage on the topics of inequality and poverty, which he said is *"part of our national divide in a really important way…"* and it is *"not receiving the kind of sustained, imaginative, aggressive coverage that it deserves."* … *"There are basic questions about the way the country is today that aren't being addressed by the journalistic institutions …"*

The organization Fairness and Accuracy in Reporting's 2012 study of campaign reports found that only 17 of 10,489 stories addressed poverty (0.16%). This despite the facts that about one in five Americans are food insecure, the total wealth of the poorest 40% is negative, and over one-seventh of Americans are living below the official poverty line, causing widespread harm far beyond the poor.

The pressure to act on an issue increases in proportion to the number of people who see the issue as important, and the media largely determine what people see as important. One study found that people shown TV news broadcasts edited to include more coverage of unemployment increased by 65% the number of people who considered unemployment a serious problem.[367] Since the mass media are most people's main contact with society outside of their immediate environment, their views on societal issues will largely be determined by it. When public opinion is shaped to serve elite interests, public policy follows.

(But as the massive study of 1,779 policy issues noted earlier showed, even when public opinion opposes elite interests, the majority opinion is ignored in policy decisions due to our dysfunctional political system. However, when majority opinion is aligned with elite interests, it makes policymaker's actions serving elite interests a little less risky, and more certain. Also, a point exists in support levels beyond which the majority cannot be ignored.)

Philosopher and Nobel laureate economist Amartya Kumar Sen has pointed out the power of the press in determining public policy regarding famines: Countries with a free press do not experience famines because the free press draws attention to the problem, and people will view a government's failure to eliminate famine as intolerable.[368] Although we are not experiencing famines, the fact that about a fifth of our population is food insecure also requires a well-functioning media for the problem to be appropriately addressed with public policies.

The President of the United States (Obama), leaders of other major nations, the head of the International Monetary fund, at least three Nobel Prize winning economists, and even the Pope have all expressed the view that the problem of large and growing inequality is one of the most, or the most, important issue of our time. And as we have seen, for very good reason, and the problem is much more severe and faster growing in the United States than in any other developed country. We also have the lowest economic mobility of any developed country. Appropriate coverage would stimulate public debate with information that would likely result in sufficient public pressures on policymakers for major changes in the status quo that best serves elite interests, not majority interests.

Deficient mass media coverage notwithstanding, many Americans see the importance of our large and growing inequality. The Pew Research Center's 2014 Global Attitudes survey in 44 countries asked which among five dangers—Religious & ethnic hatred, inequality, AIDS & other diseases, nuclear weapons, pollution & environment, was considered the *"greatest threat to the world."* Americans chose inequality above others by a small margin, which would have been much larger if most Americans knew the facts.

Mass media reports during campaign season almost invariably emphasize a view intended to decrease the support of candidates who support policies that would serve the interests of the majority of Americans, or "populist" policies, because elites oppose these policies. Media pundits typically try to discourage support from the public and the candidates for these policies because they are "impractical," despite the majority support for them. These media advocates of "centrism" typically try to direct Democratic Party candidates away from serving the interests of groups of people who have been traditionally their supporters, often denigrating them as "special interests": unions, civil rights, feminist, environmental and consumer rights organizations, the "working class," the poor, and the elderly.

Meanwhile, the pundits present corporate-friendly policies as necessary for electoral success. The ABC News website, The Note, a daily digest of news and political gossip, expresses the latest in conventional mass media wisdom. The following is from a May 2006 issue regarding the upcoming elections. *"Democrats will be, in their hearts, for higher taxes, universal health care, a heightened emphasis on civil liberties, and a dramatic and swift reduction of troops from Iraq."* Also; *"The Democrats just have to hope that the American people don't find out until February."*

ABC's own polling or that of other media companies indicated these positions had majority support. Media pundit approved Democrats, the ones who, not coincidentally, typically get elected, frequently embrace politically unpopular ideas, from the Iraq War to NAFTA-style trade deals.

An ABC News/Washington Post poll in May 2006 found 66% disapproval for the administration's handling of the Iraq war; only 37% thought it was worth fighting. Polls vary over recent years, showing that from slightly less than half to about three-quarters of those asked want a government-guaranteed universal health insurance system—even if it means tax increases. A 2007 New York Times/CBS News poll found that nearly 8 in 10 said they thought it was more important to provide universal access to health insurance than to extend the tax cuts of recent years. A 2009 CBS News/New York

Times poll determined levels of support for tax increases for wealthier house-holds to improve access to health care and provide tax cuts for those with lower incomes: 74% supported the idea.[369]

According to a 2012 Washington Post/ABC poll, 60% of Americans support raising the marginal tax rate on income above $250,000. Even 57% of those making over $100,000 a year support a hike.[370] A poll by the New York Times and CBS News found that 68% favor raising taxes on people earning over $1 million per year.[371] And raising the age for Medicare from 65 to 67 is opposed by 67% of Americans. Polls show that broad majorities of Americans believe the rich and the corporations are not paying their fair share of taxes. A 2013 Gallup poll asked:

"Do you feel that the distribution of money and wealth in this country today is fair, or do you feel that the distribution of money and wealth in this country should be more evenly distributed among a larger percentage of the people?" 59% said it should be distributed more evenly, 33% said the distribution is fair.

To the question, *"Do you think our government should or should not redistribute wealth by heavy taxes on the rich?"* 52% said yes, 45% no.

But because of deficient media coverage, most Americans' views on how extreme economic disparities are, are far from reality. If they knew the facts, each of these poll majorities would be much larger.

The Roper organization originally asked the last question in a survey conducted for Fortune magazine near the end of the Great Depression in 1939. Current support for redistributive public policies is higher than it was in the 1939 Fortune poll, which found 35% favoring it and 54% opposed.[372] Survey methods were different in that era, so those results may not be directly comparable to today's. But this comparison suggests that Americans have become more, rather than less for government involvement in redistributing wealth since the era when many populist candidates won office. 1939 was near the end of the New Deal era when populist policies and institutions were established that most of us would now not consider living without, such as:

Social Security, unemployment insurance, federal regulations setting maximum hours and minimum wages and the abolition of child labor, the Federal Deposit Insurance Corporation protecting depositors' savings and ending the risk of runs on banks, federal requirements for disclosing the balance sheet, profit and loss statements, the names and compensations of corporate officers of firms whose securities were traded, the Securities and Exchange Commission to regulate the stock market and prevent corporate abuses relating to the sale of securities and corporate reporting, and others. The character of our mass media now is a barrier to future progress, and at election time this is more obvious than at other times.

If a candidate supports policies on which polls indicate majority support, it's an ominous sign for their future in politics, according to the mass media pundits.

A November 30, 2013 article in the Washington Post, *"More liberal, populist movement emerging in Democratic Party ahead of 2016 elections,"* expresses the consistent mass media bias that "liberals" pushing for a higher minimum wage, *"tougher financial regulations, specifically targeting massive banks they would like to break up,"* and policies to *"narrow economic inequality, to expand the safety net to help those who have lost jobs to globalization and to relieve some of the burden of student debt,"* is dangerous. Advocating for these policies *"carries political risks for Democrats, who could be accused of being reckless about the national debt or insensitive to the demands of business and economic growth. What's more, many Americans are uncomfortable with the notion of the government redistributing income far beyond what happens today in order to accomplish basic elements of the populist agenda."*

But the facts indicate quite the contrary. The majority supports all these "dangerous" ideas. An accurate, unbiased article would have stated that a groundswell of support is developing for "populist" policies that serve majority interests and that a skilled communicator seeking office and expressing support for these policies in a functioning democracy could ride the groundswell to victory.

Most Americans support stronger government regulations and enforcement to protect people from the actions of corporations that focus on their interests, regardless of the public interest, such as acquiring and abusing monopoly and semi-monopoly power and marketing products to children. A New York Times and CBS News poll found that 74% believe large corporations have too much influence on American life and politics.[373] About two-thirds of Americans support stricter regulations on the way banks and other financial institutions conduct their business, according to an April 2010 Washington Post-ABC News poll, and a 2010 Gallop poll had similar results.

A July 2011 poll by the Center for Responsible Lending found 74% favored having a single agency focus on protecting consumers from financial organizations. Variation over party lines is small—68% of Republicans feel the same. A Rasmussen Reports survey found that 50% of U.S. adults support a plan to break up the 12 megabanks. While polls show that Democrats favor breaking up the big banks more than Republicans, many Republicans point out that the big banks would fail on their own if the government stopped bailing them out. A Harris poll shows that 87% of Republicans, 87% of independents, and 81% of Democrats are against bank bailouts.[374] In other words, the percentage of Americans who favor breaking up the big banks—either directly through government intervention or indirectly by withdrawing government support, is about 90%.

A 2014 Pew Research Center poll found that 69% believe the government should do more to reduce the gap between the rich and everyone else.[375] But as in the similar Gallup Poll mentioned earlier, if most Americans knew how extreme our inequality was, the percent expressing the view that the government should do something about it would be much larger. A 2013 poll conducted by the public opinion research firm Hart Research Associates found that 80% agree that we should raise the minimum wage to $10.10 an hour and increase it periodically to account for rising costs. A Hart Research Associates and American Viewpoint poll found that 64% of adults say the federal government is doing too little to make higher education available and affordable.

On trade, polls show that the public is widely disapproving of free-trade deals that have destabilized the middle class, despite repeated exposure to media pundits expressing claims of these deals' benefits. A May 2012 Angus Reid Public Opinion poll found that U.S. respondents who believe that the United States should "renegotiate" or "leave" NAFTA outnumbered by nearly 4-to-1 those who say the country should "continue to be a member" (53% vs. 15%). Support for the "leave" or "renegotiate" positions dominated among Republicans, Democrats, and independents.

This polling research was either performed by mass media companies or was readily available to them. Their most prominent pundits' consistent efforts to divert their audience from expecting any possibility that "populist" candidates who support all the majority opinions discovered in the polls could be elected is a strange thing to witness. On first look, it seems to be clearly false propaganda. But after considering that a candidate who agrees with the majority on these issues is highly unlikely to get the necessary funding from corporations and the wealthy to run a successful campaign within our current election system one can see why these pundits are likely correct, but not for the reasons they express.

The 2016 presidential campaign had a very extraordinary candidate who has broken the rule requiring vast amounts of money from wealthy individuals and corporations to effectively compete. Bernie Sanders, with donations averaging $27 raised tens of millions of dollars for his presidential primary campaign.

His campaign was typical in another way, though. Since he a populist candidate, the mass media avoided as much as possible covering him and his policy proposals in news reports. Completely ignoring him would not be possible since his popular support levels indicated a real chance at winning the presidency. But his coverage was hugely disproportionate to his support levels. Through early December 2015, he had 20 seconds of coverage on ABC World News Tonight while they devoted 81 minutes to right-wing billionaire Donald Trump who wants to reduce taxes on corporations and the wealthy.[376]

When they covered Sanders, the reports tended to be biased against him. In a study by the media watchdog group Fairness and Accuracy in Reporting they found, "In what has to be some kind of record, the Washington Post ran 16 negative stories on Bernie Sanders in 16 hours, between roughly 10:20 PM EST Sunday, March 6, to 3:54 PM EST Monday, March 7—a window that includes the crucial Democratic debate in Flint, Michigan... All of these posts paint his candidacy in a negative light, mainly by advancing the narrative that he's a clueless white man incapable of winning over people of color or speaking to women. Even the one article about Sanders beating Trump implies this is somehow a surprise—despite the fact that Sanders consistently out-polls Hillary Clinton against the New York businessman (Trump)"

Giant media companies are in a uniquely powerful position even among wealthy corporations and industries because they can not only substantially determine who is elected and what policies are enacted through campaign contributions and lobbying, they also largely directly control the public debate and who is given significant exposure to participate in it. This is an enormous amount of power too often abused to serve narrow interests, not the best interests of the country.

As a result of report content biases, and a changing advertising environment that reduces advertising dollars for the support of journalism, media news content is serving the population increasingly poorly. So people in increasing numbers are "tuning out" the news and dropping out of civic life.

Another kind of bias typical of the mass media during campaign season relates both to their interest in not motivating forces for fundamental change and in minimizing programming costs. Campaign media reports focus an inordinate amount of discussion on "the horserace" of the campaign at the expense of substantively covering policy issues.

For example, the following Mitt Romney statement in a speech received wide coverage during the 2012 presidential campaign:

"I go across the country and I'm talking to single moms. For instance, 30% of single moms are living in poverty now under this president." (Barack Obama)

Rather than motivating detailed analysis of the issue of women and children in poverty with details on the policy solution proposals from various sources including the candidates, if any, the sound bite motivated discussion of the fact that both candidates were fighting to win over the "key group" of women voters, with polling data on who was winning the battle.

"Liberal" Mass Media Bias?

The six giant companies controlling 90% of our media content are controlled by major owners and management with politics to the right on the political spectrum to varying degrees, and generally to the far right on economic issues. This leads to reporting bias contrary to the widespread assertion of a "liberal" one. Their selections for radio "news" talk show hosts make this obvious. Almost all commercial station nationally syndicated political radio talk show hosts are right-wing ideologues. The top five commercial station owners nationally broadcast right-wing hosts 91 percent of their political talk time.[377]

Some claim this is to counterbalance left-leaning conventional news programming, but this claim is false. On some social issues a slight "liberal" orientation may exist, but on economic and other issues, mass media news and other programming related to public issues is biased to the right, or to favor economic elites. The terms "liberal" and "conservative" are now too ambiguous. A distinction that is more useful is that between majority interests and elite interests, or the one that the Occupy movement brought to widespread public awareness, between the 99% and the 1%.

For decades, our mass media have been an important force advancing economic injustice or the disparity between the 99% and the 1%. For example, beginning in the 1980s, corporate mass media participated in a propaganda campaign that served corporate and wealthy individuals' tax cutting agenda. They printed and broadcast the mythology that we have the highest tax rates among democracies worldwide.

The opposite is true. We pay 24% of GDP in taxes, the lowest of the OECD countries, whose average rate is 36.2%. And our tax rate on the highest income individuals has been reduced dramatically over recent decades with the help of the mass media pundits and prominent coverage of every politician and corporate manager complaining about "confiscatory taxes."

When Ronald Reagan was elected president in 1980, the top personal income tax rate was 70%, and by 1988 it was reduced to 28% (recently raised to 39.6%). Also, since 1980, the top corporate tax rate has been reduced from 46% to 35%, before the loopholes, which reduce it to an effective 12.1%.

Many reports appeared about ruthless auditors of the IRS allegedly harassing poor widows and small business people. Year after year, cases were exaggerated and highly publicized. As a result, policymakers under-budgeted the IRS. In 2002, the IRS said it lacked auditors to review complex accounts of large corporations, so it had to limit its audits to relatively simple audits of middle class and low-income people.[378] In 2014, the IRS budget was 7% lower than in 2010.

For every dollar that goes into IRS enforcement, about $200 is recovered in taxes.[379] And the result of the lost public revenues from high-income personal income tax cuts, corporate tax cuts, and reduced enforcement of tax laws is growing societal dysfunction.

Mass media bias is also clearly displayed in their choice of news program guests. For example: *Nightline* is one of the most widely viewed and enduring mass media news programs. The organization Fairness and Accuracy in Reporting (FAIR) found in a 1989 study that in the prior 40-month period of Nightline programming, the most frequent guests were Henry Kissinger, Alexander Haig, Elliott Abrams and Jerry Falwell, far from "liberal" or majority interest voices. Progressive and public interest voices were grossly underrepresented.

FAIR also found that economics news coverage usually looks at how events impact stockholders rather than workers or consumers. Think tanks partly funded by unions are often identified as "labor-backed," while think tanks heavily funded by business interests are usually not identified as "corporate-backed."

The character of Nightline's guest choices is typical of other news programs. Studies show that network news sources skew white, male and elite. A FAIR June 2002 study found:

".... ABC World News Tonight, CBS Evening News and NBC Nightly News in the year 2001 shows that 92% of all U.S. sources interviewed were

white, 85% were male and, where party affiliation was identifiable, 75% were Republican."

In a 1999 study published in the academic journal Communications Research, four scholars discovered a fourfold increase over the prior dozen years in the number of Americans telling pollsters that they discerned a liberal bias in their news. But a review of the media's actual ideological content over the 12-year period offered no corroboration for this view. Their conclusion: News consumers were responding to *"increasing news coverage of liberal bias media claims, which have been increasingly emanating from Republican Party candidates and officials."* A concentrated, organized propaganda effort succeeded.

More Indications of the True Bias of the Media

Media bias is displayed in how program hosts refer to people in the news. A 2002 study from the Center for the Study of Language and Information at Stanford University found that "liberal" legislators had a better than 30% greater likelihood on average of being labeled "liberal" than the "conservatives" had of being labeled "conservative." The press described U.S. Congressman Barney Frank as a liberal two-and-a-half times as frequently as it described Congressman Dick Armey as a conservative. It labeled Senator Barbara Boxer liberal almost twice as often as it labeled Senator Trent Lott conservative, and labeled Senator Paul Wellstone liberal more often than it did Senator Jesse Helms conservative. When the host uses the liberal label, the implication is that the person is not objective, or biased and out of the mainstream. With no label, the implication is no bias or more mainstream.

Would a "liberal" mass media ignore the 2011 Tar Sands protests in D.C. and the hundreds of arrested protesters, including a renowned NASA scientist? Ours did. The mass media also virtually ignored the largest anti-war protest in world history on the eve of the Iraq invasion in 2003, but have since given plenty of mostly uncritical coverage of much smaller Tea Party protests.

The mass media gave much free publicity and praise to House Budget Committee Chairman Paul Ryan's "brave," "heroic" budget plan, while they ignored the much more carefully crafted Progressive Caucus' People's Budget that would far better serve majority interests. (At that time Ryan was a likely 2016 presidential candidate; now instead he is Speaker of the House.)

The mass media had plenty of right-wing guests on the news that urged President Obama to approve the Keystone pipeline and that criticized him for delaying it, but nobody explained why there's a huge movement against it.

The pipeline reaffirms our commitment to releasing potentially catastrophic levels of carbon into the atmosphere. Despite overwhelming scientific evidence for warming of the climate, and human causes for most or all of it, little coverage of the issue exists on corporate media. The potential for catastrophic consequences is enormous, making it possibly one of the most important news stories in history.

The mass media's coverage of Occupy Wall Street was mostly hostile or dismissive, while the Tea Party is commonly treated respectfully.

Since 2000, U.S. multinationals have cut 2.9 million jobs here while increasing employment overseas by 2.4 million. This is likely just the tip of the outsourcing iceberg, as multinational corporations account for only about 20% of the labor force. This is an important cause of the unemployment and stagnating or declining wage problems. Why are so few people aware of this? When was the last time you saw a front-page headline or a top network news story about outsourcing? Jack Welch is portrayed in our media as a brilliant and successful businessman, worthy of admiration and respect. As the CEO of General Electric, Welch moved dozens of GE factories abroad, outsourced hundreds of thousands of jobs, and slashed benefits for many of his employees. To add insult to injury, after destroying the retirement dreams of so many of his workers, he received a $400 million golden parachute for himself.[380] Would a "liberal" media portray Welch as a kind of hero or villain?

If a corporate organization drafted laws and then passed them on to legislators to implement, wouldn't you think the allegedly liberal media would report on them? The American Legislative Exchange Council is such an organization, yet relatively few people know of it.

Among the most important facts in *Now Is the Time for The New Enlightenment* that the media should widely report is U.S. per capita health care costs are over double the OECD average, and we have some of the worst health care outcomes. A research report produced by Harvard Medical School affiliated researchers published in the December 2009 issue of the American Journal of Public Health found that 45,000 Americans per year died due to lack of health insurance.

Few people know these facts. Wouldn't a "liberal" or majority interest press widely report on them and the proposals to solve the problems?

As previously noted, in 2012, congressional races Democrats drew nearly 1.4 million more votes than Republicans, yet Republicans won control of the House with 234 seats to 201 seats. Wouldn't a "liberal" or majority interest press widely report on this, and the proposals to solve the gerrymandering problem that is making a mockery of what's left of our democracy?

In a 2011 Hart poll, only 22% of those polled had heard of the Citizens United Supreme Court decision. Since 77% believe that corporations have more control over our political process than people do, why wouldn't a "liberal" or majority interest mass media prominently report and offer debates on Citizens United that resulted in an explosion of corporate dollars in our election process?

Wouldn't a "liberal" or majority interest mass media prominently report that tax cuts of recent decades primarily benefited the wealthy? Wouldn't it mainly report on the economists who express the view that tax cuts for the wealthy are harmful to society, rather than those who falsely claim the opposite?

One year the estate tax was repealed, benefiting only the wealthiest of the wealthy. Many lawmakers are trying to repeal it permanently. Where is the outcry from public interest groups and economists in our mass media that we should not repeal this most progressive of all taxes? Instead, it is important to increase it, because currently it is having little impact on the development of an intergenerational aristocracy, and public funds are desperately needed. Only those seeking a permanent aristocracy would allow little exposure to opponents of the repeal of the estate tax.

The corporate mass media are largely in the hands of right-wing extremists parading as moderates while providing prominent media exposure to those who propagandize us with the lie of a "liberal" media. They know this will push the political envelope farther and farther to the right, or to serve elite interests.

On the relatively few occasions when discussions of solutions to systemic problems harming the majority of Americans broadcast media gives some airtime, the segments generally have someone present a solution with supporting facts, and then an opponent, using false supporting information, states why the proposed solution would be ineffective or harmful. Then the highly paid host or moderator abdicates any responsibility to expose falsehoods, apparently to create the false impression of impartiality. It is not impartial to let one view appear to be just as valid as another when one is based on ignorance or lies; it unfairly advantages ignorance or dishonesty. People viewing the exchange leave as uninformed or misinformed as they were before it, and believe one side or the other based on prior prejudices, often based on prior propaganda because most people do not have the time or ability to check the facts themselves. Fact checking people given media exposure and reporting the facts is one of the most important roles of the media.

Mainstream press reports that challenge conventional views when they occur, occur infrequently. Without the repetition and follow-up needed to be persuasive or of enduring interest their impact is marginal or nil.

How major owners and upper managers influence media content decisions throughout a huge mass media corporation's hierarchy

Persons of almost any political persuasion can get jobs at the entry ranks of journalism unless they are blatantly radical. The higher one goes up the corporate media hierarchy, the greater the emphasis on ideology as a hiring selection criterion. The prominent and influential columnists and commentators are selected to have views aligned with ownership and upper management views on fundamental public issues. And corporate media's hierarchical structure results in pressures, sometimes subtle, sometimes not, on all levels to ensure that elite interests are not significantly violated.

Most editors can cite examples of compromises in story emphasis or selection due to pressure from publishers, owners, and advertisers. Most often, though, limitations on reporting come from self-censorship based on cues from prior conversations with superiors or the experience of rejected ideas. Similarly, journalists design their stories to avoid disapproval from their editors. This makes direct intervention by owners and top management a less frequent necessity and leaves journalists and editors with a greater feeling of autonomy.

Many top news executives meet on a weekly or sometimes daily basis with editors and staffers to learn of, and influence when needed, story selection and emphasis. News and corporate executives can suggest, select, and veto stories whenever they choose. However, because they have other duties and they are expected to abide by the corporate division of labor, they do not normally exercise their power on a day-to-day basis. They do not need to, because the acceptable bounds have been communicated throughout the hierarchy often enough for their influence to be maintained.

Too much disagreement with superiors types people as "cranks," and even if it does not lead to dismissal there's a negative impact on career advancement. Rather than seeing this self-censorship as a form of censorship, journalists will often describe themselves as "realistic" or "pragmatic," by always being aware, if not always consciously, of what is expected. Rewards and punishments designed to induce conformity also socialize people into the existing system. Reporters and editors often start seeing things as superiors do, because their careers are at stake. In this regard, news people are no different from subordinates in other hierarchical organizations.

Also, many of the prominent and influential columnists and commentators are now multimillionaires, so elite interests are their own. They live in the same neighborhoods as top political figures and financial elites over whom they ostensibly serve as watchdogs. They attend the same functions, they have the same circles of friends and associates, their children go to the same elite private schools.

Advertisers Influence Media Content

Some constraints imposed by media executives and owners on the working press result from pressures exerted by corporate advertisers. For example, look at the New York Times' coverage of the automobile industry when the industry was pressuring Congress to repeal the seatbelt and airbag regulations soon after they were implemented, which saved over 17,900 lives in 2007 alone (according to the U.S. Department of Transportation).

The Times ran stories that were, as one Times staff person admitted, "more or less put together by the advertisers." Times publisher Arthur Ochs Sulzberger openly acknowledged that he urged his editors to focus on the industry position in coverage of safety and auto pollution. To do otherwise, he said, *"would affect the advertising."* The auto industry was a substantial source of support for newspapers, responsible for about 18% of ad revenues in 1973 and 1974 when the repeal effort was made.

The New York Times has probably the most extensive and fact-based news of any newspaper in the country. But even its unofficial credo is said by some observers to be *"Do not significantly alienate those on whom we depend for access and money."* This credo is commonly applies; its official one, *"All the news that's fit to print,"* never does.[381]

In 1972, the publisher of Vogue magazine said, *"The cold hard facts of magazine publishing mean that those that advertise get editorial coverage."* A senior vice president of the MGM movie studio told newspaper executives in 1981 that he had seen too many negative movie reviews and that this risked the withdrawal of $500 million per year in movie ads.[382]

For decades, newspapers kept smoking related deaths out of the news even after a 1927 definitive study made that inexcusable. Because tobacco companies were among the top three or four newspaper advertisers, they instead printed reports by the Tobacco Institute that smoking did not cause cancer. Even in 1980, there were more stories in the newspapers about the causes of the flu, polio, and tuberculosis than the cause of death of one in seven Americans—tobacco.[383]

With hundreds of billions per year spent on advertising, major advertisers do not leave to chance not just the number of people who will see their ads, but also their character. The preference is for a more affluent audience since they would be more able to spend money on their products. Since content determines audience, this is a way content is influenced by advertisers to favor the preferences of the affluent.

Advertisers also prefer content that is sufficiently "positive" for association with their product or service. They generally prefer to avoid placing their ads in stories about poverty, considering these stories not sufficiently "positive."

No broadcast network produces a program without considering whether major advertisers will like it. Prospective shows are discussed with major advertisers, who look at plans or tentative scenes. They reject, approve, or suggest changes.

The Federal Communications Commission (FCC) held hearings in 1965 to determine how much influence advertisers had on the content of television and radio. Procter and Gamble was the largest TV advertiser at the time; an excerpt of its testimony on its requirements for program advertising purchase makes the point: *"Where it seems fitting, the characters in Procter and Gamble dramas should reflect recognition and acceptance of the world situation in their thoughts and actions... men in uniform should not be portrayed as engaging in any criminal activity... There will be no material on any of our programs which could in any way further the concept of business as ruthless, and lacking all sentimental or spiritual motivation."* The company also testified that they applied these policies to entertainment, news and public affairs documentaries in which its ads appeared.

Brown and Williamson Tobacco Corporation also testified on the character of the programming in which it would buy ads (this was well before tobacco ads were banned), and here is an excerpt: *"Tobacco products should not be used in a derogatory or harmful way. And no reference or gesture of disgust, dissatisfaction or distaste be made in connection with them... no cigarette should be used as a prop to depict an undesirable character. Cigarettes used by meritorious characters should be Brown and Williamson brands...*[384]

Investigative reporters Jane Akre and Steve Wilson produced a report in 1997 for a Fox News, Florida TV station that included evidence of health risks from Monsanto Company produced growth hormone, rbGH, that increases milk production of cows. Monsanto threatened Fox with losing its advertising dollars—for the Florida station, the entire Fox network, and station owner Rupert Murdoch's Actmedia, a major advertising agency used by Monsanto if they ran the story. Fox pulled the series for "further review." Akre and Wilson then were repeatedly instructed to include unverified and even some false statements by Monsanto's dairy research director. For example, they were told to include a statement that milk from rbGH-injected cows is the same as, and as safe as, milk from untreated cows.

Using rbGH in lactating cows causes no increase in the concentration in their milk, but it stimulates the production of insulin-like growth factor-1 (IGF-1) by the cow, resulting in an increase in the concentration of IGF-1 in the milk of the rbGH treated cows. Some controversy exists on whether the IGF-1 can be absorbed intact in the gastrointestinal tract, but blood levels of IGF-1 are strongly associated with cancer risk. The safety of this milk is so questionable both Canada and the entire European Union ban it.[385]

Injected cows also have much higher levels of udder infections, which puts more pus in the milk. To treat this, farmers use more antibiotics, which also end up in the milk. The increased use of antibiotics to treat rbGH-induced mastitis promotes the development of antibiotic-resistant bacteria, which is a public health threat.[386] Common infections, which have been treatable for decades, may once again kill.

Conglomerate media control also creates a route for advertisers to affect the policies of other corporations or subsidiaries in the conglomerate. For example: Readers Digest Association owns the magazine Readers Digest and the Funk and Wagnalls book publishing company. In 1968, Funk and Wagnalls prepared to publish a book, *The Permissible Lie*, which criticized the advertising industry. A month before publication date, Readers Digest ordered its book subsidiary to cancel publication because it threatened to offend advertisers in the magazine.

Advertisers demands on TV programming underlie much of its superficiality and materialism. The president of Bell and Howell described, disapprovingly, to the FCC the standards applied by most advertisers "*One should not associate with controversy, ... one should always remember that comedy, adventure and escapism provide the best atmosphere for selling.*" Many outstanding programs with large audiences over the decades that did not meet these advertisers' criteria were canceled.

In recent decades, not all advertisers have considered "positive" content necessary to provide an acceptable media environment for their products or services. Some have given the media giants more of a free hand in creating the largest audiences at the lowest cost, as long as the programming did not have significant potential to disrupt the status quo, with this result:

Prime time television "reality" programs glorify some of the most revolting characteristics of the human psyche—deceit, cynical sexuality, greed, and the desire to exploit and humiliate. Programs are designed to elicit real and devastating emotional breakdowns on camera. Also, most local TV news emphasizes bloody accidents and crimes under a policy known in TV studios as *"if it bleeds, it leads."* By the time an American child is 18, he or she has typically seen 16,000 simulated murders and 200,000 acts of violence on TV.[387] TV is the most commonly used "babysitter" in the country. The character of the corporations largely controlling our media has resulted in this baby sitter being an instructor in mayhem and murder.

The Large Conglomerate Profit Maximization Imperative Is Growing More Destructive

Large conglomerate profit maximization focus has also led, along with a changing media environment, to unprecedented news programming cost cutting. On local TV, weather and traffic has risen to, on average, 40% of the content produced on the newscasts, while reporting and in-depth reporting on important public issues declines. The cable channel that has tried to brand itself around deep reporting, CNN, produced about one-half the story packages in 2012 that it did in 2007.[388] Newsrooms are shrinking and even disappearing altogether, as are full-time reporters stationed in state, national and foreign capital bureaus. And as they go, so goes the information and ideas needed for the functioning of a democratic society. Newspaper newsroom cutbacks in 2012 reduced the number of journalists by 30% since 2000.[389]

Good and wide-ranging journalism is of similar *"public good"* status as universal public education, military defense, and public health and transportation infrastructure. Over the last century, journalism's essential function seemed well supported because advertising funded much of the news in its efforts to reach consumers. Too few news consumers knew of how this produced biased content. Now, advertisers' need for journalism to connect with target audiences is disappearing, so even their corrupting source of support is being withdrawn.

Our Founding Fathers understood the importance of a vigorous press. They promoted and instituted huge subsidies for the press. Let's again be clear on the great importance of supporting a well-functioning "Fourth Estate" for a well-functioning democracy.

In addition to mostly ignoring populist candidates, reporters are acting primarily as amplifiers, rather than as investigators, of the assertions of the candidates and other political partisans they do cover, largely due to lack of support for sufficient time for investigations. Only about a quarter of statements in the media about the character and records of the presidential candidates originated with journalists in the 2012 race, while twice that many came from political partisans. In 2000, half the statements originated with journalists and one-third came from partisans.[390]

A similar loss of journalistic value exists in the reporting of news from businesses and other sources. The ratio of public relations workers to journalists grew from 1.2 to 1 in 1980 to 3.6 to 1 in 2008.[391] The gap has likely widened since. Journalists are too often given only the time to parrot the public relations workers. For news organizations, distinguishing between high-quality information of public value and agenda-driven propaganda serving corporate, government official, or candidate's interests, has become increasingly uncommon. We are in an era of massive and increasing corruption as a result of both our election and lobbying systems. This would not be occurring if our most influential "watchdogs" had not become "lapdogs."

With reporting resources in great decline, our media regularly covers fewer specialized areas, so journalists' level of expertise in any one area and the ability to report on it are compromised. About one-third of U.S. adults have stopped using a news outlet because it no longer provides them with the news report quality they were accustomed to getting.[392]

This decline of journalism is a crisis for our democracy, but even before this recent decline, media content selection biases based on the character of unrepresentative ownership and management were not serving our country well. The problems of our dysfunctional media require radical solutions.

Huge conglomerate media control having major detrimental impacts on the news coverage is most extreme at the local level. Corporate managers disconnected from the communities being served, whose overriding concern is maximizing corporate profits, have too often trivialized journalism on local issues of importance.

Providing information to allow voters to make informed judgments before casting their votes for local candidates on their policy proposals, opinions on relevant issues, and their character, with fact checks of their statements and issue analysis, is an essential role of media. However, a nationwide study conducted by the Lear Center at the University of Southern California's Annenberg School in 2004 found that only 8% of 4,333 local news broadcasts that aired in the month before Election Day contained any mention of a statewide or local race. The reports mainly included "horse race" poll numbers rather than any substantive information about the candidates or relevant issues.

A Fairness and Accuracy in Reporting study of five regional newspapers found little coverage of 2008 and 2010 races for the House of Representatives. Third-party candidates were invariably ignored.[393]

The more disconnected the ownership of the media is from a community, the less it is interested in serving it.

The Dangerous Trend of Media Consolidation Has Accelerated Since 1996

A 1996 law allowing extreme media concentration has been especially harmful to the public interest. As a result of this law one company, Clear Channel Communications, owns 1240 stations in 300 cities and dominates the audience share in 100 of 112 major markets. Its nationwide propaganda regime is detrimental to our nation's progress, and its central control character is harmful in other ways.

Most of Clear Channel's stations are remote control operated from a central location using the same pre-recorded material nationwide. It has only 200 employees. Cases exist where a major community emergency, such as a toxic chemical spill, needed to be reported to the community, but no one was at the station to get and announce the report.

The "news talk" programming that Clear Channel features, 24 hours per day has a political agenda that influences massive numbers of people's views on public issues. About 18% of Americans listen to talk radio regularly. Many support the host's views with religious zeal and refuse to hear facts to the contrary. They have likely swayed elections of major importance, including presidential elections, and will continue to do so.

Since Rush Limbaugh has been the highest rated talk radio program host for decades, with many millions of devoted listeners, his statements have been most often checked by nonpartisan fact-checking organizations. Here are some of their findings:

In a 1993 radio show, Limbaugh stated *"The poorest people in America are better off than the mainstream families of Europe."* At the time, the average cash income of the poorest 20% of Americans was $5,226; the average cash income of the four largest European nations was $19,708.[394]

In Limbaugh's April 29, 1994 radio program he stated, *"There is no conclusive proof that nicotine's addictive...and the same thing with cigarettes causing emphysema, lung cancer, heart disease."* Overwhelming evidence existed to the contrary. So many thousands of people likely have died prematurely, and many more will die, because of Limbaugh's misinformation, considering the size of his fan base. And the extent of non-fatal serious harm to health resulting from his misinformation is similarly large.

In his book *"The Way Things Ought to Be"* (p. 70), Limbaugh writes: *"Don't let the liberals deceive you into believing that a decade of sustained growth without inflation in America [in the '80s] resulted in a bigger gap between the haves and the have-nots. Figures compiled by the Congressional Budget Office dispel that myth."* CBO figures for after-tax incomes show that in 1980 the richest one-fifth of our country had eight times the income of the poorest one-fifth. By 1989, the ratio was over 20 to one.

In an April 28, 2014 radio show, Limbaugh expressed his view that things are going very well for African-Americans in the U.S. "Some of the wealthiest Americans are African-American now." But the Forbes 400 wealthiest Americans list had just one African American on it and no other close to the top 400, and the black/white per capita average wealth ratio was 1/7. The black poverty rate was 24%, 71% higher than the 14% American average, and African Americans were incarcerated at a rate more than 5 times that of whites.[395] Nearly half of black men are arrested by age 23.[396]

Stephen Hawking criticized Trump's decision to pull the United States out of the Paris climate change agreement saying "We are close to the tipping point where global warming becomes irreversible. Trump's action could push the Earth over the brink" to a disastrous level of climate change. In response Limbaugh said: "We're living in dangerous times"—not because of Trumps' actions but because "the left has ... dumbed down their professoriate, they've dumbed down their commentariat." Unfortunately, many millions of "ditto-heads" (people who agree with everything Limbaugh says) believe that one the most highly regarded theoretical physicists in history understands less about the physics of solar radiation's interaction with rising greenhouse gas in the atmosphere than Rush Limbaugh, who knows next to nothing about science.[397] Limbaugh's statement is correct "We're living in dangerous times," and he is the leader of the propagandists largely responsible for the danger.

Rush Limbaugh has a finely honed ability to distort reality and, when he likes, twist it 180 degrees. His chronic inaccuracy and his lack of accountability wouldn't be a problem if Limbaugh were just an entertainer. However, Limbaugh is taken seriously not only by many millions in his audience but also by influential people in mainstream media. He's been an "expert" on Charlie Rose and Meet the Press, and the New York Times (10/15/92) and Newsweek (1/24/94) have published his writings. A U.S. News & World Report piece (8/16/93) by Steven Roberts declared, *"The information Mr. Limbaugh provides is generally accurate."* Ted Koppel invited Limbaugh to be on Nightline as an environmental "expert."[398]

Expressing his political power: A National Review cover story declared him the *"Leader of the Opposition"* (to Democrats)[399] After Rush Limbaugh's described a woman law student as "a slut" and "a prostitute," some Republicans — including then-National Chairman Michael Steele — made disparaging remarks about him but quickly realized they must submit to his political power, and then humbly asked Limbaugh's forgiveness. (Limbaugh is among the highest paid people in U.S. media, signing a contract in 2008 for $400 million through 2016, an indication of the enormous size of his fan base.)

The dangers of blind adherence to the views of charismatic people given nationwide media exposure can ultimately lead to greater dangers than are apparent now:

In the 1920s, Germany was regarded as a model of democracy and the peak of Western civilization in the arts and the sciences.[400] As we all know, not long afterward, blind adherence to the views of charismatic people turned many Germans monstrously destructive, both internally and internationally.

Germans were propagandized to believe that the Jewish people were a race whose goal was world domination and that all of history was a fight between races which should culminate in the triumph of the "superior" Aryan race. Therefore, they considered it their duty to eliminate all Jewish people. Many were indoctrinated with the view that Jews were the Christ-killers, agents of the devil, and practitioners of witchcraft, and that their ethnic origin made them hopelessly corrupt and habitual criminals who could never be rehabilitated.[401] Ultimately, blind adherence to propaganda by a large proportion of the German population led to one of the most horrific atrocities in history, the murder of six million Jews.

Skepticism of the absurdities at the foundation of this atrocity was overcome by repetitive assertions of charismatic people. The dangers of charismatic people given nationwide exposure to sway public opinion with lies and distorted information while there is little exposure to the facts regarding their statements are real.

With some similarity to Nazi tactics, it is common among talk show pundits to denigrate people with opposing views, sometimes with loud, highly emotional tirades. The opposition is called stupid, immoral, hypocritical, disingenuous, dishonest, and devious, while they and their fans are *"great Americans,"* as one very popular host repeatedly calls his fans, and his fans call him. The implication being that all who don't accept their statements and agenda are not part of the *"in crowd"* of *"great Americans,"* and that even their motives regarding the well-being of the country are suspect.

Another very popular host nationally spends much of his airtime yelling in a rage at the top of his voice. His rants include denigrating anyone with other than a far right viewpoint who attracts his attention. Profanity is definitely not off limits, and its frequency is shocking, especially since his show airs when people of all ages are equally likely to hear it. Bastard seems to be one of his favorite descriptors. I have heard him yell it three times in less than an hour as part of an ironic and vicious verbal assault on different people.

If you are hoping that his popularity results from a similar kind of morbid curiosity that attracts many people's attention to a serious accident, you will be disappointed. Most people I have spoken to that listen to his show think he's *"great"* and believe virtually everything he says. He is an important influence on their thinking on public issues.

Calm and carefully reasoned debate between people knowledgeable on the issues in question on most right-wing talk shows is as alien as a chess match in a wrestling ring. In addition to often promulgating misinformation, they contribute to a climate of destructive and dangerous political vitriol.

Anyone listening to many of the pervasive right-wing radio talk shows resulting from media consolidation would be struck by the unanimity of views on most issues of public importance.

Former Nazi propaganda minister Joseph Goebbels said, *"What you want in a media system is ostensible diversity that conceals an actual uni-*

formity." The intentions of our right-wing talk show hosts or our highly concentrated media are obviously not those of Goebbels, but media as consolidated as ours can too easily be a propaganda tool for purposes of both lesser and similar destructiveness.

As noted earlier, advocates for serving important public needs by raising taxes on high-income people, which have been dramatically reduced over the last few decades, have been marginalized. Talk radio has been an important influence in this process. Right-wing hosts have disseminated not just misinformation, but blatant lies to get millions of people to act against their own best interest. For example: Rush Limbaugh, Sean Hannity, and Glen Beck have a total number of listeners per week of over 33 million. I have heard each of them repeatedly say that raising tax rates on high-income people does not increase government revenue. And many other widely heard hosts with a very similar agenda fill the 24 hours per day talk radio cycle. These people are intelligent enough to know that this absurd claim regarding any degree of tax increase under consideration had no basis in reality.

This and other statements these people have made indicate that there is a common source of their talking points intended to mold public opinion to serve the narrow interests of our "aristocracy." They know that many people will believe almost anything if it is repeated often enough by enough people. Millions of people believing this lie allowed tax cuts for the wealthy or *"trickle down"* economic policy to be instituted with little public dissent. On the contrary, millions then voted, and continue to vote, against their own (and the country's) best interest, for candidates who promise tax cuts on the wealthy, based on this lie.

Wealthy individual and corporate funded think tanks and conferences are likely where these hosts get some of their common talking points. For example, the Koch brothers semi-annual conference with media "pundits" and hosts began in 2003. (The Koch brothers, are tied as the fifth wealthiest people in the nation, worth a combined $81 billion.)[402] Their June 2010 event in Aspen, Colorado was attended by conservative media stars; Glen Beck; Philip Anschutz, Examiner newspapers and Weekly Standard owner; Charles Krauthammer, syndicated columnist and Weekly Standard contributor; Stephen Moore, Wall Street Journal editorial board member; Ramesh Ponnuru, National Review senior editor; and Andrew Breitbart (recently deceased), the mastermind behind Breitbart.com and Breitbart.tv.

As an indication of the kind of policies that the Koches are working to influence our political system to institute (and the philosophy at their foundation) consider: David Koch ran as the Libertarian Party's vice-presidential candidate in 1980 on a platform advocating for the following: *"repeal of federal campaign finance laws...abolition of Medicare and Medicaid programs...deregulation of the medical insurance industry...repeal of the Social Security system...privatization of the public roads and national highway system...abolition of the governmental Postal Service,"* repeal of *"all personal and corporate income taxation including capital gains taxes"* and *"the eventual repeal of all taxation"* and *"Government ownership, operation, regulation, and subsidy of schools and colleges should be ended,"* End *"all government welfare, relief projects, and 'aid to the poor' programs... repeal the Occupational Safety and Health Act...abolish the Consumer Product Safety Commission...repeal all state usury laws."*[403]

There is no indication that the Koches have changed their views on these issues in the intervening decades. The fact that a much larger percentage of Republicans advocate for some of these policies now than in 1980, when they were considered "fringe" or "crazy," is likely largely due to the Koches influence on our political system, including our media. The Koches agenda not only opposes every major law that has assisted the middle class, the elderly, the children, the sick, and the most vulnerable in this country, if implemented in its entirety, it would ultimately result in the extreme social dysfunction associated with the worst examples of "third world" countries.

To protect their oil and other businesses from the impact of a public more strongly convinced of the seriousness of anthropogenic climate change, the Koch brothers have funded think tanks that have denied the problem. Krauthammer has used the "mainstream" forum of his Washington Post column to dismiss the people basing their opinion on climate change on the scientific evidence as just members of the *"Church of the Environment."* He has appeared on Fox News to discuss why any legislation addressing climate change is *"dead on arrival."* Other attendees use their forums to deny climate change, and the significance of human actions to it, to large audiences. Certainly, a consensus on viewpoints on other issues is also developed in these kinds of forums.

The pervasiveness and persistence of propaganda serving elite interests is misguiding many millions of people, many of whom refuse to see contrary facts. Research demonstrates that the more a person consumes biased, agenda driven media, the more likely it is that he will dismiss factual, contrary information as propaganda and biased.

Monarchs or the dominant classes before the Enlightenment did not have the power to communicate messages that served their interests 24 hours per day to millions over thousands of miles and do so instantaneously. Therefore, propaganda was a far less robust tool, requiring more reliance on physical force to exert their will, which is much more costly, so was used far less often to influence the masses than propaganda is today. In this way, our current domination by economic elites is more oppressive than what existed before the Enlightenment.

Local control of mass media will eliminate or minimize the problem of nationwide propaganda regimes and best serve local community interests. The New Enlightenment media policy reforms will accomplish this.

Our media are supposed to be a check on political and economic abuse of power. But now that major corporations and conglomerates control 90% of our media content, our most influential media are integrated with economic and political elites so instead are elites' extraordinarily powerful tools.

Some other examples of stories of great import ignored or poorly reported in the mass media, due to the media's integration with political and economic elites, are:

- CBS News and the New York Times have conducted several polls on the Iraq War that have included the question *"Was Saddam personally involved in 9/11?"* In April 2003 the responses were: 53% Yes, 38% No. Hussein had no involvement with the 9/11 attacks.

     President Bush's Secretary of State, Colin Powell, said proof existed that Iraqi officials had ties with al-Qaeda, then later said no proof existed. Donald Rumsfeld, Bush's Secretary of Defense said, *"I have acknowledged since September 2002, that there were ties between al Qaeda and Iraq,"* and that there was *"bulletproof"* evidence demonstrating *"that there are in fact al Qaeda in Iraq."*

     Vice President Dick Cheney said, *"There clearly was a relationship [between al Qaeda and Iraq]. It's been testified to. The evidence is overwhelming."*

     In a State of the Union address, President Bush said Iraq had 500 tons of chemical weapons, 25,000 liters of anthrax, 38,000 tons of botulism toxin, was importing uranium for nuclear bombs, and had al Qaeda cells determined to destroy the United States.

     All claims regarding weapons and the al Qaeda connection were false. Bush eventually stated, long after the Iraq war began, that Hussein had no involvement in the 9/11 attacks. The mass media allowed the Bush administration and its operatives to propagandize us with the falsehood that Saddam was involved in 9/11 to create support for the war in Iraq. Hussein was a serious problem for the United States and the world, but invading Iraq under false pretenses would not have been allowed by a well-functioning "Fourth Estate." (At the time leading up to the Iraq war, GE, a major military contractor, also owned NBC. War would increase GE's sales and profits, so there is a reasonable concern this may have influenced NBC reporting toward a pro-war bias.)

- New York Times reporters James Risen and Eric Lichtblau were ready to report, in mid-2004, the existence of the NSA's warrantless eavesdropping program. How President Bush learned of this fact is not known, but he did. (Was his administration spying on the Times editorial staff?) He requested that the Time's publisher, Arthur Sulzberger, and its editor-in-chief, Bill Keller, come to the Oval Office to discuss the issue. Bush claimed, with no evidence, and implausibly, that they would help terrorists if they revealed that the NSA was spying on Americans, without the warrants required by law. Bush insisted that they not publish the story. The Times obeyed until after Bush's reelection. Then at the end of 2005, they reported the story. A close election was decided by voters unaware that Bush was eavesdropping on Americans without warrants, based on the New York Times decision.[404]

- The Trans-Pacific Partnership (TPP) is a massive "free trade" agreement being pushed by big corporations and negotiated behind closed doors by officials from the United States and eleven other countries—Australia, Brunei, Canada, Chile, Japan, Malaysia, Mexico, New Zealand, Peru, Singapore, and Vietnam. The agreement could result in offshoring millions of American jobs, rolling back Wall Street reforms, threatening Internet freedom, banning buy American policies needed to create green jobs, increasing the cost of medicines, exposing the U.S. to unsafe food and products, and empowering corporations to attack our environmental and health safeguards.

   Although it is called a "free trade" agreement, the TPP is not mainly about trade. Of TPP's 29 draft chapters, only five deal with traditional trade issues. Our domestic federal, state, and local policies would have to comply with TPP rules. The TPP would empower foreign firms to enforce new rights and privileges by dragging governments to foreign tribunals to demand taxpayer compensation over policies that, they claim, undermine their expected future profits.

We only know about the TPP's threats thanks to leaks; the public is not allowed to see the draft TPP text. Even members of Congress, after being denied the text for years, are now provided only limited access. Meanwhile, over 600 official corporate "trade advisors" have special access. Many groups have expressed outrage at the leaked content and the lack of transparency of, and democratic participation in, the shaping of this agreement. They have received little or no mass media attention, as have all the issues relevant to the agreement.[405]

- Where were our mass media during the period leading up to the financial crisis when dishonesty, irrationality, and fraud became the national financial culture? Investigative journalism and widespread reporting of what was occurring would have been helpful in avoiding the crash. The amounts involved in the criminal fraud committed during this period totaled many times more in value than the total value of all the bank robberies in history.

Conglomerate ownership of media also creates direct conflicts of interests with the public interest. A media corporation is unlikely to serve its "watchdog" role on corporations when a corporation in its conglomerate is involved in wrongdoing. The conglomerate's media arm is not likely to report it. Also, a conglomerate's media arm is not likely to cover issues that could motivate public policies contrary to any of the interests of a corporation in the conglomerate. For example:

- In addition to GE's possible pro-war bias possibly influencing coverage consider: Over the years, GE led the way in taking advantage of trade deals that allowed them to shut down factories in the United States and outsource tens of thousands of American jobs to low-wage countries. General Electric also very aggressively works to avoid paying U.S. taxes. Despite making billions in profits, they use hundreds of accountants and lawyers to exploit tax laws that their lobbyists helped write so that, in some years, they don't pay anything in federal taxes. Also, General Electric is a major polluter. According to *The Boston Globe,* the *"General Electric Company is sharply objecting to a new federal plan that would force it to spend hundreds of millions of dollars to remove massive amounts of toxic chemicals from the Housatonic River, which the company polluted for nearly 50 years."* NBC and other networks with similar types of conflicts either ignore or tend to give media exposure to "pundits" biased in their favor on the issues of outsourcing, lowering taxes on corporations, removing labor and environmental regulations, and reducing government expenditures. A reduction in taxes has also reduced our government's capacity to enforce regulations.

- Disney, the owner of ABC, has many thousands of low wage workers in China and in their theme parks here in the United States. As a result, ABC is unlikely to give coverage to the issue of outsourcing or the issues of low wage workers here or in China.[406]

- In 1998, Disney owned ABC News canceled a report on the hiring of convicted pedophiles at Disney World.

These kinds of conflicts of interests are inherent to corporate conglomerate media.

The major newspapers, networks, newsweeklies, and wire services compose a vast news-gathering infrastructure with correspondents and stringers throughout much of the world. The Associated Press alone operates 243 news bureaus in at least 120 countries. Despite these vast resources, many important and revealing stories have been broken by small publications with a tiny fraction of the material resources and staff available to mass media corporations.

Stories about hunger in America, the chemical poisoning of our environment and our people, the illegal activities of our government at home and abroad, U.S. sponsored torture, the dangers of nuclear power plants, and other such revelations were uncovered by small news outlets long before they were finally picked up, if ever, by the mainstream press.

A media environment where six giant companies control 90% of what we read, watch, or listen to is damaging our democracy, and far more destructive outcomes can result than we have seen. No imperial ruler in history had multiple channels that could permeate entire societies with powerfully influential video and audio messages.

The extraordinary, unified force of our corporate conglomerate media must be overcome if we are to have a true government of, for, and by the people

The economic elite leaders of the big six media companies and their companies, are close-knit and not fully competitive. They work together to maintain and expand their power. The big six have similar boards of directors, they jointly invest in ventures, lend each other money and cooperate in other important ways. According to a Columbia Journalism Review study report, the five largest media conglomerates have 45 interlocking directors (the same board member sits on the board of more than one corporation).[407]

These media corporations also have interlocking directors with many other kinds of large corporations, including banks, investment companies, oil companies, health care and pharmaceutical companies and technology companies. Several studies show that those 15 to 20% of corporate directors who sit on two or more boards, who are called the *"inner circle"* of the corporate directorate, unite 80 to 90% of the largest corporations in the United States into a well-connected *"corporate community."*[408]

Adam Smith warned of the impact of coordinated domination by a few aligned business owners and managers:

"People of the same trade seldom meet together, even for merriment and diversion, but the conversation ends in a conspiracy against the public, or in some contrivance to raise prices."

Now the danger is far greater due to interlocking directorships and conglomerates crossing industries.

The six dominant media firms, among the largest in the world, and their leaders, have the power and use it to serve the interests of the corporate world and economic elites. Their leaders' power to select content and commentators given exposure in our mass media, and to select subordinates who are socialized to have aligned interests or world views authorized to do so, is used to bias content to serve their interests. And their power in lobbying and on our election system they have used with little regard for the public interest.

Sometimes media firm managers or owners may believe they are acting in the country's best interest when they distort media content or omit important facts. Some arrogantly believe that imposing illusions to manipulate the "stupid majority" is necessary. But if the majority is ignorant, the media are mainly responsible since it is the media's most important function to educate the population on the facts at the foundation of good public policy choices. And the judgment of elites supposedly in the public interest generally serve their interests above all others.

As Noam Chomsky, media scholar and "world's top public intellectual," points out in the book and movie *Manufacturing Consent,* some see *"democracy and freedom [as] threats to be avoided"* rather than values to be treasured and preserved, so they avoid disseminating the knowledge that would bring power to those other than themselves. As John Adams wrote, *"Power always thinks it has ... vast views beyond the comprehension of the weak; and that it is doing God's service when it is violating all his laws."*[409] And almost

400 years ago John Milton, the famous English intellectual and poet, complained of essentially the same injustice: *"They who have put out the people's eyes, reproach them of their blindness."*

Mostly, though, the leaders of the mass media are under no illusion on whose interests they are best serving. The mass media have been an important part of the process that has altered regulatory, tax, and expenditure policies that better served the public interest, to ones that are now poorly serving or disserving the public, to serve their interests. And they are a barrier to the necessary fundamental reforms to our economic and political systems that are disserving the majority and resulting in great injustices.

A Media of, for and by the People Will Be A Force for Major Social Advancement

It is true that many people today are ignorant of important facts and are unwilling to seek reliable sources of facts needed to make wise public policy decisions. But social forces, including those from the media, are largely responsible for the cultural and intellectual pursuits of the "masses," including the "working class." This is clearly indicated by the results of social conditions in 19th century England when the "working class" had interests of a character far from modern day stereotypes arising from today's social forces.

The cultural and intellectual pursuits of 19th century English "masses" were studied using over 2,000 memoirs, diaries, oral histories, newspapers, surveys, polls, library and school records, and other sources. The book *The Intellectual Life of the British Working Classes,* by Jonathan Rose, reports the striking results: Weavers, miners, cooks, wheelwrights, fishermen, milk maids, mechanics, shepherds, farmers, and others in the "working class" commonly read an impressive range of so-called high-brow literature: Dickens, Milton, Tennyson, Ruskin, Marx, and Shakespeare, to name a few. They appreciated and sought the great works of intellectual and creative merit for their time, due to the social forces around them. From the book:

"Nearly fifty groups in and around London [existed] where working men and women were studying chemistry, geology, mathematics, and astronomy, with all the gravity and deliberation, and confidence, of old and experienced professors."

Today the "masses" tend to have pursuits of a different character, but our mass media has a fundamental role in creating them, and creating our divided, coarsened, and consumption driven society. In pursuing their interests, our mass media reinforce these negatives. To an overwhelming degree, they abdicate their important responsibility to educate, challenge and inspire.

We share with the people of the Enlightenment the experience of unprecedented penetration of new media (although the printing press was not new in the 18th century, the level of penetration and influence of print media was new) in our society and the essential character of other conditions described in *Now Is the Time for The New Enlightenment.* But the people of the Enlightenment era had an advantage over us: Their mass media, or the media content that reached their majority, were not mainly under the control of their wealthy ruling class. And even when a wealthy owner had control, a sufficient number of them were strongly motivated by a "social conscience" or were more able than our wealthy media owners to see that their well-being depended on the well-being of their society.

Their printing presses published ideas that stimulated the majority of people's imagination of the real possibility of a fundamentally more just way of organizing their societies. The Enlightenment's beneficial societal transformations were dependent on this process. The current character of our media, especially the mass media, whose content reaches the largest number of people, is a barrier to this kind of process. This is a critically important problem that must be solved.

We have unwisely trusted that our media corporations would place the public interest above corporate interests and the private benefits of those in control of them. Our dysfunctional media are a threat to our society. A diverse media controlled by people representative of the people being served will best serve our nation. A media of such a character is now an urgent necessity.

In Summary

A media system dominated by a few huge, powerful, and manipulative corporations that control almost all that we learn about our society is a barrier to the widespread awareness of the accurate, unprejudiced information we need. When facts are distorted or obscured, as they have been, it creates conflict and makes problem-solving impossible. We need accurate, unprejudiced information and fact-based policy solutions, clearly, widely, and commonly expressed to best deal with our many serious problems

Our media system requires radical reforms for a far more constructive content and tone of our democratic discourse, and for instilling a sense that we all must learn about important public issues so we can best serve our role in our renewed, well-functioning democracy.

"Every government degenerates when trusted to the rulers of the people alone. The people themselves, therefore, are its only safe depositories. And to render even them safe, their minds must be improved to a certain degree."[410]

Thomas Jefferson

"Their minds must be improved," largely, by a greatly improved media.

The Structure and Support of a New Fourth Estate

The media are called the *"Fourth Estate"* or the fourth branch of government, because of their essential role in democratic governance, so our mass media enterprises are not just business enterprises. New Enlightenment policies require broadcast media, and motivate other media, to have a different organizational structure than that of conventional companies, one that is more appropriate because this structure is internally democratic and, largely as a result, the structure will inherently best serve its role in a democratic society.

The current structure not only is not best serving the public interest; its design inevitably results in serving it poorly. A media owned, managed and controlled by a small and privileged elite cannot well serve the public interest.

The following major organizational structure solutions will serve important social ideals. They are guided by the principle that a well-functioning government of, for, and by the people requires a vigorous media of, for, and by the people. They include policies in these categories:

- Require, and offer financial supports for, local community members' ownership and control of all communities' broadcast media.
- Promote by offering financial supports for local community members' ownership and control of all communities' print mass media.
- Promote by offering financial supports for worker-ownership and control of national content producing media enterprises, including Internet media.

Broadcast Media

Our ownership of the airwaves allows us regulatory control over air media companies to ensure that they are used in a way that best serves the public, but this enormous potential has been far from realized. We will be best served by media corporations controlled by people far more representative of the majority. Federal financial resources and regulations should ensure that media corporations of such a character predominate. This New Enlightenment media policy will support and require a gradual worker takeover of all broadcast media thereby greatly enhancing broadcast media corporations' ability and desire to best serve the public interest.

Broadcast licenses come up for renewal every eight years and are generally automatically renewed for another eight years. With the availability of sufficient financing, workers of local stations could take ownership and management control of their stations. Corporations owning more than one station we will require to divest to local worker-owners. The *Commonwealth Bank* will provide loans at the Federal Reserve Discount Rate for the worker buyouts at the eight-year license renewal time.

New Enlightenment financial supports also include company federal subsidies of $18,000 per year per full-time journalist and editor. This is approximately one-half the median salary of reporters and correspondents in 2015.[411] Eligibility requirements for the subsidy include worker-ownership and worker self-direction (Worker owned and self-directed enterprise (WSDE) structure policy 3 describes), and that the company is a non-profit organization. The non-profit status allows tax deductible donation support from community members. All citizens over 18 years of age will be encouraged to at least donate federally supplied news media vouchers.

To avoid undue influence from a donation source, we will establish blind trusts where all donations will be made anonymous, and to limit dependence on any one source, donation amounts will be limited (possibly to about .1% of a media company's annual budget or $5,000 whichever is less). On WSDE media that has news and other types of programming, revenue from regulated advertising will be allowed to support programming other than news programming. In some cases, tax deductible donation support will be sufficient to support this programming without ad revenue, freeing the company to choose non-commercial status, for the public relations value, to be free of any possibility of influence from advertisers in programming decisions, and to not have to devote resources to dealing with advertisers.

When advertising revenue is necessary, stations will raise funds with sponsor content similar to what occurs on public media. Slightly more extensive content will be allowed if it has accurate informational value. Sufficient public support for most WSDE media companies will likely exist to eliminate the need for advertising revenue and, when needed, its relatively minor role will minimize advertisers influence, and the kind of ad content allowed could have public value, unlike the deceptive or devoid of accurate or useful information in most ad content now.

The broadcast media journalist subsidies, plus the subsidies described later for other journalists, and other news media subsidies will total about $6.3 billion per year ($1.3 billion in direct journalist subsidies and $5 billion in citizen news media vouchers). This amount is small compared to the $30 billion per year we spent in current dollars supporting journalism during the country's early decades. And we spent $621 billion in 2011–12 on public education in total from all levels of government. A well-functioning press able and willing to be devoted to its fact-finding and educational role serves a basic and essential public educational purpose of similar importance. Even several multiples of this expenditure for this purpose is justifiable.

The New Enlightenment's large subsidy per journalist will be a motive for ownership transfer to workers since it gives a competitive advantage to worker-owned media companies. However, due to the great importance of local worker-ownership and control of media companies, we will also require it at broadcast station license renewal time. All newly licensed stations and stations renewing licenses will have this license requirement. If the workers and owners cannot agree on a price, an independent appraisal will determine the price.

This policy would be comprehensive, so it would include the major networks and other large corporations that own local stations. They will also be required to divest their stations to local owners at license renewal time.

The network's central news content producing operations that supply content to their affiliates would also be eligible for journalist subsidies if these operations were sold to workers who instituted a non-profit, WSDE structure. Worker-owner financing also will be available through the Commonwealth Bank for these national enterprises. The resulting competitive advantage the subsidies will create will motivate divestiture and WSDE establishment.

As the few examples noted earlier indicate, divestiture is important because, in addition to the news content problem resulting from current ownership and management being unrepresentative, the interests of other enterprises within a conglomerate may harmfully influence news content.

Any group of ten or more journalists who seek to establish a new central news producing WSDE to supply content to local stations and/or other media outlets, or to establish a new local station WSDE, will also get subsidy support based on the following condition: They meet eligibility requirements for start-up financing described in *The Way to Prosperity for All, Facilitating the Establishment of Worker-Owned Enterprises*, Policy 3.

Existing companies supplying news content to local outlets, such as Associated Press and Thomson Reuters, will also receive the $18,000 per year subsidy per journalist and editor for any that become independent worker-owned, WSDE structured enterprises, also supported by Commonwealth Bank loans.

Currently, a board of directors determines mass media corporations' policies, usually fewer than 20 people selected by controlling shareholders who are exclusively very wealthy. They are poor representatives of the population demographic being served. In the recommended WSDE structure, policies would be determined either by workers, based on a one person, one vote democratic process, or by a board of directors elected from among the workers, depending on the policy and the size of the company. Greater freedom for journalists and other content creators to work on content of their choosing would result from this system.

An elected board of directors will choose managers when needed to manage and coordinate distinct operations, such as story production, clerical, technology, communications, public relations, and general maintenance. For more details on WSDE governing structure, see *A System to Facilitate Widespread Establishment of Worker-Owned Enterprises,* Policy 3.

New Enlightenment WSDE media will be financially better able to serve the public interest due to the subsidies and larger audiences which will generate direct audience and other funding source support. Also, serving the public interest will be a higher priority of more representative democratically controlled media enterprises. Good journalism will thereby flourish. Our renewed Fourth Estate will be an integral component, as it should be and needs to be, in a new well-functioning democracy.

The New Enlightenment's subsidy policy will also require air media companies to have semi-annual public forums where representatives of the company will take questions and comments from community members. New license renewal periods will be reduced from the current eight-year period to four years, and licenses could be challenged by any outside group that selects ten provisional board members with an alternative policy platform to that of the current company. Public hearings and a petition signature standard will initiate a public vote to determine whether the existing ownership is to be significantly altered or replaced on the license renewal date.

Due to the regular input from the community, and the more democratic policy making by media corporation decision-makers more representative of the community, it would be rare for local worker-owned and WSDE media outlets to have a license challenged, despite the systemic facilitation of this process that our policy would offer. In any rare case when the majority of voters choose to replace the licensee, the ten provisional Board members would decide on maintaining or replacing some current journalists or content creators, and within six months WSDE governance processes would be reestablished, including board of director elections every four years. Any worker not continuing would get reemployment assistance, his or her portion of the value of the company, and the amount available in his capital account (described in Policy 3) at the time of separation.

The ten provisional board members and any other new workers would have to purchase a proportional share of the company. Commonwealth Bank funds would be available for those who need to finance their purchase if the WSDE has insufficient funds for these loans.

The Fairness Doctrine

To further ensure a diversity of views on issues of public importance, we would reinstitute the Fairness Doctrine with additional provisions. Under the Fairness Doctrine, stations issued broadcast licenses had to devote some of their programming to controversial issues of public importance and had to allow the airing of opposing views on those issues. Stations could provide contrasting views in various ways: news segments, public affairs shows and/or editorials. It did not require that each program be internally balanced, nor did it mandate equal time for opposing points of view.

The Fairness Doctrine simply prohibited stations from broadcasting from a single perspective, day after day, without presenting opposing views, as is common today, especially on "news talk" radio stations. Typically, when an individual or a citizen group complained to a station about imbalance, the station would set aside time for an on-air response for the omitted perspective. Only a "reasonable opportunity for presentation of opposing points of view" was required. If a station disagreed with the complaint, feeling that an adequate range of views had already been presented, the decision would be appealed to the FCC for a judgment. If one view received a lot of coverage in primetime, then at least some response time would have to also be in primetime.[412]

The Fairness Doctrine depended on the vigilance of listeners and viewers to notice imbalance. It provided occasional remedies to violations, but most importantly it codified the principle that broadcasters had to present a range of views on controversial issues. Stations generally behaved based on the knowledge that they might have to account for violations, and that gross violations would be unacceptable. Additionally, the rule mandated that broadcasters alert anyone personally attacked or subject to an attack in their programming and give them a chance to respond. The Fairness Doctrine also required any broadcasters who endorse political candidates to invite other candidates to respond.

The demise of the Fairness Doctrine is part of the anti-regulatory trend of more recent decades. This pro-industry trend in the FCC, and in Congress, has ended the right of access to broadcast television by any but the moneyed interests. What has not changed over this time though, despite the rise of other media, is that air media remain the dominant force affecting public opinion, especially on local public issues.

Broadcasters have a responsibility to use the airwaves to inform the public on a diversity of issues and views. A Fairness Doctrine, in addition to a diverse and more representative ownership, will ensure this responsibility is met.

The New Enlightenment's Fairness Doctrine policy will require air media to provide free equal time immediately following a purchased public policy related ad for an opposing view. This would effectively reduce the total ad rate for view and counter-view to one-half the standard rate—a reasonable and necessary air media public service responsibility in exchange for the use of our airwaves. Also, if the ad advocates for the election of a particular candidate, all other candidates will be given equal time.

Since the demise of the Fairness Doctrine, we have had much less coverage of issues of public importance. Also, it has resulted in an era where there is one right-wing host after another, and little else, on some stations. Disney owned KSFO in liberal San Francisco is one such station, and almost every city in the country has one; some have two. In Eugene, Oregon, the local daily newspaper, the Register-Guard, reported the results of a study: The two commercial talk stations had "*80 hours per week, more than 4,000 hours per year, programmed for Republican and conservative talk shows, without a single second programmed for a Democratic or liberal perspective.*" Eugene is an uncommonly progressive city, yet the uniformity of programming from the opposite viewpoint on the air was extreme. From the article: "*Political opinions expressed on talk radio are approaching the level of uniformity that would normally be achieved only in a totalitarian society. There is nothing fair, balanced or democratic about it.*"

In a challenge to the constitutionality of the Fairness Doctrine, the Supreme Court ruled unanimously that while broadcasters have First Amendment speech rights, the fact that the spectrum is owned by the government and merely leased to broadcasters gives the FCC the right to regulate news content. The Supreme Court ruling stated: *"There is nothing in the First Amendment which prevents the Government from requiring a licensee to share his frequency with others... It is the right of the viewers and listeners, not the right of the broadcasters, which is paramount."* In the 1970s, the FCC called the doctrine the *"single most important requirement of operation in the public interest—the sine qua non for grant of a renewal of license."*

The necessity for the Fairness Doctrine is due to the extraordinary power of the broadcast media, and to the fact that many fewer broadcast licenses exist than people who would like to have them. Unlike print and Internet media, which are unlimited, broadcasting licenses are limited by the finite number of available frequencies. As trustees of a limited public resource, licensees must accept public interest programming obligations in exchange for the public giving them the use of the resource and semi-monopoly status.

However, large companies of other media types have semi-monopoly status also, since barriers to entry for their level of influence are, for all practical purposes, prohibitive. The power of the major newspapers is in a different class than that of a small local newspaper, so any biases they may have are far more influential. The New York Times alone prints about one million papers per day. The major national newspapers are important agenda setting institutions that determine what is covered and how it is covered by other newspapers and media. No real competitors exist for the major newspapers, nor can they exist without huge sums of money and long periods of time, so they too have extraordinary public interest obligations.

First Amendment restrictions on "abridging... the freedom of the press" put constraints on print media regulation that do not exist to the same degree for air media. The public ownership of the airwaves allows more regulatory control. (The possibility also exists for similar regulatory control of Internet media as air media since Internet infrastructure uses public right-of-ways.) However, New Enlightenment print and Internet media policy, described next, will motivate and facilitate a beneficial transformation in the character of the ownership and management of print media. Without mandates, our print and Internet media policy will result in a more diverse, fair and fact-based print and Internet media that will advance the content and tone of our democratic debate.

After New Enlightenment reforms are instituted, broadcast license denials will be very rare for an entirely different reason than the reason they are rare now: a dysfunctional FCC. The reason will instead be that air media will be structurally designed, supported, and regulated to serve the public well. FCC reform is also necessary, as detailed in Policy 33.

Print and Internet Media

The following policy would apply to all existing print and Internet media companies supplying news and educational content on policy related issues that adopt a WSDE structure and a non-profit organizational status with a circulation greater than 10,000 for print media, or access by 20,000 unique IP addresses monthly for Internet media. (These minimums seem reasonable but are open to adjustment based on public input.)

These companies will receive a federal $18,000 per year salary supplement or support per journalist or editor to motivate worker-ownership and the WSDE structure. We will also offer Commonwealth Bank funds at the Federal Reserve Discount Rate for print and Internet media companies seeking worker-ownership with the WSDE structure and non-profit status.

The subsidies to, and better performance of worker-owned print media in the service of the public interest for the other reasons noted, will create competitive pressures sufficient to motivate many current owners to sell to workers.

Existing media companies would have previously defined who journalists are; it is unlikely that they would fraudulently claim that other employees are journalists after we initiate the subsidy. Criminal penalties for doing so will be enforced.

New WSDE print or Internet media companies formed by ten or more journalists will also be eligible for the journalist subsidy based on this condition: They meet eligibility requirements for start-up financing described in Part 2, Policy 3. We financially incentivized local lending institutions or city governments to supply part of the funding in the eligibility systems. They would be in the best position to judge the likelihood of success of the proposed media WSDE and would not risk their portion of the WSDE funding requirements if they believed the company founders did not have the necessary level of competence, or if the demand was insufficient. Both the grouping of ten people and the oversight during WSDE formation requirement by local lenders and the Commonwealth Bank for new media companies would minimize the possibility of fraud to get the journalist subsidy. We will establish peer review and minimum consumer subsidy requirements that are lower than that of preexisting companies, which we will periodically increase.

These policies will motivate the widespread transformation of media companies to democratic worker self-directed enterprises, eliminating media domination by a narrow, unrepresentative segment of our population.

In the case of large Internet based news service companies, such as Yahoo and Google that provide services other than news, the journalist subsidy would motivate divestiture of their news operations for it to meet the requirements for receiving the subsidy. The subsidy would allow them to better compete with the new subsidized competitors in the market. (Other requirements for large search engine companies are necessary and described later.)

Public Media

Public television and radio broadcasting is the most consistently trusted major news source, with Americans telling pollsters it deserves far greater public funding. Although it has sometimes been a superior source of information compared to commercial media, similar management biases existing in commercial media are also influencing the selection of report subjects or emphasis to an unacceptable degree. Wealthy and corporate interests or the interests of government have had a disproportionate influence. For example:

After the recent death of British Prime Minister Margaret Thatcher, reporter Margaret Warner on PBS declared that Thatcher *"brought a free market revolution to Britain, lowering taxes and privatizing state industries... Britain's economy rebounded from her tough medicine."* Thatcher was by most accounts an extreme "conservative," so she had similar praise on Fox News. However, the British newspaper The Guardian listed economic indicators during Thatcher's tenure: Inequality increased—the wealthy got much wealthier and the poor got poorer. Poverty increased from 13.4% in 1979 to 22.2% in 1990, and when she left office in 1990, unemployment was higher than when she took office. PBS and Fox News did not mention these facts.

Corporate and wealthy donors have influenced content, and the political whims of congressional party leaders serving elite interests influenced content using the threat of withdrawal of funds for the Corporation for Public Broadcasting.

The Koch brothers have been especially aggressive in using their vast amounts of wealth to influence public media and our political system in general. David Koch and his brother Charles own Koch Industries, a huge energy and chemical conglomerate. David Koch contributed $23 million to public broadcasting, and he is on the boards of the public broadcasting stations WGBH and WNET.[413] This enables him to exert influence over the network, including its news operation. Also, by having Koch as a trustee, they were establishing a defense against a coordinated campaign's false charge of "liberal bias," and positioning themselves to receive substantial new donations from wealthy donors. Less pressure from congressmen on the far right to further remove public funding resulted from Koch's public media position.

For decades, federal funding for public broadcasting has been dwindling; the government's contribution now makes up only 12% of PBS' funds. Affiliates such as WNET depend almost entirely on gifts, some of which are enormous. For example, in 2010, WNET received fifteen million dollars from James Tisch, the CEO of Loews Corporation. (Tisch is now the chairman of WNET's board.) Some bias to avoid content that would offend wealthy donors is unavoidable in these circumstances. For example:

A controversial film, *Citizen Koch,* focused on the aftermath of the Supreme Court's Citizens United ruling, which allowed unlimited corporate spending on issue and candidate campaigns, was intended for PBS broadcast. But the public broadcasting funded production company ITVS withdrew funding for the project. The film correctly expressed that the Citizens United ruling had endangered democracy by drowning out ordinary voters' concerns in a surge of corporate cash and that many working-class Republicans felt betrayed by the Party's attack on public-employee unions in Wisconsin.

Citizen Koch mentions the Koches multiple times as using the ruling to make major contributions to promote conservative candidates and causes. Officials at ITVS claim they pulled the funding for *Citizen Koch* because they didn't like the film, and not because of pressure from the Koch brothers. No hard evidence exists regarding the cause, so we all have to use only our judgment to decide on the likelihood that Koch money played a role in the funding withdrawal, or at least had the power to play a role.

More public funding and a more democratic and representative management structure are needed in public broadcasting as well. We will institute a WSDE governance structure and a $36,000 per year per journalist subsidy on the local and central content producing level. We will also establish fixed ten-year budgets for the federal support of public broadcasting to remove the continual defunding threat by hostile members of Congress. Public Broadcasting employs about 3,500 journalists, so the total public broadcasting subsidy would be about $126 million. However, a primary objective of this policy is to stimulate and support the hiring of more journalists. We will support a doubling of the number of public media journalists, so the subsidy would be $252 million, an increase of about 57% over 2014 funding levels of $445 million.[414]

The number of journalists will increase further based on the citizen news media voucher funding.

The larger per journalist subsidy is offered since public media depend on public funding and no advertising revenue is permitted. The large increase in public support will substantially diminish corporate influence. Income from individuals, public interest groups, state governments, colleges and universities, syndication and other sources will likely increase also, due to content improvements.

Except for those policies related to worker-ownership, since we will maintain public ownership, the WSDE governance structure described in The Way to Prosperity for All, Policy 3, will be instituted. Workers will determine policy on the local station and the central content producing level using democratic processes. Local public broadcasting stations will send, or otherwise involve, representatives to public media's national content producers to participate in programming decisions.

Rather than a small, elite group of managers having disproportionate influence, as is currently the case, journalists would have greater freedom to pursue stories of their choosing. In-depth reporting on a greater diversity of issues would result from these policies, and reports will not be biased in favor of elite interests.

News Media Vouchers

The essential "public good" character of journalism New Enlightenment policy will further support with public funds by giving each citizen over 18 years of age a $20 News Media Voucher.[415] The cost to the federal government to further support journalism would be $5 billion—voluntarily supplied by 248 million citizens using a $20 voucher if all eligible citizens use it. All news media would be eligible to receive vouchers.

The system gives a news media outlet support in proportion to the number of citizens who see its value. Likely, WSDE news media and public media will get a disproportionate share of the vouchers, which will rapidly increase their dominance. Voucher funds not used in a year will be used to increase the journalist subsidy and voucher amount the following year.

The average (mean) annual income of the 54,400 journalists in the U.S. is $46,560 (greater than the median noted earlier), so journalists' financial compensation now totals $2.5 billion, so the vouchers alone could triple it.[416] However, the news media could use the voucher funds for any news content related expenses including increases in office space, equipment, travel expenses, or number of journalists. Ideally, the number of journalists would nearly double in the first year of the subsidies. News outlets heavily supported with news media vouchers would have much larger increases and some outlets will have none.

In many communities, few journalists remain, and those that do remain cannot cover all that needs to be covered. Elections are going uncovered, and city, county and state government exercise power and allocate funds with no or little public knowledge. Far more journalists are needed.

As the citizen news media vouchers increase the number of journalists in the early years of supplying it, and therefore the journalist subsidy funding, we will reduce the voucher amount so that the total news media subsidy remains at $6.3 billion per year.

Media Subsidies: An Important Part of a Well-Functioning Media Here and Elsewhere

Washington, Jefferson, Hamilton and their contemporaries instituted postal and printing subsidies that were an essential part of the functioning of the free press of their time. They guaranteed what Madison described as *"a circulation of newspapers through the entire body of the people...[that] is favorable to liberty.* "[417] Subsidies made possible much of the abolitionist press that led the fight against slavery. From the days of our founding to the mid-nineteenth century, enormous printing and postal subsidies were instituted.[418]

If annual U.S. expenditures to subsidize journalism were the same percentage of GDP in 2009 as in the 1840s, it would have been $30 billion, 67 times the $445 million federal subsidy in 2014 for public broadcasting, and there was no other public support for journalism.[419] Postal and printing subsidies remain important today, but air media and the Internet have made them less important than the direct support of journalists.

Some may be concerned that government funding will lead to government influence on content, but the system of funding we will use will ensure that it does not. International experience indicates this is easy to accomplish. The Freedom House, the pro-private media organization, annually ranks international press freedom. Freedom House prioritizes the importance of having no government infringement of private press freedoms and ranks the nations with the largest subsidies—the nations of northern Europe—in the top six on its 2008 list of nations with the most free news media. The United States ties for twenty-first. Research has found that increases in subsidies in northern Europe led to media that more vigorously pursued their "watchdog" role.

The Economist magazine annually evaluates nations on the basis of the functioning of government, civic participation, civil liberties, political culture, and pluralism using its Democracy Index. It found that the six top-ranked nations maintain some of the most generous journalism subsidies. If the United States, No. 18 in the index, spent the same per capita on public media and journalism subsidies as Sweden and Norway, which rank 1 and 2, we would spend as much as $30 billion a year, about our expenditure in the 1840's. Sweden and Norway are also in the top tier of the pro-business Legatum Group's Prosperity Index, which measures health, individual freedom, security, the quality of governance, and transparency, in addition to material wealth. The United States ranks ninth.

We will establish an analogous organization to the Corporation for Public Broadcasting (CPB), the Corporation for Democratic Media (CDM), to distribute the subsidies to media companies with the required WSDE structure, worker-ownership, and non-profit corporation status. The CDM will develop and publish for public review and comment guidelines for performance for maintaining subsidies to specific media companies based on peer review and number of consumer criteria.

These organizational and policy changes would be radical changes in the service of the public interest, but they will also serve well the financial interest of the owners of media companies. Media outlets controlled by people who are more representative of the majority will serve the majority more beneficially, leading to larger audiences, and media revenues from all sources are based directly or indirectly on audience size.

The New Enlightenment WSDE policy (Policy 3) describes ways we will motivate and support the gradual transfer to WSDE's of other kinds of business enterprises. The especially vigorous support of media enterprises' transformation not only serves the purpose of beneficially transforming enterprises essential to the functioning of our democracy that are currently serving their role poorly, it also offers prominent examples of the operation of WSDEs. The character of its operations and their beneficial impact on the workers and community will become obvious and help motivate the establishment of WSDE's throughout the economy.

Search Engines

Search engines potentially have a great impact on the public discourse because information is filtered through them that reaches billions of people. In just one month, December 2012 there were 175 billion search engine searches worldwide.[420] Although the algorithms that create search results, as far as I know, have been designed based on objective, not politically biased, analyses of data, public oversight of the function of these search engines is justified due to their enormous power. With no oversight, unscrupulous management could make algorithm changes to bias search results for political purposes. Because of the extraordinary, widespread impact of these search engines on information flow, we will require public oversight by a division within the FCC obligated to maintain any proprietary secrets, with criminal penalties if violated by any individual responsible.

Even without intentional abuse for political purposes, existing targeted search result technology and practices have potentially dangerous implications. Search results based on prior search and other Internet activity can lead to reinforcing biases and reducing common understanding of the issues. This can further divide an already too divided country. Advantages also exist from targeted search results and advertising. This is a complex and controversial issue that requires far more public knowledge and debate. (Campaign microtargeting and Internet privacy policy of the New Enlightenment Citizens Union, and ultimately Party, is in development)

The \$18,000 commercial and \$36,000 public broadcasting per year salary support per journalist would cost about \$1.2 billion per year. This expense assumes subsidies for all 58,500 journalists in the United States, of whom 3,500 are in public broadcasting and subsidies for 50% more public broadcasting journalists. Corporation for Democratic Media administrative costs for the subsidy program will likely be somewhat higher than the administrative costs for the Corporation for Public Broadcasting: 5% of managed funds. If it were 40% higher, or 7%, this would raise the total cost to about \$1.3 billion. The current number of non-public media journalists would not initially be in WSDEs. However, we will budget for the eventual condition where the number journalists in WSDE media equals the current number in all media. When this number is exceeded, additional subsidy funds will be sourced from the \$5 billion voucher budget unless we democratically determine to increase total public support for WSDE media in the future.

The \$1.3 billion plus the \$5 billion in News Media Voucher subsidies totals \$6.3 billion per year for news media subsidies.

I repeat for emphasis: We spent about \$30 billion in current dollars during the country's early decades supporting journalism. And we spent \$621 billion in 2011–12 on public education. A well-functioning press, able and willing to be devoted to its fact-finding and educational role, serves a basic and essential public educational purpose of similar importance, so this, and even several multiples of this expenditure amount for this purpose is justifiable.

James Madison expressed the importance of a well-functioning media to our government:

"A popular Government, without popular information, or the means of acquiring it, is but a Prologue to a Farce or a Tragedy; or, perhaps both. Knowledge will forever govern ignorance: and a people who mean to be their own Governors, must arm themselves with the power which knowledge gives."[421]

This policy will arm us with the "means of acquiring" "popular information." It creates the vigorous media of, for, and by the people necessary for a well-functioning government of, for, and by the people.

> *The New Enlightenment: Ideals of Democracy,*
> *Human Rights, Reason, and Progress * Policy 29*

Lobbying Reform

Corporations spent $3.31 billion on over 12,000 lobbyists in Washington in 2012. This is $119,000 per congressperson per week. They made these massive expenditures because in prior years they received far more value in tax savings and rebates, regulatory advantages, and favoritism in government contracts.

As I noted in Part 1, between 2008 and 2010 thirty large corporations spent more money lobbying Washington than they paid in taxes. Twenty-nine paid zero in taxes and instead received tax rebates over those three years. General Electric received $5 billion, while it had profits of $10.5 billion. The total value of the rebates received by the thirty corporations was near $11 billion. Combined lobbying expenses during the period were $475 million, so they received a 2,216% rate of return on their investment. Combined profits during the same period were $164 billion.

The Sunlight Foundation determined the 200 corporations most active in Washington and analyzed for the years 2007-2012 what these companies received in federal contracts and other federal support, what they spent on lobbying, and how much their executives and political action committees gave in campaign contributions. They found that the top 200 corporations spent nearly $5.8 billion on lobbying and campaign contributions—an insignificant amount compared to what they received: $4.4 trillion in federal contracts and assistance. Federal business contracts totaled $1.28 trillion and federal assistance $3.17 trillion. The federal assistance included loans, loan guarantees, and grants. The $4.4 trillion may not have all resulted from their lobbying, but likely a substantial fraction did. If it all did, and they profited by just 10% of the $4.4 trillion, their lobbying resulted in a 7,500% return on investment.

Lockheed Martin, the nation's largest contractor and world's largest military equipment company, received over $19 billion in federal contracts in 2011 and spent millions in lobbying for these and future contracts. The ten biggest government contractors are defense contractors, and they are also big suppliers of lobbyists. The defense industry lobbied our government using 384 lobbyists and $43 million from January through November 2013, and $59 million in 2012.[422] This is one reason our defense budget is as large as it is, and goes up despite having no military rival remotely close to our level of military power.

Allowing corporate managers to use the huge financial resources of corporations to influence our political and policy-making systems disadvantages members of the general public. It commonly results in unnecessary governmental or consumer costs to serve corporate managers' exclusive goal of maximizing corporate profits.

Our current lobbying system facilitates what could be considered to be veiled bribes, but sometimes it's veiled extortion. Members of Congress may implicitly threaten businesses with not renewing a federal contract or not approving a new one, or with removing regulatory or tax advantages they have, if they're not spending money to support them. A far more transparent policy making process is needed to minimize corruption or undue influence originating from either side.

Lobbyist influence derives from two sources: money for lawmakers' campaigns and access to provide information to lawmakers. Under our current election system, lawmakers are desperate for campaign cash because of the enormous advantages large amounts of money provide in campaigns. Direct campaign cash promises, and indirect ones through outside groups, such as super-PACs, and fundraising assistance promises from lobbyists, are used to influence policy to serve the narrow interests of wealthy corporations and individuals. New Enlightenment's election system reforms will eliminate the need for large amounts of campaign cash, so after we institute the reforms this source of influence will no longer be important.

However, the other source of influence, access to provide information may be even more commonly decisive. Influence comes from an ability to become an essential part of the policymaking process by flooding understaffed, under-experienced, and overworked congressional offices with enough information and expertise to shape their thinking. A recent Policy Council survey found that two-thirds of staffers say that lobbyists are "*necessary to the process*" as either "*collaborators*" or "*educators.*" House staffers keep track of hundreds of issues, and they are ill equipped to do so for several reasons.

Since a 1974 law, all House offices are limited to 18 staff members, split between the home district and Washington, DC. This has stayed the same even though a substantially higher degree of legislative complexity commonly exists now compared to 1974, and the population of most districts is larger, resulting in more constituent correspondence and services. In 1974, the population of the U.S. was 214 million; now it is 317 million. Also, an important support institution, the Congressional Office of Technology Assessment, has been eliminated.

Most House and Senate staff persons are inexperienced, and their relatively poor pay results in high turnover rates. Most Senate staffers have worked in their job for less than three years. For most, it is their first job. In House offices, one-third of staffers are in their first year, while only one in three has worked there for five years or more.[423] Congressional offices handicapped with staff of little policy knowledge due to high turnover make them extraordinarily vulnerable to lobbyists' influence.

Sixteen lobbyists representing business overrun policymakers' offices for every one representing a union or public interest group. From 1998 through 2010, business interests and trade groups spent $28.6 billion on lobbying, compared with $492 million for labor, nearly a 60 to 1 business advantage. Business lobbyists flood Congress with the most people and the most reports, and pay attention to the most details. What they provide serves their corporate clients' interests, generally in disregard of the public interest. No requirement exists for lobbyists to disclose which lawmakers they are meeting with and what information they provide in their materials or personal contacts, so important sources of influence are hidden from view.

In his famous essay, *On Liberty,* John Stuart Mill (1859) wrote that subjecting arguments to public scrutiny is unconditionally beneficial and provides the best way of sorting out good arguments from bad ones. Secrecy provides fertile ground for policy harmful to the public interest to serve special interests and undermines the ability of the press to provide an effective check against the abuses of government. As the expression goes, *Sunshine is the strongest antiseptic.*

Special interests exerting influence in secret dominate our policymaking system. The public, the media, and competing advocates often cannot discover which lobbyists are meeting with whom, what they are advocating for, and how they are advocating for it.

When constituents wish to express their opinion to their senator or congressperson they write a letter, call the office, or email. Congress receives over 200 million messages a year from constituents. Most offices have a list of generic responses and responding using the current system uses large amounts of staff time and results in little influence or, most commonly, no influence by average citizens.

The Solution

New Enlightenment policy uses modern technology to solve the problem of lack of transparency, while also serving the important purpose of leveling the playing field between wealthy interests and the general public in the ability to access lawmakers with information and advocacy on policy issues. The following solution will also reduce burdens on congressional staff.

The Library of Congress will create a website that will become the online forum for all public policy advocacies. Currently, every time a piece of legislation is introduced, the Library of Congress makes that legislation available online through the "THOMAS" System (named after Thomas Jefferson). The new web-based system, "JAMES" (named after James Madison), will be the forum for lobbyists, constituents, and other interested parties to publicly and transparently debate legislation. The JAMES system is a modified version of a Brookings Institution proposal. It is modified to further level the playing field between corporate lobbyists and the general public or public interest groups, and expand its functions.[424]

JAMES will provide congressional staff, journalists, and the public, with access to arguments, information, and ideas about public policy. All information will be searchable and sortable.

We will require that registered lobbyists state the organization they are representing and briefly state their clients position on a bill (or amendment or section of the bill). Also, they can provide a simple up or down vote that will make it easy for anybody, including congressional staff, to see who is for and who is opposed to particular policies. Every U.S. taxpayer would also get an account based on his or her Social Security number. Each account holder could also state his or her position and provide one up or down vote on a bill or section of the bill or amendment. Comments will require citizens to use their real names, which can also be determined by the Social Security number, but name and Social Security number would not be publicly disclosed (unless a citizen chooses to reveal name). Identification encourages a high-level civic debate, which often does not occur in anonymous forums.

Both the Executive Office of the President and the administrative agencies responsible for implementing and enforcing the laws have valuable expertise relevant to policy proposals, including insights into costs and feasibility. So the Executive Office and administrative agencies also may post pages for comments on a particular bill, section, or amendment and provide useful information, including any foreseeable problems with implementation or enforcement.

JAMES would have a hub page for each bill proposed by Representatives. You could see which organizations oppose and which are in favor; each of those organizations could detail their arguments and respond to one another's arguments, and would include contact information should someone want to learn more. All positions and arguments being made public will result in more democratic and more thoroughly vetted public policy. Everybody— members of Congress and their staffs, journalists, and the public—will be better informed, and everybody will be empowered to participate.

Corporate lobbyists and lobbyists for public interest groups receiving more than a low, yet to be determined, maximum amount or percentage of funding from corporations will be required to use the JAMES system as their sole contact route to lawmakers' offices. We include a restriction on some public interest groups because they are often used by corporations to advance their interests.

The restriction on corporate lobbyists' personal meetings with lawmakers should not be seen as a First Amendment violation; The JAMES system allows full expression by all, just the form is restricted for efficiency, transparency, and equal access reasons. The restriction is important in the service of the public good, and it is not for persons representing themselves. We accept a requirement for more extensive separation of church and state than this minor separation of corporation and state for the public interest. But will the current Supreme Court consider this reasonable and important restriction to be constitutional? Probably not, so a change in the Court or the Constitution will likely be necessary.

Lobbyists could update their pages as much as they like as new information becomes available, or in response to ongoing information input by other participants. They can also post separate pages for each state and congressional district if they wish, to provide more targeted information to help individual offices better understand how their constituencies might be affected.

Personal meetings access on public policy issues would remain available for individual citizens and representatives of public interest groups below the maximum threshold in corporate funding. Congressional staff will be required to publicly disclose the gist of any public policy related in-person conversation between their office and citizens or public interest group representatives on JAMES (citizens can require that the disclosure be anonymous). In cases where citizens have personal issues, such as being mistreated by a government agency where they seek the assistance of their representative in resolving the problem, these discussions not directly related to public policy development would not require public disclosure.

The ideal of citizen or organizational input on government policy intended to influence policymakers being done in public before the Internet was not practical in our large society. The JAMES system will make best use of the opportunity provided by this powerful technology for transparent public policy communications with policymakers. Individual citizen's potential for influence would likely be greater in this forum than through any other communication route, and lawmakers' offices would prefer it for the efficiency advantages.

This new system will eliminate the unjust and often socially destructive policy influence advantages resulting from the wealth of corporations. The average citizen and true grassroots funded interest groups cannot hire armies of lobbyists to develop relationships with many lawmakers and their staffs to provide information and advocacy within a nontransparent system, as corporations now can.

In addition to legislation introduced by their representatives, members of the public would also be given the opportunity to include their own policy proposals in a separate section of the website. Unorganized, unrestricted suggestions, comments, and data would not likely be productive, though. So the system requires policy proposal input in an organized way to facilitate the evaluation of the likely large number of entries.

Five sections per policy proposal submission will be created where these maximums could be entered as needed: A 50-word summary, a 500-word summary and up to a 2,000-word description, then up to a 20,000-word description; then, if necessary, content up to 100,000 words could be included in the fifth section. Participants would have to input content successively up the levels as necessary. If further details are needed, the content in the five sections will be used to determine whether sufficient interest exists to provide it.

Website viewers could indicate whether they approve any policy proposal, and proposals will rise in rank based on their number of approvals. The higher the rank of a policy proposal, the higher the likelihood it will attract the attention of legislators for further evaluation. As a result, some proposals originating from citizens may be introduced as bills for consideration by the legislature.

The proposed system offers prizes for proposals that get introduced and become law. In addition to the incentive value of the prestige associated, the prize will provide a substantial financial reward. The reward would essentially be in compensation for the time it would take to develop an innovative, valuable public policy proposal, with some compensation for the risk of expending large amounts of time with no reward if the proposal is not adopted. Possibly $300,000 would be a reasonable average award amount. The award would vary based on the level of importance or complexity of the policy.

Prizes will encourage people with valuable knowledge and ideas not currently recognized by elite power holders and experts to offer valuable policy innovations that otherwise would not have been given consideration. Many people have high levels of expertise in areas where they do not have professional training or university credentials whose knowledge and skills in these areas we currently waste. This system will use this expertise, and will substantially increase public officials' very limited access to the most innovative ideas for solving problems. It will help close the growing disconnect between the potential and practice of citizen participation.

It is widely acknowledged that people do not get involved in politics because of few opportunities for involvement, and current opportunities provide little power to make a difference. Millennials feel particularly disenfranchised; their age group is voting in historically low percentages. This policy will be especially useful to them since they are the most Internet savvy generation; it has been an important part of most of their lives. Also, millennials' unemployment rate has been consistently higher than the national average (the national unemployment rate was 5.5% in February 2016, while millennials had an unemployment rate of 7.8%), so a disproportionately large percentage is not involved in productive work, despite high average education levels. (However, New Enlightenment policies will eliminate the unemployment problem.)

Proposals input into the JAMES system, either from constituents or from legislators, will be organized by state and congressional district, and like lobbyist input, would be updatable. The JAMES system will offer a forum for a kind of national debate on public policy issues. All parties will be able to respond to one another's input.

The JAMES system will substantially increase efficiency and transparency of communications with lawmakers. Congressional offices will be able to tally, track and respond to constituent opinion, and citizens will be able to see how their views compare to others by district, state, or for the entire nation.

When a representative supports a policy contrary to the majority of those constituents expressing their opinions, he or she will be held accountable by the press, and by the voters at election time. The will of the people, or at least those motivated to express their wishes, will be more transparent on a wide variety of issues.

Public interest groups would generally also prefer to use JAMES as their contact route. Most public interest groups can't afford to hire enough lobbyists to schedule multiple meetings with every office, as corporations now can. JAMES will allow a more level playing field on which to compete. They will also be able to see what corporations are arguing and respond to their arguments and allegations. Likewise, corporations will be able to respond to their critics.

Members of Congress will also be able to post policy proposals that they have not yet formally introduced as bills to get public feedback to improve the proposal before writing the legislation. They will be able to post to their individual district/state sub-pages to target comments to their constituencies. The search and sort functions will make it easy for constituents to find out where their senators and representatives stand on issues.

JAMES would be of immense help to congressional staffers and members of Congress who need to learn something quickly about an issue. The large volume of information that congressional staff has to deal with, as well as the high turnover rates, results in inadequate time to research issues sufficiently. The JAMES organizational and ranking system would help them do this more systematically, potentially transforming some staffers' jobs.

Journalists would be able to learn more quickly and easily of all the groups and many of the people who are interested in a particular issue, giving them more choices on whom to interview and the ability to easily find a broad range of perspectives on the issue.

Most people will be able to use the JAMES system based on website instructions because we will design it to be as simple to use as possible. However, to ensure that everyone, or as many people as possible, can use the system, we will create a nationwide online training program for local librarians to prepare them for offering local citizens classes on the all the functionality of JAMES. The classes will be offered at local libraries periodically. An online training course designed for the public will also be available. JAMES system use will also be a recommended part of senior year high school social studies curriculum.

Further Supporting Unbiased Well-Informed Policymaking

To further increase the ability of lawmakers to make unbiased, well-informed decisions, New Enlightenment policy provides funding for increases in congressional staff numbers and pay. As previously noted, both constituent size and legislative importance and complexity warrant more and higher paid staff. (The Dodd-Frank financial regulation law and the Affordable Care Act were each thousands of pages long.) Except for high-level congressional staff, annual salaries are between $30,000 and $60,000, with most about $45,000, while having to live in high cost of living Washington, DC. [425] Legislative assistants specialize in specific legislative fields. They assist with the development of, and monitor, legislation, and they devise strategies to pass legislation—clearly work of potentially enormous consequence.

The people working on issues worth billions, hundreds of billions and ultimately even trillions of dollars earn less than the average surveyor ($59,180), and most often less than a third of what the average dentist makes ($163,240).[426] With a thriving market for talented lawmaker staff, low salaries, and difficult working conditions, inevitably, talented congressional staff members commonly leave the public sector for employment in the private sector. The average age of a DC-based House personal office staffer is 31. Ex-staffers who became lobbyists often increased their earnings by multiples, a value derived from their congressional employment. Higher legislative assistant pay is needed to maintain longer term and more knowledgeable assistants.

New Enlightenment policy doubles the budget for congressional staff. In addition to reducing turnover rates, this will help attract better-qualified staff. The increased funds will also support staff increases, with each office deciding the division between staff number and pay increase. Each congressional office is currently allotted $945,000 to hire up to 18 staff members. Doubling this per member allotment results in a total increase in spending on staff of $506 million per year.

Each senator's legislative assistance budget is about $478,000.[427] We will double Senate legislative assistance budgets to serve the same purpose as the funding increase for congressional staff, again with each office deciding the division between staff number and pay increase. This increase amounts to $48 million total per year.

In 1995, Congress defunded the Congressional Office of Technology Assessment (OTA). This left Congress with no experts to advise committees and members of Congress regarding decisions on national security, offshore oil drilling, transportation, energy, health, computer, biotech, nanotechnology, and many executive branch programs in science and technology worth trillions of dollars. Instead of decisions based on information and analysis provided by the impartial OTA, decisions have often been based on lobbyist supplied information designed to serve their clients' needs.

For a budget of about $20 million a year, OTA produced over 700 peer reviewed, high-quality reports and many more congressional testimonies by its staff between 1972 and 1995.[428] Representative Amo Houghton (R-N.Y.) commented when the OTA was defunded that *"we are cutting off one of the most important arms of congress, when we cut off unbiased knowledge about science and technology."*

The Union of Concerned Scientists (UCS) strongly supports reinstating the OTA. After OTA was defunded, the UCS asserts, *"The Department of Homeland Security spent three years pushing for a costly radiation detection system for smuggled nuclear material that did not work as promised, while neglecting to upgrade existing equipment that could have improved security."* Billions of dollars were wasted.

American Physical Society, the world's largest organization of physicists, has condemned the missile defense project as unworkable but the funding for these boondoggle contracts continues year after year, wasting billions. Risks of nanotechnology, biotechnology, and numerous medical devices continue to not be impartially assessed.

In 1985 an OTA report cautioned about the lack of preparedness and knowledge regarding potentially *"catastrophic oil spills from offshore operations."* If the OTA wasn't defunded it may have followed up on this report with more specific warnings, and we may have averted the *Deepwater Horizon* disaster. The Minerals Management Service of the Interior Department, one of the worst examples of a *"captured"* regulatory agency of industry, did not advise Congress truthfully about the risks.[429]

Congress needs an independent, impartial technical adviser, devoted to serving the needs of members of Congress and congressional committees. Separating valuable information from lobbyist spin is time-consuming and often requires a level of expertise that even the best and most well-trained congressional staff is not likely to have.

Fortunately, the office itself was just defunded, not abolished. In its last year of operation, the OTA had a budget of $21.9 million. We will restore its budget, adjusted for inflation, to $34.5 million.

The Congressional Research Service (CRS) budget of $107 million New Enlightenment policy we will increase by 30%, also to support more and higher paid research staff to better serve lawmakers' research needs. The cost for the House and Senate staff funding support increase will be about $554 million, for the CRS funding increase about $32 million, and for the OTA $34.5 million, totaling about $621 million per year.

"Grassroots" Lobbying and Political Advertising

If grassroots lobbying is left poorly regulated, lobbyists will shift their resources to the tactic of influencing public opinion to influence legislation, so it will be even more important than it is now to better regulate grassroots lobbying. As noted previously, the New Enlightenment's Fairness Doctrine will require air media to provide free equal time immediately following a purchased public policy related ad for an opposing view. If the ad advocates for the election of a particular candidate, all other candidates will be given equal time. And to further level the playing field needed for a true democracy, The New Enlightenment's free candidate airtime policy will give candidates a large amount of airtime to respond to purchased ads.

Also, voters can better judge the reliability of the statements made when they know who is paying for them. New Enlightenment policy is that any organization that spends over $500 toward the promotion of any public policy or candidate, must disclose the amount spent and all of its $200 or more contributors. Disclosure of funding sources within 24 hours of receipt for interest groups doing public policy and candidate related advocacy will be required.

Super PACs are required under current law to file reports with the Federal Election Commission (FEC) that disclose their contributors, contribution amounts, and expenditures, but disclosure can be delayed up to three months. Under current law, no one will know a possibly multimillion dollar donation source until after the election, if the money is given three months or less before the election. No good reason exists for allowing a 3-month delay for disclosures; it is easy to comply with a 24-hour limit.

Also running campaign TV ads that mention candidates are non-profit 501(c4) groups. They need not disclose their contributors and do not register as political committees with the FEC by claiming that they spend less than 49% of their funds on elections. Enforcement of the 49% limitation is rare. These nonprofit groups are especially attractive to individuals and corporations who fear a public backlash due to their support for a particular candidate. The $500 expenditure disclosure rule applies to all groups, so it will bring 501(c4) group's "dark money" into the light.

Disclosure requirements will include identifying the top three contributors for any political ad on the ad. Also, we will post all disclosures with detailed identifying information on the FCC website.

Lobbying laws and political advertiser disclosure laws are poorly enforced. We will move enforcement responsibilities to the Department of Justice for more effective enforcement.

These New Enlightenment reforms will be an important part of creating a truly democratic government. They will also minimize the inappropriate use of public funds and save the public hundreds of billions in unwarranted tax breaks and costs resulting from corporate regulatory advantages, including artificially high consumer prices from semi-monopoly or monopoly power. Just considering that 30 corporations received rebates totaling $11 billion over three years averaging $3.7 billion per year, based on their nontransparent lobbying efforts, and the other examples described above, savings will be much larger than the $621 million per year cost for this policy. I do not take into account any estimate of the excess in our budget analysis, so the budget surplus will likely be larger than the estimate (for this reason among others).

*The New Enlightenment: Ideals of Democracy, Human Rights, Reason, and Progress * Policy 30*

Congressional Rules Reform

The intention in designing the House was for it to be a broad-based legislative body, more representative of widespread public opinion and responsive to the people than any other element of the federal government. This is why the House is granted exclusive power to initiate revenue bills, and to take the country to war. The last war Congress declared was in December 1941, against Germany and Japan. The many undeclared wars since constitute one important indication of a dysfunctional Congress.

Over the last several decades, legislative branch authority has become overly concentrated in the hands of a few leaders of the majority party. And these leaders have a *"pay to play"* system, where a minimum amount of fundraising for the party is a requirement for powerful committee assignments. The system most highly rewards congresspersons most corrupted by wealthy donors.

For decades, congressional rules have been such that legislation was considered by the full House or Senate only if it was supported by party leadership or the committee chairs assigned by party leaders. Legislation that would have been supported by a majority and instituted has instead not been considered by a committee or the full House or Senate. Also, for decades, majority leaders in control of committees have barred minority amendments to bills. This avoids the possibility that even members of their majority party might vote for the amended bills, despite their not serving the party's agenda, because they believe either that it is the right thing to do or that it is what the people they represent prefer.

We are allowing the will of the people to be denied by these dysfunctional processes. Rules that allow obstruction by party operatives should not exist. When these operatives are those most corrupted by the moneyed interests, the inevitable result is our *"government of the 1%, by the 1%, and for the 1%."*

The rules for House floor debate are determined anew by a Rules Committee constituted for each session of Congress that is dominated by the majority party. In our current system, a small majority may have all the power and a large minority none.

Changes in the dysfunctional internal rules of organization of Congress is a necessary part of the process of removing important institutional barriers to a government of, for, and by the people.

The Solutions

The Rules Committee and all other committees should be formed with no party controlling or influencing the process. Committees in the various policy subject areas should be composed of, to the degree practicable, members of Congress drawn together based on their interests in considering problems and their potential solutions in these subject areas. And basic rules designed to ensure democratic processes should be permanently established. The following New Enlightenment reforms will meet these ideals.

Committee chairs who have decided which bills are considered by the committee, and all committee staff members who have scheduled the hearings, invited experts to testify, and prepared background materials for committee members are, under the current system, party appointees. Under New Enlightenment policy, all these positions will be held by professional, nonpartisan career House staff obligated to serve all members equally. This staff will have no power to make the significant decisions impacting the progress of bills. They will exclusively serve the needs of committee members, whose power will be determined by democratic processes within each committee.

A nonpartisan House administrator will preside over committee hearings and offer bills for consideration based on the votes of members reaching a predetermined threshold, possibly one-third (or less, if time allows) of committee members wanting committee consideration. New Enlightenment policy is also for a House rule guaranteeing that any bill or proposed amendment receiving 150 co-sponsors in the full House will automatically be allowed a committee hearing in the appropriate committee, an up-or-down vote in committee, and then, even if it fails in committee, a vote on the House floor. Experts would be called to testify also based on committee members' votes reaching the one-third threshold. If time allows, this threshold could be reduced to one-quarter or less.

Committee members should not be chosen by party operatives or be based on party affiliation criteria, as they are now. Any congressperson who chooses membership the New Enlightenment policy will allow membership.

Membership would require attending at least 90% of all committee hearings. This would eliminate the possibility of "virtual" membership, where a member could claim membership just to influence committee outcomes based on prejudices. Attendance ensures that members know of important expert testimony, and it encourages conversations with colleagues on the issues under consideration. It also requires priority setting for the limited time available, which allows the necessary level of expertise to be gained for well-informed judgments on the laws under consideration. If the size of highly preferred committees must be limited for any reason, including to ensure adequate membership in other committees, it will be done based on seniority.

Filibuster Reform

The filibuster was intended to be a way to prevent a Senate majority from ignoring the interests of the minority. As long as a senator kept talking on the floor, a bill could not move forward unless three-fifths, or 60 senators, voted to end debate.

In the first 50 years of the filibuster, it was used only 35 times (for part of this time the minimum was two-thirds rather than three-fifths). In the last two years alone, it was used over 100 times.[430] Current rules allow senators to not even show up on the floor to explain themselves; instead just signaling their intent to filibuster stalls legislation.

As a result, the Senate has become a place that one senator described as *"non-functional,"* where even routine bills must now clear 60 votes. This means that 41 senators, representing as little as 11% of the U.S. population, could, with little effort, obstruct passage of a bill supported by 59 senators representing as much as 89% of the population. This is completely contrary to the intent of our Founders, who intended the filibuster process to be sufficiently burdensome that it would be used infrequently, and under extraordinary circumstances. They believed a supermajority should be required in select circumstances, such as passing treaties, Constitutional Amendments and motions of impeachment.

Every filibuster initiates a complex set of Senate procedures that effectively brings the institution to a stop for as long as a week, preventing other critical issues from being addressed.

The Solutions

1. Require real (not virtual) Filibusters: If senators want to halt action on a bill, they must take to the floor and hold it through sustained debate.

2. End filibusters on motions to proceed: Today, filibusters can be used both to prevent bills from reaching the floor for debate (motion to proceed) and to prevent bills from being passed. New Enlightenment policy will end the practice of filibustering motions to proceed. This will cut the number of filibusters about in half, and allow more issues to be debated.

3. Put the burden on the minority to take responsibility for the filibuster continuation by requiring 45 publicly disclosed votes daily supporting continuation, rather than requiring the majority to get 60 votes to end it.

---

*The New Enlightenment: Ideals of Democracy, Human Rights, Reason, and Progress * Policy 31*

Community Broadband

Some communities are setting up *"community broadband"* networks or high-speed Internet networks. Community broadband networks offer lower costs for the same or higher speeds than the telecom giants offer, whose rates are far above international norms, and in some communities telecom companies do not offer broadband.

Since the communication and information transfer capabilities of the Internet are vast, free community broadband will greatly enhance the ability of everyone, of all economic statuses, to be well informed on public policy issues (and many other subjects), and to participate actively in our democracy. It will also be of substantial economic importance, especially for the poor, so it will help reduce inequality. We propose a national policy supporting free community broadband.

The New America Foundation compared high-speed Internet for various download and upload speed offerings, and other telecom services, in 22 cities around the world by price. They found that our international counterparts offer much lower prices and faster Internet service.

They compared "triple play" offerings that combine Internet, phone, and television services and found that consumers in Paris can purchase a 100 Mbps bundle of television, telephone, and high-speed Internet service for the equivalent of approximately $35. In the least expensive American city, Lafayette, LA, a package with just 6 Mbps costs around $65. In the U.S., the best deal for a 150 Mbps home broadband connection from cable and phone companies is $130/month. The international cities surveyed offer comparable speeds mostly for about $50/month. In Seoul, South Korea, triple play costs $15 per month for 10 Mbps. For mobile broadband, $30 is the lowest price for 2 GB of data in the U.S., twice as much as what users in London pay. Residents of Hong Kong have access to Internet service with download and upload speeds of 500 Mbps for the equivalent price that residents of New York City and Washington, D.C. pay for maximum download speeds 1/20 as fast and upload speeds 1/250 as fast (downloads up to 25 Mbps and uploads up to 2 Mbps).

An OECD study found that the U.S. pays about 23 times the average Mbps cost of broadband service as Denmark, and about 20 times that in Korea and the U.K.[431] Most of the countries studied have much higher levels of competition.

In 2014, over 80% of Americans had no choice but one cable company for high-speed Internet.[432] With no competition, no incentive exists to lay higher capacity fiber lines, or charge a fair price. Our much higher prices and lower connectivity speeds result from monopoly and semi-monopoly power. However, the solution is not necessarily more competition. Infrastructure is best provided publicly (although associated services could be well supplied privately).

A Harvard Business School 2013–14 survey report on U.S. competitiveness, *An Economy Doing Half Its Job,* stated that businesses *"support for universal broadband connectivity was consistent across firm sizes. High-speed networks are increasingly essential to the ability of all enterprises to be competitive."* Our high prices, low connectivity speeds and lack of availability in some communities are significantly harming our economy and ability to compete internationally.

Community wireless uses unlicensed space on the public airwaves to provide dependable high-speed Internet connections, without the high cost and hassle of traditional phone and cable wires. This technology has the potential to revolutionize how we create, distribute, and access information, facilitating the transition to a new, truly democratic government. As much as 70% of the broadcast TV spectrum in some markets is sitting unused because of regulations and a misinformation campaign waged by the broadcasters' lobby that we could use for this purpose.[433]

As a result of intense lobbying by, and campaign contributions from, Internet providers and cable and telephone companies, several states have passed laws that prohibit municipal governments from setting up community broadband networks. New Enlightenment policy will affirm the rights of all municipalities to establish broadband networks and support their establishment, and we will make the best use of the unused spectrum. We will also federally support fiber supplied broadband or any combination of wireless and fiber.

Cities that supply utility services can more easily use existing conduit for fiber, which minimizes the cost of installing fiber lines. New Enlightenment policy will establish national eminent domain laws to facilitate existing conduit use for all cities. The purchase of any existing fiber lines from current providers we will also support if the cost is below that of newly installed lines. We will provide consultants to assist cities in the establishment phase of providing telecommunication services to their city residents.

New Enlightenment policy offers grants to cities of $175 per capita in the planned municipal broadband service area for municipalities to set up broadband that is free to users and supported by general funds. If all cities took advantage of this policy, the federal subsidies would cost $55.5 billion. We will grant this amount over a five-year period, or $11.1 billion per year.

We will also offer zero interest rate 20-year loans from the Commonwealth Bank to supply any additional funds needed for municipalities to set up broadband that is free to users. The loan agreement will require that the funds for the broadband services be raised by a progressive income tax, determined as follows: The tax will be the fraction of the federal income tax needed to support the loan. Taxpayers would just multiply their federal tax by this fraction for their payment to the city. (So all taxpayers with less than $50,000 in income would pay no tax.) Any overestimate or underestimate in the fraction necessary to cover the cost will be compensated for by adjusting the fraction the following year.

A city income tax, once considered a novelty, now provides substantial revenue in over 170 municipalities, including 21 cities with a population of at least 100,000. More than 18 million people live in cities that impose an income tax.[434] All cities should use a progressive income tax of this type, rather than sales taxes, as a fairer and more economically beneficial way to raise funds for all purposes.

Communities that offer free high-speed Internet will experience significant economic stimulus. In the modern era, access to free high-speed Internet is almost as economically important as access to free roadways.

> *The New Enlightenment: Ideals of Democracy, Human Rights, Reason, and Progress * Policy 32*

Community Radio

The cost of establishing a community radio station can be as little as $10,000 if volunteer labor is used in setting up the studio and transmission equipment. New Enlightenment policy will offer two $10,000 grants to each of the 601 cities with over 50,000 population for the establishment of community radio stations, with $5,000 per year operating grants. Stations could not use operating grants for salaries. Volunteer labor to support the station's programming will be a grant requirement. (Specialized labor for short periods such as for equipment repair could be paid.)

Any costs over $10,000 for establishment, and $5,000 annual operational costs will continue to need community funding, but these grants will greatly facilitate the start-up and operation of a station by community groups of small means. This will help grassroots organizations strengthen their communities and improve their governments.

Any group of ten people could offer a 5,000-word maximum statement of purpose and policy guideline description on a city website. Community members voting for their top three choices and an instant runoff voting process will determine the grant winners. At least one of the stations will devote all airtime to public issues. The other could have a cultural, scientific or another educational purpose not necessarily directly related to public policy. In either case, democratic processes will determine citizen access to the station's airwaves. Possibly a citizen elected board of directors can make the determinations, or perhaps internet based citizen voting could be used.

Community radio enables community members and groups to inform their communities on issues of concern to them, to share experiences, and become creators and contributors to media.

In some markets, lack of availability of spectrum may limit additional stations, so the grants not used in these markets we will make available to other cities, in order of highest population first.

This policy will require a one-time expenditure of $12 million, and an annual expenditure of $6 million, an insignificant amount of money compared to the value provided by 1,202 community radio stations that this policy will play an important role in establishing and supporting.

*The New Enlightenment: Ideals of Democracy, Human Rights, Reason, and Progress * Policy 33*

FCC Reform

The FCC has not regulated the practices of the communications industry in the best interest of the public. Its mission to ensure their following stated duties have clearly not been realized:

- Promoting competition, innovation, and investment in broadband services and facilities.
- Encouraging the highest and best use of spectrum domestically and internationally.
- Supporting the nation's economy by ensuring an appropriate competitive framework for the unfolding of the communications revolution.
- Revising media regulations so that new technologies flourish alongside diversity and localism.

The FCC's cooperative relationship with industry has made it *"a captive agency"* that views the industry as a more important client than the public. Another indication of this is:

Although air media cannot deny political ads of candidates, even if they contain factual errors, they are required to deny factually incorrect third-party ads (as they are for false claims in all commercial advertising) by FCC regulation. The Annenberg Public Policy Center determined that 85% of the money spent on political ads by the four biggest spending third-party groups between December 2011 and June 2012 contained deceptive information. Yet there was not a single case of TV stations rejecting a third-party political ad or even asking third-party groups to verify the claims they were making in their ads. Apparently, the only fact checked by the media companies was whether the checks they received from the Super PACs were good. Even in the instances where companies' own reporters exposed fraudulent claims in ads, companies continued to run the ads.

Large fines and license removal are possible penalties for these violations; the FCC did nothing. Since 1934 there have been well over 100,000 license renewals and only four license renewal denials. The odds are less than 4/1,000 of 1% that a broadcaster will lose its license. This despite many cases where essential public service legal requirements are not being met, and clear disservice is being done. Also, the FCC has abdicated its responsibility to give each community a say in whether a license should be renewed based on past performance.

In 2002, FCC chairman Michael Powell said he would not consider it a problem if one broadcast giant owned every station in an entire metropolitan area. If the FCC chairman was democratically elected, would he make such a statement and institute policies to support it? We think not.

Because of the importance of an effective communications media regulatory agency to our democracy, New Enlightenment policy is for the direct election of FCC commissioners for six-year terms. Five is the current number of commissioners, and we would maintain this and establish five divisions with a commissioner of each division. A democratically elected FCC leadership would be motivated to institute and enforce regulations that serve the majority.

*The New Enlightenment: Ideals of Democracy, Human Rights, Reason, and Progress * Policy 34*

Laws and institutions must go hand in hand with the progress of the human mind. As that becomes more developed, more enlightened, as new discoveries are made, new truths disclosed, and manners and opinions change with the change of circumstances, institutions must advance also, and keep pace with the times ... The only orthodox object of the institution of government is to secure the greatest degree of happiness possible to the general mass of those associated under it."

Thomas Jefferson, Founding Father, principal author of the Declaration of Independence, third President of the United States

"Human progress is neither automatic nor inevitable... Every step toward the goal of justice requires sacrifice, suffering, and struggle; the tireless exertions and passionate concern of dedicated individuals."

Martin Luther King, Jr., Activist, humanitarian, and leader in the African-American civil rights movement, 1977 Winner of Presidential Medal of Freedom, the 2014 Congressional Gold Medal, and the 1964 Nobel Peace Prize

Part 4

Information and
Arguments Supporting Policies

Note 1: The Justifications for Higher Taxes on High Incomes and Taxes on Wealth

Higher Taxes on High Incomes and Taxes On Wealth Are Morally Justified

Among the important functions of government is to ensure against extremely immoral economic outcomes within the citizenry. Without a minimum wage and other government regulations, and support systems such as unemployment insurance, social security, the EITC, and food, health care and housing subsidies, many tens of millions of Americans would be below what most Americans believe are morally acceptable minimum standards of living. And publicly supported education helps reduce unjust disparities in economic opportunities. When economic inequality is large and characterized by tens of millions of people with insufficient resources to meet their basic needs, so already below acceptable standards, they should be assisted and not further financially burdened by government. For both moral and economic reasons, government services should be supported using highly progressive taxation.

Even with existing tax-supported government services, tens of millions of Americans depend on charity assistance to meet minimum standards consistently. About one-fifth of Americans are food insecure, for example, and occasionally either go without needed food or depend on charity assistance to meet their food needs. Millions of Americans do not consistently meet what would be widely considered to be minimum acceptable living standards even with available charity assistance. These conditions exist despite the fact that if our total economic product were distributed more equitably, even maintaining large disparities, it could easily far exceed morally acceptable minimum standards for everyone. On a per capita basis, we produce over 30 times the amount of goods and services per year than when the country was founded.[435]

Even when fully employed, tens of millions of Americans do not receive a living wage for their work. And many millions of Americans are not offered the opportunity to work; they live under the economic and psychological hardship of unemployment. Although the unemployment rate is not high in 2016, official government unemployment statistics do not account for the many millions who have given up hope of finding employment. Clearly, immoral economic outcomes exist for those at the bottom of the economic hierarchy.

Since per capita income and wealth are at historic highs, that tens of millions of Americans have insufficient resources to meet their basic needs implies an unjust amount of our economic product is going to people at the top. Yet moral arguments are made claiming that very high income and wealth people "deserve" what they have because they "earned" it. These arguments succeeded in creating beliefs that cause many people to oppose higher taxes on the wealthy.

One of these widely established beliefs is that the work of the wealthy is solely responsible for their wealth. Another is the wealthy deserve what they have because our economic system well correlates financial reward and social contribution. They consider that a proper expression of appreciation for a large social contribution we limit to the degree that we levy higher taxes on the wealthy. However, these beliefs are based on faulty or insufficient information.

Our market compensation outcomes have often not well served the purpose of being proportional to the social value of the work of individuals. Many of the greatest contributors to society have been compensated little, and many people are among the wealthy as a result of socially harmful work.

As noted earlier, extreme financial rewards motivated harmful work in the financial industry where predatory lending and fraudulently selling high-risk loans and loan derivatives as low risk (among other antisocial, even criminal acts) made people very wealthy. In the process, they played an important role in the devastation of the Great Recession and would have destroyed their companies were it not for vast amounts of public funds.

The financial sector is an important source of rising inequality; worldwide, one in five billionaires comes from that sector. In the U.S. in 2005, 13.9% of the top 1% were financial professionals, up from 7.7% in 1979. Much of their activities resulting in their extreme compensations is of questionable, low, or negative social value.

Societal contribution and reward are not positively correlated at the very high end of the income spectrum, even considering the examples that do not involve illegal activity, and too weakly so elsewhere. Among the reasons are that financial incentives motivate pushing costs associated with a product onto society or people not involved in the transaction, or creating negative externalities. Negative externalities are not uncommon in market transactions and disconnect size of reward from the size of social contribution. As noted earlier, an extreme externality ignored in market transactions is the cost of greenhouse gases. The social costs of carbon could be as high as $893 per ton which would far more than eliminate fossil fuel companies' profits and the salaries of their managers and workers if they paid these costs. Of course, providing an energy source is socially valuable but if fossil fuels were appropriately priced far more alternative sources of energy would be sold instead.

Extreme and unjust compensations often result from monopoly pricing power. Better regulation, enforcement and expansion of antitrust laws, and much higher tax rates on extreme corporate profits and personal compensations are possible solutions. However, when businesses are monopolistic, such as those that benefit from network effects, a superior alternative may be for the national government to purchase and operate these businesses. Network effects occur when the larger the size of the customer base the larger the value offered so that one large company dominating the market ultimately results. For example: Microsoft Window's value is proportional to the number of people who use it because developers create more software for the platform where it will be most used.

Market forces also create monopolies when the larger the company the lower the price it can offer consumers. This occurs is when a firm has large fixed costs that are less than proportional to the amount of output. Once the firm pays the large costs necessary for a large consumer base, its cost per consumer is relatively low so its prices can be. High barriers to entry into the market and high costs per customer for new entrants results in monopolies. For example: Once an electric company pays the enormous fixed costs for power generation and distribution and has a large customer base on which to spread these costs another company entering the market would be impractical. Two (or more) similarly sized companies with their own infrastructure could compete, but costs would almost double (or more). Competition is not always desirable. Sometimes a monopoly in a strong regulatory environment or public ownership better serves the public.

Public ownership of the means to provide energy to a community can be particularly beneficial. Democratic processes could result in many communities providing energy from distributed renewable energy sources and energy conservation measures. Until energy storage technologies advance, a grid offering energy from other or outside sources will remain necessary for periods when energy from renewable sources is insufficient, such as when the sun isn't shining or the wind isn't blowing. However, on a national level, this grid can be mainly supplied by renewable sources. When parts of the country have insufficient energy from renewable sources, energy can be supplied from other places where an oversupply exists. The localized peaks and valleys in renewable energy supply can be smoothed out by a national grid with minimal need for storage capacity.

Even when a business abuses monopoly pricing power, consumer costs can be lower than they would be in a competitive market due to economies of scale. However, another form of social harm results from massive wealth and power in private enterprises that dominate a market. FDR expressed the danger:

"The first truth is that the liberty of a democracy is not safe if the people tolerate the growth of private power to a point where it becomes stronger than their democratic state itself. That, in its essence, is Fascism—ownership of Government by an individual, by a group, or by any other controlling private power." When markets are not competitive and extreme wealth and power concentrate in private enterprises our democracy is endangered.

Large, powerful companies dominate our political system and have "captured" the regulatory process. Powerful firms influence public policies that reduce threats to their market power and enhance their wealth. They can limit antitrust and health and safety regulation and enforcement, and corporate taxation; avoid state sales taxes for online retailers; get subsidies, and get patent, permitting, land-use, immigration, trade, or licensing requirement laws imposed to make it harder for competitors to enter or compete in their market, and get favoritism in very lucrative government contracts to increase their wealth and power. A political system dependent on vast amounts of money from private sources is well serving the actors with the most money.

A federal government takeover of monopoly businesses maintains and potentially expands the economy of scale advantages of the monopoly while eliminating their power to cause harm. For the federal government to take over businesses under any circumstances many people oppose based on the claim that government provides services less efficiently or at a higher cost than private businesses. This claim has been shown to be false. As I noted earlier, the Project on Government Oversight's analysis found that private contractors cost taxpayers, on average, 1.83 times more than if federal employees had done the work, wasting $145 billion in 2010 alone.

Also, a comparison of the Post Office and the private shipping services of FedEx and UPS disproves the efficiency and cost claim for government-provided services. The Post Office receives no public funds yet it provides similar services for much lower costs, in some cases over a third less.[436] This despite the fact it pays its workers substantially more than the comparable private companies pay. Medicare is another example of a government enterprise providing services more efficiently than similar private ones.[437]

Inequality is far less extreme in public relative to similar private enterprises. The top manager of Medicare services is paid $222,000; the top manager of private health insurance company Centene was paid $22 million in 2016, about one thousand times as much.[438] The CEO of FedEx was paid $16.8 million, UPS $11.8 million, while the Chief Operating Officer of the Post Office was compensated $359,000 in 2016.

Some monopolies result from the beneficial process of providing a superior product or service allowing a company to grow while gaining economy of scale advantages also. It would not be a significant disincentive for companies or individuals to create product or service innovations if democratic processes lead to a decision for the federal government to offer a market price for the company once it monopolizes the market since the company value, and so compensation to the innovators would be large. When federally operated, no public funds should be used in its operation and a price for services or products that includes a reasonable profit should be maintained or established to generate public funds for public services or to reduce taxes. Eventually, innovative competitors may offer the same product or service at a lower price, or substitutes for the product or service of a different kind that serves that same purpose.

Corporate governance deficiencies have also disconnected size of reward from the size of social contribution allowing CEOs to receive compensations far beyond their contribution to their firm or society. Also, exploitive property rents have created huge wealth and negative social consequences. Similarly for exploitive intellectual property "rents." Patent laws are abused to extract enormous sums of money from society, which depress the productive capacity of the economy and the well-being of the majority.

The prospect of vast amounts of wealth tends to corrupt people's social conscience or moral vision, and the risk of this outcome is intrinsic to a market-based economy. A social environment where community interests are integral to business decisions is necessary and requires a degree of economic inequality far less than exists. A market economy dominated by worker-owned and self-directed enterprises that is well regulated by a truly democratic political system will minimize the destructive aspects of markets and create a social environment that will raise the consciousness of community interests and the perceived value in serving it. It will also create an environment where intrinsic rewards, or the satisfaction of doing something interesting, enjoyable or socially valuable, and the rewards of status, prestige, and appreciation are more dominant motivators.

The lives of some of the most important contributors to society in history demonstrate that intrinsic rewards sufficiently motivate the creative work most responsible for our productive capacity if financial rewards are enough to support a decent lifestyle. However, intrinsic rewards are not sufficient to motivate some people to do necessary work and the prospect of larger than average financial rewards to provide a larger than average social benefit has some, but limited value in enhancing performance. Evidence for the little or sometimes even negative value of financial incentives in enhancing performance is in a subsequent section *Intrinsic and Extrinsic Rewards Impact on Productivity*. Substantially reducing the extreme degree of economic rewards in our top 1% will not negatively affect their or the nation's economic performance. On the contrary, distributing our national economic product more equitably will enhance economic performance.

If we could design a system where financial rewards were always proportional to social contribution of fundamental importance to its design would be the degree of proportionality it creates. In the New Enlightenment, however large an individual's societal contribution, the degree of compensation must be justified based on the Enlightenment ideal expressed in Article 1 of the 1789 Declaration of the Rights of Man and the Citizen: "Social distinctions can be based only on common utility." The degree incomes rise above average must be beneficial to society as a whole. The degree we have harms our economy, political system, social relations, and health.

A just system (including a tax system) must take into account that even when an individual's positive contributions play a role in creating his or her large amounts of wealth and income, enormous social resources are essential to the process. Since everyone's powerful partner is society and its vast socially created resources, the partner deserves the result of the partner's contribution. The large social resource resulting from public investments in infrastructure, R & D, and public education is widely acknowledged, but often ignored, yet far more important is the impact of many generations of accumulated knowledge. This too is a public resource.

Productivity, or the amount of goods and services produced per man-hour, advances almost every year and is now over 30 times larger than in 1800. On average, a person today using the same effort as a person in 1800 with the same physical and intellectual capacity can produce over 30 times the amount of goods and services in the same amount of time. An equivalent amount of labor and capital supplied two hundred years ago that we supply today to produce our GDP would produce far less than 20% of our GDP. The over 80% difference results from accumulated knowledge—a commonly inherited social resource.

Virtually all products and services, and the tools (including processes) we use to create them, have many past generations of knowledge advancements intrinsic to them. Since no one alive today is responsible for this knowledge, it is an unearned gift of the past. Given the level of economic inequality now, an urgent moral imperative is upon us to more widely share in the benefits produced by this enormous common inheritance.

In the short to medium term, we must institute far more progressive taxation as part of the solution. If over 80% of the difference in our GDP or personal income on average now from what it would have been just two hundred years ago with the same labor and capital results from the social resource of accumulated knowledge, then it is justified for over 80% to be returned to society for social needs—social needs best served by taking little or none from those with middle or low incomes.

Much higher tax rates on top incomes and wealth than exists is especially well justified because the greater the income and wealth an individual has, the greater percentage of his gains resulted from the productivity multiplying force of social resources. An individual separate from society using just the knowledge of a thousand years ago can produce little wealth. The social resource side of the partnership in which everyone participates is responsible for huge incomes to a much higher degree than for lesser incomes. This justifies highly progressive taxation.

However, personal use of the vast inherited social resource of knowledge and the social resources created by our society acting collectively today through governments far from fully explain the vastness of the income of our highest income people. Most results from the social resource created productive capacity of the people in their employment.

Average employee productive capacity is unprecedentedly large, but instead of receiving the value they produce, much of it goes to the employer. If a big company's average employee produces much more in value than he or she receives in pay, the total of this excess generated by all employees is very large. This huge total is being distributed among employers, who are the people with the vast incomes: upper management and company owners.

Corporations hire people if they will produce more in value than they receive in pay, and now, on average, they are producing more than ever in history above the amount they are paid. Median wages have stagnated for decades while corporate profits and upper management pay soared to historic highs. This dynamic where employees, on average, create increasingly large amounts of value but receive none or little of the gains is behind our society's huge and growing inequality since over 90% of American income earners receive their income as employees.

With the structure of our corporations and economic system as they are, higher taxes on top incomes are necessary to rectify this injustice and will make possible the social benefits that would result from New Enlightenment policies. A dysfunctional political system and media, and to an important degree even many of our educational institutions, dominated by the influence of an economic elite, makes the fact that common social resources are mainly responsible for wealth generation not commonly known. If it were widely known, it, with other moral justifications, would be a powerful force for the appropriate taxes on high incomes and wealth that will not only greatly enhance the well-being of the large majority of people, it will benefit everyone if you measure well-being using a more appropriate measure than dollars exclusively.

Especially in the last few decades, when acting on moral arguments at all, policymakers acted on a fallacious, but common, moral argument against higher taxes on high incomes and wealth. It asserts that the initiative, hard work and intelligence of people receiving extraordinary economic gains is solely responsible for their gains. Clearly, though, the facts indicate the contrary. A person's labor sometimes plays a role in the process resulting in very large incomes and wealth, but when it does, his or her initiative, work, and intelligence are not mainly responsible. Everyone has a powerful contributing partner—society. Ignoring this, policymakers reduced or restricted taxes on high incomes and wealth, unjustly, and to the detriment of society. Far higher taxes are justified in the case of inherited wealth, since the initiative, hard work and intelligence of the possessor played no role in its acquisition.

The importance of the social resource side of the partnership in which all individuals participate in creating wealth has been recognized and described by some of the most prestigious economists, sociologists, philosophers, and political theorists over more than two centuries. Their views' significance to public policy was great when they expressed them, and it is now greater than ever. Some have quantified the proportion of wealth creation today that results from inherited social resources. Below is a large sampling of some of their views on the importance of social resources in wealth creation, with a summary of some of their reasoning.[439]

Thomas Paine

Thomas Paine, English-American political activist, Founding Father, author and political theorist, who inspired the "Patriots" in 1776 to declare independence from Britain, wrote: *"It is as impossible for an individual to acquire personal property without the aid of society as it is for him to make land originally."* Everything an individual produces *"beyond what a man's own hands produce"* results from living in society so he *"owes on every principle of justice, of gratitude, and of civilization, a part of that accumulation back again to society from whence the whole came…"*

Leonard T. Hobhouse

Leonard T. Hobhouse, a British sociologist of the late 19th and early 20th century, founder of theoretical sociology, and the first professor of sociology in Britain, wrote that the *"prosperous business man"* should consider *"what single step he could have taken"* without the *"sum of intelligence which civilization has placed at his disposal"* and the *"inventions which he uses which he uses as a matter of course and which have been built up by the collective effort of generations."*

"The true function of taxation is to secure to society the element in wealth that is of social origin or… all that does not owe its origin to the efforts of living individuals. When taxation, based on these principles is utilized to secure healthy conditions of existence to the mass of the people it is clear that this is no case of robbing Peter to pay Paul. Peter is not robbed. Apart from the tax it is he who would be robbing the State. A tax which enables the State to secure a certain share of social value is not something deducted from that which the taxpayer has an unlimited right to call his own, but rather a repayment of something which was all along due to society."

"An individualism which ignores the social factor in wealth will … deprive the community of its just share in the fruits of industry and so result in a one-sided and inequitable distribution of wealth."

Frank Knight

Frank Knight, economist and one of the founders of the free market Chicago School of Economics, wrote in 1923 in "The Ethics of Competition": *"The ownership of personal or material productive capacity is based upon a complex mixture of inheritance* (meaning of knowledge and other socially created factors), *luck, and effort, probably in that order of relative importance. What is the ideal distribution from the stand point of absolute ethics may be disputed, but of the three considerations named certainly none but the effort can have ethical validity. From the standpoint of absolute ethics most persons will probably agree that inherited capacity represents an obligation to the world rather than a claim upon it.*

Individual productive capacity is multiplied by the *"total accumulated social inheritance [that] is mental or spiritual or 'cultural,' as well as 'material.' "There* is *"no visible reason,"* why anyone is *"more or less entitled"* to benefit from a personal *"capacity resulting from impersonal social processes."*

Thorstein Veblen

Thorstein Veblen, the late 19th and early 20th century American economist and sociologist, and leader of the institutional economics movement, describes the cause of economic inequality in his (and our current) time this way: The same natural right that once entitled the small farmer to the fruits of his labor were unjustly given the owners of capital. This small minority is given ownership and control of *"the state of the industrial arts, a creation of the community."*

He considered this tiny elite to be *"vested interests"* or the *"kept classes"* and expressed the view that the conditions of modern rights of ownership results are *"nothing better than a means of assured defeat and vexation for the common man."* He emphasized that traditional moral views of entitlement must be adapted to the industrial system. In primitive agricultural societies, almost all wealth creation resulted from the labor of the individual, so justifiable claims by society were small. Now a large proportion of productive power originates with commonly inherited knowledge and other societal factors.

Richard Posner

Richard Posner, legal theorist, economist, and judge on the United States Court of Appeals, and the most cited legal scholar of the 20th century, observed that in *"a state of nature people would not have much in the way of life, liberty, or property."* and *"The long life, spacious liberties, and extensive property of the average American citizen are the creation not of that American alone but of society-a vast aggregation of individuals, living and dead-and of geographical luck (size, topography, location, natural resources, climate)."*

Herbert Simon

Herbert Simon, American political scientist, sociologist, Nobel laureate economist and widely viewed as one of the most important social scientists of the 20th century, at his 2000 Gaus Award Lecture before the American Political Science Association said this regarding individual entitlements in a world increasingly dominated by societal contribution: *"If we are very generous with ourselves I suppose we might claim that we 'earned' as much as one-fifth of [our income]."* The rest *"is the patrimony associated with being a member of an enormously productive social system, which has accumulated a vast store of physical capital, and an even larger store of intellectual capital-including knowledge, skills, and organizational know-how held by all of us-so that interaction with our equally talented fellow citizens rubs off on us both much of this knowledge and this generous allotment of unearned income."*

How much of this inherited patrimonial share of output should be returned to society from individuals *"is a matter of values to be decided by political processes."* A very large share of American per capita income was due to *"the happy accident that the income recipient was born in the U.S.,"* and *"the huge gift bestowed as a patrimony."* This gift, received simply by chance of birth, Simon believed should be subject to high taxation.

Based on Simon's view that more than 80% of income is from social contributions, or individual labor earns less than 20%, a tax rate greater than 80% would be justly due, to return benefits to its source. This would be appropriately applied only where it would be beneficial to society, such as where high concentrations of wealth or income exist, not in the case of the poor or the middle class.

Robert Dahl

Robert Dahl, Yale professor and former president of the American Political Science Association, often described as *"the Dean"* of American political scientists, stated: *"It is immediately obvious that little growth in the American economy can be attributed to the actions of particular individuals...a large firm is inherently a social and political enterprise. It is inherently social in the sense that its very existence and functioning depend on contributions made by joint actions, past and current, that cannot be attributed to specific persons: the arrow of causation is released by 'social forces,' history, culture, or other poorly defined agents...without the protection of a dense network of laws enforced by public governments, the largest American corporation could not exist for a day. Without a labor force, the firm would vanish. It would slowly languish if the labor force were not suitably educated. Who then provides for the education of its skilled workers, its white-collar employees, its executives? One of a firm's most critical resources is language. Language comes free, provided by 'society' and millennia of evolution."*

"Concepts, ideas, civic orientations like the famous Protestant ethic, the condition of science and technology: these are social. Who has made a larger contribution to the operation of General Electric–its chief executives or Albert Einstein or Michael Faraday or Isaac Newton?...Insofar as a right to property is justified by the principle that one is entitled to use the products of one's own labor as one chooses ... the principle would lead to the conclusion that the control and ownership of the economy rightfully (largely) belongs to 'society.' If so, means must be found for 'society' to exercise the control to which it is entitled by virtue of its collective ownership."

Dahl proposed redistributive measures and employee-owned enterprises as ways for society to exercise this control. *"Changes in the way the economy is likely to be perceived in the future would almost certainly help to make distributive issues more salient."* The *"ill fit"* between conventional "private" views of economic institutions and their *"social and public"* nature, he observed, *"creates a discordance that probably cannot be indefinitely sustained."*

Robert Solow

In his landmark 1957 paper on economic growth, Nobel-Prize winning economist Robert Solow wrote that it is the progress of knowledge that is the primary stimulus for long-term economic growth. In his Nobel Prize lecture, he stated: *"Gross output per hour of work in the U.S. economy doubled between 1909 and 1949; and some seven-eighths of that increase could be attributed to technical change..."* He determined that an increase in capital in 1949 was responsible for one-eighth of the ability to produce twice as much per hour as in 1909. Solow found that output per hour (measured in 1939 dollars) increased from 62 cents to $1.27 between 1909 and 1949, and only eight cents of this increase could be attributed to increases in the amount of capital. All the people who contributed the knowledge and the resulting technological advancements to society over the period were responsible for the rest. This knowledge is a common social resource.

Gar Alperovitz

Gar Alperovitz, professor of political economy, University of Maryland, former Fellow of King's College, Cambridge; a founding Fellow of Harvard's Institute of Politics; a Fellow at the Institute for Policy Studies; and a former legislative director in the U.S. House of Representatives and the Senate, wrote this on who deserves what and why: *"Society's contribution is not only 'current' in the sense of active systems and institutions that facilitate everyday life, but, more importantly, it is also inherited, a 'gift of the past' in the form of material, intellectual, and cultural assets created and preserved by previous generations...."*

These *"active systems"* include the publicly funded educational system, transportation system, legal system, and the system of government research institutions that all support "private" wealth creation. All these public systems' capacity to support wealth creation result from inherited *"gifts of the past...The most important contribution of society (and of the past) is inherited and ever-expanding knowledge...since the wealth we today enjoy is largely a gift of the past, and since no one individual contributes more than a minor amount compared to the gift of the past...society as a whole (after due consideration of all other issues of policy and incentive) has a primary moral claim to that (very large) portion of wealth that the inherited knowledge"* was instrumental in creating...*the ever-growing contribution of the past inevitably becomes proportionately larger and more valuable, year by year, than the time-bound contribution of any specific 'new' generation."*

"The critical question is how long a society of extreme and growing inequality, of growing social and economic pain—and, simultaneously, of ever-advancing technological capability and productive knowledge—can ignore the distributive implications of a simple acknowledgment of the enormity of that which comes to us all from those who preceded us in history."

William Baumol

William Baumol, New York University professor of economics, ranked as among the most influential economists in the world (by IDEAS/RePEc), estimated in the 1960s that *"nearly 90 percent...of current GDP was contributed by innovation carried out since 1870."*

Many other prestigious economists, sociologists, philosophers and political leaders have made similar points. For some additional examples see the end of this Note on the justifications for higher taxes on high incomes and taxes on wealth.

Baumol estimated in the 1960s that nearly 90% of the GDP was contributed by innovation carried out since 1870. In 2000, Herbert Simon estimated, *"If we are very generous with ourselves"* we earned *"as much as one-fifth of our income."* The most generous estimate by the two to individuals today attributes 20% of their income to the individuals' efforts, 80% results from the social contribution, so 80% is justly due back to society. Solow would agree that 20% is a very generous estimate regarding individuals' contribution to their income since from his estimate for 1949 to today productivity has increased more than four-fold.

More than 80% of income on average results from the social contribution so is justly due back to its source through taxes. (Based on society's judgment of its needs in consideration of the level of the individual's income.)

Plowing, planting and harvesting one acre of wheat took about fifty-four hours of work in 1829. By 1895, innovations had reduced this figure to less than three hours.[440] From 1947 (the start of BLS data) to 2015 productivity has increased by a factor of 4.25.

As an especially significant illustrative example of knowledge-based social resources improving productivity or increasing labor's capacity to create wealth, with unjustly distributed resulting benefits, consider the following:

A secretary skilled in using the Excel spreadsheet program is given an assignment by Company A's manager to do calculations on business data and organize the results. Excel reduces the level of time and effort to accomplish this work enormously compared to that needed to accomplish it just a few decades ago. In 1960, the secretary, with pencil and paper, and possibly a slide rule, would have done the thousands of calculations assigned. Then she would have done the organization by personal observation of the results. In fact, though, a secretary would not have been given this task in 1960, it would have been given to a specialist, possibly an accountant. Today, the secretary can do this work that could have taken months and much more skill to accomplish in 1960, in hours or even less, using Excel.

The questions of fundamental importance are these: Who is receiving the economic benefit of this enormous advance in productive capacity, and who should be? Secretarial wages have declined since 1960, so secretaries have not benefited. In 1960, the median income of secretaries was $5,208,[441] which had the same buying power as $41,150 today. In 2010, the median wage of secretaries was $34,660 per year, a decline of 16% since 1960. Within the company, as in almost all companies, the economic benefits of productivity advancements, including those resulting from the introduction of microcomputer hardware and software, have gone mainly to company management and owners, who have greatly increased their income and wealth over the last few decades. Outside Company A, the economic benefits of the introduction of microcomputer hardware and software to Company A have disproportionately gone to the managers and owners of the companies that produce and distribute computer hardware and software.

Some return is justly due on Company A owner's capital investment for the hardware and software that allows the greater productivity. This investment is almost insignificant compared to the costs saved or the additional wealth resulting from the productivity advance over the lifetime of the hardware and software. The additional value created in one week's use could easily exceed the cost of the equipment, so the vast majority of the value created should be directed elsewhere.

Company A's managers contributed the same amount as the secretary did to the productivity advance—nothing. They are all fortunate, equal, common inheritors of the technology. Most of the productivity advance rewards are more appropriately given to those most responsible for the productivity advance—our common benefactors of the past—and consequently to all of us.

Some managers or owners of the software or hardware companies (or other company workers who receive far lower financial rewards) made software or hardware development contributions, but in all cases, they built on a great common inheritance with a relatively minor advance. Despite this, some of their financial rewards were vast. An appropriately large portion was not returned to society because society did not require it. If it is not required, those receiving vast economic rewards are not likely to contribute an appropriate portion voluntarily. Only a society with a mandatory tax system can exist in the modern world, and the less morally and economically justified the tax system is, the more dysfunctional the society will be.

The case of Microsoft's (the producer of Excel) Bill Gates is an extreme example of the universal truth that all modern day productivity advancements are built on an enormous inherited common social resource of knowledge. The vast wealth directed to this one individual due to his contribution to software development, including the development of Excel, is not justifiable on moral or economic grounds.

My purpose is not to diminish any actors or category of actors in the current economy, including Gates who has financially benefited most from the additional societal wealth resulting from productivity advancements from the use of microcomputers. Gates, for example, worked hard for many years, probably 70 hours a week or more. Clearly, not everyone could do what he did. (Some of his actions resulting in his vast wealth could reasonably be considered abusive though.) Many other owners and managers are similarly skilled and hard-working.

My purpose is to apply a long-standing, fundamental and commonly accepted moral principle or ideal, whose ancient roots are expressed in the biblical reference of Paul in Galatians (6:7): *"Whatever a man sows, that is what he shall reap."* In other words, only what your labor supplied should determine the degree to which you are compensated. If a partner increases someone's capacity to create wealth, the partner deserves what results from what the partner supplied. Society was and is a far greater than equal partner to Gates, so it deserves a far more than equal share of the proceeds.

The secretaries in Gates' company inherited all the enhanced productive capacity they have compared to secretaries in 1960 and contributed nothing. But generously, Gates contributed 1% to the productive capacity compared to all the scientists, engineers and others whose work he inherited and without which he would have accomplished nothing. He inherited over 99% of what was needed for the advancement, and his company's secretaries inherited 100%. Is it reasonable or just that he receives $76 billion in excess wealth above large amounts of total spent annual income in compensation, while his company's secretaries receive no additional compensation (and, in fact, lost income) due to the advancement at least 99% of which resulted from a knowledge base and other societal factors that both the secretaries and Gates inherited? Neither the secretaries nor Gates did anything to deserve what they commonly inherited, so neither is more entitled to its resulting benefits.

Just compensation for society's provision of its vast resources to individuals for their use to create additional value can be thought of using the analogy of a license fee for taxes. Society is due a license fee in an amount it considers most appropriate for the use of its assets that includes many socially created resources, the most important of which is its inherited knowledge base.

If Gates, or anyone else with vast wealth, lived isolated on a primitive wilderness island, he would have created little or no wealth. Our society allowed and was an active participant in, the creation of his wealth.

As an extension of Robert Dahl's question *"Who has made a larger contribution to the operation of General Electric–its chief executives or Albert*

Einstein or Michael Faraday or Isaac Newton?," consider: Who is more responsible for a superstar athlete's or other superstar performer's tens of millions of dollars in annual income: the star, or the people responsible for the
communications network and other technological capacities that allow the
transmission or distribution of the star's image to millions of people? Without
the knowledge and technological advancements created by generations of scientists and engineers our technological capacities would not exist, and without our technological capacities, most of their income would disappear.

Like the superstar performer, all participants in our economy benefit
from our commonly inherited knowledge base including through our publicly
funded systems that support private wealth creation such as our educational
system, legal system, the system of government research institutions, and our
roads and other parts of the transportation system. GPS, microelectronics,
computers, the Internet, and lasers all resulted from decades of public research
investment, as did many advances in aerospace, pharmaceuticals, medical devices, containerization, and agriculture. Many private corporations' owners
and managers profit greatly from public investment created advances and systems.

In conclusion, consider this allegory, which expresses the essential point:

A previously unexplored island with a high rock-cliffed shoreline is
2,000 feet from the shore in shark infested waters. The mainland population
has no boats capable of the trip to the island, which is surrounded by rapidly
flowing water. One person builds ten feet of a bridge to the island, and about
a year later another person builds a second ten feet of the bridge, and the process continues over a few generations until one ten-foot section remains to be
built to reach the island.

A person named William Bates (did you notice the hint of a similarity to
Bill Gates?) then builds the last 10-foot section. He goes onto the island,
where he finds $76 billion worth of gold, hires a crew to remove the gold for
a million dollars, and keeps all the gold. Does he deserve to keep all the gold?
What about the 199 other people who built 99.5% of the bridge without which
William Bates would have nothing? Most are no longer alive and contributed
the results of their work to all the mainland inhabitants. Should this society
insist that the gold be distributed far more equitably among all the members
of their society?

"Redistribution" is not the best term to use for a system that uses highly
progressive taxation to reduce inequalities, since the tax system is just return-

ing an appropriate portion of large economic gains to the source of its creation, society, for it to use in the best interests of society. *"Just compensation"*
more accurately describes the process. When people pay for services, we do
not use the term *"redistribution."*

For decades, prominent pundits have expressed the mistaken view in the
mass media, and even in many of our educational institutions, that redistribution of income and wealth is harmful to society and unjust. The impact of this
consistent propaganda has been that just the word "redistribution" elicits such
a negative emotional reaction that rational discussion on its true implications
becomes difficult. It's almost like "redistribution" has been made into one of
the notorious four-letter words. But just as it's obviously not a four-letter
word, it is an obvious necessity when an economic system creates gross, even
obscene inequalities—inequalities that are not only a profound moral wrong;
they also are economically damaging to our society.

Skillful marketing can get tens of millions of people to accept ideas bad for
them, just like it can for products bad for them, and in the process cause substantial harm to society, as it has in the case of cigarette marketing. Consider
that the following very effective marketing campaign may have been less
harmful than marketing the idea that minimizing "redistribution" is good for
us:

In the late 1920s, Lucky Strikes cigarettes were marketed as a way for
women to stay slim. One typical ad said, *"Reach for a Lucky instead of a
sweet."* Sales of Lucky Strikes increased by over 300% during the first year
of the advertising campaign. Sales went from 14 billion cigarettes in 1925 to
40 billion in 1930, making Lucky Strike the leading brand nationwide.

In the 1950s, the "Marlboro Man," was introduced to portray rugged
manliness in smokers of Marlboro cigarettes. In 1955, when the Marlboro
Man campaign started, sales were at $5 billion. By 1957, sales were at $20
billion, representing a 300% increase within two years. The Philip Morris
company easily overcame any possible negative impact of the large and growing evidence of smoking's serious harm to health through its Marlboro Man
campaign.

According to the CDC, tobacco use now costs the United States over
$289 billion a year, including at least $133 billion in direct medical care for
adults and more than $156 billion in lost productivity. Smoking causes cancer,
heart disease, stroke, lung diseases (including emphysema, bronchitis, and
chronic airway obstruction), and diabetes. For every person who dies from a

smoking-related disease, about 30 more people suffer from at least one serious illness from smoking.

More than 16 million Americans suffer from a disease caused by smoking. Tobacco use is the leading preventable cause of death. Very effective marketing indoctrinated people with false beliefs about cigarettes that resulted in enormous harm to them and society.

A large majority of people have been indoctrinated with the false belief that it is morally wrong (and economically harmful) for society to insist that when people are in a position of receiving very extraordinary amounts of income and wealth, that they are required to return most of it to society. They earned it; society has no right to it, is the indoctrinated belief. The wealthy, who control our mass media and influence our educational institutions, serve well their narrow self-interests by using these routes to the masses to promulgate this falsehood. As we have seen, though, they earned some, but not most of it. Most of it was created by a powerful partner, the partner who needs the result of his contribution, or payment for his services, to create a just and well-functioning society that will improve the quality of life for everyone.

Tens of millions of people are "smoking" the belief that we have been very effectively marketed—that higher taxes on the wealthy are unjust. In fact, they are just compensation and necessary. Believing that higher taxes on the wealthy are unjust is harming the health of at least tens of millions of people and damaging our society. As I noted in Part 1, negative health consequences are created even in the wealthy from the social conditions associated with large inequalities.

Let's stop using for *"just compensation"* the word marketed to elicit an adverse reaction: *"redistribution"* and require what is just and beneficial: far higher taxes on the wealthy.

"Redistribution" is also not an accurate term for using the tax and government expenditure systems to lower disparities because that word implies a *"zero-sum game,"* meaning what one party gains, the other loses to the same degree. But when disparities are large, government transfers that raise the incomes of the lower end of the income spectrum stimulate economic activity, increasing the income of the higher taxed wealthy. This compensates for the higher taxes to some degree and a potentially large one.

We should reward hard work, intelligent work, and innovative work. But all work should be rewarded to the extent that is reasonable, based on commonly accepted moral principles and more widely disseminated facts.

The world's wealthiest person in 2007, Warren Buffett, has expressed an understanding of the importance of the societal component of wealth creation: *"… society is responsible for a very significant percentage of what I've earned."* He has said that if he spent his working years in, for example, Bangladesh or Peru he would have little or nothing. *"I work in a market system that happens to reward what I do very well—disproportionately well. Mike Tyson, too. If you can knock a guy out in 10 seconds and earn $10 million for it, this world will pay a lot for that. If you can bat .360, this world will pay a lot for that. If you're a marvelous teacher, this world won't pay a lot for it. If you are a terrific nurse, this world will not pay a lot for it... I do think that when you're treated enormously well by this market system, where in effect the market system showers the ability to buy goods and services on you because of some peculiar talent, I think society has a big claim on that...If anything, taxes for the lower and middle class ... should even probably be cut further. But I think that people at the high end—people like myself—should be paying a lot more in taxes. We have it better than we've ever had it...I just think that when a country needs more income, and we do… they should get it from the people that have it."*

Wealth creation resulting from any one individual's contribution is relatively small, and growing smaller, compared to the vast social contribution resulting from continuously accumulating knowledge.

Although wealth is created mostly as a result of our commonly inherited knowledge base, some people working in our economy now contribute to its creation more than others. Within part of the income spectrum a positive correlation exists between income and societal contribution. But it does not extend to the very high end of the income spectrum. Structural defects in the corporate form is one reason.

Corporations—teams of individuals working to create economic products—tend to have people in a position of power to divide corporate income among "team" members that direct a hugely disproportionate share to serve the purpose of placing themselves well within the top 0.1%. In the process, they unreasonably and unjustly restrict the corporate income portion to everyone else on the "team." As previously noted, 60% to 70% of the top 0.1% of the income hierarchy consists of managers of large corporations. And much of the rest are members of the 0.1% as a result of capital income they receive as owners of the enterprises composed of the "teams" that are producing the income.

Also, in the product and services marketplace, market participants are generally not motivated to enhance societal well-being per se; they are motivated to make the market more profitable for themselves, so when it is possible to do so by making them less efficient, competitive or fair, some participants will. When markets are fair or competitive, profits above a normal return cannot be sustained because rivals will enter the market at a lower price yielding a more normal return. These lower priced rivals will take away customers from the participant with excess profits, forcing it to lower its prices to compete, thereby lowering its profits.

Large corporations, often through governmental policy influence, have created and abused anti-competitive market positions to sustain above normal returns, sometimes extracting large amounts of money from the public to accumulate vast wealth. This harms overall economic efficiency, in addition to being morally unjustifiable.

These far above normal returns from an excess charge to the public are effectively a tax on a product or service, except that instead of the large proceeds serving the public good, they are directed into a few individuals' pockets. Some of the most important innovations in business in the last three decades have centered not on making the economy more efficient, but on how better to ensure monopoly or semi-monopoly pricing power or how to circumvent government regulations intended to align social returns and private rewards.[442]

Monopoly or semi-monopoly pricing power in the telecommunications industry, health insurance industry, pharmaceutical industry, banking industry, by large hospital chains, and by companies such as Microsoft, Monsanto (which owns genetic traits in over 90% of soybeans planted in the U.S.) has resulted in artificially high prices and vast wealth concentrated in the hands of a few.

This problem is not just a recent one: Over a half century ago the only British prime minister to have received the Nobel Prize in Literature and the first person to be made an honorary citizen of the United States, Winston Churchill, stated that some forms of wealth, such as that gained by monopolists and derived from land appreciation and commodities speculation, is reaped *"in exact proportion, not to the service but to the disservice done."* Returning most of this wealth to society is especially well justified.

In *The Wealth of Nations,* Adam Smith stated that business owners' and managers' tendencies to seek to *"narrow the competition must always be against* [the public interest], *and can only serve to enable the dealers* [business owners and managers], *by raising their profits above what they naturally would be, to levy, for their own benefit, an absurd tax upon the rest of their fellow-citizens."* This *"order of men have generally an interest to deceive and even to oppress the public, and who accordingly have, upon many occasions, both deceived and oppressed it."*

A theory of economics, *"marginal productivity theory,"* that became dominant in the second half of the nineteenth century is the theory that supports the positive correlation view of income and social returns, and so supports high incomes, both morally and economically. The theory states that individuals with higher productivities or greater contributions to society will receive higher incomes. An individual's productivity is in theory determined by holding all other factors of production constant then adding his labor and measuring the increase in value created.

In addition to contrary evidence, the marginal productivity theory has been challenged on theoretical grounds. Nobel laureate economist George Stigler called it *"naïve productivity ethics."* One reason for that is that it does not account for the causal role of other contributing factors in enabling the marginal product. It is impossible to know what portion of total output is created by any one person, or any other individual factor. Also, the theory does not distinguish between what a person's labor produces and what is produced by what he owns.

Consider: Someone stands on someone else's shoulders to grab an apple off a tree. Was it his "marginal productivity" that allowed the apple to be eaten, so he alone deserves to eat it? Obviously not. The poor guy whose shoulders were made painful or injured in the process arguably deserves more than half the apple.

Although it is impossible to know what portion of total output is created by any one person, this theory is widely accepted by economists. Also, the theory assumes markets have perfect competition, perfect information, perfect rationality—not real world conditions. And even under ideal conditions "market failures" occur.

Market failures commonly occur due to costs to society or to any individual or individuals not directly involved in the transaction that are not paid by the business or incorporated in the consumer's price. Without government regulations, negative externalities would be far more common. For example, in a market free of government regulation competitive pressures would force manufacturers to pollute the environment to minimize pollution mitigation costs. This results in costs to society, and sometimes societal environmental and health costs can be far larger than the cost of pollution mitigation. When people make large incomes resulting from pushing costs onto society greater than their incomes, their incomes result from a negative, not from a correspondingly large, positive contribution to society. If societal contribution and reward were positively correlated, they would be taxed at rates greater than 100%.

Despite these facts, many people believe that the marginal productivity theory is valid. They believe that individuals with higher incomes are making larger contributions to society than individuals with lower incomes. Below, I summarize additional evidence indicating this theory is invalid or inapplicable to real world outcomes, and that this is most clear at very high-income levels in our economy:

- As previously noted, defective corporate governance laws and a culture that says "grab as much as you can" (and a compliant public, including shareholders) have allowed CEOs to receive a rapidly increasing share of corporate income as compensation, far in excess of their societal contribution. From 1978 to 2011, CEO compensation increased over 725%, a substantially greater increase than that of the stock market, and far greater than the 5.7% growth in worker compensation over the same period. And stock market appreciation has been extraordinarily large based on an unjust portion of the wealth created by large productivity gains since 1978 going to owners of corporations. Prior to 1978 productivity gains far more equitably benefited both workers and owners.

  Defenders of exorbitant CEO compensations claim that senior managers are largely responsible for big increases in their firms' profits and stock prices, so they earn their immense compensations. As we have seen, though, society is mainly responsible for huge economic gains and it is not possible to measure the contribution of any one individual in a large corporation.

  But is there a positive correlation between CEO pay and long-term profitability of companies? As I noted previously, an extensive study provided the answer. A study of 1,500 companies' performance compared to other companies in the same field from 1994 to 2011 found that "*The [stock value] returns are almost three times lower for the high paying firms than the low-paying firms"* and that the longer the highly paid CEOs were in office, the more their firms underperformed. Large stock options compensation was especially destructive. Also, the UKs "High Pay Centre" has found a negligible link between incentive payments to executives and shareholder returns in the UK.[443] I discuss later in the *Intrinsic and Extrinsic Rewards Impact on Productivity* why we should not be surprised by these study results.

Also, directors of large corporations have a part-time job that compensates them far out of proportion to their societal contribution. Meeting just three or four times per year, the average S&P 500 director was paid $251,000 in 2012, so they are highly motivated to be generous to the CEO, who generally strongly influence the selection of directors.[444] Mutually generous compensations also result when executives sit on one another's compensation committees of the board of directors. Since it is impossible to give a precise estimate of each manager's or director's contribution to the firm's output the compensation system yields extreme compensations limited by cultural norms and the high degree of freedom those involved have to serve their interests at the expense of the rest of the corporation.

Our corporate governance laws do not require firms to give shareholders a say in management or director compensation, which would normally be expected since they own the firm. This would be a restraint on the explosion of executive salaries and inequality. As I noted earlier, two-thirds of the top 0.1% in income consists of top managers.

- Top income levels exhibit a sharp discontinuity at the highest levels. Yet no discontinuity, other than income, exists between "the 9%" and "the 1%," regardless of criteria including years of education, selectivity of educational institution, or professional experience. One would expect a theory based on "objective" measures of skill and productivity to show relatively uniform pay increases within the top decile.[445]

- That income inequality in the United States is at a level higher than that of poor and emerging countries at various times in the past also indicates that any explanation based solely on objective inequalities of productivity is false. U.S. income inequality is higher than what existed in India or South Africa in 1920-1930, 1960-1970, and 2000-2010. Inequality of individual skills and productivities is far less in the United States today than it has been in the half illiterate India of the recent past, or in apartheid (or post-apartheid) South Africa.[446]

- The explosion of very high salaries occurred in some developed countries but not others. This suggests that institutional differences between countries, rather than individual productivity are responsible.
- CEOs often receive huge pay increases and stock option gains for stock price increases based on external events they had nothing to do with. For example: When the price of a major input falls, the stock price can soar, so their stock and stock option's (commonly received as part of their compensation) value soars, and profits soar, so pay soars.

  An extensive international historical study found that this *"pay for luck"* varies widely with country and period, *"and notably as a function of changes in tax laws, especially the top marginal income tax rate, which seems to serve either as a protective barrier (when it is high) or an incentive to mischief (when it is low). Of course, changes in tax laws are themselves linked to changes in social norms pertaining to inequality... Specifically, the very large decrease in the top marginal income tax rate in the English-speaking countries after 1980 (despite the fact that Britain and the United States had pioneered nearly confiscatory taxes on incomes deemed to be indecent in earlier decades) seems to have totally transformed the way top executive pay is set, since top executives now had much stronger incentives than in the past to seek large raises."*[447]

- Asymmetrical information, or where one party in a transaction knows valuable information related to the transaction that the other does not, also has led to income far beyond any societal contribution (if one exists). One example is the income from predatory lending, where the full cost of a loan is hidden from unsophisticated borrowers, which contributed to the recent financial crises.

This explosion of very high incomes then increased the political influence of the beneficiaries, who then used their gains to fund the campaigns of candidates who support keeping top tax rates low and depressing them further. Also, high-income individuals fund think tanks or grassroots lobbying to influence the public, which indirectly influences policymakers to support low top tax rates. And these low rates motivate abusive practices to further increase pre-tax income.

It is worth repeating ($22 trillion worth) that some CEOs of financial corporations were largely responsible for $22 trillion of losses to our economy and the destruction of their companies, were it not for billions or hundreds of billions of dollars of taxpayer bailout money. Some of these same individuals made billions in income before the crisis and were given millions of dollars in bonuses after the crisis. This is possibly the most obvious and extreme "marginal productivity theory" violation example. The top executives at Bear Stearns and Lehman Brothers were compensated $650m and $400m respectively between 2003 and 2008 – a period in which these two firms were heading for one of the most spectacular failures in American financial history.[448] Many other extreme examples exist, such as that of Hank A. McKinnell. He was CEO of Pfizer pharmaceutical firm for five years during which time its stock valuation dropped by $140 million. He then left the company, and apparently as an expression of appreciation, he received a payout of $200 million, free lifetime medical coverage, and an annual pension of $6.5 million.

If the marginal productivity theory has limited validity, at the astronomical end of the compensation spectrum we enter an anti-universe where not the higher the marginal *productivity,* the higher the compensation, but the higher the marginal *destructivity,* the higher the compensation.

Appropriate taxes and regulations and enforcement of existing regulations could have, and could in the future, alleviate or eliminate unjust economic system outcomes at the top, as would government support for the widespread establishment of worker-owned and self-directed enterprises. But government policy will continue to be determined by the current wealthy beneficiaries unless we make radical improvements to our election and policy-making process and media.

Socially valuable, hard, or least pleasant work sometimes is compensated below a living wage, like toilet cleaning, while flash trading stocks can net someone millions of dollars in an hour, without owning any stock at the end of the hour. Some people who profit the most in our system do little or no actual work, including those who live off inherited wealth.

Of course, though, many of the people who profit the most in our system do useful work. Since Gates is the wealthiest person in the U.S., it is instructive to evaluate the "deservedness" of his vast wealth in more detail. Productive capacity increases were widespread and of enormous proportions resulting from introducing microcomputers into our economy. Since most people believe that Gates made an extraordinarily important contribution to this revolutionary advance, they consider that his $76 billion in wealth "incentive" is well deserved because the added value from the microcomputer revolution is in the trillions of dollars. Bill Gates has a rare combination of a high level of technical and management skills. Let's evaluate the importance of the contribution of Gates, and consider the incentive needed for the advancement associated with him:

In 1980, Gates' new Microsoft Corporation signed a deal with IBM to supply an operating system for its new line of personal computers. This deal was the beginning of the Microsoft empire. Gates then bought the rights to Tim Paterson's of Seattle Computer Products operating system, 86-DOS, which became Microsoft's PC-DOS, later renamed MS-DOS. 86-DOS was a thinly disguised clone of the most widely used operating system of the time, Control Program/Microcomputer (CP/M) that Gary Kildall had written.

The story of how Gates outmaneuvered Kildall for the IBM deal is not fully known. Some believe that Kildall wrongly assumed that Gates would not take a clone of his program to sell to IBM on ethical grounds and that Kildall is the true founder of the personal computer revolution and the father of PC software.[449] Gate's actions could have been stopped if current legal standards for software copyright infringement existed then.

Kildall's operating system was superior to Microsoft's in one important way; it had multitasking capabilities. The availability of multitasking capabilities to the public was thus delayed for a decade, due to Microsoft being the monopoly supplier of the operating system in the market dominating IBM PC of the 1980s.[450]

Although some details of this history are uncertain, whether it was Gates or Kildall or Tim Paterson (among other competitors) who "won the race" for the PC operating software for the market dominating IBM PC in the 1980s, one would have been available when it was needed. Neither operating system development nor the demand that drove the process would have been significantly altered had Gates never been born. Gates may be an example demonstrating that sometimes those who "get there first" can inhibit advancement.

Also, it is important to note that public funds supported Kildall's development of CP/M since he developed it while teaching at the Naval Postgraduate School in Monterey, California, in the early 1970s.

Gates and his company have received vast financial rewards. Are these rewards mainly resulting from Microsoft's semi-monopoly operating system status?

Gates and his company have not been responsible for any major innovation. WordPerfect was the first widely used word processor on the market, and Microsoft developed Word to compete with it. Lotus was the first widely used spreadsheet on the market, then Microsoft developed Excel to compete with it. It destroyed Lotus by coding hidden bugs in its semi-monopoly operating system to cause Lotus to crash (*"DOS ain't done 'til Lotus won't run"* was one unofficial motto). Windows was developed to compete with the previously introduced and generally considered superior Macintosh graphical user interface. WinCe was a response to PalmPilot. Netscape was the first web browser on the market. Gates used his 90% of the market control of microcomputer operating systems to destroy Netscape by threatening to cancel Compaq's Windows license if it installed Netscape Navigator in its computers and then by bundling its essentially equivalent Explorer with its operating system for free. MSN was a response to AOL. Xbox was introduced after Sega's and Sony's home game systems. Bing is Gates response to Google. Monopolists tend not to be good innovators.

It is impractical to require judgments on a case-by-case basis of the value of contribution (or harm) that played a role in creating large financial rewards to individuals in the rules of income and wealth taxation. Clearly, though, when an individual receives extreme amounts of money, society is responsible for a major portion of any contribution associated with it (if any), so the rules of taxation can justifiably direct a major portion of the money received to serve society's needs.

Society has a right to tax using a system that best serves all its members for this important reason also: Property is a creation of law with no independent origin apart from how the law structures ownership and property rights. Since the division of property or wealth and the means to acquire it can exist only within a system of laws, including tax laws, there can be no moral claim against taxation on the grounds that property or wealth is essentially "private." It is a construct of a social system that established both property rights and the rules of taxation. Chartering corporations, buying and selling legal titles to property, making and enforcing contracts, suing for damages, and a legal system that allows people to receive paychecks and dividends from stocks, and that secures wealth in its various forms, all involve government "intrusion," as does taxation. All are equally justified to be designed to serve the best interests of society.

Maximizing total happiness is also a moral societal imperative, one implied by Thomas Jefferson's statement, *The only orthodox object of the institution of government is to secure the greatest degree of happiness possible to the general mass of those associated under it.*" And in John Adams' statement, *"The End of all Government is the happiness of the People ...the greatest happiness of the greatest Number is the point to be obtained.*"[451] However, it is also a moral imperative that the process not unjustly burden or harm a minority.

An analysis of more than 450,000 responses to the Gallup-Healthways Well-Being Index revealed that people's emotional well-being or happiness does not increase above a household income of about $75,000 per year.[452] Emotional well-being was measured based on people's frequency and intensity of experiences of joy, stress, sadness, anger, fascination, anxiety, and affection the day prior to the poll.

However, the researchers also found that "life evaluation" or the thoughts that people have about their life does increase as income rises above $75,000 at least to an amount well over $120,000, although measures of happiness do not. They also found that poverty strongly exacerbates the negative effect of adverse circumstances such as divorce, health problems, and loneliness, on happiness.

Their data only refer to differences between people with somewhat stable incomes, they do not imply that people will not be happy with a raise from $100,000 to $150,000, or that they will be indifferent to an equivalent drop in income. However, public policies should focus on maximizing stable conditions of happiness, not transient ones. The researchers also reported a possible association between high income and a reduced ability to savor small pleasures, an indication that happiness may decrease above some maximum income.

Below $75,000, additional dollars have increasing value the lower the household's income, and above $75,000, no stable value on happiness. An economic system dominated by worker-owned and self-directed businesses will greatly reduce the creation of extreme incomes both at the high and low end. It will raise the incomes of tens of millions of people at the low end where additional dollars substantially increase happiness without significantly, or at all, reducing happiness at the high end, so will greatly increase total happiness. Also, redirecting an appropriate portion of exorbitant incomes created by our currently poorly functioning economic system dominated by unjust economic enterprises to those of low income where relatively small changes in income are especially significant to happiness will serve the ideal of "*the greatest happiness of the greatest Number.*"

Another important moral justification for high taxation on high incomes and wealth exists when the resulting revenue is used to serve the ideal of equality of opportunity. When a society has large economic disparities and low economic mobility, there is a breakdown of an essential precondition for the ability of most members of the society to make important moral evalua-tions of public policy.

An important psychological basis of moral evaluations is the real possi-bility that your station in life is not certain. This motivates the desire to apply the "golden rule," or what might be considered a corollary to the "golden rule," to policy decisions. The corollary: "Do unto to others as you would have others do unto you, if you were in their situation." If your station and your children's station in life you consider certain, then an important motive is eliminated to understand the circumstances of another station because you cannot imagine the real possibility of being there.

The wealthy support policies that "do unto" the poor and middle class that they would not if they did not know that they and their children can never be or are highly unlikely to ever be, in the middle or lower economic class. If equal opportunity to rise or fall based on merit existed, there would be far greater economic mobility than there is, and a stronger motive to apply the golden rule, because you may end up in the other's shoes.

The very wealthy can buy their own education, libraries, parks, and health care services. And they know their children will be able to do so with-out working or doing anything of value to society because they will pass on most of their wealth, so they need not consider the needs of members of soci-ety who are not wealthy. Seeing the moral (and even societal economic) im-perative to be taxed to support public education, public libraries, public parks, and healthcare and other public services for people who cannot afford them is more difficult when you cannot imagine the possibility of being in a condition of needing these things.

Is it possible to see that 20% of the members of your society did not have enough money to buy the food they needed at least once over the last year, or that 40% of the nation (133 million people) in total have debts greater than their assets by an average of about -$10,600 average per household, while you have billions of dollars, indicate a moral imperative for economic system im-provements? It is possible, but it is more difficult to see when you cannot see the possibility that you or your children will ever be in need of food you can't afford, and not have vast wealth.

The society is then divided, and its moral foundation is damaged, with its most influential members opposing what is best for society. Also, as people suffer longer and greater injustices, rage can develop in the disadvantaged classes blinding them to moral considerations. This has led to violent revolts in some societies with large economic disparities, including revolts during the original Enlightenment.

Our low economic mobility also relates to the "deservedness" moral criterion on distributing the country's economic product in this way: Great economic rewards to those with inherited privilege where their labor played a role in creating it are not "deserved" to the degree they would be if people were all given an equal opportunity to advance.

Although some at the top of our income and wealth distribution rose from poverty or from no significant family economic advantages, this is relatively uncommon. The U.S. has the lowest intergenerational economic mobility of all the advanced nations. The Brookings Institution found that 42% (25% in Denmark) of men whose fathers were in the bottom fifth of the earnings distribution stayed in the bottom fifth,[453] most of whom live in poverty and are food insecure. Only 8% moved to the top fifth.

The advantage of being born into a wealthy family to be wealthy as an adult is obvious when vast wealth is inherited. But it is also obvious when more limited start-up capital for enterprises, connections to other rich and well-connected mentors, and other financing sources, and privileged educational resources are supplied. In addition to the disadvantages of being born into a family of lower economic class, racism and sexism are also important in depressing opportunities for large groups of people.

The 2013 Forbes 400 wealthiest Americans list has only one African American, Oprah Winfrey, and only 10% are women, of whom 87.5% inherited their fortunes. About 40% of those on the Forbes 400 list inherited assets of $1 million or more. Over one-fifth inherited sufficient wealth to be on the list, with only those individuals with wealth over $1.05 billion. Just this fifth alone holds $346.3 billion in combined wealth. Of those with inherited assets under $1 million, many had advantages of an upper class, such as private schooling with tuition of tens of thousands of dollars per year, private tutoring, and some startup capital for a business. It is estimated this is the case for an additional 22% of those on the Forbes 400 list.[454]

These same advantages play an important role in the wealth acquisition of many others in the top of our wealth distribution outside of just the top 400, considering our nation's low intergenerational economic mobility.

In the case of inheritance taxes, considerations of the role of unfair advantages can be included in the rules of taxation.

In Conclusion

Higher taxes on high incomes and wealth are morally justified and necessary. The resulting increase in revenues will be used in many ways to make dramatic improvements in society. We are far from realizing our ideals of equal opportunity and equal justice for all. The resulting increase in revenues will help us meet these ideals. The increased revenues will enable us to lift tens of millions of Americans out of poverty to a standard of living that now exists in the middle class and substantially improve the standard of living of tens of millions more; create a true government of, for, and by the people; widely establish a more just and better functioning corporate form; make economically stimulative and badly needed improvements to our infrastructure, and will have other important beneficial impacts on our society.

The Economic Impact of Higher Tax Rates on High Incomes and Wealth

Far higher taxes on extreme incomes, even at rates higher than 80%, are morally justified if these rates do not significantly damage national economic performance. If we reduce the pie, even if we more equitably distribute the pieces, the result could be more harmful than beneficial, with everyone with a smaller piece of pie. How important to national economic performance is the work of some of those who receive extremely high pre-tax incomes, and how much impact is likely on their work of the reduced financial rewards resulting from higher taxes?

Based on the evidence noted earlier, the marginal productivity theory is invalid or not applicable to real world conditions, at least at the extremely high end of the income spectrum. For many extremely high-income people, their income does not result from a correspondingly huge social contribution. Quite the contrary is commonly the case, especially in the financial industry, which has a disproportionate share of billionaires many of whose "contribution" has been negative, even devastating.

Independent of industry, extremely high incomes result from some people taking substantial portions of the results of the enormous socially created productive capacity of large numbers of other people. Evidence for better economic functioning resulting from using a tax and transfer system so that all people receive a more appropriate share of the results of their productive capacity is substantial. And better economic functioning will result from the more egalitarian outcomes inherent in worker-owned and self-directed enterprises.

Among the highest income people, though, are there some among the greatest contributors to our society? If so, this may suggest that extreme financial rewards, though sometimes a motive for harmful behavior, could, on balance, be important for society to maintain.

Since knowledge advancements are the most important factors in economic performance, consider the role of personal income and wealth incentives in motivating the most important of these advancements. Here are a few of the many examples of people widely recognized as being among the most important contributors to the knowledge advancements responsible for our most important economic advancements who have received relatively little financial rewards. These examples are indicative of a general principle:

- Alan Turing, widely considered the father of computer science and artificial intelligence, formalized the concepts of "algorithm" and "computation" and developed the first model of a general purpose computer. He was motivated by his intellectual curiosity, his desire to discover something new and important, and to a lesser degree, his desire for peer recognition. His only financial reward was his compensation as a British government and university employee.

- Watson and Crick's work on the nature of DNA is an essential part of many modern sciences, including medicine, genetic engineering, molecular biology, forensic science, bioinformatics, phylogenetics and genetic genealogy, and information storage (the text of a 54,000-word book was encoded in DNA). They did their work at Cambridge University, on a graduate student and research fellow salary for the thrill of discovery, rather than being motivated by the possibilities of great wealth.

- U.S. government and university employees, funded by the Defense Department, created the Arpanet, which developed into the Internet. They did it to serve the important purpose of allowing communications among computer users, motivated by the intellectual challenge, possibly peer recognition, and for their salaries as financial compensation, without expectations of great wealth.

- Nikola Tesla invented the induction motor that revolutionized industry and household appliances in the 19th and 20th century. He also invented polyphase alternating current, and with George Westinghouse built the first hydro-electric power plant in Niagara Falls, New York that started the electrification of the world. He died in poverty.

- Tim Berners Lee, the inventor of the World Wide Web and writer of the first "graphical user interface" Web browser made his inventions freely available, which greatly speeded up developing the Internet. He could have been a billionaire, but he did not need extreme wealth to motivate his work.

- All the physicists who developed quantum mechanics created the foundation of a substantial portion of our modern economy. As much as 30% of GDP is based on inventions made possible by quantum mechanics.[455] Semiconductor design relies on quantum mechanics, and semiconductors are an essential part of the design of computer and all other electronic chips. Quantum Mechanics is also of essential importance to chemistry and biology. Many modern technological inventions operate at a scale where quantum mechanical effects are important. Other examples include the laser, the electron microscope, and magnetic resonance imaging (MRI). These physicists did their work at universities for the thrill of discovery, and probably to some degree peer recognition, not great financial rewards.

These advances formed the foundation of our modern economy. None of these people were remotely close to being billionaires, and some had wealth less than one ten-thousandth of a billion dollars. Persons of great intellectual or creative capacity are driven mainly by intellectual curiosity and the excitement of seeing or developing something new, an innate desire to excel, and the desire to make an important social contribution.

The advancements that resulted in vast financial rewards, such as those associated with Gates and the founders of Google and Facebook, are relatively minor. And similar or equivalent advancements would have been accomplished by others without the need for vast financial rewards. If the people credited with these advancements had never been born, we would still have computer operating systems, search engines, and online social networks. The evidence for this in the case of Gates, the wealthiest man in America, we've seen earlier. Also, the people receiving the vast rewards associated with these advancements did not require the level of compensation they received as a motivation for their work.

Other innovators or inventors have had wealth among their motives to some degree, but the vast levels of wealth that some individuals have now are unnecessary as an incentive. And surprisingly, for many kinds of work, above some baseline, financial incentives not only make no positive contribution to performance, they are actually harmful to it, as the evidence described in the next section indicates.

But even if exceptions exist, would any inventor, even one most motivated by wealth, have not invented what he did with millions or tens of millions of dollars, rather than hundreds of millions, billions, or tens of billions of dollars as his incentive? A point exists beyond which there is no additional incentive value, even for those most motivated by financial rewards, and we are far past that point when individuals receive financial rewards in the hundreds of millions or billions of dollars.

Intrinsic and Extrinsic Rewards Impact on Productivity

Most work has intrinsic rewards—its performance is gratifying or enjoyable independent of any external or extrinsic rewards. Well over 100 studies show that extrinsic motivators, including money, praise, and other rewards, are not just ineffective in the long term, but are counterproductive regarding work that is most important: creative or problem-solving work, and learning. Extrinsic motivators are also detrimental to maintaining good values. But if a person feels he is being paid an unfairly low amount this could inhibit performance. Above this baseline, the evidence indicates that associating pay with performance inhibits the performance of the most valuable kinds of work.

In 2009, scholars at the London School of Economics—alma mater of eleven Nobel laureates in economics—analyzed 51 studies of corporate pay-for-performance plans. The economists' conclusion: *"We find that financial incentives ... can result in a negative impact on overall performance."*[456]

Harvard Business School Professor Teresa Amabile is one of the world's leading researchers on creativity. She has frequently tested the effects of extrinsic rewards on the creative process. Amabile and others have found that extrinsic rewards can be effective for tasks that depend on following an existing formula. But for work that demands flexible problem-solving, inventiveness, or conceptual understanding, extrinsic rewards can be destructive. Rewarded subjects often have a harder time seeing or developing original solutions.[457]

The drive to do something because it is interesting, challenging, and absorbing is essential for high levels of performance. But the "if-then" (such as if you do this, then we'll pay you more) extrinsic motivators used in most businesses often stifle, rather than stir, creative thinking.

One comprehensive analysis of nearly three decades of studies on the subject confirms that, *"Careful consideration of reward effects reported in 128 experiments lead to the conclusion that tangible rewards tend to have a substantially negative effect on intrinsic motivation."*[458] Studies indicate that when families, schools, and businesses focus on short-term performance enhancements with extrinsic motivators, they do considerable long-term damage to performance.

Mainstream economists considered work a "disutility" or something we'd avoid unless we receive payment in return. The research indicates, though, that it is a "utility" or something we'd pursue even if we were not paid for it.

Many of us have had the experience of having done something just because we loved doing it, until getting paid for doing it, after which we don't consider doing it again without getting paid. The phenomenon whereby extrinsic motivators destroy intrinsic motivation we ignore. But by almost universally ignoring this, we diminish national economic performance.

If an industrial designer, for example, who loves his work has his pay contingent on creating a very successful new product, he'll work harder in the short term, but become less interested in his job in the long term. As one leading behavioral science textbook puts it, *"People use rewards expecting to gain the benefit of increasing another person's motivation and behavior, but in so doing, they often incur the unintentional and hidden cost of undermining that person's intrinsic motivation toward the activity."*[459]

This is one of the most robust findings in social science, and also one of the most ignored. Human beings have an innate drive to be self-determined, productive, contributing members of their community. Intrinsic rewards are the essence of that drive. Extrinsic rewards such as financial rewards apparently are a destructive distraction. An adequate or equitable pay compared to others doing similar work is important in workplaces, but associating additional rewards for enhanced performance is often counterproductive.

Would a doctor performing heart surgery exert more care or effort if his pay depended on whether the patient survived? If it had any effect, the "incentive" would more likely be a distraction creating a negative impact on performance.

Another problem with extrinsic rewards is that some people will choose unethical shortcuts to the goal. Most scandals and misbehavior we commonly see involve extrinsic reward motivated shortcuts: Executives report false quarterly earnings to get a performance bonus. Teachers falsify test results to enhance their performance evaluations. Athletes inject themselves with steroids to get lucrative performance bonuses. Contrast that with behavior motivated intrinsically. When the reward is the activity itself, unethical shortcuts are not considered.

Google employees are given 20% of their work time to do whatever they want to. On average, half of Google's new products were created during this time, attributable to an enhanced autonomy and sense of purpose.[460]

One of the most striking examples demonstrating the relative importance of intrinsic and extrinsic motivators is Wikipedia. In the mid-1990s, Microsoft started an encyclopedia called Encarta. It employed the standard financial incentives. It paid professionals well to write and edit thousands of articles. Very well compensated managers oversaw the project to ensure the product's excellence so it would be widely used and ensure that it came in on budget and on time. A few years later, Wikipedia started using a very different production model: No one gets paid. Do it just because you find it enjoyable or gratifying to do it.

Microsoft gave up on Encarta in 2009 because it was obvious to almost everyone that Wikipedia was superior. In 2009, Wikipedia had 97% of website encyclopedia users, while Encarta had 1.27%. Ten years earlier, if you asked any economist which model would produce a superior encyclopedia, it's highly unlikely you would have found a single one who would have predicted the Wikipedia model.

Distributing income more equitably in the workplace would benefit the economy because the extrinsic reward of extreme income is unnecessary to increase performance. On the contrary, financial incentives targeted to increase performance instead are harmful to the performance of the most important kinds of work. Money directed instead to lower wage workers would enhance their sense of fairness which has been demonstrated to free up intrinsic motivation. It will also increase economic activity through increasing many unjustly low-wage workers' highly restricted purchasing power. One way to accomplish this is through a tax and transfer system.

A superior way to free up intrinsic motivation and create a more prosperous economy and more equitable income distribution is through widespread worker-ownership and self-direction. The New Enlightenment WSDE proposal (Policy 3) will, over two decades, create an economy dominated by workplaces whose structure inherently accomplishes much lower income disparity and greater worker autonomy—both important in enhancing economic performance. However, in the short to intermediate term, using the tax system for lowering disparities is necessary.

Choosing tax rates that optimize societal benefit requires these considerations, though: Financial resources are highly mobile in the modern world, so we cannot choose rates far from the norm of other developed countries even if overwhelming moral and other reasons exist to do so. International agreements on financial transparency and tax rates can eliminate the problem, but before we achieve this ideal, in designing optimal rates we must address the problem of expatriation. Tax avoidance problems and how to alleviate them are discussed further in the New Enlightenment's wealth tax proposal and in this note later regarding eliminating a capital gains tax avoidance technique. An increasingly globalized economy will eventually require international agreements on appropriate corporate and personal tax rates on high income and wealth, based on moral, worldwide economic and other important considerations, to eliminate the race to the bottom problem among countries.

How Important Is Any Individual Innovator?

Let's assume that exceptions to the rule exist regarding the impact of financial motivators on creative work and that some people credited with a significant advance have had as an important motive the prospect of vast wealth. If such cases exist, how likely is it that other persons less motivated by personal wealth would have made the same contribution soon after the persons credited with the advance? The following are some important facts not widely known regarding this question.

Although it is widely accepted and commonly taught in schools (except in some specialized college courses) that a series of *"heroic"* breakthroughs by individuals have been responsible for most discoveries and inventions, this is not true. Specialists in the historical study of the technological and knowledge advancement process have discovered that although major advancements as a result of very extraordinary intellects having *"eureka"* moments do occur, generally advancements happen in a more continuous evolutionary process. And when great leaps in knowledge occur, more often than is commonly known, more than one of the most intelligent and knowledgeable persons in the field of research are drawn to make the leap.

One way this process has been described is: Advancements are made on a moving wave of knowledge. Most often, more than one of the most intelligent and knowledgeable persons at the top of the wave can see what is coming. The following are a few of the hundreds of known examples:

- Charles Darwin rushed to complete his work on his theory of natural selection because Alfred Russell Wallace wrote him a letter indicating that he was developing the same arguments. If Darwin didn't publish his great work "The Origin of the Species," it is likely that Wallace (or possibly others) would have published work with a similar thesis in the same time frame.[461]

- James Watson and Francis Crick also raced to publish their "double helix" DNA structure analysis because they knew others, most likely Linus Pauling, would publish this conclusion soon, based on his publication of the alpha helix structure of various proteins two years earlier.

- On the same day Alexander Graham Bell filed his patent application for telegraphy ideas that suggested the possibility of the telephone, Elisha Gray filed a patent application on his apparatus "for transmitting vocal sounds telegraphically" a few hours later. But the device Bell proposed would not have worked, and the one Gray proposed would have. However, Bell secured a second patent that improved on the first soon after, and after years of litigation he emerged as the legal "inventor" of the telephone. Hundreds of other legal claims were also filed against the original Bell patents. However, the most striking fact is this:

  There is certain evidence that an Italian immigrant, Antonio Meucci, more than five years before Bell took out his patents, invented a voice telegraphy device on which he could not file a full patent application, due to his lack of the $10 fee. In 2002, Congress recognized Meucci as the inventor of the telephone.[462]

- The light bulb would have been invented at roughly the same time if Thomas Edison had never been born. At least 23 other people built prototype light bulbs before Edison, including two groups who filed patents and fought legal battles with him over the rights (Sawyer and Mann in the U.S., and Swan in England).

Simultaneous invention or discovery is very common, most often with only one person receiving the credit. This has been revealed by many researchers in this field. See "Simultaneous Invention," Note 4, for more of the hundreds of examples.

The world would have benefited from most advancements in the same time frame even if the people who got there first, and so were credited with the advancement, were never involved. Likely cases exist, though, where a person was of unusual importance, or where an advancement would have been significantly delayed without the person's involvement. We cannot know in all cases what would have occurred if a person credited with an advance was not involved.

The most important fact remains: individuals of great creative capacity do not have as an essential motivation vast financial reward. However, the many examples of simultaneous invention and discovery provide another indication that huge financial rewards are unnecessary for productivity enhancing inventions and discoveries that have been and will continue to be of great importance to economic performance.

Money Is Not Our Best Motivator, and Greed Is Not Good

Everyone who survived the 2008 financial crisis can see that a society where each person acts to maximize his own financial gains does not result in the best outcomes for society. The origin of the view that all a society needs are individuals in selfish pursuits of their own goals for the best societal outcomes, through the magic of the *"invisible hand"* of markets, is attributed to Adam Smith. However, Smith's often quoted *"invisible hand"* phrase used to express this idea is misused because Smith was not referring to markets when he used the phrase. Consider the quote from his *The Wealth of Nations* in context:

*"But the annual revenue of every society is always precisely equal to the exchangeable value of the whole annual produce of its industry... As every individual, therefore, endeavours as much as he can, both to employ his capital in the support of domestic industry, and so to direct that industry that its produce maybe of the greatest value; every individual necessarily labours to render the annual revenue of the society as great as he can. He generally, indeed, neither intends to promote the public interest, nor knows how much he is promoting it. By preferring the support of domestic to that of foreign industry, he intends only his own security; and by directing that industry in such a manner as its produce may be of the greatest value, he intends only his own gain; and he is in this, as in many other cases, led by an **invisible hand** to promote an end which was no part of his intention."*

Smith was expressing the view that it is ironic that business leaders in the circumstance of deciding whether to invest overseas or at home would inevitably choose the option of investing at home because this is in their best interest, which coincides with the best interest of their home country. He was supporting domestic investment and expressing a rationale against an aspect of free trade. But modern-day business managers and directors have proven Smith wrong; they freely invest their capital in foreign countries because they do not see their and their society's interests as coinciding.

Smith did not believe that all a society needs are individuals in selfish pursuits of their own goals for the best outcomes for society through the magic of the market's "invisible hand." He expressed an understanding of the limits of markets and the vital role of government in establishing, assisting, regulating and supplementing them.

Smith also uses the *"invisible hands"* phrase in his first published work, *The Theory of Moral Sentiments*. It also does not refer to markets and expresses that by providing a minimum standard of living for those in their employment the rich serve their self-interest:

*"The produce of the soil maintains at all times nearly that number of inhabitants which it is capable of maintaining. The rich only select from the heap what is most precious and agreeable. They consume little more than the poor, and in spite of their natural selfishness and rapacity, though they mean only their own conveniency, though the sole end which they propose from the labours of all the thousands whom they employ, be the gratification of their own vain and insatiable desires, they divide with the poor the produce of all their improvements. They are led by an **invisible hand** to make nearly the same distribution of the necessaries of life, which would have been made, had the earth been divided into equal portions among all its inhabitants, and thus without intending it, without knowing it, advance the interest of the society, and afford means to the multiplication of the species."*

Smith was implying a degree of social consciousness of the *"rich,"* which again, unfortunately, has been proven wrong. The character of the rich in his time, though *"selfish and rapacious,"* has been exceeded in selfishness and rapaciousness by many of our present-day rich who compensate those in their employment with less than a living wage.

The term *"economist"* was not used in Smith's time. He considered himself to be a *"moral philosopher."* For Smith, the market is to be regulated to be a moral mechanism of social support. For example, he explains in the early parts of *The Wealth of Nations* the great value of division of labor in improving the productivity of an economy. Business managers must employ division of labor in the production process to be competitive. However, later in the book, he writes this about its destructive aspects and the need for government regulation of businesses in their use of division of labor:

"In the progress of the division of labour, the employment of the far greater part of those who live by labour, that is, of the great body of the people, comes to be confined to a few very simple operations; frequently to one or two. But the understandings of the greater part of men are necessarily

formed by their ordinary employments. The man whose whole life is spent in performing a few simple operations, of which the effects, too, are perhaps always the same, or very nearly the same, has no occasion to exert his understanding, or to exercise his invention, in finding out expedients for removing difficulties which never occur. He naturally loses, therefore, the habit of such exertion, and generally becomes as stupid and ignorant as it is possible for a human creature to become. The torpor of his mind renders him not only incapable of relishing or bearing a part in any rational conversation, but of conceiving any generous, noble, or tender sentiment, and consequently of forming any just judgment concerning many even of the ordinary duties of private life. Of the great and extensive interests of his country he is altogether incapable of judging; and unless very particular pains have been taken to render him otherwise ... His dexterity at his own particular trade seems, in this manner, to be acquired at the expense of his intellectual [and] social ... virtues. But in every improved and civilized society, this is the state into which the labouring poor, that is, the great body of the people, must necessarily fall, unless government takes some pains to prevent it."

In other words, businesses will be driven to use a practice, division of labor, to a degree that destroys workers' humanity, intelligence and ability to participate in a democratic society, so government regulations are needed to limit the practice.

Nobel laureate Paul Samuelson, who also believes *"there is no satisfactory alternative to market systems,"* has written, *"Using markets is not the same as unregulated capitalism... [which] systematically breeds intolerable inequalities. And instead of such inequality being the necessary price to encourage dynamic progress...instead breeds dysfunctional shortfalls in what economists call "total productivity factor" ... As CEO pay rose respective to median employee pay, from ... 40 to 1 ratio up to and beyond 400 to 1, industrial progress deteriorated rather than accelerated."*[463]

We cannot build a lasting or decent society or well-functioning economy based on the beliefs that greed is good and social responsibility and civic virtue are irrelevant.

Excessive greed is largely responsible for the widening disparities and the financial company executives' behavior which caused the Great Recession, and will continue to create serious economic problems. As I described earlier, almost all the benefits of our large productive capacity advancements during the last four decades, unlike prior decades, owners of corporations and their top managers have greedily directed to themselves, rather than sharing it with workers. As a result, the restricted purchasing power of the lower and middle classes depressed their spending. It also made it more likely that they would take on debt, especially since unscrupulous and greedy bankers and financial intermediaries, freed from regulation and eager to earn good yields on the enormous savings injected into the system by the wealthy, offered credit indiscriminately. Loan originators often sold the loans, so they did not care if the borrower could pay it back because their morals were overcome by their greed. Massive values in toxic loans and loan derivatives resulted, which inevitably defaulted, devastating the economy.

Greed and the resulting economic divergence is also largely responsible for increasingly severe political system dysfunction. Only avarice can motivate people with an already hugely disproportionate share of our nation's wealth to corrupt our political system, as they are, to take even more wealth and power. A society cannot continue to function indefinitely with an extreme divergence between social groups. Greed is blinding an elite to this fact.

In addition to the very influential Adam Smith's writings, Charles Darwin's writings are also misused or misunderstood in justifying the false ideal of individual competition motivated by greed being sufficient for the best outcome for society. Darwin described empathy and cooperation, not competition, as natural traits of humans and animals, and of the greatest importance to the survival of animal species:

"In however complex a manner this feeling [empathy] *may have originated, as it is one of high importance to all those animals which aid and defend one another, it would have been increased through natural selection; for those communities, which included the greatest number of the most sympathetic members, would flourish best, and rear the greatest number of offspring"* Charles Darwin

Facts and Economists, and Their Sometimes Uneasy Relationship

Without taxation, collective action for a tolerable and stable modern society is impossible. Progressive taxation to raise revenues for this collective action is justified on both moral and economic grounds, and with the widening inequalities, progressive taxation is more important than it has been in the past. Under reasonable limits, increased taxes on high incomes and taxes on wealth will be economically beneficial, if government uses the resulting revenues in ways that experience demonstrates are beneficial, including increasing opportunity for the middle class and the poor, research and development funding, infrastructure improvements, and decreasing economic disparities.

An International Monetary Fund report on an extensive international study of the effects of inequality and redistribution on growth supports the claim that redistributive policies are beneficial.[464] It found lower net inequality resulting from the effects of redistributive policies to be *"robustly correlated with faster and more durable growth."* And it found that the flatter distribution of income resulting from redistributive policies contributed more to economic growth than the quality of the country's political institutions, its foreign debt, openness to trade and foreign investment, and its exchange rate.

The IMF recently released another, and the largest, international study on inequality and growth. It found an inverse relationship between the income share accruing to the rich (top 20%) and economic growth. If the income share of the top 20% increases by one percentage point, GDP growth is 0.08% lower in the following five years, suggesting that the benefits do not trickle down. A similar increase in the income share of the bottom 20% (the poor) is associated with 0.38 percentage point higher growth. The study is based on a sample of 159 advanced, emerging, and developing economies for the period 1980–2012.[465]

Harvard economist Philippe Aghion's research also has found a negative effect of inequality and positive effect of redistribution upon growth.

However, despite the evidence in these studies and other evidence, controversy remains among economists on redistributive policies and on how tax increases on high income and wealth will affect behaviors and the impact of these behaviors on economic performance. Considering the widely varying opinions of economists both currently and over time, not just facts, but cultural and other biases are involved in some of their determinations.

In 1934, 66% of economists polled favored taxing capital ("unearned") income at higher rates than earned income, compared to 7% of economists polled in 1994. The 1930s was a period when populist views as a response to the Great Depression were culturally dominant. This allowed the New Deal to be instituted, which significantly reduced inequality. We now tax capital income at much lower rates than income from labor, and the opinion of economists has been an important motive for doing so.

In 1919, Irving Fisher, then president of the American Economic Association, in his presidential address devoted to the subject of U.S. inequality, said that the extreme concentration of wealth was the nation's foremost economic problem, and the fact that it was increasing was *"distressing."* One possible solution he suggested was to impose an estate tax with a tax rate of *"one-third of the* [entire value of the] *estate on the first descent, two-thirds ... on the second,"* rising to 100% on the third descent.[466] It is highly unlikely a modern-day president of the American Economic Association would make a similar proposal. Fisher's concern was warranted. Not long afterward the country experienced the Great Depression, largely related to huge inequality.

In recent decades, the interests of the wealthy have been the dominant influence on economic policy, and mainstream economists have supported this trend. This has resulted not only in capital income being taxed less than earned income, but also low taxes on high income from labor and on inheritances—or nonexistent taxes with most large inheritances. This is what the wealthy believe is in their interest; however, a more just society would benefit everyone, not just the poor and middle class.

In 2004, Martin Feldstein, President Reagan's chair of the Council of Economic Advisors, devoted his American Economic Association presidential address to the subject of health insurance. Health care is an appropriate topic because health care expenditures in the United States are about 18% of GDP, and about 50 million Americans were uninsured in 2004 although most worked full-time. Even those with health insurance are often financially destroyed when they get a serious illness.

What was the solution to these problems offered by the person who has reached the pinnacle of the economics profession in 2004? (The presidency of the American Economic Association is the highest honor economists can give one of their own.) Feldstein told the audience that health insurance in the U.S. faced a problem because deductibles and co-payments were too low, and as a result people went to the doctor too often: *"They* [low co-payments] *also lead to an increased demand for care that is worth less than the cost of production."* He advocated for disallowing health care premium deductions for employers to make health care more expensive for the people needing the care, or aligned with *"the cost of production."*

Feldstein ignored the facts that when he made his address 45,000 people per year died unnecessarily because they didn't have health insurance, and that not getting care early in a treatable condition can cause more serious disease and expensive care in the future.

A significant cause of our high-cost health care system is not that people go to the doctor unnecessarily. Feldstein mentioned none of the real causes of our health care system costing over double the OECD average per capita, where citizens have easy access to health care, so easy access is obviously not the problem. Feldstein did not explicitly state that he considered that too much of the resources of the wealthy go to the health care of the poor, but this was really his main point. The wealthy can afford to go to the doctor as much as they like in our system, while everyone else needs to be restricted by price, was the essence of his message.

What are the real causes of our high health care costs? The sales, marketing, and underwriting activities of private insurance companies with diverse billing and review practices, unnecessary testing and procedures due to perverse financial incentives of caregivers, very high doctor pay, semi-monopoly power in the health insurance industry and in large hospital chains, and monopoly power in the drug industry, and other inefficient health system practices resulting from a poorly regulated privatized system.

Economists have biases, both conscious and unconscious, and it is now much more likely for them to favor the interests of the wealthy and most powerful than those of the middle class or poor.

Think tanks that play an important role in our national policy debate hire many economists. Most think tanks serve the interests of economic elites. Using money from wealthy donors, corporations, and foundations supported by wealthy donors, think tanks hire the "expert" economists produced by the graduate departments of universities. These economist's ideas and proposals are disseminated through pamphlets, books, articles in major magazines and newspapers, and through their participation in the forums provided by the think tanks and other policy discussion organizations. They also serve on the little-known federal advisory committees that are part of just about every department of the executive branch.

Corporate leaders and other wealthy donors attend discussions in these forums to express their views and to influence experts. The policy discussion organizations also give members of the upper class and corporate community the opportunity to see who seem to be the best natural leaders, by watching them in the give and take of the discussion groups. They can see who understands the issues from their viewpoint, facilitates discussions, and relates well to others.

The organizations thus serve as screening mechanisms for new leadership which the upper class and corporate community can help promote for government service. These organizations increase the status of their participants, thus the media and interested public tend to see them as knowledgeable leaders, whose views are accurate and important, and who deserve a role in government. Economists advance their position and prestige in corporate funded think tanks and their influence on government officials. When they serve elite interests in this system, it is beneficial for their careers.

Elite funding of our elections is also related to policymaker bias toward economist advisors who serve the interests of economic elites. This bias is also often self-serving based on another condition: Many of our policymakers are themselves among the economic elite. As I noted previously, 268 members of Congress (about 50%) are millionaires with an average wealth of over $4 million—including income producing assets only, so their wealth is likely far larger. At least 10 members have wealth exceeding $100 million.

Forces for bias toward the interests of economic elites also exist within universities. Many university economics departments have allowed hiring and coursework decisions to be corrupted by the prejudices and interests of wealthy donors. For example:

Between 2007 and 2012, the billionaire Koch brothers' private foundations contributed $30.5 million to 221 U.S. colleges and universities. The Koches also donated $41.2 million to 89 nonprofits and one annual conference, all of with public policy and educational missions promoting deregulation, small government and "free markets."[467]

The Koches have influenced higher education for over 30 years, beginning with what is now called the Mercatus Center and the Institute for Humane Studies, both based at George Mason University in the Virginia suburbs of Washington. The May-June 2012 issue of Academe, the magazine of the American Association of University Professors, reported that The Charles G. Koch Foundation gave the Florida State University economics department $1.5 million to hire two assistant professors and fund fellowships and undergraduate curriculum on free-enterprise topics. The foundation appointed an advisory board that would award money to faculty and ensure that the work they completed fit with the foundation's mission. In exchange for this "gift" the Koch Foundation got to assign specific readings, select campus speakers and lecture topics, shape the curriculum with new courses, name the program's director, and initiate a student club.[468] The Koch Foundation "gift" is more appropriately called a long-term investment in maintaining a social structure that best serves their interests.

$1.5 million is a substantial amount of money for the university but is insignificant for the Koches. It is less than .002% of their $81 billion, so it is very easy for them to corrupt institutions and individuals. This is even more evident when you consider that they need not use any of the $81 billion at all to do so, since their income, and economic gains more generally, are correspondingly vast. The $1.5 million is also an insignificant fraction of these gains.

The Koches corrupting influence was not just at Florida State, which was a high-profile case, but also at other universities where the Koches and John Allison, retired chairman and CEO of the financial institution BB&T, have donated money. (Allison is on the board of directors at the Koch funded Mercatus Center, and is the president of the Cato Institute think tank.) BB&T sponsors chaired professors, typically in economics departments; the universities where they sponsor a chaired professor are often ones where the Koch's donate.

Our universities should be our most important institutions for free and unbiased inquiry. Important portions of many of them—along with the other parts of the foundation of our social structure—we have allowed to be corrupted by wealthy individuals and corporations.

U.S. academic economists are the highest paid professors of all academic disciplines. (According to May 2015 Bureau of Labor Statistics, on average 36% higher than sociology, 13% higher than physics, 25% higher than biology, 34% higher than math and computer science professors.) This also motivates many economists to believe that the economy of the United States is working well, rewarding talent and merit accurately and precisely. However, some prestigious economists believe otherwise and have expressed clearly their views on the common biases of mainstream economists:

Economist James K. Galbraith, professor at the Lyndon B. Johnson School of Public Affairs and at the Department of Government, University of Texas at Austin, Senior Scholar with the Levy Economics Institute of Bard College, and a member of the executive committee of the World Economics Association, wrote:

"Leading active members of today's economics profession... have formed themselves into a kind of Politburo for correct economic thinking. As a general rule...this has placed them on the wrong side of every important policy issue, and not just recently but for decades. They predict disaster where none occurs. They deny the possibility of events that then happen...They oppose the most basic, decent and sensible reforms, while offering placebos instead. They are always surprised when something untoward (like a recession) actually occurs. And when finally they sense that some position cannot be sustained, they do not reexamine their ideas. They do not consider the possibility

of a flaw in logic or theory. Rather, they simply change the subject. No one loses face, in this club, for having been wrong. No one is dis-invited from presenting papers at later annual meetings. And still less is anyone from the outside invited in."

No mainstream economist predicted the most cataclysmic economic event in decades—the Great Recession. To believe that such a thing could occur would violate what appears to be a dictum of their common religious text, that a society with unregulated "free markets" is as close to heaven as we can get on Earth. Instead, unregulated or weakly regulated "free markets" threw tens of millions of people into hell on Earth, and required a very unfree market intervention to avoid economic catastrophe—trillions of dollars of public money.

The Financial Times, widely regarded as the most credible and influential financial and economic issues publication internationally, published the following in a September 25, 2014 editorial:

"Now the dismal science [economics] *itself is in the dock, with much soul-searching over why economists failed to predict the financial crisis. One of the outcomes of this debate is that economics students are demanding the reform of a curriculum they think sustains a selfish strain of capitalism and is dominated by abstract mathematics.*

For a subject so engaged with studying worldly behaviour, there is too much timeless abstraction and too little scrutiny of real-world events. The typical economics course starts with the study of how rational agents interact in frictionless markets, producing an outcome that is best for everyone. Only later does it cover those wrinkles and perversities that characterise real economic behaviour, such as anti-competitive practices or unstable financial markets. As students advance, there is a growing bias toward mathematical elegance. When the uglier real world intrudes, it only prompts the question: this is all very well in practice but how does it work in theory?"

Warren Buffett made a similar statement on the relative importance to mainstream economists of their theories versus reality when referring to how the academic economics community regards his investment approach. (Buffett is likely the most successful investor in history. He was ranked as the world's wealthiest person in 2008 and as the third wealthiest in 2011). He said, *"Well, it may be all right in practice, but it will never work in theory."*

Economist Thomas Piketty, who in 2006 became the first head of the Paris School of Economics, which he helped set up, is a world-renowned researcher and scholar on economic inequality. He expressed the following on the biases and disconnection from the real world of economists:

"Economists are all too often preoccupied with petty mathematical problems of interest only to themselves. This obsession with mathematics is an easy way of acquiring the appearance of scientificity without having to answer the far more complex questions posed by the world we live in… economists have an unfortunate tendency to defend their private interest while implausibly claiming to champion the general interest."

Ronald Coase, Nobel laureate in economics and a professor emeritus at the University of Chicago Law School, wrote this about economists: *"In the 20th century, economics consolidated as a profession; economists could afford to write exclusively for one another. At the same time, the field experienced a paradigm shift, gradually identifying itself as a theoretical approach of economization and giving up the real-world economy as its subject matter… it is no longer firmly grounded in systematic empirical investigation of the working of the economy… It is time to reengage the severely impoverished field of economics with the economy."*

Modern day mainstream economists' biases serving elite interests may be uncommonly extreme and pervasive, but the problem has occurred at other times. John Maynard Keynes, one of the most influential economists in history (an entire school of modern economic thought bears his name) wrote the following on others in his profession in the 1930s in England:

"For professional economists… were apparently unmoved by the lack of correspondence between the results of their theory and the facts of observation;—a discrepancy which the ordinary man has not failed to observe…" and *"* [the widely accepted theories of economists] *could explain much social injustice and apparent cruelty as an inevitable incident in the scheme of progress, and the attempt to change such things as likely on the whole to do more harm than good, commanded* [their theories] *authority. That* [their theories] *afforded a measure of justification to the free activities of the individual capitalist, attracted to* (their theories) *the support of the dominant social force behind authority."*

Keynes wrote this in his 1936 book (in the latter half of the Great Depression, an economic crisis with some similarity to our Great Recession) *The General Theory of Employment, Interest and Money.* This book is widely credited with creating the foundation and terminology of modern macroeconomics. It is striking how perfectly appropriate, and possibly even more appropriate, his statements are for the United States today, as they were when he wrote them regarding England 80 years ago.

Albert Einstein said: "*A foolish faith in authority is the worst enemy of the truth.*"

When you hear mainstream economists' continued pronouncements of their opinions, theories and study results on the benefits arising from small government and "free markets," or the harm from regulations to align corporate practices with the public good, higher taxes on the wealthy, redistributive policies and other government expenditures (especially on infrastructure, basic research, and systems to disseminate knowledge), give them the skepticism they deserve. Skepticism of pronouncements serving elite interests was one of the ideals of the original Enlightenment that we will also emphasize in the New Enlightenment.

Prior propaganda's impact is often difficult to overcome, though. The tendency to accept, rather than be skeptical of doctrine or information consistent with prior information that a person has been conditioned to believe, is strong. Psychological research has discovered that biases are self-reinforcing. Individuals process information that is consistent with their prior beliefs differently than information that is inconsistent. Information consistent is considered significant and remembered, while information that is inconsistent is discounted and more likely forgotten or ignored. This distortion is called "*confirmation bias*" and can reinforce false beliefs. When people in authority, or people given a mass media forum, express an inaccuracy or falsehood, the bias can become widespread and further culturally reinforced. Sometimes just common sense is closer to reality than the views of the "experts," and can interrupt this process of spreading propaganda, if "common sense" would be more commonly used.

Common sense applied in the case of the wealthiest man in America, Bill Gates: In 1980, if someone had told Gates he would make "only" one-hundredth of $76 billion (the amount he now has) or $760 million, after 33 years of work, it would not have affected his behavior at all.[469] (As I described earlier, the value of Gates' social contribution was far from proportional to the $76 billion "incentive.")

In the unlikely event that Gates would have decided this level of compensation was insufficient, other people would have been ready to make similar, and in one known case, likely superior contributions. Some probably would have considered not just 1% of $76 billion, but one hundredth of 1% (or one ten-thousandth, $7.6 million) sufficient compensation in excess wealth, in addition to large amounts of spent income after 33 years of work.

$75 billion, or $1 billion less than Gates' wealth, is enough to pay the average college tuition for four years for about 2.2 million students in public universities in the United States that may not have otherwise gone to college for financial reasons. The knowledge and skills gained by many of these graduates would allow them to be involved in advancements they otherwise would not have, due to the financial barrier to a college education that now exists. The higher skill levels would also enhance the abilities to economically contribute in other ways (and their higher educational level would benefit them and society in ways other than economic). This is just one example of how not returning through taxation most of the extreme financial gains of individuals to society harms our economy (and society).

As I've noted before, student debt is now massive, totaling over $1.2 trillion, more than the total national credit card debt. The United States is now ranked twelfth internationally in the percentage of young people with college degrees, an area where we once led the world. Many people are choosing not to go to college because they cannot afford it. Our poor income mobility relative to the rest of the industrialized countries (and to ours a few decades ago), implies that we are wasting a significant amount of our most valuable resources, our human resources. A primary reason is unequal quality and availability of educational opportunities.

Wastage of our human resources also occurs because of our economic system's detrimental effect on the home environment, which is critical in educational attainment. When parents must work long hours due to low wages, they are less able to supervise and motivate their children in their schoolwork. New Enlightenment policies will significantly alleviate this problem as well as other major social problems having a negative effect on the home environment. These policies require an increase in government expenditures, which require higher taxes on the wealthy.

16 million children (22%), live in poverty even though their parents are in their prime working ages. Today, most poor Americans are in their prime working years. In 2012, 57% of poor Americans were ages 18 to 64, versus 41.7% in 1959.[470] Most are food insecure, meaning that occasionally they cannot afford the food they need. Not eating well and other stresses resulting from poverty also negatively affect current economic performance and educational attainment, and so long-term economic performance.

If Walmart's founder, Sam Walton, had pursued a career as an engineer rather than a retailer, can anyone believe we would not have discount department stores? Did society need to create a $145 billion "incentive" for Walton to create his chain of discount department stores? Obviously not. And Walmart is discount in a very limited sense. Government programs pay the food, housing, health care, and energy subsidy costs of its workers to a substantial degree because of their unjustly low wages. These costs do not appear in Walmart's low prices and are very large.

A 2013 study by staff of the U.S. Committee on Education and the Workforce found that a single Walmart Supercenter in Wisconsin cost taxpayers between $3,015 and $5,815 on average per year for each of its workers. Assuming the mid-point of $4,415, multiplied by Walmart's approximately 1.4 million U.S. workers, this yields a bill that Walmart is giving to taxpayers to support their workers of $6.2 billion per year. Walmart is the country's largest private employer, and its wages are among of the lowest in the industry. (American fast food workers receive over $7 billion in public assistance.)[471]

If the Walton families instead had "only" $1 billion and the rest of their $145 billion in wealth were used to serve urgent public needs wouldn't we all be far better off? How large is $1 billion? If it was invested with a 5% return (wealth this large tends to bring higher than 5% returns), the Walton families could spend $137,000 per day and not reduce the $1 billion at all! I don't believe it is possible to spend $137,000 per day on anything they can consume or use, but if it is, it would certainly take a lot of effort.

The details of a system of income and wealth tax rates to optimize economic and social benefits require an extensive and quantitative analysis, and are not possible to determine precisely because too many variables exist, including both the details of the tax system and how the resulting revenues will be spent. But these examples indicate that we are far below an optimum for some income and wealth levels.

The New Enlightenment's tax policy will not reduce the wealth of the super wealthy anywhere remotely close to the amounts in these examples. No significant effect on the work of high income or wealth people, even with far higher than New Enlightenment tax rates, would occur. And using higher tax revenues for policies that will result in reduced inequality is of great economic importance, as much evidence indicates, including that in a Congressional Budget Office report. The economic recovery predicted in the report relies on households in the bottom 80% of the distribution accumulating debt again in line with the prerecession trend. Clearly, this process is unsustainable.[472] As I noted previously, in the years leading up to the recession the bottom 80% of the American population had been spending around 110% of its income.

Using tax revenue to reduce inequality, eliminate poverty (or nearly so) and unemployment, reduce work-hours and increase educational opportunity, as New Enlightenment policies would, will create a more stable economy and release a lot of wasted economic potential from our most valuable resources, our human resources.

Also, if higher taxes on high incomes are used to greatly increase the numbers of people able to invest in their own cooperatively owned and self-directed business enterprises, it will substantially increase their and society's overall productivity. Many studies, some of which Policy 3 describes, indicate that when workers are self-directed or have a say in enterprise decisions, including those determining how income is distributed among the workers, or own a portion of the business in which they work, productivity is enhanced. This is an important way we would use increased tax revenues.

Opponents of raising income taxes on high-income households use faulty studies indicating that high-income taxpayers responded to tax-rate increases by reporting less income to the Internal Revenue Service, or to tax rate decreases by reporting more income. More careful analysis has found that such changes in reported income primarily reflect the timing of reported income and other tax avoidance strategies, not changes in real work, savings, and investment behavior. One influential study that falsely concluded that high marginal tax rates impose significant costs on the economy Part 4, Note 4 describes. High-income taxpayers have responded to large cuts in tax rates with no or negligible changes in work-hours.[473] While avoidance strategies involve some economic costs, these costs are small and can be minimized by policies that equalize tax rates over income types, limit tax shelters and simplify the tax code by minimizing deductions.

Some claim tax rate increases motivate taxpayers to work less because the after-tax return to work declines. But some work more, to maintain a level of after-tax income similar to what they had before the tax increase. For the vast majority of high-income taxpayers, the tax rate has not affected their work level, but for the few it did, the evidence shows that these two opposing responses canceled each other out.

In addition, as we have seen, extrinsic motivators positively impact only some kinds of work, mainly in the short term, and extreme financial rewards are not used for these kinds of work. Since higher taxes on high income will reduce extrinsic motivators that have been demonstrated to be detrimental to the performance of the kinds of work that often generate high income, economic performance may be enhanced by top income tax rate increases just for this reason alone. In addition, the increased public funds wisely spent will have a beneficial impact.

Unlike our current estate tax that taxes on average only 1% of the $1.2 trillion transferred per year to heirs, a properly designed estate or inheritance tax is especially beneficial to society. Vast wealth transfers to winners of *"womb lotteries,"* as Warren Buffett calls wealthy heirs, are unrelated to any societal contribution of the recipient. (Buffett is skilled at creating colorful, concise, and precisely accurate descriptions or labels. He called mortgage derivatives *"financial weapons of mass destruction"* in 2005, well before most people knew of the label's accuracy). Multigenerational aristocracies are not justifiable on economic grounds.

The ideal of all having an equal chance "at the starting line" is receding. New Enlightenment policies are designed to help restore it, even if there is no other reason than maximizing societal economic performance requires equal opportunity for all. The New Enlightenment program replaces the estate tax with an inheritance tax that will support policies for equal opportunity.

Capital gains taxes disproportionately impact high-income people. The bottom 90% of the population gets less than 10% of all capital gains. The much lower capital gains tax rates than tax rates on labor have been an important factor in the rise of inequality that studies show is negatively correlated with economic growth across countries. Raising taxes on capital gains to support New Enlightenment policies will reduce inequality and raise economic performance.

However, a capital gains tax avoidance technique is likely to be more prevalent if the rate is increased unless unrealized capital gains are taxed to the degree practical. Instead of selling the appreciated asset, which would require paying the tax on the gains, some of the wealthy get a loan on its value which does not. Thus they get access to the cash value of the asset while avoiding the tax. A "mark-to-market" system for appreciated value on stocks will eliminate the tax avoidance problem for stock gains. The system requires paying the tax on unrealized stock gains each year. To avoid forced sales to pay the tax, taxpayers will be allowed a government loan on the tax amount with just interest due if this is necessary. All or part of the principal payment could be deferred until the asset was sold or before then when funds were available. If the asset fell in price the following year, the taxpayer could deduct the loss, and with the savings in taxes pay all or part the loan from the prior year.

We could also use this system for investment real estate when assessed values are updated. For assets whose value is not regularly updated we would require that if a loan is taken out with the asset as collateral the loan officer's assessment of the value be used to determine any gains for the capital gains tax.

Some economists claim that increases in capital gains tax rates harm economic performance by depressing private saving rates and investment. They have motivated policymakers to institute the much lower capital gains tax rate than the top labor tax rate based on this claim. But Tax Policy Center researchers found no statistically significant correlation exists between capital gains rates and real GDP growth during the last 50 years.[474]

The Congressional Research Service (CRS) has reported that most studies show that lower capital gains tax rates have a likely negative impact on saving and investment. The CRS concludes, *"Capital gains tax rate increases appear to increase public saving and may have little or no effect on private saving. Consequently, capital gains tax increases likely have a positive overall impact on national saving and investment."*[475] Also, a large difference between the tax rates on capital gains and the tax rates on other types of income is used to avoid taxes. This diverts money to relatively unproductive investments that taxpayers would not invest in but for the tax benefit. A lower capital gains rate also motivates the waste of resources on elaborate schemes to convert ordinary income into capital gains to achieve the tax benefit.

Raising the capital gains tax rate to eliminate the differential between it and the labor rate discourages tax sheltering behavior—another reason it will increase economic efficiency. Also, lower capital gains rates have encouraged corporations to pay out dividends, leaving fewer funds inside the corporation for investment.

Another common false claim that serves the interests of the wealthy to minimize their taxes is that higher top marginal income tax rates will be very harmful to small business owners. A recent Treasury Department analysis found that only 2.5% of small business owners fall into the top two income tax brackets and that these owners receive less than one-third of small business income. As a Center on Budget and Policy Priorities report, *Recent Studies Find Raising Taxes on High-Income Households Would Not Harm the Economy,* points out, even those small business owners affected by tax increases on high-income households are unlikely to respond by reducing hiring or new investment because:

- Small businesses can expense (immediately deduct in full) the cost of investment. This makes the effective tax rate on new investment zero, regardless of the statutory rate.
- If a small business can finance investment with debt, the interest payments would be tax deductible, making the effective tax rate negative.
- They can deduct wage payments in full.

Assertions of economic damage from increases in tax rates on high-income households are repeated so often that many policymakers, journalists, and ordinary citizens assume they are based on certain, well-established facts. They are not. The best research supports the fact that we are far below optimal tax rates on high incomes.

As I noted in *The Way to Prosperity for All*, Nobel Prize winning economist Peter Diamond and the American Economics Association's John Bates Clark Medal winner, Emmanuel Saez, did an analysis to determine the tax rates that would optimize economic benefits. They found that the optimum federal tax rate on incomes over $400,000 is between 48% and 76%. The higher rate applies if tax avoidance and evasion opportunities are minimized. Their analysis estimated a range of responsiveness to the higher rates that high-income taxpayers will have. The optimal top tax rate range they determined is based on the assumption that high-income taxpayers will respond at the highest level of their estimate range to the higher rates, which is unlikely, so optimal tax rates are likely to be higher. They also determined optimal rates higher than New Enlightenment rates for incomes over $100,000.

Diamond and Saez' analysis did not consider some factors that, if accounted for, also would result in higher optimal rates. Among them is the benefit of productivity enhancements from increasing the perception of fairness. The sense that our economic system is unfair undermines trust and motivation, which is essential for the functioning of our economy (and our democracy). How much people are paid affects their productivity, if they are paid unfairly low wages.

Economist Thomas Piketty has determined that *"a rate on the order of 80% on incomes over $500,000 or $1 million a year, not only would not reduce the growth of the U.S. economy, but would in fact distribute the fruits of growth more widely while imposing reasonable limits on economically useless (or even harmful) behavior."*[476] Raising top tax rates by even just a small percentage raises substantial amounts of revenue for important public needs because an extraordinarily large portion of our national income is now directed to the top.

Emmanuel Saez's analysis also revealed that top marginal tax rates are strongly negatively correlated with the **pretax** income share of national income of people with top incomes. The graph shows this strong negative correlation. His research suggests that the post-World War II reduction in top marginal income tax rates has encouraged executives and managers to bargain a higher share of total corporate income, at the expense of other workers' wages.

Top 1% Income Share (pre–tax) and Top Marginal Tax Rate

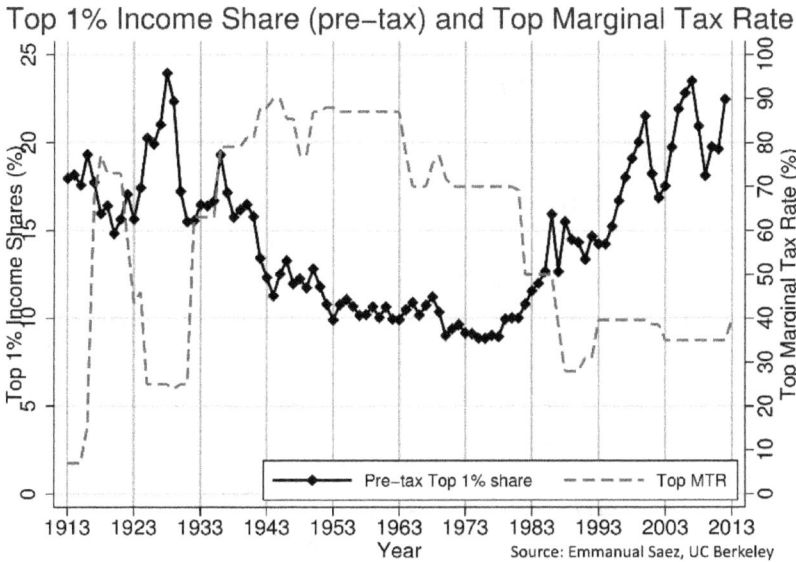

Source: Emmanual Saez, UC Berkeley

Cross-country comparisons also suggest that a substantial portion of the behavioral response to top tax rate cuts reflects this zero-sum, nonproductive shift of income from nonsupervisory workers to managers and executives.

These data may suggest the transfers are "zero-sum," meaning they merely shift income between classes with no gains to productivity. But they are more likely "negative sum." National income in total is depressed when inequality is as extreme as it is now. Tens of millions of Americans having incomes with very depressed buying power, tens of millions with even less than what is needed to meet basic needs, depresses economic activity. And their unfair compensation depresses their productivity.

High-income people save a much larger amount and proportion of their income than lower income people do, so far more consumption per dollar exists in lower income households than in higher. Therefore, using the tax system for "redistribution" will increase demand for goods and services and the workers that supply them. And when inequality is extreme, the positive impact will be correspondingly large. "Redistribution" is the conventional way to express this process. But as we have seen a better way is: Payment to society for services rendered is used to serve the greater good. This necessarily involves ensuring at least a decent standard of living for everyone, and that the majority are far more equitably compensated for society-wide enhanced productive capacity resulting from common, enormous socially inherited and created resources.

Also, the resulting higher government revenues allow expenditures that increase equality of opportunity, which increases the economic power of our most valuable resources, our human resources. And the resulting higher government revenues will increase productivity in other ways, such as through research and development, and through infrastructure improvements, both of which have greatly improved economic performance in the past.

The rise in inequality to extreme levels, both before the Great Depression and the recent (and to many, effectively ongoing) Great Recession indicates that inequality was a fundamental causal factor for both. When money is concentrated in a small fraction of society, and a large fraction has little money, the depressed demand for goods and services depresses employment and wages at the bottom creating a "vicious cycle." Then when a large percentage of people must borrow to live, the process is unsustainable.

Some Historical Evidence of the Benefits of Higher Top Tax Rates

From 1936 to 1980, the top marginal tax rate was between 70% and 94%, and it averaged 82%. Since 1987, the official top rate has remained below 40%, and the effective rate, after all deductions and credits, has been between 18% and 25%. Higher taxes on top earners are correlated with faster growth, contrary to the claims of so-called supply-side economists. The graph in Policy 2 showing the average annual growth rate in real GDP as a function of top marginal tax rate makes this clear.

As previously noted, from 1951 to 1980, when the top rate was between 70% and 92%, average annual growth in the American economy was 3.7%. Today, many of the most prominent pundits and politicians claim these tax rates cause economic disaster. Instead, they are associated with the opposite— economic boom. The growth rate over the decade 2006 through 2015 averaged 1.4%.

"Supply-siders" claim that Ronald Reagan's 1981 tax cuts caused the 1980s economic boom. But that boom followed Reagan's 1982 tax increase. (However, this boom was mostly caused by the huge decreases in oil prices and interest rates.) Similarly, most of the 1990s boom followed Bill Clinton's 1993 tax increase.

Correlation does not prove causation. Many factors are involved in economic growth. However, the positive historical correlation of growth and top tax rates proves that higher top tax rates are not incompatible with higher growth rates, as the most prominent pundits in the media would have you believe. If the resulting increase in funds from the increase in top tax rates is used to support opportunity enhancing and other economically stimulative policies including redistributive policies, as they have in the past, causal factors are involved in the positive correlation.

Until a generation ago, most Americans and their representatives argued vehemently that the wealthy should pay tax rates that to many people today are not acceptable to even discuss. Why is it that what was once considered normal and necessary, and served the country well, is now considered entirely out of bounds to many? Decades of propaganda with false information about the harmfulness of increasing taxes on high incomes has succeeded.

Taxing extreme incomes at high rates is an American invention, and it is what helped make us more egalitarian and prosperous than the rest of the world in the middle of the 20th century. The tax rates of the 1940s, 1950s, and 1960s, when the top marginal tax rate went as high as 94%, paid for the interstate highway system and research and development projects. Government funded R&D allowed us to put the first man on the moon, create the Internet, early computer hardware and software, the Global Positioning Satellite (GPS) system, and many other publicly funded technological advancements. Higher top tax rates also paid for waterworks, airports, nuclear power plants, and the benefits of the GI bill. These benefits included low-cost mortgages, low-interest loans to start a business, cash payments of tuition and living expenses to attend college, high school or vocational education, and one year of unemployment compensation.

The funds for these purposes were instrumental in the country's subsequent economic success. Tax cuts for the wealthy have greatly restricted similar investments, and greatly increased the national deficit and the debt. They have also increased inequality with all its negative consequences.

An October 1995 study by the Council of Economic Advisers found that: *"[Public] investments in R&D have rates of return...close to 50%, [which] exceed the high private rates of returns, of 20% to 30%, by a considerable amount, because of the "spillovers"—benefits that accrue as other research-*

ers make use of new findings, often in applications far beyond what the original researcher imagined.... However, such spillovers imply that private firms will not invest in enough R&D from a national perspective."

Few people know that the algorithm that led to Google's success was funded by a public sector National Science Foundation grant. Or that molecular antibodies, which provided the foundation for biotechnology, were discovered in public Medical Research Council labs in the U.K.[477] Or that many of the most innovative young companies in the U.S. were funded not by private venture capital, but by public venture capital, such as through Small Business Innovation Research. Over the last three decades, public funding was responsible for important developments in the computer industry, the Internet, the pharma–biotech industry, and many more including today's nanotech industry. None of these technological revolutions would have occurred without the leading role of the state. In 2003 alone, federal spending on computer science research totaled over $2 billion. In 2004, federal government funding accounted for nearly two-thirds of all basic research done in the United States.[478]

A 1995 MIT study found that eleven of the fourteen most medically significant drugs developed over the previous quarter century originated with research financed by the government. 70% of science citations in biotechnology patents are from papers originating in "public science institutions."[479]

In 1972, the Defense Department sought to persuade a commercial operator to take over the Arpanet, which determined that the market in data services was too small to invest in. the Arpanet has since become the Internet.[480]

In 1977, Digital Equipment Corporation's CEO, Ken Olsen, said: "There is no reason anyone would want a computer in their home" CEOs have commonly revealed a lack of vision of major negative consequence to their firms.

It has been the state, not the private sector, that has had the vision for major advancements, and for making the large, long-term investments needed. Only taxes give the state the capability to fund these investments. Large government deficits are not sustainable.

What Does International Experience Indicate?

U.S. productivity growth was higher than that of the European Union during, for example, the 1995-2004 period. But France, Germany, Norway, Belgium, Great Britain, Italy, Ireland, and Finland all had higher taxes than the United States between 1970 and 1990, with higher productivity growth than the U.S. And the advantage in GDP per capita between the U.S. and Europe as a whole predates any difference in tax systems. It goes back to the late 19th century and relates more to geography than to economic system. However, over the last several decades the rise in workhours per capita to the point where it is now almost 25% longer here is primarily responsible for the difference.[481]

America has far more land and natural resources, such as oil, gas, and coal, per person than Europe does (just as Norway's higher oil and gas earnings account for its higher GDP per person than the U.S.). We average 84 people per square mile, while Europe has 189. Although we have about the same land area as all of Europe, we have 36.5 billion barrels of proven oil reserves; Europe has 13.3 billion barrels.[482] With less than half the population of Europe, this amounts to 114 barrels of oil per capita in the United States and 18 barrels in Europe.

Despite America's vast resource advantage, we have a lower quality of life than countries in northern Europe. To improve our quality of life requires public expenditures on education, infrastructure, and to reduce inequality and poverty, and to accomplish other goals of the New Enlightenment. This requires higher taxes on those most able to pay it, those of high income and wealth.

The table shows several examples of countries with higher taxes than the U.S. with higher GDP per capita than the U.S. Most of these countries have also had higher average GDP growth rates over the last decade than the U.S.[483]

Social spending on education, health, training, research, and other services, and on infrastructure contribute to growth by promoting the development of human capital, technological advancements and by facilitating commerce. Many more "socialist" states benefit from a way of taxing and spending that is more pro-growth than the policies of more "free market" countries. The IMF and other studies clearly show this.

Country	GDP per capita 2013 estimate[484]	Tax revenue as percentage of GDP	2003-2013 average GDP growth rate %[485]
Luxembourg	127,819	37.5	2.1
Norway	100,235	43.6	1.7
Switzerland	92,796	30.3	1.8
Sweden	71,322	46.4	2.3
Denmark	66,474	48.2	0.7
Australia	53,568	27.1	3
Canada	54,225	31.1	1.9
United States	50,144	24	1.7

Our "Free Market" Is Not Free

As we have seen, many people's contributions throughout history are largely responsible for our "free market" economy today. Their efforts and intelligence largely paid for our "free market" economy. And our "free market" is interwoven with, and cannot function without, systems created by our society acting collectively today.

Government protects property rights and civil liberties. Businesses move their goods to market on the public roads, hire publicly educated workers and use other valuable public services. The systems that provide these services are not free. Should the 40% of the country with a total wealth less than zero pay the costs for a functioning economy or those at the top of our income and wealth distribution who have benefited most from the enormous value derived from working in our society? The over $2.3 trillion of the wealthiest 400 Americans exceeds the total GDP of 121 of the 189 nations for which the World Bank records GDP, yet they strive to reduce their taxes. [486]

In addition, our so-called "free market" is often characterized by the economically powerful abusing market conditions and rules to dominate the economically weak, so it is not truly "free." The rules that markets require to function the economically powerful are corrupting our political system to adjust to serve their interests, and the rules enforcement mechanisms they also often strongly influence to serve their interests. And many of the wealthiest corporate participants in the so-called "free market" receive by far the greatest financial benefit from the huge amounts of socialized costs for research and development, infrastructure, and educating the workforce.

Also, our "free market" law of supply and demand that says that supply equals demand is violated or has failed when the supply of investment to bring the poor out of poverty is not being met by the demand.

New Enlightenment tax rate increases on high incomes are moderate, and some individuals will still have after-tax annual incomes in the hundreds of millions, possibly even billions of dollars, as some have had in the recent past. I am not implying that it seems to me that incomes this large are justifiable, but at least currently, many people do think so. New Enlightenment tax increases are sufficient to fund New Enlightenment programs and are to levels lower than at other times in our history. (The most extreme example in U.S. history of a tax policy proposal to serve the common good is described in Part 4, Note 5)

Higher tax rates on high incomes and taxes on large amounts of wealth are well justified on moral and economic grounds. A more comprehensive vision of how to serve the best interests of our country includes seeing their necessity in serving the cause of democratic governance.

Higher Taxes on High Income and Wealth Can Rescue a Democracy in Peril

At least since the time of Aristotle, it has been well known that economic inequality plays a central role in political instability. As I noted in Part 2, Aristotle wrote 2,400 years ago: *"Good government is attainable in those states where there is a large middle class—large enough ... to be stronger than both of the other classes...The reasons why democracies are generally more secure and more permanent than oligarchies is the ... middle class.... is more numerous and is allowed a larger share in the government than it is in oligarchies."*

The classical historian Plutarch in the first century observed that *"An imbalance between the rich and the poor is the oldest and most fatal ailments of all republics."*

Throughout much of our history, federal policy was based on a recognition that a democratic republic must be free from concentrations of economic power that characterized England in the eighteenth century. To help meet this ideal, our income and estate taxes have been the most progressive in the world. In addition to an income tax rate on high incomes over 60% from 1932 to 1981, our estate tax was 60% or larger on large estates from 1934 to 1983.[487] Policymakers determined that tax burdens should lie mostly on those with the greatest ability to pay, based not just on economic and moral considerations but also to reduce gross concentrations of wealth and entitlements through birth that characterized an aristocratic society, not a free and democratic society. Great wealth can buy political favors and elections with relatively small expenditures compared to the gains, destroying meaningful democracy. And it has largely purchased another essential component of a functioning democracy, our Fourth Estate.

In modern society, narrowly viewed self-interest has motivated some of the very wealthy to use their power to influence government to minimize taxation of extreme personal income and eliminate from consideration taxing extreme personal wealth. Their influence has also reduced the regulation and taxation of corporations (from which most derive their wealth), and the support of public goods or services. The wealthy can buy their own services rather than support widely beneficial public services. Their power is commonly used politically to oppose what is best for society.

In *Now Is the Time for The New Enlightenment* I describe the impact of our large "democracy deficit" resulting from our large economic disparities. The higher taxes of The New Enlightenment will support economic policies that will reduce it by giving tens of millions of people both more time and money to participate in our political system. They will also support The New Enlightenment political system and media policy reforms that will greatly improve democratic functioning.

Vast inequality of wealth is also socially destructive because it degrades relationships among people (cultural, social, political) and eventually undermines the sense of community needed for participation in a democratic society. This is particularly true in the United States, which is not bound by ties of ethnicity and culture.

When a progressive income tax was instituted during the Progressive Era (1890s to 1920s), its purpose was far more than to raise revenue in the most economically efficient manner. It was to serve the cause of social justice and to create a more democratic social order by curbing economic power. This Progressive Era had many of the wealthy and lower economic classes join together to serve this cause. They shared a view that wealth was being unjustly concentrated from causes related to the character of their newly created industrial economy.

The first income tax was instituted to fund the Civil War; it was abolished soon after. The income tax was reinstituted in 1894 and exempted the first $4,000 of income, which is equivalent to $110,000 in 2013. Although it had wide popular support, the Supreme Court declared it unconstitutional. A popular movement supporting the income tax eventually led to the 16th Amendment allowing the institution of the third income tax in 1913. It provided exemptions of $3,000 for singles and $4,000 for couples, $70,900 and $94,500 respectively in 2013 dollars. We were a much poorer country then, so it affected only about the top 2% of Americans.[488]

Unlike today, an important, influential fraction of the wealthy agreed that the great productivity advancements of their "progressive" era created unprecedented amounts of wealth that were being unjustly concentrated in a narrow economic elite, so they supported a tax that impacted only higher income households. Edward Filene, owner of the largest department store in the world in the early 1900s, said, *"Why shouldn't the American people take half my money, I took it all from them."* (Unfortunately, the probability that the owners of the largest department store in the world today, the Walmart heirs, who own the majority of Walmart stock and have wealth of $145 billion, will make a similar statement is zero.) Theodore Roosevelt said, *"The man of great wealth owes a peculiar obligation to the state, because he derives special advantages from the mere existence of government."*

The country today is facing a similar concentration of wealth and power, partly resulting from similar unjust characteristics of our new kind of rapidly advancing economy. In our case, great productivity advancements have resulted from the computer, automation, and other technological advancements. As we have seen, these advancements mostly result from commonly inherited knowledge and other social resources. Our percent concentration of wealth is similar to then, but the far larger amounts of wealth in our elite is resulting in a greater challenge to reduce our inequalities.

Although economic disparities are a cause of other disparities, other disparities also cause economic disparities, leading to a vicious downward spiral. In the Progressive Era, a larger proportion of the wealthy than today recognized this spiral and realized that *"we are all in this together."* This more common, culturally determined sentiment of the time resulted in an important fraction of the wealthy seeing the value of the government using the tax system to reduce disparities and serve the common good. The motivating principles of maximizing personal gain and minimizing any obligations to society are more dominant than they were in the Progressive Era. The degree of their dominance now is an ominous sign for the future well-being of the country.

Ronald Reagan's famous statement that *"government is the problem,"* was not sufficiently specific. *Bad* government is the problem. Good government is the solution to many problems and is a necessity for many reasons. Among the reasons is that without good government, we will be exposed to powerful harmful forces from corporations and individuals acting irresponsibly, even criminally.

Corporate managers of conventional corporations serve only one purpose: maximize corporate profits. Harming the public in the process, with any associated negative public relations value can be, and often is, considered just part of the cost of doing business. Harm can sometimes be hidden from public view when dysfunctional regulatory agencies and a dysfunctional press exist. Without government regulations of corporations, with fines for violating them whose costs are much larger than the savings resulting from ignoring them or criminal penalties when appropriate, exposure to harm by corporations would be far more prevalent. Among the harmful impacts will be those resulting from monopoly power and the abuse of extreme economic power to corrupt our political system to serve the few at the expense of the majority.

Recent Supreme Court decisions have greatly advanced the injustice of "free speech" being meaningfully available almost exclusively to wealthy individuals and corporations. These decisions have further degraded a political system corruptible by an economic elite. As a result, huge corporations and wealthy individuals are dominating both our economic and political systems to a significantly larger degree than they have in the past. If vast corporate wealth and the wealth of our top 0.1% continues to increase we will continue to diverge from a truly democratic society, eventually to where no check on private power will exist. We must correct a corporate form whose design flaws are a largely responsible for this ominous trend.

The compensation process for, and behavior of, CEOs of large corporations is one important driver of the dangerous rise in vast economic power in a small elite over the last few decades. In the 1950s, CEOs who laid off workers were seen as failures. Today, when they lay off workers, it is not uncommon that they are rewarded with higher salaries, higher stock option wealth, and bonuses. Also, if they hire effective lobbyists to reduce their company's taxes or get some regulatory advantage that harms the public, their pay typically increases.

CEOs in the 1950s would have been embarrassed to receive 350 times the salary of the average worker, as is common for S&P 500 corporations today. In 2011, Apple's Tim Cook received $378 million in salary, stock, and other benefits, 6,258 times the wage of an average Apple employee. A typical worker at Walmart earns less than $25,000 a year; Michael Duke, the retailer's former chief executive, was paid about a thousand times as much, over $23 million in 2012.

When cultural mores are not sufficient to control and are now even motivating behavior harmful to society, better laws, including those that would improve the structure of our economic system and the enterprises that comprise it, are needed to ensure more shared prosperity and motivate an awareness of our interdependence and shared destiny. New Enlightenment policies are designed to accomplish this and to create systems to facilitate further advancement.

Without a change in our priorities as a society, we will descend into conditions of far greater injustice and dysfunction. Sufficient numbers of the wealthy in the Progressive Era acknowledged the large degree of societal contribution to their wealth and worked to increase the support requirements of the very wealthy to society so that obstruction by others was a surmountable barrier. The motives for sufficient numbers our wealthy to do so are as com-pelling now as in the Progressive Era, due to the similarly large and increasing economic disparity resulting in great hardships in a substantial fraction of the population, and the growing economic and political system dysfunction.

It is not unreasonable to expect that a similarly important fraction of our wealthy as in the Progressive Era are intelligent and decent enough to see and act on the fact that without society they would have little or no wealth and that *"we are all in this together."* A widespread cultural focus of attention on these fundamental truths is needed. This will occur if The New Enlightenment Citizens Union or Party rises to prominence because promoting the awareness of, and acting on, these fundamental truths are their essential purposes, and there are currently no prominent cultural actors similarly focused.

Other Important Benefits That Will Result from Higher Taxes on High Income and Wealth

As I noted in Part 1, many studies suggest that a strong correlation exists be-tween income inequality and health, and inequality and social problems. Some have shown that inequality has a causal relation to health and social problems. One study suggests that the loss of life from income inequality in the U.S. in 1990, well before the much larger disparities we experience today, was the equivalent of the combined loss of life due to lung cancer, diabetes, motor vehicle accidents, HIV-related causes, suicide, and homicide.[489]

One explanation for income inequality's apparent effect on health and social problems is *"status anxiety."* Wide economic disparities exacerbate status competition and cause stress, which can lead to poor health and other negative outcomes. Some research has compared different groups in various countries and found that those in lower socioeconomic groups in more income equal countries sometimes do better than those in higher socioeconomic groups in more income unequal countries.

As noted previously, as inequality rises, societies tend to experience pro-portionately greater negative impacts on life expectancy, math proficiency, literacy, and trust, infant mortality rates, homicide rates, imprisonment rates, teenage births rates, obesity, mental illness, drug and alcohol addiction rates and social mobility.

Higher taxes on high income and wealth are necessary for the New En-lightenment programs to substantially reduce inequality.

Social Contribution to Wealth Creation: Additional Testimonies (continued from earlier in note 1):

Douglass North

Douglass North, Nobel laureate economist, also expressed the view that *"growth in the stock of knowledge"* is the fundamental underlying determinant of modern economic growth. *"Successful economic development will occur when the belief system that has evolved has created a 'favorable' artifactual structure* [knowledge, culture and their transmission mechanisms] *that can confront the novel experiences that the individual and society face and resolve positively the novel dilemmas...the beliefs that individuals, groups, and societies hold which determine choices are a consequence of learning through time-not just the span of an individual's life or of a generation of a society but the learning embodied in individuals, groups, and societies that is cumulative through time and passed on intergenerationally by the culture of a society."*

Kenneth J. Arrow

Kenneth J. Arrow, American Nobel laureate economist wrote: *"There are large gains to social interaction above and beyond what ... individuals and subgroups could achieve on their own... a surplus (is) created by the existence of 'society' as such which is available for redistribution."*

George Akerlof

Nobel laureate economist George Akerlof agrees that *"Our current standard of living ... is due almost entirely to the cumulative process of learning that has taken us from Stone Age poverty to twenty-first-century affluence"*

Brian Barry

Brian Barry, Professor Emeritus of Political Philosophy at Columbia University and Professor Emeritus of Political Science at the London School of Economics, emphasizes that this insight is especially important in advanced countries, where people are born into a wealth of *"productive capital, good systems of communications, orderly administration, well-developed systems of education and training, and so on...any claims that those now alive can make to special advantages derived from the efforts of their ancestors [are] quite limited."*

Theodore Roosevelt

President Theodore Roosevelt, in his groundbreaking "New Nationalism" speech of 1910 stated that the just and reasonable resolution of the *"conflict between the men who possess more than they have earned and the men who have earned more than they possess is the central condition of progress...The really big fortune, the swollen fortune, by the mere fact of its size acquires qualities which differentiate it in kind as well as in degree from what is possessed by men of relatively small means. Therefore, I believe in a graduated income tax on big fortunes, and ...a graduated inheritance tax on big fortunes...increasing rapidly in amount with the size of the estate."*

Joel Mokyr

Joel Mokyr, economic historian and former president of the Economic History Association, summarizes what should result in the good fortune of all of us this way: *"Knowledge is a pure public good...Increases in the stock of human knowledge, technological progress and changes of institutions has provided us with a 'free lunch'"* or *"an increase in output that is not commensurate with the increase in effort and cost necessary to bring it about."*

Joseph Stiglitz

Nobel laureate economist Joseph Stiglitz expressed this view: *"Just as the importance of land in production changed dramatically as the economy moved from agriculture to industry, so too does the movement to a knowledge economy necessitate a rethinking of economic fundamentals."* But as Gar Alperovitz (like many other scholars in this field) points out: *"We must now add the judgment that such a rethinking must include the question of what is contributed and what is inherited, what is earned and what is unearned, and, accordingly, who deserves what, and why?"*

Benjamin Franklin

Benjamin Franklin, one of the Founding Fathers of the United States has been called "The First American." A renowned political theorist, politician, scientist, inventor, civic activist, statesman, diplomat, author, and printer. As a scientist and political theorist, he was a major figure in the American Enlightenment. As I noted in The New Enlightenment wealth tax proposal he wrote on this subject as well:

"*All the Property that is necessary to a Man, for the Conservation of the Individual and the Propagation of the Species, is his natural Right, which none can justly deprive him of: But all Property superfluous to such purposes is the Property of the Publick, who, by their Laws, have created it, and who may therefore by other Laws dispose of it, whenever the Welfare of the Publick shall demand such Disposition. He that does not like civil Society on these Terms, let him retire and live among Savages. He can have no right to the benefits of Society, who will not pay his Club toward the Support of it.*"

In Summary

On moral and economic grounds, and to establish a well-functioning democratic republic, from those with large amounts of income and wealth a justifiable large debt is owed to our society, much of which is not now being paid. If it is paid to support New Enlightenment economic and social policies, transformative beneficial impacts beyond and including the economic and political will result. After we enact New Enlightenment taxes the contribution from the wealthiest in our society will have no significant impact on their privileged lifestyle, which is unprecedented in all of human history. Their contribution will be used wisely and for great benefit to all of society.

Now is the time to correct our course because our extreme, and growing, economic and political inequality is an existential threat. The ancient Greek philosopher Plutarch was correct when he wrote "*An imbalance between the rich and the poor is the oldest and most fatal ailments of all republics*"

Among the following notes are calculations required for selected New Enlightenment policies, where the required dataset is small.

Note 2: Economic Stimulus Including Employment Impact of All Policies

Dr. Mark Zandi of Moody Analytics estimates a GDP increase of $1.55 for every dollar spent on unemployment benefits. (Dr. Zandi is Moody's Analytics' chief economist and director of economic research. Moody's Analytics is a leading provider of economic research, data, and analytical tools. Dr. Zandi is a co-founder of Economy.com and is a commonly used advisor to policymakers.) The basic reason GDP increases more than the amount spent is expressed in this example: Assume that households consume 80% of any increase in their income and that the government increases its expenditure by

$20 billion. Any government spending is income of households in the form of wages, interest, rent, and profit. Since households will consume 80% of the increased income, they will increase their consumption by $16 billion (0.8 × $20 billion). The resulting $16 billion increase in incomes which will trigger another round of consumption amounting to $12.8 billion (0.8 × 0.8 × $20 billion), and so on. The resulting effect is that the GDP increases by more than the initial increase in government expenditures.

Dr. Zandi's 1.55 multiplier estimate is used for New Enlightenment additional federal expenditures, which mainly benefit people with the most restricted buying power. Based on the author's communication with Dr. Zandi's staff, the multiplier assumes the spending is not accompanied by tax increases. This multiplier is often used while ignoring this fact. But since New Enlightenment policies are designed to not increase the deficit (instead, they create hundreds of billions in surplus to eliminate the debt and the interest on it), an approximation of the countervailing impact of the required tax increases is needed. Increased taxes on the high income and wealth households will have a much smaller negative impact on GDP because it will reduce their consumption by far less than the tax amount, and for many people not reduce their consumption at all. For households with very high income most or all of the taxed amount is not used for consumption and instead is saved in banks or invested. Also, a substantial amount of the public revenues generated from New Enlightenment taxes is sourced from high levels of savings which are not being used for consumption.

The economy now needs increased demand for goods and services far more than investment or savings to increase GDP and demand for workers. Corporations have $4.75 trillion idle; they have no reason to invest it or to hire more workers because of the existing depressed demand for goods and services.

Even for people at the lower end of the income scale with increased taxes, the taxed amount will mainly reduce their savings, not spending (and so will not significantly affect their lifestyles).[490] Therefore, transfer payments through the New Enlightenment EITC to people with less than $50,000 per year income, most of whom spend all or almost all their income, will substantially increase consumption.

In the case of the inheritance tax, on average, little change in consumption will occur. It is possible that the distribution of the wealth of large estates will increase consumption despite the much higher average tax rate compared to that of inheritances under the current estate tax because it motivates distributing large numbers of relatively small inheritances to minimize the total tax paid that does not exist under the estate tax. A larger number of relatively small inheritances will result in a greater portion of the total value used for consumption than a few large inheritances.

Also, an increase in taxes on inherited wealth will induce some of the wealthy to increase their consumption because they can give to heirs less of what they save, and this will stimulate the economy.

The additional New Enlightenment taxes on corporate profits (directly and indirectly) will reduce consumption relatively little. Corporate profits have mainly been used for share buybacks, dividends, and cash reserves.[491] None of the consumption associated with investment in new facilities is involved in share buybacks. And about 75% of dividends go to just 1% of households, who save the majority of their income.

Some of the amount in various taxes and subsidy eliminations will likely be paid through a reduction of corporate profits. For example, taxes on pollution will put competitive products produced by businesses that do not create the pollution (or the products that create the pollution) at a relative advantage, forcing polluting businesses to reduce their profits.

Other increased taxes also are progressive, and overall the stimulus impact of all tax and expenditure policies would yield in total about a $1.35 trillion increase in GDP based on estimates I detail in the following table. There is about $109,000 GDP per employed person, so this GDP increase would result in hiring about 12.4 million full-time workers. But after accounting for the increase in the full-time workforce after the work-hour reduction, only 4.3 million workers would be officially unemployed. The 3.5 million unemployed "missing workers" are also available for full-time work, though. The total 7.8 million workers would not be sufficient to supply the needs, so unemployment would be eliminated, and a labor shortage may exist. Some companies may need to employ some workers over 36 hours per week at the overtime rate. More likely, though, more than the 3.5 million "missing workers" would enter the workforce. 14 million more workers would if the labor-force participation rate was the same as it was in 2000.[492]

The stimulus estimate has a significant degree of uncertainty, but surely the negative impact of the higher taxes on demand for goods and services will be substantially less than the positive impact of government expenditures they allow, which will be targeted in ways that will strongly stimulate the economy.

(The demand for goods and services increase that New Enlightenment government expenditures create will be in more environmentally sustainable ways. Eventually we will need further advancements in public policy focused on environmental considerations and resource limit considerations.)

Estimate ($billions)	Description	% negative impact on stimulus dollars	Negative impact on stimulus dollars
Tax increase or spending reduction, Stimulus reduction dollars estimate, (product of first and third column)			
-758	Income tax increase	60	-454.8
-516	Wealth Tax	10	-51.6
-241	Inheritance Tax	25	-60.3
-189	Eliminate $133,700 income Social Security tax cap	70	-132.3
-15.8	Fossil Fuel Subsidy Elimination	70	-11.1
-7.8	Nuclear Industry Subsidy Elimination	70	-5.5
-17.7	Agricultural Subsidy Elimination	70	-12.4
-2.5	Public Lands Policy Reform Revenue Savings and Gains	70	-1.8
-300	Financial Transactions Tax	50	-150.0
-8.1	Real Estate Transfer Tax	80	-6.5
-84	"Too Big to Fail" Bank Fee	25	-21.0
-350	Corporate Tax Reform Including Ending Tax Haven Abuse	20	-70.0
-161.5	Military Spending Reduction	80	-129.2
-70	Mortgage Interest Deduction Elimination	70	-49.0
-210	Carbon Tax	90	-189.0
-123	Anti-Poverty Program Expense Reduction Due to Poverty Reduction	100	-123.0
-40	Federal Unemployment Compensation Savings	100	-40.0
-2.8	Cigarette Tax	90	-2.5
-4.8	Alcohol Tax	90	-4.3
-24.1	Equal Charge Tax for Nuclear Power	70	-16.9
-7.9	Toxic Releases Tax	70	-5.5
-3.1	Airline Fees	90	-2.8
	Total stimulus reduction dollars		-1539

($billions)	Expenditures, Full stimulus dollars
Estimate	**Description**
6.3	Journalism subsidies
904	Income Supplements
420	Worker half payroll tax elimination
300	Infrastructure, Public Works (Estimate Per Year for 10 Years.)
3	Reemployment System
143	Grants, Tax and SBA Expenditures to Promote Worker-ownership
382	Social Security Plus
138	Free College Education
90	Elementary and Secondary Education
8.7	Public Defenders and Inmate Rehabilitation
2.3	Candidate Postage Cost Subsidy
1.7	"Primary" Candidate Newspaper Subsidy
2.2	New Democratic Forms
11.1	Free Municipal Broadband Subsidy
2412	**Total stimulus dollars**

Total stimulus dollars (billions)	Total stimulus reduction dollars (billions)	Total effective stimulus dollars	GDP increase (multiplier times effective stimulus $)
2412	-1539	873	1353
	(Stimulus multiplier)	1.55	
GDP increase		**Revenue increase from GDP increase**	
1353	0.2	271	
$109,000 GDP per employed person so this GDP increase would increase employment by this much:		**million people**	
1.353×10^{12}	1.09×10^{5}	1.24×10^{7}	12.4
(dollars)	(dollars/person)		

Note 3: Simultaneous Invention

A study published in the Academy of Political Science's Political Science Quarterly by William Ogburn and Dorothy Thomas in 1922 found 148 major inventions and discoveries that had been made independently by two or more individuals or groups at the same time. In 1960, a similar study by Columbia University sociology professor Robert Merton led him to conclude that *"the pattern of independent multiple discoveries in science is in principle the dominant pattern, rather than a subsidiary one."* 90 to 98% of patent lawsuits are filed against independent inventors and not copiers. Even the idea that multiple simultaneous invention is the norm was advanced by multiple independent groups at the same time.

Isaac Newton and Gottfried Leibniz independently invented calculus. Three mathematicians "invented" decimal fractions. Logarithms were invented by John Napier and Henry Briggs in Britain and by Joost Bürgi in Switzerland. Other simultaneous discoveries in mathematics include the law of inverse squares, the principle of least squares and non-Euclidean geometry (an essential part of Einstein's general theory of relativity). Oxygen was discovered by Joseph Priestley in Wiltshire, England in 1774, and by Carl Wilhelm Scheele in Uppsala, Sweden a year earlier. Other simultaneous discoveries in chemistry include the: the law of gases, the discovery of boron and other elements (aluminum was "discovered" by a few different people over the centuries) and molecular theory. In addition to the light bulb, other simultaneous inventions related to electricity include the Leyden jar (precursor to capacitors), the induction coil, electric motors, and electric trains. Color photography was invented at the same time by Charles Cros and by Louis Ducos du Hauron, in France. There were four independent discoveries of sunspots in 1611, by Galileo in Italy, Scheiner in Germany, Fabricius in Holland and Harriott in England.[493]

The law of the conservation of energy, so significant in science and philosophy, was formulated four times independently in 1847, by Joule, Thomson, Colding and Helmholz. It is recognized now, though, that Robert Mayer "discovered" the law in 1842. There were at least six inventors of the thermometer and nine of the telescope. Typewriters were invented simultaneously in England and in America by several individuals. The steamboat is claimed as the "exclusive" discovery of Fulton, Jouffroy, Rumsey, Stevens, and Symmington. Some simultaneous discoveries in medicine include the germ theory of disease, anesthetics, and MRI technology.

Simultaneous independent inventions and discoveries also include the airplane, photography, the telegraph (five people), pendulum clock, microscope, sewing machine, phonograph, and microphone.

An "invention" is generally a combination of previously existing technology in new ways. These new ways are often not great leaps. Sometimes genius can make great leaps, but even then, the leap is modest compared to what was built upon. And these great leaps are motivated intrinsically, not extrinsically.

Note 4: Response of High-Income Taxpayers to Tax Rate Changes

In a 1995 paper, Martin Feldstein, Harvard economist and President Reagan's chair of the Council Of Economic Advisors, (whose faulty analysis of our health system cost problem I described previously) concluded that cuts in marginal tax rates in 1986 led to a *"dramatic increase in taxable income,"* particularly for high-income taxpayers. Feldstein relied on a Wall Street Journal op-ed arguing that a deficit-reduction package should cut marginal income tax rates, rather than raise them. More recent literature has pointed out major flaws in Feldstein's 1995 paper and others like it:

Former Congressional Budget Office and Office of Management and Budget director Peter Orszag noted that Feldstein's study overlooked that high-income taxpayers' incomes were rising substantially for other reasons, such as a large drop in energy prices and interest rates over the study period.

Tax scholar Reuven Avi-Yonah has summarized the more recent literature as showing:

- The compensation of the rich can easily be moved to a different taxable year, so observed changes in taxable income reflect timing rather than long-lasting behavioral responses to tax changes.
- The rich have incomes that tend to surge in times when demand is increasing. The tax cuts of the 1986 Tax Reform Act were enacted in a period of strong economic growth resulting from energy price and interest rate declines and other factors unrelated to tax rates. Income increases for the rich appeared as tax responsiveness, but other factors were involved.

The former chairman of the President's Council of Economic Advisors, Austan Goolsbee, estimates that these factors cut the estimates of how much high-income taxpayers respond to tax changes by over 75%.

Similarly, economists Roger Gordon and Joel Slemrod suggest that natural experiments around the 1986 Act are misleading because they reflect shifting of income from corporations, whose rates went up, to individuals, whose rates went down. They also emphasized that studies like Feldstein's track changes in taxable income over short periods of time and thus cannot ascertain whether a short-term increase in reported income is due to an increase in actual income or to a change in when income is derived and in how much of it is reported.

In addition, the 1986 tax reform law not only cut marginal rates but also broadened the tax base significantly, so the subsequent increase in reported taxable income also reflects that the new tax rules required more complete reporting of income. The Congressional Research Service suggests that insufficiently adjusting for this base broadening is another important reason some studies have shown that changes in taxable income were much greater after the 1986 tax reform than after other tax changes.

Note 5: Most Extreme Tax Increase Proposal

In 1942, to pay for the war effort, President Franklin D. Roosevelt said, *"No American citizen ought to have a net income, after he has paid his taxes, of more than $25,000* (about $358,000 in 2013 dollars).*"* Imagine the reaction if a modern president said that no American should have an income, after taxes, over $358,000, or a tax rate of 100% for amounts over $358,000. (Would a modern day president want to risk seeming so cruel as to make a proposal that predictably might send many members of Congress (and most of our talk show hosts) into a fatal apoplexy?)

President George W. Bush went to war twice without once calling for shared sacrifice to pay for it. Obviously, World War II was of a different scale but why is asking a relatively small increase in taxes from our citizens most able to pay them for the common good now out of bounds for most of our policymakers? Decades of false propaganda on the harmfulness of higher taxes on high incomes has succeeded.

With New Enlightenment income tax rates, some individuals will still have after-tax annual incomes in the hundreds of millions, and some in the billions of dollars (as some have had in the recent past). The proposed rates are below prior rates enacted, and maintained for decades.

Note 6: Revenue Resulting from Proposed Corporate Tax System Estimate

(billions)   **Rough, "ballpark" estimate based on data below**

540	Trade deficit 2012
16,600	The United States' GDP estimate 2012
17,100	Total value of all final goods and services sold in U.S.
85,000	GWP (gross world product) estimate 2012
.202	Fraction of world final goods and services sales in U.S.
.061	2012 profit rate of corporations taxable at the corporate level *
22,300	Total sales of US corporations taxable at the corporate level*
1.34	Total sales of US corporations corporate level taxable/GDP
114,000	Total world sales corporate level taxable assuming same ratio as U.S.
6,960	Total world profits corporate level taxable businesses assuming U.S. rate
1,400	Total profits U.S. taxable
492	.35 X above
772	.55 X above
201	Actual tax paid
291	**Additional tax for 0.35 tax rate**
572	**Additional tax for 0.55 tax rate**

* Based on IRS Table 1. Number of Returns, Total Receipts, Business Receipts, Net Income (less deficit), Net Income, and Deficit by Form of Business Tax Years 1980-2012

Detailed District Economics Group's (DEG) 2010 estimate results

550	.35 tax revenue estimate
864	.55 tax revenue estimate based on DEG
204	Actual tax paid
346	**Additional tax for 0.35 tax rate**
660	**Additional tax for 0.55 tax rate**

Note 7: Descriptions of Some Well-Studied Worker-Owned and Controlled Enterprises

Below I describe, with New Enlightenment recommendations, the most studied WSDE examples. During the debates on how best to proceed with the transformation to an economic system where worker controlled and owned business enterprises are the predominant business enterprise structure in the country, it will be important to understand the basic character of these well studied and other well-studied examples. The examples described include the Plywood Cooperatives in the Pacific Northwest, the Mondragon Cooperatives of Spain, and the Lega Cooperatives of Italy.[494] (In most cases, I use co-op and WSDE interchangeably here.)

Plywood Cooperatives

In the period 1942-57, the plywood industry cooperatives in the Pacific Northwest of the U.S. accounted for about 20% to 25% of total national plywood industry production capacity. Although their numbers have declined substantially, in line with the decline of this industry in the Pacific Northwest generally, some continue to operate.

These co-ops in most cases train all workers to do every job in the plant except for specialized functions, such as machine maintenance and accounting, and all worker-owners normally receive an equal hourly wage. Most jobs do not require an amount of training that would lead to significant productivity losses due to the training time. It is likely that because of the skills acquired allowing individuals to have varying work experiences or the reduction of burdensome monotony, productivity was enhanced.

[We recommend that co-ops formed as a result of New Enlightenment policies consider implementing a similar practice for jobs that would not require large amounts of training of some workers to be able to perform the work of others. We do not recommend equal pay as a general practice in co-ops that require worker skills, training, and sacrifices of varying levels, as would most often be the case. Democratic processes described in Policy 3 will determine worker wages.] The plywood co-ops made exceptions to their equal pay rule, for the general manager and others not directly involved with production, to reduce the wage disparity with conventional firms.

The plywood co-ops rely on mutual monitoring among members to ensure that all workers give their best efforts in their work performance. Mutual monitoring and sharing the economic benefits of their work resulted in a substantially reduced need to employ supervisors compared to similar conventional mills.

In a typical coop's governance structure, authority is shared equally by all worker-owners who meet annually to elect directors from among the worker-owners and to approve large capital expenditures, admission of new members, and other proposals. Every worker-owner has an equal vote regardless of invested capital. [New Enlightenment Policy 3 associates equal power sharing with equal ownership.]

The directors hire the general manager, who has authority over day-to-day operations. There are usually committees dealing with innovation, grievances, and other matters. Members may see whatever data or documents they wish and routinely exercise this right. In all plywood co-ops, any resale of shares is limited to potential mill workers. Usually, the firm has a first right to buy a departing owner's share at the current market price. If the firm chooses not to exercise this right, the transfer to a new owner must be approved by a majority either of the board of directors or a meeting of the membership. A probationary period is normally required unless the new member is already working in the mill. [I recommend all of these practices as guidelines; most are similar to the other well studied and successful cooperatives.]

The typical size of the co-op is similar to conventional mills, 200-300 workers. This figure includes hired non-owners, which according to one study was 16-36% of the workforce, which included newcomers planning to buy a share, and a few highly skilled (and paid) tradespeople, such as electricians and specialists in machine maintenance. [In the New Enlightenment's recommended structure, non-owner workers are limited to 10% of the workforce comprised of specialists whose services would not be needed on a full-time basis or needed temporarily excluding workers in their probationary or trial period of nine months.]

Some researchers found that managers sometimes had a difficult time because members sometimes felt free to ignore their instructions, causing high manager turnover rates and an inability to plan for the future. So more cooperative management decision-making and clear guidelines must be established to allow the disciplining of workers acting destructively or unproductively. Better functioning decision-making and disciplinary policies are described in the following section on the Mondragon Cooperatives.

The plywood co-ops deserve to be counted as a success story. Their decline in numbers does not reflect deficiencies in their organizational form, but rather a long-term contraction of the regional industry. The remaining co-ops have survived for several decades in competition with unionized mills run by large corporations (Weyerhaeuser, Georgia-Pacific. Boise Cascade), and numerous smaller mills owned by individual proprietors.

Mondragon Cooperatives

The renowned Mondragon Cooperative Corporation (MCC), an umbrella organization for a group of cooperatives, has developed into the world's first transnational worker cooperative, and it's the tenth largest private firm in Spain, with 2012 revenues of 14 billion euros ($19.3 billion). It has grown from about 30,000 workers in 1997 to over 83,000 full-time workers and over 15,000 part-time workers in 289 cooperatives in four sectors: industry, finance, retail and knowledge, in 2013. Each year, MCC teaches about 10,000 students in its education centers, and it has roughly 2,000 researchers working at 15 research centers in the University of Mondragón and its industrial cooperatives.

MCC's bank, Caja Laboral Popular (CLP), is its pivotal institution. Other cooperatives apply for membership by signing a Contract of Association with the CLP, and receive financial and technical assistance. The contract requires a co-op to submit a balance sheet and annual budget to the CLP, with monthly updates in a standard format. Each co-op is comprehensively audited at least once every four years. Affiliated co-ops conduct all banking and financial operations through the CLP, and deposit their surplus funds there.

[Community credit unions and banks, local citizen bond purchasers, and the city and federal governments will serve the financial needs of cooperatives in the New Enlightenment WSDE establishment systems. The important advisory role of the CLP we will substitute with an expansion of Small Business Administration services, bondholders and other community members at the annual bondholder meetings, and the Council of Cooperatives.]

Authority within a Mondragon Cooperative is vested in the General Assembly of its worker-owners, which meets at least once per year. All decisions are based on one vote per person, with no one other than a worker-owner having a vote. The Assembly elects a "Governing Council" (board of directors) from within its ranks to four-year terms. Although nine members is common, the size of the board can vary from three to twelve members. The council is composed of regular workers, generally from a wide variety of job categories, who perform their directorship duties on their regular work time for no extra pay. The Council meets at least once per month and appoints managers for a term of four years, with renewal contingent on a performance review.

Managers cannot be dismissed except for extraordinary reasons and with the approval of the General Assembly. Mutual monitoring and the fact that workers share in the economic benefits of their work has resulted in a greatly reduced need to employ supervisors, as in the plywood cooperatives. Only in exceptional circumstances was a cooperative allowed to employ non-members, and these were limited to 10% of the workforce (usually people with special skills needed temporarily).

The governance structure also includes several bodies that are mainly advisory. A Social Council elected by the membership deals with safety, wages, grievances, and related issues. Serious disciplinary problems are reportedly rare. Penalties can include suspension, loss of income for up to sixty days, or in extreme cases, expulsion. [These practices are good guidelines, and used in the New Enlightenment system.] At Mondragon, there are agreed-upon wage ratios between executive work and field or factory work, which earns the coop's minimum wage. These ratios range from 3:1 to 9:1 in different cooperatives and average 5:1.

The general manager of an average Mondragon cooperative earns five times as much as the theoretical minimum wage paid in his or her cooperative. In reality, this ratio is smaller because few Mondragon worker-owners earn minimum wages, as most jobs are somewhat specialized and classified at higher wage levels. The highest to lowest wage ratio of a cooperative is decided periodically by its worker-owners through a democratic vote.

The Management Council, which consists of top managers and executives, sometimes augmented by outsiders, advises to the Governing Council. A "Watchdog Council" consists of three elected members of the general assembly. It monitors everyone else.

Applicants are screened carefully not only for skill and education, but also for their degree of social integration into the community, with a six-month probationary period. A strong emphasis is on socialization into the ethics of cooperation.

Wages are formally viewed as advances on anticipated profits. The position of any individual member on the wage scale depends on a system of points awarded for qualifications, responsibility, hard or dangerous work, and social integration. The precise weights vary across co-ops, depending on circumstances.

After deducting wages, interest, and depreciation from net income, a minimum of 20% is allocated to a Collective Reserve Fund, which is used for reinvestment or to help support the co-op in down times. 70% is credited to the individual capital accounts of the members in proportion to their wages and 10% is allocated to a social fund for community projects. As the level of profit increases, the fraction set aside for mandatory reserves grows. When losses occur, no more than 30% of these losses is covered out of reserves; any remaining losses are debited from individual accounts. On voluntary departure, workers are given their individual account balance, but if the capital withdrawal is a threat to the enterprise it could result in a penalty of up to 30%.

In 1974, conflicts over co-op management led to the conclusion that future cooperatives in the group should not grow past 500 members, to preserve the desired level of democratic participation by all workers. Instead, scale economies are gained by gathering individual co-ops into groups based on geography or product line.

Most observers agree that because of international competition, the Mondragon cooperatives have commonly imitated workplace organizational trends practiced in traditional firms, such as division of labor and a management hierarchy. But their more democratically determined management structure, ongoing feedback mechanisms, and participatory decision-making on major proposals provide important advantages, some that manifested in the worldwide recession of the early 1980s. The co-ops accepted low margins, and workers agreed to cut wages, which helped in gaining international market share. Studies have found that cooperatives can react more quickly and equitably to crises, such as the recent financial crisis, because workers decide *themselves* to cut wages, or cut hours, or take unpaid leave, to avoid layoffs. Also, the delays of formal negotiations with labor unions are eliminated.

For the purpose of greater integration of all co-ops in 1984, a new supervisory body was created, the Cooperative Congress, along with a new top management body, the Council of Groups. These new institutions facilitated organizing co-ops according to both geographic region and product line to achieve economies of scale and other synergies. Some of these changes were controversial because some felt they separated top management from the workforce. Mondragon has retained democratic internal structures at the level of the individual co-ops though, and in a less direct way at the level of the MCC as a whole.

For cultural and historical reasons, and due to the different funding mechanism of co-ops in our proposal, the extent or method of the cooperation of the co-ops in the Mondragon structure would likely not be practical here, at least initially, but I suggest an integrative mechanism of similar advantages. One "Council of Cooperatives" (CC) will be established per city, or region if city size is inappropriately small, to serve some integrative purposes.

Also, after establishing WSDEs under our policy for two years, we will promote the establishment of additional support institutions: An annual National Cooperative Congress and a national cooperative research and development institution. For more details on these institutions, see The Way to

Prosperity for All, Policy 3.

Researchers have found that one of the most important reasons for the success of the Mondragon cooperatives is that even the smallest of them is both assisted and disciplined by various sources of management services. Another reason for Mondragon's explosive growth in its first decades appears to be that the CLP had too much capital, rather than too little. Spanish banking laws of the 1950s allowed cooperative banks to pay a slightly higher interest rate to depositors than other banks, giving it an advantage in attracting savings. The result was that the group's growth in the late Sixties and early Seventies was bank driven. The cooperatives probably would not have been able to finance their development from other, more conventional sources.

The governmental grants and loans and the interest-free bond policy, which essentially allows the co-op to pay a slightly higher interest rate to investors than other corporations and banks, support New Enlightenment WSDEs. Also, supports include the lower FED funds rate to credit unions and WSDE banks for supplying funds to WSDEs. These supports will give New Enlightenment co-ops larger advantages than the Mondragon co-ops have for expansion and development. The CC, bondholder meetings, the CDA, SBA, and possibly credit unions would be sources of management advice in our proposal. Established WSDEs seeking expansion, including through absorption of conventional firms, could offer bonds to finance the expansion with the same tax advantages as in our WSDE establishment proposal.

Lega Cooperatives

In contrast to the plywood cooperatives and Mondragon, which developed with little state involvement, the Italian cooperative movement has been supported with tax advantages, preferential access to public land and contracts, job creation programs, loans and grants, and the financial expertise of public banking and research institutions. The National League of Cooperatives and Mutual Aid Societies, the Lega, had 11,398 member co-ops in 1989 (including consumer co-ops not generally under workers' control) and 3.4 million individuals as members. It directly employed 230,734 workers and accounted for 2.73% of national GDP. By the mid-1980s, the Lega, had become the fourth-highest export earner in Italy after Fiat, Montedison, and Olivetti. It now has 14,500 member co-ops.

Manufacturing activities include ceramics, machinery, rubber products, furniture, and high-tech equipment. Non-manufacturing activities include construction, food catering, and health services. The larger manufacturing and construction cooperatives in the Lega have 500 to 3,000 workers, but even in these fields, smaller firms are more common. Lega's construction cooperatives averaged 269 employees, and engineering and metalworking cooperatives averaged 135, with most other manufacturing activities in the 40 to 75 range. Among Lega service firms, cleaning and maintenance co-ops averaged 267 workers, restaurant co-ops averaged 188, and the rest were much smaller.

The Lega Cooperatives are in Italy's Emilia Romagna region, home to a population of 3.9 million people (7% of the national population). At the end of the Second World War, the region lay in economic ruin. The formation of cooperatives transformed the region from one of the poorest to one of the most prosperous in Italy and Europe. Per capita income is 50% higher than the national average. The unemployment rate was 4% in 2003, and after the international financial crisis in 2009, it was 5.7%, the lowest in Italy.[495]

As in the Mondragon cooperatives, after deducting wages, interest, and depreciation from net income, the Lega cooperatives allocate a minimum of 20% to a Collective Reserve Fund, which is used for reinvestment or to help support the co-op in down times. These funds cannot be recouped by individuals leaving the firm. No more than 20% can supplement wages, and the remainder is used for social security. Within these rules, Lega co-ops are governed by a general assembly of the membership that meets annually. The general assembly elects a "council" or board of directors for a 2-year term and approves the firm's budget and decides on other major proposals. This council chooses a president from among its members and appoints a management board to implement its decisions.

The council meets weekly or every other week to oversee the activities of the management board. Workers can join the co-op after a probationary period. All employees, whether or not they are co-op members, also vote for a separate works council to represent them in wage and working condition negotiations. In the larger cooperatives, base pay is set through collective bargaining involving an industrial union.

The Lega supervises, monitors performance and provides legal and accounting services to member co-ops. It also facilitates sharing technical information, lobbies government on behalf of member co-ops, and assists in creating of new co-ops or the creation of co-ops from conventional firms. Each cooperative elects representatives to regional congresses, and there is a hierarchy of congresses and officials system that would likely not be applicable in the U.S., at least initially. Individual cooperatives are autonomous and may join or leave the Lega. Lega lacks strong authority over member co-ops.

Studies have found that Lega co-ops have far lower wage disparities relative to private firms and fewer managers as a fraction of the workforce, higher value added per person per hour worked and per unit of fixed capital, many fewer strikes and days per worker lost to absenteeism, and lower quit rates.

The Lega experience proves that it is possible to create a large, vibrant cooperative sector using government legislative and financial support. The Mondragon and Lega cases both indicate that a successful workers' cooperative sector requires an institutional mechanism for the routine creation of co-ops, either new or through conversion of capitalist firms. No such mechanism existed after the initial burst of cooperative formation in the U.S. plywood industry, and this contributed to the decline in the population of plywood co-ops during the last half century. The New Enlightenment Policy 3 provides such mechanisms.

Note 8: The Postal Service

The Postal Service is an example of a public institution that is more efficient than private ones. It remains financially solvent without public subsidies while continuing to offer services at low rates, despite its mandate to serve all of the public, no matter where they are. Unlike private corporations that operate only in areas where they can make a profit, the Postal Service serves everyone. The USPS is the second-largest employer in the United States, after Walmart. It has about 550,000 career and 100,000 non-career employees. At its peak, there were nearly 900,000 employees.

In some rural and low-income urban areas, the post office is the only institution that connects those communities to services and to the rest of the world. It provides services such as money orders where there are no banks and copying where there are no office stores. Through the Carrier Alert program, postal carriers even look after members of the community. Disabled and elderly residents can register with the program, and their local postal carrier will check in with them six days a week. If a problem is noticed, carriers can connect them to local service agencies for help. In rural communities, the local post office often serves as a lifeline.

The Postal Service is one of our oldest institutions; it's the only one explicitly mentioned in the Constitution, in Article 1, Section 8, the Postal Clause. For most of its history, it was funded through taxes and income. Postal subsidies for the press were of essential importance to our democracy in its early history.

In addition to requiring self-funding since the early 1980s, in 2006, Congress passed a bill that mandated that the USPS pre-fund 75 years of retirement funds, including health benefits, within a ten-year period. At the same time, Congress restricted the rates that the USPS could charge. This amounts to $5.5 billion that must be put aside during that period. No other business or institution is required to pre-fund retiree benefits that far in advance, and only about one-third of Fortune 1000 businesses engage in any pre-funding.

If the pre-funding mandate did not exist, the USPS could have invested in expanding its services and creating more jobs with living wages and benefits. And the USPS also could have modernized and moved in a more sustainable direction by transitioning to a "green" fleet of vehicles.

E-commerce depends on the USPS because it is the only entity that has the physical infrastructure in place to deliver to every home and business in the country.

The goal for some policymakers is to privatize the Postal Service to enhance the profits and wealth of the corporate interests in the mail industry. In Europe, this trend progressed for 15 years, and now all government Post Office services have been privatized. A report by Global Research, "Deregulating and Privatizing Postal Services in Europe," described the results: "With few exceptions, the new competitors emerging from the liberalized market never opened post offices or installed letter boxes. Instead, they pick up mail directly at the premises of their mostly large corporate customers. As for mail delivery, they typically deliver only two or three days a week, and only in highly populated areas." For the public, services declined and prices increased.

Note 9: "Government of the People Act" (GPA) Defects:

The GPA allows unlimited contributions from parties

Although required to come from a separate party fund that accepts only small contributions, the major political parties will be able to focus relatively huge amounts of money collected nationally to the candidates in the minor fraction of the general election congressional races that are truly contested, thereby unfairly and extremely diminishing third-party and independent candidate opportunities. Historically, third-party candidates have played critical roles in our democracy by introducing popular and groundbreaking issues eventually co-opted by major parties, only because these candidates and their parties were a real threat to the major parties.

Presumably, reducing the influence of money in elections to the degree the Act does will somewhat reduce our "democracy deficit," but not sufficiently, because third-party candidates and other candidates will remain unjustly disadvantaged. As I noted previously, a 2013 Gallup poll found that 60% of Americans believe that the Republican and Democratic parties "*do such a poor job that a major third-party is needed.*" That's the highest Gallup has measured in the 10-year history of this question. Our Founders were opposed to the government and political system being organized into parties of the kind we have in the major parties.

The GPA subsidy qualifying requirement to get a minimum of 1000 contributions totaling at least $50,000 in a 180-day period disadvantages third parties

The Act proposes no system that will equitably give all candidates the opportunity to be evaluated by voters to determine those most worthy of this support. In the general election, an incumbent and the opposing major party candidate have the organizational resources and media access to relatively easily get this level of support, again disadvantaging third-party and independent candidates. An excellent third-party or independent candidate with superior policy proposals, generally cannot get mass media coverage and is less likely to get the organizational support that major parties can provide to gain the level of financial support needed to qualify for the subsidies.

The GPA multiplies the mass media exposure and the organizational size advantage of major party candidates

Even where third-party candidates qualify for the subsidy, they would be disadvantaged because the subsidies are six or nine times (depending on other restrictions) the amount of contributions under $150. Due to the far greater mass media exposure and the organizational size advantage, major party candidates will be able to get larger numbers and total amounts of contributions under $150. Either the six or nine times subsidy will proportionately multiply a disparity in donation amount, so it multiplies the disparity in the power between the major party and other candidates to communicate with voters.

For example, if a major party candidate gets $500,000 in donations and an independent or minor party candidate gets $50,000, after the subsidies, if each qualified for the nine times subsidy, the major party candidate would get $4.5 million and the other candidate $450,000 in subsidy. That's over a $4 million advantage for the major party candidate. If the initial donation amounts were doubled or tripled, the advantage would be over $8 million or $12 million. When dollars are proportional to power to communicate the current power structure will be maintained.

The GPA primary election subsidies often will unfairly advantage major parties:

Primary elections are also subsidized under the Government of the People Act. This will unfairly advantage major parties by giving the winner mass media exposure, both throughout the primary campaign and after winning that some third-party nominees will not have because third parties often do not have primaries.

The bill does not address ballot access

For reasons described in The New Enlightenment ballot access policy, we need national ballot access standards that are fair and reasonable as part of any election system reform. Currently, ballot access requirements unfairly limit third-party candidates' access.

New Enlightenment election system proposals have fair and reasonable national ballot access regulations, and an equitable system to evaluate candidates for generous allotments of airtime, postage, and other subsidies. The generous allotment of airtime system does not require government funds.

Note 10: Analogous Examples to 400 People Having the Wealth of 190 Million People

The following are proportional analogies to our situation of 400 people having the wealth of 190 million people. On average, a person in the top 400 has wealth 475,000 times that of a person in the bottom 190 million. In all of these examples, the same proportions exist.

Analogy 1

A government receives international aid of 475,000 pounds of rice to help alleviate famine in a population of 475,010 people. The government distributes it, giving ten people 431,818 pounds of rice or 43,181.8 pounds per person, then distributes the remaining 43,182 pounds to the remaining 475,000 people. So each of these 475,000 people on average receives 0.091 pounds, or 1.5 ounces. This provides well under one-tenth of minimum daily caloric requirements. Not one of the ten people receiving 431,818 pounds can eat 43,181.8 pounds of rice. This situation would not be sustainable. It could be sustained only as long as people tolerate being taxed to support a non-democratic government that creates these conditions and maintains them with a system of laws, law enforcement personnel, and prisons.

Analogy 2

A ship goes out to sea on a 20-day voyage with 28,620 pounds of food rations, three pounds per person per day for 477 people. The captain stashes 28,605.7 pounds of the food rations for himself and his wife and the rest of the ship has access to 14.3 pounds, or .03 pounds (.48 ounces) each for the trip. The 28,605.7 pounds of the food for the captain and his wife allows each to eat 715.1 pounds of food per day. The captain cannot eat 715.1 pounds of food per day, neither can his wife, and many of the other people on the ship will not survive on their less than about .0015 pounds, or .024 ounces per day. The social structure of this ship will not be stable. (How is that for an understatement?) Obviously, 475 people on board would not tolerate these conditions.

Analogy 3

Visualize the distance of one inch and let this represent the wealth of a person with the average wealth of the least wealthy 190 million Americans. Then the wealth of a person with the average wealth of the wealthiest 400 Americans is a distance of 7.5 miles.

Analogy 4

Here is a proportional analogy by weight:

Imagine lying down with a nickel on your chest. If you are wearing a shirt, you would barely feel it. The nickel's weight represents the wealth of a person with the average wealth of the least wealthy 190 million Americans. If you then put the weight representing the wealth of a person with the average wealth of the wealthiest 400 on your chest, you could feel it, but not long because you would be crushed by 5,236 pounds, about the weight of two Toyota Corollas.

"There should exist among the citizens neither extreme poverty nor, again, excessive wealth, for both are productive of great evil . . . Now the legislator should determine what is to be the limit of poverty or of wealth."

Plato, "Father of Western Philosophy"

"Happy for us, that when we find our constitutions defective and insufficient to secure the happiness of our people, we can assemble with all the coolness of philosophers, and set it to rights."

Thomas Jefferson, Founder, fourth president of the United States, Enlightenment philosopher

Afterword

The Princeton University researcher's analysis of the governmental response on 1,779 policy issues over recent decades indicates that we are in the midst of an emergency if we care about living in a democracy. Even when large majorities of Americans favor a policy change, if elites oppose it, they generally do not get it. America now is a society ruled by, and exclusively serves the interests of, the wealthy and corporations. We do not live in a true democracy or a society organized in the interests of its people. And as our political system has increasingly poorly served the majority, so have our economy and our media.

Some of our Founders and greatest presidents, and many scholars and visionaries throughout history, warned against highly concentrated economic power as a threat to democracy, and even an existential threat. We did not heed their warnings, and now the threat is real. Our mutually reinforcing historic levels of political and economic inequality are resulting in a vicious cycle downward. Already major injustices and systemic dysfunctions have manifested, and the trends are ominous. Now, to save our nation, we must break the vicious cycle and create a true democratic republic. A democratic republic will achieve Jefferson's stated ideal for governments: *"The greatest good for the greatest number,"* so we never fully had one, but we face uniquely powerful forces diminishing what we have had, and obstructing advancement.

This time is especially dangerous because of the historic levels of wealth in our modern day economic elite. And this wealth is even greater than official statistics indicate because unreported financial assets held in tax havens are as much as $32 trillion or a third of all global wealth. In the U.S., historic top incomes are also larger than official statistics show because a significant amount of capital income is not reported because it is tax exempt.

John Adams pointed out over 200 years ago the universal truth we see manifest today, *"Power always follows property,"* or financial resources in the modern world. Other than essentially buying the election of policymakers and otherwise directly dominating our public policymaking process, with just a tiny fraction of the wealth available to them, this power is wielded through media with historic levels of concentration in the hands of a segment of this elite, with interests commonly far removed from majority interests. Control a nation's media, and you largely control the nation's social structure—another reason ours is serving elite interests, at the expense of the majority.

And certainly the power of concentrated wealth as vast as it is now in one-tenth of our "1%" is harmfully wielded in other ways, both known and unknown.

Many people have not been exposed to the facts, others have and refused to see their significance, and others knew major change was needed but felt powerless because a direction to a superior society was unclear. This book provides a clear direction. You may consider it an invitation to a more prosperous and far more just and democratic society. But for us to get to it, we will have to take the journey together.

Only a mass movement can accomplish major change, and our mass media are not likely to be helpful, so the journey will be long before we reach our destination. The first step is to use your real and virtual social networks to tell others about this book, the policies described in it, and the organization devoted to seeing them instituted.

Let this time of crises be a time of opportunity to revitalize and reinvent institutions to serve our ideals of Democracy, Human Rights, Reason, and Progress—a time for a New Enlightenment.

Robert Bivona

It is time for a New Enlightenment.
Will you be a part of it?

THE NEW ENLIGHTENMENT

The Stakes Are Too High for You Not to Join Us

Innovative, Effective, Efficient Ways to a New Day	**Our Time for Greatness**

Be a part of the
New Enlightenment Citizens Union
Only a mass movement can result in the institution of New Enlightenment policies.
The New Enlightenment Citizens Union will be the organizational foundation of this movement.
It needs your support.

www.newenlightenment.us

Endnotes

[1] http://www.gallup.com/poll/1600/congress-public.aspx

[2] Congress Still Ranks Low in the Public's Eyes, Rasmussen Reports, 1/3/15 http://www.rasmussenreports.com/public_content/archive/mood_of_america_archive/congressional_performance/congress_still_ranks_low_in_the_public_s_eyes

[3] More Americans Struggle to Afford Food, 9/12/13, Alyssa Brown http://www.gallup.com/poll/164363/americans-struggle-afford-food.aspx

[4] Household Wealth Trends In The United States, 1962-2013:What Happened Over The Great Recession? Edward N. Wolff, National Bureau Of Economic Research, pg.14

[5] Inside The 2013 Forbes 400: Facts And Figures On America's Richest http://www.forbes.com/sites/luisakroll/2013/09/16/inside-the-2013-forbes-400-facts-and-figures-on-americas-richest/

[6] Fortune magazine, America is the richest, and most unequal, country, Erik Sherman 9/30/15, http://fortune.com/2015/09/30/america-wealth-inequality/, U. S. Census data http://www.census.gov/newsroom/press-releases/2015/cb15-157.html

[7] Striking it Richer:The Evolution of Top Incomes in the United States (Updated with 2013 preliminary estimates) Emmanuel Saez, UC Berkeley,1/25/15. The data in Saez's document is determined using income tax statistics. Based on the authors communication with Emmanuel Saez, about 2% additional income share would likely result from taking into account income directed to tax havens.

[8] Letter from Thomas Jefferson to Thomas Cooper, 10 September 1814

[9] Letter from George Washington to Richard Henderson, 19 June 1788

[10] Democracy In America, Introductory chapter, Alexis De Tocqueville

[11] NY Times, America, Land Of The Equals By Chrystia Freeland, 5/3/12

[12] American Enterprise Institute: Life Expectancy v. Real GDP Per Capita, 1800-2007 Mark J. Perry. In 1800, in the U.S. per-capita real GDP was $1,343 by 2007, it was $42,952. https://www.aei.org/publication/life-expectancy-v-real-gdp-per-capita-1800-2007/. Worker hours per capita are much lower now than in 1800, so the GDP/capita ratio is an underestimate of the productivity gains.

[13] U.S. Department Of Health & Human Services, Information On Poverty And Income Statistics: A Summary Of 2013 Current Population Survey Data 09/18/2013 https://aspe.hhs.gov/basic-report/information-poverty-and-income-statistics-summary-2013-current-population-survey-data

[14] From Building a Better America—One Wealth Quintile at a Time Michael I. Norton1 and Dan Ariely, Harvard Business School, Department of Psychology, Duke University

[15] The State of Working America's Wealth, 2011, Table 2, Economic Policy Institute

[16] How Some CEOs Cheat Their Way To Higher Pay, Alan Pyke 9/13/13 http://thinkprogress.org/economy/2013/09/13/2620121/ceo-pay-performance-based-cheating/

[17] Chinese Struggling Less Than Americans to Afford Basics, 10/12/11, Rajesh Srinivasan and Bryant Ott, http://www.gallup.com/poll/150068/chinese-struggling-less-americans-afford-basics.aspx

[18] Transitioning In and Out of Poverty, Urban Institute, 9/09, Signe-Mary McKernan, Caroline Ratcliffe, and Stephanie R. Cellini

[19]http://newlaborforum.cuny.edu/2012/08/02/the-working-poor-a-booming-demographic/#sthash.ST8nQLLW.dpuf

[20] The Working Poor: A Booming Demographic, PERI, University of Massachusetts, Amherst, Dr. Jeannette Wicks-Lim

[21] The Book of Jobs, Joseph Stiglitz Vanity Fair Jan 2012

[22] Washington Post, Who are the 1 percent? Suzy Khimm October 6, 2011 https://www.washingtonpost.com/blogs/ezra-klein/post/who-are-the-1-percenters/2011/10/06/gIQAn4JDQL_blog.html

[23] Adam Smith, The Wealth of Nations: An Inquiry into the Nature & Causes of the Wealth of Nations, Book 5, pg. 316 and Book 3, Chapter IV, pg. 448

[24] Saving Capitalism, Robert Reich, 2015, pg. 99

[25] Capital In The Twenty First Century, Thomas Piketty pg. 302

[26] Thomas Piketty suggested this more appropriate (and amusing) metaphor in Capital In The Twenty First Century

[27] Our Revolution, Bernie Sanders, 2016, pg. 249

[28] Coming Apart, Charles Murray, pg. 70

[29] The decline of the American public good By Robert Reich, Guest blogger / January 5, 2012, The Christian Science Monitor

[30] The Price Of Inequality, Joseph Stiglitz, pg. 72

[31] Leonard E. Burman, Daniel Patrick Moynihan, Professor of Public Affairs Maxwell School Syracuse University, Testimony Before the House Committee on Ways and Means and the Senate Committee on Finance, http://www.finance.senate.gov/imo/media/doc/092012%20Burman%20Testimony.pdf

[32] Progressive Taxation and the Subjective Well-Being of Nations, Psychological Science December 8, 2011, Shigehiro Oishi, Ulrich Schimmack, Ed Diener

[33] Reuters, The fortunate 400, David Cay Johnston, http://www.reuters.com/article/us-column-dcjohnston-top-idUSBRE85500720120606

[34] Senate September 2012 Unemployment Report

[35] Income and wealth data: Online Appendix of Wealth Inequality in the United States since 1913, Emmanuel Saez, Gabriel Zucman, PDF version, Table B, Table A0, and World Top Incomes Database, Table A3, Emmanuel Saez, Thomas Piketty

[36] Consumer Expenditure Survey, 2012, Table 1400. Size of consumer unit: Annual expenditure means, shares, standard errors, and coefficient of variation. Household and consumer unit are treated synonymously since their numbers are insignificantly different.

[37] http://www.zillow.com/home-values/

[38] Economic Policy Institute, The State of American Retirement, How 401(k)s have failed most American workers, Monique Morrissey, 3/3/16

[39] GDP data from US. Bureau of Economic Analysis, https://research.stlouisfed.org/fred2/series/GDPMCA1/downloaddata

[40] Based on BLS data, 142,228,000 employed persons, Feb 2013 and Gross National Income of $16.4 trillion, 2012 http://databank.worldbank.org/data/download/GNI.pdf

[41] PBS NewsHour, What the Founding Fathers Believed: Stock Ownership for All, Paul Solman, 11/15/13, http://www.pbs.org/newshour/making-sense/what-the-founding-fathers-beli/

[42] How Much More (Or Less) Would You Make If We Rolled Back Inequality? Quoctrung Bui, 1/22/15, NPR Planet Money report on a calculation by Larry Summers.

[43] Wall Street Journal, Tax Rate for Top 400 U.S. Taxpayers Climbed in 2013, Josh Zumbrun, 12/30/15   http://www.wsj.com/articles/tax-rate-for-top-400-u-s-taxpayers-climbed-in-2013-1451497056

[44] A Rise in Wealth for the Wealthy; Declines for the Lower 93% An Uneven Recovery, 2009-2011, Pew Research Center, Richard Fry and Paul Taylor

[45] The ETS Center for Research on Human Capital and Education, Poverty and Education: Finding the Way Forward, Richard J. Coley, with Bruce Baker, Rutgers University http://www.ets.org/s/research/pdf/poverty_and_education_report.pdf

[46] AlterNet, The Real Numbers: Half of America in Poverty -- and It's Creeping Upward, Paul Buchheit

[47] Based on data from The U.S. House Budget Committee report, War on Poverty 50 years later, March 6, 2014, and Forbes survey data. The wealth of the top 400 is not for all the same people each year, but this is an indication of the vast amount of wealth being directed to a tiny economic elite.

[48] America's Poverty Tax, pg. 211 Gary Rivlin, from Divided, David Kay Johnston

[49] Rewriting the Rules of the American Economy, 2016, Joseph Stigliz, pg.154

[50] http://abcnews.go.com/blogs/politics/2011/12/1-out-of-45-children-homeless-says-report/

[51] Bankruptcy: Past Puzzles, Recent Reforms, And The Mortgage Crisis, Michelle J. White, Working Paper 14549 National Bureau Of Economic Research, 12/08

[52]Statistic Brain http://www.statisticbrain.com/home-foreclosure-statistics/

[53]https://feedingamerica.org/newsroom/~/media/Files/research/local-impact-survey-009/economic-impact-2009.ashx

[54] Bureau Of Labor Statistics http://data.bls.gov/pdq/SurveyOutputServlet

[55] Business Insider, Amazing Charts Show How 90% Of The Country Has Gotten Shafted Over The Past 30 Years, Oct. 15, 2011, Henry Blodget   http://www.businessinsider.com/income-inequality-charts-2011-10

[56] Based on Bureau Of Labor Statistics data http://data.bls.gov/pdq/SurveyOutputServlet

[57] Striking it Richer: The Evolution of Top Incomes in the United States (Updated with 2011 estimates) Emmanuel Saez January 23, 2013.

[58] Capital In The Twenty First Century, Thomas Piketty, pg. 327

[59] USA Today online "U.S. household wealth reaches record high" http://www.usatoday.com/story/money/business/2013/12/09/household-wealth-thirdquarter/3932563/

[60] FED Report on the Economic Well-Being of U.S. Households in 2014, May 2015

[61] Saving Capitalism, Robert Reich, 2015, pg. 134

[62] See Capital in The Twenty First Century, Thomas Piketty for the results of a large international historical study showing this relationship.

[63] Wealth, Income, and Power, G. William Domhoff, University of California Santa Cruz, sociology department

[64] http://www.gallup.com/poll/159728/say-politics-washington-cause-serious-harm.aspx

[65] The Huffington Post, Call Time for Congress Shows How Fundraising Dominates Bleak Work Life Jan 08, 2013, Ryan Grim, Sabrina Siddiquihttp://www.huffingtonpost.com/2013/01/08/call-time-congressional-fundraising_n_2427291.html

[66]http://www.rasmussenreports.com/public_content/politics/general_politics/february_2012/43_say_random_choices_from_phone_book_better_than_current_congress

[67] Opensecrets.org, Millionaires' Club: For First Time, Most Lawmakers are Worth $1 Million-Plus, Russ Choma 1/9/14

[68] The Center for Responsive Politics, Cost of Election, https://www.opensecrets.org/overview/cost.php

[69] Billion-Dollar Democracy, Blair Bowie, Adam Lioz, U.S. PIRG and Dēmos 2013 report

[70] Affluence and Influence: Economic Inequality and Political Power in America, Martin Gilens

[71] Testing Theories of American Politics: Elites, Interest Groups, and Average Citizens, preview April 2014, Martin Gilens, Princeton University.

[72] Pew Research Center, U.S. voter turnout trails most developed countries Drew Desilver http://www.pewresearch.org/fact-tank/2015/05/06/u-s-voter-turnout-trails-most-developed-countries/

[73] Forbes, "New Study: Trust in Both Business and Corporate Leaders Plummets" 1/22/13

[74] Gallop poll, 9/21/12, http://www.gallup.com/poll/157589/distrust-media-hits-new-high.aspx

[75] For Hire: Lobbyists or the 99%? How Corporations Pay More for Lobbyists Than in Taxes A report by Public Campaign December 2011

[76] James Madison, Detached Memoranda, http://press-pubs.uchicago.edu/founders/documents/amendI_religions64.html

[77] Center for American Progress, Using Public Lands for the Public Good

[78] http://www.who.int/healthinfo/paper30.pdf Measuring overall health system performance for 191 countries Ajay Tandon, Christopher JL Murray, Jeremy A Lauer, David B Evans, GPE Discussion Paper Series: No. 30 World Health Organization

[79] Our Revolution, Bernie Sanders, 2016, pg. 332

[80] Estimated Financial Effects of the "Patient Protection and Affordable Care Act," Pg. 15, Center for Medicare and Medicaid services, 3/30/2011

[81] http://www.thefiscaltimes.com/Articles/2013/09/10/Secret-Reason-Doctor-Shortage By Beth Braverman

[82] Healthcare-Now.Org, Health Insurance CEO Pay Skyrockets in 2013 https://www.healthcare-now.org/blog/health-insurance-ceo-pay-skyrockets-in-2013/

[83] Letter from Thomas Jefferson to George Logan, 12 November 1816 http://founders.archives.gov/documents/Jefferson/03-10-02-0390

[84] New Scientist, 10/19/11, Revealed – the capitalist network that runs the world, Andy Coghlan, Debora MacKenzie

[85] Income inequality and mortality in metropolitan areas of the United States. J W Lynch, G A Kaplan, E R Pamuk, R D Cohen, K E Heck, J L Balfour, and I H Yen, American Journal of Public Health. 1998 July; 88(7): 1074–1080

[86] Fragmentary Notes for "A Dissertation on the Canon and the Feudal Law", May – August 1765 http://founders.archives.gov/documents/Adams/06-01-02-0052-0002

[87] An Essay on Man's Lust for Power, 1807, http://founders.archives.gov/documents/Adams/06-01-02-0045-0008

[88] John Adams letter to James Sullivan, 26 May 1776 Papers 4:208--12

[89] Letter from John Adams to Boston Patriot, 31 October 1810

[90] James Madison, Parties, 23 Jan. 1792, Papers 14:197--98

[91] Letter To Thomas Jefferson from James Madison, 8 August 1791

[92] Letter from Thomas Jefferson to William Branch Giles, 26 December 1825

[93] Thomas Jefferson: Autobiography, 6 Jan.-29 July 1821, 6 January 1821

[94] Letter to James Madison from Thomas Jefferson, 28 October 1785

[95] Thomas Jefferson letter to James Madison 28 Oct. 1785

[96] The Works of Theodore Roosevelt: American ideals and other essays, social and political, 1/1/1906, pg.10

[97] Franklin D. Roosevelt's Message to Congress on Curbing Monopolies, April 29, 1938

[98] The writings of Thomas Jefferson: Volume 8, pg.104

[99] Letter from Thomas Jefferson to Edward Rutledge, 25 August 1791

[100] The Real Thomas Jefferson, Andrew M. Allison, M. Richard Maxfield, K. DeLynn Cook, and W. Cleon Skousen, National Center for Constitutional Studies, 2008, pgs. 167,168

[101] Financial Crisis Cost Tops $22 Trillion, GAO Says Eleazar David Melendez, 02/14/13 http://www.huffingtonpost.com/2013/02/14/financial-crisis-cost-gao_n_2687553.html

[102] CNBC, NYC total property value surges over $1 trillion, setting a record, Javier E. David, 1/16/16

[103] Politics in the Slump: Polarization and Extremism after Financial Crises, 1870-2014 Manuel Funke, Moritz Schularick, Christoph Trebesch, 9/23/15 Free University of Berlin, John F. Kennedy Institute, University of Bonn, University of Munich

[104] Our Revolution, Bernie Sanders, 2016, pg. 298

[105] Ibid. pg. 317

[106] American Society of Civil Engineers, 2013 Infrastructure Report Card http://www.infrastructurereportcard.org/a/documents/2013-Report-Card.pdf

[107] Federal Reserve of San Francisco, Highway Grants: Roads to Prosperity? 11.26/12 Sylvain Leduc and Daniel Wilson http://www.frbsf.org/economic-research/publications/economic-letter/2012/november/highway-grants/

[108] U.S. Infrastructure Investment: A Chance To Reap More Than We Sow, Credit Market Services: Beth Ann Bovino, U.S. Chief Economist Standard And Poors Report

[109] The Bush tax cuts are here to stay, EPI report, Rebecca Thiess

[110] Our Revolution, Bernie Sanders, 2016 pg. 250

[111] Forbes, 9/12/13, Six Reasons Why Another Financial Crisis Is (Still) Inevitable, Alan Blinder

[112] Forbes, Big Banks and Derivatives: Why Another Financial Crisis Is Inevitable, 1/8/13, Steve Denning

[113] Opensecrets.org, http://www.opensecrets.org/industries../indus.php?ind=F06++

[114] Rewriting the Rules of the American Economy, 2016, Joseph Stigliz, pg.Vll

[115] Wall Street Journal, U.S. Homeownership Rate Hits 48-Year Low, 7/28/15, Laura Kusisto

[116] CNNMoney, What the foreclosure settlement means for you Les Christie February 9, 2012

[117] Saving Capitalism, Robert Reich, pg.77

[118] Our Revolution, Bernie Sanders, 2016, pg. 303-305

[119] New York Times, 9/23/10, "Report Finds Low Graduation Rates at For-Profit Colleges," Tamar Lewin

[120] NY Times, With Lobbying Blitz, For-Profit Colleges Diluted New Rules Eric Lichtblau, 12/9/11

[121] The Price of Inequality, Joseph Stiglitz, pg. 196

[122] The Real Thomas Jefferson, Andrew M. Allison, M. Richard Maxfield, K. DeLynn Cook, and W. Cleon Skousen, National Center for Constitutional Studies, 2008, pgs. 459, 460

[123] New York Times, Rikers Island Struggles With a Surge in Violence and Mental Illness, 3/18/14 Michael Schwirtz

[124] The New Yorker, The Caging Of America, 1/30/12, Adam Gopnik

[125] http://solitarywatch.com/facts/faq/

[126] New York Times, Rikers Island Struggles With a Surge in Violence and Mental Illness, Michael Schwirtz, 3/11/14

[127] State Spending for Corrections: Long-Term Trends and Recent Criminal Justice Policy Reforms, The National Association of State Budget Officers, 9/11/13

[128] The Impact of Mass Incarceration on Poverty, H. DeFina, Lance Hannon Villanova University - College of Liberal Arts and Sciences February 23, 2009

[129] Our Revolution, Bernie Sanders, 2016, pg. 383

[130] Huffingtonpost, Author and Legal Scholar, Michelle Alexander, Talks about the War on Drugs and Mass Incarceration (Part 1) 12/9/15 http://www.huffingtonpost.com/kathleen-wells/interview-with-author-and_b_1469260.html

[131] Schools and the New Jim Crow • An Interview With Michelle Alexander By Jody Sokolower (Michelle Alexander is an associate professor of law at Ohio State University and author of the New Jim Crow Mass Incarceration in the Age of Colorblindness http://www.rethinkingschools.org//cmshandler.asp?archive/26_02/26_02_sokolower.shtml

[132] Incarceration in Fragile Families Christopher Wildeman Bruce Western The Future of Children, Volume 20, Number 2, Fall 2010, pg. 157-177

[133] USA Today online http://www.usatoday.com/story/money/business/2013/12/09/household-wealth-thirdquarter/3932563/, "U.S. household wealth reaches record high")

[134] Based on the Federal Reserve 2013 Survey of Consumer Finances data

[135] Based on BLS data, 142,228,000 employed persons, Feb 2013 and Gross National Income of $16.4 trillion, 2012 http://databank.worldbank.org/data/download/GNI.pdf

[136] Striking it Richer: The Evolution of Top Incomes in the United States (Updated with 2011 estimates) Emmanuel Saez January 23, 2013.

[137] Capital In The Twenty First Century, Thomas Piketty, pg. 327

[138] The Working Poor: A Booming Demographic 2012, Political Economy Research Institute, Jeannette Wicks-Lim

[139] The Overworked American Family: Trends and Nontrends in Working Hours, 1968-2011 Michael Hout and Caroline Hanley University of California, Berkeley

[140] UTNE reader, Less Work, More Life, John de Graaf, 12/22/10

[141] Eurofound, European Observatory of Working Life, Law on the 35-hour week is in force, Alexandre Bilous, 1/27/00 http://www.eurofound.europa.eu/observatories/eurwork/articles/working-conditions/law-on-the-35-hour-week-is-in-force

[142] Our Revolution, Bernie Sanders, 2016 pg. 240

[143] New York Times, Skilled Work, Without The Worker, John Markoffaug, 8/18/12

[144] Inequality Kills, Stephen Bezruchka, MD from Divided: The Perils of Our Growing Inequality, 2014 ed. David Cay Johnston

[145] The New Enlightenment wage subsidy, income tax and reemployment proposals are modified versions of proposals by Robert Reich, PhD., Chancellor's Professor of Public Policy, Univ. of Ca. at Berkeley, Former U.S. Secretary Of Labor, from Aftershock pgs. 129-134

[146] www.bls.gov/lpc/special_requests/nfbbardata.txt

[147] The Obama administration has recently proposed a new overtime regulation where, starting on December 1, 2016, most salaried workers earning up to $47,476 a year will receive time-and-a-half overtime pay when they work more than 40 hours during a week. However, Republicans and their corporate allies have already begun their effort to overturn the new rules. Speaker of the House, Paul Ryan, has said he is "committed" to passing legislation in Congress to stop implementation.

[148] The Unemployment Insurance System, William Carrington April 1, 2013 https://www.cbo.gov/publication/44041

[149] Economic Policy Institute website, "Missing workers" http://www.epi.org/publication/missing-workers/

[150] Bruce D. Meyer and James X. Sullivan, "Winning the War: Poverty from the Great Society to the Great Recession," National Bureau of Economic Research, NBER Working Paper Series, Jan. 2013

[151] The President's Proposal To Expand The Earned Income Tax Credit, Executive Office of the President and U.S. Treasury Department, 3/14

[152] Committee for a Responsible Federal Budget, The Tax Break-Down: Child Tax Credit, 2010

[153] Bureau of Labor, https://www.dol.gov/featured/minimum-wage/chart1

[154] Bureau of Labor, http://data.bls.gov/pdq/SurveyOutputServlet

[155] The $904 billion estimate accounts for the number of 2013 married filing jointly filers that would have had the husband and wife employed increasing by about a 26%, and their reported incomes being reduced by half when filing separately. More will be motivated to work based on the new EITC. The estimate also accounts for the fact that many earning less than $10,000 per year in 2013 would have increased their work-hours to meet the $10,000 per year requirement for the expanded EITC. This and other New Enlightenment policies would result in sufficient work opportunities being available. We use the estimate that 50% will do so in determining the expanded EITC cost, and that their new incomes will be heavily skewed toward the lower end of the $10,000 to $50,000 income spectrum, and to be conservative none will be employed above $50,000. This estimate also accounts for the savings from eliminating the $57 billion per year child tax credit.

[156] The word "radical" to many has a negative connotation of being too extreme, but its original root meaning is "of or relating to the origin" or "root" (of a problem in this case) and "very basic and important"

[157] NY Times editorial, Putting Corporate Cash to Work, March 9, 2013

[158] Capital In The Twenty First Century, Thomas Piketty, pg. 513, 358

[159] Multiyear average growth rates based on Bureau of Economic Analysis, Percent change from preceding period excel file data

[160] What Ideas Are Worth: The Value of Intellectual Capital And Intangible Assets in the American Economy Kevin A. Hassett and Robert J. Shapiro

[161] Capital In The Twenty First Century, pg. 256 (PDF version) by Thomas Piketty

[162] http://www.epi.org/publication/ib364-corporate-tax-rates-and-economic-growth/

[163] Capital In The Twenty First Century, Thomas Piketty, pg. 435

[164] Can They Do That, Lewis Mathy, pg 58

[165] Can They Do That, Lewis Mathy, pg 25

[166] In 1845, at the beginning of the industrial system when many people left their farms to be employees in factories women factory workers produced a publication, Factory Tracts. Here is

how they described in it the employer-employee social order. "When you sell your product, you retain your person. But when you sell your labour, you sell yourself, losing the rights of free men and becoming vassals of mammoth establishments of a monied aristocracy that threatens annihilation to anyone who questions their right to enslave and oppress. Those who work in the mills ought to own them, not have the status of machines ruled by private despots who are entrenching monarchic principles on democratic soil as they drive downwards freedom and rights, civilization, health, morals and intellectuality in the new commercial feudalism." (as quoted in Requiem for the American Dream, Noam Chomsky, pg. 121. I first heard the appropriate phrase "little tyranny" applied to the conventional corporate structure in a speech by Noam Chomsky.)

[167] The Citizen's Share: Putting Ownership Back into Democracy by Joseph R. Blasi, Richard B. Freeman , Douglas L. Kruse, 11/ 4/13 pg.21

[168] In his opinion in Supreme Court case, Standard Oil Co. Of California And Standard Stations, Inc. V. United States. 337 U.S. 293 (69 S.Ct. 1051, 93 L.Ed. 1371) Decided: June 13, 1949.

[169] It is possible for an enterprise to be worker owned, but not worker self-directed, as is currently generally the case in ESOP corporations, described later in the proposal. Worker-ownership without worker self-direction is an unnatural combination though since owners would normally insist on control, especially if they spend a large part of their waking hours involved with the enterprise. Worker self-direction can also exist without worker-ownership, and I recommend this arrangement in a couple of specialized cases. However, as a general rule I will use WSDE to mean enterprises that are both worker self-directed and worker owned, except in cases I will specify. For more information on WSDEs see Democracy at Work, by Richard Wolff.

[170] The Citizen's Share: Putting Ownership Back into Democracy by Joseph R. Blasi, Richard B. Freeman , Douglas L. Kruse, 11/ 4/13 pg.83

[171] National Center for Employee Ownership, Employee Ownership Report, March April 2015

[172] Default Rates on Leveraged ESOPs, 2009-2013, The National Center for Employee Ownership

[173] The National Center for Employee Ownership, Research on Employee Ownership, Corporate Performance, and Employee Compensation, https://www.nceo.org/articles/research-employee-ownership-corporate-performance

[174] Why Thomas Jefferson Favored Profit Sharing, David Cay Johnston, Newsweek, February 4, 2014

[175] Research on Employee Ownership, Corporate Performance, and Employee Compensation, The National Center for Employee Ownership

[176] The Citizen's Share: Putting Ownership Back into Democracy by Joseph R. Blasi, Richard B. Freeman , Douglas L. Kruse, 11/ 4/13 pgs.168-187

[177] Governing the Firm: Workers' Control in Theory and Practice, 2003, Gregory K. Dow, Cambridge University Press, pgs. 226, 227

[178] Luc Labelle, "Development of Cooperatives and Employee Ownership, Quebec-Style," Owners at Work (2001), http://dept.kent.edu/oeoc/PublicationsResearch/Winter2000-2001/CooperativesQuebecStyle.htm (accessed May, 2010).

[179] The Relative Survival of Worker Cooperatives and Barriers to Their Creation, Advances in the Economic Analysis of Participatory & Labor-Managed Firms vol. 14 December 2013, Erik K. Olsen

[180] CECOP-CICOPA, Business Transfers to Employees Under the Form of a Cooperative in Europe: Opportunities and Challenges, 12 (June 2013), http://www.cecop.coop/IMG/pdf/bussiness_transfers_to_employees_under_the_form_of_a_c ooperative_in_europe_cecop-4.pdf

[181] http://www.co-oplaw.org/special-topics/worker-cooperatives-performance-and-success-factors/#fn-9170-3

[182] CECOP-CICOPA, Business Transfers to Employees Under the Form of a Cooperative in Eu-rope: Opportunities and Challenges, 12 (June 2013)

[183] International Labour Organization, Resilience of the Cooperative Business Model in Times of Crisis, 29 (2009), http://www.ilo.org/wcmsp5/groups/public/—ed_emp/—emp_ent/documents/publication/wcms_108416.pdf

[184] Katrina Berman, "A Cooperative Model for Worker Management," in The Performance of Labour- Managed Firms, ed. Frank Stephens (New York: St. Martin's Press, 1982), pg. 80.

[185] http://online.wsj.com/public/resources/documents/CEOperformance122509.pdf

[186] Jackall and Levin, Worker Cooperatives in America, pgs.26, 27.

[187] Hendrik Thomas, "The Performance of the Mondragon Cooperatives in Spain," in Partici-patory and Self-Managed Firms: Evaluating Economic Performance, ed. Derek Jones and Jan Svejnar (Lexington: Lexington Books, 1982), 149

[188] Greg MacLeod and Darryl Reed, "Mondragon's Response to the Challenges of Globaliza-tion: A Multi- Localization Strategy," in Co-operatives in a Global Economy: The Challenges of Co-operation Across Borders, ed. Darryl Reed and J. J. McMurtry (Newcastle: Cambridge Scholars Publishing, 2009), 127–13

[189] Eurostat, "Emilia-Romagna: Economy," http://circa.europa.eu/irc/dsis/regpor-traits/info/data/en/ itd5_eco.htm (accessed May, 2010) as referenced in Worker Cooperatives and Revolution: History and Possibilities in the United States, Christopher Wright, University of Massachusetts Boston, ccwwgd@gmail.com

[190] Emilia-Romagna – Economy, The combination of traditional products and technological innovation, http://archive.today/AD9Y#selection-79.0-85.68

[191] The Tax Foundation, Corporations Make Up 5 Percent of Businesses but Earn 62 Percent of Revenues, 11/25/14 Andrew Lundeen, Kyle Pomerleau

[192] If the price to sales ratio of all businesses is the same as that of the Standard and Poors 500, 1.76, according to Bloomberg News, Bottom Line for S&P 500 Is Top Line as Price-Sales Expands, Lu Wang, 1/9/15

[193] Italy's economy has been more negatively impacted by the international banking system caused financial crisis than most countries. Its economic problems now are not indicative of a failure of its efforts to promote successful worker-ownership of businesses through this and other government support programs.

[194] Insolvency, Employee Rights & Employee Buyouts, A Strategy for Restructuring, Ithaca Consultancy, 8/06, Anthony Jensen

[195] Using Goldratt's Thinking Process to Improve the Success Rate of Small Business Start-ups, Lloyd J. Taylor, The University of Texas of the Permian Basin, Elizabeth Seanard, Mid-land College Business and Economic Development Center

[196] Limitations On Credit Union Member Business Lending Compared To The Commercial Loan Powers Of National Banks, Credit Union National Association

[197] https://www.frbdiscountwindow.org/en/Pages/Discount-Rates/Current-Discount-Rates.aspx

[198] http://www.bondsonline.com/Corporate_Bond_Yield_Index.php?fa=yield_curve&fileDate=4%2F1%2F2014&sector1=C_AAA&sector2=&sector3=&sector4=&fa2=Export#

[199] Global Financial Crisis: Further Action Needed to Reinforce Signs of Market Recovery: IMF, Peter Dattels and Laura Kodresin

[200] Ensuring a sustainable future: Making progress on environment and equity, Magda Barrera, Jody Heymann, 10/13, pg. 20. The wealth transfer projection referenced is $4.8 trillion over the 20-year period from 2006 to 2026 or $240 billion/year

[201] Default Rates on Leveraged ESOPs, 2009-2013 By Corey Rosen and Loren Rodgers, National Center for Employee Ownership, July 2, 2014

[202] If community member bond purchases supported 25% of the $60 billion and 20% that would qualify for the tax-free interest income, and the bond interest averaged 4.5%, the tax exemption cost would be about $162 million per year. Based on the assumption that retiring owners will take back in loans half the value of the transferred businesses, their tax exemption costs would be about $46 million. This assumes the same distribution of sales prices as sales over the years 2013 and 2014 recorded in the private company merger and acquisition transaction database of "Pratt's Stats," a 4% interest rate, and an average income tax of 40% for retiring owners. The bond purchaser's tax exemption cost is based on an assumed 30% average tax rate.

[203] 2011 Corporate Bankruptcy Recap, bankruptcydata.com, New Generation Research Inc.

[204] CEO data from: Trends in CEO Pay at S&P 500 Index Companies, AFL-CIO report, Median wage data from Social Security Administration, http://www.ssa.gov/oact/cola/central.html

[205] Alternatives to Economic Globalization, John Cavanagh and Jerry Mander, pg. 142

[206] The Story of Kmart's Reorganization, Jon Fisher, Justin Wolbert, 5/4/2011, pg. 64

[207] This assumes a bondholder average income tax rate of 30%.

[208] Wall Street Journal, Apr 25, 2014, Fact Check: Does Private Equity Kill Jobs? Lauren Weber

[209] Survey of Terms of Business Lending, 11/15 https://www.federalreserve.gov/releases/e2/current/

[210] http://tweakyourbiz.com/finance/2015/02/12/what-is-a-typical-interest-rate-on-a-small-business-loan/

[211] This assumes sociable takeovers of 5% of public companies per year and 10% of their stock holders will accept the conversion of their stock value to bond value, and the 2010 Survey of Consumer Finances distribution of ownership of stock values.

[212] Credit Union National Association Monthly Credit Union Estimates February 2016

[213] Is Local Democracy Possible in the Global Era?, Gar Alperovitz, 9/15/12, http://www.truth-out.org/news/item/12757-is-local-democracy-possible-in-the-global-era

[214] What Then Must We Do?: Straight Talk about the Next American Revolution, 2013 pg. 53, Gar Alperovitz

[215] The Great American Jobs Scam, Greg Leroy, pgs. 38-40

[216] http://www.nytimes.com/interactive/2012/12/01/us/government-incentives.html?_r=0

[217] Using the SCF data and the taking the difference between the $495,000 average in wealth per household and the wealth of each household (treating households with negative wealth as having zero wealth) and summing these amounts for all households below average in wealth, yields $38.6 trillion. Five percent of this amount, $1.9 trillion, will be subsidized through the expenditure of one-twentieth of it for 20 years or $96.5 billion per year

[218] New England Journal of Medicine 2003;349:768-75. Costs of Health Care Administration in the United States and Canada

[219] Computed Tomography — An Increasing Source of Radiation Exposure David J. Brenner, Ph.D., D.Sc., and Eric J. Hall, D.Phil., D.Sc., N Engl J Med 2007; 357:2277-2284 November 29, 2007

[220] Full-Body CT Screening Found to be Risky, Columbia University report http://www.cumc.columbia.edu/publications/in-vivo/Vol3_Iss10_sept_04/radiology.html

[221] The purpose of patent law is to benefit society by encouraging innovation. Current patent laws are abused now in ways harmful to society, sometimes even through stifling innovation. For example, the White House intellectual property advisor Collen Chien noted in 2012 Google and Apple have been spending more money acquiring and litigating over patents than on doing research and development. Also, patent laws allow patent renewal on the basis of small and insignificant changes which harmfully extends monopoly pricing power and market domination beyond what are arguably too long original patent periods.

[222] The Citizen's Share: Putting Ownership Back Into Democracy, Joseph R. Blasi, Richard B. Freeman, Douglas L. Kruse, pg. 40

[223] Letter from John Adams to James Sullivan, 26 May 1776

[224] To James Madison from Thomas Jefferson, 28 October 1785

[225] The Citizen's Share: Putting Ownership Back into Democracy by Joseph R. Blasi, Richard B. Freeman , Douglas L. Kruse, 11/ 4/13, pg.30

[226] After the Revolution: Profiles of Early American Culture Joseph J. Ellis, pg. 192

[227] Why Thomas Jefferson Favored Profit Sharing, Newsweek, 2/4/14, David Cay Johnston

[228] Proposals to Revise the Virginia Constitution: I. Thomas Jefferson to "Henry Tompkinson" (Samuel Kercheval), 12 July 1816

[229] Saving Capitalism, Robert Reich, pg.41

[230] Who Stole The American Dream, Hendrick Smith pg. 386

[231] The "Ripple Effect" of a Minimum Wage Increase on American Workers, Brookings Institution, 1/14

[232] Oxfam, The cost of inequality: how wealth and income extremes hurt us all

[233] A Burger King worker paid $7.25 per hour if able to save his entire income would have to work full-time 2,137,931 years to have the wealth of his employer

[234] https://www.oxfam.org/sites/www.oxfam.org/files/file_attachments/bp210-economy-one-percent-tax-havens-180116-en_0.pdf

[235] Capital in The Twenty First Century, 2014, Thomas Piketty, pg. 466

[236] https://www.reuters.com/article/us-offshore-wealth/super-rich-hold-32-trillion-in-off-shore-havens-idUSBRE86L03U20120722

[237] The Washington Post, Democrats' 'Better Deal' for workers leaves a tough question unanswered, 7/26/17, Max Ehrenfreund

[238] Changes in the Distribution of Income Among Tax Filers Between 1996 and 2006: The Role of Labor Income, Capital Income, and Tax Policy, Congressional Research Service, Thomas L. Hungerford

[239] Review of Income and Wealth Volume 42, Issue 4, 1996, Edward N. Wolff, CIA World Factbook https://www.cia.gov/library/publications/the-world-factbook/rankorder/2172rank.html, Factor Components Of Inequality: A Cross-Country Study, Cecilia Garcia-Penalosa Review of Income and Wealth Series 59, No.4, 12/13/2013,

[240] New York Times, To Reduce Inequality, Tax Wealth, Not Income, Daniel Altman, 11/18/12

[241] Capital In The Twenty First Century, Thomas Piketty, pg. 517

[242] Property tax played a role in the debates surrounding the constitution, and the national government levied a property tax in 1798 which raised about 89% of its revenue from real estate and 11% from the "property" tax on slaves. Source: "A History of the Property Tax in America," Pg. 11,12 John Joseph Wallis, Department of Economics University of Maryland & National Bureau of Economic Research

[243] Columbia Law Review, Vol. 99 January 1999 No. 1, Taxation and the Constitution, Bruce Ackerman, Yale Law School

[244] A shockingly large amount of the "wealth" of the country in Thomas Jefferson's day was in the form of human "property" – slaves. The value of slaves ranged between two and a half and three years of national income, which would be about $45 trillion today! see Capital In The Twenty First Century, Thomas Piketty, pg. 160

[245] Benjamin Franklin letter to Robert Morris, 25 Dec. 1783, http://press-pubs.uchicago.edu/founders/documents/v1ch16s12.html

[246] U.S. Census Bureau, Survey of Plant Capacity Utilization, http://www.census.gov/manufacturing/capacity/index.html

[247] Bureau of Labor Statistics Long Tem Unemployed Fact Sheet

[248] Missing Workers, The Missing Part of the Unemployment Story, Economic Policy Institute

[249] Based on estimate in the book Aftershock, Robert Reich, pg. 134. It would be somewhat less since Reich's proposal does not have an upper limit on the prior wages.

[250] Our Revolution, Bernie Sanders, 2016, pg. 348

[251] http://www.northeastern.edu/news/2014/11/generation-z-survey/

[252] Washington Post, National student loan default rate dips to 13.7 percent; still 'too high,' official says, Nick Anderson, 9/24/14

[253] Center for American Progress, The High Return on Investment for Publicly Funded Research, Sean Pool and Jennifer Erickson, 12/10/12

[254] Center for College Affordability and Productivity, 25 Ways to Reduce the Cost of College Center for College Affordability and Productivity, September 2010

[255] Center for College Affordability and Productivity, 25 Ways to Reduce the Cost of College

[256] U.S. Department of Education National Center for Education Statistics Table 105.20 http://nces.ed.gov/programs/digest/d14/tables/dt14_105.20.asp?current=yes , Trends in College Pricing 2013 report http://trends.collegeboard.org/sites/default/files/college-pricing-2013-full-report.pdf

[257] Federal Investment in Public University Infrastructure to Stimulate the Economy, Increase Bachelor's Degree Attainment in the Workforce, and Enhance National Competitiveness December 2008, Michael M. Crow, President, Arizona State University

[258] John Adams Historical Society, http://www.john-adams-heritage.com/quotes/

[259] Teddy Roosevelt's New Nationalism, Speech in Osawatomie, Kansas, August 31, 1910

[260] The Aging Networks, 8th Edition: A Guide to Programs and Services By Kelly Niles-Yokum, PhD, MPA, Kelly Niles-Yokum, Donna L. Wagner, PhD, pg. 124

[261] Center on Budget and Policy Priorities, Top Ten Facts About Social Security

[262] Social Security Administration Publication No. 13-11785, Fast Facts & Figures About Social Security, 2015

[263] Employment-Based Retirement Plan Participation: Geographic Differences and Trends, 2009 By Craig Copeland, Employee Benefit Research Institute

[264] Social Security Bulletin • Vol. 69 • No. 3 • 2009, The Disappearing Defined Benefit Pension and Its Potential Impact on the Retirement Incomes of Baby Boomers by Barbara A. Butrica, Howard M. Iams, Karen E. Smith, and Eric J. Toder

[265] Social Security Reduces Inequality- Efficiently, Effectively and Fairly, Nancy Altman and Eric Kingston, from Divided: The Perils of Our Growing Inequality edited by David Cay Johnston, pg. 250

[266] Secure Retirement For All Americans, New America Foundation, Steven Hill August 2010

[267] The New York Times, One in Every 31 Adults in Prison; Prison Spending Outpaces All but Medicaid, 3/2/09, Solomon Moore

[268] The New Jim Crow: How the War on Drugs Gave Birth to a Permanent American Undercaste, Michelle Alexander, Huffington Post, 03/08/10, See Michelle Alexander's book The New Jim Crow for more details

[269] Michelle Alexander on the Irrational Race Bias of the Criminal Justice and Prison Systems 8/1/12, By Mark Karlin,http://www.truth-out.org/opinion/item/10629-truthout-interviews-michelle-alexander-on-the-irrational-race-bias-of-the-criminal-justice-and-prison-systems

[270] The Impact of Mass Incarceration on Poverty, H. DeFina, Lance Hannon Villanova University - College of Liberal Arts and Sciences February 23, 2009

[271] The Pew Charitable Trusts, 2010. Collateral Costs: Incarceration's Effect on Economic Mobility. Washington, DC: The Pew Charitable Trusts.

[272] The National Institute of Mental Health website, Inmate Mental Health, http://www.nimh.nih.gov/statistics/1DOJ.shtml

[273] Rikers Island Struggles with a Rise in Violence: Schwirtz, Michael. New York Times, 3/11/14

[274] Incarceration in Fragile Families, Christopher Wildeman, Bruce Western, The Future of Children, Volume 20, Number 2, Fall 2010, pgs. 157-177

[275] http://www.nytimes.com/2012/03/11/opinion/sunday/go-to-trial-crash-the-justice-system.html

[276] National Legal Aid & Defender Association, website http://www.nlada.org/Defender/Defender_Gideon/Defender_Gideon_5_Problems

[277] State, County and Local Expenditures for Indigent Defense Services, Fiscal Year 2008, Prepared for: The American Bar Association, Standing Committee on Legal Aid and Indigent Defendants, Bar Information Program, Prepared By: Holly R. Stevens, Colleen E. Sheppard, Robert Spangenberg, Aimee Wickman, Jon B. Gould

[278] Mother Jones, How Many Innocent People Are in Prison? Beth Schwartzapfel, Hannah Levintova, 12/12/11, http://www.motherjones.com/politics/2011/12/innocent-people-us-prisons

[279] Innocence Project website http://www.innocenceproject.org/Content/How_many_innocent_people_are_there_in_prison.php.

[280] National Institute on Drug Abuse website, http://www.drugabuse.gov/publications/principles-drug-addiction-treatment-research-based-guide-third-edition/frequently-asked-questions/drug-addiction-treatment-worth-its-cost

[281] Time magazine, The Swiss Difference: A Gun Culture That Works, Helena Bachmann 12/20/12

[282] Estate Tax Reform: Issues and Options, Lily L. Batchelder, New York University School of Law, 2/27/09

[283] "How to target untaxed wealth" December 17, 2012, By Lawrence Summers, Economist, President Emeritus and Professor of Harvard University, Secretary of the Treasury, Clinton administration, Director of the National Economic Council for President Obama, 1/09- 11/10

[284] Common sense, Thomas Paine, 2005 Penguin edition, first published 1776, pg. 85

[285] Ibid, pg. 89

[286] Ibid, pg. 89,90

[287] Center on Budget and Policy Priorities, Myths and Realities About the Estate Tax, August 29, 2013 By Chye-Ching Huang and Nathaniel Frentz

[288] Saving Capitalism, Robert Reich, pg.146

[289] *Impact of Estate Tax on Small Businesses and Farms Is Minimal,* Center on Budget and Policy Priorities

[290] Mckinsey Research Brief, Who Should—and Shouldn't—Run the Family Business Dorgan, Stephen J.; Dowdy, John J.; Rippin, Thomas M. 2006

[291] Educational Quality And Equality, Linda Darling·Hammond, From All Things Being Equal: Instigating Opportunity in an Inequitable Time, ed. Brian D. Smedley and Alan Jenkins.

[292] OECD, Centre for Educational Research and Innovation, Education at a Glance 2014, Table A4.2.

[293] Saving Capitalism, Robert Reich,2015, pg. 140

[294] U.S. Department of Education, Institute of Education Sciences, National Center for Education Statistics https://nces.ed.gov/fastfacts/display.asp?id=66

[295] The potential for massive improvements in administrative efficiency was revealed in a Dan Rather report: The Finnish government oversaw more than a million students, from primary school to university, with about 600 administrators. In comparison, Rather noted, the city of Los Angeles oversaw some 664,000 students with about 3,700 administrators.

[296] Madison Papers, Detached Memoranda, ca. 31 January 1820

[297] Adam Smith, Lectures on Jurisprudence, Constitutional Law Foundation, http://www.conlaw.org/Intergenerational-II-2-4.htm

[298] Tax Policy Center Statistics, Source of Revenue as Share of GDP, 1934 to 2020

[299] U.S. Corporate Tax Rate Plunges To 40 Year Low Of 12.1 Percent, Pat Garofalo, 2/3/12 https://thinkprogress.org/u-s-corporate-tax-rate-plunges-to-40-year-low-of-12-1-percent-283868e14367#.8edywltk4 and CBO, The Budget and Economic Outlook: 2014 to 2024, pg. 86

[300] NY Times editorial, Putting Corporate Cash to Work, March 9, 2013

[301] Senate September 2012 Unemployment Report

[302] A Decade of Flat Wages, The Key Barrier to Shared Prosperity and a Rising Middle Class, Heidi Shierholz, Lawrence Mishel, 8/21/13, Economic Policy Institute

[303] Offshore Cash Hoard Expands by $183 Billion at Companies, Richard Rubin, 3/8/13, http://www.bloomberg.com/news/articles/2013-03-08/offshore-cash-hoard-expands-by-183-billion-at-companies

[304] U.S. Government Accountability Office "International Taxation: Large US Corporations and Federal Contractors with Subsidiaries in Jurisdictions Listed as Tax Havens or Financial Privacy Jurisdictions" GAO-09-157, 12/08

[305] Thomas Jefferson to Horatio G. Spafford, 17 March 1814

[306] USPIRG The Hidden Cost of Offshore Tax Havens State Budgets Under Pressure from Tax Loophole Abuse January 2013

[307] US PIRG The Hidden Cost of Offshore Tax Havens, 2/5/13

[308] Sales Factor Apportionment of Global Profits as an Alternative Construction of a Corporate Income Tax Base, Michael Udell and Aditi Vashist, District Economics Group, July 14, 2014

[309] https://www.irs.gov/uac/SOI-Tax-Stats-Integrated-Business-Data

[310] Stockholm International Peace Research Institute, http://www.sipri.org/media/pressreleases/2014/nuclear_May_2014

[311] Analysis and estimates from the Project On Government Oversight and Taxpayers for Common Sense

[312] Rebalancing Our National Security, October 2012, Center for American Progress report

[313] How Much Does It Hurt? The Impact Of Agricultural Trade Policies On Developing Countries, 2003 IFPRI, Michael Rubinstein, Janet Hodur

[314] National Center for Policy Analysis, Farm Subsidies: Devastating the World's Poor and the Environment 11/24/06, Max Borders, H. Sterling Burnett

[315] Agricultural Subsidies, Cato Institute, Chris Edwards

[316] Sourced from NASA, Climate change: How do we know? http://climate.nasa.gov/evidence/

[317] National Energy Information Center http://www.eia.gov/oiaf/1605/ggccebro/chapter1.html

[318] Department of Energy, Technical Support Document: Social Cost of Carbon for Regulatory Impact Analysis Under Executive Order 12866 (February 2010), www.epa.gov/oms/climate/regulations/scc-tsd.pdf.

[319] U.S. Energy Information Administration, https://www.eia.gov/dnav/pet/pet_move_impcus_a2_nus_epc0_im0_mbblpd_a.htm

[320] Aftershock, Robert Reich, pg. 250

[321] Washington Monthly Why Are Harvard Grads Still Flocking to Wall Street? September/October 2014 Amy J. Binder

[322] Rewriting the Rules of the American Economy, 2016, Joseph Stigliz, pg.116

[323] Rewriting the Rules of the American Economy, 2016, Joseph Stigliz, pg.41

[324] Wealth Inequality Rising Fast, Oxfam Says, Faulting Tax Havens, By Patricia Cohen 11/18/15 http://www.nytimes.com/2016/01/19/business/economy/wealth-inequality-rising-fast-oxfam-says-faulting-tax-havens.html?_r=0

[325] Stiglitz, J. E. "Using Tax Policy to Curb Speculative Short-Term Trading," Journal of Financial Services Research, 3(2/3), December 1989, pg. 101-115.

[326] Thoughts on Tax Rates and Revenue Potential for Financial Transaction Tax in U.S. Financial Markets, Robert Pollin and James Heintz, Political Economy Research Institute University of Massachusetts-Amherst

[327] National Association of Realtors, Existing Home Sales Data, https://store.realtor.org/product/report/existing-home-sales-historical-data-file?sku=e186-ehs-01-16, Commercial total of $363 billion from authors personal communication with George Ratiu, Director, Quantitative & Commercial Research, National Association of Realtors

[328] Income mean and upper limit from 2011 Tax policy center http://www.taxpolicycenter.org/taxfacts/displayafact.cfm?Docid=330

[329] Average annual savings per taxpayer calculated based on CBO "Distribution of Selected Major Tax Expenditures, by Income Group" http://www.cbo.gov/sites/default/files/cbofiles/attachments/43768_DistributionTaxExpenditures.pdf

[330] Center on Budget and Policy Priorities, Mortgage Interest Deduction Is Ripe for Reform, Will Fischer, Chye-Ching Huang, 6/25/13

[331] Rewriting the Rules of the American Economy, 2016, Joseph Stigliz, pg.41

[332] Saving Capitalism, Robert Reich, pg.41

[333] Revenue estimates from "Job Creation Tax Options" by Get America Working! workgroup

[334] "Effective Marginal Tax Rates for Low- and Moderate-Income Workers," Congressional Budget Office, Nov. 2012.

[335] Rights of Man, Thomas Paine

[336] Thomas Jefferson letter to Samuel Kercheval, 1816, ME 15:42

[337] Thomas Jefferson to Spencer Roane 6 Sept. 1819, http://press-pubs.uchicago.edu/founders/documents/a1_8_18s16.html

[338] http://www.cnn.com/2010/POLITICS/02/21/poll.broken.govt/

[339] Los Angeles Times, 2012 campaign set to cost a record $6 billion,10/31/12 By Matea Gold

[340] Dollarocracy, John Nichols and Robert McChesney, 2013 pgs. 104,153

[341] The families funding the 2016 presidential election, New York Times, Nicholas Confessore, Sarah Cohen and Karen Yourish, 10/10/15

[342] New York Times, Koch Brothers' Budget of $889 Million for 2016 Is on Par with Both Parties' Spending, Nicholas Confessore, 1/ 26/15

[343] Demos Report, The Money Chase: Moving from Big Money Dominance in The 2014 Midterms to a Small Donor Democracy, 1/14/15 Adam Lioz, Karen Shanton

[344] Call Time for Congress Shows How Fundraising Dominates Bleak Work Life http://www.huffingtonpost.com/2013/01/08/call-time-congressional-fundraising_n_2427291.html

[345] America the Possible, James Justave Speth, pg. 172

[346] http://www.businessinsider.com/these-6-corporations-control-90-of-the-media-in-america-2012-6

[347] Media and polarization Evidence from the introduction of broadcast TV in the United States Filipe R. Campante, Daniel A. Hojman. Journal of Public Economics 100 (2013) 79–92

[348] TV Basics, http://www.tvb.org/media/file/TV_Basics.pdf

[349] This is not to imply any other similarity between these two very different candidates. The mythology exists that Trump, like Sanders, is a populist candidate. However, one important indication otherwise is his income tax proposal. According to an analysis by the Tax Policy Center, although the proposal would cut taxes at every income level, high-income taxpayers like himself would receive the biggest cuts, both in dollar terms and as a percentage of income. The highest-income 0.1 percent of taxpayers (those with incomes over $3.7 million in 2015 dollars) would experience an average tax cut of more than $1.3 million in 2017, nearly 19 percent of after-tax income. Middle-income households would receive an average tax cut of $2,700, or 4.9 percent of after-tax income. The proposal would reduce federal revenue by $9.5 trillion over its first decade and an additional $15.0 trillion over the subsequent 10 years, before accounting for added interest costs.

[350] The simple algebra showing this is below:

$$\text{Total } V = V1 + V2 + V3 \ldots + V336$$
$$= 6A1 + 6A2 + 6A3 \ldots + 6A336$$
$$= 6(A1 + A2 + A3 \ldots + A336)$$

[351] National Journal, Ad Rates Spiking as Candidates, Groups Scurry to Get On Air By Reid Wilson July 26, 2012

[352] thestreet.com, TV Political Ad Spending Will Break Records in 2016, and These Broadcasters Will Cash In, Chris Nolter, 6/8/16 https://www.thestreet.com/story/13594342/1/tv-political-ad-spending-will-break-records-in-2016-and-these-broadcasters-will-cash-in.html

[353] Wesleyan Media Project, Advertising Volume Up 122% Over 2012 Levels; Spending in Presidential Race Over $400 million, 5/12/16

[354] This assumes on average candidates would choose audiences of about average size in their three minute time slot selections. Another perspective on this is ad revenues would be reduced by these percentages if ad rates were proportional to audience size, as is candidate V.

[355] Letter from John Adams to Jonathan Jackson, 2 October 1780

[356] Letter From Thomas Jefferson to Francis Hopkinson, 13 March 1789

[357] Fairvote.org, Seven Ways to create 100% Voter Registration, http://archive.fairvote.org/?page=857

[358] Citizens Without Proof: A Survey Of Americans' Possession Of Documentary Proof Of Citizenship And Photo Identification, Brennan Center For Justice At NYU School Of Law

[359] Waiting to Vote in 2012, Charles Stewart III, MIT Political Science Department Research Paper No. 2013-6

[360] 2013 Report Card for America's Infrastructure, American Society for Civil Engineeers http://www.infrastructurereportcard.org/a/#p/overview/executive-summary

[361] Smart Citizens, Smarter State, Beth Simone Noveck, pg. 259

[362] See, for example, Putting the Public Back into Governance: The Challenges of Citizen Participation and Its Future Archon Fung; When the People Speak, James Fishkin; Democratic Imperatives: Innovations in Rights, Participation, and Economic Citizenship Report of the Task Force on Democracy, Economic Security, and Social Justice in a Volatile World April 2012 American Political Science Association; Fostering Citizen Participation Top-down, Lyn Carson and Rodolfo Lewanski, The Tao of Democracy, Tom Atlee.

[363] The Federalist Papers : No. 71

[364] Opinion on the Treaties with France, 28 April 1793, Thomas Jefferson

[365] The Working Poor: A Booming Demographic, PERI, University of Massachusetts, Amherst, Jeannette Wicks-Lim

[366] U.S. Census, https://www.census.gov/hhes/www/poverty/data/historical/people.html, How Many People Experience Homelessness?, July 2009, National Coalition for the Homeless http://www.nationalhomeless.org/factsheets/How_Many.html

[367] News that Matters, Shanto Iyengar and Donald Kinder, University of Chicago Press, 1987, pg. 20

[368] "Famines." World Development 8(9): pgs. 613–21, 1980. Amartya Kumar Sen,

[369] http://www.cbsnews.com/news/polls-show-longtime-support-for-tax-hikes-on-rich/

[370] http://www.langerresearch.com/wp-content/uploads/1144a3FiscalCliff.pdf

[371] http://www.nytimes.com/interactive/2015/06/03/business/income-inequality-workers-rights-international-trade-poll.html

[372] Gallop politics website, http://www.gallup.com/poll/161927/majority-wealth-evenly-distributed.aspx

[373] New York Times, Americans' Views on Income Inequality and Workers' Rights, 6/3/15

[374] Overwhelming Majority of Americans Want to Break Up Big Banks, 4/4/13, WashingtonsBlog, http://www.washingtonsblog.com/2013/04/only-23-of-americans-opposed-to-breaking-up-big-banks.html

[375] Pew Research Center, Most See Inequality Growing, but Partisans Differ over Solutions, 1/23/14

[376] ABC World News Tonight Has Devoted Less Than One Minute To Bernie Sanders' Campaign This Year, 1/11/15, http://mediamatters.org/blog/2015/12/11/abc-world-news-tonight-has-devoted-less-than-on/207428

[377] The Structural Imbalance of Political Talk Radio, John Halpin, James Heidbreder, Mark Lloyd, Paul Woodhull, Ben Scott, Josh Silver, S. Derek Turner 6/20/07

[378] The New Media Monopoly, 2004, Ben H. Bagdikian, pg. 112

[379] Saving capitalism, Robert Reich, 2015, pg. 71

[380] Our Revolution, Bernie Sanders, 2016 pg. 260

[381] Ex-New York Times reporter Chris Hedges in his book Unspeakable

[382] Ibid, pg. 250

[383] The New Media Monopoly, Ben H. Bagdikian, pgs. 250,251

[384] Ibid, Pg. 239

[385] The Cancer Cow: A study of the risks associated with milk from rbGH treated cows, Nutrition Bytes, University of California, Los Angeles, Malawa, Zea

[386] Monsanto Forced Fox TV to Censor Coverage of Dangerous Milk Drug, 5/25/11, http://www.huffingtonpost.com/jeffrey-smith/monsanto-forced-fox-tv-to_b_186428.html

[387] Ibid, pg. 261

[388] Pew Research Center, State of the News Media 2013, http://www.stateofthemedia.org/2013/overview-5/

[389] Pew Research Center, State Of The Media, 2015 http://www.journalism.org/2015/04/29/state-of-the-news-media-2015/

[390] Pew Research Center, State of the News Media 2013, http://www.stateofthemedia.org/2013/overview-5/

[391] Pew Research Center, State Of The Media, 2013 http://www.stateofthemedia.org/2013/overview-5/

[392] Pew Research Center, State Of The Media, 2013 Americans Show Signs of Leaving a News Outlet, Citing Less Information, Jodi Enda and Amy Mitchell

[393] Congress's Missing Coverage: Local papers little help in casting an informed vote, Chad Rosenbloom, http://fair.org/extra/congresss-missing-coverage/

[394] FAIR, The Way Things Aren't, Rush Limbaugh Debates Reality, http://fair.org/extra/the-way-things-arent/1896/

[395] http://www.naacp.org/criminal-justice-fact-sheet/

[396] http://www.nydailynews.com/news/national/black-men-arrested-age-23-study-article-1.1586000

[397] Limbaugh dropped out of college after failing all his classes to become a disc jockey. There is no indication he has educated himself on science to any significant degree since.

[398] Ibid.

[399] http://www.nationalreview.com/article/207702/rush-leader-opposition-james-bowman

[400] Power Systems, Noam Chomsky, pg. 27

[401] 36 Questions About the Holocaust - Simon Wiesenthal Center http://motlc.wiesenthal.com/site/pp.asp?c=gvKVLcMVIuG&b=394663

[402] The Koch Brothers Have Gotten Much, Much Richer Under Obama, 01/23/2016, The Huffington Post, Sam Levine, http://www.huffingtonpost.com/entry/koch-brothers-net-worth_us_56a3ac86e4b076aadcc6d1f4

[403] http://www.sanders.senate.gov/koch-brothers

[404] No Place To Hide, Glen Greenwald, pg. 55

[405] Trans-Pacific Partnership (TPP): Job Loss, Lower Wages and Higher Drug Prices, 2014 Public Citizen, https://www.citizen.org/TPP

[406] Our Revolution, Bernie Sanders, 2016, pg. 434

[407] The New Media Monopoly, 2004, Ben H. Bagdikian, pg. 9

[408] The Class-Domination Theory of Power, G. William Domhoff, UCSC

[409] Letter from John Adams to Thomas Jefferson, 2 February 1816

[410] Thomas Jefferson: Notes on Virginia Q.XIV, 1782. ME 2:207

[411] Occupational Employment and Wages, May 2015, Reporters and Correspondents, http://www.bls.gov/oes/current/oes273022.htm

[412] http://fair.org/extra/the-fairness-doctrine/

[413] Alternet, 'Citizen Koch': The Movie About Our Sick Democracy PBS Tried to Kill, Andrew O'Hehir, http://www.alternet.org/election-2014/citizen-koch-movie-about-our-sick-democracy-pbs-tried-kill

[414] Corporation for Public Broadcasting http://www.cpb.org/aboutcpb/financials/budget/

[415] This is similar to a proposal by Robert McChesney, Professor, Department of Communication, University of Illinois at Urbana-Champaign. The voucher amount in the McChesney proposal is $200, which seems unnecessarily large since it would increase current journalist support by a factor of twenty. 248 million citizens with a $200 voucher each supplies a total $49.5 billion. The total of all pay to journalists in 2015 is about $2.5 Billion

[416] The number of journalists includes all Reporters, Correspondents, and Broadcast News Analysts, http://www.bls.gov/ooh/media-and-communication/reporters-correspondents-and-broadcast-news-analysts.htm The average or mean wage is for Reporters and Correspondents http://www.bls.gov/oes/current/oes273022.htm

[417] James Madison, Public Opinion, 19 Dec. 1791, Papers 14:170

[418] Don't Let Murdoch Rewrite Our Media History Josh Stearns, quoting Robert McChesney, http://www.freepress.net/blog/10/01/22/don%E2%80%99t-let-murdoch-rewrite-our-media-history

[419] How to Save Journalism, John Nichols and Robert W. McChesney, January 25, 2010 edition of The Nation.

[420] Google Handles 115 Billion Searches a Month, Felix Richter, 2/12/13 https://www.statista.com/chart/898/number-of-searches-handled-by-search-engines-worldwide/

[421] James Madison to W. T. Barry, 4 Aug. 1822, Writings 9:103--9

[422] The Center for Responsive Politics, http://www.opensecrets.org/lobby/

[423] Congressional staffers, public shortchanged by high turnover, low pay, by Luke Rosiak-The Washington Times Wednesday, June 6, 2012

[424] Brookings Institution, A Better Way to Fix Lobbying, Lee Drutman

[425] http://www.theopenhouseproject.com/2009/12/02/whats-the-average-salary-of-house-staff/

[426] May 2012 National Occupational Employment and Wage Estimates, BLS and The Open House Project http://www.theopenhouseproject.com/2009/12/02/whats-the-average-salary-of-house-staff/

[427] Congress and Senate staff budgets: CRS, Congressional Salaries and Allowances, Ida A. Brudnick January 7, 2014

[428] The Nader Page, Time for OTA, https://blog.nader.org/2010/05/28/time-for-ota/

[429] https://blog.nader.org/2010/05/28/time-for-ota/ The proof of MMS's "capture" is as appalling as it is abundant: staff failing to collect millions of dollars in royalties; oil and gas companies allowed to revise their own multi-million-dollar leasing bids; gifts and money from oil and gas companies to agency employees with whom the Service was conducting official business; social events with industry representatives that included illegal drug use and sex; an MMS inspector conducting inspections of oil drilling platforms while negotiating a job for himself with the company that owned those platforms (and finding no violations during those inspections), oil and gas company employees filled out official inspection forms in pencil to allow easy erasing and replacement of entries in pen by MMS inspectors; the industry cut and pasted Environmental Assessments from drilling projects in other parts of the world with no oversight from MMS (as evidenced by the inclusion of walruses - a cold water species which lives in Alaska - as a species of concern in the Gulf of Mexico); and MMS adopted wholesale a set of "best practices" for oil and gas drilling straight from the American Petroleum Institute, and then made these best practices only suggestions. Unfortunately, this phenomenon is not limited to MMS: during the Bush years financial regulators ignored dangerous practices on Wall Street and the world paid the price.

[430] Fix the Filibuster, No Labels, https://www.nolabels.org/fix-the-filibuster/

[431] OECD Communications Outlook 2013 http://dx.doi.org/10.1787/comms_outlook-2013-en

[432] Saving Capitalism. Robert Reich, pg. 32

[433] New America Foundation, Measuring the TV "White Space" Available for Unlicensed Wireless Broadband, 1/5/06

[434] http://taxfoundation.org/article/city-income-taxes

[435] American Enterprise Institute: Life Expectancy v. Real GDP Per Capita, 1800-2007 Mark J. Perry. In 1800, in the U.S. per-capita real GDP was $1,343 by 2007, it was $42,952. https://www.aei.org/publication/life-expectancy-v-real-gdp-per-capita-1800-2007/. Worker hours per capita are much lower now than in 1800, so the GDP/capita ratio is an underestimate of the productivity gains.

[436] http://online-shipping-blog.endicia.com/fedex-ups-usps-shipping-rates-comparison-chart-2015/

[437] https://krugman.blogs.nytimes.com/2009/07/29/medicare-versus-insurers/?mcubz=0 Medicare versus insurers Also see, http://www.politifact.com/truth-o-meter/statements/2011/may/30/barbara-boxer/barbara-boxer-says-medicare-overhead-far-lower-pri/

[438] http://www.fiercehealthcare.com/payer/health-insurance-ceo-pay-tops-out-at-22m-

[439] Gar Alperovitz's and Lew Daly's important book "Unjust Deserts," is the source of many of the quotes in this Note on the moral justification of higher taxes on high incomes and wealth.

[440] Unjust Deserts, Gar Alperovitz, Lew Daly, 2008 pg. 35

[441] U.S. Bureau Of The Census, Current Population Report, Consumer Income, 1960, pg. 32

[442] Some of these are described elsewhere in this book, but for more details see The Price Of Inequality, Joseph Stiglitz, "Rent Seeking And The Making Of An Unequal Society" and "Markets And Inequality" chapters

[443] High Pay Centre (2015) 'No Routine Riches: Reforms to Performance-Related Pay'. http://highpaycentre.org/pubs/no-routine-riches-reforms-to-performance-related-pay

[444] Can CEO Pay Ever Be Reeled In? The Atlantic, Susan Holmberg, Mark Schmitt, 10/29/14

[445] Capital In The Twenty First Century, Thomas Piketty pg. 314

[446] Ibid, pg. 235

[447] Ibid, pg. 335

[448] Oxfam, The Wages of Failure: Executive Compensation at Bear Stearns and Lehman 2000–2008 Bebchuck, A. Cohen and H. Spamann (2009).

[449] Seattle Times, Judge says PC-system allegations not libel, 7/26/07, Benjamin J. Romano

[450] They Made America: From the Steam Engine to the Search Engine, Harold Evans, Gail Buckland, David Lefer, 2004, Chapter on Gary Kildall

[451] Letter from John Adams to the President of Congress, 25 October 1781

[452] High income improves evaluation of life but not emotional well-being, Daniel Kahneman and Angus Deaton

[453] Getting Ahead or Losing Ground: Economic Mobility in America By Julia B. Isaacs, Isabel V. Sawhill, And Ron Haskins, Pg. 40 The Brookings Institution

[454] Born On Third Base Report, United For A Fair Economy September 17, 2012 (www.faireconomy.org)

[455] 100 Years Of Quantum Mysteries, Scientific American, Feb 2001, pg. 69 Max Tegmark and Archibald Wheeler

[456] When performance-related pay backfires, http://www.lse.ac.uk/newsandmedia/news/archives/2009/06/performancepay.aspx

[457] Drive: The Surprising Truth About What Motivates Us, Daniel H. Pink, http://www.obooksbooks.com/books/3597_6.html

[458] Drive: The Surprising Truth About What Motivates Us, Pg. 37, Daniel H. Pink

[459] Understanding Motivation and Emotion, 2015, Johnmarshall Reeve, pg. 133

[460] The Puzzle Of Motivation, TED summaries, Dan Pink: https://tedsummaries.com/2014/06/06/dan-pink-the-puzzle-of-motivation/ Also mentioned in Pink's book, Drive

[461] Unjust Deserts, Gar Alperovitz, Lew Daly, 2008, pg.59

[462] Ibid. pg. 60

[463] The Dynamic Moving Center Paul Samuelson 11/12/08

[464] International Monetary Fund, "Redistribution, Inequality, and Growth" by Jonathan D. Ostry, Andrew Berg, Charalambos G. Tsangarides, February 2014

[465] IMF Report: Causes and Consequences of Income Inequality : A Global Perspective, Era Dabla-Norris ; Kalpana Kochhar ; Nujin Suphaphiphat ; Frantisek Ricka ; Evridiki Tsounta, June 15, 2015 http://www.imf.org/external/pubs/ft/sdn/2015/sdn1513.pdf

[466] The Book of Jobs, Joseph Stiglitz, Vanity Fair, Jan 2012

[467] Koch Millions Spread Influence Through Nonprofits, Colleges, 7/1/13, Investigative Reporting Workshop, American University School Of Communications, Charles Lewis, Eric Holmberg, Alexia Fernandez Campbell, Lydia Beyoud

[468] Ibid

[469] Would some of the extreme "supply siders" and anti-tax "pundits" the mass media uses deny this, and claim that Bill Gates might have reacted this way?: "Only $760 million! Why bother continuing. I think I'll go surfing, and see if I can get on welfare and food stamps instead"

[470] Pew Research Center, Who's poor in America? 50 years into the 'War on Poverty,' a data portrait, Drew Desilver

[471] Saving Capitalism, Robert Reich, pg.137

[472] Levy Economics Institute of Bard College, Strategic Analysis, April 2014, Is Rising Inequality a Hindrance to the US Economic Recovery?

[473] "Stop Coddling the Super-Rich," New York Times, August 14, 2011, http://www.ny-times.com/2011/08/15/opinion/stop-coddling-the-super-rich.html.

[474] Troy Kravitz and Leonard Burman, "Capital Gains Tax Rates, Stock Markets, and Growth," Tax Policy Center, 11/7/05.

[475] Thomas L. Hungerford, "The Economic Effects of Capital Gains Taxation," Congressional Research Service, June 18, 2010 and "An Analysis of the "Buffett Rule," Congressional Research Service, October 7, 2011.

[476] Capital In The Twenty First Century, Thomas Piketty, pg. 513

[477] The Guardian, On capitalism we lefties are clueless – it's not just a rightwing caricature, Zoe Williams, 2/29/12, https://www.theguardian.com/commentisfree/2012/feb/29/capitalism-left-ies-clueless-emma-harrison

[478] Unjust Deserts, Gar Alperovitz, Lew Daly, 2008 pg. 76

[479] Key facts from the book Unjust Deserts published on Demos website http://www.demos.org/publication/unjust-deserts

[480] Ibid.

[481] http://fortune.com/2016/10/18/americans-work-hours-europeans/

[482] The Status of World Oil Reserves, 10/11 James A Baker lll School Of Public Policy, Rice University, US Energy Information Administration http://www.eia.gov/naturalgas/crudeoilreserves/pdf/table_1.pdf

[483] GDP is a poor measure of societal economic or societal well- being. I use it because it is the most commonly available and long-term measure. Several attempts have been made at better measures: Genuine Progress Indicator (GPI), which includes consideration of environmental and social factors and the Index of Sustainable Economic Welfare, which factors in both pollution and income distribution. Other alternative efforts try to supplement or replace traditional income-based measures with happiness-based measures include the Happy Planet Index, and the National Well-Being Accounts.

[484] Based on 2013 GDP estimates, IMF World Economic Outlook Database, September 2011

[485] Data from Global finance   http://www.gfmag.com/component/content/article/119-economic-data/12368-countries-highest-gdp-growth.html#axzz2fjudQvFx

[486] World Bank GDP ranking http://data.worldbank.org/data-catalog/GDP-ranking-table

[487] The exemption was never less than $644,000 in 2015 dollars on an estate. However, in the case of five heirs, the New Enlightenment total in exemptions will be $1.5 million.

[488] Carolyn Jones, a law professor at the University of Iowa as quoted in A Brief History Of The Income Tax by Tracey Samuelson, 2/1/13, http://www.marketplace.org/topics/wealth-poverty/brief-history-income-tax.

[489] Income inequality and mortality in metropolitan areas of the United States. J W Lynch, G A Kaplan, E R Pamuk, R D Cohen, K E Heck, J L Balfour, and I H Yen, American Journal of Public Health. 1998 July; 88(7): 1074–1080

[490] Business insider article on UBS's U.S. economics team findings on savings rate Chart Of The Day: Rich People Really Love To Save Their Money
 http://www.businessinsider.com/chart-savings-rate-by-income-level-2013-3#ixzz2fjIIHimA, top 5% has savings rate averaging 37.2% and our income tax increases are on mainly the top 5%.

[491] https://hbr.org/2014/09/profits-without-prosperity

[492] People Get Ready, Robert Mcchesney, John Nichols, 2016, pg.57

[493] The New Yorker, In The Air, Who says big ideas are rare? 5/12/08, Malcolm Gladwell

[494] Most of this information is from: Governing the Firm: Workers' Control in Theory and Practice, 2003, Gregory K. Dow, Cambridge University Press

[495] Italy's Emilia Romagna, Clustering co-op development, By David Thompson and http://ec.europa.eu/enterprise/policies/innovation/policy/regional-innovation/monitor/base-profile/emilia-romagna

Index

About the Author

Robert Bivona has a degree in physics, did graduate work in physics and engineering, and has decades of professional experience in physics, math, and engineering. He applied his analytic skills to his lifelong interest in public policy because our nation urgently needs fresh policy solution ideas from outside professional political and economics orthodoxy. Our political problems and resulting economic problems—largely caused by current political and economic professionals—are resulting in great injustices and unnecessary hardships for tens of millions of our fellow citizens, and are an existential threat to our nation.

The New Enlightenment policies were developed and
the book written over approximately five years, from
December 2011 through October 2016.

www.ingramcontent.com/pod-product-compliance
Lightning Source LLC
Chambersburg PA
CBHW060302030426
42336CB00011B/909